...han a workbook, this text shows students how to become successful writers through detailed explanations and motivational activities.

The Elements of Basic Writing

by Audrey J. Roth
Miami-Dade Community College

The Elements of Ba ic Writi.ıg effectively combines textbook and workbook formats into an innovative writing resource that will help your students learn the complex elements of writing. Through proven, innovative pedagogy and class-tested activities, students learn how to write grammatically correct sentences, coherent paragraphs, and well-structured essays.

With special attention paid to pre-writing, this text provides detailed coverage of the entire writing process. The author carefully builds on concepts and introduces principles in a logical, easy-to-follow manner, making steady progression simple. Most important, the text develops and encourages the critical thinking skills necessary for students to become accomplished writers — during college and throughout their professional careers.

The Elements of Basic Writing helps to demystify the writing process through a series of incremental activities based on subjects the student selects.

Motivating students to begin writing immediately is the primary focus of this text. To do that, the author speaks to the reader not as a student, but as a writer. Sensitive to students of different ages, cultures, and economic backgrounds, the author presents the basics of writing in small steps using clear, uncomplicated language. This, combined with incrementally challenging reinforcement exercises and extensive examples, helps students more readily master the skills of good writing. Best of all, the text is designed to be flexible, and can be used within a classroom environment or as a self-teaching, self-paced resource.

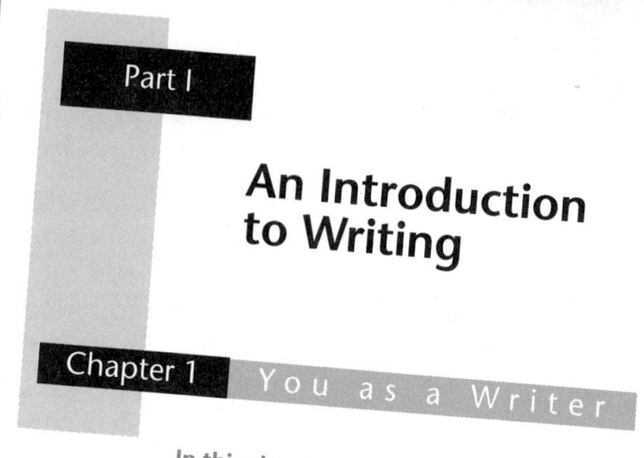

Part I

An Introduction to Writing

Chapter 1 You as a Writer

In this chapter you will

- begin to think of yourself as a writer
- recognize your present writing skills
- focus on improvements you want to make
- discover how you (and others in the class) view writing
- create your own "Writing Profile"

Writing may occupy only a very few hours in your life, but some of that time can be particularly important. Perhaps you will write a cover letter to an application or résumé for a job you particularly want. Or you may be away from a parent or child you love, and decide to write a letter to that person. You may have to demonstrate writing skill on a test so you can pass a course. Some colleges even require students to prove their writing ability in order to earn a degree.

The higher one moves in government or corporate America, the more important writing is likely to become to an individual. In a "communication society," such as ours, much of the communication is through writing. Even phone conversations are often confirmed by letter or memo. There are also all sorts of reports and proposals and presentations being written every day by people whose chief work is not writing, but who must be able to communicate their thoughts to others through written words. People in the social sciences and natural sciences also find themselves doing unexpected amounts of writing as they share their research, experiences, and ideas with others in their fields. So important is writing beyond school that every day there are probably hundreds of classes, seminars or workshops being given around the country to help full-time employees become better writers.

1

The Elements of Basic Writing is divided into six parts, each clearly focusing on a specific aspect of writing.

Carefully written and strategically organized, this text provides students with the structure they need, while offering instructors the flexibility they demand. In Part I, chapters on the writing process are closely integrated, providing a cohesive, sequenced overview. Subsequent chapters are presented as complete, separate units, allowing them to be covered in any order.

Chapter 2

Getting Started

In this chapter you will

- consider the various forms of writing
- examine how you start writing
- see how audience affects writing
- understand the purposes of writing
- examine the writing process

Think for a moment about how many words are used around you in just one hour. How about the number of words that you *don't* hear—across the hall, down the street, in the next county? The number of spoken words in even a moment of time is staggering!

Now think about how many words are *written* in an hour. Not as many as are spoken, but the number still is probably one that only mathematicians and high-powered computers can calculate.

Who are the millions of people writing something at this very second, as you read the words on this page? Maybe little children in school learning how to form the letters that spell their names. Maybe lawyers preparing cases to get their clients released from jail. Maybe students taking notes for the next class. Maybe a parent leaving a note for a child with a reminder to do a household chore. You could add more and more to the list if you spent just a few minutes trying.

What People Write

People write to communicate, to transmit ideas from one person to another (or to a group). How well the writer succeeds depends on how accurately the reader can understand the writer's intentions.

13

Part I: An Introduction to Writing

The text begins with an eight-chapter sequence covering the many processes of writing. Chapters 1 and 2 set the tone by showing students how to view themselves as writers and how to begin writing. Chapters 3 through 8 lead students through a series of writing steps, including selecting topics, pre-writing, drafting, and revising.

Critical thinking activities are built into each of the eight separate chapters on common rhetorical strategies.

Part II: Kinds of Paragraphs

This section covers the common rhetorical strategies: Description, Narration, Process, Classification, Definition, Comparison and Contrast, Cause and Effect, and Persuasion. Students learn how to write eight different types of paragraphs — a separate chapter for each type — while also discovering how to think critically about their purpose and audience. In addition to clear explanations and samples, every chapter features a special section highlighting the keys to mastering each particular paragraph type.

202 Kinds of Paragraphs

8. A vacation at ________ and a vacation at ________ **have in common:**

9. My ________ instructor and my ________ instructor **have in common:**

10. The movie ________ and the movie ________ **have in common:**

Key #2 to Comparison and Contrast: Finding Specifics

When you have identified the two people, things, or ideas that are going to be compared and/or contrasted, you must be sure that they really do have several characteristics that will make it possible for you to write about them in this way.

Developing a list of characteristics will give you ideas to work with in a convenient form. If you don't immediately think of what to put on such a list, try discussing the subjects with someone, try mapping, or try brainstorming.

Since an example of Key #1, finding something in common, was about "Nightline" and "The Oprah Winfrey Show," two very popular television shows, the example Key #2, finding specifics, will use the same subjects.

SPECIFIC SIMILARITIES

Begin by listing in the left column those qualities which both shows have in common. (They are in italics here, as they were in the examples earlier in this chapter.)

Next to each common quality, note ways in which the two shows are *similar*:

moderator	strong leader is always in control of show
format	has selected guests
	interviews guests
content	about people or ideas audience is interested in
timing	-------
popularity	gets top ratings
longevity	broadcasting more than five years
audience	closed captioned for hearing impaired

Students apply their newly acquired writing skills to each subsequent chapter of the text.

Part III: Longer Forms of Writing

In this section, students apply the principles of Parts I and II to complete longer, more complex forms of writing, such as essays. Students are instructed in combining rhetorical forms of paragraphs into well-written and structured essays. Furthermore, an extensive chapter on essay tests teaches students how to analyze expectations of essay test questions and develop strategies for dealing with this common assignment.

274 Longer Forms of Writing

Linking Paragraphs for the Body of an Essay

An essay is a series of connected—or linked—paragraphs. The first paragraph of a short essay is usually enough to introduce readers to the author's main idea (thesis statement), and an ending paragraph is usually enough space to bring all the ideas together. Between those, however, is the series of paragraphs called the "body" of the essay.

You must have at least one paragraph as the body, but there is no ideal number or upper limit on how many paragraphs the body can be. The number depends on how much you have to say on the subject, how complicated the subject is, and how much time you have for writing. Naturally, anyone limited to an hour of in-class writing can produce only a few paragraphs (especially if there is no prewriting in advance), while the same person will probably write many more paragraphs for the body of an essay prepared thoughtfully outside of class.

As you have already seen (in Chapter 7, on page 94), the sentences of a single paragraph read much more smoothly when they are connected by transitions rather than being plunked down on paper one after the other. Connecting the ideas of one paragraph with those of another is as important as connecting sentences. Because the essay is longer than one paragraph, the author has more to lead the reader through.

An essay should supply the reader with two kinds of links or connections:

1. The whole essay should be so linked that a paragraph can't be moved (or removed) without damaging the content.
2. One paragraph should be so linked to what comes before and after it that the reader cannot imagine any order of content other than the one on paper.

LINKING THE WHOLE ESSAY—COHESION

When everything in an essay fits together well—the words, the paragraphs, the ideas—it is called a "cohesive" essay. The word "cohesion" means to stick or hold together. It also means logically organized.

Your essays will be cohesive if you do everything you have been studying in this book and this chapter so far. That is, you should:

1. Select a subject narrow enough to be written about in the time available.*
2. Limit what you will say by writing a focused thesis statement.**
3. Make a plan for the content and stick to it. Even if you have a great deal of additional information, you may have to omit it for the sake of a cohesive essay.***

The payoff is an essay in which all the parts are linked—which a reader recognizes as cohesive.

* See Chapter 4, "Narrowing Subjects", pages 35-48
** See pages 262-264 in this chapter
***See pages 265-267 in this chapter

Part IV: Sentence Grammar
Part V: Mechanics
Part VI: Words

These three separate sections are designed to help students learn grammatical writing principles through highly focused chapters. Each chapter contains many diverse, skill-building exercises that students can tackle either in class or as individual assignments.

The Annotated Instructor's Edition provides additional support and quick, easy reference throughout the teaching experience.

To assist you in your teaching efforts, the **Annotated Instructor's Edition (AIE)** offers complete instructor's annotations throughout the text. In it, you will find a range of support material that is useful both in the classroom and for creating student assignments. The first three parts of the text contain succinct boxed annotations that appear in the margins in a second color. Each offers additional teaching strategies, references, or supplemental information to help clarify and enhance key concepts. Equally important, there are answers to all activities found in the text — both definite and suggested — as well as extra "**Sharing**" activities throughout.

Annotations appear only in the AIE. They do not appear in the student text.

Finding Subjects 27

Winning

COMMENT: No. Winning what? By whom? From whom? The subject is vague. It is also complex. On both counts, it won't do as the subject of a paragraph and needs more elaboration as subject for an essay.

You can make the same point about magazines. Most of them use narrow columns for all but feature articles.

CAUTION: Don't use newspaper paragraphs as a guide to paragraph length. There, paragraphs are extremely short, often only a single sentence. But there is a special reason: columns are narrow and a reader's eyes need the constant break of the indentation that marks a paragraph. Even this paragraph—short on a book page—would show up in a newspaper as a long block of type that looked too hard to read.

Activity 3-2

DIRECTIONS: Put a **P** on the line next to each of the following words or phrases that might be a paragraph subject. Leave blank the lines in front of those subjects that could have more than one idea and therefore not be suitable for a paragraph.

EXAMPLE ▶ P **how to hold chopsticks for eating**

The purpose of the *Activity* is to show that some subjects are broader than others, but without using such technical terms.

___ 1. Freud's contributions
___ 2. New methods of recycling
P 3. A good filing system for a two-person office
___ 4. Being a good parent
P 5. Registering to vote
P 6. My favorite chair
P 7. Starting a fresh-water aquarium
P 8. The octopus and its ink
P 9. Definition of a nuclear family
___ 10. Trusting neighbors

Sharing

This is a precursor to narrowing activities in Chapter 4.

1. Form a group with three or four classmates.
2. Let everyone share responses to *Activity 3-2.*
3. Discuss why you felt each item was or wasn't suitable for a paragraph. Suggest ways in which those believed unsuitable could be changed to make them into subjects for paragraphs.

Three Considerations in Choosing a Subject

Students seldom think about these things, so you may want to encourage them to think of all three when they choose various subjects.

Successful writers are those who give careful thought to the subjects they choose. Writing even something as short as a paragraph takes time, so don't choose a subject unless you are willing to stick with it, even through several revisions and readings by your classmates. Here are three more considerations in choosing a subject.

1. **Choose a subject you care about.** Otherwise, you may have a hard time "getting into" your subject.
2. **Choose a subject you won't get tired of.** Even if the writing takes a while, you need to choose a subject you can stick with for as long as it takes to write a piece you feel is successful.

Innovative pedagogy and outstanding organization help make it easy for students to access and assimilate information more readily .

This new text incorporates several unique pedagogical features designed to enhance the presentation of the subject's many sophisticated concepts. Moving from relatively simple to more complex, the material in each chapter delivers information in small increments, making it easier for readers to grasp and retain. Individual and group activities are interspersed throughout, enabling students to practice what they have learned. Each chapter opens with clearly stated "**Chapter Objectives**," and concludes with "**Recap**" sections reinforcing these same goals. And, in certain chapters, color-enhanced "**Highlight**" boxes feature key principles for fast, easy reference.

400 Sentence Grammar

Indefinite Pronouns and Verb Agreement

Indefinite pronouns got that name because they don't necessarily require an antecedent noun or pronoun.

EXAMPLES ▶ **Everybody** made fun of me.
Someone is knocking on the door.
Nothing moved!

However, indefinite pronouns may refer to a noun or pronoun that comes after it in the sentence, or even in the paragraph.

EXAMPLES ▶ **Everybody** may collect his or her pay later.
Few playwrights see their work produced on Broadway.

Verbs must agree in number with indefinite pronouns that are the subjects of sentences. Singular indefinite pronouns take singular verbs.

Plural indefinite pronouns require plural verbs. Some indefinite pronouns are considered either singular or plural, depending on their meaning in a particular sentence.

The charts below show singular, plural, and either singular or plural indefinite pronouns. Compound words ending in *-body,-one,* or *-thing* make up most of the list of singular indefinite pronouns. However, there are others, as this chart shows:

SINGULAR INDEFINITE PRONOUNS

-body	-one	-thing	Other
anybody	anyone	anything	any
everybody	everyone	everything	another
nobody	no one	nothing	each
somebody	someone	something	either
			every
			much
			neither
			none
			one

OTHER INDEFINITE PRONOUNS

Singular or Plural	Plural
all	both
any	few
more	many
most	several
none (occasionally)	
some	

A wide variety of interesting topics help make the text's activities more informative and challenging for students.

The Elements of Basic Writing includes an extensive collection of activities and assignments that teach and reinforce the principles of writing. These exercises cover a full range of topics — from personal and academic to vocational and special interest — to maintain high student interest. Each activity is preceded by *several* examples, so students understand what is expected of them. Students can also choose their own writing subjects for specific activities, helping to create a stronger sense of ownership and pride in their writing.

"Sharing" activities encourage learning from others.

In addition to individually performed exercises, this text also features "**Sharing**" activities. Each suggests group or two-person projects, along with instructions, encouraging students to discuss subjects, review each other's writing, and participate in collaborative writing exercises.

Punctuation 459

Activity 29-12

DIRECTIONS: On the line to the left of each sentence, write a C if parentheses or dashes are used correctly in the sentence, and an I if they are incorrect. If you write an I in the space, make the proper corrections in the sentence.

EXAMPLE ▶ I **The designer's newest line (spring sportswear) was in the catalog.**

___ 1. Parents' jobs are never done not even when their children have children of their own.
___ 2. My birthplace (Chicago) is known for its very severe winter weather.
___ 3. Our family doctor—the one who we've used for the past 30 years is retiring in March.
___ 4 The most popular mall in the city Shops at the Sea is going out of business.
___ 5. Only one player—Hank Aaron—has hit more lifetime home runs than Babe Ruth.
___ 6. Only one U.S. president Richard Nixon has resigned.
___ 7. I predict the winner will be the horse starting on the inside Dutchman's Calling Card.
___ 8. If you get to work late again as you have the last six days— you will be fired.

Activity 29-13

DIRECTIONS: Write a paragraph, on your own paper, on any *one* of the following topics:

My favorite songs and music
Newspaper articles I've read on topics of interest
Books, stories, and poems I enjoyed reading

Write the paragraph for other students in your class to let them know something about you. Pay particular attention to what you have learned in this chapter about using apostrophes, quotation marks, end punctuation marks, quotation marks, colons, and parentheses or dashes.

Sharing

Share the paragraph you wrote for *Activity 29-13* with at least one other person in the class. Help the author of the paper you read by editing it for the punctuation marks listed in the *Activity* directions.

Activity 29-14

DIRECTIONS: Put quotation marks and end punctuation in the following dialogue where they are needed.

I overheard the most frightening conversation today while I was riding on the subway. A woman said to a man, I'm really worried about Eva The police found the gun in her house

The complete teaching package includes exceptional teaching tools to facilitate instruction and student learning.

The Elements of Basic Writing provides a full range of custom-designed supplemental materials to support instructors and students throughout the course.

Annotated Instructor's Edition

Test Bank

Comprised of two 20 item tests and two Mastery Tests of 75 items for each of the sentence grammar chapters (19-32), the Test Bank provides a total of 710 items that can be used for in-class or homework assignments or for preparing exams.

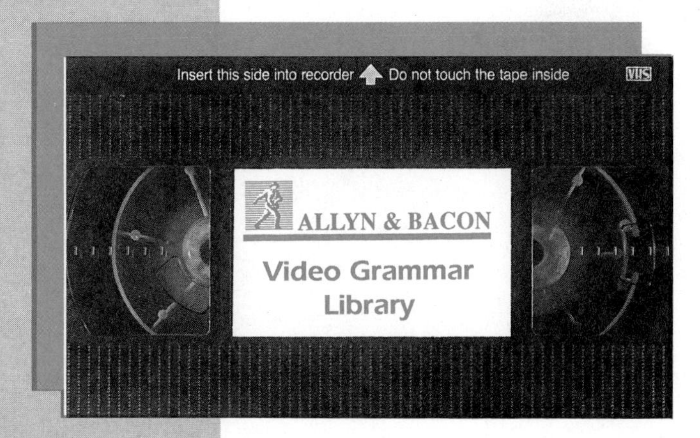

Allyn & Bacon Video Grammar Library*

This series of 5 videotapes, free to adopters, includes 10 brief (12 minute) lessons on common grammar and mechanics problems such as subject-verb agreement, sentence fragments, and run-on sentences. Two special lessons discuss how to avoid sexist language and plagiarism.

Software is available for both the IBM and Macintosh. Please contact your Allyn & Bacon representative for details.

* Some restrictions may apply. See your Allyn & Bacon representative for details.
All informations is accurate as of date of printing. Subject to change without notice.

Annotated Instructor's Edition

The Elements of Basic Writing

Audrey J. Roth
Miami Dade Community College

Allyn and Bacon
Boston London Toronto Sydney Tokyo Singapore

Executive Editor: Joseph Opiela
Editorial-Production Supervisor: Elaine Ober
Cover Administrator: Linda Dickinson
Buyer: Louise Richardson
Text Designer: Donna Merrell Chernin
Copy Editor: Sandra Sizer Moore
Editorial-Production Service: DMC & Company

A Division of Simon & Schuster
160 Gould Street
Needham Heights, MA 02194

Printed in the United States of America
10 9 8 7 6 5 4 3 2 1   95 94 93 92 91

ISBN 0-205-13380-0

Brief Contents

Contents of Student Text

A detailed table of contents begins on page iii of the student text.

To the Instructor

That students need the support of their teachers and their classmates may be especially true in writing classes. The textbook should also be supportive, and so *The Elements of Basic Writing* encourages students to write effectively by showing them how to be successful.

This text is more than a workbook, although the numerous *Activities* in each chapter involve students in practicing the principles of good writing. Through the explanations, interwoven with the *Activities*, students are led to comprehend the complexities of writing; the *Activities* are skill builders and practice for writing paragraphs and longer pieces. Students come to understand, in this book, that instead of being handed simplistic formulas that don't apply to all the writing situations they encounter, even in school, each individual can develop a repertoire of writing skills that can be called upon for different audiences and varying purposes.

How to encourage the students in your class is something only you can decide; I have no way of knowing, as I sit here in front of the computer, how you like to teach your classes. Therefore, I have tried to make *The Elements of Basic Writing* flexible and comfortable for you. My guides have been the many students and classes I've taught, the professional books and articles I continue to read carefully, and the thoughtful, committed colleagues I have talked with and listened to around the country at a variety of conventions, workshops, and conferences.

I have been mindful, in writing both the text and the *Activities*, that this book will be used by students representing a diversity of races, ethnicity, age, and economic strata.

Finally, my belief that leading students to think critically is a prime way to help them become better writers is not just a matter of jumping on a currently popular bandwagon. I have tried to teach that belief for a number of years, and hope that you will see how it has been incorporated into this book.

Organizing The Course

Writing classes ought to involve people in writing. Therefore, beginning with the first chapter, this book speaks to students as writers and immediately sets them to writing. In the first chapter there is also a questionnaire from which additional writing topics can be developed throughout your course.

You may choose to begin your course with Part One, which describes writing as a process of learning and self-expression. The chapters in this part will start students writing without the self-consciousness, and lack of self-confidence, they often bring to a composition class.

Each chapter in Part Two focuses on a different rhetorical form of increasing difficulty, from description and narration to persuasion. You may want to have students begin to work on some, or even all, of these chapters immediately after finishing Part One.

On the other hand, you might choose to begin the course with assignments of chapters from Part Two, moving to Part One as students experience specific difficulties, such as finding subjects for writing, organization, or proofreading. The focus in this part is on having students write paragraphs because they are single-idea units and students who feel overwhelmed by writing multi-paragraph papers will feel more comfortable with the shorter form.

Part Three treats the longer forms of writing: essays and essay tests. In it, students will study how to apply the principles of Parts One and Two to these more complex kinds of writing. They will have the chance to combine rhetorical forms of paragraphs into essays and will be shown how to analyze the expectations inherent in essay test questions. You will probably not want to assign these chapters until students are able to deal with paragraphs adequately.

Each chapter in Parts Four (Sentence Grammar), Five (Mechanics), and Six (Words) is also self-contained and has many skill-building *Activities*. The chapters are meant to help you teach these principles in the classroom. Or, you may find them most useful to you as individualized assignments when students have difficulty with the aspects of writing covered in these sections.

Writing In and Out of Class

Though there is much to be said for in-class writing, many students do not do well in it. The person who feels she or he is a slowpoke, and sees out of the corner of one eye that others are finishing, is prompted to rush through the writing in order to keep up with those who are faster. Of course, the thought that perhaps those others finish quickly because they are not giving enough attention to the work at hand usually doesn't figure in the thoughts of someone who feels slow.

Therefore, my own preference is for writing to be started in class, often by group discussion or initial drafting, but polished outside of the classroom. Writing should then be brought back for small group responses before the author completes revision. Even proofreading a piece of writing can be a cooperative venture, with students helping other students. Since most business writing is done cooperatively, students usually welcome the chance to start practicing this skill early in their course work.

Using This Textbook

The premise of this book is that writing isn't a mystery. Rather, it's a series of elements that can be mastered because they are presented in small steps and in understandable language. *The Elements of Basic Writing* shows students how to write and encourages them to do so.

Other books for basic writers often expect students to analyze what others have written in an effort to find "right answers." Not this book! Instead, you will see that from the beginning it helps students write on their own and on subjects of their own choice.

The chapters in Part One are related because they are about a process, and moving through them sequentially will be most helpful to students. After that, each chapter is a separate unit. Thus, you aren't locked into somebody else's notion of what your course should be, but can choose whatever order you want to follow. Or, you can use the book as a self-teaching, self-paced text for students who have better skills or are more mature than others.

In the **Annotated Instructor's Edition**, you will find answers, both definite and suggested, to all the *Activities* except those in which student selection of original writing subjects is paramount. While those *Activities* in which answers will vary may take a bit longer to look over, they are very useful to students because they come closest to modeling out-of-class writing situations.

You will also find margin notes in the first three parts of the Instructor's Edition. I hope these comments and strategies will complement your own teaching techniques. (Such notes are omitted from the last three parts of the book, because the content of those chapters is sure to be very familiar to you.)

Process, Rhetoric, and Edited American English

All three are in *The Elements of Basic Writing.* Eight chapters on the processes of writing show students that there are many routes to the finished paper. The rhetoric chapters that follow focus on paragraphs, because they are writing tasks that can be accomplished more easily than longer pieces. You can assign them in any order you choose, and may omit any that you wish. Similarly, if students report that they are being given essay tests in other classes early in the term, you can assign that chapter when you deem it necessary.

The chapters on grammar and mechanics are carefully designed not to overload students with minutiae and academic terminology. Besides, many basic writing students have been given this work repeatedly, under the guise of teaching them to write. Not all such instruction registers with all students and, in fact, it alienates many of them from writing. So, in presenting or assigning work on grammar and mechanics, you will probably place it in the context of writing according to the conventions of our time and the expectations of an audience.

Chapter Structure

Every chapter is predicated on the idea that there should be no secrets from the students and no surprises about expectations. All present information in small increments, and with frequent stops for *Activities* that enable students to practice what they have just read about.

The content of each chapter moves from the relatively easy to more complex material. In those on grammar and usage, mechanics, and language, the principles are shaded in color so that they stand out for students and are easy to locate. Writing expectations begin with the personal, but soon change to the transactional.

Chapters 9 through 16, which are about different kinds of paragraphs, follow the same format. Each begins with a statement of objectives and an introduction to the rhetorical form. Then, students are reminded of the importance of writing for an audience and a purpose, thus reinforcing principles presented in Part One. Following an example of the rhetorical form, there is a unit of "keys" to writing that particular kind of paragraph. These are meant to unlock any secrets to successful writing that students may think are hidden from them and thus impede success. Finally, students prepare to write a paragraph in the rhetorical form presented in that chapter by formulating a topic sentence—another reinforcement of Chapter 5.

Each chapter in this Part concludes with a "Recap," thus reminding students of the opening objectives and framing the chapter.

Activities and Assignments

I have tried to make the sentences and paragraphs of the *Activities* throughout *The Elements of Basic Writing* as varied and interesting as I can. They cover a range from personal and academic to vocational/professional and various kinds of special interests.

Each Activity begins with an example, so students will know what is expected of them. In the Annotated Instructor's Edition are answers to most *Activities* and suggested responses to others.

Students using *The Elements of Basic Writing* choose their own writing subjects, so you should not expect to find lists of "canned" ideas. When students select what they write about, they have a greater sense of "ownership" and pride in what they produce. They feel more comfortable than with an assigned subject and produce better writing. After all, students ought to write about what they know best—and what that is, no teacher or author could possibly guess at.

Sharing Writing, Sharing Ideas

From time to time within the chapters you will see a headline that says, "Sharing." In that section are instructions for students to work in pairs or small groups, either discussing subjects or looking at each other's writing. A few also suggest writing together. Many researchers have shown the efficacy of this approach, of such collaboration. Far from being an invitation to parrot another's work, we know that this way is helpful and supportive, qualitie needed by all writers and particularly important to basic writers.

The marginal notes occasionally suggest other sharing activities that will supplement those you have found successful in the past or think of in conjunction with this text.

Evaluating Student Writing

To grade or not to grade each time a student produces something is a philosophical question I assume you have thought through. Certainly, most students like some indication of their accomplishment on a particular assignment or up to a certain part of the term.

As students read their classmates' paragraphs and other pieces of writing, the authors receive valuable response (though they may not see such reading and response as evaluation). As a teacher, you can also respond to writing without attaching a grade—and I hope you will do so regularly.

Analytical readings of student writing are necessary so you can direct students to work on needed sections of Parts Four through Six and make their next try meet reader expectations. Although you shouldn't give this kind of reading to everything that everybody writes, you will certainly want to give such close readings to several almost-final pieces of work during a term.

Many teachers also find it effective to tell students in advance which one characteristic of writing they are reading for in each paper. One time it could be subject and verb agreement, another time misplaced modifiers, another time parallelism. By mastering just that one characteristic, students feel they have a better chance of a mark-free paper than if they had to remember a dozen things at once.

Few things are as disheartening as a paper returned with red marks all over it citing all sorts of "wrongs" the individual has committed. I prefer making comments in plain pencil (since papers I read are always typed, word processed, or written in ink). And, of course, even a little bit of encouragement goes a long way!

If your school has a rubric for holistic scoring that is applied to entering (and other) writing assessments, you know that applying it to course work is helpful for students. If you do not have one ready-made, a good exercise near the beginning of the term is to have students in a class devise one. They will then be able to fulfill their own expectations of writing quality.

As a convert to the portfolio assessment of writing, if you are not already using this method, I urge you to at least investigate it. What goes into a final portfolio can easily be governed by your course competencies. When students have a chance to select their own revised work to be read holistically in a portfolio, you help make them responsible for their own learning.

Further, the end-of-term grading, rather than averaging what was done throughout the course, rewards students for their accomplishment rather than penalizing them for what they didn't know or couldn't do earlier. Since few of us would be willing to have every stage of everything we write be graded by the eagle eye of someone who we are convinced is expert in what we are not, you can readily understand why students like to make their own choices of writing they have had the chance to revise. It makes for better reading for me, too.

Acknowledgments

Top place on this list of acknowledgments is shared by many people. There are all my students over the years, of course, because I have learned much from listening to them and reading what they wrote. There are also many colleagues in all parts of the country to whom I am indebted for the same reasons. Being with these teachers and researchers at the professional meetings through the years has been exceptionally instructive. Those who published books and articles have enabled me, additionally, to consult with them time and again. My gratitude goes to these students and colleagues who have taught me so much about writing and teaching.

To Joe Opiela of Allyn and Bacon: I never should have had breakfast with you in Seattle! It was Joe's idea that I write this book and he has been as helpful as he promised to be. Moreover, he has always been patient with me and only badgered gently and infrequently.

Elaine Ober at Allyn and Bacon oversaw production with aplomb and Amy Capute was an ideal Editorial Assistant. Extra special thanks are due to Donna Chernin of DMC & Company for quickly understanding the ideas behind this book and doing everything she and her computer could to bring you these pages looking even better than I envisioned them.

Judith Matz has been a sounding board and scientific resource person *par excellence*; she knows, I hope, how grateful I am for her contributions. My departmental colleagues Barbara Asbury, Don Geffner, and Sue Lewis were most helpful, as were these people whose comments on the manuscript led me, I hope, in the right directions:

Carolyn M. Birden, Community College of Philadelphia; Mary Boyles, Pembroke State University; Leslie Bradley, Pennsylvania State University; Peter Carino, Indiana State University; Sigrun Coffman, Truckee Meadows Community College; Patricia E. Connors, Memphis State University; Sally Fitzgerald, University of Missouri, St. Louis; Donna Gorrell, St. Cloud State University; Eric Hibbison, Virginia Commonwealth University; C. Jeriel Howard, Northeastern Illinois University; Joseph Labriola, Sinclair Community College; Timothy Miank, Lansing Community College; Janice Neulieb, Illinois State University; Joanne Pinkston, Daytona Beach Community College; Don Sieker, New Hampshire College; Betty Jean Wallace, Sinclair Community College.

To my family—Ray, David, and Jason—go love and gratitude for making this project seem worthwhile. And, yes, the book is finally finished!

Activity Answers

Answers to *Activities* that do not fit on text pages are in this section. Page numbers show where each *Activity* appears in the text.

8-8

Pages 127-128

SPELLING

Everybody should get more interested in the environment because the air, earth, and waters are all being polluted. The ozone layer above us is disappearing and so the kind of weather we have on earth is changing for the worse. Less rain is one result of what has happened and that has meant not enough water to grow food in many parts of the world. On earth we see many results of pollution in land stripped for mining or whole forests cut down so beef can be raised to supply hamburger restaurants. Pollution is also caused by the careless way people throw out paper, cans, and bottles as they drive along the highways. A very serious way the earth is being polluted is by careless disposal of toxic wastes. Some of such waste disposal gets into the water supply on land or goes through rivers so eventually the pollution reaches into the oceans where it is killing plant life and fish. If enough people get involved in stopping these kinds of pollution, maybe we can begin to improve our environment.

8-9

Pages 128-129

Sports Illustrated named Greg LeMond "Sportsman of the Year" for 1989 and his picture were on the front cover of the magazine. When you heard his story, you will understand why, which shows great determination. Greg LeMond began competitive bicycle racing when he was 14 and turned pro at 19. He was only the second American to enter the Tour de France, the most famous bicycle race in the world. Two years later, in 1985 at the age of 25, LeMond became the first non-European ever to win that race. Which is 2,025 miles through France and lasts 23 days. A few months later he was injured in a hunting accident by a relative and ends up with 60 shotgun pellets in his back and side. 30 of them are still in him, including two in his heart lining. They thought he would never recover then they thought he would never race again. LeMond had other setbacks because of illness and in difficulties in training , but he never gave up hope of racing again. By making a remarkable physical recovery, using his skill as a cyclist, and follow good strategy, he won the Tour de France again in 1989. Now you know why *Sports Illustrated* think LeMond is such a great sportsman.

Activity

8-10

Page 129

When I was in 11th grade, I worked one period a day in the school library. My job was easy and I tried to do it well. One thing I had to do was shelve books that had been returned, which meant that I had to put them in order by call numbers and by author's last names. The numbers were pretty easy to follow, but after a while I found myself walking around singing the children's Alphabet Song that goes, "A, B, C, D, E, F, G. H, I,..." so I could alphabetize the ones that went on the shelf that way. I also had to check out books for the other students; it meant taking out the white title card to file and stamping the due date on a blue card that then went in the pocket inside the back cover. When I wasn't busy, I listened to the answers our librarian gave to questions from students, so I was learning information without realizing it. I was sorry when the end of the term came, but I was proud that the librarian said to me, "You've done a great job! I hope you come back to work here next year."

9-1

Pages 132-133

Descriptive words that students are asked to underline once are underlined, underline twice are in italics, circle are in boldface, one wavy line is both italics and boldface, two wavy lines are underlined and boldface.

Every afternoon when the sun streamed into the window of grandmother's kitchen and shone bright white on the porcelain sink below it, she came into the room and closed the clean white plastic vertical blinds. Every little breeze set the ***vanes clicking*** against each other, sometimes just slowly, and other times with ***great speed and noise***. Even in the year-round warm weather we had, closing the blinds kept the *white tile counters* on either side of the sink *cool*. A white porcelain refrigerator stood at a right angle to the counter and to my right when I walked into the room. Facing the refrigerator, on the opposite wall, was a pale yellow stove, a remnant of some years before when colorful appliances were popular. The shiny surfaces of both these appliances added to the coolness of the room and made me want to sample the good food always out on the round, whitewashed pine table for us children. In late fall there were **tangy oranges** piled in bowls, ready for us to peel and eat, even enjoying the *sticky*, **sweet juice** that covered small hands and dribbled down chins. Sometimes the smell of *freshly-baked bread* beckoned us from the TV set in the living room, and there were small loaves with *crispy* brown crusts cooling on a rack on the table, ready to be spread with yellow butter from a white plastic tub next to them. In early summer, grandmother sometimes peeled mangoes picked from the backyard trees, and put out a bowl of the *slippery*, pale orange wedges for the children. These we had to spear with forks, because we couldn't hold onto them with our hands. Of course, before and after the snacks, our meals were served on the round pine table. A cloth or place mats protected it from the dishes, and usually the eight chairs were filled with family members anxious to eat grandmother's good cooking.

9-3

Page 136

If you walk into the south door of my living room, you will be able to tell a lot about my interests and how I live just by looking around. On the north wall, facing the entrance, is a double window with textured light and dark beige drapes that are usually pulled back. In front of the window, so I can get good light, are my art supplies: a paint-splattered easel that usually has a canvas on it, a high, light-colored wooden stool, and a table holding a lot of paints, brushes in jars, and a palette with every color imaginable on it. Some of the more colorful pictures I like are hung on the wall on the east side of the window, and more pictures and blank canvases and other things lean against the wall. On the west side of the window is a bookcase with seven shelves overflowing with the colorful bindings of hard-cover and paperback books, some put in straight, and some stacked on top of each other. On top of the bookcase are seven beer mugs from different colleges I visited, and two gold metal team basketball trophies with wooden bases and players holding basketballs. A shiny metal magazine rack on the floor in front of the bookcase is overflowing, and around it are all the magazines that don't fit in: copies of *Sports Illustrated, Golf Digest, Running, Psychology Today, Art News, TV Digest,* and more. On shelves against the west wall are my television set in a black cabinet, a VCR on top of it, and a CD player to the right of them. Speakers for the CD are on each side of the wall, about six feet up. Between them are posters of my favorite cities of New York, San Francisco, and New Orleans. Doors to the kitchen and bedroom are on the east wall facing the stereo, and the wall between them is just the right size for my weight bench to be against it. The beige, green, and brown jungle cotton print couch is pulled forward from the wall so I can walk behind it to the doors and the weight bench. Underneath the couch you can see some of the exercise stretchers and weights I work out with. The floor of the room is beige square tiles, so I only have a rectangular blue rug in front of the couch.

17-13

Pages 276-277

Transitional words that students are instructed to underline twice are shown in italics.

Look at the development of job titles over the past fifty years and you will see a circular movement that changed unpleasant-sounding jobs into nice-sounding ones, *formerly* sexist job titles into gender-free titles, and *now* ordinary or unpleasant-sounding job titles into important or nice-sounding ones. The changes reflect the attitudes of workers and the society of the time. The jobs themselves haven't really changed, *but* calling them by other titles makes people feel better about themselves and their work.

Being called a "garbage collector" doesn't sound very nice, *even if* what you do is collect garbage. *But* if you are called a "waste management worker," you can feel better about the job. In the years that job titles changed, "janitors" turned into "building superintendents", and "undertakers" became "funeral directors."

In the 1960s and 1970s, as more women moved into the work force, everybody's consciousness was raised about who did what work. Jobs that were once only held by men, such as "policeman," "fireman," or "postman" began to go to women, *also. Clearly,* the job titles had to change. *Now* we have "police officers," "fire fighters," and "postal workers" or "mail carriers." *Instead of* attaching a person's gender to the job of serving food in a restaurant, "waiter" and "waitress" are being discarded in favor of "server."

In times of tight money, people can't always get the salary raises they want or deserve. *But* surveys show that they do want to be considered important on their jobs. *As a result,* employers are now giving people important-sounding job titles, which is very much like changing unpleasant-sounding job titles into nice-sounding ones. A college graduate who doesn't want to be a "secretary" will accept a job as "administrative assistant." In some businesses, a supply clerk is being called a "technician coordinator" and a "salesperson" is called a "sales consultant." These people are no longer hired by "personnel departments" but by "human resources consultants."

The matter of job titles seems to have come around again to making people feel good about who they are, *even* if the salary doesn't improve or the job itself get any better. *At least* a person can now hold an important-sounding job that doesn't hinge on gender.

Activity

17-17

Pages 283-285

With the development of sensitive scientific instrum ents and computers setup to analyse both present and past information, specialists are now beginnning to be able to warn poeple about the most scary natural disasters: hurricanes volcanoes tornadoes, and earthquakes. All are still dangerous but at least whether and other reports can tell people to get to safety, sometimes before they are hit by these disasters.

Hurricane forcasting is quite accurate now whereas in the not too distant past, people didn't know when a hurricane was going to start There is now all kinds of evidnce gathered about these storms. When a hurricane forms forms, usally the U.S. Weather

Service sends its planes to fly into the storm and threw the eye to collect information about winds and directions. Radio and televiision stations broadcast Details about the developement and progress of hurricanes now, and poeple who live in the path have time to get ready. They can take steps to save there property and they have time toget away from the hurricane if thats what they want to do

Scientists are increasingly able to tell when certain volcanoes are goeing to become active enough to blow. There are 540 volcanoes that have been active in the world. Three-fourths of them are in the so-called Ring of Fire" that stretches around the Pacific ocean. It run from islands north of Australa through Indonesia and Malaysia, through the Phillipines and Japan along all the Aleutian Islands of Alaska, down the West coast of the United States, and along the Pacific coast of south America. Sensitive Instruments and and computerized Information tell specialiststhat these volcanoes are likly to become active when one of the earths plates slides over another. the lower plate begins to melt and break through week parts of the earth's crust to come out through volcanoes that may not have been active for many hundrids of years.

Tornadoes are very unpredictable. Weather specialists now no enough to spot areaes were conditions are right for tornadoes to frm. But they still don't know enuf to tell exactly wen and where the torndoes will take shape or if they will stay in the air Or touch down. On of the scariest things about tornadoes is that come up very fast, so many people dont get any advance warning at all. Another is that most poeple just don't have any place to take shelter Also, there is no way to protect proprty from a tornado.

earthquakes are recorded constantly all over the world but nobody hasyet figured out how to predit them. Most of the small earthquakes or "tremors" don't cause any damage, but one strong quake, espesially in a populated aria, can wipe out buildings and kill thousands of people. In china, there is a whole network of rural farmers who watch their animals, specially the chickens, for unusual behavior; that methid hs turned out to be surprising accurate in determining if an earthquake was going to occurr. But in most of the world, and certinly in the United States, we depends on specialists with delicate scientific instrments to moniter earth movements. Maybe soon they will be successsful infinding what they are looking for: a way to predict earthquakes.

With all the information now Available in advance about hurricanes volcanoes tornadoes and earthquakes, scientists continue trying to develope better instruments, and information to give people advance warning. Their is know way to save property or even the land in faceof these four kinds of natral disasters, but at least lives are being saved asmore is learened about them.

18-1

Pages 291-292

1. Describe and discuss the effect of the roof overhangs for the building design shown at the beginning of this exam paper.
2. Compare the methods and events used by Cavour in uniting Italy to those of Bismarck in uniting Germany.
3. Contrast the characteristics of alcohol addiction with those of heavy drinking.
4. Was Napoleon a Corsican monster, a French Emperor, a tyrant, a lawgiver, a sawed-off egomaniac, a great man, a military genius, or a butcher? Defend your answer with specific references.
5. Under what circumstances do we on earth see a total eclipse of the sun?
6. Look at this famous photo of a Chinese man standing in front of an advancing tank in Tiananmen Square, Beijing. Account for its impact on people around the world who see it.
7. Studies show that the greatest number of trauma cases occur between 6 p.m. and midnight. Can you account for this finding?
8. Enumerate and discuss the ways in which community service could help high school students feel more civic responsibility.
9. A proposal was made to the local school board that children should be taught by teachers of their own race and ethnicity. Do you agree or disagree with the proposal? Defend your position.
10. Compare the behavior of social insects, such as honeybees, with the social structure found among higher animals, such as baboons.
11. Explain how the invention of Hadley's sextant made ocean exploration safer and more successful.
12. List the factors which led to the rapid growth of the textile industry in New England. Discuss both natural resources and sociological factors.
13. While most people agree that science and technology have enriched our lives, others believe the problems they bring outweigh the benefits. Give at least three examples of inventions which have brought both good and bad into our lives.
14. Imagine that you have been asked by a manufacturer to write directions for using an abacus. What would you write to explain how to use the abacus to add?
15. Briefly trace the history of the Hate Crime Statistics Act signed by President Bush.

16. Analyze the use of Native American rhythms in the music of Aaron Copland.
17. While Impressionism is thought of as a movement in painting, its influence extended into music, literature, and architecture. Describe examples in each of these fields and identify their common elements.
18. Summarize post World War I events which led to the 1929 stock market crash.
19. Use examples to prove that introduction of exotic species of plants harmed the ecological balance of South Florida.
20. Argue for or against calling up for active duty the mothers who are in the military reserves and who have young children.

19-9

Page 307

Verbs that students are instructed to underline twice are shown in italics.

Armadillos *are* small American mammals with rough, bony shells. Several kinds of armadillos *exist* in Texas, Louisiana, and along the southern Atlantic coast. Armadillos *have* long, sharp claws to dig tunnels in the ground. The armadillo *may decide* to live in it. Insects, earthworms, snails, and spiders *are* their chief foods. Their hard shells, which look like suits of armor, *are* a protection for these little animals to hide inside of. The armadillo *cannot bite* in self-defense. Armadillos' mouths *are equipped* with only small back teeth.

19-13

Page 310

Verbs that students are instructed to underline twice are shown in italics.

Are you *choosing* a career for the first time or ~~think~~ *thinking* of changing one? You *should look* for help. Counselors in schools and colleges ~~has~~ *have* a lot of information available to you. Computer programs *print* out suggestions based on answers you give to many questions. People who have jobs you are considering ~~is~~ *are* also good sources of information. Most of them happily *talk about and* ~~shares~~ *share* their interest in their jobs.

19-22

Page 311

Direct objects that students are instructed to underline twice are shown in italics.

1. A change in Soviet power gave citizens (IO) a *taste* (DO) of democracy.
2. Reading has always given me (IO) great *pleasure* (DO).
3. The winning runner always breaks the *tape* (DO) first.
4. Please give me (IO) the *keys* (DO) before you leave.
5. If you take a *course* (DO) in psychology, you will learn about human behavior.
6. The intended receiver snagged the *ball* (DO) and scored a *touchdown* (DO).
7. The suspect offered a *confession* (DO) in exchange for a plea bargain.
8. Electronics repair courses teach students (IO) marketable *skills* (DO).

Activity 20-1

Pages 314-315

Prepositions that students are instructed to circle are shown in italics; objects are underlined.

1. The parade *down* Main Street ended *near* the post office.
2. Did Juan put water *in* the radiator when he went *to* the gas station yesterday?
3. The crackling *of* the fire brought back memories that made my mouth water *for* roasted marshmallows.
4. The flight does not leave today, but it will depart early *in* the morning tomorrow.
5. Is that a police cruiser *behind* our car?
6. This room is excellent *for* our needs, which are to practice *in* the mornings and evenings and to sleep *in* the afternoons.
7. Hillary crawled slowly *from* the sleeping bag and began to hunt *for* firewood.
8. *In* the winter when ice is *on* the lake, I like to sail my ice boat *across* the lake and *along* the shore.

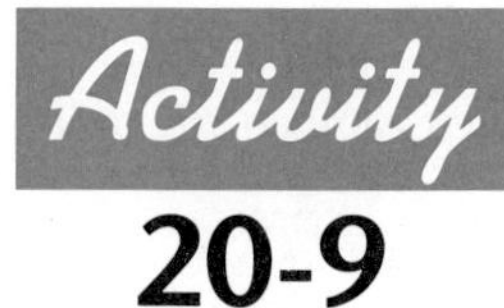

20-9

Pages 322-323

Dependent clauses that students are instructed to circle are shown in italics; independent clauses are underlined.

1. My father served in the Navy for twenty years, and his knowledge of the sea is amazing.
   compound
2. *Because the Wisconsin team has not lost a game in three years,* it has been chosen for the post-season championship play-off.
   complex
3. Helmut worked in the post office every Christmas season for fifteen years and knows every zip code in the state.
   simple
4. *If you want to mail a package* and *have it arrive at any time in the near future,* you have to send it by Priority Mail.
   complex
5. Either I am going to watch television all evening and enjoy being a couch potato, or I am going to the jazz concert with my cousin.
   compound
6. Tonight I have to wash my hair and wash the cat, too.
   simple
7. *Because no one else volunteered,* Jason drove the car to the airport.
   complex
8. It is very strange *that the phone did not ring all day*, but tonight I can get nothing accomplished *because it rings every five minutes.*
   compound-complex

21-4

Page 332

Answers will vary. These are only suggestions. The part of the sentence that should be added is in parentheses next to each number.

1. (Add an independent clause) Peter read the newspaper every day as he was riding the bus.
2. (Add a subject and a verb) Sally, an only child, was encouraged to have playmates.
3. (Add a subject) The only important issue is to preserve wildlife.
4. The sentence was complete.
5. (Add an independent clause) I stopped to admire the garden at the point where the two paths joined, in the intersection where the wild flowers were blooming.
6. (Add an independent clause) Harvey cried whenever he was sleepy.
7. (Add a predicate) The test results showed the experiment was a success.
8. (Add a subject) The governor declared a disaster area because the tornado destroyed 300 homes.

21-5

Page 332

Cats make perfect pets because they are very quiet and clean, and they do not chew up your shoes. They are easier to take care of than dogs, who need more attention and special treatment. If you ever wondered how the expression "cat nap" came about, it is probably because cats take an average of sixty-five naps a day. Furthermore, cats only need about twenty minutes of petting each day, unlike dogs, who require a great deal more attention and exercise. Recent studies show that cats are increasing in popularity as pets, since more people live in apartments today and lack space. It is nice to have a cat sleeping around your house in odd places and coming to you to be petted, now and then, while never demanding very much.

21-8

Page 338

PARAGRAPH 1:

Landscaping your lawn can do more for the environment than just adding beauty in fact, a new type of landscaping, called xeroscaping, can conserve water and require less maintenance than traditional methods. Xeroscaping requires rock or bark, not grass with this method less water wasted in summer Which is especially important in areas where there is little rainfall.

PARAGRAPH 2:

Living in a climate where winters are cold and snowy presents problems that require special advance planning for example, buying snow tires, sealing up windows, and cleaning the furnace are just a few of the things that should be done before winter actually begins. Waiting until needed items are no longer available Can make winter unpleasant buying in advance can make a cold winter easier Indeed preparing for winter can make it a pleasant time An opportunity to spend time indoors with your family getting to know one another better.

22-3

Page 343

This is a suggested rewriting and not necessarily the only way to write the paragraph in the active voice.

In the early days of Arizona, many townspeople built their city jails of adobe. Inmates dug out of them and escaped often and easily. The town of Clifton hired a miner named Margarito Verala to build an escape-proof jail. Verala carved the jail out of solid rock. When the job was finished, Verala took his pay to a saloon. He wanted everyone to drink a toast to him for what he did. The other drinkers didn't want to do that, so Verala shot a hole in the ceiling. For doing that, Verala became the first inmate in the jail he built.

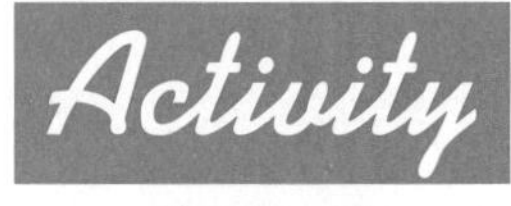

22-8

Page 349

Verbs that students change and are asked to circle are underlined.

Helmut was surprised that his geology course turned out to be so interesting. The teacher lectured, showed slides and movies, and tested the class fairly and often. The section of the course about how great land plates moved and therefore changed the appearance of the earth's surface was new information to him. Helmut learned about how large land masses lifted to form mountains and plateaus. Other land masses pressed together until they buckled and became mountains. As glaciers moved slowly toward the sea and rivers cut through mountains, the surface of the earth also changed. Helmut also discovered that rocks, coal, and minerals developed because of great heat and pressure within the earth.

23-4

Page 355

Monument Valley, Utah, was an almost unheard-of place in the 1930s when the film director John Ford learned about it. Ford decided he had to set some of his westerns in that beautiful place. So he did what any other film director would do: he had scripts written that took place in Monument Valley. Then there was only one location on which to shoot them: in Monument Valley itself. So he did that. However, first he had to arrange for the Navajo nation to give permission to shoot film on their land. Ford also found he needed many Native Americans for the big scenes that showed off the valley landscape so well. So that the scenes were accurate, Ford hired many of the Navajo people for his films.

Activity 24-1

Page 372

Many people identify with cartoon characters. Surprisingly, the characters that are special favorites are usually losers, not winners. Mickey Mouse was a big hit from his first animated cartoons created by Walt Disney in the 1920s. Even today, he continues to chased by characters bigger and stronger than he is, and he is often on the losing end. Having a girlfriend, Minnie Mouse, is one of the few ways in which he is more fortunate than some other characters in his films. Fred Flintstone, supposedly living in the Stone Age, usually ends up doing what his wife, Wilma, and the children want. That suggests that he, too, is a loser. His counterpart of the future, George Jetson, is always having run-ins with his boss that make him seem like a loser. Charlie Brown, who began life as a character in a comic strip, had a stage musical written about him, and is now featured in film specials is also a loser. In fact, psychologists and philosophers have written about Charlie Brown. They have tried to analyze his appeal to people of all ages. The latest in this long line of cartoon characters the public has made a big favorite is the Simpson family. Bart Simpson often gets in trouble with his father, but he may be most popular because he says things many people think but don't say out loud.

24-2

Page 373

The proper nouns that students are asked to underline twice are shown in italics.

1. By studying hard, the engineering student passed all the exams by a small margin.
2. The growth of home businesses is possibly a result of the weak economy and the fact that many people are tired of commuting.
3. The flowers that bloom in *May* after a long cold winter uplift the spirits after the long, dreary grey days.
4. "In-line skates," a type of roller skate but with the wheels all in a single row, are rapidly replacing traditional skates in popularity.
5. *Alphonse* was surprised to meet his high school friends *Ricardo* and *Beatrix* in the cafeteria of the college.
6. Wallpaper is not so difficult to hang, and the look it can add to a small bedroom or kitchen makes the effort worthwhile.
7. Vandals drove around the streets last night breaking car windows and knocking down mailboxes.
8. When fighting began, the name *Operation Desert Shield* was changed to *Operation Desert Storm.*

Activity 24-10

Page 382

The corrected nouns that students are asked to circle are underlined.

If you're already separating newspapers from cans and bottles and sending all of them for recycling, maybe you feel that you can't do more to help the environment. That may not be true. One of the best things you can do is plant a tree. A program called Global ReLeaf is sponsored by a well-known organization, the American Forestry Association. It encourages people to improve the earth's environment by having more and better trees and forests. Of all the trees that die or disappear because they are cut down or removed by developers, only one in four is replaced. We need trees because they produce life-giving oxygen. They also filter air pollution, prevent soil from washing away, provide a place for wildlife to live, and reduce noise pollution. Properly planted trees can reduce air conditioning costs 10 to 50 percent and serve as windbreaks that cut heating costs. In cities, concrete and dark surfaces hold heat and are 6 to 10 degrees hotter than their surroundings. Planting trees in places such as parking lots and along streets can make the city cooler.

25-8

Page 396

When Pat and *I* decided to take a vacation together, *our* children objected. *They* said that *we* would be away from home too long, and that *it* would cost more money than we should spend. However, *we* said that *it* was for *us* to decide, because *we* would be spending *our* time and *our* money. Besides, *we* told *them* that *we* would bring home presents for each of *them* .

25-10

Page 399

Responses will vary. The following paragraph is one possibility for rewriting in the third person point of view.

The study of ancient people can reveal an understanding of the problems of modern cities. As ancient people progressed from separate groups of nomadic tribes to living together in cities among other family units, it is evident that modern cities have different kinds of problems from those in ancient cities. The most important difference between ancient and modern cities is that cities no longer have unity in a centralized local government which, ideally, addresses problems on a local level. Lack of a strong local government in which all residents participate could be the single factor responsible for the increase in crime, the feeling of isolation, and the lack of safety often felt in large cities.

26-1

Page 406

In *Activity 26-1* and *26-2*, the essential words are underlined; the modifiers that students are asked to underline twice are in italics.

1. *Most* parents insist *on good manners.*
2. The *school* bus had a *flat* tire.
3. *Male* birds are *often the most* colorful.
4. A *rainy* day can be a *good* time *for reading.*
5. Fishing is a *healthy outdoor* hobby.
6. The *12-car passenger* train was late.
7. *Electronic home* games have improved *in recent years.*
8. *Wash-and-wear* clothes make ironing *unnecessary.*

INSTRUCTOR'S SECTION

26-2

Page 406

1. Snorkeling is *a safe* and *inexpensive* hobby *for all ages.*
2. *Some young* parents take *parenting* classes *to learn how to take better care of their children.*
3. *College* students should learn the basics *of note taking and study skills.*
4. *Old* quilts have become *popular collectors'* items.
5. *Car* maintenance *often* prevents *expensive* problems.
6. *Air* travel is safer and quicker *than travel by car.*
7. *Fresh-water* fish do *not* taste *like salt-water fish.*
8. *Professional basketball* players seem taller *each year.*

26-3

Page 407

Answers will vary. These are possibilities.

1. My large, brown dog usually runs through the neighbor's rose garden.
2. At gymnastics camp we sometimes played card games that were fun.
3. The rose garden contained many lovely blossoms that made the neighborhood attractive.
4. If you visit the zoo, be sure to see the koala bear, because it has very unusual habits.
5. A scary book that I read recently is about witches.
6. Boat motors need regular maintenance if they are to work properly.
7. Vacationing is fun, especially when things go as planned.
8. Wood floors may be better to have than carpeted floors, depending on individual taste.

26-4

Pages 407-408

Adjectives that students are asked to circle are underlined. The word the adjective modifies is in bold face.

1. We had ham **sandwiches** for lunch today.
2. In fall the beautiful maple **trees** show flashy **colors**.
3. Some drivers fail to obey stop **signs**.
4. Young children at play are **very** imaginative.
5. A good basketball **player** shows speed and agility.
6. Better income-tax **laws** might benefit everyone.
7. She is the girl with the nice **smile**.
8. The salt-water **crocodile** is smaller than its cousin, the fresh-water **crocodile**.

26-13

Page 417

This is only a suggestion. Student revisions will vary.

As I drove down the highway on my way for a job interview as reporter for the local newspaper, I saw a deer along the side of the road. Right away I knew I was going to like this small city! I got the job and have been happy ever since because I get to meet such interesting people. For instance, Harriet Sullivan's business is painting houses and she has three assistants. She is the first female house painter I have ever met. Then there is Mike Wilson who, I think, is a very fair person. He is the owner of the condemned building who discussed with the tenants the plan to demolish it. The only thing I haven't liked since moving here happened three days ago. When I walked through the park after the rock concert, I was amazed at the amount of trash people left behind.

29-14

Pages 459-460

I overheard the most frightening conversation today while I was riding on the subway. A woman said to a man, "I'm really worried about Eva. The police found the gun in her house!"

Startled, the man replied, "But they still haven't found the body, have they?"

"Well, that's just the thing," the woman said as she squirmed in her seat. "Victoria knows where they dumped it, and I think she's going to go to the cops."

"We all know what will happen to her if she does that," the man said. "She'll get rubbed out the same way Naomi did after she went to the police."

"Well," the woman said with a hint of doubt, "can Eva risk killing someone else at this point?"

"Maybe you're right," her male friend said. "If she asked me, I'd tell Eva to quit while she's ahead."

"Eva's not looking for anyone's advice right now," the woman responded, "not yours, mine, or anyone's."

The man responded, "You're right. But I'm beginning to worry because there's too much evidence that looks pretty bad. I wouldn't be surprised if all of our friends are in for some time in prison. What do you think?"

"I have no idea what's going to happen," the woman said. "I can't wait to see tomorrow's episode on TV of *Life Goes On.*"

Activity

29-15

Page 460

I've got many hobbies, but my favorite is traveling. In the past ten years, I've been to Europe, Japan, the Middle East, the Soviet Union, and across the United States. It's difficult for many people to believe, but I'd say that my favorite trips weren't the ones I took across the sea. They're the ones I took to see different parts of the United States I'd never seen before. New Hampshire and Vermont's foliage in the autumn are something you shouldn't miss! As for history, Philadelphia's Independence Hall and Liberty Bell are "must-sees." So are many of Boston's sights. My brother-in-law's apartment in New York City overlooks one of the world's greatest cities. Florida's and California's beaches provide year-round fun in the sun. Mountain lovers' desires can be met in both the east and the far west. There are even deserts in the United States! So, if you plan any trips across the United States, I'm sure yours will be as fascinating as mine were.

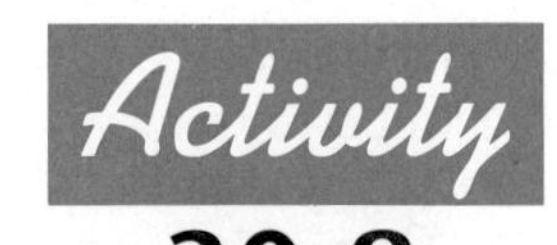

30-8

Page 468

This week's copy of *Sports Illustrated* arrived at my house on Monday. I enjoyed one article in particular about Chicago Bulls star Michael Jordan. A native of Wilmington, North Carolina, Jordan attended the University of North Carolina. At UNC, Jordan set many university records and helped the Tar Heels win the national championship. After leaving the university, he played on the 1984 United States Olympic team, leading the Americans to the gold medal in Los Angeles. The Bulls drafted him that year, and Jordan was on his way to becoming possibly the most popular athlete in the country. His spectacular slam dunks gained him world-wide fame; there are Jordan fans as far away as the Soviet Union and Japan. He is also renowned for his clean style of living off the basketball court. This popularity has led to his becoming a spokesperson for many of America's most famous companies, from Nike to McDonald's to Chevrolet and Coca-Cola. I think it is difficult to turn on a television set and not see a Michael Jordan commercial. Jordan has said that because of his position, he can influence many people, especially kids. That's why he thinks it's important to keep his clean image and help people any way he can. I think Michael Jordan is one of the greatest basketball players ever!

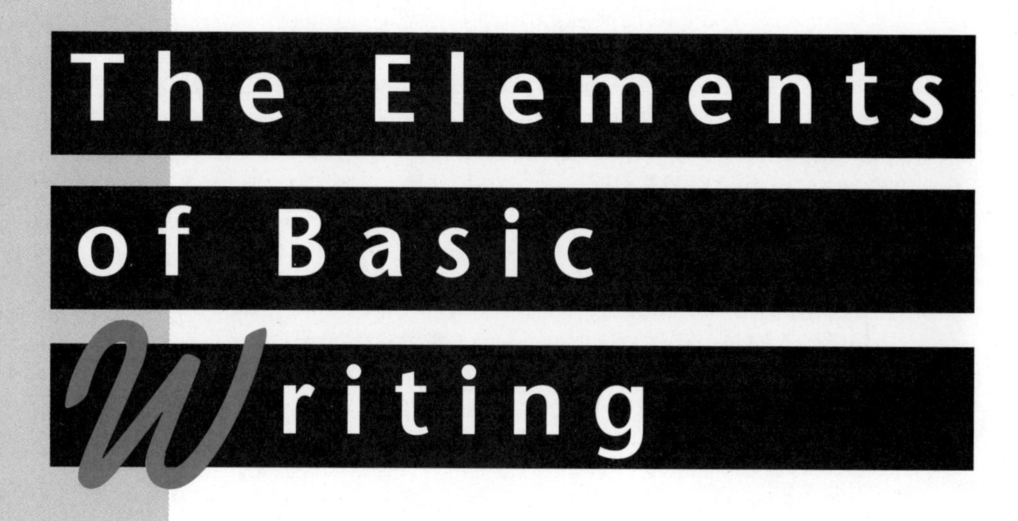

Audrey J. Roth
Miami Dade Community College

Allyn and Bacon
Boston London Toronto Sydney Tokyo Singapore

Executive Editor: Joseph Opiela
Editorial-Production Supervisor: Elaine Ober
Cover Administrator: Linda Dickinson
Buyer: Louise Richardson
Text Designer: Donna Merrell Chernin
Copy Editor: Sandra Sizer Moore
Editorial-Production Service: DMC & Company

A Division of Simon & Schuster
160 Gould Street
Needham Heights, MA 02194

ISBN 0-205-13379-7

Printed in the United States of America
10 9 8 7 6 5 4 3 2 1   95 94 93 92 91

Contents

A Message to Students

If writing is not always been easy for you, take heart: it's not easy for many professional writers. If you believe you don't measure up to teachers' expectations of what writing should be, take heart: thousands of other students, including many in your class, feel exactly the same. If you avoid writing because you're afraid of making mistakes, take heart: lots of other people do, too. What's more, almost nobody—including the professionals and the teachers—gets writing right the first time.

My message to you here, and throughout *The Elements of Basic Writing*, is that you can write! You have been writing throughout school and in your personal life, increasing in skill every time you do. Your work may not have the polish right now that is demanded of publishable work, but you can work at writing the same way published writers do. And you can publish what you write—for your classmates, friends, and family, if not for a wider audience.

I have no magic formula for you to follow, because there isn't any. Instead, writing requires that you practice, practice, practice, just as you would any skill from baking a cake to playing a top-notch game of football. This book and the class you are in will give you plenty of opportunity to practice writing, to talk about writing, and to read about it. I hope it will also give you enough insight into what makes writing that you will find the practice gets easier and more pleasurable.

Each chapter in this book is a self-contained unit on a specific aspect of writing. Each has text for you to read, then *Activities* that let you practice the principles that lead you, in easy steps, to trying particular kinds of writing or the skills you need to write.

I hope you will accept the reassurance of Chapters 1 and 2 that you have a great deal that's worthwhile to commit to writing. For the next six chapters of Part I, you will either be introduced to processes in writing or you will be reviewing them. This series of chapters will lead you from finding writing subjects to revising and proofreading your work. The emphasis is on paragraphs, because that's a unit of writing big enough to let you say something important, yet small enough to handle even in a tight time limit.

Part II shows you how to write eight different kinds of paragraphs, one for each chapter. After the explanation and sample in each chapter, you'll find a section that gives you the "key" to unlocking the secret of that particular kind of writing. The text is easy to follow, and the *Activities* lead you gradually and painlessly to practice the skills that go into each kind of paragraph writing. No guesswork for you, either; an "Example" at the beginning of each *Actvity* shows what you are expected to do.

In the chapters on essays and essay tests, you will have a chance to write longer pieces, and to use in one composition perhaps several of the individual kinds of paragraphs you learned about.

Furthermore, if you read the opening of each of the first 18 chapters, you'll get a preview of the content. Then you can check the "Recap" at the end of the chapter and find a summary of what you've learned.

An additional feature of *The Elements of Basic Writing* is that you're not expected to accomplish everything by yourself. Throughout the first three sections there are opportunities for sharing your ideas with classmates, getting responses from them, and working together to improve each other's work. Talking does, indeed, help writing.

Finally, you know that there are many conventions to master in writing the English language: matters of grammar, mechanics, and word choice and spelling. Not sticking to those conventions or customs doesn't mean you're a poor student or a terrible person. It just means you are putting stumbling blocks in the way of a reader trying to understand your ideas. Just as you like to be able to read with ease, your readers would like to do the same. Therefore, chapters in the last three sections of this book take up grammatical and mechanical principles that, if followed, will make your writing easier for others to follow. Most of these items you probably already know and practice. Some may be new to you, but you can learn them quickly by repeating the customs (to yourself or other students) and doing the *Activities* that take up most of each of these last chapters.

I hope you will find the *Activities* in this book interesting, as well as helpful, to do. Some have definite right-or-wrong answers, but many depend on your own ideas and they will be different from the responses of your classmates. However, if you do the *Activities* carefully and thoughtfully, you will soon be a better writer than you are today.

Writing this book has been an instructive adventure for me. I hope that using it will be one for you.

Part I

An Introduction to Writing

Chapter 1 You as a Writer

In this chapter you will

- begin to think of yourself as a writer
- recognize your present writing skills
- focus on improvements you want to make
- discover how you (and others in the class) view writing
- create your own "Writing Profile"

This chapter sets the stage for the book and for the classroom. It is supportive of students; it takes for granted that the students can write and can accomplish their assigned work. To help achieve an open classroom feeling, you might get students talking about what they do, other than attend school, and about their attitudes toward academics and toward writing.

Writing may occupy only a very few hours in your life, but some of that time can be particularly important. Perhaps you will write a cover letter to an application or résumé for a job you particularly want. Or you may be away from a parent or child you love, and decide to write a letter to that person. You may have to demonstrate writing skill on a test so you can pass a course. Some colleges even require students to prove their writing ability in order to earn a degree.

The higher one moves in government or corporate America, the more important writing is likely to become to an individual. In a "communication society," such as ours, much of the communication is through writing. Even phone conversations are often confirmed by letter or memo. There are also all sorts of reports and proposals and presentations being written every day by people whose chief work is not writing, but who must be able to communicate their thoughts to others through written words. People in the social sciences and natural sciences also find themselves doing unexpected amounts of writing as they share their research, experiences, and ideas with others in their fields. So important is writing beyond school that every day there are probably hundreds of classes, seminars or workshops being given around the country to help full-time employees become better writers.

Use *Activity 1-1* as a good ice breaker at the beginning of the course. After students have filled in their lists, have auto owners find other auto owners, spaghetti lovers find other spaghetti lovers, etc. in the classroom. Be sure students get the names of people they meet. If there's time, you might have students go around the room introducing people they have something in common with to others in the class.

One way to move toward becoming a better writer is to start thinking of yourself as a writer. A person who sets out to improve at swimming changes mental attitude with the move from saying, "I swim," to thinking, "I am a swimmer." So it is with writing. It is one thing to say "I write," but a different mindset that enables you to say, "I am a writer." When you begin to focus on writing and begin to perceive yourself as a writer, you will make progress toward becoming a much-improved writer.

For example, think of the many ways you can describe yourself. You could say you are:

- a student
- a person with brown eyes
- a child
- a parent
- a TV watcher
- a reader
- a spaghetti lover
- an automobile owner
- a caring person

Activity 1-1

DIRECTIONS:

1. If any of the items on the list above don't apply to you, cross them out.
2. Then, fill in the blanks below with additional words or phrases that describe yourself.

______________________ ______________________

______________________ ______________________

______________________ ______________________

______________________ ______________________

______________________ ______________________

______________________ ______________________

Did you include the word "writer" in describing yourself? Perhaps you don't yet think of yourself as a writer, but you *are* one. Being a writer doesn't just mean that you write for publication—such as a novelist or a newspaper reporter. Nor does being a writer mean that you have to write plays or poems.

If you have ever written anything for yourself, your friends, your family, your boss, your teachers—for anyone at all—you are a writer. Everyone who writes may be called a writer, and you must certainly have done some writing in your lifetime. In fact, you have probably done a lot of writing!

Most students have written more in school than out of it. School (or academic) writing may have been

- essay tests
- summaries of reading assignments
- class notes

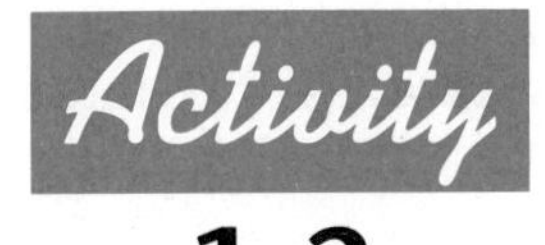

1-2

Students who have been out of school for a while may have trouble recalling these and need some prompting from you and other students.

DIRECTIONS: On the lines below, add other kinds of writing you recall doing in school or for homework.

(You may want to begin with the last year or two you were in school, but try to think back to other, earlier years when you make your list.)

___________________ ___________________

___________________ ___________________

___________________ ___________________

___________________ ___________________

You may find yourself having to act as an "idea starter" for students to make this list. Reviewing these listed items with the class is a start.

Now think about writing you have done that is not related to school. Here's a start:

- shopping list
- thank-you notes
- diary or journal
- letter of complaint

1-3

DIRECTIONS: Cross off any of the four above that you have not written. Then add to the list of writing that you do in your personal life that isn't related to school in the spaces below.

___________________ ___________________

___________________ ___________________

___________________ ___________________

___________________ ___________________

Sharing

You may have your own favorite ways of forming such groups. If not, you may let students make their own groups, work with classmates they've just met (vs. those they have known earlier), grouping by first or last initial, by birth month, by assigning each a number from one through six and letting all with the same number work together, etc. When individual writing strengths and weaknesses become apparent, you may want to group students so they can help others.

1. Form a group with two or three other people. Read aloud to each other the lists you wrote for *Activities 1-2* and *1-3*. (That is, the kinds of writing you have done both in and outside of school).
2. If someone jogs your memory, and mentions something you have written but didn't put down, add it to your list. You can write in the margins if you run out of lines.

Ease and Difficulty in Writing

Like everyone else, some things are easy for you to do and some are hard. One person may find skiing a snap but another can't keep balanced on skis. Doing math may be easy for you, but hard for your best friend. On the other hand, the friend may be able to draw and sketch very well, but you can never make a picture look like anything recognizable.

Writing is like that. For some people it's hard; for others, it's easy. Even if you feel that writing is easy for you, there are some elements of writing that are easier for you than others. For example, getting ideas may be easy for you, but putting commas in the "right place" might be hard.

Activity 1-4

DIRECTIONS: Under each heading below, list the things about writing that you find easiest, and those that seem hardest, or that give you the most trouble. (You will probably have a different number of items in each list.)

Easy	Hard
________________	________________
________________	________________
________________	________________
________________	________________
________________	________________

Sharing

This *Sharing* can also be done with the entire class.

1. Form a group with two or three other students. Read aloud to each other your lists for *Activity 1-4*.
2. When you hear someone read an item you may have overlooked, add it to your own list. You may write in the margins or add lines if you need more space.

1-5

DIRECTIONS:
1. Look at your listing of what you find easy and hard about writing. Put a star or an asterisk next to the *one* item you find easiest.
2. Then, put a star or an asterisk next to *one* of the items that you find hard and would most like to improve as you develop your writing skills.

Have each student give you a note about the selection. You can then use the student's choice as a guide to comments on that person's writing and as a check on the individual's progress.

You can use this information in assigning students to work together.

Keep both those items in mind. Or write them on a special slip of paper, or somewhere in this book. Then, as you work with other students in the class during this term, you will be able to help them with the one element of writing that you find easiest. It's often said that the best way to learn something is to teach it to someone else. Therefore, you will get better at what is already easy for you when you help friends. Perhaps you will even move on to helping others with other elements you find easy about writing.

Take the elements you now find difficult one at a time. Begin with the item on your list that you have marked as the one that you would most like to improve. As you write in response to activities in the rest of this book, work to improve that element. Once it becomes an easier element of writing, you can move on to conquer the next item you want to improve or make easier for yourself.

Writing does seem to call upon you to do many things all at once. Actually, though, you are doing a number of small tasks, and bringing individual skills to each piece you write. Therefore, you can work on each activity that seems difficult, and eventually make all of them easier for yourself.

Seeing Yourself as a Writer

Reading occupies only a very small part of anybody's day, and writing even less. We spend most of our time looking at shapes and colors, at people and objects. We are all more likely to remember a picture in a newspaper than its caption. Most people find that visuals are powerful, that they call up memories and ideas. While it may not be *exactly* true that one picture equals a

This section is designed to let students draw on the right side of the brain. Stress that art work "doesn't count," that the ideas behind the sketches are important. If you're not a very good artist, you can illustrate with your own work on the chalk board—perhaps by drawing your own picture of yourself in relation to writing—that drawing ability is not important.

thousand words, it is certainly true that pictures have an impact on people that words do not always have.

Have you ever pictured yourself in relation to writing? Perhaps not. Here is how one student saw herself when she knew she had to write something:

The mazes aren't only in Nintendo games! This student thought of writing as a maze that she was lost in, so that's what she drew.

Another student saw himself as being chased by a monster representing writing, and he drew this:

A man who feels comfortable writing drew another kind of picture.

Now you will have a chance to make a picture of how you see yourself as a writer. As you have seen from these examples, you don't have to be an artist to make this picture; stick figures will do. Nobody who looks at your picture will be worrying about the art work, only about the idea it illustrates.

1-6

DIRECTIONS: On a separate piece of paper, draw a picture of how you see yourself in relation to writing tasks.

Sharing

The need to supply supporting statements for generalities or conclusions is a crucial writing activity.

You will find it both entertaining and instructive to look at the students' pictures as well as to read their writing.

1. Exchange with another person the pictures each of you drew.
2. On the basis of the picture, write several sentences telling how you believe your partner perceived herself or himself in relation to writing tasks. Describe what you see on the picture that supports each idea you write about.
3. When you have finished the writing, let the person who drew the picture read your work.
4. Discuss how close you have come to understanding each other's perceptions.

Your Writing Profile

Thinking about writing, answering questions about it, and focusing on it help you get into the role of a writer.

The next unit gives you a chance to think about the writing you did when you were a child and about your present writing attitudes and habits. There are also a few questions about reading, because reading and writing are closely related; they are like two sides of the same coin. Each is a way of getting you to think more specifically about the experiences you have had, and about the beliefs you bring to writing.

None of these questions has a "right" or "wrong" answer. Please follow directions for each item. Some are blanks that need to be filled in, and some are letters to circle or spaces in which to put checks. Answer each item honestly in order to gain the most profit from developing "Your Writing Profile."

Part 1 WHEN YOU BEGAN TO WRITE

If there are people in the class for whom English is not a first language, this is the chance to have them discuss how they learned to write English. What differences were they aware of? This might be an instructive discussion if the other language does not use the same alphabet we do.

DIRECTIONS: Think back to the time you first learned to write. Then answer each question by filling in the space, or checking the space next to an answer, based on your memory. If you can't recall, leave the item blank.

1. What do you remember about learning to form letters and words when you were a child?

   ____

2. Where did you learn to write?

   ____

3. About how old were you when you learned to write?

   ____

This section should be easy for students to talk about because it's in their past. It also helps to establish the continuity of writing.

4. Do you recall this learning as
   ☐ easy ☐ hard ☐ challenging ☐ satisfying
   ☐ other ______________________________

5. When you were a child, did you play with pencils, crayons, a typewriter, a computer?

   ____

   ____

6. When you were young, did you scrawl on a page and call it words or writing or stories?
   ☐ Yes ☐ No ☐ Don't remember

This section is included because it establishes the close relationship between reading and writing.

You may want to build on this section by treating some of the text in this book as lessons in reading comprehension such as establishing main and supporting statements.

Most of the items in this section make good discussion and short writing subjects any time during the term. For example, what's here can be augmented with other questions. What's your favorite part of the paper and why? Which magazines do you read and what do you like about them? Write a summary of a book you've read recently. Convince a classmate to read the same book or magazine you do.

Part 2 READING

DIRECTIONS: Circle the letter of each response that describes your own reading. You may have more than one response to a question. If none of the printed responses describes an answer you would give, circle "other" and write your response after it.

1. I found that learning to read was
   a. easy
   b. hard
   c. other
2. Today I usually find that reading is
   a. enjoyable
   b. difficult
   c. slow-going
   d. other
3. I usually read at least part of a newspaper
   a. daily
   b. every few days
   c. at least once a week
   d. hardly ever
   e. other
4. I usually read magazines
   a. daily
   b. every few days
   c. at least once a week
   d. at least once a month
   e. hardly ever
   f. other
5. If I read a magazine regularly, it is likely to be about
   a. news
   b. sports

c. fashion and beauty
d. a hobby
e. a special interest (such as cars, astronomy, etc.)
f. other

6. I usually read from non-school books
   a. daily
   b. several times a week
   c. weekly
   d. at least once a month
   e. hardly ever
   f. if somebody recommends a book

Part 3 OVERVIEW OF YOUR WRITING

DIRECTIONS: Put a check next to the response that most accurately describes you. If another question follows, fill in the blank with an answer to it.

1. I like to dictate what I have to write, and let somebody else type it or do it on a word processor.
   ☐ Yes ☐ No ☐ Sometimes

This relates to reading technique and can be mentioned with Part 2 reading queries.

2. When I'm reading, I underline or make notes.
   ☐ Always ☐ Usually ☐ Sometimes ☐ Never

3. I write for my own pleasure.
   ☐ Often ☐ Sometimes ☐ Hardly ever ☐ Never

4. If I *do* write, it's likely to be

   ____

You may want to point out how items 5 through 10 are writing problems that inhibit success but that can be overcome.

5. When I write something, I have a "picture in my mind" of the person or group of people I am writing to.
   ☐ Yes ☐ No ☐ Sometimes ☐ Usually

6. I am very aware of my own problems in writing every time I start writing.
   ☐ Yes ☐ No ☐ Sometimes

7. I stop to make spelling corrections when I write a first draft.
   ☐ Yes ☐ No ☐ Sometimes

8. I try to get punctuation and capitalization correct when I write a first draft.
   ☐ Yes ☐ No ☐ Sometimes

9. I believe I write slower than I should.
   ☐ Yes ☐ No ☐ Sometimes ☐ Usually

10. I get attacks of anxiety when I have to do a writing assignment for school or work.
☐ Always ☐ Usually ☐ Sometimes ☐ Hardly ever

11. Right now, I think my writing skills for my immediate needs are adequate.
☐ Agree ☐ Mostly agree ☐ Partly disagree ☐ Disagree

12. Right now, I think my writing skills for my future needs are adequate.
☐ Agree ☐ Mostly agree ☐ Partly disagree ☐ Disagree

Part 4 WRITING ATTITUDES

Discussing some of these attitudes in groups or in class is helpful to some students

DIRECTIONS: Fill in the blanks to complete each statement about yourself and your writing.

1. When I write, I feel

____

This item makes a good "quickie" in-class writing assignment.

2. The best writing I ever did was

____

because

____

3. The thing that I like best about writing is

____

4. The thing I like least about writing is

____

This is also good for a short, positive piece of writing.

5. The writing I am proudest of is

____

because

____

6. The writing I would most like a chance to do over is

____

because

____

7. The place where I am most comfortable writing is

____

because

____

8. If I could have one wish about my writing (in school, out of school, on the job, required, not required), it would be

____

9. I think I could improve my writing if

____

Students may need prompting on possibilities here: novel, screenplay, song, something for work (not necessarily for school).

10. If I could produce one really good piece of writing, it would be

____

Part 5 WRITING HABITS

DIRECTIONS: Circle the letter of the response (or responses) that most closely describes the way you write. Write in your own answer after "Other" if none of the choices suits you.

1. When I have to write something, I usually
   a. get to work right away
   b. put it off as long as I can
   c. work at it in little pieces I hope will fit together
   d. make a plan and then do it part by part
   e. other

Here's a good time to talk about the importance of talking about writing before, in-process, and after. You may want to use this to air your views about collaborative efforts.

2. When I know I have to write something, I usually
   a. like to talk about what I will write before I start doing it
   b. don't want to bother people with my problem
   c. ask for advice from friends, family, teachers, or co-workers
   d. try to think about it by myself
   e. other

3. I feel better about a piece of writing if I
   a. have somebody I know go over it with me before I turn it in
   b. check the grammar by myself according to a book
   c. other

Point out that this is pre-writing.

4. When I have writing to do, the time I spend thinking about what to say and generally how to say it.
   a. a lot
   b. a small amount
   c. moderate

d. dependent on how much time I have to write
e. dependent on how important the writing is to me
f. other

A class discussion on how people write will relate to material on the subject in Chapter 2.

5. My favorite writing implement for first drafts is a
   a. pen
   b. pencil
   c. typewriter
   d. computer
   e. other

6. If I write something at home, I usually
   a. do it myself
   b. ask a friend to help
   c. ask somebody in the family to help
   d. get somebody to do it for me
   e. other

7. After writing a first draft, I usually
   a. figure I've said what I want to say and there's no sense going over it
   b. spend very little time going over it
   c. spend some time going over it
   d. spend a lot of time going over it
   e. other

8. I view writing as something that
   a. has to be done for school
   b. will help me get ahead in jobs
   c. a boss forces me to do
   d. I enjoy
   e. I wish I didn't have to do
   f. other

9. When I write, I usually
   a. take my time doing it
   b. do it as quickly as possible to get it over with
   c. make a quick start and then slow down a lot
   d. other

Obviously, this is not the kind of quiz for which someone can provide the "correct" answers. Nor can you give youself a score that proves something. However, by answering these questions, you should have focused on some aspects of yourself in relation to reading and writing that you may not have thought about before. Such awareness is very important to you as a writer. (It may even be the subject of writing you want to do.) And after you have worked through this book, come back to Parts 4 and 5 to see if your answers change a few months from now.

Sharing

1. Share one or more sections or individual items of "Your Writing Profile" with classmates. Discuss how your responses are different or similar.
2. Write a paragraph about your response to any one of the items. You may use the statement as the first sentence, and give details or specifics about your response in the remaining sentences.

RECAP—YOU AS A WRITER

- Start thinking of yourself as a writer.
- Recognize your present writing skills.
- Plan to work on skills you know now you'd like to improve.
- Be aware of the closeness of reading and writing.
- Focus on your writing attitudes, habits, and processes.

MORE IDEAS

1. Have students interview family or friends using all or some of the same questions as those in the "Writing Profile." Then ask them to write a summary of the answers they receive.
2. Ask students to write a comparison of their own answers to those they receive from other people on a few questions in the "Writing Profile."
3. Ask students to interview a teacher of first, second, or third grade about how he or she teaches children writing. Queries can range from how they teach forming letters to the kinds of writing assignments they give. (Children usually write simple "essays" by the time they're in third grade.)

Chapter 2

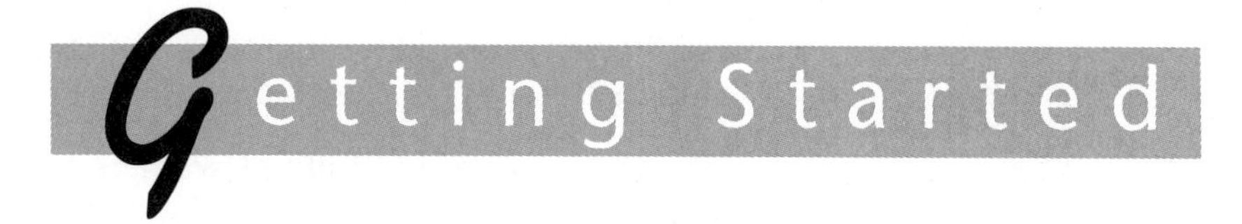

Getting Started

In this chapter you will

- consider the various forms of writing
- examine how you start writing
- see how audience affects writing
- understand the purposes of writing
- examine the writing process

Think for a moment about how many words are used around you in just one hour. How about the number of words that you *don't* hear—across the hall, down the street, in the next county? The number of spoken words in even a moment of time is staggering!

Now think about how many words are *written* in an hour. Not as many as are spoken, but the number still is probably one that only mathematicians and high-powered computers can calculate.

Who are the millions of people writing something at this very second, as you read the words on this page? Maybe little children in school learning how to form the letters that spell their names. Maybe lawyers preparing cases to get their clients released from jail. Maybe students taking notes for the next class. Maybe a parent leaving a note for a child with a reminder to do a household chore. You could add more and more to the list if you spent just a few minutes trying.

What People Write

People write to communicate, to transmit ideas from one person to another (or to a group). How well the writer succeeds depends on how accurately the reader can understand the writer's intentions.

Many students seem to confuse fiction and non-fiction. You might want to clarify the terms.

There are two broad categories of writing: fiction and non-fiction.

Fiction is material an author makes up; what is written never *really* happened, although something close to the fiction may, indeed, have occurred.

Novels, short stories, most plays and film scripts, and many TV programs are fiction. They come from the mind of the writer. Although the *idea* for the fiction may come from reality, the writer shapes it and what results is not what occurred.

Poetry is not quite the same as fiction, but because of its creative nature and its closeness to the realm of the imagination, it is closely related.

Non-fiction is writing about what *is* or what actually happens. It is reality transformed through the art of writing to the page. A newspaper is non-fiction, as are many magazine articles. Reports, letters, memos, essays, biographies and autobiographies, and some dialogues are non-fiction. In fact, most of the writing done in the world is non-fiction. It is the kind of writing you will be concentrating on in this book.

Starting to Write

Starting to write isn't very easy for most people. If you are in the group that finds it hard to begin, even when you know that you have something important to write, you are among millions of others. People in all sorts of jobs who don't particularly like to write, but who must do it for their work, often have trouble starting. Students who must write "on demand" often have trouble getting started. As a matter of fact, so do professional writers!

Discuss such rituals with the class. If you have your own, you may want to share them.

Let students vent their feelings about on-demand writing (tests, timed in-class) and writing at home.

How do people who *have* to write go about doing so? Many develop their own tricks. Some spend a lot of time cleaning off the desk before getting around to writing. Others sharpen a lot of pencils or line up a dozen pens—even if they're going to compose on the computer. Some clean closets just to avoid facing that blank piece of paper. Lots of people talk about the writing task with others before actually tackling it. Others just won't start writing until they are sitting in a particular chair with a cup of coffee next to them at a certain spot. Still others slouch down on a couch or in a car and do deep breathing exercises before they actually start writing.

Here is what two students wrote about how they start writing:

> **STUDENT A:** I start to write by using an outline. I use an outline to organize my thoughts. If I have an outline, then it's easier to know what I want to say in the writing. That makes me write faster.

> **STUDENT B:** When starting to write an essay or a story, or any type of paper I feel it necessary that I have no distractions. The library has too many people talking, so sometimes I sit in my car and write what I have to do. If I decide to write a paper at home, I can go to my room and shut the door and not turn on the TV or the stereo. Then it is easier to start writing.

You can see that Student A thought about the *method* of starting a piece of writing, while Student B thought about the *place* where writing was done most easily. Both are good answers to the question, "How do you go about starting to write?"

2-1

DIRECTIONS:

1. Think about writing tasks you do often, whether they're for yourself, for a school assignment, or because they're part of your job.
2. In the space below, name one such writing task.

____

3. Describe for someone in the class how you usually go about beginning that writing task. (Use additional paper if you need more room.) If you have any rituals, such as those mentioned above, be sure to include them.

____

____

____

Everybody writing right now is doing so for an audience and for a reason or purpose. How people *start* to write may, indeed, be affected by who they are writing for and why they are doing so.

Audience

Students have not usually thought of any audience for their writing. Or, at best, only of the teacher as reader. Thus, talk about audience should be continued through the term. It is included in each chapter in Part II.

Nobody writes in a vacuum. That is, everyone who picks up a pencil or sits in front of a computer keyboard to write is doing it for somebody to read—for an audience. If the writing is a journal or an errand list, the intended reader may be only the writer. Or the writing may be for another person or a small group of people, such as the office manager, an aunt, a committee, a project group. Some people write for even wider audiences: readers of the school newspaper, or company stockholders.

As you get ready to write, the *first step is to decide who you are writing for.* That audience, whether one reader or many, will play a part in helping you decide what you will write and how you will write it.

Here are two examples of how one friend might write to another, in a different city, about the same store:

Use these two paragraphs as models for additional writing: "A new _______ store opened ___________. You'd love/hate shopping there. They have...best/worst of all..." Let students share their work in groups and with the whole class.

Version 1

A new gift and home furnishing store, Dan's Discount Dishes, opened on Gulliver Road near Third Avenue a few weeks ago. You'd love shopping there. They have earthenware, china, and porcelain starter sets and serving pieces. Of course, you can get individual place settings in Lenox, Wedgwood, Rosenthal, Mikasa, and others. Best of all, the salespeople are knowledgable and helpful.

Version 2

A new gift and home furnishing store, Dan's Discount Dishes, opened on Gulliver Road near Third Avenue a few weeks ago. You'd love shopping there. They have all kinds of dish sets with great designs and in all the terrific colors we're seeing in magazines these days. You can even get some of the square-shaped sets you and I like. Best of all, the prices really are lower than in most other stores.

The difference in content of the two paragraphs, which might even have been written by the same person, tells you about the audience for which each is intended.

Knowing the audience helps you determine:

- what kind of vocabulary to use
- what the audience already knows about the subject
- what the audience is interested in
- what you believe the audience needs or wants to learn from what you are writing

VOCABULARY *Version 1* contains specialized words: "earthenware, china, and porcelain" are kinds of ceramic ware achieved by differences in clay and firing methods. "Starter sets and serving pieces" describe groupings of dishes. This writer knew the reader of the letter, a friend, would understand the language.

AUDIENCE KNOWLEDGE The author(s) of both versions knew that the location of Dan's Discount Dishes was recognizable to the readers, so it didn't need any elaboration. The author of *Version 1* knew that the reader would know about "place settings" and the names of the well-known companies "Lenox, Wedgwood, Rosenthal, Mikasa." The author of *Version 2* knew the reader was knowledgable about style ("great designs," "terrific colors you're seeing"), read the same magazines, and had talked about "square-shaped sets."

AUDIENCE INTEREST The authors of both versions emphasized what each reader was most interested in by putting the information in the last sentence: service in one and price in the other. In both paragraphs, those important points are introduced by the phrase, "Best of all."

WHAT AUDIENCE SHOULD LEARN The writer(s) of each paragraph wanted the friend to know about merchandise in the new store.

You can now see the basis for the difference of content in the two paragraphs. *Version 1* is for somebody who knows about dishes ("earthenware, china, and porcelain, "starter sets and serving pieces," "Lenox, Wedgwood, Rosenthal, Mikasa"), and who cares about service in a store. *Version 2* is for somebody who knows about style ("great designs," "terrific colors you're seeing in the magazines these days," "square-shaped sets you and I like"), and cares about prices in a store.

When you have written in the past, you may not always have thought consciously about the audience before writing, but somewhere in the back of your mind there was, most likely, a sense of who was going to read your words.

Activity 2-2

DIRECTIONS: Here is your chance to recall five pieces of writing you have done, and who you wrote for. (You may want to refer to your responses to *Activities 1-2* and *1-3* in Chapter 1.) Now you are also asked to recall what you knew about the audience.

EXAMPLE ▶

What I wrote: *history exam*

Intended audience: *teacher*

Vocabulary:

was expected to use terms learned in class and

teacher is an expert in subject

Audience knowledge:
lots—or he wouldn't be teaching the course

Audience interest:
likes the subject—wants students to be informed about it

I wanted audience to know:
I learned the work in the course

You may need to use these as prompts for students working on this *Activity.*

1. What I wrote: letter

   Intended audience: friend away at school

   Vocabulary: same as mine

   Audience knowledge: same as mine

   Audience interest: same as mine

   I wanted audience to know:
   news about some of our high school friends

2. What I wrote: note in suggestion box

   Intended audience: my boss

   Vocabulary: a very smart person

   Audience knowledge: knows a lot about this business

   Audience interest: improving things at work

   I wanted audience to know:
   a better way to move supplies into our work area

3. What I wrote: ______

   Intended audience: ______

   Vocabulary: ______

   Audience knowledge: ______

   Audience interest: ______

   I wanted audience to know:
   ______

4. What I wrote: ______

   Intended audience: ______

   Vocabulary: ______

   Audience knowledge: ______

   Audience interest: ______

   I wanted audience to know:

   ______

5. What I wrote: ______

   Intended audience: ______

   Vocabulary: ______

   Audience knowledge: ______

   Audience interest: ______

   I wanted audience to know:

   ______

Purpose

Discuss such daily activities to emphasize purpose.

You do very few things in your life without a reason. The reason you get out of bed after you've been partying the night before and would rather sleep is that you are thirsty and need a drink of water, or that you can no longer put off mowing the lawn, or that somebody is making so much noise you can't sleep any more. Think about several things you did this morning and you will easily find the reasons—or purposes—you did each of them.

Writing is also the result of a purpose. That is, every time you wrote the things you put on the lists in Chapter 1, you were doing so because you had a purpose. It may have been so you could remember something, or because your boss requested it of you, or because you wanted to impress somebody—but, like all writing, it had a purpose.

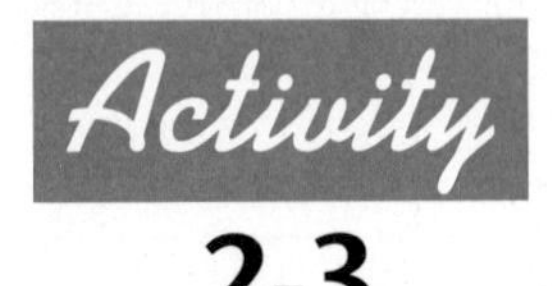

2-3

DIRECTIONS: Note the five kinds of writing you've listed in *Activity 2-2* and the purpose or reason you wrote each one.

EXAMPLE ▶ **Kind of writing:** *history exam*

Purpose: *to pass the course*

You may need these for prompts to help students recall purposes.

1. Kind of writing: letter to friend

   Purpose: tell what's been going on at home

2. Kind of writing: suggestion at work

   Purpose: get good evaluation from my boss and maybe a bonus

3. Kind of writing: ____________________

   Purpose: ____________________

4. Kind of writing: ____________________

   Purpose: ____________________

5. Kind of writing: ____________________

   Purpose: ____________________

You had some definite reasons or purposes for the writing you noted above. But the purposes for which people write can also be divided in another way. That is, you could write:

> You will recognize these as James Britton's expressive and transactional categories.

- to express yourself
- to accomplish something

What you wanted to accomplish can be further divided into writing that aims mainly:

> Let people think of other purposes such as to uplift, to annoy, etc.

- to inform
- to persuade
- to amuse

You might also be writing to astonish or surprise your audience, but for purposes here we will call that sort of writing informative, persuasive, or amusing.

If you are writing to express yourself, to get some of your thoughts and feelings onto paper as poetry, fiction, or non-fiction, you don't have to worry about what other people think unless you plan to share your writing. Then, of course, you have to think about your audience.

Most of the writing that people do, in school or out, is done to accomplish something. In both school and business, most writing is designed to inform the reader and, in a more limited way, to persuade. (See the comments at the beginning of Chapter 16, Persuasion, (page 231) about the belief of some people that all writing is persuasive.)

> Students may not know Allen as a writer, except of films. Let them supply other names, such as Bill Cosby.

Comedy, or writing aimed only at amusing people, is not in generally large supply. Even articles by Woody Allen, who makes many movies that continue to amuse us, often have the underlying serious purpose of making people look more closely at themselves and their society.

Look back at the Table of Contents of this book, and you will see that each chapter in Part Two is about a different kind of paragraph. Each of them is primarily to inform the reader. Description (Chapter 9), Narration (Chapter 10), Process (Chapter 11), Classification (Chapter 12), Definition (Chapter 13), Comparison and Contrast (Chapter 14), and Cause and Effect (Chapter 15) are ways you can write informatively. Only Chapter 16 is specifically on "Persuasion." You can, however, use any of these kinds of writing as part of persuasion, and you can combine these methods in various ways whenever you write to be informative.

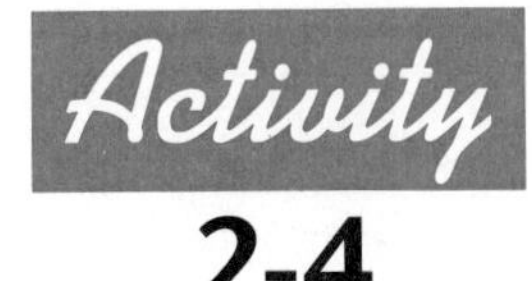

2-4

DIRECTIONS: Put yourself in the position of having to write each of the following. Determine what the *main* purpose of such writing is. On the line to the left of the item, write an **E** if you think its main purpose is expressive, an **I** if you think it is mainly to inform, a **P** if it is mainly to be persuasive, and an A if it is to amuse.

EXAMPLE ▶ A **A co-worker has been away from work for several weeks because of illness.**

If students disagree with any of these answers, let them discuss and support their alternate responses.

E 1. You have a great idea for the school drama department, and write it down in your *Idea Journal.*

P 2. The cafeteria at work doesn't seem to you to have a big enough selection of foods for vegetarians, so you write a memo to the manager.

I 3. The manager of the department where you work has requested everyone in the section to evaluate the work flow.

I 4. Your research paper for English class is due. The audience for the paper is supposed to be others in the class.

A 5. You are writing your parents about the day their only grandchild took her first steps alone.

P 6. You read something in the paper today that you disagree with, and decide to write a letter to the editor.

I 7. A material shortage is delaying manufacture of an item your biggest customer is expecting.

I 8. Your company just bought two new pieces of machinery. You are pleased with the installation and the way it is working, and decide to write the manufacturer of the machines.

I or P 9. You have had to circle the parking lot daily for two weeks looking for a place to park, and even then you've been late for classes every day. As confirmation of a conversation you had with the dean about the problem, you were asked to write a memo about the discussion.

P 10. You received a C in a course. You thought you deserved a B. Write a letter to the instructor.

Sharing

1. In a group with two or three other students, read aloud to each other your lists of kinds of writing, audiences, and purposes.
2. If someone has written information you overlooked on your own list, add it now. If your list gets longer, add lines for writing to those already on the page.

Your Writing Process

Discuss different ways that people might write. This is a good time to reveal your own writing processes and how they may change, depending on purpose.

You have probably already developed a way of writing. If it works for you, fine. Stick to it. If it doesn't give you results as good as you'd like, reading this section and following some of the guidelines may help you improve.

Some people jump right in and start writing as soon as they have an assignment. Chances are, what comes out of the pen or the printer is more like freewriting (which you'll practice in Chapter 3, pages 23-34). If you are a thoughtful person and a careful writer who concentrates on communicating as accurately as possible, you won't be satisfied with this method.

Many who start writing immediately are "writing their way into" a good piece of work. That is, within the often crazy, mixed-up work that comes out there is actually a main idea and support for it. People who work this way know that they have to aim at organization; the process by which it's reached is full of curves along the way.

Other people do some (even a lot of) thinking and planning before they put a draft of the work on paper. They make notes. They may even make a formal outline. They may start with some specific things they want to say, and later arrive at a statement that includes them all. Or they may start with generalities and fill in the specifics as they go.

THE ELEMENTS OF WRITING

Writing starts with the need to write something. You may know what you have to write about because you got an assignment from a teacher, or a boss or yourself. Or you may have to pick your own subject, in which case, Chapters 3 and 4 (pages 23-48) will be helpful. Most kinds of writing also start after you have a time limit and, perhaps, a given length.

Sometimes you have an audience and a purpose before you start thinking about the subject. Otherwise, decide on them when you choose the subject. In that case, the deciding is part of "pre-writing."

From then on, writing goes through four stages:

You may have variations in these terms that you are comfortable with.

- pre-writing—thinking, jotting, using different ways of getting ideas—may include decisions about audience and purpose
- drafting—putting the content together and writing it all out so you can see what you're saying
- revising—trying chunks of text in different places, looking for better order or sequence, improving wording and sentence structure
- proofreading—"prettying up" the paper, making it conform to current notions of what is "right" in grammar, spelling, and mechanics.

Good writers don't move through this as a rigid sequence. Instead, you should think of these four stages as a circle and you, as the author, moving from one place to another around the circle.

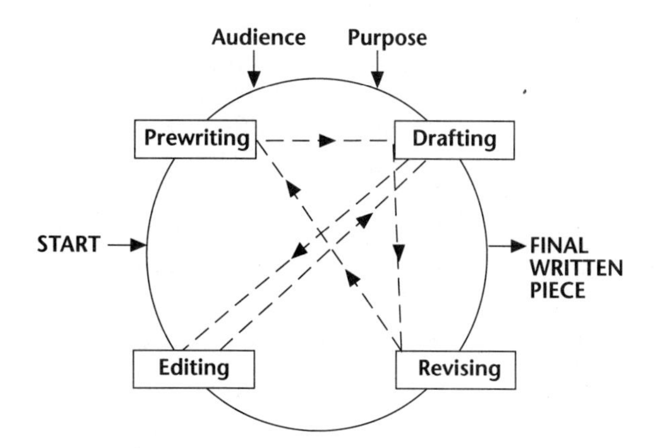

When you write, you zig and zag, test and try, move back and forth across and around the circle. The process is called "recursive," meaning that it follows a course that curves around and doubles back on itself.

Furthermore, you do not always write the same way. If you are dashing off a note, you won't go through revision. If what you are writing is really important to you, you will spend a great deal of time on the work and make a great many stops on the circle. If you write the same kind of letter again and again, as people often do for their jobs, you will skip around the circle in different ways, perhaps omitting most of the pre-writing and much of the revision. These are your writing processes.

What follows is the retelling of a student's process in writing an essay to share a point of view (inform) with classmates (audience). The subject was left up to the student. Numbering what was done is the student's way of showing the process followed.

1. Looked through the newspaper for ideas. See gang grafitti on many walls around town. Police have latest protective fighting gear but gangs don't. I don't jog in the park any more because gangs have started showing up there. Writing about gangs might be good idea. Listed what came into my head and didn't worry about writing sentences.
2. Good phrases kept popping into my head at odd times. Keep paper and pencil in car to write them down any time.
3. Words started to flow when I sat down to work on assignment.
4. I can see lots of ideas in here. Need to organize them to be able to write easily. Do it. Sort of.
5. Tinker with words. Mostly follow organization but move things around.
6. On TV news saw something about gangs and police. Was it a few weeks or months ago? Add notes about it to other notes.
7. Finally! A main idea. Police don't seem to be able to control gangs very well. Other things I've written out or ideas played with will support that. Can follow it with examples on the TV show.
8. The full paper pretty much wrote itself out. Two days left before paper is due.
9. Changed some words. Took out the few parts that weren't about local gangs. Things fit better now.
10. Made some word and sentence changes when I typed.
11. No time to put this away before going over it again like teacher says. Checked spelling, punctuation, etc. Time to hand this in.

Not everyone who received the same class assignment would follow it through this same way. The process just described worked for one person on one assignment. There was hesitation, moving forward and backward, but no indication of how much time the student spent doing any of these things. Writing doesn't come quickly or easily for most people, not even for many professional writers.

Sometimes ideas seem to be in your head all at once, but you have to separate them out to do one at a time. We can't write in exactly the same way that thoughts occur; we can only put them down in a line, one after the other. Just know that the only way to describe the back and forth movement of writing is to call it a process, something that keeps happening.

MORE IDEAS

1. Writing for different audiences is difficult for many students to become accustomed to. Try assigning writing on the same subject for two very different people such as teacher and first grader, parent and friend.

2. The jargon of different jobs is usually interesting to students, and knowing about it will help get across the idea of vocabulary specific to an audience. Have members of the class share lists of words special to their jobs. Some colorful phrases, for instance, are used in restaurants for giving orders: Adam and Eve on a raft, cow juice, etc. Tank-truck drivers returning empty are "hauling sailboat fuel."

RECAP—GETTING STARTED

- Consider how what you write fits into what all authors write
- Review how you have usually gone about writing
- Understand the influence of audience on writing
- See how the purpose of writing controls it
- Review the purposes
- See writing as a recursive process

Chapter 3

Finding Subjects

In this chapter you will

- look at three kinds of writing subjects
- get an overview of writing situations
- consider the stages that subject selection goes through
- learn three considerations in choosing a subject
- differentiate between personal and impersonal subjects
- list many possible writing subjects
- try freewriting
- start an *Idea Journal*

The chapter deals with selecting a broad subject for writing. The next chapter is about narrowing the subject selected.

Almost everything in writing hinges on choosing a good subject. Decide on one that suits the writing situation, and you are likely to have a good piece of writing result. Make a bad subject choice, and you will have a hard time overcoming the mistake.

Kinds of Writing Subjects

There are three kinds of writing subjects in school, in business and industry, in government, and on your own:

1. Assigned subjects
2. "Area" subjects
3. Free choice subjects

Occasionally the lines separating the three blur slightly, but it's helpful to consider them separately.

ASSIGNED SUBJECTS

When somebody tells you what to write about, you are spared the problem of picking your own subject. Some people consider this a blessing because they don't have to worry about something as important as making the choice. Others consider assigned writing a curse because they don't get to exercise their originality or do what they want to do.

Assigned writing takes place both in school and in the workplace. Teachers often assign students students a subject to write about. The essay test (see Chapter 18 on pages 287-289) is an example of such assigned writing. Other classroom writing is often given to you. In a literature class, you may be asked to compare characters in two plays. In humanities class, you may be asked to write about the impact a painting makes on you. In any class, you may be asked to write the most important point you learned that day.

Students usually don't think of these as assignments.

Working often requires people to write on specific matters—a kind of assigned subject. Social workers who must write up their clients' cases after each visit are responding to an assignment. The letters that inspectors send to citizens who violate local building, electrical, or other kinds of codes are written as assigned subjects that are part of their jobs. The memo a manager has to write to the people in her or his department about using the copying machine for personal paperwork has an assignment.

RELATED AREA SUBJECTS

These tend to be mainly school assignments.

Students are sometimes told, "Write about anything you want to in relation to this course." That's being given almost a completely free hand in choosing a subject. Only the minor limitation of relating the writing to the subject under study in a classroom is put on the subject choice.

Most people who write as part of their jobs are writing about a particular subject area: whatever goods or services their employer sells. For example, insurance claims processors write about insurance, of course. But in a way it can be called a related area subject because they may need to figure out what to write a claimant (a sort of free choice situation), or there may be a rule or procedure to cover that particular situation (as rigid as an assignment).

FREE CHOICE SUBJECTS

Have students discuss how they feel about free choice subjects. Do they have different attitudes depending on circumstances?

People seem to have the same attitudes toward free choice subjects as they do toward assigned subjects. They consider the freedom either a blessing or a curse. Some welcome the chance to make their own decisions about what to write. Others are overwhelmed by the need to make still another decision about writing.

Anyone who sets out to write a song or a poem, a story, a novel, or an article needs the freedom of choosing the subject. A nervous student who worries more about pleasing a teacher than about making writing pleasurable is usually unhappy with the openness of free choice. On the other hand, a student who sees in a free choice subject the chance to play with ideas, demonstrate originality, and prove ability to work through the writing process in order to learn will welcome the chance to choose the subject for writing.

3-1

DIRECTIONS: Think back over writing you have done in school, at home, and on the job. Be as specific as you can in stating what you wrote, and then check the appropriate box to note if the subject was assigned, an area-related choice, or a completely free choice.

Recall may be easier in schools with a "Writing Across the Curriculum" program. Reiterate the first sentence of "Directions."

EXAMPLE ▶ The writing was

a paper for growth and human development class

☐ Assigned ☐ Area Related ☐ Free Choice

1. The writing was

____

☐ Assigned ☐ Area Related ☐ Free Choice

Students may need prompting for this *Activity*. They might include thank-yous, project status reports, essay tests, etc.

2. The writing was

____

☐ Assigned ☐ Area Related ☐ Free Choice

3. The writing was

____

☐ Assigned ☐ Area Related ☐ Free Choice

Continue the list on your own paper as you think of more writing you have done.

The rest of this chapter and the next one are written on the assumption that you have the choice of selecting a subject to write about. However, you may find that much of what follows is also applicable to assignments and to choosing related area subjects.

What Affects Subject Choice

Four elements of writing play a part in choosing a subject:

- the audience
- the purpose
- the time you have
- the length of the piece

You may need to remind students of these four in setting up their writing subjects during the term. You may also want to use them as a framework for your own writing assignments to the class.

You already know, after reading Chapter 2 (especially pages 15-20), that audience and purpose determine a lot about what and how you write. The other two elements also play a part.

The time you have for writing may control your choice of subject in several different ways. If you must produce writing to turn in at the end of a class period or a test, you know that you must limit the subject to what you can handle in the allotted time.

Less restricting is the school assignment you must turn in one or more class periods away. Then the matter is how much time outside of school you are willing or able to devote to the writing. If the writing isn't very important to you, you will choose to spend relatively little time on it. If you have a sick child at home who requires a lot of care, you will not have the time for homework that you otherwise might.

All workplace writing is done on a timetable. The report is due in a month; company policy is to answer every letter within 48 hours; the proposal has a due date. The time allowed for writing always seems to be set—and much of it feels as if it had to be done yesterday.

Sometimes you have a stated length for the writing you are about to start. Some teachers assign a minimum number of words or pages. There's no sense in trying to write about "the environment" in five pages or 1000 words. You couldn't say anything in that space specific enough to have meaning, so that's when you start narrowing or limiting the subject. (See Chapter 4, pages 35-48.)

Newspaper writers usually have some idea of how much space their story will be given. Syndicated columnists know exactly how much space they're allowed. Many executives will not read more than a page on any subject, no matter how much money it involves, so the people writing for them know they must either condense complicated matters, or write a series of one-pagers by breaking down big projects.

This book helps you concentrate on writing paragraphs in Part Two and on essays in Part Three. Yet a paragraph can be anywhere from one sentence to ten or twenty or more. Because you can deal with only one main idea in a paragraph, you have to choose the subject for it very carefully.

Stages of Choosing a Subject

> This section points out that most subjects students think of will need narrowing. See Chapter 4.

Writers choose their subjects in one of two ways. Either they immediately zero in on a particular part of a general subject, or they get a sense of a larger subject they want to deal with, and then limit or narrow it (see Chapter 4, pages 35-48). If it is the first of these, writing can begin. Choosing a subject this way may be a matter of practice and skill, or a matter of luck. Those who depend on their skill in identifying a topic limited enough to write on in the time and space allowed probably have a good deal of subject-choosing and writing practice, so they know almost instinctively what will and what won't work.

Paragraph writing subjects must be so limited that they are sometimes harder to choose than subjects for longer writing. (You can get about 250 words of double-spaced typing on a page, and most paragraphs you write will probably be shorter than that.) Because a paragraph is limited to a single idea, you must select a subject about which you can say something useful to the reader in limited space.

EXAMPLES ▶ Choosing a picture frame

COMMENT: Yes. This subject is probably all right for a paragraph because it could give the principles in a few hundred words.

> Other examples: Distractions when studying. Pesky neighborhood children.

Wearing a life preserver while boating

COMMENT: Yes. Another probable candidate for a paragraph subject, if you limit the writing to reasons for wearing the life preserver without elaborating on any of them.

> If this name is unfamiliar, try Bush, or another U.S. president. Or try any local mayor or a state governor.

Maxmilian as a ruler of Mexico

COMMENT: No. A serious judgment about the leader of a government can't be made in a few hundred words, and you shouldn't be satisfied with making some obvious surface statements on such a complex subject. It's probably a better subject for a book, or at least for a very long article or paper.

Winning

COMMENT: No. Winning what? By whom? From whom? The subject is vague. It is also complex. On both counts, it won't do as the subject of a paragraph and needs more elaboration as subject for an essay.

You can make the same point about magazines. Most of them use narrow columns for all but feature articles.

CAUTION: Don't use newspaper paragraphs as a guide to paragraph length. There, paragraphs are extremely short, often only a single sentence. But there is a special reason: columns are narrow and a reader's eyes need the constant break of the indentation that marks a paragraph. Even this paragraph—short on a book page—would show up in a newspaper as a long block of type that looked too hard to read.

3-2

DIRECTIONS: Put a **P** on the line next to each of the following words or phrases that might be a paragraph subject. Leave blank the lines in front of those subjects that could have more than one idea and therefore not be suitable for a paragraph.

EXAMPLE ▶ P **how to hold chopsticks for eating**

The purpose of the *Activity* is to show that some subjects are broader than others, but without using such technical terms.

___ 1. Freud's contributions
___ 2. New methods of recycling
P 3. A good filing system for a two-person office
___ 4. Being a good parent
P 5. Registering to vote
P 6. My favorite chair
P 7. Starting a fresh-water aquarium
P 8. The octopus and its ink
P 9. Definition of a nuclear family
___ 10. Trusting neighbors

Sharing

1. Form a group with three or four classmates.
2. Let everyone share responses to *Activity 3-2.*
3. Discuss why you felt each item was or wasn't suitable for a paragraph. Suggest ways in which those believed unsuitable could be changed to make them into subjects for paragraphs.

This is a precursor to narrowing activities in Chapter 4.

Three Considerations in Choosing a Subject

Students seldom think about these things, so you may want to encourage them to think of all three when they choose various subjects.

Successful writers are those who give careful thought to the subjects they choose. Writing even something as short as a paragraph takes time, so don't choose a subject unless you are willing to stick with it, even through several revisions and readings by your classmates. Here are three more considerations in choosing a subject.

1. **Choose a subject you care about.** Otherwise, you may have a hard time "getting into" your subject.
2. **Choose a subject you won't get tired of.** Even if the writing takes a while, you need to choose a subject you can stick with for as long as it takes to write a piece you feel is successful.

3. **Choose a subject you know something about.** The premise of this book is that you have enough to say in writing without doing library research or any special study to gather information. Don't ever choose a subject because you think it will impress somebody or because a friend convinced you it was a good one.

Personal and Impersonal Subjects

You may want to start the term with personal writing, but should try to move students away from it. Many students are reluctant to do so, reflecting their anxieties. Also, occasionally students won't write about themselves, so alternate assignments are helpful.

When you write about yourself, the writing is called personal. When you write about ideas or events removed from you, the writing is called impersonal. Many writing classes begin with personal writing because most people feel they have more knowledge about themselves than they have on other subjects. This is especially true of people who are not very comfortable about writing.

However, college students must learn to go beyond themselves and quickly move into impersonal writing. Some writing courses demand only impersonal writing with not an "I" on the whole paper. Also, the writing required for many subjects you take in school is expected to be impersonal.

Job-related writing is impersonal also, because it isn't about the person doing the writing. Although you might know the individual you address in a memo or a letter and occasionally use "I," the wording and the tone of the writing is impersonal.

When you choose a subject for writing in classes, write about yourself only if that is the assignment. If no specific instructions are given, check with the teacher to make sure you are expected to produce either personal or impersonal writing.

Sources of Writing Subjects

The starting place for finding writing subjects is yourself. That doesn't mean you will end up *writing* about yourself, just that you find subjects by thinking about yourself, your knowledge, and your interests.

You may need to urge students to believe this paragraph. Some are reluctant to.

You need to feel loose when you start looking for writing subjects. Don't worry about the audience or the purpose. Forget, for now, about restrictions of time or length. Don't even worry about whether or not you have enough information to write on a subject; you can always go to books, articles, people, films, videos, or records that can give you information you need. Concentrate here on just developing some subjects you could write about. The sources for the subjects will be:

- experiences you have had
- special interests you have
- what you read, hear, or study
- people you know or have known
- your beliefs and ideas
- what you have seen

The activities that follow will give you a chance to see how many subjects for writing you have available right now.

Activity 3-3

DIRECTIONS: On the spaces below, list at least five experiences you have had. They don't have to be exotic, just usual things you have done.

EXAMPLE ▶ *washing a car*
being sent to Saudi Arabia
get kids ready for school in morning

1. ______
2. ______
3. ______
4. ______
5. ______

Use your own paper to add other experiences, if you wish.

Activity 3-4

DIRECTIONS: On the spaces below, list at least five special interests you have or have had. These may be hobbies or things you like to do and know about.

EXAMPLE ▶ *electronics*
flower arranging
astronomy

1. ______
2. ______
3. ______
4. ______
5. ______

Use your own paper to add other special interests, if you wish.

Activity 3-5

DIRECTIONS: On the spaces below, list at least five topics that you have read, heard, or studied about and that interest you. They may be ideas you got from newspapers, books, TV, people you know, or classes.

EXAMPLE ▶ *danger of national park destruction*
censorship directed at MTV
sports

1. ______
2. ______
3. ______
4. ______
5. ______

Use your own paper to add other topics that interest you, if you wish.

3-6

DIRECTIONS: On the spaces below, list at least five people you know or have known that you think other people should know about. Tell the person's position or relationship to you.

EXAMPLE ▶ *my mother*
Mr. Simmons—high school math teacher
Alice—my sergeant

1. ______
2. ______
3. ______
4. ______
5. ______

Use your own paper to add other people you know or have known, if you wish.

3-7

DIRECTIONS: On the spaces below, list at least five beliefs or ideas you hold that you think you could write about.

EXAMPLE ▶ *am underpaid at my job*
like to help other people
believe in honesty

1. ______
2. ______
3. ______
4. ______
5. ______

Use your own paper to add other beliefs and ideas, if you wish.

3-8

DIRECTIONS: On the spaces below, list at least five things or events you have looked at closely and that you could write about.

EXAMPLE ▶ *my home country*

subways

wheat silo

1. ______
2. ______
3. ______
4. ______
5. ______

Use your own paper to add other things or events you have looked at closely, if you wish.

3-9

DIRECTIONS: Look back at all the possible writing subjects you have listed in *Activities 3-3* through *3-8*. Look back over your lists and put a check mark next to two items in each *Activity* that you would be willing to write about.

Sharing

This is an important group activity because it reinforces the assurance that each student has much to write about.

Item 3 is a summary of this chapter.

1. Form a group with three or four classmates.
2. Let each person read aloud the items from the six lists checked as possible writing subjects. Others in the group should respond to which they would like to read and what kind of information they'd like to know about each.
3. As the group discusses the various subjects, consider if they are general or limited, how they might meet the three considerations for choosing a writing subject, and if they would probably be personal or impersonal.

Freewriting

Here, freewriting is introduced as a general way to find a subject. In the next chapter, it is used as a device for narrowing a subject.

Freewriting is a way of getting ideas out of your head and onto a piece of paper, a typewriter, or a computer screen. From the mass of material you can write in three minutes or five minutes (or longer) will come several ideas that can become subjects for writing.

Furthermore, **only the writer sees freewriting.** Nobody will look at a freewriting unless the author chooses to share it. Freewriting is a way of thinking on paper. There is no right or wrong, good or bad, in freewriting.

The rules for freewriting are simple:

- Write as fast as you can.
- Write down anything that pops into your head.
- You may want to forget everything you ever learned about thinking in sequence or relating each idea to the one before.

- If they will slow down your writing, ignore the "rules" about spelling, grammar, punctuation, and capitalization.
- If you run out of something to say, write the last word or words over and over until you start thinking/writing again.
- Start writing when a timekeeper says "start" and stop as soon as the person says "stop," even if you're in the middle of a word.

If you are writing on a computer, try turning the screen off, so you can't see what you are writing while you are doing it.

Here is what one student wrote during a freewriting session.

> This is about the craziest thing anybody ask me to do it just don't make sense. What shoudl I say? I don't no it is so crazy. The basketball game last night was great. I wonder if there'll be any party this weekend. I should be thinking about school, not basketball and partys. Well, I don't feel like writing about basketball or partys. I will go to the computer lab to get the paper for my science class done done done done. Then the paper will look good and hopefully teacher like will like it better. It will be easier to read if I do it on the computer. I wonder how the computer really works, how it can get everything down so fast and changed around fast. The best part about the computer is the spelling because you can have the computer tell you which words are spelled right and which aren't. Then when it find a word you spelled wrong, it tells you how to fix it. The rain hasn't stopped yet. I hope it stops when I have to go out to my car so I can get to work. The job is

You can see that the student moved from one idea to another in this passage, that there was a place he got stuck and repeated one word, that there are spelling mistakes, and words left out. All these are acceptable! Only the writer sees freewriting. Its only purpose is to get you started at writing, so you are doing it for ideas, not for looks.

3-10

DIRECTIONS: Freewrite for five minutes while someone times you. Use as a starting point anything that pops into your head. Save what you write.

Sharing

This discussion will also lead to writing.

1. Form a small group with one or two classmates.
2. Discuss your experience in freewriting. Do not talk about the content of the writing unless you want to. Concentrate on sharing how you felt while you were doing the freewriting, and how you feel now that the timing is over.

Activity

3-11

DIRECTIONS: For four days this week, practice freewriting at home. Write for five minutes at a time on each of the first two days, and ten minutes at a time on each of the next two days. Ask someone to be the timekeeper, or set a clock or timer for the freewriting. Save what you write.

Help students explore how they feel about keeping a journal, and about writing regularly. Have they ever kept a journal or diary? For what reasons?

Keeping an *Idea Journal*

Many professional writers keep journals—notebooks in which they record what they see, do, or think. Many people in all walks of life also keep journals. Individuals use journals to follow an inward journey, or to see the development of the self. For example, many people undergoing treatment for drug addiction are asked to write their innermost thoughts in a daily journal so that they can come to understand themselves better.

Many people keep journals as a record of business dealings or of vacation trips. Others use them to write occasional poetry or lines from songs they find appealing. People in fashion designing often keep journals in which to sketch design details or costumes they may later use for inspiration.

There are "general" journals that many people write in regularly about their thoughts and experiences. Some people keep such specifics as dreams journals, or journals that record ideas they will later use for songs, short stories, or articles they plan to write.

An *Idea Journal* will work well for you in a writing class, and especially one in which you have a free choice of subjects to write about. As you follow this book, your *Idea Journal* will be a good source of writing ideas and inspiration.

Get a separate, spiral-bound notebook that you can carry with you easily. That will become your *Idea Journal.* Note in it, every day:

Point out that these are possibilities, not requirements. There may be other possibilities, too.

- funny things you hear
- unusual sights you see
- interesting characteristics you note about people
- anything that makes you become thoughtful
- words you hear or read that interest you
- what you hear that makes you angry, sad, or happy
- ideas you read or hear that you disagree or agree with
- outstanding features of places you go
- strange signboards or ads you notice
- anything else about people, places, events, things, or ideas that catches your interest

These should just be notes, best written at the time you see, hear, or think what you write down. They might be complete quotations, single-word lists, or parts of sentences. What's important is writing down these ideas as soon and as often as you can.

Short freewritings are excellent class starters during the term.

At least once a day, look through the notes you've written, and circle one that interests you. Then, write a dialogue, a poem, an essay, or a letter to someone real or imaginary. Or you may choose to freewrite, or do a focused freewrite (see Chapter 4, pages 39-40), on what you have circled. The important point is to *write daily in some extended form.*

3-12

DIRECTIONS: Do the following two things:

1. Get the notebook that will be your *Idea Journal.* Begin your notes and daily writing as soon as you have the journal.
2. Bring your *Idea Journal* to each class meeting. (Your instructor may ask you to write in it or to share parts of it with others.)

Sharing

> You may want to start each class by having one student share something from her or his *Idea Journal*, and let others ask questions or talk about it.

1. In a group with two or three other people, take turns reading aloud three or four parts from your *Idea Journal* that you are willing to share.
2. Have others in the group tell you which parts they would like to hear more about or what they would especially like to know. Mark those passages by underlining them or by putting a line down the margin next to them.
3. Write an extension of any part of your *Idea Journal* chosen by your group.

Some of what you've written for the *Activities* for this chapter will be interesting enough for you to work with further; some will not. Occasionally, you may start writing about one of the ideas and decide it's not working out successfully enough to continue with. However, after completing this chapter, you will have more than enough free choice subjects to write about for this, and other, courses.

RECAP—FINDING SUBJECTS

- Recognize that there are three kinds of writing subjects.
- Figure in what you know about audience, purpose, time available, and length when you choose a subject for writing.
- There may be two stages for you to choose a subject.
- Pay attention to the three considerations in choosing a subject.
- Differentiate between personal and impersonal writing.
- Your knowledge and interests are sources for many writing subjects.
- Freewriting is a way of finding a subject.
- Start and keep an *Idea Journal*.

Chapter 4

Narrowing Subjects

In this chapter you will

- see the differences between a general and a narrowed subject
- practice narrowing subjects by
  - focused freewriting
  - brainstorming
  - clustering
  - questioning
  - tree diagrams
  - circle diagrams

Opening text reinforces explanations in Chapters 2 and 3 about how subject choice and coverage are tied to considerations of audience and length.

Some subjects require a book to cover them. Every library is full of them: American history from 1800 to the Civil War, geology of North America, Thomas Jefferson, survey of psychology, and on and on. In fact, there are many books on the subjects named, just as there are on other such broad subjects.

Any writer setting out to do an article on Thomas Jefferson would obviously limit that subject a great deal. Perhaps "Jefferson as an Architect" or "Jefferson's Role in Writing the Declaration of Independence." That is, an article could only be about one aspect of Jefferson's life. Even at that, the writer would have to figure out how much could or should be included. The choice will depend on the same elements you read about in Chapter 3 as affecting your own subject choice : audience, purpose, time, and length.

Anyone who decided to write a Jefferson article for a particular magazine would be sure about the audience and, probably, the purpose before starting work. If the magazine editor either requested the article or accepted it on the basis of the author's inquiry, the writer would be told an expected length and, possibly, a due date.

Students may not know that authors often write on speculation and, in seeking publication need to query editors.

On the other hand, anyone about to write an article about Jefferson in hopes of getting it published somewhere would make personal decisions about audience, purpose, time and length. If an editor later decided to publish it, the author might have to make changes so the article would be suited to the readers of the magazine and would fit the length allowed.

Now, suppose you had studied Jefferson as part of a history course and the instructor assigned you to write a paper about him to be due next week. You know the audience (instructor), the time (one week), and the purpose (to show you know enough about Jefferson to get a good grade). The length depends on how much you think you can do in that week when you have a math test and a design project also due. You know that you have to narrow or limit (the words are used interchangeably) the subject, Thomas Jefferson.

Books, Articles, and Short Essays

These lists tie in with Chapter 3 where items were given as examples for students.

Some of the examples you saw at the beginnings of *Activities 3-3* to *3-8* of Chapter 3 would take a book to write about. In fact, they *are* the subjects of books:

electronics
flower arranging
astronomy
sports
my home country [that is, a particular country]
subways

Some of the other examples in those *Activities* might make an article or a paper of at least six or eight pages:

being sent to Saudi Arabia
danger of national park destruction
censorship directed at MTV
honesty
helping other people

The last two were actually written as "[I] like to help other people" and "[I] believe in honesty." They indicate personal writing and might make papers of fewer than six pages.

Other examples in *Activities 3-3* to *3-8* were already limited enough to make a short essay—that is, six or fewer typewritten pages. They are:

washing a car
getting kids ready for school in the morning
my mother
Mr. Simmons—high school math teacher
Alice—my sergeant
am underpaid at my job

[I] like to help other people

[I] believe in honesty

wheat silo

The differences among these three groups—items listed that would take a book to cover, those that could be an article at least six pages long, and those that could be written about in a short essay—are probably already visible to you. The ones that take up a book are very general and can be divided in many different ways, including into chapters in a book.

The subjects that might be a mid-length article are more limited. However, you might think of the one on national parks as being a book, and the ones on honesty and helping others as being more than a dozen pages long. (So could the one on Saudi Arabia, depending on the writer's length of service there.)

The subjects shown as probable short essays are limited; they don't try to cover too much. Being underpaid, helping other people, and believing in honesty lend themselves to personal writing. The others could be impersonal. The three about individuals could be written either personally or impersonally, depending on the author's choice.

Activity 4-1

Students work from their own materials generated in Chapter 3 and follow the models above.

DIRECTIONS: Look back at your own listings in *Activities 3-3* to *3-8* and divide what you wrote there into the same three categories you've just been reading about.

1. Items I listed that could be books:

______________________ ______________________

______________________ ______________________

2. Items I listed that could be mid-length articles or long papers:

______________________ ______________________

______________________ ______________________

3. Items I listed that could be short essays:

______________________ ______________________

______________________ ______________________

Narrowing for Paragraphs

A paragraph is a series of related sentences on one subject that makes a single point. Most paragraphs have a topic sentence that contains the main idea of the paragraph. There are also usually other sentences that support the main idea. As you read in Chapter 3 on page 26, paragraphs may be from one to several dozen sentences long, and from a few words to several hundred. You can see this variation if you open any book, count the number of paragraphs on a page and the number of sentences in each paragraph.

You can readily see that the subject you choose for a paragraph must be very narrow or limited. In *Activity 3-2* you made some choices about subjects that could be written about in single paragraphs. Now look again at the lists in this chapter of examples given in *Activities* in Chapter 3 that might make short essays. This time, consider which of them are limited enough to make paragraphs:

washing a car
getting kids ready for school in the morning
my mother
Mr. Simmons—high school math teacher
Alice—my sergeant
am underpaid at my job
[I] like to help other people
[I] believe in honesty
wheat silo

Probably "washing a car" and "wheat silo," if the writer only described its appearance, would make good subjects for paragraphs. Maybe the ones on getting kids ready and on the job are also limited enough, depending on what the author chose to say, for whom, and why.

In *Activity 4-2*, Students are dealing here with their own ideas as sources of writing, not just letting instructors hand out lists of subjects.

Writing about each of the three people on this list could yield subjects for paragraphs if the author focused on just one characteristic of each person. Telling about one incident of helping others or of doing something honest are also possible paragraph subjects. And the one about being underpaid would make a paragraph explaining just one reason the person felt that way.

4-2

If you spot items in this list not yet narrow enough for paragraphs, have students come back to them for revision after working through some of the narrowing techniques in this chapter.

DIRECTIONS: Do the following three things, in order:

1. Write here your own list for #3 of *Activity 4-1* showing items you believe could be short essays.

____

____

____

2. Put a check next to each item on the list that could probably be a paragraph subject without further narrowing.
3. Write the remaining items on your own paper and next to each note a way of narrowing it to paragraph length.

EXAMPLE ▶ **am underpaid at my job—narrow: *times I worked late without pay and without being asked***

Sharing

The group work gives students a chance to be challenged and to support what they do.

1. Form a group with two or three classmates.
2. Let each person in turn read aloud his or her responses for *Activity 4-2*.
3. Let other members of the group tell the reader if they agree with the choices of already narrow subjects and newly narrowed ones. If there are disagreements, the proposer of change and the author should air their views. The author has the final say on a subject choice.

In Chapter 3 you read a section titled "Stages of Choosing a Subject." You have just demonstrated what that section showed: how you can arrive at a subject for writing by moving from a broad area to a narrower one suitable for writing in a limited time and length. In the remaining parts of this chapter, you will read about and practice a number of ways to narrow subjects to those that will fit the time and space requirements students usually have. Whether you have to produce a paragraph in fifteen minutes, an essay in an hour of class time, or a revised draft of a longer paper in two weeks, one or more of the following methods will help you get to suitably narrowed subjects.

Focused Freewriting

This is a close relative of the freewriting you read about in Chapter 3. However, then you read about and practiced writing that just "spilled out" when you put pen to paper or hands to keyboard. You started with whatever popped into your head.

Focused freewriting starts either with a new freewriting or with one you have done before. You then zero in on some word or words that interest you enough to follow up in another freewriting session.

The "rules" for focused freewriting are the same as those for other freewriting:

- Write as fast as you can.
- Write down anything that pops into your head.
- You may want to forget everything you ever learned about thinking in sequence or relating each idea to the one before.
- If they will slow down your writing, ignore the "rules" about spelling, grammar, punctuation, and capitalization.
- If you run out of something to say, write the last word or words over and over until you start thinking/writing again.
- Start writing when a timekeeper says "start" and stop as soon as the person says "stop," even if you're in the middle of a word.

Here is a small section of the freewriting illustrated on page 32. The student author chose it as the starting place for a focused freewriting:

> I wonder how the computer really works, how it can get everything down so fast and changed around. The best part about the computer is the spelling because you can have the computer tell you which words are spelled right and which aren't.

This is the resulting focused freewrite:

EXAMPLE 

> The computer class in high school toght me about how the computer works. It's a system of different combinations of 1 and 0. You could have 00001101 be one letter or number and 01000100 be another letter or number I forget what thats called. I remember that 1 and 0 stand for open or closed circuits. We learned things about bits and bytes. No, I don't think I remember enough about how a computer works to write a paper about it. What about the spelling checker. I am glad theres one on all the computers in the lab I use at school for writing my papers. It tells me which words i don't spell right and if one is wrong I can ask for it to spell the word. The teacher in the lab keeps telling us to watch out because the computer can't tell which word we want in which place. Red is a word the computer will say is spelled right but if you mean read the computer won't know the difference. Like if you put or and mean of the spell checker will say it's OK. Maybe there is the beginning of a paper on spell checkers on computers if I can find enough information.

The example is offered as a model. You may want to point out to students that in freewriting, mechanics and grammar are less important that getting the thoughts on to paper.

COMMENT: This focused freewriting began with one fairly broad subject—computers—and a more limited one—spell checkers. After spending a little time on how computers work, the student realized a lack of memory about the subject was going to make writing on it hard. He then switched to thinking on paper about spell checkers. That may prove to be a suitable writing subject for a paragraph.

Activity 4-3

You may want to look at this passage to make sure it's useful as a basis for focused freewriting.

DIRECTIONS: Do 1, 2, and 3 below and in that order.

1. Choose one of the freewritings you did in *Activity 3-10* or *3-11.* Circle a short section in that freewriting that interests you particularly and record it here.

____

____

____

____

____

____

2. On your own paper, do a focused freewrite for five minutes on the section of an earlier freewriting that you copied above. Save your work.
3. If you think you could write a paragraph from an idea in this focused freewrite, stop now. If you still don't believe you have arrived at any idea you could write about in a paragraph for classmates, circle a short section of the focused freewriting and spend another five minutes freewriting.

Point out to students that focused freewriting can continue in order to narrow an idea. It's called "looping."

Another kind of focused freewriting begins when you or someone else gives a word or phrase. You must then begin writing immediately, using it as an idea starter, just as you used the written passage earlier as a way of starting a focused freewrite.

Activity 4-4

You may want to have students write a paragraph from one of these focused freewrites.

DIRECTIONS: Do a focused freewrite for five minutes using one of the subjects below as a starting point. Don't stop to consider which subject you can best write about. Just close your eyes and point to a word on the page. (Try more than one, if you wish.)

losing things	fish
restaurants	song lyrics
children	job
a book I read	best friend(s)
history	diamonds
frustration	the environment

Within the focused freewriting you have just done, you will probably find at least one subject you can write a paragraph about. If not, start from a word or phrase within the focused freewriting and do another focused freewriting.

Brainstorming

Brainstorming is a technique often used for solving problems in business. It's used by a group of people to deal with anything from customer dissatisfaction with delivery dates to long-range planning and future directions. The object of brainstorming is to get lots of ideas out before any of them is accepted or rejected.

Brainstorming works well orally. People in the group all deal with the same subject and can say what they wish. Hearing other people's ideas stimulates everybody's own thinking and those in the group are able to say what comes to them at the moment.

The five rules of brainstorming are:

1. You (and others in the group) keep throwing out ideas on the subject at hand.
2. Nobody can respond to or judge an idea during a brainstorming session. That is, nobody can say, "That's a great idea," or "That's lousy," during brainstorming.
3. Someone must act as recorder and keep a list of ideas generated during a brainstorming session.
4. Stay on task. Resist picking up on one idea and talking about it.
5. Stop when the ideas slow down.

EXAMPLE ▶ **Here is a brainstorming list recorded by one group of students. They began with *noise pollution*:**

comes from machines used in tearing up streets
rock concerts
people driving by with radios turned up high
can make you go deaf
buildings—new building
make people pay fine for it
need legal definition first
people who yell on street
or in houses—families
factory machines
what's difference between noise and other sounds?
measuring it
wear earplugs
big crowds in stadium yelling
sound-absorbing building materials

You can see that the people in this group had ideas about what created noise pollution and about how to deal with it. From this list, members of the group could each select a subject to write about. (They decided, however, that each would write a paragraph on one or two of the items and put them together to see if they could make an essay. It worked out pretty well.)

This is an idea for a brainstorming group. See next *Sharing* on page 44.

1. Form a group with three or four classmates.
2. Let one member of the group select an item from the following list for the group to brainstorm. The person who makes the selection may participate in the brainstorming, but will also serve as recorder.

achieving recognition	volunteering
heroism	dishonesty
water pollution	television programs
an important task	being helpful

other: ______________________________

3. Let the group follow the brainstorming "rules" above.
4. When conversation stops, the recorder should read aloud the list to be sure everyone's contribution has been recorded.
5. Rotate the topic-selecting/recording until each member of the group has had a chance to serve in those ways.
6. Let the group decide if it wants to write (now or later) about any of the subjects generated, either individually or as a group.

Students usually enjoy this sort of cooperative essay writing with everyone participating—especially if they can make it silly, should they wish.

You can adapt the brainstorming method of getting ideas, even if you are alone. Just write out your own brainstorming list. That is, start with a subject and put down every idea that occurs to you. Don't worry about details or logic. Aim at keeping ideas flowing and writing down enough about each one that you can choose from among them for a writing subject.

Activity 4-5

DIRECTIONS: Practice brainstorming by yourself. Do 1 and 2, in order.

1. Choose one of the topics from the following group and write it at the top of a piece of paper. Remember to follow the five brainstorming rules. Then make your brainstorming list.

a local problem	used cars
global warming	attending college
collecting (things)	respect
pets	health

other: ______________________

2. When you have finished brainstorming, put a check next to those items on your list you think you could write a paragraph about. Put an X next to those items you could write about if you narrowed them a little more.

You should ask to see this brainstorming list. You may want to have students write paragraphs from among those checked.

Clustering

When you are brainstorming (either orally with others or in writing by yourself), one idea prompts another. That's the key to both ways of brainstorming. When the ideas are coming to you one after another, they may not seem to be connected. Later, when you look at a brainstorming list, you may start to notice connections.

Many students who have recently been in high school are already familiar with clustering, though they may not have used it for narrowing subjects. Almost unanimously, they like using it to develop specifics of content for writing.

Clustering is an adaptation of brainstorming on paper that does two things:

1. It helps you get ideas from your head onto paper.
2. It helps you organize those ideas while you write them down.

These things happen because **clustering is a *picture* of ideas and relationships** rather than just a list of words. In fact, many people find that clustering is easy to work with because they can note things as they think of them.

Begin clustering by writing down a subject and drawing a circle around it. Then, as ideas come, connect them with lines either to the beginning subject or to each other. Here is an example of one student's clustering of professional sports.

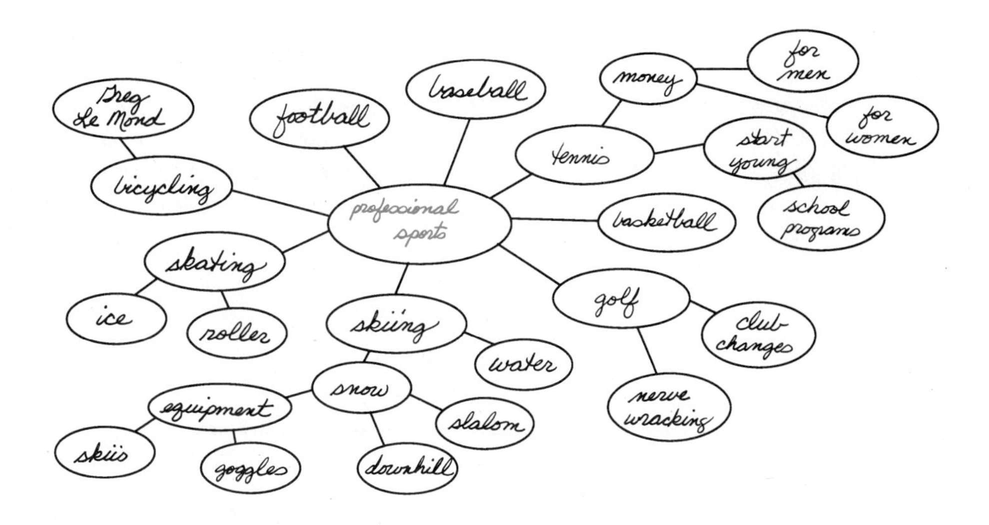

The man who did this started by thinking of different kinds of professional sports. He followed through on some of them, abandoned them, and moved on to another circle naming a sport.

Note that the "arms" or lines of the clustering are uneven and that some have more circles on them than others. That's the way clustering works. You should never feel that anything in clustering has to be "evened up."

By looking at this cluster, you get a picture of the many relationships the man who drew it saw among ideas that came to his mind about professional sports. Although narrower than the starting point, only some of the items in this cluster could be a subject for writing. Given the assignment of writing a paragraph, this student decided to focus on professional tennis—still far too much to write about—and do more clustering as a way of narrowing the subject.

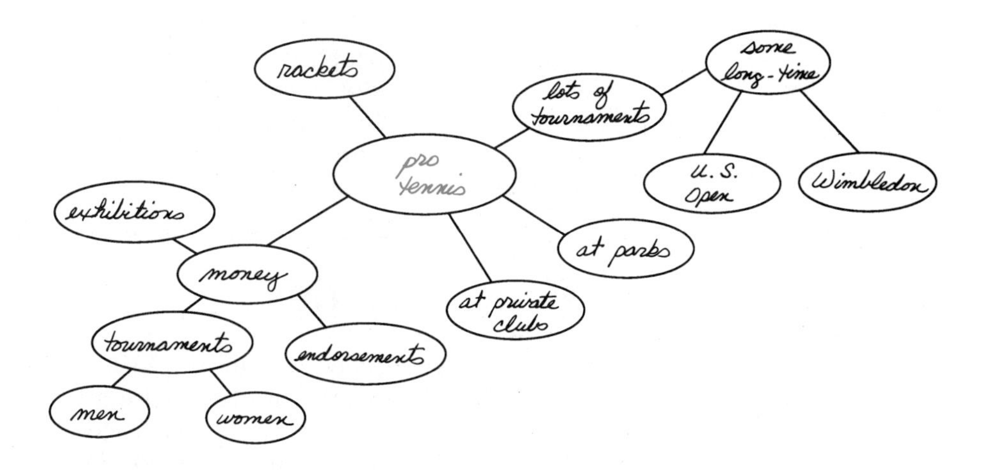

This time the subject of the money for professional tennis players came out of the clustering for further narrowing. The branching of that cluster will give you an idea about the content of the paragraph.

Activity 4-6

DIRECTIONS: Choose one of the following subjects as the start of a practice cluster. On your own paper, write your selection in the center circle. Use it as the start of a cluster and make as many connections (branches) as you wish in whatever order is comfortable.

relatives	hobbies
music	annoyances
junk food	X-rated movies
success	punishment

other: ____________________________________

Sharing

Hearing others explain their clusters and then having to give a personal explanation is good reinforcement for students.

1. Join with two or three classmates to form a group.
2. Let each person in the group share the cluster done for *Activity 4-6*. While examining each person's cluster, group members should ask the originator about the wording or flow of ideas the cluster shows.
3. Each member of the group should receive suggestions from the others about which branch or item in the cluster they would be interested in reading about.

4-7

This returns to student-generated subjects.

DIRECTIONS: Look back at lists you wrote for 1 and 2 in *Activity 4-1*. Choose one of the broad items on either list to use as a starting point for narrowing to a writing subject using clustering.

Write that broad subject here:

____

____

On your own paper, narrow it by clustering. When you have finished the cluster, use a color pen or pencil to circle a unit or a branch that is narrow enough to write a paragraph from. (If necessary, do an additional clustering. Use your own paper but keep it with this cluster to show your instructor or other students.)

You may need to remind students that this is only a model of the general kinds of questions that can be asked and no one should feel that success will follow from its slavish imitation. Again, students may be familiar with asking questions to elicit specifics for writing, but not with doing so for narrowing.

Asking Questions

The story goes that reporters are taught to ask five questions in order to get all the information they need to write a news item: who? what? where? when? why? These questions are also a good way to narrow a writing subject. You might also add three more: how? what if? so what?

- **Who** are the important people in this field? Who is involved in this event or in others like it? Who do you want the audience to know about?

- **What** is going on in this field? In this location? Is there something new about it my audience would be interested in learning?
- **Where** does this occur? Can it take place anywhere, or just in a limited place?
- **When** did this happen? When will it happen?
- **Why** did the person behave in this way? Why did this happen? Why will this happen? Why is it made this way?
- **How** did this happen? How did the person come to this conclusion? How did the person develop this way?
- **What if** you changed one element? What if you rearranged the parts?
- **So what?** Why does this matter?

Now let's see how these questions can serve you as a way of narrowing a broad subject and lead you to one limited enough to use for writing. Each question you ask is a narrowing of that broad subject. Answering any of them could be at least a paragraph.

Start with a broad subject: fishing. You'll find book after book on the subject in libraries, bookstores, and sporting equipment stores. Next, ask the eight questions about the broad subject.

EXAMPLE 

You may have to show students how these kinds of questions can be asked about their own topics. Note, also, that these specific questions may differ from those in the general model because of the influence of the broad subject.

Who is fishing these days (freshwater or salt water)?
What does the sale of state or local licenses reveal? Who are commercial fishermen today? Who are some well known people who have shown their interest in fishing (as Hemingway did)?
What do people find so great about fishing as a hobby? A sport? What kind of living do commercial fishermen make? What sort of life do they lead? What effect has water pollution had on sport or commercial fishing? What changes, if any, have there been recently in fishing equipment?
Where are good local fishing areas? For what kind of fish? Where are the best sport fishing locations in the world and how did they get that reputation?
When is the best time to go after certain fish? When is a good age to teach children fishing? When did people start to go sport fishing? When did states start to require fishing licenses?
Why is fishing such a popular pastime? Why did states or communities start regulating fishing? Why is stocking lakes and rivers practiced? Why are different kinds of rods and reels constructed the way they are?
How can I learn to fish if I don't know anybody who does it? How are rods made? How are lures selected? How are flies tied?
What if commercial fishing for certain species were to be stopped? What if all edible fish came from fish farms? What if the government prevented fishing in the Great Lakes?
So what? Why so much interest in fishing, anyway?

Any of the many questions coming from those first eight words and phrases is a narrowed subject for writing. The answer to the one you choose will result in at least a paragraph.

4-8

Here, and elsewhere in this chapter, students are asked to write on their own paper to save space in the book. You may want to have those papers kept at this page.

You may need to prompt students with the first few questions on some of these subjects.

Students can be asked to write a paragraph on one of their three selections.

DIRECTIONS: Do number 1 on your own paper. Then write the answers to numbers 2 and 3 below.

1. Choose one of the following subjects about which to ask as many questions as you can. Write the questions in a list, using the example above as a guide.

   computers　　boats
   equality　　heroes
   betting　　space flight
   other: ______________________

2. What did you select as your broad subject to ask questions about?
3. On the lines below, note three of the questions you wrote that are narrow enough to answer in a paragraph.

   a. ______________________
   ____
   b. ______________________
   ____
   c. ______________________
   ____

Sharing

1. Form a group with three or four classmates. Read aloud your starting broad subject and your list of questions.
2. Let others in the group suggest additional questions on the subject that they would be interested in hearing answers to.
3. Continue so that each person has a turn in reading and receiving more questions from others in the group.
4. Make sure that each question asked really does narrow the broad subject.

Activity 4-9

Students can be asked to write a paragraph on one of their three selections.

DIRECTIONS: Do 1, 2, and 3 in sequence.

1. Choose one item from the lists you wrote for 1 and 2 of *Activity 4-1* that could be narrowed by asking questions. Write that broad subject on your own paper.
2. Using your own paper, write as many questions as you can that will narrow that subject.
3. On the lines below, note three of the questions you wrote that are narrow enough to answer in a paragraph.

   a. ______________________
   ____
   b. ______________________
   ____
   c. ______________________
   ____

Tree Diagram

Tree diagrams are generally familiar to students. They appear in a number of natural science and social science textbooks, However, they are somewhat harder to develop for narrowing topics than are other techniques in this chapter, because they require more logical thinking.

A tree diagram—so called because it looks very much like a modernistic tree with branches or the horizontal and vertical lines used to show a family tree—is still another way to narrow a subject. When you make a tree diagram, you are held to a particular sequence and must make one idea follow from another.

The fact that you must follow a sequence when you make a tree diagram makes it different from a cluster, which allows you to write down ideas in whatever order they occur to you. The tree diagram acts as a prompt to make you think in a given order.

Start with writing the broad subject on the top line. Each division that comes from it rates a word or two as branches of the vertical lines coming from it. As you go further down in the diagram, you are dividing and narrowing the elements.

The student who made this tree diagram started with cars.

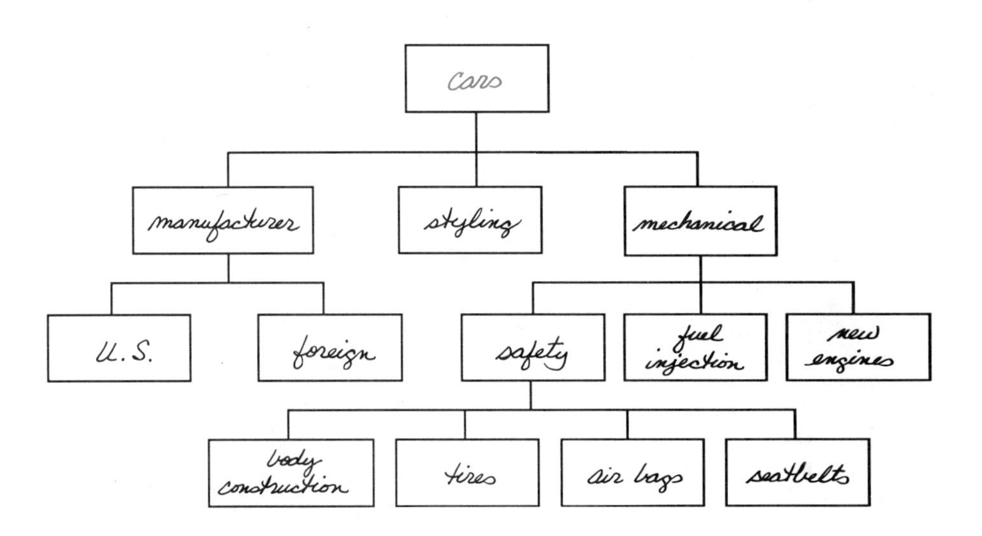

You can see how the person who made this tree diagram seems to have narrowed the broad subject of cars to safety features. Because other branches from the original subject are not divided still further, we can infer that the student either didn't know enough to take them further or didn't want to. At any rate, the tree served its purpose in leading to the narrowed subject of auto safety features for writing.

Circle Diagram

This is the most difficult and most limiting of the methods for narrowing shown in this chapter.

Another way of narrowing broad writing subjects is to make a circle diagram. Start by drawing a fairly large circle and labeling it with the broad subject. Inside it, draw a series of successively smaller circles, giving each a label of more and more narrow aspects of the broad subject. The resulting circle diagram looks like a target with writing in each circle.

The circle diagram is probably most helpful if you have a fairly definite sense of narrowing the broad subject but want to see how to get to the narrowed part—the inside circle—most quickly. To use this method, you must follow through from the starting subject without letting yourself even think about related ideas. Sometimes, such a forced focus is very helpful.

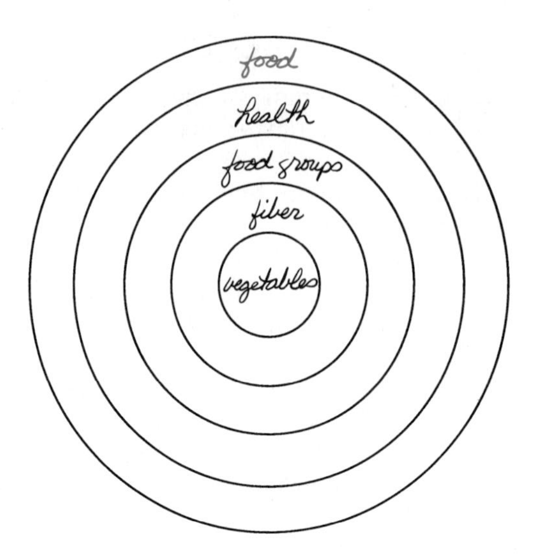

Activity
4-10

DIRECTIONS: On your own paper, make *either* a tree diagram or a circle diagram on one of the following broad subjects:

vacations	job security
shopping	responsibility
college	city planning
other:	

4-11

Note that this makes use of the *Idea Journal* students, mentioned near the end of Chapter 3 were asked to start keeping.

DIRECTIONS: On your own paper, do 1, 2, and 3 in order.

1. Look in your *Idea Journal* to find a writing subject that interests you but would turn out to be longer than a paragraph. Write that subject first.
2. Narrow it to make it suitable for a paragraph by using one of the methods described in this chapter. Check the box next to the one you will use: ☐ focused freewriting ☐ brainstorming
   ☐ clustering ☐ questioning
   ☐ tree diagram ☐ circle diagram
3. Write a paragraph based on the narrowed subject you developed.

RECAP—NARROWING SUBJECTS

- Know when a writing subject is suited to a book, a long paper, a short essay, or a paragraph.
- Focused freewriting is a way of narrowing subjects.
- Brainstorming, orally with a group or on paper by yourself, is a way of narrowing subjects.
- Clustering shows a picture of how you think through narrowing a subject.
- Questioning a broad subject is a way of narrowing.
- A tree diagram is a fairly direct way of narrowing a broad subject.
- A circle diagram is the most direct way of narrowing a subject for writing.

Chapter 5

Topic Sentences

In this chapter you will

- learn what a topic sentence is
- put ideas together for topic sentences
- examine the five requirements for topic sentences
- learn three ways to write topic sentences
- practice writing useful topic sentences
- consider three places topic sentences appear in paragraphs
- identify stated topic sentences in paragraphs

Once you have a subject narrow enough to write about, you are ready to construct the series of related sentences about it that will make a paragraph. As you already know from Chapter 4 (page 37), the paragraph makes a single point, usually called a main idea. All the sentences in it support the one main idea.

The statement of the main idea in a paragraph is called its **topic sentence.** It gives a reader (that is, the audience) two important pieces of information.

1. It tells the subject or what the paragraph is about.
2. It tells what the author wants the reader to know about that subject.

Because the topic sentence states what the audience should get out of reading a paragraph, it is important to each reader. The topic sentence is also important to the writer because *it sets out the information to be included in the paragraph.* For that reason, you should practice writing a topic sentence before you start writing the paragraph for which it is the main idea. The topic sentence is a *general statement*. The rest of the sentences in a paragraph support or elaborate on it; they are all more specific than the topic sentence.

The subject/predicate = narrowed subject/telling audience gives students two ways of looking at topic sentences.

Like all sentences, the topic sentence will have two parts: a subject and a predicate. (See Chapter 19, pages 300-312, to refresh your memory on subjects and verbs/predicates.) You can probably use the narrowed subject you arrived aT as the subject of the topic sentence, or what the paragraph is about. Then, decide what one, main thing you want the reader (audience) to know about that subject. That becomes the predicate (which includes the verb) of the topic sentence. Put the two parts together and you have a topic sentence.

EXAMPLES 

Narrowed subject: seat covers for my new car
I want audience to know: I had a really hard time finding them.
Topic sentence: Seat covers for my new car seemed impossible to find.

Narrowed subject: delivering meals to the elderly
I want audience to know: it's a way to feel helpful
Topic sentence: Delivering meals to the elderly is a way to feel that you are helpful to people.

Activity 5-1

DIRECTIONS: You will recognize most of the subjects below as examples of narrowed subjects given in Chapter 4. Each has been supplied with something an audience should know. Based on those two pieces of information, write a topic sentence for each item. You may need to add or change a few words to make a sensible sentence.

EXAMPLE 

Using subjects that appeared in Chapter 4 establishes the continuity of the writing process. It also lets students see how to go from subject to topic sentence.

Subject: packaged food labeling
Audience should know: will start meeting new government standards
Topic sentence:

Packaged food labeling will gradually start to meet new government standards.

This rather simple exercise eases students into actually writing topic sentences without worrying about the information to include.

1. **Subject:** washing cars
   Audience should know: makes a good part-time job for teens
   Topic sentence:

   Washing cars can be a good part-time job for teens.

2. **Subject:** getting kids ready for school in the morning
   Audience should know: depends on organizational ability
   Topic sentence:

   Getting kids ready for school in the morning depends on an adult's organizational ability.

3. **Subject:** work late without extra pay
   Audience should know: I have strong sense of responsibility
   Topic sentence:
   I often work late without extra pay because I have a strong sense of responsibility about my job.

4. **Subject:** computer spell checkers
   Audience should know: they can't check spelling as well as a person can
   Topic sentence:
   Computer spell checkers still can't check spelling as well as a person can.

5. **Subject:** noise pollution in factories
   Audience should know: should stop because workers can have hearing loss
   Topic sentence:
   Factories should stop noise pollution because it can cause workers to have hearing loss.

6. **Subject:** attending this college
   Audience should know: has already given me a start on a vocation
   Topic sentence:
   Attending this college has already given me a good start on the vocation I'm aiming for.

7. **Subject:** fishing for snook
   Audience should know: brings many anglers to the mangroves of south Florida
   Topic sentence:
   The chance to fish for snook brings many dedicated anglers to the mangroves of south Florida.

8. **Subject:** my Uncle Bill
   Audience should know: is my idea of a hero
   Topic sentence:
   My Uncle Bill is my idea of a heroic person.

These topic sentences were mostly written for you because both the subject and predicate parts were supplied. In the next two sections, you will learn the requirements of a topic sentence and some ways to develop them from your own information.

Have students analyze the topic sentences in *Activity 5-1* according to these criteria.

Five Requirements of a Topic Sentence

A topic sentence must be one that you, as a writer, can work with to build a paragraph. Therefore, it must:

1. Be limited to a single idea
2. Be a complete sentence (not a question)
3. Express an attitude or belief (or make a statement that needs explanation)
4. Contain specific words
5. Be broad enough to allow support

Although there are several examples for each of the five requirements, you may want to have the class (or small groups) generate their own additional examples.

1. The topic sentence must be limited to a single idea. That is, it must be narrow enough to be about only one thought. It can't have a compound subject or verb.

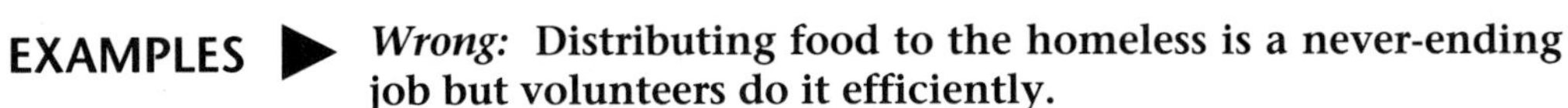

EXAMPLES ▶ *Wrong:* **Distributing food to the homeless is a never-ending job but volunteers do it efficiently.**

COMMENT: One idea is that the job is never-ending. Another is that volunteers do it efficiently. Both can't be in the same sentence.

Right: **Distributing food to the homeless in our community is a never-ending job.**
Right: **Volunteers in our community efficiently distribute food to the homeless.**

Wrong: **Water pollution and lack of managed building growth almost destroyed Everglades National Park.**

COMMENT: The compound subject, "water pollution and lack of managed building growth" means the subject hasn't been limited enough. Only a single subject, not a compound one, can be used in a topic sentence.

Right: **Water pollution almost destroyed Everglades National Park.**
Right: **Lack of managed building growth almost destroyed Everglades National Park.**

2. The topic sentence must be a complete sentence. It can't be a fragment because that would be only part of an idea. Phrases and clauses may be part of the topic sentence, but not a substitute for it. (To refresh your memory about fragments, please turn to Chapter 21; see Chapter 26 about phrases and clauses.)

The topic sentence also can't be a question. In the definition of a topic sentence (in the second paragraph of this chapter), you read that it makes a statement, so it can't ask a question. It might, however, answer a question.

EXAMPLES ▶ *Wrong*: **Witnesses who are eager to cooperate at a trial.**

COMMENT: This is a fragment, even though it begins with a capital and ends with a period. Because it isn't a complete sentence, it can't be a topic sentence.

Right: **Witnesses who are eager to cooperate at a trial will often "remember" whatever seems helpful.**

Wrong: **When is the right time to teach children responsibility?**

COMMENT: A question can't be a topic sentence. Try answering it.

Right: **A child should start being taught about responsibility as soon as it begins to understand spoken language.**

3. The topic sentence must express an attitude or belief, or make a statement that needs explanation. Some of the more successful topic sentences tell the audience what you believe or how you feel about something. That is, they communicate information that only you have available to share with readers. Also possible are topic sentences that state facts or transmit information, but only if they can be supported. That is, if you can build a paragraph around them.

Never use as a topic sentence a statement that "goes nowhere." It's a dead end and you will have nothing more to write than the one sentence.

EXAMPLES ▶ *Wrong:* **The rug in my bedroom is blue nylon.**

COMMENT: That's fine. But so what? Where do we go from there? It's a dead-end statement that can't be a topic sentence.

Right: **The colors you choose for your home reflect your personality.**

Right: **Smuggling antique art objects into the U.S. for illegal sale is big business.**

COMMENT: Although these two sentences state information, they make acceptable topic sentences because they require support. Reading them almost makes you say, "Tell me more about that."

Right: **Freewriting is a good way to get your thoughts on paper.**

Right: **Science fairs are an excellent way for young people to get interested in science.**

COMMENT: Each sentence expresses a belief the writer is obviously going to explain and support. Therefore, each would make a good topic sentence.

4. The topic sentence must contain specific words. As in all writing, specific words give more information than vague ones. Because a topic sentence is written to give readers information about the content of a paragraph, you should give it to them straightforwardly and without guesswork.

EXAMPLE ▶ *Wrong*: **Some environmental groups are very active.**

COMMENT: Which groups? How active is "very active"? The statement needs to be more specific if it is to be a good topic sentence.

Right: **Earth First! and Sea Shepherd Conservation Society use aggressive nonviolence to protest environmental destruction.**

5. The topic sentence must be broad enough to allow support. Paragraphs have some sentences that give details and support the main idea. The topic sentence acts as an umbrella over all of them because it is a broad or wide-ranging statement.

EXAMPLE ▶ ***Detail:*** **The moon appears 30% larger when it is close to the horizon than when it is higher in the sky.**
Detail: **Near objects appear larger than distant ones.**
Broad: **Many examples of optical illusion are all around us.**

COMMENT: The detailed statements are specifics. Both are examples of the broad statement and therefore support it.

Activity 5-2

Additional *Activity:* Have students revise those which are not now acceptable topic sentences so that they become acceptable.

DIRECTIONS: Write "Yes" on the line before each of the following items that could be the topic sentence of a paragraph. If the item could not serve as a topic sentence, write "No" on the line. If you write "No," give the reason for your judgment.

yes **The number of people with eating disorders appears to be increasing.**
no **The number of people with eating disorders.**
REASON: *It's a fragment.*

Yes 1. Every snowflake has a different shape.
REASON: ____

No 2. Learning mathematics.
REASON: It's a fragment

No 3. Her patent on in-line roller skates expired in 1985.
REASON: Not general enough

No 4. Food and medical labeling should be improved and government standards set for them.
REASON: Not limited enough

No 5. "Willing Ally" has been a top-selling record for 16 weeks.
REASON: Dead-end statement

No 6. A helpful teacher in school influenced many students.
REASON: Words aren't specific enough

Yes 7. Arson destroyed 400 homes.
REASON: ____

No 8. Is a winning combination.
REASON: It's a fragment

No 9. What would make a good photograph?
REASON: It's a question

Yes 10. A clock that chimes every quarter hour can be very annoying.
REASON: ____

Three Ways to Write Topic Sentences

When you set out to write your own topic sentences, you will start with only the subject part. You need to decide what you want the audience to know, the predicate part. You may know that right away, deciding on it either while you are narrowing the subject or as soon as you have one. Or, you may have to do some more thinking, such as in 2 or 3 below. You can develop a topic sentence in one of three ways:

1. Immediately thinking of a general statement
2. Listing or clustering details that lead to a general statement
3. Doing a focused freewrite leading to a general statement

You need to be familiar with all three of these because you may not always decide on a topic sentence in the same way.

1. You may immediately think of a general statement about a selected subject because you know what you want to tell the audience about it. For example, suppose you decided on the subject of "a job I had." As soon as you chose it, you knew that you wanted to tell the audience "the one in the local hamburger shop was the worst." Together, those two ideas lead you quickly to a topic sentence: "The worst job I ever had was working in the local hamburger shop."

You know that is a general statement because you can support it by telling the various things that made that job the worst you'd had.

2. You may list or cluster details about the subject and from them arrive at the general statement. Suppose you don't think in generalities. Many people don't. They are more likely to consider the details they want to write. That, too, is a way to arrive at a topic statement.

For instance, given the same subject—"a job I had"—you may make decide to cluster or to make a list that looks something like this:

- package carry-out
- hamburger shop
- delivering phone books
- sports store cashier

Since the assignment is to write about a job you've had, you must choose one of them. Three were repetitive and boring, but OK. They hardly seem worth writing about. But the other one—that job in the hamburger shop—calls to mind a number of things about it:

- sloppy people
- messy kids
- never got to rest
- paper on floor
- clean trays
- salt and pepper on table
- mopping
- sweeping

Looking at all these details about the job, you may have decided that you not only didn't like working at the hamburger shop, but that it was probably the worst job you ever had. (Clustering could bring you to the same place these lists do.)

These details in the cluster or the list will become the supporting points or the content of the paragraph. Taken together, they lead to the general statement and topic sentence, *"The worst job I ever had was working in the local hamburger shop."*

3. You may do a focused freewrite leading to a general statement. In a freewriting, you let your mind wander and can mix specific with general statements or relate one subject to another. Here is an example of such a freewrite based on the subject, "a job I had."

> I've had lots of jobs—part-time because I've been going to school—package carry-out boring, easy. Delivering phone books wasn't too bad. The hours were short but I had to drive and stop, drive and stop a lot. And the phone books got heavy to carry after a while. My father says they're bigger now than when he moved to town. Jobs. Job—-When I was cashier in the sporting goods store I met a lot of people. The ones that worked in the store plus all the people I waited on. After a while I started making pretty good money there, too. Then there was the few months I stuck it out working in the hamburger shop. Lots of sloppy people leaving papers on the floor, spilling over their drinks and expecting me to mop them up. Kids terrible. Especially the ones that were always dropping salt and pepper on the table for trying to put salt in the pepper shaker and pepper in the salt shaker. I can't believe they were so awful. sweeping and mopping. never got a chance to rest. What a lousy job. worst I ever had.

At that point the freewriting can stop because so much of it focused on the hamburger shop job, it's apparently what most concerns the writer. The general statement and topic sentence will therefore be, *"The worst job I ever had was working in the local hamburger shop."*

5-3

This *Activity* lets students go back to the work they did in Chapter 4. Again, this emphasizes process, and the relation between narrowing subjects and taking them a step further into devising topic statements.

DIRECTIONS: Please do the four parts of this *Activity*. When you complete the *Activity*, you will have tried the three ways of arriving at topic sentences.

1. Look back at the narrowed subjects you developed for *Activities 4-2, 4-3, 4-5, 4-8, 4-9,* or *4-10*. Choose five such narrowed subjects about which you could write paragraphs and note them here.

   1. ______________________________
   2. ______________________________
   3. ______________________________
   4. ______________________________
   5. ______________________________

2. Choose one of the above subjects about which you have an immediate idea for a general statement.

   Subject: ______________________________

   Audience should know: ______________________________

   ____

   ____

Topic sentence: ______________________________

____

____

(If you can't think of a general statement quickly, move to part 3.)

3. Choose another of the five subjects you listed in #1, above, and write it here.

   ____

   List or cluster details or specifics on that subject until you arrive at a general statement that can serve as a topic sentence. (Use your own paper, but keep it with this *Activity*.)
   Topic sentence:

   ____

   ____

4. Choose another of the five subjects you listed in #1, above, and write it here.

   ____

   On your own paper, **do a focused freewrite on that subject** until you arrive at a general statement that can serve as a topic sentence. (Keep that paper with this *Activity.)*
   Topic sentence:

   ____

   ____

Sharing

1. Form a group with two or three other people.
2. Let each person take a turn reading the three topic sentences developed in *Activity 5-3*. The author may want to explain how any or all of them were arrived at.
3. Others in the group should decide if these are topic sentences around which paragraphs could be written. If any one is not, suggest ways the author could vary it to make a good topic sentence.

5-4

This exercise helps students differentiate between general and specific statements.

DIRECTIONS: Each group of sentences below includes both broad and detailed statements. Circle the letter of the broad statement that could be a topic sentence the others would support.

EXAMPLE 

a. **Oranges and grapefruits ripen from November through January.**
b. **Watermelons are a summer treat.**
(c.) **Fresh fruits are each available for only a short time during the year.**
d. **Apples are always associated with the autumn season.**

Point out that not all groups of sentences automatically make a paragraph. Most sentences need additional information; what's here is merely a framework.

1. a. A candle flame can be seen from 30 miles away on a clear night.
   b. People can taste sweetness if a teaspoon of sugar is put in two gallons of water.
   c. A drop of perfume can be detected all through a six-room house.
   (d.) The human senses are so acute that most people can detect amazing things by using them.
   e. If all is quiet, a watch can be heard ticking from 20 feet away.

2. a. Ernest Hemingway wrote 15 novels.
   (b.) Ernest Hemingway wrote for many different kinds of publications.
   c. Ernest Hemingway wrote dozens of short stories.
   d. As a World War I foreign correspondent, Ernest Hemingway had many of his news reports published.

3. (a.) Higher-order animals have skin, eat, can breathe, and move around.
   b. Mammals are the only animals that give birth to live young.
   c. Birds have wings and feathers, can fly, and lay eggs.
   d. Fish have fins and gills, and they can swim.

4. a. Unusual conditions in the atmosphere have been responsible for turning on some auto alarms.
   b. This morning, two auto alarms were blaring in the school parking lot, but nobody went to look at the cars.
   c. I hear auto alarms going off in my neighborhood often but never see anybody going out to shut them off.
   (d.) People don't seem to pay attention to automobile alarms going on.
   e. Two of my friends had cars stolen, even though there were alarms in them.

5. a. Many large companies consider gyms as important as cafeterias and libraries in their buildings.
   b. An indoor jogging track offers people in high-stress jobs a year-round place to exercise.
   c. Many tennis clubs in cities have courts reserved all during the day because people feel better when they take time off to play.
   d. Playing handball or racquetball a few times a week is very relaxing for most people.
   (e.) Exercise is a good way for an individual to reduce stress.

6. (a.) A children's science museum is a wonderful place to teach youngsters about the universe.
   b. Children learn some laws of physics by "playing" with different machines.
   c. Many children's science museums have a powerful telescope, and demonstrations are given by astronomy club members.
   d. Many children's science museums have exhibits showing the life cycles of different animals.
   e. Children's science museums encourage class field trips and have people available to lead the class tours.

7. a. My cousin Juanita borrowed two scarves from me, but hasn't given them back even though I often ask her for them.
   (b.) My cousin Juanita is an ungrateful person.
   c. She expects her mother to make her bed for her.
   d. My cousin Juanita hardly ever says "Please" or "Thank you."
   e. Juanita almost never will do a favor for a person.
   f. My cousin Juanita is always borrowing money from her parents but never seems to pay it back.

8. a. In a traditional Cambodian wedding ceremony, a sheathed sword is laid across the folded hands of the bride and groom.
   b. Only 20% of the cultures in the world insist that marriage be a matter of one man and one woman.
   c. At the end of a traditional Jewish wedding, the groom stamps on a glass and breaks it.
   (d.) Marriage customs differ greatly around the world.
   e. Only a few societies allow young people to choose their marriage partner.

9. (a.) Most weekly television programs about families are unrealistic.
   b. Arguments are never really serious, and everything is always settled within a half-hour.
   c. In *The Bill Cosby Show*, both the Huxtable parents have prestigious careers, but their work never seems to interfere with their home life.
   d. For the Simpsons, battling each other is a way of life.
   e. The houses of TV families always look in perfect order, but you never see anybody really cleaning them.

10. a. Boys are not really any better at math and science than girls are.
    b. Girls do not have any particular skills at cooking or entertaining guests.
    (c.) There is almost no evidence for the differences between boys and girls that people often assume exist.
    d. Boys are not really any better at analyzing ideas and tasks than girls are.
    e. Girls are not really less motivated to achieve than boys are.

5-5

Point out to students that most of these supporting sentences require expanding before they can comprise a paragraph.

DIRECTIONS: Each group of sentences states details that could support the topic sentence of a paragraph. Write such a topic sentence below each group. (The detail sentences and the topic sentence will not necessarily make a complete paragraph for each item in this *Activity*.)

EXAMPLE 

a. Present household light bulbs could be replaced by those that use less energy to give the same amount of light.
b. Businesses could replace present incandescent lights with energy-saving fluorescent ones.
c. Sales of more fuel-efficient cars aren't being pushed.
d. More efforts at recycling can be started.

Topic sentence:

The U.S. already has many energy-saving methods that aren't being used to advantage.

1. a. You will need a picture hanger or hook, a hammer, a measuring tape, and a pencil.
   b. Stand on a safe step ladder or step stool.
   c. Choose the exact location for the picture to hang.
   d. Mark on the wall the spot where the center of the hanger or wire will be when the picture is properly placed.
   e. Hammer the picture hanger into the wall at the marked spot.
   f. Hang the picture and straighten it.

   Topic sentence:

   Hanging a picture is easy.

2. a. Don't stand under a tree.
   b. Get out of the water, if you've been swimming, and dry off.
   c. Stay in your car if you are traveling.
   d. Don't use the phone or operate electrical appliances in the house.

   Topic sentence:

   Everyone should observe some simple safety measures during an electrical storm.

3. a. Tropical forests are being destroyed for fuel wood and timber to export.
   b. When anything starts growing where the forests used to be, it is eaten by grazing cattle grown for export.
   c. Mining is also taking place where once there were forests, preventing their regrowth.
   d. Trees that purify the air and make it breathable are not being replaced after they are cut.
   e. Global warming and climate changes will surely follow.

   Topic sentence:

   Cutting down the tropical forests has severe consequences for everyone in the world.

4. a. It begins with moisture from land and bodies of water that evaporates as water vapor.
   b. When the vapor condenses to rain, snow, or sleet, it falls back to the earth.
   c. Plants absorb some of this moisture, and it becomes groundwater that slowly moves to the surface.
   d. Surface water runs off into large bodies of water from which it then evaporates as water vapor.

Topic sentence:

Water follows a cycle from bodies of water through air and land, back to bodies of water.

5. a. Computers make it easy to record and store very large amounts of information.
   b. Nobody can imagine a business office without telephones.
   c. We wonder how anybody in an office got along without copying machines before they were invented.
   d. The fax machine has made it possible to send and receive print and pictures almost anywhere in the world within minutes.
   e. Early office workers thought a typewriter was a wonderful addition and time saver.

Topic sentence:

The modern office runs on machines that early office workers would hardly have believed.

6. a. Famine occurs when the people of an area do not have enough food to live on.
   b. Rapid population growth means the land cannot support the people.
   c. Poor land use leads to lowered or failed food production.
   d. Civil and other wars keep civilian refugees from getting food sent to them from the outside.
   e. Arguments between countries over water rights makes growing food even more difficult.

Topic sentence:

Human beings are responsible for many conditions that lead to famine.

7. a. Can openers are generally made for right-handed people to use with ease.
   b. The arrangement of large and small holes on the handles of scissors makes them better suited for right-handed than for left-handed people.
   c. The face of a standard watch will be upside down if a left-handed person wears it on the wrist of the non-writing hand.
   d. Knitting and crocheting is hard to learn because the instructions are for right-handed people.
   e. Strings on instruments such as the violin and guitar are arranged for right-handed people.

Topic sentence:

Being a left-handed person in a right-handed world is hard.

8. a. What we call today the "Swiss Army Knife" got the name because it was adopted by the Swiss army in 1891, soon after being developed by a Swiss knife maker, Karl Elsener.
   b. It has since been carried by expeditions to the North Pole, Mount Everest, and the moon.
   c. The basic model controls six blades with only two springs.
   d. There are 40 models available.
   e. Besides blades, the knives may contain can openers, screwdrivers, reamers, saws, wire cutters, scissors, tweezers, toothpicks, needles, fish scalers, key rings, and more.

   Topic sentence:

   The Swiss Army Knife is a very versatile tool.

9. a. Wearing masks at Halloween probably comes from an ancient idea that a mask could fight off an evil spirit.
   b. Masks are used in Eskimo and Northwest Indian cultures as symbols during rituals.
   c. In many African cultures, masks are emblems of power worn during chief installations and during hunting.
   d. Actors in ancient Greek and traditional Japanese theater wore masks.

   Topic sentence:

   Masks have a long and varied history of use.

10. a. Somewhere, floating in space, is a camera dropped by an astronaut during a space walk.
    b. Landing vehicles were left behind on the moon after the first Americans to land there blasted off.
    c. Rockets and satellites circle through space when they are no longer useful.

    Topic sentence:

    People are leaving garbage in space just like they do on earth.

Emphasize that the topic sentence is usually first in academic writing. That is not true of other kinds of writing, especially the many published paragraphs that have unstated topic sentences. Basic writing students are usually more comfortable in putting the topic sentence first or last.

Three Possible Places for Topic Sentences in Paragraphs

When a topic sentence appears in a paragraph, it is most often the first sentence. But sometimes it is the last sentence, and occasionally it appears somewhere in the middle of a paragraph. In the following examples, the topic sentence in each paragraph is underlined.

Topic sentence is first in the paragraph:

Ancient Egyptians used the papyrus reed that grew along the Nile River to make a material they could write on. The reeds were cut and gathered into bundles that were flattened by beating. The process was slow and took a long time. Then, individual reeds were beaten until they were very flat and thin. Presses were used to squeeze the water out of them. When there were enough flattened reeds, they were woven into sheets by alternating the reeds over and under each other. Naturally, the length of the reeds controlled how long or wide a sheet could be. Still more water had to be squeezed from the sheets by presses. Then the papyrus sheets were ready to be dried in the sun. The result was a sheet something like our paper, but very strong and ready to be written on.

Topic sentence is last in the paragraph:

Dolphins are gentle animals that get along well with people. Many dolphins are kept in water parks on exhibition and are trained to swim with people who can pay the money it costs to do it. The dolphins will even let people hold on to their fins and be pulled along through the water. That may be fun for people to do, but it doesn't do much good for the animal. For one thing, people can carry diseases that dolphins catch. In fact, many dolphins have already died from germs and viruses that don't even make people sick but that are deadly to dolphins. For another thing, people can get rough with the dolphins without realizing they are doing it. It is bad enough to keep dolphins penned up and exhibited, but it is dangerous to these gentle animals to let people swim with them. For these reasons, people should not be allowed to swim with dolphins that are on exhibition.

Topic sentence is in the middle of the paragraph:

I once worked in a long-established, well-respected law office that fit the image of what that kind of place should be. Everybody sort of tip-toed around, and there were soft rugs and deep furniture in dark colors. The company had a dress code that fit the image. It was that the women had to wear just that: dresses. We could wear plain skirts with blouses, but we were not allowed to wear colors that were too bright or anything with big prints. The dress code for men was that they had to wear shirts with ties (and dress slacks or suit trousers, of course) and, in order to fit the image of that law office, anyone going out of the office or meeting a client had to wear a jacket .

For *Activity 5-6*, you may want to have students pick out the principal supporting ideas for each topic sentence.

5-6

DIRECTIONS: Underline the topic sentences in each of the following paragraphs.

1. The first hour I was on the job the manager handed me a bucket and a mop, and showed me where to get water and cleaning fluid to put into the bucket. The broom and dustpan were kept in the same place. She also showed me where the cloths were to clean off the tables, where to put the plastic and paper that people left behind, and how to wipe and stack the trays. Then I was on my own. In all the time I'd eaten at that hamburger place, I never realized how sloppy people were. Maybe I'd been guilty, too. Little kids spilled food on the floor and threw things around. They poured salt all over the table instead of on their fries. Adults were sloppy about how their table looked, and when stuff fell on the floor they'd just kick it out of the way. For the rest of my shift, I was cleaning tables, sweeping up, and mopping the floor. That job at the local hamburger place is the worst one I have ever had.

That job at the local hamburger place is the worst one I have ever had.

It is more like a miniature computer than anything else.

2. It is more like a miniature computer than anything else. It is small enough to fit into your purse or suit pocket, yet it stores an amazing amount of information. You can use it to store your appointments, important days, all the information about people, such as their addresses and phone numbers, and even more. Then you can call up what you need when you need it, and the information is displayed on a small screen.

However, the switch to computers in my office was not as bad as I expected.

3. I imagined rows of big eyes watching me and all the other people in the office. I heard that the managers could tune in on you and watch what you were doing on the computer. That didn't appeal to me. However, the switch to computers in my office was not as bad as I expected. The top management sent in some people to explain how the computers worked. These people were very good because they also showed how the computers would help us do our jobs better and faster. Afterwards, everybody in the office got as much individual help as they needed to be able to work the computers. It didn't take very long to get used to using them .

The "floating" quality of the pure new "White Soap" developed by Procter & Gamble in 1878 was an accident.

4. The "floating" quality of the pure new "White Soap" developed by Procter & Gamble in 1878 was an accident. An employee at the firm's plant in Cincinnati left the soap vats churning one day while he took a lunch break. After this batch of soap was shipped out to market, the public began to place orders for the "soap that will float." The floating ability was due to the lengthy beating, which whipped extra air into the soap liquid.

I still take my kids out on Halloween because too many people do crazy things, and I want to keep an eye on the kids.

5. Every Halloween since they could just about walk, my kids have always liked to go out to "Trick or Treat." Even though they are bigger now, I still take them out on Halloween. It's not because they can't walk around by themselves or don't know how to cross the streets safely. I still take my kids out on Halloween because too many people do crazy things, and I want to keep an eye on the kids. Crazy people do things like put razor blades inside apples and then give them to kids. Sometimes they also do things like that to candy. After they're finished getting their bags filled, I don't let the kids eat anything until I take them over to the hospital and get a free x-ray of what they get in the trick-or-treat bags. By being with them, I'm sure the kids don't eat stuff that isn't checked first.

RECAP—TOPIC SENTENCES

- A topic sentence states the main idea of a paragraph.
- The subject of a topic sentence tells what the paragraph is about and the predicate tells what the author wants the reader to know about it.
- There are five requirements for a topic sentence.
- A topic sentence may be arrived at by three methods.
- A topic sentence may appear at the beginning, middle, or end of a paragraph.

Chapter 6

Planning Paragraphs

In this chapter you will

- differentiate between general and specific statements
- distinguish between main and supporting ideas
- organize paragraphs by
  - time
  - space
  - importance
- plan a paragraph for a specific audience

Developing a topic sentence, which you did in Chapter 5, is an important step in writing a paragraph. Next, you need to plan the complete paragraph. Most writing is planned out before the author starts the actual work. Such planning will help you use your time and effort to advantage. Instead of false starts, long pauses while you think of what to write, and lots of crumpled papers, having a plan in advance of the writing lets you get to work immediately.

Planning doesn't mean you have to make a formal outline. None is really needed for a short piece of writing such as a paragraph. But you should at least have a numbered list of specific, supporting ideas next to you when you start writing. It will show the order in which you will write the content that makes up the paragraph.

General and Specific Statements

In most of Chapter 5, and especially in *Activities 5-4* and *5-5*, you worked with general and specific statements. But they were all on paper for you to see. Now it's time to look at the difference between the two kinds of statements and then see how they are used for supporting the general statement that is a topic sentence. Then you will create your own specific statements for support.

A **general statement** is one which a listener or reader must ask questions about in order to understand completely.

> Have students select general and specific statements from writing they've done so far for this class. Let them write the statements in a list and work in a group to check each other's perceptions of what makes these two kinds of statements.

EXAMPLES ▶ **Books are a good source of information for students.**

QUESTIONS:

What kind of books?
What sort of information?
For all students?
What is "good"?

A **specific statement** is limited or narrowed enough that it doesn't leave questions in the mind of the listener or reader. The author has anticipated, and answered, them.

An astronomy book will show the location of stars in the night sky.

A math book will show how to solve stated problems.

A literature textbook will contain examples of short stories.

You can see that these specific statements have answered some of the questions left by the general statement. Not just "books," but an astronomy book or a math book or a literature book. Not just "information," but "the location of stars in the night sky," and so on. Additional specific statements can be about the other questions, if it's important for the writing that they be answered.

The specific statements above are called **"first level"** specifics. They can be narrowed, to a **"second level,"** to be even more specific.

Page 95 of the book *New Looks at Astronomy* shows the stars that make up the constellation Orion.

Instruction on long division is in Chapter 10 of *Basic Mathematics.*

"The Lottery" is in the literature textbook for this course.

The page, the chapter, and the story in these examples tell specifically what kind of information is in each book. In some kinds of writing, the first level of specific statement is called for; in others, the second level is needed. Often, you will use both.

Here are some other general statements and specifics that illustrate how they can be narrowed.

General: Eating vegetables is important to everyone's nutrition.

Specific: Nutritionists recommend eating at least three portions of vegetables daily in order to get enough vitamins, minerals, and complex carbohydrates to stay healthy.

General: Computers make many tasks easier for people.

Specific: I use the spreadsheet on the computer daily to figure commissions for the salespeople this company employs.

Activity 6-1

DIRECTIONS: Put a **G** next to each of the following statements that is general and an **S** next to each that is specific.

EXAMPLE ▶

 **Everyone should take at least one general psychology course.**

 **Pavlov's famous experiment on conditioning is included in Chapter Two of the psychology book this class uses.**

S 1. M&Ms are advertised not to melt in your hands.

G 2. When you finish painting, we will have time to do other things.

G 3. Swimming can be dangerous.

S 4. I studied for a history test for three hours last night.

S 5. You can go scuba diving at two of our national parks, but only Biscayne National Park in Florida is on the U.S. mainland.

G 6. Auto racing is a fast sport that is exciting to watch.

G 7. Lots of good movies are available on videotape these days.

G 8. Roberto is an excellent artist.

S 9. Half the people in the drum and bugle corps can play either instrument.

G 10. The city road department should install more traffic lights in our neighborhood.

6-2

DIRECTIONS: On the lines below, write the number of each general statement in *Activity 6-1*. Next to it, write a specific statement on the same subject. Begin each number and its statement on a new line.

EXAMPLE ▶

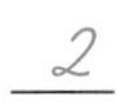 **When you finish painting the bedroom, you and I will have to go out for a walk and get an ice cream cone.**

Next, have students turn the specific statements into general ones.

Let students compare their responses to this *Activity* either in a group or with the class as a whole.

3 Always swim with at least one other person or where there is a lifeguard.

6 Some people watch auto racing because they are exciting by the danger of the sport.

7 All the best-picture Academy Award movies of the last ten years are now available on videotape.

8 Roberto Ruiz won the first prize for oil paintings this year in the college art department's competition.

10 The city road department should install traffic lights on the corner of Elm and Maple Streets because there have been three accidents there and many near-misses in the last three months.

Supporting Topic Sentences

This part again acknowledges there are different ways of approaching writing. Students should never feel there's just one "right way."

As you already know, the topic sentences of a paragraph must be supported, or explained, by specifics in the other sentences. These supporting sentences are not as individually important as the topic sentence, but they are necessary for the reader as a way of understanding the topic sentence fully.

If you wrote the topic sentence after listing or clustering some specifics, you already have most of the supporting information you will need for a paragraph.

If you arrived at the topic sentence by focused freewriting, you probably also have most of the supporting specifics. (See Chapter 5, pages 49-64.)

If you wrote the topic sentence directly, now is the time to decide how you will support it. To help decide what specifics to include, think of the topic sentence as a statement you make to someone who doesn't know you very well. That person will then ask you questions. Write down the questions. Your answers to them can then be brainstormed, and they will be the support you need for the topic sentence.

You might want to alert students to the fact that in brainstorming there's no need to write full sentences, just to keep up with thoughts.

EXAMPLE ▶ **Topic Sentence:** Careful shopping will keep your grocery bill down.

Thoughtful Questions:
What does "careful shopping" mean?
Will that interfere with what I want to buy?
How much will my grocery bill go down?

Answers to Questions:
"Careful shopping" means going to the store with a list.
Sticking to the list.
Reading ads for specials and buying them.
Not overbuying.
Using coupons.
Choosing fresh fruits and vegetables that won't spoil quickly.
Can buy all or most of what's wanted.
Can't tell how much bill will go down.

An alternate to the question/brainstorm method of finding supporting ideas is clustering that begins with your topic sentence. Here is an example.

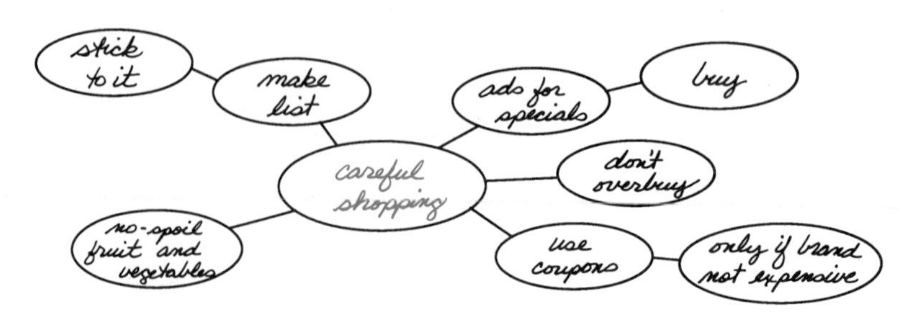

By turning the brainstormed answers or the cluster into sentences and linking them, you can write a paragraph that supports the topic sentence.

You will recognize that the topic sentence opens the following paragraph.

EXAMPLE  Careful shopping will keep your grocery bill down. You should go to the store with a shopping list and stick to it. Then you won't buy on impulse, because every item added to the shopping cart adds to your grocery bill. Read ads in the newspaper or give-away ads for the store you will shop at to find out what specials are in effect. Include them in your shopping list if you need the items or expect to buy them within the next two weeks. You should also look for in-store specials that are on your list. The pennies you save by buying such store specials add up to savings. Clipping and using coupons for foods and household items you need will also save you money. Finally, you should choose fresh fruit and vegetables that will last until you need to use them, even if that is a few days after your trip to the grocery store. You can be sure that with such careful shopping, you will certainly save money.

Brainstorming and clustering, introduced in Chapter 4 as narrowing techniques, are here noted as good techniques for getting information to write from.

Activity 6-3

DIRECTIONS: Read each of the following general statements and think of questions your classmates might ask. On your own paper, write out the questions and brainstorm answers. Then write at least four specifics to support each general statement. If you prefer, you can cluster to find at least four specifics.

EXAMPLE  **All students should be assigned homework.**
1. Doing it helps you remember what you learn in class.
2. It teaches responsibility.
3. It will help you progress faster.
4. There is always more you can learn about any subject.

Students are asked to write at least four specifics here in order to get away from the erroneous notion that all main ideas have to be divided into three parts.

A. Regular exercise will help you stay healthy.

1. It helps the body digest and absorb food nutrients.
2. It tones the muscles.
3. It is good for the heart at any age.
4. It will help you stay alert.

Others: ______

B. I like to keep my prized possessions in certain places.

1. My favorite photos are on the chest in my bedroom.
2. My best clothes are hung away neatly.
3. My car key is always with me or in a secret place.
4. The book I won is on a shelf.

Others: ______

C. I admire people who ___are honest___.
(name a quality or activity)

1. They never get caught in their own lies.
2. "Honesty is the best policy."
3. They can always stand up and look people in the eyes.
4. They don't have to put on a front for anybody.

Others: ________________

D. When I have spare time, I like to ___watch TV___.
(name an activity)

1. You don't have to do much thinking for yourself if you don't want to.
2. It's cheap.
3. It's entertaining.
4. I can learn a lot from watching some programs.

Others: ________________

E. Keeping up with daily news is very important.

1. You ought to know what's going on in your town.
2. What happens in other parts of the world can affect you.
3. It will give you something to talk about with others.
4. Intelligent people are expected to keep up with things.

Others: ________________

Sharing

1. In a group with two or three other people, share your responses to *Activity 6-3.*
2. Group members should discuss any other information they would like to have as specifics in support of the general statements.

Activity 6-4

The *Idea Journal*, introduced in Chapter 3 as a device for students to use for writing ideas, is put to use in this chapter, as it will be throughout the text.

DIRECTIONS: Do each of the following, in order.

1. Select a subject from your *Idea Journal* that you could write a paragraph about. Narrow it if necessary. Write it here.

   Subject: ________________

   ____

2. Assume that the audience for this paragraph will be the people in the last *Sharing* group you worked with in this class.

3. Develop a topic sentence for your subject that will be suitable for your audience. Write it here.

   Topic sentence: ______________________________

   ____

4. List what you believe that audience would like to know about your topic sentence, or what questions it (they) would ask. Write them here:

   ____

   ____

   ____

   ____

5. On your own paper, brainstorm or cluster answers to the questions to get specifics that support the topic sentence.
6. Write a paragraph on your own paper using your topic sentence and the supporting information.

Sharing

1. Form a group with one or two other people. Share your paragraphs written for *Activity 6-4*.
2. Let the group discuss with each author, in turn, the supporting information for the topic sentence of the paragraph. If group members want more information or specific kinds of support, let the author add it to the paragraph as appropriate. If any ideas do *not* support the topic sentence, cross them out.

Order of Support

As you have been writing paragraphs in response to assignments so far, you may find that you are arranging your supporting ideas in certain ways. Most likely, the arrangement has been in one of the ways you are going to read about now.

Writing is a matter of giving order and shape to your ideas. Therefore, once you have decided on a topic sentence for a paragraph and thought about information that supports that main idea, you have to arrange what you will write. As you have already seen in this chapter, the topic sentence can be placed anywhere in a paragraph, but it is usually easiest to begin with it. Then you and your reader can get ready for the specifics that support it.

Emphasis throughout this text is that a topic sentence be written at the beginning of a paragraph. Students usually find that learning structure is easier because of this dependable location. Chapter 5, however, showed that topic sentences can appear in different places in a paragraph.

Three arrangements of supporting sentences are often used:

- time order
- space order
- emphasis order

TIME ORDER

When you write a paragraph that has to do with something in time, you will probably want to use a time arrangement for the supporting specifics. That is, you tell what happens (or happened) earliest, then next, and bring the reader to the present, or to the last thing that happens (or happened).

For example, suppose you are going to write to someone who doesn't attend your school about how to register for classes. Experience has taught you that doing some things in advance will save a lot of trouble at actual registration. After deciding what you have done in the past, you might develop a numbered list like this:

1. decide on courses
2. watch for registration date
3. get class schedule
4. choose times for courses
5. get advisor's OK

Working from such a list, you might put the topic sentence at the beginning and write the following paragraph.

EXAMPLE  To register for classes with the least amount of hassle, you should do everything possible before registration starts. Decide at the beginning of the term which courses you want to take the next term. Watch for an announcement of registration dates, so you will be ready. Get a class schedule as soon as it's available, and then choose the times you want to take the courses. You will have to see a counselor to OK your schedule, so do that next. Then you will be ready to stand in line the first day registration for the next term opens.

Activity 6-5

DIRECTIONS: Following each topic sentence is a group of supporting ideas, but in scrambled order. Unscramble them, and put each in time order-of-support by writing a number showing the correct order in the space at the left of each idea.

EXAMPLE  **My brother and I planned a surprise anniversary party for our parents at our home.**

__6__ **welcomed guests**
__3__ **decided on music**
__1__ **selected date and time**
__2__ **made out guest list**
__5__ **brought in food**
__4__ **got parents out of house**

(Note: You may have made out the guest list before choosing the date and time, but other ideas would have to be in the time order shown.)

A. Candidates for city council are ready for the election being held today.

__4__ file for a place on the ballot
__2__ decide to run for vacant council seats
__5__ campaign among voters
__3__ get eligibility petitions signed by voters
__1__ be aware of city issues

B. Operation Desert Storm was a quick victory for the U.S. and its allies.

__2__ many countries decided Iraq had to leave Kuwait
__5__ Iraq was finally told to leave Kuwait by January 15, 1991
__3__ The United Nations announced sanctions against Iraq to try to get its military to leave Kuwait

(continued on next page)

1 Iraq invaded Kuwait
4 Operation Desert Shield started with the U.S. and other countries sending arms and personnel to staging areas in Saudi Arabia
8 Iraqi troops began surrendering
6 Iraq didn't move troops out of Kuwait
9 cease fire between Iraq and allies ended fighting February 28, 1991
7 bombing of Iraq began and name changed to Operation Desert Storm

C. I finally got the job I wanted!
2 considered other job possibilities
4 filled out many applications
3 decided on job I wanted to look for
1 was unhappy on old job
5 was called in for a few interviews

D. This time I organized things before I moved.
2 painted new apartment
4 served breakfast to friends who came to help me move
1 started far ahead by packing seldom-used things
6 removed the last of my possessions
5 carried out bigger pieces of furniture first
7 swept out the old apartment
3 finished last-minute packing

E. Becoming an architect takes a long time.
5 serve an apprenticeship with an architectural firm
3 be accepted in architecture school
1 decide to get the needed education
2 pass required pre-architecture courses
4 earn degree in architecture

Activity 6-6

DIRECTIONS: Using the unscrambled information from one of the items A through E in *Activity 6-5*, write a paragraph using time order. Make the supporting ideas into sentences, and add whatever wording you need to make the paragraph be complete and readable. Begin with the topic sentence.

Activity 6-7

DIRECTIONS: Select an idea from your *Idea Journal* and develop a topic sentence that lends itself to a paragraph in which the supporting ideas are in time order. Write such a paragraph on your own paper, beginning with the topic sentence.

Sharing

1. Form a group with two or three other students.
2. Share the paragraphs you wrote in *Activity 6-7*. Check each other's work to make sure that the topic sentences really do lend themselves to support using the time order.
3. Help each author to provide enough support by pointing out information you'd like to have, but that may have been omitted.
4. As an author, make your paragraph complete enough to satisfy the others in your group.

SPACE ORDER

Some writing subjects haven't got much to do with time order, and trying to use such support in paragraphs wouldn't accomplish anything. However, the subject may lend itself to organizing support according to space.

Describing a room is one such subject. You could write about what someone entering the room might see by beginning at one point and then going around the room. That is, you could show how each item in the room occupies space next to the previously-mentioned one.

When you use space order for writing, think of yourself as an observer and use one of eight different paragraph structures for supporting information:

- left to right
- right to left
- near to far
- far to near
- top to bottom
- bottom to top
- most dominant or important to least
- least impressive to most dominant

The student who wrote the following paragraph drew a diagram of the space he was going to describe. He then decided to begin the supporting sentences by telling of the most dominant feature in the main entrance: the tall display case.

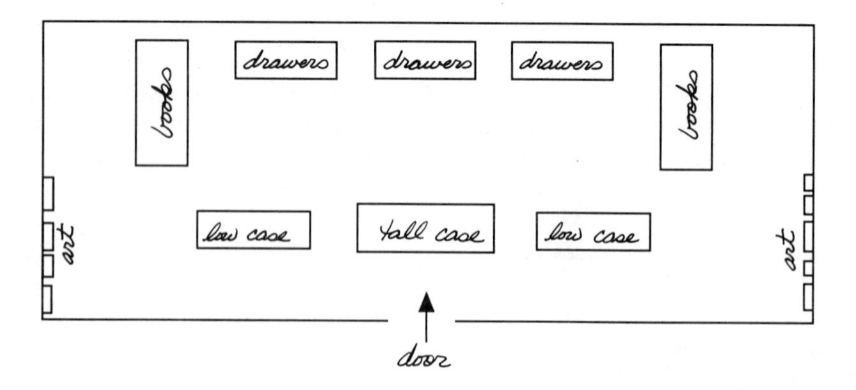

That this student drew a map for guidance in writing—which may be interpreted as a plan—will probably be a novelty to most students. It's another technique some may choose to try.

You can see how space order is used in the paragraph. The smaller cases on either side of the tall ones are mentioned, then the two side walls with details about them emphasize the topic sentence idea of the entrance being like a museum or art gallery.

EXAMPLE 

Walking into the main entrance of my school library is more like walking into a museum or art gallery than into a library. The first thing that meets your eye is a glass display case, taller than I am and at least six feet wide. Sometimes the case has clippings and books about a news event, and often it has books on a certain subject with pages opened to big pictures that catch your eye. If the subject of the books is something like ceramics or model airplanes, there will also be real examples along with the books. Objects like that help the library look like a museum. On either side of the big case are low glass display cases, also with clippings and books in them. You can just about see the library books and catalog drawers beyond the cases, but they don't seem to catch your attention. Instead, your eyes will be drawn to the two side walls of the entrance area. Here, art students show their works. Sometimes there are big paintings or collages and sometimes photographs are displayed.

Activity 6-8

DIRECTIONS: Each of the following topic sentences can be supported by using the space order. On the lines provided, tell what details the paragraph for the topic sentence should contain and the space order in which the information should be given.

 **EXAMPLE**

Topic sentence: The parade of athletes into a stadium at the opening of the Olympic games always begins with Greece, because that was where the first games were held.

Support organized by space should:

tell the order in which athletes of different countries

then march into the stadium.

> You may need to remind students that in doing this *Activity*, they're not asked to provide supporting sentences, just to suggest how to go about looking for support.

A. **Topic sentence:** The earth is only one of nine planets in our solar system.

Support organized by space should:

name the planets in order leading to or

from the sun (Pluto to Mercury or Mercury to Pluto)

B. **Topic sentence:** On my trip from home to school, I watch out for several important landmarks that tell me where to turn.

Support organized by space should:

tell the route taken and the things or places used

as landmarks along the way

C. **Topic sentence:** The room in my house that seems to have the most in it is the kitchen.

Support organized by space should:

start at left or right of entrance door and go around the room describing what is seen.

Or, can begin with table in middle and then get to other things around room in order.

D. **Topic sentence:** The painting has people, boats, a river, and trees in it.
Support organized by space should:

tell where each thing is in the picture, from foreground to background

E. **Topic sentence:** This is the route to follow if you want to get quickly from this classroom to the Registrar's Office at this school.
Support organized by space should:

begin at door leaving room and tell which stairs, halls and buildings to go along to get to office

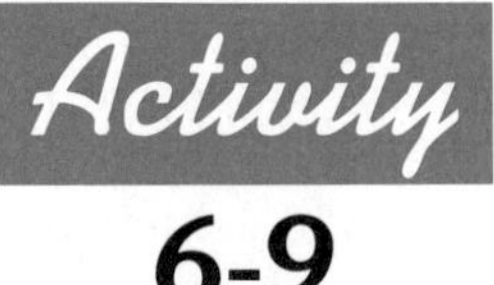

Activity 6-9

DIRECTIONS: Using the information from one of the items A through E in *Activity 6-8* that you said should go into a paragraph using the space order, write the paragraph. Make the supporting ideas into sentences, and add whatever wording you need to make the paragraph be complete and read smoothly. Begin your paragraph with the topic sentence.

Activity 6-10

Students may need help finding a usable subject from their *Idea Journals*. Also, students may need to be reminded that they are to write a paragraph for this *Activity*, not stop where the lines on the page do for listing supporting statements.

DIRECTIONS: Select an idea from your *Idea Journal* that could be developed into a paragraph with supporting ideas using space order. Write a topic sentence below and list the order of support. Write the paragraph, beginning with the topic sentence, on your own paper.

Topic sentence:

Supporting ideas:

Sharing

1. Form a group with two or three other students.
2. Share the paragraphs you wrote in either *Activity 6-9* or *6-10*. Check each other's work to make sure that the topic sentences really do lend themselves to support using the space order.
3. Help each author to provide enough support by pointing out information you'd like to have but that may have been omitted.
4. As an author, make your own paragraph complete enough to satisfy the others in your group.

This is probably the most widely used order, though students have not, til now, seen order of importance in this light.

ORDER OF EMPHASIS

Usually, the most important point you have to communicate is the one you want to emphasize. The idea will be one of several supporting ones, but what you want to emphasize is up to you. It may be the largest or smallest, the cheapest or most expensive, the one that interests you most or least, the one that is most important or least important. When you are writing, *you* decide what to emphasize.

Two places in a paragraph where readers pay particular attention are the beginning and the end. **Therefore, to emphasize or call attention to one particular supporting idea, you should put it either first or last in a paragraph.**

The following examples show how you can use order to give emphasis by placing a supporting idea in either of these two important places.

The topic sentence of both paragraphs is the same: being a good parent is a tough job, so it's something you should really work at. The supporting statements, numbered in order for each example, are in a different order in each paragraph.

Example 1		Example 2
2	do things together	1
3	do what child wants	2
1	give your attention	4
4	be good example	3

In these examples, the topic sentence is in italics. The supporting idea the author wants to emphasize most is underlined.

EXAMPLE 1 

The most important thing you can do for your child is to give your attention to her or him by really listening when the child talks to you. You should also try to do things together, even if it's only household chores. Also important in being a parent is to try to spend time doing some things the child wants to do. You should also set a good example for a child and not do things that are wrong and the child will then copy. *You can see that being a good parent is a tough job, so it's something you should really work at.*

EXAMPLE 2 

Being a good parent is a tough job, so it's something you should really work at. You should try to do things with your child, even if it's only household chores. Also important in being a parent is to try to spend time doing some things the child wants to do. Being a good parent also means you should set a good example for a child and not do things that are wrong and the child will then copy. Finally, the most important thing you can do for your child is to give your attention to her or him.

As a reader of these two example paragraphs, you are made further aware of which supporting idea the writer wants to emphasize because the words "the most important thing" appear within the sentence. Such wording need not always appear; the location of the information would draw your attention to it.

Planning the paragraphs for both examples was probably just the same. The difference came in designating which idea the author wanted to emphasize, and then selecting a position for it within the paragraph. In the following activity, see for yourself how that works.

6-11

The information in each item can be made into a paragraph, if you want students to write them.

Here, the text comes back to the importance of audience, already introduced in Chapter 2. A fruitful class discussion about audience can be developed from this *Activity*. Students may occasionally need nudging to get them to deal with the reasons for choices.

DIRECTIONS: Below each of the following topic sentences are several supporting ideas. An audience for each is also stated. Put a check mark next to the one supporting idea you would choose to emphasize. Then, in the space provided, tell why you made the choice you did.

EXAMPLE 

Audience:
10- to 12-year olds going on their first camping trip
Topic sentence:
A great camping trip requires a lot of planning.
Supporting ideas:
make up menus ✓
get the right kind of tents
choose good companions
take right clothing
get best equipment possible
I would emphasize this because:

10- to 12-year olds are usually interested in food.

1. **Audience:** Group of social friends

   Topic sentence:

   The first time I went to a rock concert was almost a disaster.

   Supporting ideas:

   couldn't find seats
   got separated from friends ✓
   sound system wasn't very good

   I would emphasize this because:

   being with friends is important and we all hate
   to be separated

2. **Audience:** Teen sports enthusiasts who wanted to see the Olympic Games in person

   Topic sentence:

   Watching the Olympic Games on TV is better than going to see them in person.

   Supporting ideas:

   can see more events
   doesn't cost anything
   get better views of the action ✓
   can see replays
   is more comfortable
   can flip off what gets boring

   I would emphasize this because:

   if they are so interested in sports, they'd want to see everything as closely
   as possible

3. **Audience:**
   Working adult planning to attend college
   Topic sentence:
   Holding a job while going to school isn't easy.
   Supporting ideas:
   always tired ✓
   not enough time to study
   requires tight scheduling
   not enough free time
   I would emphasize this because:
   being tired at work and during free time isn't good for the person or people
   on the job or at home

4. **Audience:** High school students about to enter college
   Topic sentence:
   Paying close attention in class has helped me to pass tests.
   Supporting ideas:
   learn by hearing information
   can tell what teacher wants to emphasize ✓
   cuts down on out-of-class study time
   am actually spending more time on the subject
   I would emphasize this because:
   they probably would want to know how to get by but spend the least
   amount of time doing it

5. **Audience:** Group of older office workers
   Topic sentence: Exercise is good for everyone.
   Supporting ideas:
   gives energy
   releases tension
   keeps heart healthy ✓
   I would emphasize this because:
   office workers probably sit a lot and if they are older, they probably
   aren't into exercise

Audience and Planning

In the following activity, you will have a chance to do three things necessary for planning a paragraph: write an original topic sentence, list some ideas that will support it, and choose the order in which the support will appear. You may do these three in any order you choose, writing the topic sentence either before or after you list the support. List as many items of support as you think your topic sentence requires for the audience, and then number them according to which you would put first, second, etc. The audience for each is stated.

6-12

You will probably want to look at the topic sentences developed for this *Activity* to be sure students are selecting suitable general and specific ideas for the purposes of the purposes here.

DIRECTIONS: Fill in the blanks to show a topic sentence for a paragraph, supporting ideas, and the order you would use for these ideas. You must designate one for each order or presentation: time, space, or emphasis. Write numbers next to each showing in which order you would present the supporting ideas.

1. **Audience:** A kindergarten class

   Topic sentence:

   ____

   ____

   Supporting ideas: **Order**

   ______________________________ ________

   ______________________________ ________

   ______________________________ ________

   ______________________________ ________

   ______________________________ ________

   ______________________________ ________

   Order of presentation: Check one:

   ☐ time ☐ space ☐ emphasis

2. **Audience:** A teacher you once had and who you admire.

   Topic sentence:

   ____

   ____

   Supporting ideas: **Order**

   ______________________________ ________

   ______________________________ ________

   ______________________________ ________

   ______________________________ ________

   ______________________________ ________

   ______________________________ ________

   Order of presentation: Check one:

   ☐ time ☐ space ☐ emphasis

3. **Audience: A friend**
   Topic sentence:

   ____

   ____

   Supporting ideas: **Order**

   ________________________________ ________

   ________________________________ ________

   ________________________________ ________

   ________________________________ ________

   ________________________________ ________

   ________________________________ ________

   Order of presentation: Check one:
   ☐ time ☐ space ☐ emphasis

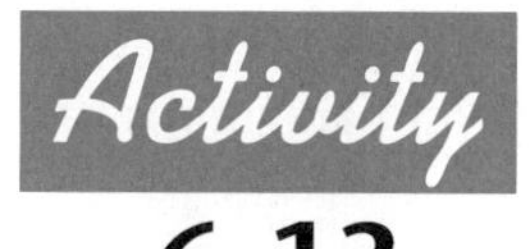

6-13

DIRECTIONS: Choose one of the topic sentences with supporting ideas and order of presentation you developed in *Activity 6-12.* Write a paragraph using the information you created, but adding whatever details you think necessary and whatever wording will make the paragraph read smoothly. Use your own paper for writing.

Sharing

1. Form a group with two or three other students.
2. Share your paragraph written for *Activity 6-13* by reading it aloud to others in the group.
3. Let others in the group note if the order of presenting information was clear to them. If there is any question of the order, revise the paragraph to satisfy others in the group.
4. Repeat 2 and 3 until each person in the group has had a chance to read a paragraph and get the response of others.

Activity 6-14

This is similar in some ways to *Activity 6-5*, but here students are dealing with full sentences, and by writing the information into paragraph form they get a more complete sense of writing as a process of making meaning.

DIRECTIONS: Each of the following sentences is numbered, but they are not arranged in one of the planned orders you have just been studying.

1. Cross off the printed number and next to it write the correct order number for each sentence to appear in the planned paragraph. Begin the paragraph with the topic sentence.
2. Write the paragraph properly on the lines below.

__4__ 1. Later, people choose foods by how they believe the food will taste.

__2__ 1. Yet most people develop such strong food preferences that they will not try a new food even if they are very hungry.

__6__ 3. All through life, people are careful about eating foods they are unfamiliar with.

1 4 Food is one of the most basic needs of all people.

5 5 By the time a child is 10 years old, he or she will give you reasons for food choices, though they do not all make sense.

3 6. Such preferences are developed partly by learning what not to eat when we are very young.

____

____

____

____

____

RECAP—PLANNING PARAGRAPHS

- Differentiate between general and specific statements by questioning/brainstorming or by clustering.
- Main ideas are supported by specifics.
- The time order works well to support some topic sentences.
- A space order organizes supporting statements in paragraphs on some subjects.
- Decide whether to put the point you want to emphasize most at the beginning or at the end of a paragraph.
- Your knowledge of audience affects the plan you will make for a paragraph.

Chapter 7

Drafting Paragraphs

In this chapter you will

- see why specific words are better than vague ones
- expand statements for detail
- write examples
- use transitions to connect ideas in a paragraph

For most writers, the "moment of truth" comes when they actually set pencil or pen to paper—or when they see their own words on the typewriter paper or the computer screen. No matter how much thinking, planning, or jotting down of words or phrases has been done, many people feel that until they actually see a paragraph or report materialize in front of them, they haven't done any *real* writing.

This takes into account that people work in different ways. You may want students to think about, and discuss, their own ways of writing.

The way to get that writing onto paper or screen varies from one individual to another. Some people like to write as fast as they can, capturing everything on paper very much like free writing, and then go over and over the work, revising it a great deal. Other people are more comfortable if they work slowly, figuring out sentences—even phrases—one at a time and polishing as they go, so they don't need to make a lot of changes in preparing to show their work to another person. Still other people write quickly at some times, rather slowly at others.

Some people want to change everything they write several times; others have no desire to vary even a word from what they record the first time. And lots of people change their first writing according to the reason they are writing, a business report or letter written as a variation on what they've done many times will certainly be quicker to write than something totally different from what has been written before.

Definition

If you've done the writing *Activities* so far in this book, you've been drafting. If group members suggested changes that you've followed, you've been drafting. If you've worked on a memo with someone at work, you've been drafting. If you've changed the wording on a report during a bus ride, you've been drafting. Drafting is at the heart of writing. In fact, what some people refer to as "writing" is almost entirely drafting—getting all those thought-about and planned ideas from jotted notes into a readable form on paper or the computer screen.

The object of writing drafts is not so much to get a piece "right" or "final," but to sharpen your own sense of what you want to say and how you want to say it. Some people call the first writing-out of a piece, whether a business letter or a formal essay, a "zero draft." Calling it "zero" means that version is just a start; it hasn't yet reached the first draft stage. How many drafts the writing goes through after that depends on your time and the importance of the writing.

Students need to get over the notion of a first draft, a fix-up for mechanics, then a final copy.

You will also spend more time drafting (and therefore redrafting or changing) what is important to you than you will on writing what you consider unimportant or of no consequence. For example, the memo a boss asks for, and on which a promotion may hinge, is certainly going to receive more time and attention in the writing than would a routine response to the customer who wants to know why a shipment is late. One draft (or none but the one to send out) may be all you want to bother with on that routine response, but you may draft and rewrite several versions of the important memo.

Drafting occupies much of a writer's time. If you don't set out to write already knowing the audience and purpose, you will decide on them before you can go much further. You may pick a subject quickly, even without narrowing as an extra step. A topic sentence may come to mind almost instantly. Even the plan for a piece of writing may be easy to decide on. But then you have to actually start writing—start drafting.

The way you write drafts and the amount of redrafting you do will vary according to the prewriting you have done. However, there are some elements that go into all writing, and you will consider them in this chapter:

- the words you choose
- the details in sentences
- the examples or illustrations, if you use them
- the transitions that connect ideas within the paragraph

Chances are that when you write drafts you won't think about all these elements at the same time, but good writing demands that you think about, and act on, each of them one or more times, whether you are drafting paragraphs or long essays, letters or proposals, memos or reports.

Using Specific Words

Does this sort of conversation sound familiar?

"Somebody called while you were out."

"Oh? Who?"

"I don't know."

"Was it a man or a woman?"

And there you are—still in the dark.

But suppose you received this message:

> "The tailor called at 10:30 to say your suit is ready, and to pick it up as soon as you can."

The word "vague" is used here. It could as well have been "general."

No question now. The message tells you who called, when, and why. It is specific; it is definite. Instead of the vague "somebody," you know that the caller was the tailor, and you know the time the call came in. Furthermore, the person who answered the phone took time to ask one or two questions, so you could have specific information about the purpose of the call.

Vague writing is rather like that first conversation, except that you can't ask questions. All that your readers have to go on is what's on the page; they can't question you to fill in missing details. Therefore, in order to leave fewer questions in the minds of your readers, **you should select words that are as specific as possible for your writing.**

In the left column below are some examples of vague words we all use frequently. Under each is a simple question that might be asked about it. The answer to that question appears in the right column as a specific word or phrase.

EXAMPLES ▶

Vague	*Specific*
tall	
How tall is tall?	6 ft. 8 inches
everybody	
Everybody in the whole world?	students in my psychology class
car	
What does it look like?	blue 1990 Ferrari
went	
How?	ran
sit	
Straight upright?	lounge

Students usually are able to add vague words to those here and work in groups or as a class to make them specific.

Sometimes you can substitute a specific word for a vague one. But often you need to substitute (or add) several words to be specific. However, see the difference that using specific words in a sentence makes, compared to using vague ones. The underlined words will remind you that they are the specifics in the list above.

EXAMPLES ▶

Antoinne is <u>6 ft. 8 inches tall</u>.

<u>All the students in my psychology class</u> were present on the day of the last test.

I just bought a <u>blue 1990 Ferrari</u>.

Thersa <u>ran</u> home with the her report card.

I couldn't wait to get home and <u>lounge</u> on the front porch.

These sentences with specific words and phrases are better than those using the vague words in the left-hand list, because when you read them you don't have to ask questions (or, at least, so many questions) about the author's intended meaning. They are examples of the sort of good writing—that is, **specific writing**—you can produce by changing vague words to specific ones when you are drafting even for a second or third time.

7-1

DIRECTIONS: Underline the vague words in each of the following sentences. Rewrite the sentence on the lines below it, making it more specific; underline your changed wording twice. (You may also choose to change the order of information slightly so your rewritten sentence reads more smoothly.)

EXAMPLE ▶ *The cat sat out front.*

The Persian cat sat outside my front door.

Vague words, and suggested word changes are shown in boldface and italics.

Students are usually interested in comparing their responses to this *Activity*.

1. Alfredo carried the heavy package upstairs.

   Alfredo carried the ***heavy*** package upstairs.

   Alfredo carried the ***50 pound*** package upstairs.

2. A lot of students in the class got As.

   A lot students in ***the class*** got As.

   Fifteen students in the ***advanced math class*** got As.

3. I received a box of candy.

   I received a box of ***candy.***

   I received a box of ***salt water taffy.***

4. Get ready quickly!

   Get ready ***quickly!***

   Get ready ***in three minutes!***

5. Boxers in training often eat big breakfasts.

   Boxers in training ***often eat big*** breakfasts.

   Every day boxers in training eat ***three eggs, six ounces of steak, and six slices of bread*** for breakfast.

6. Bad roofs should be fixed.

   Bad roofs should be ***fixed.***

   Leaky roofs should be ***made waterproof.***

7. Prices have gone up.

   Prices have ***gone up.***

   Prices on butter, sugar, flour, canned tomatoes, and spaghetti have gone up ***by 13%.***

8. The new carnival in town has some great rides.

   The new carnival ***in town*** has some ***great*** rides.

   The new carnival ***on route 27 north of town has breathtaking roller-coaster, spinning cage, and double spinning ferris wheel*** rides.

9. Use a strong light for a reading lamp.

   Use a ***strong light*** for a reading lamp.

   Use a ***150 watt bulb*** in a reading lamp.

10. The factory laid off some workers recently.

    The ***factory*** laid off ***some*** workers ***recently.***

    The ***computer keyboard assembly factory*** laid off ***300 workers*** last ***Friday.***

7-2

DIRECTIONS: On your own paper, copy out five sentences you have written so far that contain vague words you can make more specific. These sentences may come from your *Idea Journal*, or be parts of paragraphs for the various *Activities* you are doing in this book.

Underline once the vague words in the present sentences.Underline twice the more specific wording in the rewritten sentences.

You may need to oversee the sentence selections to be sure they are useful for *Activity 7-2.*

Most of the words you have made more specific in *Activity 7-1*, and probably some of those in *Activity 7-2,* are nouns. That is, they are words representing people, places, things, or ideas. But, as the example of the words "went" and "sit" at the beginning of this section show, some verbs, (words that show action) can also be made more specific.

You may be able to think of changing "went" to "ran" without much problem. If you don't immediately think of a more specific verb when you need one, try a standard dictionary. Look for the word you think may be vague; often you will find at the end of the definition words that are closely related or that supply the specific you want. For example, instead of "take," you may decide that "snare" or "capture" is more specific.

CAUTION: Don't substitute one word for another just because you found the new word in a dictionary or a thesaurus. Unless you are sure of the meaning and know that a word *really* expresses just what you want to say, stick with the more familiar one, even if it is more general (that is, vague) than you'd like.

7-3

DIRECTIONS: Underline once the vague words in the following paragraph.

To improve the paragraph, rewrite it on the lines below and double underline the words and phrases you make more specific.

pretty good
sometimes not, One day, really good
meat, potatoes, vegetables, low price
another day
really bad
good food that is healthy
lettuce and some other fixings

Eating in the school cafeteria is sometimes pretty good and sometimes not. One day last week I had a really good meal of meat, potatoes, and vegetables for a low price. On another day, all I ordered was a hamburger, but it was really bad. I discovered that most of the time the salad bar has good food that is healthy. If nothing else appeals to you, there is always lettuce and some other fixings.

More specific:

Eating in the school cafeteria means sometimes you *get tasty food at prices up to 40% lower than elsewhere* but sometimes *the food is badly prepared. On Monday* of last week I had a *hot, attractive-looking meal* of *moist, lightly browned slices of roast beef, scalloped potatoes in a creamy cheese sauce, and crisply cooked broccoli* for *$1.95.* On *Wednesday* all I ordered was a hamburger, but it was *dried out, tough, and served on a stale roll.* I discovered that most of the time the salad bar has a *wide variety of foods that are recommended for healthful eating.* If nothing else appeals to you, there is always *crisp green lettuce, red tomatoes, sliced mushrooms, onion rings, three-bean salad, bacon bits, pumpkin seeds, croutons, grated cheese, and at least French, bleu cheese, and Italian dressings.*

7-4

DIRECTIONS: Start a paragraph with a topic sentence. Use one of the sentences you made more specific in *Activity 7-2,* or a sentence in *Activity 7-1* that you believe can be the basis for a pargraph. Or use a topic sentence you developed for any other *Activity.* Write the full paragraph, paying special attention to using words as specific as possible in all the sentences.

Students may wish to use an original topic sentence developed for *Activity 7-4.*

Expanding Sentences for Detail

Making vague words specific is just one way of improving writing when you are drafting. Another way is to expand on the ideas in sentences by giving more details.

EXAMPLES ▶ My cousin Arnold likes to watch football.

It is about a specific person: *My cousin Arnold.* The rest of the sentence makes a statement about Arnold: [He] *likes to watch football.* The first part is called the subject (that is, who or what a sentence is about) and the second part (which tells what the subject does or is) is called the predicate. (See Chapter 5, pages 50-51) When you expand a sentence, *you can add information to the subject, to the predicate, or to both.* In the following example of expanding a sentence, the underlining shows additions to the original sentence:

My <u>first</u> cousin Arnold, <u>who lives with us</u>, likes to watch football <u>on TV every Monday night</u>.

Expanding a sentence gives the reader more information. Instead of having somebody ask questions about how close a cousin Arnold is, and whether he likes to attend games or watch them on TV, the expanded sentence above gives that information.

You may want to have students contribute some original examples for the class to work on.

Here are some other examples of sentences that are expanded. The underlined wording, in each of them, was added to answer questions a reader might have asked.

EXAMPLES  **This book puts me to sleep.**

Possible questions:
What book?
Why does it put you to sleep?
Does it always do that?
If it puts you to sleep, why are you reading it?

EXPANDED:
The book I was assigned to read for Humanities 111 is called *Shelter Now*, and the combination of small print and long sentences puts me to sleep every time I try to read it.

Recycling will save resources.

Possible Questions:
Recycling what?
By whom?
What resources?

EXPANDED:
The natural resources that go into making paper and containers of glass, metal, and plastic are being used up, but if everyone who uses those things separates them from garbage and trash, recycling will save the resources we now have.

COMMENT: That's an extreme example! The sentence is probably longer and more detailed than you'd want to write, but it shows what can be done by expanding. With the additional details, a reader is better able to visualize or understand exactly what you, the writer, want to communicate.

Activity 7-5

DIRECTIONS: In the following sentences, the subject is separated from the predicate by a vertical line. Expand the subject, the predicate, or both parts of the sentence, on the lines below each one. Underline the details you add when you expand the sentence.

EXAMPLE  **Sylvia | was awarded a scholarship.**

My neighbor, Sylvia Hernandez, | was awarded a volleyball scholarship for her last two years at college.

> You may find it necessary to get students started on this *Activity* so they will expand the sentences adequately.

1. The rain | was more than we expected.

   The *sudden* rain | was *three inches* more than we expected.

2. The job market | has improved.

   The job market *for service workers* | has improved *in this city over the last two months.*

3. Snow | made the roof collapse.

   A four-foot snowfall *last night* | made the roof *of my garage* collapse *early this morning.*

4. I | am taping my favorite song.

   I | am taping my favorite song, *"Hello, Hello, You There", on the new cassette player-radio I received for my birthday.*

5. My co-workers | gave me a party.

   My co-workers *in the office* | gave me *a surprise birthday* party *last Tuesday during afternoon break.*

6. Ice cream | is my favorite.

   Chocolate chip ice cream *covered with fudge sauce and whipped cream* | is my favorite *snack when watching TV.*

7. The telephone | keeps me in touch.

   The telephone | keeps me in touch *with my grandchildren who live in Central City.*

8. Bugs | are everywhere.

   Ants, spiders, mosquitoes, and other kinds of flying bugs | are everywhere *when I set foot outside the house in summer.*

9. Athletes | broke world records.

   Six athletes | broke world records *at the last Pan American games.*

10. Richard | enjoys reading the newspaper.

    My husband, Richard, | enjoys reading *the news and sports sections of the daily* newspaper *we get.*

7-6

DIRECTIONS: Choose a sentence you have written so far for any *Activity* in this book. Or, choose one from your *Idea Journal.*
Write the sentence here:

____

Make it a topic sentence if it's not yet suitable. and write it here:

____

Start a paragraph with this sentence. In the remaining sentences of the paragraph, give details that support the topic sentence. Use the order of time, space, or emphasis for the supporting sentences. Write on your own paper.

Check all the sentences in the paragraph to be sure they contain specific (rather than vague) words, and that the sentences are expanded to give details to readers.

Sharing

This procedure of multiple readings may be new to students. Urge them not to be impatient, but to follow through as suggested. Listening to the repeated readings aloud aid student listening skills.

1. Form a group with two other people.
2. Let one person read aloud twice the paragraph written for *Activity 7-6*. During the first reading, other people in the group listen carefully to the reader. During the second reading, they make notes—actually write down—three kinds of information:
   1) Noticeably specific words that make the writing come alive, or vague words that could be made more specific.
   2) Ideas or sentences that give complete information, or those that could be expanded.
   3) Recognition of the time, space, or emphasis order, or instances where such order does not come across clearly.

   Let the author read the paragraph aloud a third time, if requested by group members, so they can write the details.
3. Each person, in turn, should read aloud the notes on the three kinds of information recorded for the work of one author, discuss it, and then give the notes to the author.
4. Others in the group should then take turns reading their paragraphs
5. After the group session, each author should revise the paragraph on the basis of comments written by members of the group.

Writing Examples

Throughout this book you have been reading examples, and they have been so labeled. There have been examples of paragraphs written for specific audiences (in Chapter 2), examples of different ways to narrow subjects (in Chapter 4), examples of different ways to write topic sentences (in Chapter 5), and of organizing a paragraph (in Chapter 6). Almost every *Activity* has shown an example of what you are expected to do in it.

Most books just talk about using examples. This is an attempt to explain what the term means.

If an adult shows a child how to hit a nail straight on the head to drive it through a board, the person's action is an example the child can copy. If somebody says to you, "The people treat the customers like dirt. Let me tell you what happened to me in there the other day..." the speaker is about to give you an example.

As a matter of fact, the last two paragraphs have been examples of examples! The first paragraph was about examples that tried to use something familiar to help you, the reader, understand something that may have been unfamiliar. The second paragraph was about using actions or stories to illustrate points that one person wants another to know about.

An example is a specific, a detail. Writers use examples to help the audience understand information more clearly and more fully. They use examples, therefore, to:

1. Make familiar what may be unfamiliar.
2. Paint a word picture to aid understanding.

Although a writer doesn't always give specific warning that an example is coming, often the words "for instance," "for example," or "such as," signal that illustrations will follow. In fact, you will do your reader a favor by indicating that you are going to give one or more examples.

When you are writing drafts, you must decide whether or not to use examples. That choice is based on answering the question:

"Will my audience understand this information better if I write one or more examples?"

If the answer is "No," you should move on to the next part of the draft. Here are some statements that may not need examples. They probably do need support for full explanations.

EXAMPLES  **Math 101 and English 101 are courses required for graduation at this school.**

TV commercials about being able to see your reflection in the clean dishes seem silly to me.

However, if the answer to the question above is "Yes," or "Probably," you must then answer a further question: "What kind of example(s) will help make the information clearer?" That is, you must select instances to serve as examples or illustrations.

Burning off calories will lead to faster weight reduction.

Helpful examples: Naming some of the ways to burn off calories.

The 10% of the population that is left-handed has to accommodate itself to a right-handed world.

Helpful examples: Telling some of the things that left-handers have to do differently from right-handers.

Activity 7-7

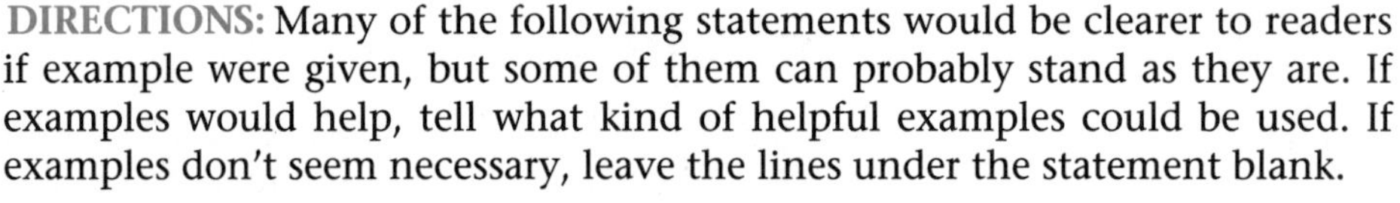

DIRECTIONS: Many of the following statements would be clearer to readers if example were given, but some of them can probably stand as they are. If examples would help, tell what kind of helpful examples could be used. If examples don't seem necessary, leave the lines under the statement blank.

EXAMPLE ▶ **In order to have a balanced diet, you should eat foods from the grain group daily.**

Helpful Examples:

name some of the foods in this nutritional group

This *Activity* makes a good collaborative experience. Also, have students discuss which items didn't seem to need examples and why.

1. Protective goggles are now required to be worn by all racquetball players.

   Helpful Examples:

   giving REASONS for wearing goggles is NOT the same as giving examples

2. Comparative shopping will show that prices on bread, milk, canned peas, margarine, and peanut butter vary at grocery stores in my neighborhood.

   Helpful Examples:

   give prices on those items from two or three different stores

3. I saw lots of old friends at Twyla's party last Saturday night.

   Helpful Examples:

   name some of the friends seen

4. Marcus complained that his office job was just as boring as his factory job was.

   Helpful Examples:

   give examples of what's boring about the office job (answering phone, filing, answering same questions, being with same people)

5. The Number 10 bus leaves from the downtown station at five minutes after every hour, from 6:05 a.m. to 11:05 p.m. weekdays.

   Helpful Examples:

6. This year, as usual, there are several new fashion fads being played up by TV, magazines, and newspaper ads.

   Helpful Examples:

   give examples of some of the fashion fads (neon colors, frayed jeans, men's partially-shaved heads)

7. Keeping up a car is more expensive than I thought it would be.

   Helpful Examples:

   tell what the unexpected expenses are turning out to be (gas, oil, engine repairs, new tires, insurance)

8. Hernando finds great satisfaction in doing volunteer work in his community.

   Helpful Examples:

   tell what that work is (running errands for a neighbor, delivering "meals on wheels", coaching boys' basketball team)

9. RosaMae was an hour late delivering the newspaper this morning.

   Helpful Examples:

   no examples needed

   giving REASONS for late delivery is NOT the same as giving examples

10. Studying the night before is just one example of effective preparation for a test.

    Helpful Examples:

    give other ways to prepare for a test (reviewing material daily, doing all required homework, taking effective notes, marking reading passages)

7-8

DIRECTIONS: Choose one of the sentences in *Activity 7-6* for which you listed examples that would be helpful explanations. Write the paragraph on your own paper, using one or more sentences for each example. Add other examples if you think of them while drafting the paragraph.

Transitions

Drafting is not only putting down a series of ideas for the audience, it is also connecting those ideas so the reader can see relationships among them. These "connections" are called the transitions. They are words and phrases within sentences and between sentences; they are also used between paragraphs.

Look at the differences in the following two paragraphs and see how the transitions underlined in one of them not only connect ideas, but also make reading seem smoother.

EXAMPLES ▶

***No* transitions:**
The duties of most cashiers include receiving money, making change, and filling out charge forms. They need to have good arithmetic skills. They must often handle a lot of money in a single day. They must be honest. Cashiers meet the public.They should look neat, act friendly and be helpful.

With transitions underlined: The duties of most cashiers include receiving money, and filling out charge forms. Therefore, they need to have good arithmetic skills. They must also be honest, because they must often handle a lot of money in a single day. In addition, since cashiers meet the public, they should look neat, act friendly, and be helpful.

Note the underlined words—the transitions—and how they signal a reader that a connection between ideas is being made:

therefore shows cause and effect
(cause=cashiers' duties)
(effect=need good arithmetic skills)

also shows addition
(addition=another quality [honesty])

because shows cause and effect
(cause=handling much money)
(effect=be honest)

in addition shows addition
(addition=more qualities of cashiers)

since shows cause and effect
(cause=meeting public)
(effect=be neat, friendly, helpful)

You can see that by connecting ideas, transitions signal your reader what to expect, or how to understand what you have written. As a writer, you have hundreds of transitional words and phrases available to you. Nobody expects you remember all of them, but by practicing and seeing how different *groups* of transitions help your writing, you will be better able to use what you need as you draft.

The groups of transitional words or phrases that follow will be listed as showing

- addition
- comparison
- contrast

- causality (cause and effect)
- time
- summary or restatement
- example or illustration
- purpose
- emphasis
- location

TRANSITIONS SHOWING EQUAL IMPORTANCE

Three groups of words are used with ideas of equal importance. They show

- addition
- comparison
- contrast

Addition, obviously, shows more of the same or equivalent ideas.

Transitions Showing Addition

again	also	and	and then
besides	equally	finally	first
further	furthermore	in addition	in the first place
last	likewise	moreover	next
nor	then	third	too
second (or any other numerical listing)			

The transition in this example is underlined.

EXAMPLE ▶ **I like to eat fish <u>and</u> I also like to eat chicken.**

EXPLANATION: Chicken is as satisfactory to eat as fish. Therefore, the transitional word and simply adds one idea (liking chicken) to another of equal importance (liking fish).

Comparison shows similarities between ideas of equal value or importance.

Transitions Showing Comparison

also	as well as	at the same time
equally important	in like manner	in the same way
likewise	similarly	

The transition in the example is underlined.

EXAMPLE ▶ **Mathematics, <u>as well as</u> English, is required for graduation.**

EXPLANATION: Mathematics is of equal importance to English as a graduation requirement.

Contrast shows differences between ideas that are basically of equal value or importance.

Transitions Showing Contrast

although	and yet	at the same time	but
conversely	despite	even so	even though
for all that	however	in contrast	instead of
in spite of	nevertheless	nonetheless	regardless
notwithstanding	on one hand	on the contrary	yet
on the other hand	otherwise	rather than	
still	whereas	while	

The transition in this example is underlined.

EXAMPLE ▶ **Helen didn't have a nibble all day; <u>however</u>, Wilma caught enough fish for three meals.**

EXPLANATION: The result of the day's fishing was different for the two women. The connector "however" signals a reader that a difference will be pointed out.

Activity

7-9

Bracketed word at the end of each sentence shows the kind of transition each is.

DIRECTIONS: Underline the transitional words or phrases that show addition, comparison, or contrast in the following sentences or groups of sentences.

EXAMPLE ▶ **More people than ever before in this country are watching or playing soccer. <u>Even so</u>, it is not yet considered a major sport by most colleges. [*contrast*]**

Transitional Words

1. I thought about studying law or medicine, but I decided both require too many years of schooling. [contrast] — but
2. Our school has a big department of furniture design. It also has a large department of upholstering. [addition] — also
3. Sharonella stayed up unusually late on Saturday night. Nevertheless, she would get up at 5 a.m. Sunday to go fishing. [contrast] — Nevertheless
4. First you need to assemble to ingredients for the cake. Then you must mix them in the order shown on the recipe. Finally, you pour the batter into a pan and bake the cake. [addition] — First Then Finally
5. Children under ten, as well as senior citizens, are charged a reduced entrance fee at the zoo. [comparison] — as well as senior citizens

TRANSITIONS SHOWING CAUSE AND EFFECT (CAUSALITY)

Many ideas are related because a cause (or causes) produces a result or effect. The familiar saying "April showers bring May flowers," shows a cause (that is, the showers) producing a result (that is, the flowers). Sometimes, however, you will not be able—or want—to write such a sentence. Rather, you will decide that a causality can be established most effectively by using transitional words or phrases to make the relationship.

Transitions Showing Causality

accordingly	as a result	because	consequently
evidenced by	for this reason	hence	if
providing that	since	so	so that
that	then	therefore	thereupon
thus	unless	whenever	

In the following example, the transition showing causality is underlined.

EXAMPLE  **The weather report on TV this morning said it would rain today, <u>so</u> I took my umbrella to work.**

EXPLANATION: Taking the umbrella to work was the result (effect) of the expected rain (cause) announced on the weather report.

TRANSITIONS SHOWING TIME

Sometimes you will want readers to be aware of the relationship of actions or ideas according to the time when they have happened or will happen. Or you will want readers to know that they are happening at the same time.

Transitions Showing Time

after	afterwards	and then	as long as
as soon as	at last	at length	at present
at the same time	before	currently	
during	eventually	ever since	finally
gradually	immediately	in the future	in the meantime
in the past	later	meanwhile	now
soon	suddenly	then	until
when	whenever	while	

In the following example, the transition showing time is underlined.

EXAMPLE ▶ It rained until noon today. <u>Afterwards</u>, the sun came out.

EXPLANATION: The relationship between the rain and the sun coming out is that of a time sequence: the events followed each other and therefore show a time difference.

7-10

DIRECTIONS: Circle the transitional words or phrases that show causality or time in the following sentences or groups of sentences.

EXAMPLE ▶ **I forgot to stop at the store on the way home and buy food for dinner. Therefore, I decided to eat out tonight [*causality*]**

Bracketed word at end of each sentence shows the kind of transition each is.
Transitional Words
Formerly
Later
Because
Hence
Subsequently

1. Spencer is now an attorney. Formerly, he was a paralegal aide in the same office. [time]
2. Many meals can be prepared in advance and kept refrigerated. Later, when guests arrive, they can be cooked, heated, or otherwise prepared for serving. [time]
3. Because the roof leaked during the last rainstorm, I am getting estimates on having it repaired. [causality]
4. If you examine the record of insurance claims, you will find that Central County has the highest number of auto accidents in the state. Hence, insurance companies will be permitted to charge higher rates to drivers in Central County. [causality]
5. The movie scene had to be shot 14 times before the director was satisfied. Subsequently, it was edited so that only six seconds appeared on the screen. [time]

TRANSITIONS SHOWING SUMMARY OR RESTATEMENT

When you are getting near the end of a series of ideas (or near the end of what you are writing), you can often help your reader to connect ideas by offering a summary that brings ideas together or by restating the principal points you have been making. Rather than simply tacking on a summary or restatement, or launching into one without warning to the reader, careful writers use one or more transitions to connect such ideas.

Transitions Showing Summary or Restatement

again	as has been noted	as you have read
for these reasons	in brief	in conclusion
in fact	in other words	in sum
of course	on the whole	that is
to be sure	to sum up	

Underlining shows the transition in this example.

EXAMPLE ▶ **You have seen the reports of expenses and the market analysis for sales. You already know that the market is soft, and changes suddenly and easily. In other words, you have seen that you should be careful about investing your money at this time.**

EXPLANATION: The second sentence states the same material, though in a slightly different way, as the first two sentences. Therefore, the transition used is a phrase that summarizes.

TRANSITIONS SHOWING EXAMPLE

As a writer, you will often use examples in your writing to make ideas clearer or more visual to a reader. However, it's important that you "tie together" these examples (if you are using more than one) and that you connect such examples with the main idea of a paragraph or longer work that you are writing. (See also Chapter 6).

Transitions Showing Example

an example is	an illustration is	for another thing
for example	for instance	for one thing
in fact	one such	some examples are
specifically	such as	

The transition signaling an example is underlined in this example.

EXAMPLE  **Many people believe that dreams have meaning. <u>For instance</u>, a dream about being lost in a forest is supposed to mean you can't decide about something you are thinking about doing.**

EXPLANATION: The second sentence gives a specific that is an example of the first sentence.

Activity 7-11

DIRECTIONS: Underline the transitional words or phrases that show summary or example in the following sentences or groups of sentences.

EXAMPLE ▶ I stopped at the store on the way home and bought tomato sauce, ground meat, two kinds of cheese, flat noodles, and onions. <u>Of course</u>, that means I'll make lasagna for dinner.

On the whole
specifically
In other words
Examples
For one thing

1. On the whole, this looks like a good year for my business. [summary]
2. My boss told me that two of my suggestions, specifically those about a new loading order and about a revised loading list form, had already resulted in cost savings for the company. [example]
3. In other words, all this means we are likely to have a new football stadium built on the property. [summary]
4. More careful driving can bring about better gas mileage. Examples of what you can do are to make gradual starts and stops, and to keep your engine tuned. [example]
5. Neighbors decided to protest the rezoning. For one thing, it would bring additional traffic to the area. [example]

TRANSITIONS SHOWING PURPOSE

To show your readers that what you've written has a reason or purpose, transitional words and phrases are available to you.

Transitions Showing Purpose

by the way	for this purpose	for this reason
if	in order to	lest
so that	to this end	whenever
with this object in mind		

In this example, the transition is underlined

EXAMPLE ▶ **Install a fish finder so that you can locate schools of fish.**

EXPLANATION: The statement shows that if your purpose is to find schools of fish, installing the fish finder will help achieve it.

TRANSITIONS SHOWING EMPHASIS

To emphasize something is to bring it to your reader's attention and to point it up as being of more importance than other ideas. You can do this by choosing transitions that not only connect ideas, but also show what you want to emphasize.

Transitions Showing Emphasis:

above all	especially	indeed
in any event	in fact	in particular
most important	to tell the truth	

Such a transition is underlined in the example.

EXAMPLE  **Improved reading skills will enable you to get homework done faster and more effectively. They will make you a more confident reader. Above all, the reading skills you learn today will serve you a lifetime.**

EXPLANATION: Several qualities of improved reading skills are shown in these sentences. The one the author believes most important and particularly wants to bring to the attention of the reader is introduced by the transitional wording for emphasis.

TRANSITIONS SHOWING LOCATION

In some pieces you write, the place or location of one element or one thing in relation to another is important to point out. You may visualize that location yourself; but good writing requires that you make that connection of location for readers so that they, too, can "see" what you know. To do so, you should use transitions to alert readers that you are going to make such a connection.

Transitions Showing Location

above	adjacent to	below	beside
beyond	closer	further	here
inside	nearby	next to	outside
north (south, east, west) of	on the opposite side	opposite to	
there	where		

The transition showing location is underlined in this example.

EXAMPLE  **I parked my car in Section B2 of the garage. Nearby, in Section B3, was one that looked exactly like my car. I even put my key in the car I didn't own.**

EXPLANATION: The word "nearby" connects the ideas of the look-alike cars by showing a location that accounts for the confusion stated in the third sentence. The transition also makes reading smoother.

7-12

Bracketed word at end of each sentence shows the kind of transition each is.

DIRECTIONS: Underline the transitional words or phrases that show purpose, emphasis, or location in the following sentences or groups of sentences.

EXAMPLE  **A couch took up most of one wall. Opposite it was a wide-screen television set. [location]**

For this purpose

1. Putting the shelves together is easy because all materials except tools are already in the package. For this purpose, you will need only a screwdriver and pliers. [purpose]

beyond

2. I could see a police car coming, and beyond it an ambulance. [location]

Indeed

3. One should always try to be truthful. Indeed, honesty is really the best policy. [emphasis]

above all

4. Sticking to a diet requires, above all, a change in eating habits. [emphasis]

To that end

5. You can save money on your clothes if many different shirts and slacks go together. To that end, choose related colors and styles that aren't too far out. [purpose]

RECAP OF TRANSITIONS

You have just studied and practiced with ten different groups of transitions. So that you don't have to keep flipping pages back and forth, here is a summary of transitional words and phrases in each group:

This summary is offered as a convenient reference for students.

- **Addition**: again, also, and, and then, besides, equally, finally, first, further, furthermore, in addition, in the first (second, third, etc.) place, last, likewise, moreover, next, nor, second (or any other numerical listing) then, third, too
- **Comparison:** also, as well as, at the same time, equally important, in like manner, in the same way, likewise, similarly
- **Contrast:** although, and yet, at the same time, but, conversely, despite, even so, even though, for all that, however, in contrast, instead of, in spite of, nevertheless, nonetheless, notwithstanding, on one hand, on the contrary, on the other hand, otherwise, rather than, regardless, still, whereas, while, yet
- **Causality:** accordingly, as a result, because, consequently, evidenced by, for this reason, hence, if, providing that, since, so, so that, that, then, therefore, thereupon, thus, unless, whenever
- **Time:** after, afterwards, and then as long as, as soon as, at last, at length, at present, at the same time, before, currently, during, eventually, ever since, finally, gradually, immediately, in the future, in the meantime, in the past, later, meanwhile, now, soon, suddenly, then until, when, whenever, while
- **Summary or Restatement:** again, as has been noted, as you have read, for these reasons, in brief, in conclusion, in fact, in other words, in sum, of course, on the whole, that is, to be sure, to sum up

- **Example or Illustration:** an example is, an illustration is, for another thing, for example, for instance, for one thing, in fact, one such, some examples are, specifically, such as
- **Purpose:** by the way, for this purpose, for this reason, if, in order to, lest, so that, to this end, whenever, with this object in mind
- **Emphasis:** above all, especially, indeed, in any event, in fact, in particular, most important, to tell the truth
- **Location:** above, adjacent to, below, beside, beyond, closer, further, here, inside, nearby, next to, north (south, east, west) of, on the opposite side, opposite to, outside, there, where

Activity 7-13

You may want to have students work in pairs for this *Activity*. Most like to compare notes after they've done the paragraphs.

DIRECTIONS: Write an appropriate transition on each of the lines in the following paragraphs. The word in parentheses under the line suggests the kind of transition to use.

Paragraph 1.

Anybody who wants to prepare for a career as an opera singer must __also__ be prepared for a great deal of learning and
(addition)
lifelong practice. __For instance__ the person must
(example)
__first__ learn several languages in addition to English. Most operas
(time)
are sung in French, Italian, or German, __so__ the individual must learn
(causality)
one or more of those languages. __Another example__ of the learning
(addition, example)
required is that vocal techniques have to be studied and practiced.

__Still another example__ of learning is that both the words and
(addition; example)

the music of many roles must be memorized __because__ opera singers
(causality)
are expected to know ten or fifteen different roles at all times.

__Sometimes__ a singer is called on to perform a role with only a day
(time)
or two's notice. Operas are plays that are sung, __so__ people who
(causality)
perform in them must also know how to act. __To that end__ ,
(purpose)
anyone who decides to be an opera performer must

also learn acting. ___Above all___, anyone who decides to be an
(emphasis)
opera singer must be prepared to devote a lifetime to studying and

keeping these skills. ___As you can tell___, being an opera singer isn't easy!
(summary or restatement)

Paragraph 2.
Reading and writing skills are so closely connected ___that___ it's hard to
(causality)
know which is more important. ___Although___ you need to have
(contrast)
something in writing ___in order to___ read it, you could not write if
(purpose)
you could not read. ___Indeed___, reading is easier to learn than writing,
(emphasis)
as ___evidenced by___ the fact that children learn to read a little
(causality)
before they start learning to write. ___Specifically___, it's harder to
(example)
hold a pencil for writing ___than___ to recognize letters and words
(contrast)
for reading. You could probably get along pretty well if you knew

how to read ___but___ not how to write. ___However___, once
(contrast) (contrast)
you learn to read, it's not too hard to learn to write.

Paragraph 3.
Two points of view exist about doing volunteer work.

___On one hand___ are those who believe people should be paid for
(contrast)
the work they do. ___For example___, if a volunteer helps admit
(example)
patients to a hospital, that person should be paid as much as one

whose salaried job is admitting patients. ___On the other hand___,
(contrast)

many believe that volunteers undertake the jobs they do

___because___ they want to spend their spare time usefully
(causality)

___and___ because it makes them feel good to know
(addition)

they are making a contribution to their community ___or___ to their
(contrast)

society as a whole. To offer money to these people who volunteer

their time and energy would be an insult and would ___also___
(addition)

deprive them of a psychological necessity.

7-14

DIRECTIONS: Copy a paragraph you wrote in *Activities 7-1, 7-3, 7-6,* or in your *Idea Journal*. Underline each transitional word or expression you have used. Add other transitions that will help readers understand the connections you meant between ideas and circle them, also. In the margin next to each circled transition, write what kind of transition you have used. The list below is a reminder of the kinds of transitions available to you.

- addition
- comparison
- contrast
- causality (cause and effect)
- time
- summary or restatement
- example or illustration
- purpose
- emphasis
- location

7-15

DIRECTIONS: Be silly! Write an original paragraph using as many transitions as you can, as long as what you write makes sense. Underline the transitions you use. Use your own paper.

There's no limit to the number of transitions to be used. Students have enjoyed outdoing each other on this writing. Or, you may want to have students work in groups on this.

Sharing

1. Form a group with two or three other people.
2. Read aloud a paragraph you wrote for *Activity 7-13* or *Activity 7-14* while the others listen. Then read it again, letting others in the group signal each transition they spot. Show the paragraph to others in the group if they need to see it in order to recognize the transitions.
3. If others in the group can suggest more or better transitions, consider following their advice and making appropriate changes to what you have written.
4. Let others in the group repeat 2, 3, and 4 so that each author has the same opportunity to work with everyone on transitions.

RECAP—DRAFTING PARAGRAPHS

- Drafting is writing on the basis of prewriting (audience, purpose, subject, topic sentence, and a plan).
- Drafting includes attention to words, details, examples, and transitions.
- Using specific words and phrases lets readers know precisely what you mean.
- Expanding sentences to add detail is another way of helping your readers understand your intent.
- Use examples to make the unfamiliar familiar and to paint word pictures.
- Transitions connect ideas within and between sentences.

Chapter 8

Revising and Proofreading

In this chapter you will

- arrange paragraph ideas so that they are orderly and stick together
- include all required information in a paragraph
- watch for consistency in person and tense
- eliminate wordiness in sentences
- rework sentences for variety
- improve word choices
- proofread for spelling, grammar, punctuation, and capitalization

Direct students to Chapters 19 through 30 and 32 for practice on these matters.

Students may not believe that revising occurs all during drafting, so it pays to emphasize the point.

To revise a piece of writing means to look at it again with the intention of making changes that will improve it. Because writing is an on-going process, you probably revise *during* drafting as well as *after* it. Some activities included in revision are:

- Moving parts of the composition to another location
- Removing sections of the composition completely
- Adding new ideas
- Changing words
- Changing sentence structures
- Shifting a tense or pronoun for consistency

Revising, in short, is what you do before you proofread and then let go of what you are working on. "Letting go" may mean that you turn the piece of writing over to a teacher, a superior at work, a colleague, a mail box, or a fax machine for transmission. It may also mean that you decide you don't want to work on the piece any longer, and then you simply put it away or destroy it.

Students usually find that a discussion of ways of distancing oneself from writing is useful.

Whether it's a paragraph for class, a memo to the boss, or a ten-page report, if you have time to put away the piece of writing briefly before letting it go, you have the advantage of looking at it as a fresh work when you attend to the final revisions. After you have moved away from it, you will find it possible to look at the writing less as a piece of yourself, and more as words on paper.

As a member of a group sharing the writing of your colleagues, you move away from a written piece. That writing isn't your own, so you can evaluate it on the basis of how it comes across to you. The trick for revision is to get that same sense of distance from writing that you, yourself, produce!

Revising for Logic and Coherence

Every sentence and every idea in a paragraph must follow the one before it in an orderly way. Sometimes the word "logic" is used to describe the progression of one thought following another.

Another word used to describe a well-written paragraph is "coherence," or all the thoughts in a paragraph sticking together and without interruption. Therefore, when you read for revision, make sure the thoughts in a paragraph are put together with order and coherence.

Writers may also revise a sentence that doesn't quite fit in. However, here deletion is recommended as more appropriate for basic writing students.

Any ideas that don't fit tightly into a paragraph should be deleted (cut out). Don't feel you have to hold onto them! You should never worry about losing words and then not having enough. You have so many thousands of words inside to call up as you need them that it's unlikely you will ever run out of words!

In the following examples, the wording that doesn't belong in the paragraph is underlined and there is an explanation of why it ought to be deleted.

EXAMPLES 

Travelers often use battery-operated alarm clocks because the batteries weigh less than an ounce and they are light to carry. These clocks are very reliable because the batteries last a long time. Also, these clocks are noiseless and therefore will never keep anyone awake. The loud "tick-tock-tick-tock" of wind-up alarm clocks is very annoying next to the bed when you are trying to sleep. Finally, the price of battery-operated alarm clocks is now comparable to wind-up or electric clocks, which are not as good for traveling.

COMMENT: The sentence underlined is about sound, but *not* about the sound of battery-operated alarm clocks, the subject of the paragraph. It should be deleted.

I have found that rubber cement is the best thing to use for gluing one piece of paper to another. My son uses it when he has to cut out and paste down magazine pictures for notebooks and posters for school. I use it for gluing pictures into my photo albums. If either of us leaves the jar standing uncovered or doesn't screw on the lid tight, air gets into the rubber cement and makes it thicken. Rubber cement can't be used to glue broken dishes together. I buy a special liquid thinner to put in the jar and make the rubber cement usable again.

COMMENT: The underlined sentence is about repairing dishes, rather than about gluing one piece of paper to another, as announced in the first sentence. It should be removed.

Snorkeling is a way of looking at life in the ocean that can be enjoyed by people of all ages. If you can swim, you can learn to snorkel in an hour or less. <u>That is in contrast to scuba diving, for which you must take a course and be certified.</u> You will need a face mask or goggles so that water will not distort the things you look at. You will also need a snorkel, through which you breathe. Fins on your feet will help propel you through the water with less effort than if you don't wear them. With this simple equipment, you can see amazing fish under the sea that never fail to thrill snorkelers.

COMMENT: The underlined sentence is about another way to view sea life under water. However, it doesn't belong in the paragraph, because the sentence before it and those following it are about snorkeling, not scuba diving.

8-1

DIRECTIONS: In some of the following paragraphs you will find at least one sentence that doesn't fit into the content. If you find such a sentence, cross it out and write a **D** (for delete) in the space to the left of the paragraph number.

D
According to a dictionary, a gadget is a small mechanical device.

_____ 1. A new kind of gadget that many people consider a necessity is on the market now. According to a dictionary, a gadget is a small mechanical device. It is an information organizer that is like a miniature computer, and it's small enough to fit into a handbag or suit pocket. It can store appointments, phone numbers, addresses, important days, and a lot of other information. Then you can call up what you need from the information organizer when you need it.

D
On the other hand, rain is a natural weather phenomenon that isn't a bit scary.

_____ 2. Many natural weather phenomena are scary because they happen with little or no warning. An earthquake is one such scary happening. One minute the ground under your feet is solid and stable, but the next minute it could be shaking. On the other hand, rain is a natural weather phenomenon that isn't a bit scary. Tornados are frightening because individual ones usually occur without warning, and because nobody can predict their path.

_____ 3. I always like to have my apartment look nice, so two weeks ago I bought three framed posters. I didn't hang them until last weekend because I had a hard time deciding where to hang each one. Finally, I put the poster of the auto show on the east wall. The country scene is restful, and I hung it over the couch. The wall over the table seemed the proper place to hang the salad poster. Now my apartment looks more attractive because of the posters.

D
The Olympic games give me a chance to see other kinds of sports.

_____ 4. I like to have sports shows on the TV when I do homework. I can watch them or not, depending on what my homework is. Sometimes I turn down the sound so I can hardly hear it, so that doesn't bother me. I am enough of a sports nut to watch any kind of sports show. I like football and baseball and basketball. I watch volleyball and soccer and tennis. I will watch golf when it is on. None of these sports on TV distract me or interferes with homework. The Olympic games give me a chance to see other kinds of sports.

_____ 5. Going to the food market with a shopping list will keep you from spending too much money. Research shows that many items in the shopping cart are bought on impulse. That is, people put into the cart items they don't really need, but pick up because they remember an ad for the product, or because they get a sudden urge to eat something. Items bought on impulse will make your shopping bill go up when they are checked out at the cash register. Therefore, you should always go to the market with a shopping list, and force yourself to stick to it.

D
As more personal video cameras are sold, people will take more films.

_____ 6. Letter-writing is almost a lost art, and that is going to make a difference to future historians. We have interesting and useful information about the Revolutionary and Civil Wars because letters that soldiers wrote home were kept by their families and handed down through the generations. In this century, people seem a lot more hurried; they don't take time to write long letters, either during war or peace times. As more personal video cameras are sold, people will take more films. Most recently, people have been sending audio tapes and even VCR tapes back and forth among family and friends who are separated. They will be like "letters" to future historians. Many people would rather telephone than write or send tapes, and that is information that will be completely lost to later generations and to historians.

D
However, music is an entirely different matter.

_____ 7. Artists have always relied on wealthy patrons to provide them with money to live on while they created painting and sculpture, and designed buildings. Some of the greatest examples of the arts that we have to enjoy today were sponsored by such individuals. People who say we don't have great art because artists no longer are employed by the wealthy are wrong. Instead of individuals, the wealthy patrons of the arts in the U.S. today are corporations. They are having new buildings designed for their offices, and decorative arts created to beautify them; they are paying artists to create these useful and attractive work places. However, music is an entirely different matter.

D
When they make this decision, they have more money to spend on themselves.

_____ 8. The so-called "nuclear family," consisting of a husband, wife, and children, is not as wide-spread as it once was. Many married adults have decided not to have children. When they make this decision, they have more money to spend on themselves. Single-parent households are increasingly common. So are extended family arrangements in which other family members, such as grandparents, aunts, uncles, and cousins, live together. Single people often choose to live alone. Alternate life styles such as two people of the same sex setting up a household, or heterosexuals living communally, seem to be on the increase.

_____ 9. Getting into the recycling habit is a positive step everyone can take at home to help preserve the environment. Many cities now have recycling contracts with private companies that will pick up newspapers, cans, and bottles weekly at private homes and apartment buildings. You are expected to separate the newspapers from the other trash, and sometimes to also separate the cans and bottles from each other. You could save the newspapers for school paper drives or to sell on your own to paper recycling companies. People can still make a little money by collecting tin cans and selling them to a recycler. The same is possible for bottles and plastic containers that you can gather and take to a recycling company instead of allowing them to be tossed away with garbage and other trash.

____ 10. The idea of "micro-lending" is a proven alternative to help people without a credit rating borrow up to about $2000 to start their own businesses. Loans are usually much less than that, and are made by a foundation or other group. They go to people who have no credit rating and could not get the money from a bank, but who have good ideas, are of good character, and are willing to work hard. People who receive the loans form groups and learn together about accounting and management while starting their businesses. I learned about micro-loans from a magazine article. While learning, and afterwards, the new business owners act as a support group for each other. They also contribute a little each week to a fund which micro-lends to more new business-people. The repayment rate of such business-starting loans has been 98%, which surprises traditional bankers.

D
I learned about micro-loans from a magazine article.

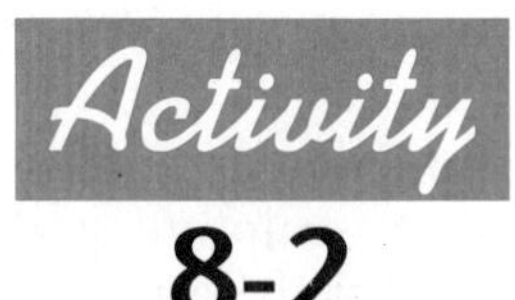

8-2

DIRECTIONS: In each of the following paragraphs, all the sentences are numbered. In some paragraphs one sentence is out of order. That is, it doesn't fit in logically with the sentences before and after it. The sentence does, however, belong in the paragraph, and only needs to be moved to its proper place.

If any of the sentences don't fit logically on the line below, write the numbers from left to right representing the correct sentence order. Then, write out the paragraph properly in the space provided. If the paragraph is all right as it stands, write the sentence numbers but do not recopy it.

EXAMPLE 

[1]Keep a dictionary handy when you write because it gives you many kinds of information. [2]You will use it most often to it to find the correct spelling of a word. [3]Finally, the dictionary gives you synonyms and antonyms for many words and that information can help make your writing better. [4]You can also find the pronunciation in the dictionary, which will help if you have to read out loud what you have written.

Although students may feel that just unscrambling the order of the sentences is adequate, writing the complete paragraph in order is worthwhile, for it gives one's hand the "feel" of complete writing.

The proper order of the sentence numbers is:

1 2 4 3

Write the sentences in correct order on these lines:

Keep a dictionary handy when you write because it gives you many kinds of information. You will use it most often to find the correct spelling of a word. You can also find the pronunciation in the dictionary, which will help if you have to read out loud what you have written. Finally, the dictionary gives you synonyms and antonyms for many words and that information can help make your writing better.

1. [1]I know I would have to do a lot of comparison shopping to find the telephone company with the best long distance rates. [2]The telephone companies seem to be in a war of prices. [3]If you watch the television commercials, one company and then another will tell you that its long distance charges are cheaper than anybody else's. [4]My father said it's true that the cost of a long distance phone call is cheaper than he remembers it was when he was my age, but that there is less variation than the ads want us to believe. [5]If I had a business and had to choose a long distance company to use, I think I would have a hard time.

   The proper order of the sentence numbers is:

   2 3 4 5 1

   Write the sentences in correct order on these lines:

   The telephone companies seem to be in a war of prices. If you watch the television commercials, one company and then another will tell you that its long distance charges are cheaper than anybody else's. My father said it's true that the cost of a long distance phone call is cheaper than he remembers it was when he was my age but that there is less variation than the ads want us to believe. If I had a business and had to choose a long distance company to use, I think I would have a hard time. I know I would have to do a lot of comparison shopping to find the telephone company with the best long distance rates.

2. [1]Getting together mailing lists and selling them to all kinds of advertisers is big business. [2]If that one list is sold to five companies, you are immediately on six different lists. [3]Your name can be on just one list because you bought a product or joined an organization, and all of a sudden you are on a lot more mailing lists and you get a great deal of unexpected mail. [4]If those six are each sold to six other companies, you are instantly on 36 mailing lists.

   The proper order of the sentence numbers is:

   1 3 2 4

   Write the sentences in correct order on these lines:

   Getting together mailing lists and selling them to all kinds of advertisers is big business. Your name can be on just one list because you bought a product or joined an organization and all of a sudden you are on a lot more mailing lists and you get a great deal of unexpected mail. If that one list is sold to five companies, you are immediately on six different lists. If those six are each sold to six other companies, you are instantly on 36 mailing lists.

3. [1]My family and I try to pick different places to eat. [2]That way we get to try different kinds of food and don't always eat the same familiar kind. [3]One of my family's favorite ways to celebrate a birthday or anniversary is by going out for dinner. [4]Luckily, we have many kinds of restaurants in our city. [5]We have been to Chinese, Thai, Indonesian, Indian, Cuban,

Spanish, Armenian, Norwegian, Japanese, and French restaurants. [6]One of the kinds of restaurants we have missed is an American restaurant, so I asked to go to one for my next birthday.

The proper order of the sentence numbers is:

3 1 2 4 5 6

Write the sentences in correct order on these lines:

One of my family's favorite ways to celebrate a birthday or anniversary to going out for dinner. We try to pick different places to eat. That way we get to try different kinds of food and not always eat the same familiar kind. Luckily, we have many kinds of restaurants in our city. We have been to Chinese, Thai, Indonesian, Indian, Cuban, Spanish, Armenian, Norwegian, Japanese, and French restaurants. One of the kinds of restaurants we have missed is an American restaurant, so I asked to go to one for my next birthday.

4. [1] The international Olympic games are held every four years. [2] In between Olympics, athletes from this hemisphere have a chance to compete in the Pan American games. [3] The United States usually sends several hundred men and women to compete in various water and track sports, as well as in such team sports as baseball and basketball. [4] These athletes look forward to the competition that will put them into the Pan American games as practice for what they will face trying for a spot representing the U.S. at the Olympic games. [5] They also view competing with athletes of other countries as a preview of what they will face if they are chosen two years later for the international games.

The proper order of the sentence numbers is:

1 2 3 4 5

Write the sentences in correct order on these lines:

5. [1] Many people enter contests as a hobby. [2] Some contests are phone-ins to local radio stations. [3] Other contests require people to mail in a form or coupon, and the winner is picked from among the responses received by the sponsor. [4] A variation of that is coupons with scratch-off spots that win prizes if pictures or words under them match. [5] Those who enter such contests don't necessarily have to buy the product that sponsors the contest. [6] If the caller identifies a song, answers a question, or is just the designated number caller, the person wins a prize. [7] Still other kinds of contests require the entrant to finish a sentence or write a poem about a product, and the best ones win prizes. [8] Hobbyists say that the more contests a person enters, the better chance there is of winning.

The proper order of the sentence numbers is:

1 2 6 3 4 5 7 8

Write the sentences in correct order on these lines:

Many people enter contests as a hobby. Some contests are phone-ins to local radio stations. If the caller identifies a song, answers a question, or is just the designated number caller, the person wins a prize. Other contests require people to mail in a form or coupon, and the winner is picked from among the responses received by the sponsor. A variation of that is coupons with scratch-off spots that win prizes if pictures or words under them match. Those who enter such contests don't necessarily have to buy the product that sponsors the contest. Still other kinds of contests require the entrant to finish a sentence or write a poem about a product, and the best ones win prizes. Hobbyists say that the more contests a person enters, the better chance there is of winning.

Revising Content for Information

You may want to have students turn back to Chapter 2 and review material there on audience.

This section emphasizes how the audience affects content, so an audience is stated for each example and *Activity*.

A fresh re-reading of a paragraph sometimes shows that a detail or explanation is missing, and therefore the sense of the work is interrupted. It's as if *you* know what you mean, but you didn't let the reader know—so the reader has to stop and think "I need more information here." Thinking of the reader as somebody other than yourself may seem confusing, but if you put yourself in the place of the intended audience, you are likely to pick up such gaps when you revise. Then you can add the needed information before your work gets to the audience.

Here is an example of writing that is suited for someone who knows the author. However, if the same sentences opened a piece meant for a different reader, that person wouldn't get past the first sentence without asking for information.

EXAMPLE  AUDIENCE: ***Classmates.*** **One weekend Sylvia, Jack, Kim, and I went to our usual hangout to have fun. Little did we know that we would run into trouble...**

COMMENT: The first sentence will stop any reader who doesn't know the author.

Which weekend?

Which day—or evening—of the weekend?

Who is Sylvia?

Who is Jack?

Who is Kim?

What or where is the "usual hangout"?

What is your idea of "fun"?

REVISION: **Last Saturday morning my cousin Sylvia, our high school friends Jack and Kim, and I went to our favorite spot at Countyline Beach for a day of swimming and surfing. Little did we know that we would run into trouble...**

COMMENT: The revised content answers the questions that came to mind after reading the first version of this paragraph opening. Now the reader no longer has to guess what the writer means. (Guesses are sometimes wrong, too.)

The next example is quite different. Although it, too, depends on the reader having some information, it's widely known information.

EXAMPLE ▶ AUDIENCE: ***Student who has taken psychology.*** **I've just started seeing a new psychologist. She is mainly a follower of Rogers and Maslow, but I believe she has also been influenced by Jung and Adler.**

COMMENT: This audience would need no further explanation. Using the names alone is a kind of "short-hand," a way for the writer to communicate with a reader that shares this knowledge. Otherwise, many questions would need to be answered, both about the people and their theories.

Who is/was Rogers?

Who is/was Maslow?

Who is/was Jung?

Who is/was Adler?

Any author who answered all those questions would end up writing a treatise on psychology, instead of something about seeing the new psychologist.

Here is yet another example of how important the audience is in determining what information may have to be added when you revise your writing.

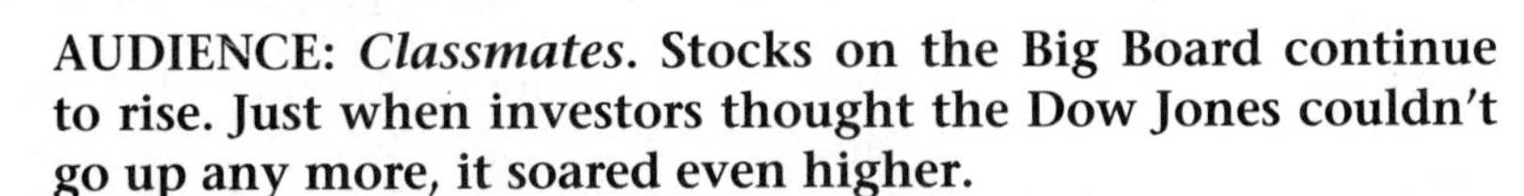

EXAMPLE ▶ AUDIENCE: ***Classmates.*** **Stocks on the Big Board continue to rise. Just when investors thought the Dow Jones couldn't go up any more, it soared even higher.**

COMMENT: Whether or not information is missing depends on the knowledge of classmates. Some may understand this terminology and need no further explanation. Others may need to have some questions answered by having the passage rewritten.

Is this about "stocks" as in the "stock market"?

What is the "Big Board"?

Who or what is Dow Jones?

What "soared even higher"?

Unless the author is sure that almost all classmates will understand the passage, it ought to be revised. Here is one possibility.

REVISION: **The prices of stocks for businesses listed on the New York Stock Exchange continue to rise. Just when investors thought the Dow Jones Industrial Average had reached its highest point, it went up even more, showing a general rise in stock prices.**

8-3

DIRECTIONS: Some of the following groups of sentences (not all are complete paragraphs) lack information, and therefore will interfere with audience understanding. If there is such a lack, underline the passage that needs further explanation. Then, on the lines, rewrite the whole sentence in which it appears. (Add other sentences, if doing so seems appropriate.) Find information or depend on your own imagination to fill in what's missing.

If the group of sentences has all the information necessary, write "No Revision Needed" on the lines below it.

Activities such as this carry the danger of stereotyping, but that seems preferable to ignoring the importance of audience.

EXAMPLE  **AUDIENCE: *Teacher.* My high school grades weren't very good. That's why I decided to join the Marines after graduation instead of trying to get into a college.**

REVISION:

My high school grades averaged only a low C.

all the things I learned in the first year

1. AUDIENCE: *Relatives.* Now that I'm in my second year of college, I can look back at all the things I learned in the first year that are making life easier for me now. My grades have gone from Cs to Bs and I even got an A in Sociology.

   REVISION:

   Now that I'm in my second year of college, I can look back at what I learned in the first year that is making life easier for me now. I learned to study effectively, waste less time, pay more attention in class, and not be distracted so easily.

I read several books.

2. AUDIENCE: *High school students.* I learned that daily reading will improve my reading skill, so over last summer I read several books. Now I feel better about doing reading required in school this term.

   REVISION:

   I learned that daily reading will improve my reading skill, so over last summer I read four books. Two of them were about my hobby of tropical fish, one was *A Tale of Two Cities*, and the other was *1984*.

so much bad news on television that I recently

3. AUDIENCE: *Classmates.* There has been so much bad news on television that I recently decided to stop watching the TV news programs. Mostly, now, I get my news out of the paper, and that way I can skip what I don't want to know about.

   REVISION:

   There have been so many rapes, murders, hold-ups, wars, and reports of toxic waste dumping reported on television that two weeks ago I decided to stop watching the TV news.

phenomenal food. There are the usual Italian standbys, in addition to American picnic foods.

4. AUDIENCE: *Students in another country.* The annual picnic of my large Italian family always features phenomenal food. There are the usual Italian standbys, in addition to American picnic foods.

REVISION:

The annual picnic of my large Italian family always features more food than we can eat in one day. There are the usual Italian standbys of cheese-laden lasagne, spicy salami, and pungent cheeses. In addition, we have such American picnic foods as hot dogs, hamburgers, and potato salad.

cut out coupons
a little bit of savings,
adds up.

5. AUDIENCE: *Members of a budgeting club.* I always cut out coupons to help save money at the supermarket. Last week I had only a little bit of savings, but over a year every little bit adds up.

REVISION:

I always cut out food coupons from the newspaper to help save money at the supermarket. Last week I only saved $2.37, but over a year every little bit adds up and I saved more than $120 this way last year.

6. AUDIENCE: *Third grade class.* One secret of how nature works is the way you and I get food and fresh air. The sun releases great amounts of energy that plants use to live on and grow. Some of those plants we use as food. Besides taking in the sun's energy, plants change it to a chemical energy that they release into the air. That, in turn, gives humans and other animals fresh air to breathe.

REVISION:

No revision needed.

a reflecting or a refracting telescope.

light-years.

7. AUDIENCE: *Scouts about to start working on an astronomy badge.* If you are thinking of getting or making a telescope for this badge work, you first need to decide if you want a reflecting or a refracting telescope. Then, if you want to start thinking like an astronomer, you have to begin understanding distances in light-years.

REVISION:

If you are thinking of getting or making a telescope for this badge work, you first need to decide if you want a reflecting or a refracting telescope. In a reflecting telescope, the image of what you want to look at appears on a large curved mirror and it is then reflected onto another mirror. You then look at the image from beneath that mirror or from the side of it. In a refracting telescope, the image that comes through the objective lens is viewed by the eyepiece lens. Then, if you want to start thinking like an astronomer, you have to begin understanding distances in light-years. A light-year is approximately 5,878 trillion miles.

codes

lightning rods

8. AUDIENCE: *Beginning architecture students.* Always check the building codes of the area for which you are designing a structure. In addition to electrical, plumbing, sewer, and structural codes, most communities now include lightning rods in their regulations.

REVISION:

Always check the building rules of the area for which you are designing a structure. In addition to electrical, plumbing, sewer, and structural rules, most communities now require that a metal rod or rods be placed high on a structure to conduct lightning to the ground and prevent damage to the structure.

short showers
use water only when necessary.

9. AUDIENCE: *People who want to save on water bills.* Take short showers instead of baths, and use water only when necessary. Also, don't keep water running while you are brushing your teeth, shaving, or washing your hands and face.

REVISION:

Take showers of less than five minutes instead of baths, and use water only to wet down and rinse off after soaping. Also, don't keep water running while you are brushing your teeth, shaving, or washing your hands and face.

a good car right price

10. AUDIENCE: *Someone thinking of buying a car.* Look at car ads and ask friends or acquaintances if they know of any cars for sale. Before long, you are bound to find a good car at the right price.

REVISION:

Look at car ads and ask friends or acquaintances if they know of any cars for sale. Before long, you are bound to find a car that runs well, has the equipment on it that you want, is a color you like, and has less than 75,000 miles on it, at the price you can afford to pay.

Only item 6 does not require revision.

8-4

Students are again sent back to their *Idea Journals* as sources for writing.

DIRECTIONS: Select an audience for each of two different paragraphs on any subjects you choose from your *Idea Journal,* from the listings you made in Chapter 1, or from discussions with friends or in class. Name the intended audience in parentheses at the top of each paragraph. Develop the paragraphs according to what you learned in Chapters 6 and 7 about planning and drafting paragraphs. Revise your paragraphs to make sure the sentence order is logical, and that you have included all necessary information for your readers.

Revising for Consistency

Once someone starts reading your work, you draw that person along what you have to communicate. If what you've written doesn't surprise the reader by suddenly changing wording, the writing is called "consistent." If, on the other hand, some elements of the writing change or shift when the audience isn't expecting them to, you make reading awkward or confusing for your audience. Two common problems you can spot in revision are:

- shifts in person
- shifts in tense

To keep **person** consistent in your writing means that you carry through each paragraph with the individual you mean to be writing about. A common sort of inconsistency is to shift from "I" to "we" or "you." That is, shifting from the first person singular to the first person plural or to the second person. The remedy for such a shift is to revise the paragraph by eliminating the changed person.

In the following example of shifts in person, the personal pronouns are in boldface type so you can see the inconsistency easily.

EXAMPLE  **I** have a part-time job of putting up metal fences. It isn't an easy job, but **I** am making enough money to stick with it. Putting up a fence takes two days. The first day **we** go to a job, **you** have to dig holes for the posts and set them in concrete. When **you** go back the second day, **you** put out the top rails between posts and attach the metal fencing to these rails. **We** have as many jobs as **we** can handle, so **I** keep making good money.

The revision shows how the person remains consistent through the paragraph:

REVISION:

I have a part-time job of putting up metal fences. It isn't an easy job, but **I** am making enough money to stick with it. Putting up a fence takes two days. The first day **I** go to a job, **I** help dig holes for the posts and set them in concrete. When **I** go back the second day, **I** help put out the top rails between posts and attach the metal fencing to these rails. My boss has as many jobs as he and **I** can handle, so **I** keep making good money.

In good writing, the **tense** remains consistent throughout a paragraph. That is, if you start writing about the past, you should keep verbs in the past tense. Or, if you start writing in the future tense, you should stay in it to be consistent.

Boldface in the following example shows inconsistency in verb tense within a paragraph.

EXAMPLE  Last week I **read** an article about people being injured in sports they were good at. The next day I **meet** a whole team of wheelchair basketball players. I **see** them twice that day, at the game and at interviews afterwards. None of these players was injured while playing basketball.

REVISION:

Last week I **read** an article about people being injured in sports they were good at. The next day I **met** a whole team of wheelchair basketball players. I **saw** them twice that day, at the game and at interviews afterwards. None of these players was injured while playing basketball.

Students who take very literally the admonition not to shift tenses may need to have reinforced the principle that tenses may change for a reason.

Although it is a good "rule" to keep tense consistent within a paragraph, occasionally there is a reason for changing tenses. If you are, indeed, talking about different times and the wording gives readers different senses of time, you cannot help but change tenses.

I planted a garden last spring,
past tense
and now I am eating fresh vegetables from it.
present tense

The word "now" signals that you are going to change tense. Also, the relationship of cause (planting a garden) and effect (eating its vegetables) indicates good reason for a change of tense in this sentence.

Without such good reason for changing tense, being consistent is a good custom to follow in revising your writing.

8-5

DIRECTIONS: Only some of the following sentences, or groups of sentences, shift person or tense. If there is no shift, write "No" in the space below the sentences. If there *is* a shift, put a double line under the words that show the inconsistency. Indicate the kind of shift by writing either "Person" or "Tense" in the space at the end. Then, write the sentence correctly in the space provided. (Hint: Not all the revisions will be simple word substitutions.)

EXAMPLE ▶ **Enrollment increased at my school so much that the registrar hires more people to take care of the crowd.**

Shift:

Tense—Enrollment increased at my school so much that the registrar hired more people to take care of the crowd.

you

1. I took advantage of living in different countries when I was in the service by learning how you could prepare special dishes from those places. Now when I want to have friends over for a meal, we can prepare one of those dishes.

   Shift:

   Person—I took advantage of living in different countries when I was in the service by learning how *I* could prepare special dishes from those places. Now when I want to have friends over for a meal, I can prepare one of those dishes.

2. Please put the books on the shelves. Then take one whenever you wish, as long as you put it back when you are finished.

   Shift:

   None

we

3. You can earn a pilot's license either by taking private lessons or by taking a course at the college. If you take lessons through the college, we will give you the needed ground course, but you will have to take the ground course as an addition if you take lessons privately.

   Shift:

   Person—You can earn a pilot's license either by taking private lessons or by taking a course at the college. *You* will get the needed ground course if you take lessons through the college, but you will have to take the ground course as an addition if you take lessons privately.

will have

4. My family's favorite holiday is Thanksgiving. We will have a big turkey and trimmings such as sweet potatoes, cranberry sauce, at least two kinds of vegetables, and pumpkin pie. Then we always sit around, too full to move.

Shift:

Tense—My family's favorite holiday is Thanksgiving. We *have* a big turkey and trimmings such as sweet potatoes, cranberry sauce, at least two kinds of vegetables, and pumpkin pie. Then we always sit around, too full to move.

5. Looking for a new car is half the fun of buying one. Trying out possible cars is the other half of the fun.

Shift:

None

says

6. Mark Twain was very much alive when he says that stories about his death were exaggerated.

Shift:

Tense—Mark Twain was very much alive when he *said* that stories about his death were exaggerated.

your you

7. Latin dances are the favorites of my friends and me. We can hardly sit still when we hear the records or go to see a live band. The rhythm will get your feet tapping and in no time at all you want to stand up and dance. Our parents say all that dancing is what keeps us thin.

Shift:

Person—Latin dances are the favorites of my friends and me. We can hardly sit still when wehear the records or go to see a live band. The rhythm will get *our* feet tapping and inno time at all *we* want to stand up and dance. Our parents say all that dancing iswhat keeps us thin.

We

8. If you live in a warm climate where there is often high humidity, you need to be very careful that books and furniture don't get mildew on them. We can solve the problem by having plenty of air circulation. You can also get a dehumidifier to put in a room.

Shift:

Person—If you live in a warm climate where there is often high humidity, you need to be very careful that books and furniture don't get mildew on them. *You* can solve the problem by having plenty of air circulation. You can also get a dehumidifier to put in a room.

9. I used to think that one person's vote couldn't make a difference in any election. Now I know that sometimes it can, because the mayor of my city was elected by only two votes.

Shift:

None

10. Stress is very bad for your physical and mental health. Therefore, you should find ways to relieve stress. Swimming and jogging help most of us. We also know that playing games such as racquetball, tennis, or basketball get you involved in ways that relieve stress.

us We

Shift

Person—Stress is very bad for your physical and mental health. Therefore, you should find ways to relieve stress. Swimming and jogging help most *people*. [First four words of next sentence deleted] Playing games such as racquetball, tennis, or basketball also [word added] get you involved in ways that relieve stress.

This item requires changing and deleting words, not just substituting them.

Sharing

1. Choose a partner to work with.
2. Write two paragraphs now or select two original ones you have written while using this book.
3. Exchange your two paragraphs with your partner. Let each person pretend to be the designated audience for the other person's paragraphs. Point out to the author any places that need re-ordering, additional information, or revision for consistency.
4. As the author, make whatever changes you think will improve the paragraphs.

The role-playing activity of being another's audience should emphasize that a writer may revise for several reasons.

Remind students that the author has control and that all suggestions need not be acted on.

Revising to Eliminate Wordiness

While you are drafting paragraphs, you have many things to concentrate on. That's why it's important to take time to revise after you complete drafting. Sometimes, in the revision, you will find that you have used more words than you needed to, that passages in the writing are wordy. Three kinds of wordiness often show up in writing.

1. Using more words than are needed to say something.

EXAMPLE ▶ **Everyone should start studying for exams at this point in time.**

***Wordiness:* "At this point in time" means "now."**

REVISION:

Everyone should start studying for exams now.

Here are some phrases that people often write, even though they are repetitious. Next to each is the revised wording.

Repetitious	***Revised***
attach together	attach
basic essentials	essentials
both together	both - *or* - together
long in size	long

Repetitious	*Revised*
maximum amount	maximum
mix together	mix
1989 model car	1989 car
past experience	experience
personally, I think	I think
refer back	refer
repeat again	repeat

2. **The ending of one sentence is repeated at the beginning of another,** not to emphasize something important but without considering how such repetition will keep the reader from moving forward. (Some writers also repeat wording to make their papers look longer—a particularly bad reason for such repetition!)

EXAMPLE ▶ **In high school I played soccer and volleyball.**
By playing soccer and volleyball, I learned a lot about teamwork.
***Wordiness:* Playing "soccer and volleyball" are in both sentences, so one can be eliminated.**

REVISION:
By playing soccer and volleyball in high school, I learned a lot about teamwork.
or
I learned a lot about teamwork by playing soccer and volleyball in high school.

3. **Repeating the obvious.**

EXAMPLE  **The color of my new shirt is blue.**
***Wordiness:* Blue is a color.**

REVISION:
My new shirt is blue.

Here are some other common expressions showing how wordiness creeps into writing and how it can be revised.

Wordy	*Revised*
by means of	by
due to the fact that	because
in order to	to
in spite of the fact that	although
in the field of	in
in the not too distant future	soon
in this modern world	now
in today's world	today
of a peculiar kind	peculiar
puzzling in nature	puzzling
such that	so
the reason is because	because
two different reasons	two reasons

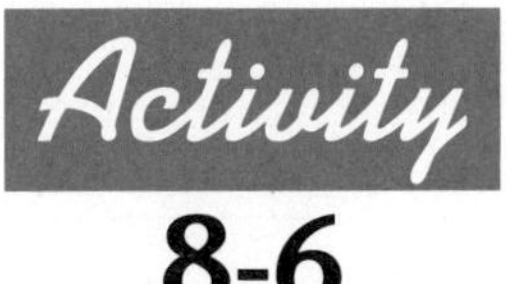

8-6

DIRECTIONS: Some of the following sentences or groups of sentences contain one or more of the three kinds of wordiness just described. Cross out any unnecessary words, and write the revised sentences in the spaces provided. You may revise some wording in the interest of better writing, but do not change the ideas. Remember, though, that some sentences are *not* in need of revision.

EXAMPLE ▶ **The builder aimed at July 15 for the ~~final~~ completion date.**

The builder aimed at July 15 for the completion date.

1. You must always endorse a check ~~on the back~~ before cashing it. That way, you show acceptance of the money from the person who wrote the check.

   You should always endorse a check before cashing it to show acceptance of the money from the person who wrote the check.

2. I was lucky enough to find a good 1987 ~~model~~ car for a price I could afford.

   I was lucky enough to find a good 1987 car for a price I could afford.

3. ~~In my opinion~~, I think the idea of opening the cafeteria a half hour before classes start is a good one.

   I think the idea of opening the cafeteria a half hour before classes start is a good one.

4. Many people came into the store during ~~the period of~~ the sale. ~~The sale~~ lasted from September 10 through ~~September~~ 12.

   Many people came into the store during the sale, which lasted from September 10 through 12.

5. Wilbur ordered ~~three~~ executive desks for the ~~new~~ offices of the three new vice presidents.

   Wilbur ordered executive desks for the offices of the three new vice presidents.

6. ~~Past~~ experience indicates that writing ~~of an~~ indefinite ~~nature~~ will not be as successful as writing ~~of a~~ specific ~~nature~~.

   Experience indicates that indefinite writing will not be as successful as specific writing.

7. ~~It will be noted~~ that records for the past year show a steady increase in business ~~for the period of time~~ between April 1 and May 1.

   Records for the past year show a steady increase in business between April 1 and May 1.

8. The supervisor is ~~of the opinion that~~ all employees are working ~~to the full extent of their capacities.~~

   The supervisor believes all employees are working their hardest.

9. My friend's new dog was so small ~~in size~~ that I almost tripped over it.

   My friend's new dog was so small that I almost tripped over it.

10. We have an ~~unexplainable~~ mystery on our hands. ~~The mystery~~ is to find out who has been taking ~~office~~ supplies from this office.

    We have a mystery on our hands: to find out who has been taking supplies from this office.

Revising for Sentence Variety

You have probably heard jokes or unkind remarks about the kind of books some children used to have when they learned to read, books that contained a series of simple sentences. That kind of writing is often referred to as "Dick-and-Jane writing" because in some famous sets of such elementary reading books the characters were Dick and Jane, and the writing went something like this:

> See Dick run. See Jane run. See Dick and Jane run. See Dick run up the hill. See Jane run up the hill. See Dick and Jane run up the hill.

Although Dick and Jane books may not have been a part of your students' reading instruction, most have heard of them.

The material which follows is sentence combining without calling it by that name.

The sentences all have the same form (subject-verb-object), and the writing is repetitious. It is *very* boring to read. How much better the passage would be if all but the last sentence were omitted, and it read:

> See Dick and Jane run up the hill.

Sometimes people who feel insecure about writing "correctly" narrow down their options so much that they end up with Dick-and-Jane sentences. Even though the thoughts are more mature, the writing is little improved:

EXAMPLE  **I rented a video. The video was Return of the Killer Tomatoes. It was meant to be serious. It was science fiction. It was very funny**

The simple, repetitious sentences make this boring to read. By combining some of the wording, instead of repeating it, those five sentences could become one:

REVISION:

> **I rented the Return of the Killer Tomatoes video that was meant to be serious science fiction, but it turned out to be very funny.**

Or, the ideas in those five sentences could be written in another way.

Two revisions show the range of possibilities.

ANOTHER REVISION:

> **I rented a video titled Return of the Killer Tomatoes. It was meant to be serious science fiction, but it was very funny.**

Here is another example of simple sentences that repeat the same structure and end up sounding dull. Combining and revising them gives the sentence the variety that makespeople want to readit.

EXAMPLE  **Textbooks have a table of contents. It is usually detailed. They have an index. Some textbooks contain study questions. Some textbooks contain a glossary. Some textbooks have colorful illustrations. All these things are designed for a reason. The reason is to help students learn.**

REVISION:

Textbooks usually have a detailed table of contents and an index. Some also contain study questions, a glossary, and colorful illustrations. All these things are designed to help students learn.

COMMENT: The move from eight sentences to three makes reading smoother and easier. It also gives variety to the sentence structure that makes the ideas more readable.

Activity 8-7

DIRECTIONS: Combine the sentences in each numbered item to make fewer sentences of more variety. Move around ideas and wording as needed. Write your new version on the lines provided.

EXAMPLE  **The Olympic Games are held every four years. They are for athletes. The athletes represent many sports. The athletes are from almost every country in the world. The athletes compete in the sports.**

REVISION:

Every four years, athletes from almost every country in the world, and representing many sports, meet for the sports competition that is the Olympic Games.

1. Some Olympic sports are only performed on snow or ice. Athletes whose sports require snow or ice meet in the winter. They meet at a place where there is snow and ice. Other sports can be played indoors. Other sports can be played outside in weather that is not too cold. Athletes in these sports meet in the summer. Summer and Winter Olympic Games are held in the same year.

   REVISION:

   Olympic athletes whose sports require snow or ice meet in the winter at a place where both are available. Those whose sports can be played indoors or outside in weather that isn't too cold meet in the summer. Summer and Winter Olympic games are held in the same year.

2. Fishing is a good hobby. You have to be near water to fish. You don't have to spend much money to get started fishing. You can buy a rod or get a cane pole. You need some line. You need a hook. You can fish by just dropping a line and hook in the water. You need some real or artificial bait.

REVISION:

Fishing is a good hobby if you are near water. You don't have to spend much money to get started fishing. All you need is some line with a hook on the end, but most people attach the line to a rod or a cane pole. Put some real or artificial bait on the hook and you're ready to fish.

3. A community school opened in my neighborhood. It is in the high school. It begins every day after high school is over. It offers all kinds of classes. Some classes help adults pass the GED. Some classes teach useful subjects. Some useful subjects are auto mechanics, woodworking, flower arranging, sewing, computers, and better parenting. Some classes are for enjoyment. Some classes for enjoyment are photography, music, ESP, creative writing, and dancing.

REVISION:

A community school opened in the local high school, and begins every day after high school ends. It offers useful courses, such as passing the GED, auto mechanics, woodworking, flower arranging, sewing, computers, and better parenting. It also offers classes for enjoyment, such as photography, music, ESP, creating writing, and dancing.

4. Word processing makes writing seem easier. Seeing your words printed on the screen makes them look nice. The words may not look so nice when you write them out. You can make corrections quickly when you use a computer for word processing. You can make corrections neatly when you use a computer for word processing. You can try out words in different places. You can move words around. When you are finished writing, you can print out a whole essay.

REVISION:

Word processing makes writing seem easier because words on the screen look better than when you write them out. On the computer, you can make corrections neatly and quickly. You can also move words around, trying them in different places. When you are finished writing, you can print out a whole essay.

5. The United States government has three branches. One branch is the legislative. One branch is the judicial. One branch is the executive. The elected president heads the executive branch. The head of the judicial branch is the Supreme Court. The two houses of Congress are the legislative branch. The government was set up this way. One branch checks on another. That way, everyone can be sure that what the government does is for the good of the country.

REVISION:

The United States government has three branches: the executive, headed by the President; the judicial, headed by the Supreme Court; and the legislative, which consists of both houses of Congress. The government was set up this way so that one branch checks on another, and everyone can be sure that what the government does is for the good of the country.

Sharing

1. Form a group with three other students.
2. Let each in the group, in turn, read aloud revised versions of items in *Activity 8-7.*
3. Let others in the group select which version of each person's work they like best and tell why.

Proofreading for Spelling, Grammar, Punctuation, and Capitalization

You may choose not to have students do proofreading when they have studied material in the appropriate chapters. Or, you may want to use the *Activities* here as diagnostic tests for making individual assignments in Chapters 19 through 30 and 32.

What many people mean by "good" writing is that it follows current customs of spelling, grammar (word order and usage), punctuation, and capitalization. Actually, "good writing" is effective for the audience and purpose for which it was composed. Matters of spelling, grammar, punctuation, and capitalization are simply customs that we have come to expect.

If a word isn't spelled as we have seen it in previous reading—and therefore expect it to be spelled—the writing isn't any worse than if the word were spelled in a more familiar way. However, the unfamiliar spelling causes a reader to stop and try to figure out what the author means—and that interference with the smooth flow of reading is not comfortable for the reader.

The same is true for grammar, punctuation, and capitalization that don't fit expectations we have about what writing should look like. When readers have to stop and figure out such matters, they are, rightfully, annoyed.

Fortunately, following the customs of spelling, grammar, punctuation and capitalization are not difficult. You have been taught most of them since starting school. If you don't recall some of them, dictionaries and handbooks are available to help you.

They are the last matters to attend to in revision, because you only need to be concerned about them when you are sure that they will appear in the final piece of writing. If you delete a word from what you've been writing, it doesn't matter whether that word was spelled "correctly" or not! If a sentence structure is changed, you only have to be concerned that the final structure (and not the one in an earlier draft) is properly punctuated. Therefore, spelling, grammar, punctuation, and capitalization are usually left for last in revision. Attending to them is called "proofreading."

You can learn more about spelling in Chapter 32, about grammar in Part 4 (Chapters 19 through 27), about capitalization in Chapter 30, and about punctuation in Chapters 28 and 29. However, here are some exercises in the skills of proofreading, just to get you started thinking about them.

SPELLING

8-8

The answers to this *Activity* are in the Instructor's Section.

DIRECTIONS: Cross out the misspelled words in the following paragraph and write the conventional spelling above each of them. (You may want to refer to Chapter 32, or to a dictionary for help.)

> Everybody should get more intrested in the environment because the air, erth, and waters are all being polluted. The ozone layer above us is dissappearing and so the kind of whether we have on earth is changeing for the worse. Less rain is one result of what has

happened and that has ment not enough water to grow food in many partss of the world. On earth we see mony results of pollution in land striped for mineing or whole forests cut down so beef can be raised to supply hamburger restrants. Pollution is also caused by the careless way people throw out paper, cans, and bottles as they drive along the highways. A very sereous way the earth is being poluted is by careless disposal of toxic wastes. Some of such waste disposall gets into the water supply on land or goes through rivers so eventally the polution reaches into the oceans were it is killing plant life and fish. If enuf people get involved in stoping these kinds of pollution, maybe we can begin to improve our enviroment.

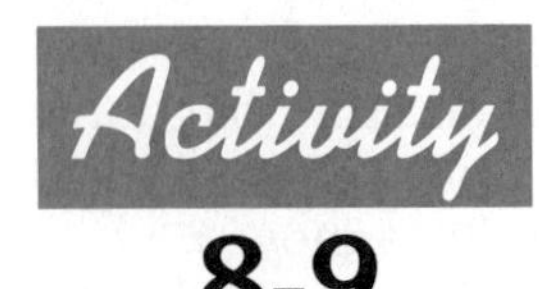

8-9

GRAMMAR

DIRECTIONS: The following paragraph contains some of the main grammatical errors that writers should be able to spot. Underline one or more examples of **subjects and verbs that don't agree**, of **sentence fragments** or **splices (run-ons)**, of **verb tenses that need changing**, of **pronouns that don't have, or don't agree with, antecedents**, of **misplaced modifiers**, or of **lack of parallelism in a sentence**. (Chapters 19 through 27 will help you find and correct these errors in grammar.)

The answer to this *Activity* is in the Instructor's Section.

Sports Illustrated named Greg LeMond "Sportsman of the Year" for 1989 and his picture were on the front cover of the magazine. When you heard his story, you will understand why, which shows great determination. Greg LeMond began competitive bicycle racing when he was 14 and turned pro at 19. He was only the second American to enter the Tour de France, the most famous bicycle race in the world. Two years later, in 1985 at the age of 25, LeMond became the first non-European ever to win that race. Which is 2,025 miles through France and lasts 23 days. A few months later he was injured in a hunting accident by a relative and ends up with 60 shotgun pellets in his back and side. 30 of them are still in him, including two in his heart lining. They thought he would never recover then they thought he would never race again. LeMond had other setbacks because of illness and in difficulties in training , but he never gave up hope of racing again. By making a remarkable physical recovery, using his skill as a cyclist, and follow good strategy, he won the Tour de France again in 1989. Now you know why *Sports Illustrated* think LeMond is such a great sportsman.

8-10

The answers to this *Activity* are in the Instructor's Section.

PUNCTUATION and CAPITALIZATION

DIRECTIONS: Correct the punctuation (commas, quotation marks, end marks, apostrophes) and capitalization in the following paragraph by adding, taking away, or changing what appears here. (Refer to Chapters 28 through 30, if you need help.)

When I was in 11th grade I worked one period a day in the school library. My job was easy. And I tried to do it well one thing I had to do was, shelve books that had been returned. Which meant that I had to put them in order by call numbers and by authors last names. The numbers were pretty easy to follow, but after a while I found myself walking around singing the children's Alphabet Song that goes, A, B, C, D, E, F, G. H, I,...so I could alphabetize the ones that went on the shelf that way. I also, had to check out, books for the other students it meant taking out the white title card to file. And stamping the due date on a blue card that then went in the pocket inside the back cover. When I wasn't busy I listened to the answers our librarian gave to questions from students so I was learning information without realizing it. I was sorry when the end of the term came, but I was proud that the librarian said to me, "Youve done a great job I hope you come back to work here next year."

RECAP—REVISING AND PROOFREADING

- Revising writing is looking at it again with the intention of making changes to improve it.
- Revising occurs during drafting as well as after it.
- Every sentence in a paragraph should be related to those which come before and after it.
- Ideas and sentences not on the same subject as others in a paragraph should be deleted.
- The author's knowledge of audience determines how much information must be included in a piece of writing.
- Person and tense should be consistent within a piece of writing, unless the content allows for change.
- Eliminating wordiness will make writing more coherent.
- A variety of sentence structures is more interesting to read than repetitions of structures.
- Proofreading is the last stage of writing.

Part II

Kinds of Paragraphs

Chapter 9 Description

In this chapter you will

This chapter seeks to make students aware that writing description includes all the senses.

- identify the characteristics of descriptive writing
- use words for the five senses
- use similes for sense perceptions
- choose a focal point for a paragraph
- write paragraphs of description

Our senses give us all the information we have. That is, through the senses of seeing, hearing, touching, tasting, and smelling we learn about the world around us and make order of it. To share something of that world with another person (or with a group of people), individuals try to recreate what they have gained through their own senses. Painters or photographers may share their own perceptions visually, hoping that others notice what they noticed. But writers use words to recreate—to describe—the world.

Explanation

Emphasize that such abstractions as personality and emotions can be described specifically by using sensory details.

You may describe an object, a place, or a person. You may also describe the atmosphere or "feel" of a place or event. Or you may have occasion to describe a feeling or emotion you experience, or the personality of a person. Naturally, nobody can "see" an emotion or a personality, but you can describe each by telling what *can* be observed of someone experiencing an emotion or having a certain personality.

For example, if you wanted to describe holiday shopping at a mall, you would tell what the place looked like. But you would also try to recreate the atmosphere by telling of the sounds and smells of the mall. If you had words for various textures of floor, walls, decorations, and so on, they would add to the description. All the sensory words you could find, therefore, would help the reader recreate, or "see in the mind's eye", the holiday-decorated mall filled with busy people.

Many people think of description only in terms of what can be seen, and then arranged in space. However, as you start to focus on writing description, remember to observe with *all your senses*, and try to find words that can describe sounds, odors, textures and weights, and tastes, as well as appearances. These are the sensory details that will make your descriptive writing come alive for everyone who reads it!

Audience and Purpose

Before you start to write a paragraph of description, think about who your audience will be, and why you are going to write this particular piece. Then you can decide what to focus on, and what will most interest the audience.

If the writing is a recommendation for a former co-worker applying for a new job, you know that you ought to focus on describing characteristics that make the person a good employee. If you are trying to convince a friend to share an apartment, telling what the place looks like may be most important. Or, describing its location near a park and close to public transportation may be most important. Underlying every descriptive paragraph are the author's decisions about how to make the subject come alive for the reader.

Sometimes you will have an audience for your description stated: other students in the class, visitors to your city, an absent friend, a kindergarten class, and so on. Remember that what you choose to describe must be written in language the audience understands and, if possible, be on a subject the audience will care about reading.

The reason for writing most description is to help your audience recreate what you experienced. Using detailed language to tell what you saw, heard, smelled, felt, or even tasted, helps readers do that. Sometimes, you may even describe what you only imagine, whether based on your past experience, or coming entirely from your own creativity.

Example of Description

If you can think of a main idea, or topic sentence, before beginning to gather information for the paragraph, write it out, and then make a list of what you will include in the paragraph. If pictures or sounds or other sensory details come to you most readily, start by listing them, and then write the topic sentence on the basis of what you have already thought about. (See Chapter 5 for ways to arrive at a topic sentence.)

The following example was written in response to an assignment to describe a place that held a pleasant recollection from childhood. Students in the class were writing for each other for a class publication about various kinds of memories.

EXAMPLE 

TOPIC SENTENCE: I always felt welcomed in my grandmother's kitchen, because its coolness held the promise of delicious food.

PARAGRAPH: Every afternoon when the sun streamed into the window of grandmother's kitchen and shone bright white on the porcelain sink below it, she came into the room and closed the clean white vertical plastic blinds. Every little breeze set the vanes clicking against each other, sometimes just slowly, and other times with great speed and noise. Even in the year-round warm weather we had, closing the blinds kept the white tile counters on either side of the sink cool. A white porcelain refrigerator stood at a right angle to the counter and to my right when I walked into the room. Facing the refrigerator, on the opposite wall, was a pale yellow stove, a remnant of some years before when colorful appliances were popular. The shiny surfaces of both these appliances added to the coolness of the room, and made me want to sample the good food always out on the round, whitewashed pine table for us children. In late fall there were tangy oranges piled in bowls, ready for us to peel and eat, even enjoying the sticky, sweet juice that covered small hands and dribbled down chins. Sometimes the smell of freshly-baked bread beckoned us from the TV set in the other room, and there were small loaves with crispy brown crusts cooling on a rack on the table, ready to be spread with yellow butter from a white plastic tub next to them. In early summer, grandmother sometimes peeled mangoes picked from the backyard trees, and put out a bowl of the slippery, pale orange wedges for the children. These we had to spear with forks, because we couldn't hold onto them with our hands. Of course, before and after the snacks, our meals were served on the round pine table. A cloth or place mats protected it from the dishes, and usually the eight chairs were filled with family members anxious to eat grandmother's good cooking.

Some of the words in this paragraph are what you can see: plastic vertical blinds; the colors of the tile counter, refrigerator, stove. Other words describe what can be touched, heard, or smelled. All of them work together to create a word picture for you, the reader, of a cool kitchen holding the promise of good foods to eat.

Key to Description: Sensory Words

Beginning here, and continuing through Chapter 16, students are given rhetorical "keys" to writing different kinds of paragraphs.

The more accurate the words you can use in writing description, the more specifically—and the better—you communicate to readers precisely what you want to share through your writing. It pays off to spend a few extra minutes to think up just the right word—or consult a dictionary or thesaurus to help you find it.

Think in terms of sensory words: what you want to reader to see, hear, touch, taste, and smell. Saying that a street reflects the heat of a hot day is not as effective as writing of the "shimmering black street with the faint odor of old tar rising from its slightly melted spots where the sun has beaten down on it for the past six hours." After you identify the sensory words in the sample paragraph, you will read about words for the five senses and participate in *Activities* that will help you use them as you write description.

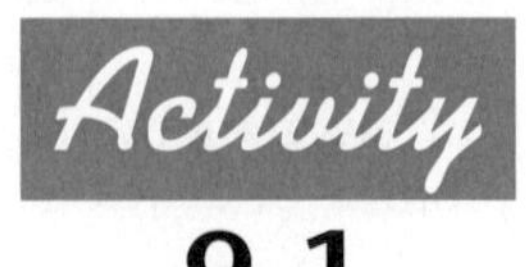

9-1

DIRECTIONS: Show yourself how many kinds of descriptive words were used in the paragraph above. It is reprinted below so you can do the following:
Underline once the words that tell what can be **seen. Underline twice** the words that represent what can be **touched.**
Circle the words that represent what can be **tasted.**
Put **one wavy line** under words that tell what is **heard.**
Put **two wavy lines** under words that tell what can be detected by **smell.**

This exercise is meant to let students discover how sensory words are used.

Every afternoon when the sun streamed into the window of grandmother's kitchen and shone bright white on the porcelain sink below it, she came into the room and closed the clean white plastic vertical blinds. Every little breeze set the vanes clicking against each other, sometimes just slowly, and other times with great speed and noise. Even in the year-round warm weather we had, closing the blinds kept the white tile counters on either side of the sink cool. A white porcelain refrigerator stood at a right angle to the counter and to my right when I walked into the room. Facing the refrigerator, on the opposite wall, was a pale yellow stove, a remnant of some years before when colorful appliances were popular. The shiny surfaces of both these appliances added to the coolness of the room and made me want to sample the good food always out on the round, whitewashed pine table for us children. In late fall there were tangy oranges piled in bowls, ready for us to peel and eat, even enjoying the sticky, sweet juice that covered small hands and dribbled down chins. Sometimes the smell of freshly-baked bread beckoned us from the TV set in the living room, and there were small loaves with crispy brown crusts cooling on a rack on the table, ready to be spread with yellow butter from a white plastic tub next to them. In early summer, grandmother sometimes peeled mangoes picked from the backyard trees, and put out a bowl of the slippery, pale orange wedges for the children. These we had to spear with forks, because we couldn't hold onto them with our hands. Of course, before and after the snacks, our meals were served on the round pine table. A cloth or place mats protected it from the dishes, and usually the eight chairs were filled with family members anxious to eat grandmother's good cooking.

The answers to this *Activity* are in the Instructor's Section.

DIRECT WORDING

Some of the words you can use in writing description tell directly what the senses observe. The trick, of course, is to find the right words to tell a reader what you saw (or see)—words that the reader understands and enough of them to develop a sensory picture.

Words for Sight

"Sight" words are usually easiest for students to find.

When you describe what can be seen, use words that tell readers details of:

- size
- shape
- color
- surface appearance
- action

Except for "action," words based on this list are modifiers (adjectives), words that change the nouns they work with; the added information makes the nouns more specific. (Occasionally, a modifying word, such as "Ford" in "Ford car" may replace the noun itself. "I bought a Ford" is perfectly understandable as generally meaning a "car"—unless you were writing about trucks, in which case the noun would still make sense to a reader.)

Last on the list are the verbs (and their modifiers, the adverbs) you need in order to make a sentence more specific, and thus help a reader visualize what you write about.

Words about SIZE are not very useful if they are as general as "big," or "small." Far more helpful is to be specific in the description. Use measurements, such as *6 ft. tall;* or *28 x 45 inches* to give the reader accurate information.

Some SHAPES are well defined, such as *square* or *rectangular* or *hour glass.* If the shape you are describing doesn't fit a category for which you know a particular word, try to find words that will lead the reader to visualize. For example, you may have to explain that the shape "begins as a four-inch square at the bottom but as the sides rise to eight inches from one side of the square and ten inches from its opposite side of the square, the basket top is a slightly off-center oval."

COLORS are particularly hard to describe because there are so many of them. One computer color program advertised that it could show 10,000 colors! The only accurate way to describe a color is by its wave length—-which would mean leaving most of us without understanding. However, we normally can think in terms of the basic colors (red, blue, yellow, and green), in addition to black and white. (Black and white, by the way, have so many variations they are among the hardest colors to match.) Beyond that, you could call a color *blue-green,* or *rust with a touch of darker red,* or some other combination of colors from among the better-known ones.

SURFACE APPEARANCE may also help a reader understand the description you write. A *wet* street looks different from a dry one. *Parched* lips and *sweaty* palms give outward appearances you might use to show an abstract idea or an inward feeling, such as fear, that can't be described adequately in other ways.

ACTION can be made more specific by choosing words that come as close as possible to meaning you intend. Anybody can write *walk,* but you will tell more if you can describe it as an *amble,* a *stroll,* a *saunter,* or a *strut.*

Look at the obvious difference between these two sentences:

Sentence A

I put the flowers in the vase.

Sentence B

I arranged the flowers in the 12-inch-tall, octagonal white porcelain vase.

Sentence B gives you information about what the subject of the sentence is doing, and about the appearance of the vase: its height and shape, its color and texture. (Porcelain is usually smooth and shiny.) Sentence B also lets you visualize the vase, while Sentence A leaves the "vase" completely to your own imagination—and that may or may not be what the writer of the sentence meant you to "see".

9-2

DIRECTIONS: Practice making your writing fit more readily into descriptive paragraphs by adding visual details to each of the following words.

Be sure details are limited to the visual (and don't include other senses, at this point).

EXAMPLE ▶ **broom:**
red, wooden-handled with bristles worn to a wedge

1. typewriter:
   ancient manual typewriter with half its letter keys missing
2. new shoes:
   shiny new black moccasin-style loafers with tassels in front
3. slice of pizza:
   triangular slice of pizza oozing strings of cheese, and studded with slices of onions, slivers of black olives, and pepperoni on red sauce
4. coffee mug:
   oversize brown coffee mug decorated with a flying mallard duck
5. notebook:
   tattered blue fabric notebook covered with pencil scratchings, and with rings that don't snap completely shut
6. bracelet:
   narrow silver band bracelet handcrafted by Hopi Indians, and bearing their symbols for lightning and thunder
7. truck:
   sleek black Chevy half-ton pickup with chrome stripping and flashy hubcaps
8. picture:
   8 x 10 picture of my mother in a 2-inch brown wooden frame
9. puppy:
   sleek brown mixed-breed puppy with white paws and floppy ears
10. suitcase:
    brown and white tweed fabric under-the-seat suitcase with brown leather trim and handle

9-3

This is a complex assignment. You may decide it's more suitable for group than for individual work. Any artists in the class may want to draw what others can then put into words.

The answers to this *Activity* are in the Instructor's Section.

DIRECTIONS: The following paragraph describes a living room in an apartment, but it doesn't give much of a picture, because words to make a reader "see" the room are omitted. On your own paper, write the paragraph again, but adding as many **visual** words as you can to improve the paragraph. Underline clearly the wording you change or add, so another person can spot it easily.

If you walk into the door of my living room, you will be able to tell a lot about my interests and how I live just by looking around. On the wall, facing the entrance, is a double window with drapes that are usually pulled back. In front of the window, so I can get good light, are my art supplies. Some of the pictures I like are hung on the wall on the side of the window, and other things lean against the wall. On the side of the window is a bookcase. On top of the bookcase are mugs and two trophies. A magazine rack is overflowing, and around it are all the magazines that don't fit in. On shelves against the west wall are my television, a VCR, and a CD player. Speakers for the CD are on the wall. Between them are posters of my favorite cities. Doors to the kitchen and bedroom are on the wall, and the wall between them has my weight bench against it. The couch is pulled forward from the wall so I can walk behind it to the doors and the weight bench. Underneath the couch are the exercise stretchers and weights I work out with. The floor of the room is tiled so I only have a rug in front of the couch.

Words Showing Spatial Relationships

What people with normal vision see around them is **three-dimensional**: it has **depth** as well as **width** and **height.** So strongly is this sense of dimension a part of thinking, that even looking at a picture, or reading a word picture, makes the mind supply all the dimensions.

In order to write about what is arranged in space—a key element of writing description—words have to give the reader clues about the dimensions of space. Words such as "near" or "far away" are of limited help when the reader doesn't have the same sense of space the writer does. "The waterfall in the photo was near where I stood," could mean that it was 500 feet away—or 2500 feet away in a picture taken with a telephoto lens. Here are some words you can use to tell where visual elements are in a description. Most of them will work well as transitions to connect ideas.

LOCATIONS	
north, south, east, west	
left, right, center	front, back, middle
above, on top of	behind, in front
above, below	toward, away from
in front of, in back of, straight ahead	here, elsewhere
inside, outside	opposite to, on the same side

GROUPS OF WORDS CLOSELY RELATED	
away from, beyond, far, further, there	
adjacent to, beside, next to	near, nearby
close to, here	under, underneath

9-4

DIRECTIONS: To the paragraph describing the room, add whatever spatial relationship words you wish to help the reader better imagine details. Circle all the words in the paragraph that show spatial relationships.

south
north
front
east
lean west
On top of
on the floor in front of
around
against west
on top of it
to the right each side of
about six feet up. Between
east facing
between them
against
pulled forward behind
Underneath
in front of

If you walk through the south door of my living room, you will be able to tell a lot about my interests and how I live just by looking around. On the north wall, facing the entrance, is a double window with textured light and dark beige drapes that are usually pulled back. In front of the window, so I can get good light, are my art supplies: a paint-splattered easel that usually has a canvas on it, a high, light-colored wooden stool, and a table holding a lot of paints, brushes in jars, and a pallette with every color imaginable on it. Some of the more colorful pictures I like are hung on the wall on the east side of the window, and more pictures and blank canvases and other things lean against the wall. On the west side of the window is a bookcase with seven shelves overflowing with the colorful bindings of hard-cover and paperback books, some put in straight, and some stacked on top of each other. On top of the bookcase are seven beer mugs from different colleges I visited and two gold metal team basketball trophies with wooden bases and players holding basketballs. A shiny metal magazine rack on the floor in front of the bookcase is overflowing and around it are all the magazines that don't fit in: copies of *Sports Illustrated, Golf Digest, Running, Psychology Today, Art News, TV Digest,* and more. On shelves against the west wall are my television set in a black cabinet, a VCR on top of it, and a stereo set and turntable to the right of them. Speakers for the stereo are on each side of the wall, about six feet up. Between them are posters of my favorite cities of New York, San Francisco, and New Orleans. Doors to the kitchen and bedroom are on the east wall facing the stereo, and the wall between them is just the right size for my weight bench to be against it. The beige, green, and brown jungle cotton print couch is pulled forward from the wall so I can walk behind it to the doors and the weight bench. Underneath the couch you can see some of the exercise stretchers and weights I work out with. The floor of the room is beige square tiles, so I only have a rectangular blue rug in front of the couch.

Sharing

1. Form a group with two or three other people who have done *Activity 9-3* and *Activity 9-4*.
2. Share with each other the paragraphs written for that activity.
3. Discuss the differences in what each person added and circled,and try to account for the particulars you put in that others didn't.

9-5

DIRECTIONS: Write an original paragraph describing a place you know well. (Do not choose a place so large or complex that you can't describe it in one paragraph.) Consider selecting a place you go to often, such as a classroom, a room in your home, a store, a place you work, or some location you have written about in your *Idea Journal*. Include as many details and visual words as you can. Use your own paper for this activity.

Words for Sounds

> Senses other than sight (i.e., hearing, touching, smelling, and tasting) are in the following sections.

After words that tell what things (or people or places) *look* like, probably the greatest number of descriptive words people have in their vocabularies are about sounds. Particularly common are words used to describe

- volume
- sound

We ordinarily write about sounds as being "loud" or "soft," according to the volume we are aware of. Of course, the reader may, rightfully, wonder just how loud "loud" is. A heavy-metal record that sounds just fine to a teenager may be "too loud" to parents three rooms away in the same house. The most accurate way to describe volume is in decibels. However, since only a few people have access to the instruments that take such measurements, each writer must search for suitable words.

Describing the sounds themselves will add liveliness to writing. Is the person *wailing, howling, bawling,* or *sobbing*? Is the bell *jangling* or *tinkling*? What you write makes a real difference to the person who will read your words.

Activity 9-6

DIRECTIONS: Fill in each blank in the following paragraph with wording that describe sounds.

> boomed jangled tinkled
> blared
> honked
> high and low notes
> crinkly - or - crackling
> clink
> buzz

Sue and Dave needed some sound effects for a film they made for a class, so they searched through some sound effects records in the film lab. They needed a bell sound, but couldn't decide if it should be one that ______________ or__________ or __________. Looking for the sound of a horn was also difficult. They wanted one that but had to settle for one that _________, even though Dave would have liked to use one that had _______________________. The next problem was finding the ________________ sound of paper being balled up and thrown into a wastepaper basket. They also looked for the sound of a ________ of a coin being put into a vending machine. Sue chose a ____________for the sound indicating someone was at the front door of the house.

Words for Smells

Every year, beginning a few months before Christmas and going right up to the holiday itself, you are besieged by perfume ads in magazines and newspapers, on radio and TV. Copywriters for all those ads have a real problem: how to distinguish one scent from another, and then have readers and listeners not only *recognize* the differences, but also convince them to buy this fragrance over that one. If you read or listen carefully, you will discover that relatively few words describing odors, beyond *light* or *flowery* or *spicy* appear in the ads.

Instead, we are told this is a *man's fragrance* or that has a *fresh* scent. Sometimes we're told nothing at all. Instead, the advertiser relies on a picture, perhaps one of a woman running in slow motion across a lawn, or of a swan gliding across a pond at sunset.

There is good reason for even experienced copywriters to avoid words that attempt to describe what we perceive with our sense of smell. It's hard to find words to describe them!

Even though we're told that an average person can smell 2,000 different odors and a trained person can recognize twice that number, most of us have trouble finding words to describe the odors our noses can identify. *Acrid* or *stale* applied to the odor of smoke, or *musty* to describe papers stored for a long time, are used widely.

Imagine, however, the problem of a copywriter who had to describe fragrant soaps in an ad for their manufacturer. Here are a few of the descriptions that appeared. Try to imagine what is being described for each:

> *Lavender*: Oriental. Classic. Regal. Gently heavy. Dense. Rich and moody.
>
> *Fougere*: Green. Fresh. Sparkling. Outdoorsy, mossy undertones but light and airy.
>
> *Jasmine*. Romantic. Floral. Resonant, not heavy. Delicately spicy.
>
> *Vetyver*: Woodsy. Musky. Tangy green and fresh, not sweet. Rounded not heavy.

Activity 9-7

DIRECTIONS: Choose something that is *not* food, but that has a definite (perhaps) strong odor or smell. Fill in the blank to tell which odor you are describing. Then use whichever of the lines below that you can to list words describing it.

In describing the odor of ___a full ashtray from last night___, I can use the following words:

acrid	smoky
stale	sweet
dusty	

Words for Taste

People can detect only four basic tastes: sweet, sour, salt, and bitter. However, when we eat a meal, we probably think we have tasted more than just those four. Such a belief occurs because taste depends on other senses.

The temperature of food—hot, cold, lukewarm, and so on—is closely associated with the sense of taste. If you almost burn your mouth with a spoonful of hot soup, you won't be able to taste much flavor in the soup. Only after the soup cools enough to keep it in your mouth for a moment can you differentiate the kind of soup it is. Similarly, without looking to see if the glass full of ice cubes held water or ice tea, many people would get only a sensation of cold, rather than the taste of either liquid.

So is the sense of smell, which works in complex ways with the taste buds to produce what we believe we are tasting. A freshly poured cup of hot coffee will seem to taste different from that same cup of coffee if it were left standing for half an hour. The difference actually comes more from the heat and the coffee aroma than from minute differences in flavor.

Color also has something to do with taste. For example, blue carrots just wouldn't have a "carrot taste" to most people. Nor would purple mashed potatoes, or other foods that might appear in colors we are not accustomed to.

Describing specific taste, then, poses quite a problem. People who need to have words to describe taste, either because it's their job or because they have some other important reason, become inventive. For instance, those who take wine tasting seriously are likely to use words such as *delicate body, foxy, robust, dry, noble,* and many others. (In fact, wine lovers have separate words to describe how the wine smells and how it seems in the mouth.)

Words for Touch

Texture, temperature, weight, shape, and density are all characteristics that can be determined by your sense of touch. The skin, especially at the fingertips, gives some information from the sense of touch. But to say something is *smooth* may still not be specific enough. Glass, metal, ceramics, paper, wood, silk—all can be called "smooth," yet each feels different. The solution for a writer is often to name both the texture and the object.

For other textures there are words that make differentiations, such as *lumpy, waffled,* or *abrasive.*

The pressure of a hand against an arm might be gentle, and thus described as *stroking,* or it might be sudden and sharp enough to be called *slapping.*

You can determine the weight of something, but only by touching it enough to lift. For instance, a series of metal balls in graduated sizes may appear to have different weights, and yet they may be all the same weight, a characteristic that (except by using a scale) can only be determined by holding them in your hand—and therefore by touch.

Indirect Wording: Similes

When individual words aren't enough to describe something, or if the writer can't find just the right word to use, we can resort to an indirect method. Primarily, it is a comparison, a way of saying something unfamiliar is the same as something familiar. Of course, that depends on the reader being familiar with the same information as the writer. Otherwise the comparison wouldn't make any sense.

EXAMPLE ▶ **The velvet feels like rose petals.**

That statement depends on the reader knowing the *feel* of rose petals.

Something in the car engine sounds like metal hitting metal.

If you'd never heard metal hitting metal, you would have to find another way to describe the sound in the car engine.

Be sure students understand the difference between a simile and an inference (such as "the person looks tired").

The examples you just read are **similes**, comparisons of two different things in a statement containing the word "like" or "as." A simile is an indirect way of describing, because instead of telling what something **is**, it tells what something **is similar to.**

This indirect method is particularly helpful with difficult descriptions, especially those of sound, smell, taste, and touch. It is also useful in writing about what can be seen. However, before using a simile in a description, think again of the audience you are writing for, and be sure you will be understood. There would be no sense, for instance, in writing that a "room was as bright as a Van Gogh landscape" unless you felt fairly certain the reader would know that the artist Vincent Van Gogh often used yellows and other bright colors in painting many sunlit pictures of outdoor scenes.

Another helpful characteristic of the indirect method of describing sensory perceptions is that you can be as imaginative as you wish. Suppose you wanted to describe the sound of a jack-hammer breaking concrete on a sidewalk. You might compare it to standing in front of a loud speaker at a heavy-metal concert. Not the same sounds, of course, but the simile would certainly get across the idea of loudness.

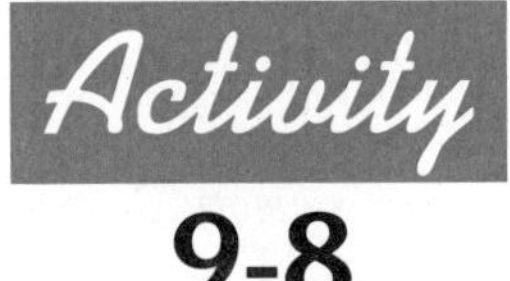

9-8

DIRECTIONS: Here are some sensory details that might be hard to describe with direct wording. Therefore, supply as many comparisons as you can for each. (You may fill all the lines, part of them, or add more lines.) Assume that you are writing for other members of your class.

EXAMPLE  **The sound of an auto horn is like**

an owl hooting

an old man blowing his nose

Students will probably need help with this *Activity*, so you may want groups or the whole class to work on it rather than individuals.

1. Dishes being stacked sounds like
   the clinking of coins
   shaking square of plastic in a basket

2. The bread tasted like
   a mouthful of feathers
   biting into a sponge

3. The wet newspaper smelled like
   shoes drying in the hallway
   a soggy meat sandwich

4. The tree bark felt like
   an alligator's skin
   a lumpy wall with paint peeling from it

5. The old, crumpled hat looked like
   a tired person slumped in a corner
   a souffle that collapsed

Sharing

Form a group with three or four classmates. Decide on several objects (a tissue, a toothbrush, a brick, etc.) or events (a wedding, graduation, etc.) or abstractions (happiness, worry, etc.), and together make up as many similes for them as you can.

Topic Sentences in Description

You have been looking separately at the five senses because they are the keys to writing good description. Now it is time to think of how you can make the senses work together for you in writing description. You can do that best either by observing or imagining the details to include in a paragraph that describes a person, place, object, or event. If you try to put *everything* you see and observe with your other four senses into the same paragraph, you will overwhelm your audience with unnecessary detail. After all, you are making many observations at the same time, but when you write them out, you can only put one after the other, and that will result in a very long paragraph with no way for the audience to know what is most important.

The solution is to choose a *focal point*, the one outstanding characteristic you want to emphasize in the descriptive paragraph. Make that one point the topic sentence. Then, use the other details you choose to include as support and development for the topic sentence.

9-9

DIRECTIONS: Below each topic sentence, write *at least four sensory details* that could be used in a paragraph supporting it with description.

EXAMPLE  ***Topic Sentence:*** **Yesterday, studying in the library was particularly hard for me.**

1. *sound of people talking all around me*
2. *wooden chairs are uncomfortably straight*
3. *newspapers rattling near where I sit*
4. *person next to me smelled of tobacco*

Encourage students to stick with words that tell what can be observed through the senses.

1. *Topic Sentence:* Waiting for someone at the airport (or bus station, or train station, or subway station) is not something I enjoy.
   1. people are sitting or standing around
   2. smell of stale food
   3. seats are hard
   4. noise of people talking and of loud speaker

2. *Topic Sentence:* Martha keeps her room very clean and neat.
   1. smell of freshly-laundered clothes
   2. furniture free of dust
   3. everything put away or in place
   4. furniture polish smell

3. *Topic Sentence:* My favorite dessert is chocolate cake with vanilla ice cream.
   1. cold ice cream
   2. fluffy cake
   3. smooth white ice cream
   4. ribbons of ice cream melting through the cake

4. *Topic Sentence:* This morning I awoke with a sore throat and a cold.
   1. sniffling sound
   2. gargling sound
   3. no sense of smell
   4. crumpled tissues on bed around me

5. *Topic Sentence:* I remember how good it felt to be held in my mother's arms.
   1. warm
   2. soft, fleshy arms
   3. smell of powder
   4. freshly-laundered clothes smell

6. *Topic Sentence:* Speaking in front of the class makes me nervous.
   1. hands sweat
   2. underarms perspire
   3. rattling of note papers when I shake
   4. choking voice

7. *Topic Sentence:* Shaneeka is so attractive that she represented her state in the Miss America contest.
   1. 5 ft. 8 inches tall
   2. sprayed hair kept it from blowing or bouncing
   3. dark brown eyes
   4. slightly pointed chin

8. *Topic Sentence:* The vacant house next door caught fire last night.
   1. flames coming through windows
   2. sound of sirens
   3. at least 25 people in front of my house watching
   4. probably 50 degrees outside

9. *Topic Sentence:* The children enjoyed the circus because it was colorful and had a lot of action.
   1. clowns tumbling in front of us
   2. elephant smell
   3. smell of popcorn
   4. clapping when group of horses entered ring

10. *Topic Sentence:* In order to get tickets to the concert, Fernando stood in line from midnight until the store opened at 10 a.m.
    1. chilly enough at night to wear jacket
    2. people in line talking quietly
    3. squeaking chair
    4. radios playing on different stations

9-10

DIRECTIONS: On your own paper, develop five topic sentences for descriptive paragraphs based on what you have written in your *Idea Journal,* or from what you have experienced and observed. You can describe a person, place, or object. Write four specifics with sensory details to support each topic sentence.

9-11

DIRECTIONS: On your own paper, do the following:

1. Use the information from any of the items you wrote in *Activity 9-9* or *Activity 9-10* to develop a **paragraph of description.**
2. In your planning work, do not limit yourself to just four supporting details, but use as many as you wish.
3. Write out a topic sentence.
4. Then, write the paragraph containing **all the sensory details** you can include to make your writing lively and readable. Use transitions and words for spatial relationships where you believe they are appropriate.
5. Underline the topic sentence when it appears in the paragraph.

RECAP—WRITING DESCRIPTION

- Decide on an audience and a purpose.
- Use as many words as possible that help the audience see, hear, touch, taste, and smell the subject you are describing.
- Help the reader's imagination by using similes for the senses
- Choose a focal point as the topic sentence for a paragraph of description.
- Use transitions and words that show spatial relationships to connect ideas.

Chapter 10

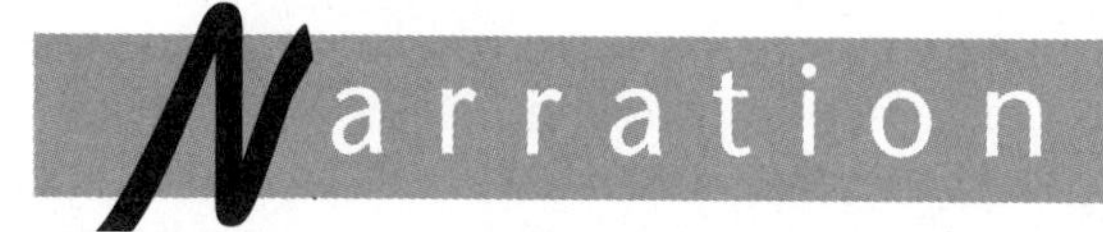

Narration

In this chapter you will

- recognize that narration has different purposes
- practice time sequencing
- choose a point of view for a narration
- review transitions appropriate to narration
- use narration for illustration
- practice writing narration

People of all ages love stories. They love to listen to stories (in person, on the radio, or on audio tape), to see them (on television or videotape, in the movies or in person), and to read them (in magazines and books). The stories may be true ("I broke my ankle in gym class last week."), or fanciful ("Let me tell you about my trip in a flying saucer."); they may be original (*Wizard of Oz*) or traditional (*Cinderella*).

Explanation

If someone asks, "What did you do today?" your response will be a narrative. ("Narrative" and "narration" are different forms of the same word.) When someone asks "What was the movie about?" the questioner probably expects a narrative. Children asking for a bedtime story are asking for a narration. Therefore, you are often called upon for oral narrations.

Narration is used in single paragraphs or in a series of paragraphs. Usually, it is to tell about an event (what happened); often several such

You may want to emphasize the point that narration can be used in the service of other modes as well as by itself.

events are incorporated into writing about a person in order to reveal the character of that individual. Narration is also used with other kinds of writing (such as classification, comparison, persuasion, and so on). For example, you might write to explain a popular belief, and include a narrative to illustrate one of the points you want to make in the explanation.

Audience and Purpose

As you can see from the varied kinds of narration mentioned in the three paragraphs above, almost everyone you can think of listens to and enjoys narratives. That is true of people around the world, and has been so for many thousands of years. Long before writing, there were stories about ancestors and beliefs, as well as about current events, told around fires or dinner tables.

Now, as in the past, some narratives are meant simply as entertainment. Traditional ghost stories, and many modern movies, are meant to scare people. Other narratives have as their purpose building pride or impressing others, astonishing people or calming them. A great many narratives give information; some also provide a way of giving instruction. Narratives that tell of a scientific experiment or an historical event do both.

With so many possibilities, you would be wise to decide what purpose you want to achieve as a first step in planning a narrative. You need to have that purpose firmly in mind, and preferably written on the paper you use for planning, in order to be guided in your choice of what to include in the narrative.

Have students think of possible narratives for different audiences, and how the same one would change if the audience did.

Audience, too, has much to do with the narrative you write. If it is for very young children, you can use only a limited vocabulary, and certainly not the same wording you could use for college students. If you are writing a narrative for race car enthusiasts, you would choose words and phrases familiar to them. If your narrative were for people who knew nothing about auto racing, you could tell the same story, but would have to select different wording.

Examples of Narration

Here are two examples of an event narrated:

EXAMPLES ▶

Have students give their own examples of narratives orally such as the worst thing/best thing/most surprising thing that ever happened to them, a film or TV episode, a family story, a sports event they took part in, etc.

EVENT A

I got up at 8 A.M. on graduation day, even though graduation wasn't until 8 p.m. I watched a lot of television that day before going to the auditorium for the actual ceremony. In the morning, I was also on the telephone a lot, because all my friends kept phoning each other. Graduation day was one time that the whole family ate together, too. I watched TV programs in the afternoon, because I was always complaining about missing them when I was in school. I also got together with some of my friends in the early afternoon. After a while, I got tired of watching TV, so I straightened up my room and got out my clothes for the evening. One reason the whole family ate dinner together was so we could leave early for the graduation...

EVENT B

I got up at 8 A.M. on graduation day, even though graduation wasn't until 8 p.m. For most of the morning I was on the telephone, because all my friends kept phoning each other. I was allowed to lounge around and not go in to work that day, so I got together with some of my friends in the afternoon. Then I came home and watched some of the TV programs I always complained about missing because they were on when I was in school. After a while, sitting in front the TV set got boring. By late afternoon I was tired of watching TV, so I straightened up my room and got out my clothes for the evening. Finally, it was time for dinner, and the whole family ate together so we could leave early...

Which of the two paragraphs is easier to read? Paragraph B, of course, because the events are unfolded in a **time sequence.**

The Key to Narration: Time

Note that this "key" is different from the literary or film flashback or flash forward.

What sets writing narration apart from other kinds of writing is that you must **keep events in the order in which they happened.**

Even if you are telling a story and want to let the reader know near the beginning what the main point is that you intend to make, you will still find that most of what you write will be a series of events: First this happened, then that occurred, then something else took place. Stories, after all, happen in time, even though they take place somewhere, and there may be many people involved. Therefore, to write a successful narration, you will do best by using a time sequence for the overall organization of the paragraph.

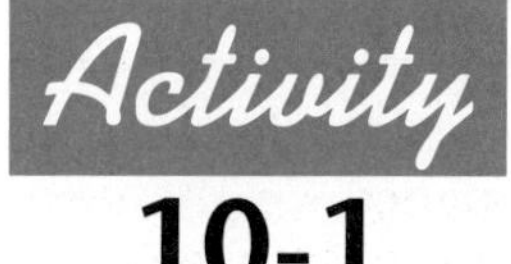

10-1

DIRECTIONS: Each of the following lists records the specifics of an event, but they are in scrambled order. Put them into proper sequence for the event by writing the letter (beginning with a) that shows where each statement belongs in time order.

EXAMPLE ▶ **A Marathon Race**

__b__ The marathon route is laid out.
__d__ Helpers and support people go to their assigned stations along the marathon route.
__c__ Runners sign up for the race.
__a__ A date and time are set for the marathon run.
__e__ Winners receive their prizes.

1. An Operation

__c__ A friend drove me to the hospital.
__a__ I woke up with severe abdominal pains.
__e__ Two days later I felt fine and went home.
__b__ My doctor suspected appendicitis and sent me to the hospital.
__d__ A surgeon operated on me and removed the appendix.

2. A Trip by Plane

__a__ We drove to the airport through heavy traffic.
__d__ The view out the window, especially over the mountains, was wonderful.
__c__ We got on the plane and fastened our seat belts.
__b__ Our luggage was tagged and sent through.
__e__ We landed at our destination and picked up our luggage.

3. Election Day

__b__ The polls open at 7 a.m.
__d__ The polls close at 7 p.m.
__a__ Candidates finish their last full day of campaigning.
__f__ The winner is declared.
__c__ Citizens go to their voting precincts.
__e__ The ballots are counted.

4. Finding a Job

b She enters a store and asks for a job application
a She scans the stores in the mall for help wanted signs.
d The interview with the manager is a success.
f She starts work that afternoon.
c She fills out the job application and gives it to the manager.
e She is offered the job.

You may want to have students do the next *Sharing* activity (that is, devise a scrambled event) now rather than later.

5. The American Revolution

c Colonists protested taxation without representation.
a Settlers landed.
d Colonists fired shots against the British army.
b American colonies were founded.

Each of the time sequences you arranged in *Activity 10-1* concluded with a particular event, with something important that happened. In the next *Activity*, you will have a chance to decide on the event, and to state the decisions or actions that led to it taking place.

Be sure to select a single event, not something that has many equal (or almost equal) elements. For example, as you saw earlier in the chapter, it's possible to write out a sequence of events about a high school graduation day—provided you don't begin when you started school, or even when you began the senior year! Although you may think of a vacation as a single event, it's really made up of a series of smaller events. To tell about the whole vacation will not be as effective as detailing one part of it—for instance, how you met a new friend at the pool, or what happened when you realized your travelers' checks were gone.

You may need to keep an eye on students' writing plans; they tend to want to write too much too superficially.

You will be most successful if you choose an event that took place within a fairly short period of time. Don't try to tell everything you did on the day you spent in Washington, D.C. Instead, focus on one part of the day, such as going to look up some information at the Library of Congress. You can then state the time sequence of activities that made up, or led to, the event.

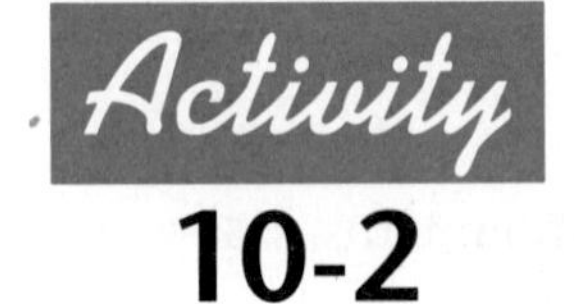

10-2

DIRECTIONS: On your own paper, write the name of five events for which you are writing the sequence of actions. Look in your *Idea Journal* for ideas. On lines below the event, and in the correct time sequence, letter and write actions or other events leading up to the event you named. Try to use at least letters **a** through **d**. Add additional letters and lines for the event if you need more space.

EXAMPLE  **Winning the MVP Award for a basketball game**

a) *Practicing many hours a week*
b) *Following coach's orders*
c) *Playing hard as a team member in the game against our traditional rival*
d) *Hearing my name announced as MVP after the game*
e) *Receiving the trophy*

Sharing

Students may work in larger groups also.

1. On a separate paper, write out one of the events and—in scrambled order—the specifics leading up to it that you noted in *Activity 10-2.*
2. Find a partner to work with, and exchange your scrambled time sequences with each other. Let each person unscramble the order of events or actions presented by the partner.
3. Discuss with your partner whether the sequence leading to the event comes across clearly or if any adjustments would make it clearer.

The Point of a Narrative

As you may have realized, just listing a sequence of actions or activities doesn't make very interesting reading—or writing. For instance, look at the two paragraphs that follow.

PARAGRAPH A

Last Monday I got up at 7 A.M. when the alarm rang and took a shower and shaved. Then I had breakfast while I read the newspaper. When I got to the office, the boss asked me to pick up a package at the post office, so I did that. When I got back to the office, I found some work left on my desk and it involved making a lot of phone calls. I made all the calls and did most of the work by lunch time. I went to our usual "hangout" to meet some friends for lunch. When I got back to the office, everyone else was already back from lunch and the boss led them all into my office She carried a birthday cake for me. Somebody had told her that it was my birthday and they all arranged for a surprise party.

PARAGRAPH B

Last Monday turned out to be a different and special day—the first time anybody gave me a surprise birthday party! It started out for me like any other day. When I first arrived at the office, the boss sent me to the post office to pick up a package. I worked at my desk from the time I returned until lunch, when I went to our usual "hangout" to meet some friends. Instead of continuing the work on my desk when I got back, I was surprised to see my boss carrying a birthday cake with my name on it and leading everybody into my office. Someone had told her that it was my birthday and they all arranged for a surprise party. Sending me to the post office was how she got me out of the way so the people could bring in the cake and party trimmings without me seeing anything. That birthday party is an event I know I will never forget because it was really so unexpected.

Which of these two paragraphs is more readable? Obviously, Paragraph B is. Instead of being a dull listing of first-I-did-this-then-I-did-that-then-I-did-this, you know at the beginning of Paragraph B that there is a reason for telling whatever story is to follow, that it is, in fact, about a first-time surprise birthday party. The paragraph has a focus, a point to make. Furthermore, the author lets you know the point near the beginning of the paragraph, and then organizes the narrative to help you get ready to receive the information that leads up to that point or focus.

Many students continue to believe that all stories must have morals; you may need to dissuade them of the notion.

Every story has to have a *point* or focus to it. That doesn't mean it must always have a moral, or be intended to teach something. But it *does* need to have a reason for being told, just as all pieces of writing must have a purpose. That reason or focus is called the **point** of a narrative. To make particularly sure that your narrative has a point, be careful that the beginning of the action is stated, that you relate a series of actions that occur in sequence, and that you conclude by referring to the event the sequence led up to.

Topic Sentences in Narratives

When you decide on the point of a narrative you will write, you have made a good start toward deciding on the topic sentence for that paragraph. (See Chapter 5 for more on developing topic sentences.)

Narratives are usually about people (though sometimes about animals). They tell **what happened to who.** Short narratives are often about just one person; as narratives get longer, more people may be a part of them.

Anyone reading (or hearing) a narrative will also want to know **where and when** the events took place. How much detail you write about the location and time of the events depends on two things:

1) how important place and time are to the narrative,
2) how long your narrative is (whether one paragraph or several)

This important information is not necessarily in the topic sentence of a narrative, but, like the sequence of events that is the key to narration, it should be included.

EXAMPLE  Three weeks ago last Saturday, I chose a cat at the Humane Society that I thought was the only perfect one there for me. I went to the front desk to make out a check for medical care for the cat, but the man in attendance said only cash was accepted. He promised to hold the kitten until I returned the next day. But when I returned, the people working at the front desk discovered another person had taken my "perfect" white kitten. Although I was discouraged and not sure I would be able to find another cat that suited me, I looked in the cages of some of the older cats, because they needed homes, too. I finally found a beautiful black cat with white paws and, as soon as I picked her up to hold, I knew this was the ideal cat for me. Because she was five months old, the Society kept her to spay her. However, this time I was cautious, and before I left the building I warned everyone I could find that this was definitely my cat, and that nobody should let her go home with any other person. Three days later I went back to bring her home. Ever since she came into the house, she has been a loving pet. Now I know that sometimes a second choice can be as good as, or better than, a first one, because there couldn't be a better cat for me than the one I have now.

Notice that although the first sentence of this paragraph suggests the point that will be made, the actual topic sentence does not appear until the end. You are, however, given information about what happened to whom, where, and when, all through the narrative.

Activity 10-3

DIRECTIONS: Do each of the following, in order:

1. Choose two of the events that interest you and for which you wrote a time sequence in *Activity 10-2,* and choose two that interest you from among those you developed in *Activity 10-1.* Write the topics or headings of all four events at the top of the next page.

____

____

____

____

2. Select one of the four events you could write a narrative paragraph about. Copy it from above, and then copy the events in time sequence that you already did for the other activities.

   Event: ____

   Time Sequence: ____

   ____

   ____

3. Complete this sentence: The point of my narrative will be

   ____

   ____

4. Write a topic sentence for your narrative paragraph.

   ____

   ____

5. Write the narrative paragraph on your own paper. Use appropriate details so the audience can clearly tell what happened to who, where, and when.

NARRATIVE TRANSITIONS

Since narratives connect a series of events occurring one after the other, writing a narrative calls for using words that signify the sequence of events. Many people have a tendency to join ideas and sentences with just a few transitional words. Here is how the story of "Cinderella" would look if it were written that way. (Transitional words showing time are underlined.)

EXAMPLE ▶ Cinderella had to help her stepmother and two step-sisters dress for the party the prince was giving. After they left, Cinderella sat near the fireplace and cried. And then her fairy godmother heard her sobbing, and then appeared before her carrying a magic wand. She knew that Cinderella wanted to go to the party, too.

So she waved her magic wand, and Cinderella was wearing a beautiful dress. And then she waved her wand again, and the pumpkin next to Cinderella turned into a coach. And then she waved her wand again, and the mice turned into horses to pull the coach. The fairy godmother told Cinderella to go to the party, but to be home by midnight.

So Cinderella went to the party, and then she met the prince and danced with him all evening...

Dull reading, isn't it? Now see the same story with other transitions showing time sequence substituting for some of the underlined words and phrases. (Substitute transitions are in bold type.)

> Cinderella had to help her stepmother and two step-sisters dress for the party the prince was giving. **After** they left, Cinderella sat near the fireplace and cried. **As soon as** her fairy godmother heard her sobbing, she **suddenly** appeared before her carrying a magic wand. She knew that Cinderella wanted to go to the party, too.
>
> **Immediately**, she waved her magic wand and Cinderella was wearing a beautiful dress. **Before** Cinderella realized what was happening, the fairy godmother waved her wand again and the pumpkin next to Cinderella turned into a coach. **When** she waved her wand again, the mice turned into horses to pull the coach. The fairy godmother told Cinderella to go to the party, but to be home by midnight.
>
> **Soon** Cinderella went to the party where **finally** she met the prince and danced with him all evening…

This time the story is the same, familiar one. (You will recognize that a lot is omitted, especially the end of the story.) The variation in wording makes it a bit more lively to read, and certainly more interesting to write.

In the section headed "Transitions Showing Time" in Chapter 7 (p. 97), you learned many words that show time relationships. They are reprinted here for your convenience. Notice how many of them are used in the Cinderella story above.

TRANSITIONS SHOWING TIME

after	at the same time	immediately	soon
afterwards	before	in the future	suddenly
and then	currently	in the meantime	then
as long as	during	in the past	until
as soon as	eventually	later	when
at last	ever since	meanwhile	whenever
at length	finally	now	while
at present	gradually		

By using these words, when they are appropriate, to make connections between one event and another in a narrative's time sequence, you can make your writing smoother and therefore easier, and more interesting, for your audience to read.

10-4

DIRECTIONS: Each item below gives specifics in time order about a particular event. Write the sentences as a paragraph that reads smoothly by using a variety of appropriate transitional words, especially those for time sequence. You may delete what seems repetitive, and may choose other transitions to get the sentences to work together as a single piece of writing. Underline the transitional words you add.

EXAMPLE  My father and I decided to go fishing. I got out my fishing tackle. My father put it in the car. He put his tackle in the car. I packed a lunch. We put the food and tackle in the car. We drove to a good fishing spot. We caught fish there before. We unloaded the car. I started fishing. My father decided to read. He started fishing. I hooked a fish. I had to fight to get the fish on shore. My father had to help land it. We weighed and measured it. It was the biggest fish I ever caught.

With Transitions

My father and I decided to go fishing. First, I got out my fishing tackle and my father put it in the car. Then, he put his tackle in the car while I packed a lunch. As soon as the food and tackle were in the car, we drove to a good fishing spot where we had caught fish before. First, we unloaded the car, and immediately I started fishing. Meanwhile, my father decided to read. However, soon he started fishing, also. Before long, I hooked a fish so big I had to fight to get it on shore. Almost immediately, my father had to stop his own fishing and help land it. Later, we weighed and measured my fish, and it turned out to be the biggest fish I ever caught.

1. Marching with the school band in the Cotton Bowl parade meant hard work. We practiced the music. We practiced walking on pavement and playing our instruments. We had car washes. We had candy sales. We published a "Booster's Book" with ads. We raised money for the trip. I had to polish my instrument. I had to polish my shoes extra well. I had to make sure my uniform was clean. I had to wash my uniform gloves. We left home for New Orleans. I marched with the school band in the Cotton Bowl parade. The practice paid off.

Transitions are shown in bold face.

Marching with the school band in the Cotton Bowl parade meant hard work. **First** we practiced the music. **Then** we practiced walking on pavement and playing our instruments. **Also**, we had car washes **and** candy sales. **In addition**, we published a "Booster's Book" with ads. Finally, we raised money for the trip. I had to polish my instrument and polish my shoes extra well. **Then,** I had to make sure my uniform was clean. **Last of all**,I had to wash my uniform gloves. **At last** we left home for New Orleans **and finally** I marched with the school band in the Cotton Bowl parade. The practice paid off.

2. On Career Day, I got permission to ride a rescue vehicle with the paramedics. I arrived at the fire station. The alarm went off. We jumped into the rescue truck. The driver turned on the siren. We arrived at the proper address. The paramedics took boxes of equipment from the truck and ran inside. They began examining the patient, who was complaining of chest pain. They quickly determined she was not having a heart attack. In a few minutes, she felt better. I stood in a corner, feeling useless. I have decided I would like to become a paramedic myself.

On Career Day, I **finally** got permission to ride a rescue vehicle with the paramedics. **As soon as** I arrived at the first station, the alarm went off. **Immediately**, we jumped into the rescue truck **and** the driver turned on the siren. In a few **minutes** we arrived at the proper address. **Immediately**, the paramedics took boxes of equipment from the truck and ran inside. **Then**, they began examining the patient, who was complaining of chest pain. They quickly determined she was not having a heart attack, **and** in a few minutes, she felt better. **Meanwhile,**I stood in a corner, feeling useless. **Since then**, I have decided I would like to become a paramedic myself.

3. An uphill hike in the desert could be dangerous. We took time to prepare for it. We bought hiking boots, hats, sun screen, and large water bottles. We spent several days getting in shape by carrying packs on short walks. We were ready. We set out very early, before the sun got too hot. The walk was easy. Gradually the trail became steeper and walking was more difficult. We reached the summit and agreed the view from the top was well worth all the effort.

An uphill hike in the desert could be dangerous. **Therefore**, we took time to prepare for it. **First**, we bought hiking boots, hats, sun screen, and large water bottles. **Then**, we spent several days getting in shape by carrying packs on short walks. **Finally**, we were ready. We set out very early, before the sun got too hot. **At first**, the walk was easy **but** gradually the trail became steeper and more difficult. **Finally**, we reached the summit and agreed the view from the top was well worth all the effort.

4. My cousin asked me to take care of her three young children for an afternoon. I agreed. As long as they were busy, things were fairly calm. One child was crying. One was climbing on the piano. The baby needed her diaper changed. I didn't know what to do first. I was able to handle each little emergency. I know what to do before babysitting. I will have plenty of toys ready for them.

When my cousin asked me to take care of her three young children for an afternoon, I **immediately** agreed. As long as they were busy, things were fairly calm. **Soon**, one child was crying **while** another one was climbing on the piano. **Then** the baby needed her diaper changed. **At the beginning**, I didn't know what to do first. **Gradually**, I was able to handle each little emergency. **At last**, I know what to do before babysitting. **Next time**, I will have plenty of toys ready for them.

You may want to have students read their paragraphs in the *Activity* aloud and discuss individual reasons for the choice of transitions.

5. Our golf game was almost over. It began to thunder. We knew we should take cover. It wasn't raining. We continued to play. A bolt of lightening struck a tree just ahead of us. The tree was split down the middle. It came crashing to the ground. I realized we could have been killed. I stop playing golf at the first sign of an electrical storm.

Our golf game was almost over **when suddenly** it began to thunder. **Immediately**, we knew we should take cover **but** it wasn't raining. **Therefore**, we continued to play **until suddenly** a bolt of lightening struck a tree just ahead of us. **Immediately**, the tree was split down the middle **and** it came crashing to the ground. **At that moment**, I realized we could have been killed. **Now** I stop playing golf at the first sign of an electrical storm.

NARRATION AS ILLUSTRATION

Once you are familiar with a narrative as a sequence of events, you will find that occasions arise when a story is appropriate to illustrate or support some information other than the event itself.

For example, you might use a story to show the character of a person. If you were trying to illustrate someone who was nasty, you might use a narrative about several behaviors that showed this side of the person's character, and include the following paragraph.

EXAMPLES  Harvey's nastiness was nothing new. At the age of six, when he lived on my street, he was observed teasing animals by not letting them eat in peace. When he was ten, he stole a blanket from a playmate in order to keep himself warm, and with complete disregard for how the other boy would feel. At fifteen, Harvey usually laughed at and made fun of people on the street collecting for various charities, and he made a point of behaving that way in front of disabled people. No wonder that by the time he was 25, he teased, stole from, made fun of, or otherwise behaved badly toward anyone he felt could not help him get ahead financially.

Although this example lists a series of events in a person's life at different ages, you can just as easily use narration as illustration of a person's character by selecting a *single* event, and show how that is the point of a story supported by individual happenings leading up to it.

This shows how narration can be used with other modes.

Ricardo's helpfulness really came through the last time the Helping Hands Club had a rummage sale. For three weeks before, he volunteered his time and car to collect clothing and small items for the sale. Even after making dozens of trips several days a week, he unloaded everything into the warehouse, where he helped log in the merchandise and mark the prices on things. Two days before the sale, when many people were working in the warehouse in the last rush, he quietly went out without telling anybody. Imagine our surprise when he came back with pizza for everyone at his own expense. On the day of the sale, Ricardo came two hours before he was supposed to just in case he was needed. He spent the rest of the day carrying merchandise out for customers, moving things as needed in the warehouse, and filling in for people who went on break. If ever there was a person who was a helping hand for the Helping Hands Club, it's Ricardo!

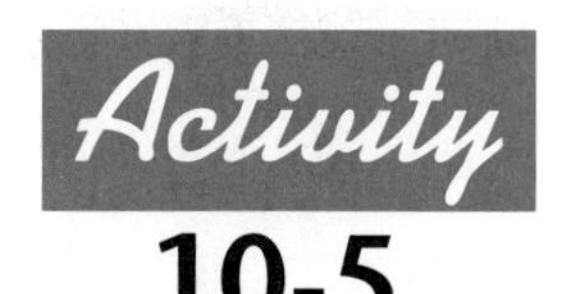

10-5

DIRECTIONS: This activity consists of several steps. Complete each of them in order.

1. In the spaces below, write the names of five people you know well enough to write about.

   a. ______________________________

   b. ______________________________

   c. ______________________________

   d. ______________________________

   e. ______________________________

2. Next to each name, write one or two words that tell something about that person's character—what sort of individual he or she is, such as "fault-finding," "generous," "irritable," and so on.
3. Circle the name and description of one person listed above that you think you could write about in a paragraph.
4. On the line below, name one event that illustrates the quality of the person's character you wrote for #2.

   ____

5. Use the lines below to list, in time sequence, events that show the quality of the person's character selected in #4.

   ____

   ____

   ____

   ____

   ____

6. Using the information you have just developed, write a paragraph that focuses on an event, and uses narration to illustrate the character of a person you know. Be sure to include the name of the person, and tell the audience how you came to know that individual.

   ____

   ____

   ____

   ____

   ____

   ____

   ____

   ____

RECAP—WRITING NARRATION

- Choose an event to tell about.
- Decide on an audience and purpose.
- Record the time sequence of the parts of that event.
- Be sure your narrative has a point.
- Write a topic sentence.
- Write a narrative paragraph.
- Use transitions showing time to make your writing smooth.

Chapter 11

In this chapter you will

- recognize two kinds of process writing
- see how audience and purpose are basic to process writing
- apply sequencing as basic to process writing
- specify steps or tell what is needed for the process
- write a process paragraph
- use transitions appropriate to sequencing

Setting up a Christmas tree safely, training a dog, or learning to use a desktop publishing program on a computer all require instructions, and a series of activities that must be done one after the other, sequentially, in order to accomplish each objective. Sometimes it's not a person, but a machine, that performs a series of actions, or an element in nature that, once begun, moves sequentially, step after step. They are all processes.

Explanation

People who write instructions for various purposes, such as those in the first sentence of this chapter, must know how to do the activity, of course. Furthermore, the writer must be able to break down the activity into a series of steps that occur in a time sequence.

Differentiating the two kinds of process writing will help student comprehension and clarify writing forms.

One kind of process writing tells others **how to do something**, such as making furniture slipcovers or taking inventory in a store. Obviously, the ability to write paragraphs (or essays) of this sort has many practical applications, both in school and out.

A second kind of process writing tells **how something works,** that is, what sequence of actions take place. Describing a process as complex as how a car works (beginning with turning the key in the ignition), or as simple as how a pinwheel spins are examples of process writing.

Notice that the two kinds of process writing tell "how to." They are similar in that both require you to write:

- a series of actions or steps
- that take place in the same sequence, and that
- result in accomplishing an objective.

In addition, many processes that tell **how to do something** require that those being instructed use **equipment** to accomplish the objective. Perhaps it is something as simple as a sponge used in the process of washing dishes, or as numerous and varied as the tools needed to tune up an auto engine. Be sure to include them in your writing so that any reader can follow your instructions.

If you are telling **how something works,** chances are that no matter what your subject, it consists of a number of **parts or separate pieces** of equipment. These need to be identified in your writing.

Audience and Purpose

You may want to encourage some students to try the humorous writing.

Writing a process paragraph (or several paragraphs) gives information to the reader(s). Unless you are a comic writer, or set out to make a comedy routine of how to do something or how something works, your writing will probably be serious and straightforward.

You may have other purposes in mind, beyond just giving information when you describe *the process of doing something*. For example, in writing about how to do something, such as folding paper to make a bird with moveable wings, you may want another person to follow the process and make a bird. Or you may want your reader to appreciate the difficulty of making such a bird. Each purpose calls for slight differences in the writing.

Writing to tell *how something works,* such as a VCR, may be just to inform the readers. Or, the information could be used to set up a troubleshooting program for someone learning how to repair VCRs. The latter, of course, requires much more technical knowledge on the part of both writer and reader.

Knowledge of what the audience knows is particularly important in process writing. Does the reader know special terms or activities associated with the process you are writing about? If so, you may be able to pass over some explanations or terms. On the other hand, you will use different language if you are writing for a person with no knowledge of the subject at all. You may also be able to show relationships between the process you are writing about and others you can expect the reader to be familiar with.

This method of starting to draft is helpful for all modes of writing and for many purposes.

Before you write a process paragraph, note the audience and your purpose for writing at the top of the scratch paper you use for planning your work. Keep referring to it, and you will be able to work efficiently.

Examples of Process

Here is an example of a process paragraph that tells how to do something. The intended audience is adult students, and the purpose of the paragraph is to teach them an important skill. The first sentence is the topic sentence of the paragraph.

EXAMPLE 

Adding new words to your vocabulary may seem to be a great deal of trouble, but the effort will pay off as you become a better speaker and writer. When you read or hear a new word you want to learn, write it down. If you only hear the word and don't know how to spell it, write down the way it sounds. As soon afterwards as is convenient, look up the word in a dictionary. (Finding it will give you the spelling, if you weren't sure.) Write the word on a 3x5 file card, and below it copy the pronunciation shown in the dictionary. Repeat the word aloud several times, following the pronunciation symbols. (If you are not sure of how to say the word, ask someone to pronounce it correctly.) On the other side of the card , write the definition—in your own words. This is a very important step, because you must deal with new words on your own terms, not those of a dictionary writer. Below it, put some word or picture association that will help you remember the definition of the new word. For example, drawing a ladder or stairway with an arrow pointing upward is a picture that can help you learn the word "ascend." Keep this card, and others like it for other new words, with you and ready to look at whenever you have a few minutes of privacy. Review each card by looking at and saying the new word, and by recalling the picture or the associated word until you can give the definition—or by looking at the definition and pronouncing the word. Finally, use your new vocabulary word at every opportunity in speaking or writing, and you will demonstrate how you improved both those skills.

Here is an example of a process paragraph that tells how something works. The purpose this time is to refresh the memory of adult students about information they must certainly have learned earlier in their education. This time, the topic sentence is the last one in the paragraph.

EXAMPLE 

The right side of the heart receives blood from the body through the vena cava, and pumps it through the pulmonary artery to the lungs. There, the blood picks up needed oxygen. The blood returns via the pulmonary vein to the left side of the heart. The left side then pumps the oxygen-rich blood through the aorta to the body, where oxygen is released for the use of the tissues. Therefore, the heart acts as a pump to carry oxygen to all parts of the body.

The Key to Process: Sequence

> Having students analyze what they, or others, have written helps them see the structure of a written piece.

Notice the sequence of steps in the paragraph explaining the process of how to do something, that is, to add new words to your vocabulary:

- write down the new word
- look it up in the dictionary
- write information on a file card in specific order
- practice memorizing the contents of the card
- use the new word

Here is the sequence of steps explained in the paragraph about the process of how something works, that is, how the heart acts as a pump for blood in the body:

- blood enters the right side of the heart
- blood is pumped to lungs for oxygen

- oxygen-rich blood goes to left side of heart
- heart pumps blood to body

Certainly neither of these processes would work if the order of the steps were changed. Nor could any audience understand either how to learn new words or how the heart works if the order of the steps were changed in the writing.

WRITING A PROCESS PARAGRAPH

Planning and preliminary work are always part of writing. They may sometimes take longer than the actual drafting, but you should take the time to do such "start up" work. For good process writing, that means you should follow a four-step process yourself:

1. choose the right subject
2. list all the steps in the process
3. include information about equipment or parts, if they are relevant to the process
4. develop a topic sentence

Choosing the Right Subject

You may want to have students turn back to Chapter 4, Narrowing Subjects, for affirmation.

The "right subject" is one that you know enough about to be comfortable sharing with others, with your audience. Take enough time to choose something that can be written about in a short space. That means you should limit the subject.

Explaining the process of building an ocean-going passenger ship is far too complex to deal with in limited time and space. Instead,you could tell how to build a model sailboat from a hobby kit, a more limited and reasonable subject.

Or you may want to write about an intellectual process, that is, one that requires thoughts or ideas to be set in a sequential order. How to get settled in a new city is extremely complex, but how to choose a dentist when you arrive in a new city is a process that is limited and that you can write about in a paragraph.

In the same way, you should limit an explanation of the process of how something works. The principle of how differences in air pressure enable an airplane to fly may seem simple enough to you, but explaining the details of an airfoil and the mechanics of air flow, velocity, and lift may be more than you have time or space to write. As an alternative, consider explaining how blowing across the top of a piece of paper causes the paper to rise.

You may want to write about a much more complex process, such as "how democracy works." Words that represent abstract ideas (that is, something you can't see, touch, smell, taste, or hear) are interesting and challenging to deal with if they represent a process, but they are more difficult to write about. Ordinarily, you will not want to tackle such a subject until you become a more confident writer. Besides, if you are asked to write only a paragraph, you may not be able to do justice to the subject in such a short space.

You may think of a subject you would like to write about, but there is no "how to" in your thinking about it. Try rewording the subject. If you can do so with a "how to," you probably have a process paragraph in the making!

A Warning: Under most circumstances, avoid writing out food recipes, except for friends who request them. A recipe is, itself, a process. It gives any reader both the ingredients and the steps in the process of putting them together to make the food dish. Therefore, recipes don't give you any chance to show your original thought or creative writing abilities.

Also, avoid writing out any other process for which you already have (or have memorized) an instruction sheet, such as how to reset a watch, or how to use the tire jack for a car. Relying on the work of whoever wrote such instructions takes away the chance to demonstrate your own thinking and planning.

A Go-ahead: You learn about many processes in your schooling and in personal experience. Perhaps the process of photosynthesis or of printing a photograph stick in your mind. You may even have learned about them through reading or watching a film. Share that information by writing about such a process, provided you work from what you have already learned, and not from rushing out to check up on the sequence from another source.

11-1

DIRECTIONS: Only one subject in each of the following pairs would be suitable for writing a process paragraph. Circle the letter of the suitable subject.

EXAMPLE ▶ **(A.) Making a patient's bed in a hospital**
B. Training to be a Nurse's Aide

A — 1. A) How the acetylene torch works
B) Uses for the acetylene torch

A — 2. A) Balancing your checkbook
B) Principles of accounting

B — 3. A) How a calculator works
B) Using a calculator to figure gas mileage for a car

B — 4. A) Every citizen should vote
B) Becoming a registered voter

A — 5. A) Changing the oil in your car
B) Dangers of not changing oil in your car

B — 6. A) Educational toys are good for a young child
B) An educational toy you can make for a young child

B — 7. A) Knowing how to do CPR can save lives
B) The ABCs of CPR

B — 8. A) Famous basketball players
B) Improve your basketball dribbling skills

A — 9. A) How a bill becomes law
B) The history of democracy

A — 10. A) A cast is often indicated for treating a broken bone
B) Putting a broken ankle into a cast

Sharing

1. Choose a partner to work with. Write one or more paired statements such as those in *Activity 11-1.* Each pair should contain one possible process paragraph subject and one on the same or a closely related subject that is too broad to be written about in a paragraph.
2. Put all the paired statements together in a box or other container and let each set of partners, in turn, choose one of the written pairs. The partners who pick each paper should read the statements aloud and state which is a process that could be written about in a paragraph. The authors of the paired statements will determine the correctness of the decision.

Everyone can tell other people how to do something, or knows enough about how something works to explain it to others. The next *Activity* will help you start thinking about writing those processes that are familiar to you.

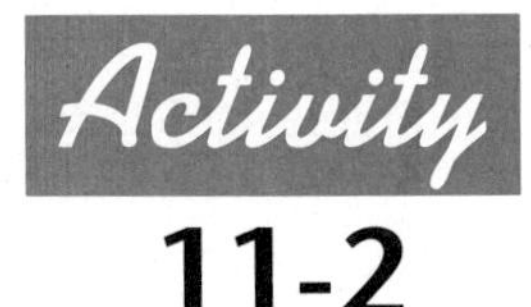

11-2

Items in both lists ought to become subjects for future process writing.

DIRECTIONS: In each column below, list as many subjects for process paragraphs as you can. Think of activities or other sequenced processes familiar to you or that you have mentioned in your *Idea Journal.*

How to Do Something	How Something Works
______________	______________
______________	______________
______________	______________
______________	______________
______________	______________
______________	______________

Specify Steps in a Process

Even if they are very familiar to you, write out the sequence of steps in a process as part of your notes. Numbering them is especially helpful. Then you can check off each step as you finish it. This method also helps keep you on target as you write.

11-3

DIRECTIONS: The sequence for each process paragraph has been scrambled. To return them to the proper order, write the number in the space to the left of each statement, showing the order in which they should appear.

EXAMPLE ▶ **An Internal Combustion Engine**

_2_ piston rises in cylinder, compressing the mixture

_4_ piston rises again, forcing exhaust gases out of cylinder

_3_ spark plug fires, creating explosion that forces piston down, producing power

_1_ piston moves down in cylinder, drawing in vaporized mixture of fuel and air

1. Washing a Car

_3_ Wash car with soft sponge
_1_ Gather pail, soap, sponge, rags, hose
_5_ Dry car with clean rags
_4_ Hose off all traces of soap
_2_ Fill pail with mild soap and water

2. Making a Bed

_1_ Place a pad over mattress
_3_ Put on top sheet and tuck in at bottom
_2_ Put on bottom sheet and tuck under mattress
_5_ Put on bed spread
_4_ Put blanket over both sheets

3. A Hair Dryer

_5_ Heated air is blown out the front by the same fan
_2_ Motor drives a high speed fan
_4_ Air passes over heated wire coils
_1_ Electric motor is turned on
_3_ Fan draws air into back of the blower

4. Making a Clay Pot

_6_ Fire the pot
_3_ Build up sides by coiling the strip on top of widest part of circle
_2_ Beginning at one end, coil strip around itself to form a wider and wider circle
_4_ Use your thumbs to smooth the coiled rings
_1_ Roll clay into long, snake-like strip
_5_ Decorate finished pot by scratching design into clay

5. Getting Emergency Help

_4_ Police complaint officer decides whether to send police or fire rescue, and gives information to dispatcher
_1_ Person calls 911 on any phone and reaches police complaint office
_5_ Dispatcher calls closest police or fire rescue unit to give address and nature of emergency
_2_ Police complaint officer answers, and asks for description of emergency and address of person needing help
_3_ Caller describes emergency and gives address
_6_ Police or fire rescue is on the way

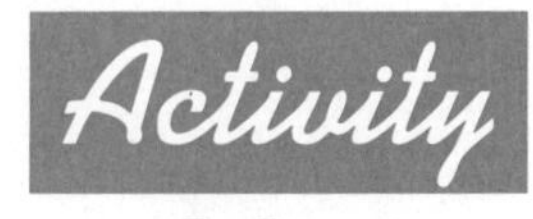

11-4

Responses will vary

DIRECTIONS: Choose two items from each of the lists you made in *Activity 11-2* that you would feel comfortable writing about. Write them in the space below, and under each one number the steps in sequence telling how to do two things and how two things work.

1. How to (do) ______________________

   requires these steps: ______________________

   ____

   ____

2. How to (do) ______________________

   requires these steps: ______________________

   ____

   ____

3. ______________________ works because

   it follows this sequence: ______________________

   ____

   ____

4. ______________________ works because

   it follows this sequence: ______________________

   ____

   ____

Determine What is Needed to Describe the Process

List any equipment needed so that someone following your directions for how to do something will be aware of what is needed. Or, if you are going to tell how something works, **list the parts or objects** that will be referred to.

When you write a paragraph explaining a process, you should be sure to include the information in the lists you make. Sometimes it is presented first, as in instructions for assembling a bookcase, so the audience will know what to get ready in order to follow the directions. Often, however, the equipment, parts, or objects are named as the paragraph proceeds.

Activity 11-5

DIRECTIONS: If you were writing to explain each of the processes listed below, you would tell the audience what equipment is needed to perform the task. Complete each such list under the process noted. (Use more or fewer lines than shown for each task.) One is done for you as an example.

EXAMPLE ▶ **How to play golf**

golf clubs

shoes with cleats

golf balls

golf glove

tees

bag for carrying clubs, etc.

1. How to give a child's birthday party
   a guest list
   invitations
   games
   birthday cake
   drinks
   other food
   prizes
   party hats

2. How to build a lamp table
   wood
   sandpaper
   saw
   nails
   hammer
   glue
   varnish

3. How to get a baseball game started
   markers for bases
   bat
   ball
   gloves
   mask for catcher

4. How to clean your teeth
   toothbrush
   toothpaste
   water
   dental floss
   gum stimulator

5. How to re-pot a plant
   plant
   pot
   potting soil
   trowel
   water
   plant food

11-6

DIRECTIONS: Assume that you are going to write a paragraph explaining the process of how something works or how something in nature happens. On the lines below each subject, *complete the list of parts or objects* that will be referred to in a paragraph that explains the process. Some answers may require you to find information from a book or a person who knows.

EXAMPLE ▶ **How a camera works**
Parts or objects to refer to:
film
view finder
lens
shutter release
shutter

1. How an electric buzzer works
   Parts or objects to refer to:
   electrical source
   buzzer
   electrical wiring

2. How photosynthesis occurs
   Parts or objects to refer to:
   plant
   sun
   soil
   water

3. How a home aquarium stays clean for the fish
   Parts or objects to refer to:
   pump
   tubing

filter material

filter

razor blade

water test kit

4. How an audio tape player works

   Parts or objects to refer to:

   tape recorder/player

   audio tape

   tape heads

   controls—stop/start/eject/fast forward/rewind

5. How a flashlight works

   Parts or objects to refer to:

   batteries

   bulb

   switch

   ______

11-7

Student responses will vary.

DIRECTIONS: Look back at *Activity 11-4* and the four possible processes you said you could write about, and list the steps for each of them. Rewrite here the two you would be most comfortable writing about. Then, under each, add a list of equipment needed, or parts that you would have to include, in a paragraph describing each of these processes.

1. How to do ______

   requires these steps: ______

   ______

   and this equipment or parts: ______

   ______

2. How to do ______

   requires these steps: ______

   ______

   and this equipment or parts: ______

   ______

How you deal with the information in this step is a matter of choice. You may decide to list all the equipment or parts at the opening of your paragraph, and then refer to them at each step of the process. Or, you may choose to introduce each at the appropriate time. However, writing such lists on your scratch paper before drafting will remind you to include the equipment or parts as you write each step of the process.

Before writing a process paragraph, you should complete your planning by writing a topic sentence that gives shape and direction to your writing.

Topic Sentences in Process Writing

Specificity is again emphasized here because most students constantly need encouragement or reminding to be specific.

In order to put all these preliminary thoughts and lists together, and to give a point or direction to a process paragraph, decide on a topic sentence that states the information your paragraph will give. Write it down and keep it before you when you are drafting and revising. Then you will have a focus and a reason for giving the audience the information you include.

Be sure your topic sentence gives specific information.

VAGUE: Washing the windows in a house can be made easy.

SPECIFIC: Dividing and pacing the job of washing windows in a house will make the work seem less tiring.

The vague statement is not nearly as helpful to both writer and reader as the specific one. Further, the specific statement is a guide to the audience, telling it the focus of the writing. It also helps the audience read accurately by telling what to look for, in this case, to be alert for "dividing and pacing the job."

11-8

DIRECTIONS: Each of the process topics below is followed by a topic sentence that may be acceptable because it is specific, or unacceptable because it is vague. On the line to the left of the topic sentence, write an **A** if it is specific and acceptable, or a **U** because it is vague and unacceptable. If you write a **U** on the line, rewrite the sentence to make it acceptable.

EXAMPLE ▶ **Topic:** How the body digests food

U **Topic sentence:** Digestion is a complex process.

Food goes from the mouth to the stomach and through a number of organs before it is fully digested by the intestines.

1. **Topic**: Preparing for an exam

A **Topic Sentence:** Doing homework regularly and taking careful notes in class are the best preparation for an exam.

2. **Topic:** How a car engine works

U **Topic Sentence:** When the car engine works, the car will move.

The internal combustion engine is also known as the four-stroke engine, because each series of motions builds up energy that causes the car to operate.

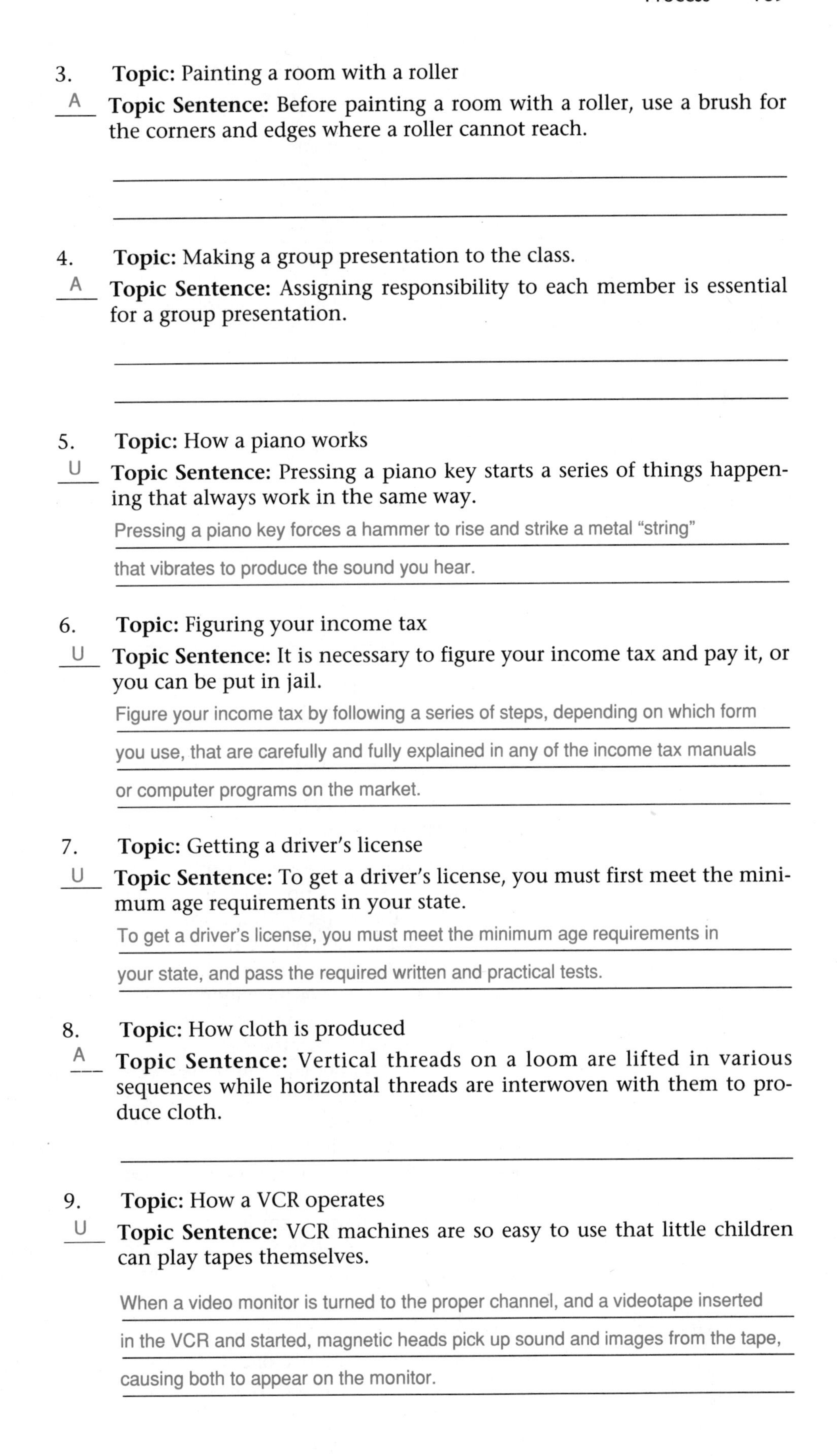

3. **Topic:** Painting a room with a roller

A **Topic Sentence:** Before painting a room with a roller, use a brush for the corners and edges where a roller cannot reach.

4. **Topic:** Making a group presentation to the class.

A **Topic Sentence:** Assigning responsibility to each member is essential for a group presentation.

5. **Topic:** How a piano works

U **Topic Sentence:** Pressing a piano key starts a series of things happening that always work in the same way.

Pressing a piano key forces a hammer to rise and strike a metal "string" that vibrates to produce the sound you hear.

6. **Topic:** Figuring your income tax

U **Topic Sentence:** It is necessary to figure your income tax and pay it, or you can be put in jail.

Figure your income tax by following a series of steps, depending on which form you use, that are carefully and fully explained in any of the income tax manuals or computer programs on the market.

7. **Topic:** Getting a driver's license

U **Topic Sentence:** To get a driver's license, you must first meet the minimum age requirements in your state.

To get a driver's license, you must meet the minimum age requirements in your state, and pass the required written and practical tests.

8. **Topic:** How cloth is produced

A **Topic Sentence:** Vertical threads on a loom are lifted in various sequences while horizontal threads are interwoven with them to produce cloth.

9. **Topic:** How a VCR operates

U **Topic Sentence:** VCR machines are so easy to use that little children can play tapes themselves.

When a video monitor is turned to the proper channel, and a videotape inserted in the VCR and started, magnetic heads pick up sound and images from the tape, causing both to appear on the monitor.

10. **Topic:** Why model rockets fly.

U **Topic Sentence:** Model rockets fly because they are built to do that.

An electric charge from a battery heats the solid fuel inside the nozzle of a model rocket engine, releasing gases that push out through the nozzle and create the thrust that propels the rocket upward.

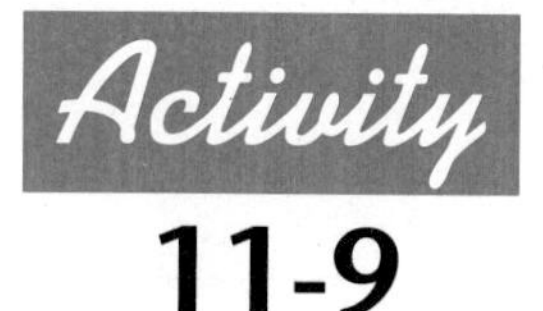

11-9

Answers will vary.

DIRECTIONS: Write a topic sentence for each of the two subjects you listed information about in *Activity 11-7.*

1. How to ______

   Topic Sentence: ______

   ______

   ______

2. How to ______

   Topic Sentence: ______

   ______

   ______

CONNECTING STEPS OF A SEQUENCE

Here are two versions of the beginning and ending of a paragraph on a process familiar to most people:

If you want to make the job of washing dishes as easy as possible, you should follow these steps. Scrape the dirty dishes. Stack them on the side of the sink. Fill one side of the sink with clear water. If you do not have a double sink, fill a dishpan with the clear water and put it on the other side of the sink. Put dishwasher liquid into the other side of the sink. Fill the sink with water. Wash the glasses with a sponge in the soapy water. Rinse them in the clear water. Put them on the side of the sink to drain. Wash the dishes in the soapy water. Rinse them in clear water. etc....You will finish washing the dishes.

If you want to make the job of washing dishes as easy as possible, you should follow these steps. First, scrape the dirty dishes and stack them on one side of the sink. Then, fill one side of the sink with clear water or, if you don't have two sinks, put the clear water in a dishpan. Then, put dishwasher liquid into the other side of the sink and fill it with water. First, wash the glasses with a sponge in the soapy water and rinse them in the clear water. After they are rinsed, put them on the side of the sink to drain. Then, wash the dishes in the soapy water and rinse them in the clear water. etc....Finally, you will finish washing the dishes.

The column on the right side reads more smoothly because there are words showing a sequence of activities in the process: *first, then, after, finally*. These are **transitional words showing sequence.** Therefore, as you write any paragraph showing a process, consider using some of these words to help readers see the progression of actions:

Refer to Chapter 7 on drafting and how transitions can be used advantageously.

TRANSITIONS SHOWING SEQUENCE

again	besides	meanwhile
also	during	moreover
and	finally	next
and then	initially	still
at last	furthermore	then
before	last	too
begin by	later	while
first, second, third, etc.		

11-10

DIRECTIONS: Choose one of the topics you worked with in *Activity 11-9.* Using all the transitions you need to show the sequence of the process, write a paragraph that either tells how to do something, or that tells how something works. Use your own paper.

RECAP—WRITING PROCESS

- Choose a "how to" subject that tells the audience in sequential steps either how to do something or how something works.
- Decide on the steps in the process you will write about.
- List any equipment, parts, or objects that are needed for the process.
- Write a specific topic sentence that presents the full process.
- Write a paragraph detailing a process.

Chapter 12

Classification

In this chapter you will

- understand classification as grouping
- determine the influence of audience and purpose
- practice classifying
- develop categories from classifications
- subdivide categories
- give direction to a paragraph with the topic sentence
- practice writing classification paragraphs

One of the ways we learn is by relating what is new to what we already know. Most often, that occurs by putting the new information (object, place, person, experience) into a group with other, related information we already have. By fitting the new information into a group, we automatically tell how it is similar. Together, the new and the old are part of the process of classifying.

Students may be able to supply other such common examples of classification.

Classifying isn't always applied to new learning. Everyone classifies dozens of times a day, usually without noticing it is happening. Walk into a drug store and even if there are no identifying signs, you can readily see that its merchandise is grouped by cold medicines, hair preparations, shaving creams, toothpaste, stomach remedies, and a host of other products. Or, look at people eating in a restaurant and you will see those who are neat eaters, those who are sloppy, those who are eating alone, those who share a table with friends, and those with other characteristics. By labeling, you have classified or grouped those in the restaurant.

Explanation

Students should particularly note that classification depends on successively smaller groupings of shared characteristics.

Classification divides a group into smaller groups, as in the examples of products in a drug store or people in a restaurant in the previous paragraph. Such division helps to divide a large group into smaller units that make more sense, that can be studied separately, or that can be dealt with in individual ways.

Classification depends on shared characteristics. As you look at a group of items to classify, you will usually find that different classifications can be made for the same group, depending on which characteristic is selected. For example, the products in a drug store are divided by *use* in the example: cold medicines, hair preparations, shaving creams, and so on. They could also be divided by their *composition:* that is, whether they are creams, powders, liquids, capsules, or tablets. Or they could be divided by their relationship to a *person's well-being:* by whether they are considered beauty aids or medicines. Such divisions are called classifications.

Because there are often different kinds of classifications possible for a particular group, you start making choices and getting ready to write as soon as you decide on the subject to classify.

Audience and Purpose

The way you classify a group depends mainly on why you are making the classification (purpose), and for whom you are doing it (audience). That is, what classifications meet the needs of the audience for ease of getting information, for selling, or for another reason. Additionally, how much you write about each classification depends on who is to read your composition (audience), and how much you want them to know (purpose).

If you have ever taken a zoology or general science course, you probably remember that animals are divided into various classes or groups according to shared characteristics. Mammals are one such group of animals: their shared characteristics are that they all breathe air and give birth to live young (rather than laying eggs). Yet mammals can be classified in several ways: some are land-living mammals (humans, dogs), and some are water-living mammals (whales, dolphins). That amount of information might be enough to identify mammals if you were writing a children's picture book, but obviously it wouldn't be enough for a junior high school science article.

Examples of Classification

Walk into a video rental store and you are likely to see films grouped into classifications such as recent releases, westerns, horror, comedy, children's, classics, X-rated, and more. The contents of the store, in fact, could be divided or classified on the basis of several reasons. Some of them are according to:

- when films were released
- audience ratings (such as "G," "PG-13," etc.)
- what types of films they are (western, horror, comedy)
- directors

You may also think of other reasons for grouping or classifying the contents of the video store.

In order to write a paragraph of classification, you must first divide the subject into groups based on reasons, such as those shown above.

This section will develop the idea of classification at two progressively more specific levels.

The following paragraph classifies films from a video rental store on the basis of what type of films they are:

> I have found that watching videos either changes or reinforces the way I feel, so I have begun renting video films based on my various moods. If I want to have some laughs or make my mood better, I will choose a comedy. Another kind of up-beat movie I like is the expensive color musicals. These movies seem to have been made mostly in the 1940s and 50s. I have always liked movies, and often I will feel nostalgic enough to want to rent movies that are now called "classics" because they were filmed 30, 40, or even 50 years ago. Romantic movies suit me at other times, mostly if they follow the boy-meets-girl, boy-loses-girl, boy-gets-girl formula. Sometimes when I want to be completely removed from all the frustrations of work, I am in the mood to watch historical movies, because they are about other times and places. I also like to watch Westerns as escape from pressures of work, because everything in them seems simpler than things are now. Many people don't like to watch horror films, but I almost always enjoy them. All I have to do to achieve all these moods is to rent a video movie.

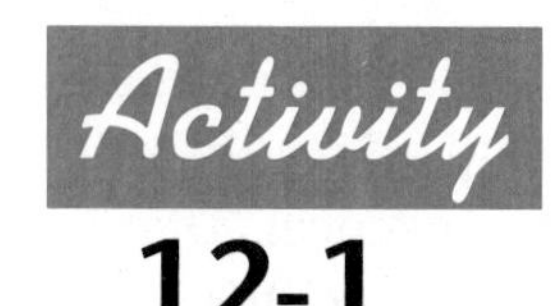

12-1

DIRECTIONS: The preceding paragraph is about different *types of video films the author rents*. The videos in that classification have been categorized into seven groups. List them here:

comedies	musicals
classics	romances
historical	Westerns
horror	

This second example shows subdivision of categories.

The next paragraph develops those classifications a bit further than the one you just read. After categorizing types of video movies, it subdivides many of them. That is, the paragraph illustrates more specific writing:

> I have found that watching videos either changes or reinforces the way I feel, so I have begun renting video films based on my various moods. If I want to have some laughs or make my mood better, I will choose a comedy. Some comedies are based on clever wording, or otherwise make me think as they entertain, while some show people acting in such silly ways that I will laugh out loud, even though I'm alone in my apartment. Another kind of up-beat movie I like is the expensive color musicals. These movies seem to have been made mostly in the 1940s and 50s. They usually involve romantic situations and often include comedy, but they are a separate group because of the singing and dancing in them. I have always liked movies, and often I will feel nostalgic enough to want to rent movies that are now called "classics" because they were filmed 30, 40, or even 50 years ago. Romantic movies suit me at other times, mostly if they follow the boy-meets-girl, boy-loses-girl, boy-gets-girl formula. I don't usually want to look at the so-called "tear jerker" romantic movies, because they were supposed to make women cry, but other romantic movies are pleasant to watch because they are about people just being in love. Sometimes when I want to be com-

> pletely removed from all the frustrations of work, I am in the mood to watch historical movies, because they are about other times and places. Some such films are based on fact, but many of them come from the imagination of the film writer, and they are pure escapism. I also like to watch Westerns as escape from pressures of work, because everything in them seems simpler than things are now. Many people don't like to watch horror films, but I almost always enjoy them because some are so far out and unrealistic, and at other times I just feel in the mood to have a few thrills and a few chills facing me from the TV screen. All I have to do to achieve all these moods is to rent video movies.

The paragraph is longer, of course, but is more complete because of the subdivisions. You can point them out in the following activity.

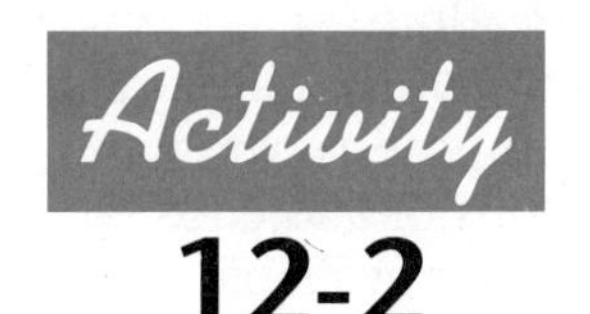

12-2

DIRECTIONS: Write the topic sentence of the second example paragraph here:

I have found that watching videos either changes or reinforces the way I feel,

so I have begun renting video films based on my various moods.

In the left column list the main categories of videos types that you identified in *Activity 12-1*. If the main category has subgroups specified in the paragraph directly above, list them in the right column.

Categories	Sub-Groups
comedies	clever wording
	make me think
	silly behavior
musicals	romances
	comedies
classics	
romances	tear jerkers
	people in love
historical	factual
	imaginative
Western	
horror	unrealistic
	thrills & chills

Notice that in both paragraphs, the topic sentence is the same. However, instead of saying only that there are different types of movies available for rental at the video store, the topic sentence of the second paragraph gives direction to the writing by relating the categories of films to personal moods.

Key to Classification: Grouping

As you have already seen, classification depends on dividing a group into further groups. However, you must start with one element that is, itself, a group—that is, you must start with a plural word. Otherwise, you cannot make classifications that come from that word.

For example, you can divide *dishes* (or a *set of dishes*) into groups: dinner plates, cups, saucers, dessert dishes, and so on. However, you cannot divide a single plate into a group.

Realize, also, that a group must contain two or more items. If you can't find two items for a group (or any subdivision of one), then you should back up and rethink what you are trying to do.

After you settle on one group as a subject, you list reasons for dividing it into other groups. We will call this first division **classifying members** of the subject group. (The resulting groups are called the classifications.)

Terminology may be confusing to some students. Principally, they need to understand the movement to progressively smaller groupings.

You could start writing a paragraph directly, telling something about each classification within the subject That is, you could compose a paragraph about movies available for rental based on the classifications of audience rating, release dates, and directors, as well as on the types of films available.

Or, you could select one of these classifications and limit the paragraph to just one level of dividing, the categories, as in the first example paragraph above. It would look like this if diagramed:

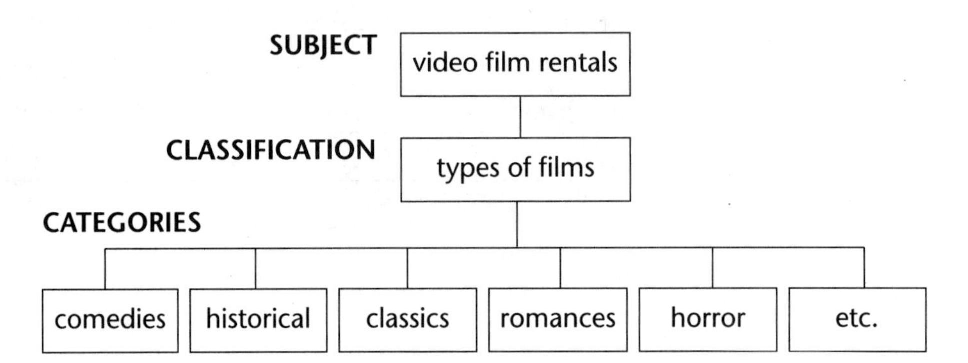

Many paragraphs of classification, however, are based on further grouping of a category into what we will call subgroups in this book. For example, the second paragraph in the above example began with a classification divided into categories which were then divided into subgroups. It can be shown this way:

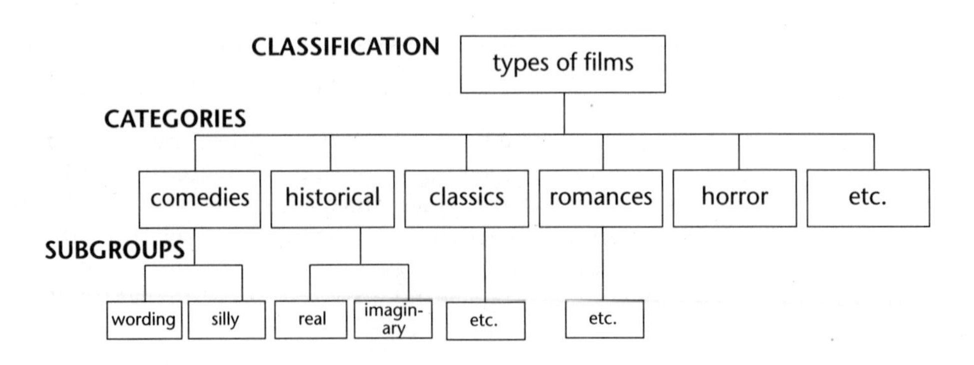

These are called **tree charts**, and each horizontal row of words is called a different **level.**

If you are going to work with the second level of grouping, that of the categories, don't mix the classifications or the first level. Rather, settle on one category so you can develop a good paragraph.

A reminder that first tries are not always successful.

You may find that the group you start leads to useful classifications to write a paragraph from. For example, you might classify the shoes in your closet. Or, you may think of so many kinds of classifications that you either have to severely limit what you write, or choose a different subject altogether. To classify "shoes" in general would probably be too much to put into a single paragraph because there are so many possible categories: by color, style, heel height, by material they're made from, by use, whether meant for men, women, or children, by designers, and so on. The paragraph might end up sounding like nothing but a listing. (You could, however, write a series of paragraphs about "shoes," perhaps by writing a paragraph about each category you made.)

Students who don't heed this advice will probably produce weak and dull writing.

CAUTION: Be sure the groupings you make are sensible, and have some significance worth writing about. Videotapes of movies originally meant for theatrical distribution and viewing might be divided according to when they were produced (such as 1920 to 1925, 1926 to 1930, 1931 to 1935, and so on). But such a division would make no more sense than grouping books by the color of their covers, or past events by the countries in which they occurred. There are too many years, colors, and countries. The groups, therefore, would end up being lists that could go on and on, yet never get anywhere.

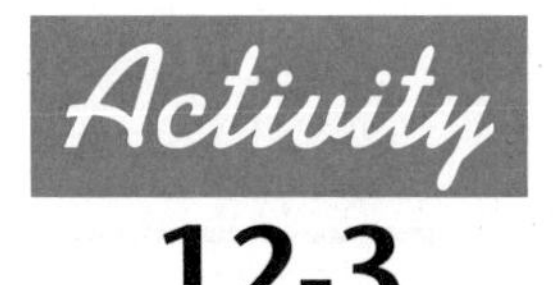

12-3

DIRECTIONS: Each of the following lists represent categories that have been made from a subject. On the line above each list, write the subject from which it was probably divided.

EXAMPLE ▶ *ways to serve ice cream*

cones **sodas**
sundaes **a la mode**

1. breads

whole wheat rye
white pumpernickel

2. writing implements

pencil typewriter
pen computer

3. timepieces

watch
sundial
clock

4. circus animals

elephants tigers
lions horses

5. winter sports

skiing
snowshoeing
tobogganing
sleigh riding
ice skating

6. track & field events

high jump
broad jump
low hurdles
100 yd. dash

7. jewelry

necklace
tie pin
ring
bracelet
earrings

8. breakfast foods

cereal
pancakes
toast
eggs

9. plays by Shakespeare or Shakespearean plays made into movies

Hamlet
Romeo and Juliet
Julius Caesar
Richard III

10. sports that don't use a ball

swimming
fencing
ice hockey
rock climbing
sailing

Answers will vary, depending on each individual's knowledge of the specified subject.

The categories you just titled in *Activity 12-3* are not the only ones possible. Most of the groups might have additional categories you can think of. For example, there are ways to serve ice cream not listed in the example: in a dish, in an ice cream roll, and in a Baked Alaska are other possibilities.

12-4

DIRECTIONS. In the space next to each list of categories in *Activity 12-3*, list other categories possible for the heading you have supplied.

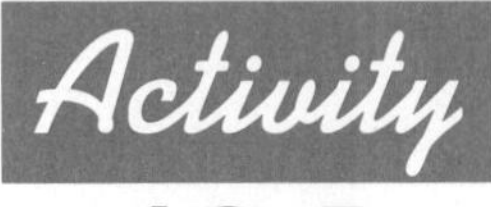

12-5

DIRECTIONS: A writing subject can be classified in several ways, and the resulting categories will differ. In this exercise, you will have a chance to demonstrate these qualities of classification.

First, think of a subject you could divide by classification. (Two subjects have been supplied below. Start with them, if you wish, or cross them off and substitute your own.) Refer to your *Idea Journal* for possibilities.

Second, write the reasons for the classifications.

Third, list categories based on the classifications you've noted.

It is not necessary for you to write on every line provided. However, you can add lines if you need to write more than the space allows.

EXAMPLE ▶ **Subject:**

Thursday nite TV programs

A. Reason for classification:

intended audience

Categories:

children	*singles*
older people	*adults*
young marrieds	

B. Reason for classification:

stations

Categories:

networks	*independents*
cable	

C. Reason for classification:

kind of program

Categories:

games	*sitcoms*
news	*sports*
interviews	*serious drama*

Remind students that they do not need to fill every line on the page, and that they may add other lines as needed. Many possibilities are shown here to assist you should some students require additional coaching to complete the assignment. Or, you may ask groups to work through this *Activity*.

1. **Subject**: musical groups

A. Reason for classification:

type of music played

Categories:

heavy metal	punk rock
jazz	Dixieland
classical	disco

B. Reason for classification:

leader's role

Categories:

guitarist	singer
trumpet player	keyboarder

C. Reason for classification:
combination of instruments

Categories:
piano, bass, drums
guitars, keyboard, drums
strings, woodwinds, reeds, timpani

D. Reason for classification:
where performance available

Categories:
CDs
concerts
videos

2. **Subject:** neighbors

A. Reason for classification:
family relationships

Categories:
married couple
parents and child
unmarried couple
parents, 2 children, 2 grandparents

B. Reason for classification:
home improvements made

Categories:
paint rooms
redecorate bedroom
new built-in stove
plant trees
re-sod

C. Reason for classification:
interests

Categories:
gardening
restoring cars
sewing
playing cards
partying
fishing

D. Reason for classification:
attitudes to me

Categories:

friendly	
mind own business	
rejecting	

Students must provide the next three subjects. The following responses are possibilities if students run dry and need coaching to reach any of them.

3. **Subject:** holidays

A. Reason for classification:
religious

Categories:

Christmas	Teachers' Day (Confucianism)
Easter	Shivaratri (Hindu)
Hanukkah	Declaration of the Bob (Baha'i)
Rosh Hashanah	Niiname Festival (Shinto)

B. Reason for classification:
proclaimed by government

Categories:

Martin Luther King, Jr.'s Birthday	Bill of Rights Day
Thanksgiving	July Fourth
Washington's Birthday	

C. Reason for classification:
personal/family

Categories:

birthdays	
anniversaries	
arriving in the U.S.	

D. Reason for classification:
honoring people

Categories:

Columbus Day	Mother's Day
Veterans Day	Father's Day

4. **Subject:** books

A. Reason for Classification:
non-fiction

Categories:

texts for classes	biographies
home improvements	sports
how-to books	travel

B. Reason for Classification:
fiction

Categories:

romances	science fiction
historical	Westerns

C. Reason for Classification:
favorite authors

Categories:

Dickens	
Stephen King	
Hemingway	

D. Reason for Classification:
"coffee table"

Categories:

"A Day in the Life of..." series	racing cars
museum collections	Ansel Adams

5. **Subject:** foods

A. Reason for Classification:
eat raw or cooked

Categories:

vegetables	
fruits	
shellfish	

B. Reason for Classification:
usually cooked for eating

Categories:

meats	turnips
fish	beets

C. Reason for Classification:
color

Categories:

green (lettuce, beans, spinach)	purple (eggplant, grapes)
yellow (squash, peppers, grapefruit)	red (cranberries, strawberries, beets)
orange (oranges, carrots)	

D. Reason for classification:
used for juice

Categories:

apples	pineapples
carrots	apricots
tomatoes	pears

Sharing

1. Form a group with two or three other people in the class.
2. Select the item in *Activity 12-5* that you feel you did the best job on, and share your responses with other members of the group.
3. Select one item in *Activity 12-5* that you would like help on, such as more reasons for classification, or more categories in a classification. Let others in the group help you put the information where you need it.

The more you know about subjects and classification, the more dividing and subdividing you can usually do. Therefore, in the next *Activity* you will have the chance to show you ability at subdividing. One easy and graphic way to do that is to draw a tree chart—such as the ones you saw on page 176 called "Key to Classification: Grouping."

Activity 12-6

DIRECTIONS: Select three of the subjects, reasons for classification, and categories you developed in *Activity 12-5* that could be subdivided to make more groupings. They may be for different subjects, or for different classifications of the same subject. Then follow these directions in order.

Although a tree chart is not the only possible way to make the information visual, it lends itself to the order required to plan classification.

1. Next to each number in the space below, copy the subject, reason for classification, and categories you selected. Each will comprise a set of information.
2. For each set of information, draw a tree chart on your own paper.
3. Subdivide any of the categories you can by extending parts of the chart to the fourth level.

This *Activity* summarizes most of the chapter. You may want to work through another example with students, or have them do an example in small groups.

EXAMPLE ▶ **1. Subject: cars**
Reason for classification:

body style

Categories:

sedan *convertible*
hard top *station wagon*

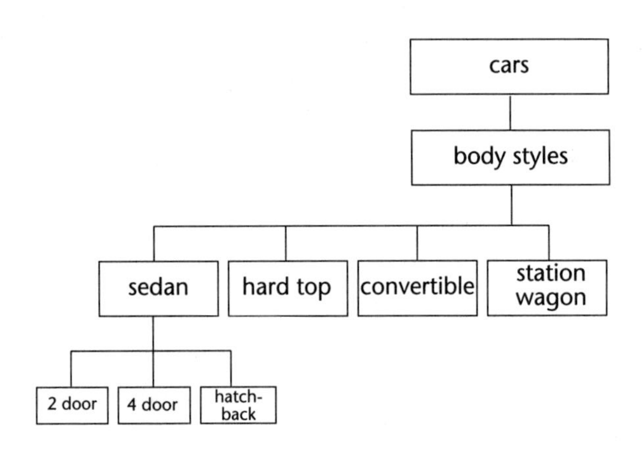

1. Subject: ______
Reason for classification: ______
Categories: ______
______

2. Subject: ______
Reason for classification: ______
Categories: ______
______

3. Subject: ______
Reason for classification: ______
Categories: ______
______

The examples here show the flexibility of topic sentences.

Topic Sentences for Classification

As you already know, the topic sentence gives direction to a paragraph by telling readers what to expect. Several topic sentences are available to you when you make classifications. The more classifications you make, the more topic sentence possibilities you give yourself about a subject.

For instance, using the subject of "Thursday night TV programs," which was the example at the beginning of *Activity 12-5*, a different kind of topic sentence could easily be developed for each of the four classifications and their categories. See how the classification is included in each of the following examples. Remember that the subject for each is the same.

EXAMPLE  **Classification A.**

intended audience

Possible topic sentence:

The television sets in my house are usually busy Thursday nights, because there are enough programs to appeal to the different people who live there.

Classification B.

stations

Possible topic sentence:

The philosophy of each television station is certain to be reflected in its Thursday night programming.

Classification C.

kinds of programs

Possible topic sentences:

So many kinds of programs are available on television on Thursday nights that I can find several I want to watch.

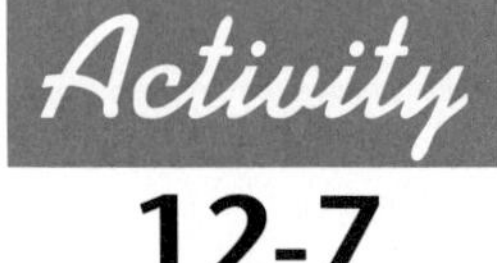

12-7

DIRECTIONS: In *Activity 12-5*, you noted five subjects and several classifications and categories for each of them. Choose three of the subjects to be the basis of possible topic sentences. Complete each of the items below, using those subjects and one classification for each. The examples just before this will show you how to do each item.

1. Based on the subject ______________________
   and this reason for classification: ______________________
   this is a topic sentence for a paragraph of classification:

   ____

2. Based on the subject ________________________________
   and this reason for classification: ____________________
   this is a topic sentence for a paragraph of classification:

   ____

3. Based on the subject ________________________________
   and this reason for classification: ____________________
   this is a topic sentence for a paragraph of classification:

   ____

12-8

This *Activity* is a culmination of all the steps in the chapter and ends with each student writing a paragraph.

DIRECTIONS: Do the following in order:

1. Circle one of the subjects in *Activity 12-5* that you believe you could write a paragraph about. (Choose a different subject from those you did in *Activity 12-6*.)
2. Circle one of the classifications and its categories under that subject.
3. On your own paper, make a tree chart for the information just circled. Add any subdivisions you believe will make a better paragraph.
4. Write a topic sentence for the paragraph. Assume that your audience is the other people in this class.
5. Write the paragraph of classification on your own paper. Add appropriate information and details to the categories.

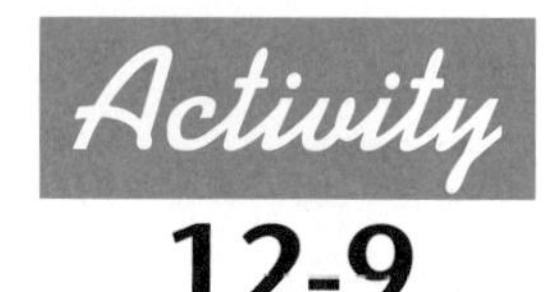

12-9

DIRECTIONS: In this *Activity* you will write a paragraph of classification, but this time the subject will be one you choose from your *Idea Journal,* or on your own. Make sure you begin with a plural word (or words) that can be divided in several classifications. Then follow the steps in this *Activity*.

1. Write the subject at the top of a page of notebook paper. Under it list at least four reasons you could make classifications. Make as many additional classifications as you can.
2. Draw a tree chart showing one of these classifications with as many categories as you can divide it into.
3. Continue the diagram by subdividing several of the categories.
4. Decide if you will write a paragraph only through the second-level categories, or if you will include subdivision in your paragraph. Circle that part of the diagram you will write about.
5. Compose a topic sentence that will give direction to the paragraph you will write. The sentence does not have to include every classification, category, or subdivision; be selective.
6. Write the paragraph of classification.

RECAP—WRITING CLASSIFICATION

- Decide on an audience and a purpose.
- Choose a plural subject.
- Divide it into several classifications.
- Subdivide classifications further into categories to be more specific.
- Write a topic sentence.
- Write a paragraph of classification.

Chapter 13

Definition

In this chapter you will

- learn the elements of simple definitions
- decide what to include in an extended definition
- discover how an audience affects wording
- learn three additional requirements of a definition
- use a topic sentence to direct paragraph content
- practice the skills of writing definitions

In Lewis Carroll's book *Alice in Wonderland,* Humpty Dumpty boasted to Alice, "When I use a word, it means just what I choose it to mean—neither more nor less." Can you imagine what confusion there would be if everyone chose personal meanings for words! Communication would be impossible.

You may want to explore denotation and connotation with certain classes. "Definition" here is close to "denotation."

Being able to communicate with others depends on both speaker or writer and listener or reader sharing a common understanding of the ideas that words represent. For convenience, most of us call that common understanding the "definition" of a word. Sometimes the definition takes just a sentence or two (a simple definition), but writers may find it necessary to write a paragraph or more (an extended definition) in order to explain a word or a phrase.

Explanation

This terminology gets away from the Latinate genus and differens.

Definition sets the limits of meaning for a word or phrase. In fact, the word *definition* comes from the Latin root meaning to set boundaries or limits. So a definition tells not only what a word includes, but also what it excludes.

Here, for example is a definition of the word *"beater:"*

EXAMPLE ▶ **A beater is a kitchen utensil in which rotating blades are activated by a hand-turned gear or by an electric motor.**

EXPLANATION: A beater is included in those items called "kitchen utensils."

A beater is excluded from kitchen utensils that don't have blades activated by a gear or motor.

SIMPLE DEFINITION

That is a **simple definition,** because it only identifies the term. Such a definition can be represented visually as a series of circles.

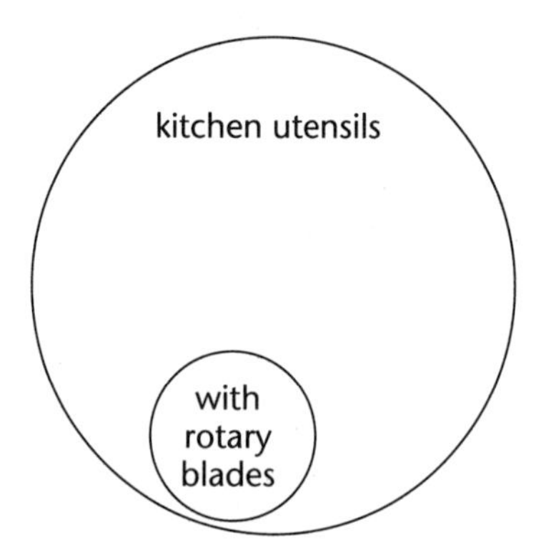

The large circle identifies the group that "beater" is included in; the smaller one shows how it is excluded from that large group of items by how it differs from them.

When you set out to write a definition, try to limit the large circle—the one that shows what group the word being defined is included in—so that you don't have such a general group as "people," "things," or "places." They include too much and make it hard to finish the definition by finding exactly what the term excludes.

Some words have very specific definitions that are easily explained in one or two sentences. For example, an "inpatient" is included in the group of people who receive hospital treatment but excluded from those who live outside the hospital while doing so. The definition of an inpatient, then, is a patient who remains or lives within the hospital while receiving treatment. It is, therefore, a simple definition.

Simple definitions are also used for many scientific and technological terms because they must be precise and are, therefore, short. (They also often contain specialized words that are perfectly clear to the scientific and technological community.) For example, "argilite" is a metamorphic rock, between shale and slate, that doesn't have the cleavage of slate. Or, a "stamen" is the pollen-producing reproductive organ of a flower, and usually consists of a filament and an anther.

EXTENDED DEFINITION

An **extended definition** is one or more paragraphs and gives additional information or explanation about the term being identified. For example, an extended definition might tell about some uses for beaters, such as whipping cream and blending ingredients, and may also deal with different designs of the blades or with different materials used to make beaters.

Words that represent what we can know through our senses, (that is, "concrete" words) are usually easier to define than those which represent

Not much is made here of concrete and abstract words, though you may want to treat the subject further.

ideas, beliefs, and feelings ("abstract" words). For example, like "beater," *carburetor*, a concrete term, represents just one sort of object, even though it comes in different sizes and may have slight variations according to its use and manufacturer. But ask a few people to define genius, an abstract word, and you are likely to get a variety of answers—and none may agree.

Definitions of more complex terms may be several paragraphs long. In at least one case, the author took a whole book to define an abstract term: Plato's *Republic* is his definition of "justice."

SYNONYMS

Sometimes a synonym is acceptable as a definition.

A synonym is a word that means almost the same as another word. Sometimes the synonyms are close enough that one word is acceptable to show the meaning of another. The synonym, of course, should be more familiar than the word it is defining.

EXAMPLE-ACCEPTABLE: *Obstreperous,* which means *unruly, boisterous, unmanageable.*

You might write: "The museum guard warned parents to control their obstreperous (that is, unruly, noisy and unmanageable) children because they might annoy others."

However, often there are very slight differences between a word and its synonym, enough so that they aren't interchangeable.

EXAMPLE-NOT ACCEPTABLE: *Meticulous* means *careful.*

The statement is not acceptable because *meticulous* means more than just "careful." It carries the notion of being very particular and paying special attention to or exaggerating small details.

Although a synonym isn't really a definition, sometimes it may fit into your writing in place of a more formal (or more complete) definition.

Audience and Purpose

If you are writing for an audience familiar with some basic terminology of biology, and your purpose is to remind them of something they already know, you might say "synapsis" is "the conjugation of homologous chromosomes...during early meiosis."

On the other hand, if the audience knew nothing of science and your purpose was to help it understand this term, you might do better to define *synapsis* as "the fusing of similar paternal and maternal chromosome pairs during cell division in sexually reproducing organisms." Many people who needed to know the term would find that definition understandable. They know about chromosome pairs and cell division. However, another audience might need to know that, plus have "fusing" changed to "blending", and "paternal and maternal" rephrased as "father and mother."

You may want to relate these examples to context.

The simple definition of "beater" earlier in this chapter was just one of several possibilities. "Beater" is one of a number of words in English whose definition is determined by how the writer (or speaker) uses it. Consider these other examples of definitions for the word "beater."

EXAMPLES ▶ A beater is a person who flushes animals from hiding, usually so the animals can be hunted.

EXPLANATION: A beater is <u>included</u> in all people.

A beater is <u>excluded</u> from people who don't perform this particular function with animals.

A beater is an implement having a handle attached to a flat metal or bamboo head of three or four joined, open work circles.

EXPLANATION: A beater is included in implements, especially those with handles.
A beater is excluded from such implements with a different kind of head or different composition.

A beater is a person who hits another person frequently and repeatedly, with the intent of harming the body of the other individual.

EXPLANATION: A beater is included in all people. Or, rather, included in those people who hit another person frequently and repeatedly.
A beater is excluded from either of these groups because of the intent to cause harm. That is, a boxer (who frequently and repeatedly hits another person) is not in the same group as a "wife beater" or a "child beater," and, in fact, is excluded from the definition given.

Have students find other words in the dictionary with multiple meanings, such as *fly*, *guard*, and *run*. Ask for the various simple definitions.

As these several meanings of "beater" show, when you read or hear an unfamiliar word and look in a dictionary for its definition, be certain to choose the one that makes sense according to the way it is used (that is, according to its "context").

In the same way, when you need to write a definition, you may have to make it specific to a particular use of the word in order to fit the context of your writing. A "gutter" as a channel for draining water at the edge of a street is different from a gutter that means the white space between facing pages of a book, magazines, newspaper, or other printed material.

An *extended definition* may begin with a simple definition, but be enlarged to at least a paragraph, usually because the complexity of the term being defined calls for more explanation.

"Drug abuse" seems to be a simple enough term. The words alone mean to misuse narcotics or other substances normally applied to the medical treatment of disease. Yet "misuse" suggests more that just a mistake. Instead, it has to do with incorrect handling, and if drugs are being incorrectly handled, the result is also harmful to people. People who misuse drugs almost always do so knowingly, because enough information has gone out for a long time about the subject. There has also been a lot of information available about the kinds of drugs that are included in the term "drug abuse." Besides narcotics and other addictive drugs which are used under closely watched conditions for medical purposes, there are street versions of them that are misused and harmful. There are mind-altering drugs, and a whole group of drugs, used in medical treatments, that affect a person's behavior, but without medical supervision they can be used by the wrong people and for the wrong reasons. When research began to show the harmful effects of tobacco on the human body, it was also classified as a drug. As a result, heavy smoking can now be called "drug abuse." The non-medical use of even such simple, non-prescription items such as rubbing alcohol and cough syrup can be labeled "drug abuse." In all, the meaning of the term has had to be expanded to cover many drugs, substances, and situations that were probably not considered in the original sense of those two words.

Such a paragraph of extended definition may be all you need for a writing purpose. However, you may also use paragraphs of definition as part of a longer piece of writing that also includes other kinds of paragraphs.

Three Keys to Writing Definition

Besides telling **what a word includes and excludes,** a definition must also meet three other requirements:

1. A definition must use words different from itself. If a reader or speaker doesn't understand the word and therefore must have it defined or explained, it doesn't help to use that word in another form.

For example, if you didn't know what a "miser" was, you'd be no further along in reading "A miser is someone who acts miserly." Often this sort of definition is described as circular, because it takes the reader around in circles without getting anywhere.

2. A definition must be understandable. A definition that uses words harder to understand than the term being defined will certainly cause trouble.

The classic example of a definition more complex than the word being defined appeared in the first dictionary (by Samuel Johnson in 1755). It said that a "net" is "any reticulated fabric decussated at regular intervals, with interstices at the intersections." If you knew all those words, you'd probably also know what a "net" was! Unfortunately, some dictionaries continue to define words with others you can't understand, such as a more recent dictionary that said "runcate" means "pinnately incised."

3. A definition must be stated in positive terms. That is, a definition must say what something *is,* rather than what it is not.

For example, if you tried to define a "book" for someone by saying "Well, you don't sit on it, and you don't write with it. It isn't something you wear, or drive in or eat, or..." you could go on almost without end in saying what a book *isn't,* and the person who wanted to know what a book *is* still would know nothing more. However, if you stated that a book is "a volume of printed or handwritten pages fastened together at one side and encased between protective covers," there is far greater understanding of the term.

Activity 13-1

You may want to have students turn unacceptable definitions into acceptable ones.

DIRECTIONS: Some of the following simple definitions are acceptable and some are not. Put an **A** (for acceptable) on the line to the left of each acceptable definition, and a **U** (for unacceptable) next to those that are not. On the lines below the definitions you find unacceptable, give reasons for your choice.

A 1. A letter is news or information that is written on paper and usually enclosed in an envelope by one person who wants to communicate it to another person or to several people.

____

U 2. A tomato is a fruit, usually red, but you can't sit on it, use it for rowing a boat, or read it.

It contains negatives instead of positives

U 3. A back pack is a pack you carry on your back

It goes in a circle, uses definition within itself

A 4. A remora is a fish that lives in the ocean and has a disk on its head by which it attaches itself to the underside of sharks or whales.

____

U 5. Endothelium is any of the several different neoplasms derived from endothelial tissue.

It contains words not likely to be understandable

Now it is time to write your own simple definitions.

13-2

This *Activity* and the *Sharing* that follows illustrate the difficulty of simplifying definitions and of defining abstractions.

Examples are of first definitions or most widely used meanings of a word.

DIRECTIONS: Write a **simple definition** for each of the following words by stating a group the term belongs to (or includes) and how it differs from (or excludes) other members of that group. (Be sure your definition also meets the three other requirements.)

EXAMPLE ▶ **Word:** fork

Belongs to the group

utensils people eat with

It differs from them because

it has two to four tines or prongs attached to a handle

1. Word: **broom**

   Belongs to the group:

   brushes of twigs, straw or synthetic bristles bound together and attached to a handle.

   It differs from others in the group because:

   the handle is long enough for a standing person to hold it at one end and sweep with it.

2. Word: **automobile**

   Belongs to the group:

   a land vehicle for passengers

   It differs from others in the group because:

   it is self-propelled by an internal engine and usually seats several people, one of whom drives.

3. Word: **snow**

   Belongs to the group:

   precipitation

   It differs from others in the group because:

   it is frozen particles of water vapor formed into solid white or translucent crystals in the upper atmosphere before falling to earth.

4. Word: **cup**

   Belongs to the group:

   cylindrical containers

It differs from others in the group because:

it is small enough to hold in the hand, usually by a handle, has an open top, and a flat bottom on which it can rest.

5. Word: **peace**
   Belongs to the group:
   a relationship between individuals or countries

   It differs from others in the group because:
   it is without war or other forms of hostilities.

6. Word: compact **disk**
   Belongs to the group:
   thin, disk-shaped devices

   It differs from others in the group because:
   on it is recorded music that is activated by a laser so it can be heard.

7. Word: **dictatorship**
   Belongs to the group:
   types of national government

   It differs from others in the group because:
   the ruler or leader has absolute authority in governing the country.

8. Word: **quilt**
   Belongs to the group:
   bed coverings

   It differs from others in the group because:
   it is a layer of cotton, wool, feathers, or down held in place between two layers of fabric firmly stitched together.

9. Word: **fax machine**
   Belongs to the group:
   machines used for communication

   It differs from others in the group because:
   it transmits and receives facsimiles or exact copies of documents over telephone lines.

10. Word: **ice cream**
    Belongs to the group:
    food

    It differs from others in the group because:
    it is prepared from a frozen mixture of milk products, sugar, flavoring and sometimes small amounts of other ingredients.

Sharing

You may want to have students share in a larger group, or with the entire class.

1. Exchange your definitions for *Activity 13-2* with another person in the class.
2. Read your partner's responses to be sure they are clear, accurate, and tell what the term includes and excludes. Be sure each definition uses words different from the term being defined, uses understandable words, and is in the positive.
3. Discuss differences with your partner and see if you want to agree in cases where you may disagree.
4. You and your partner should share the results of your work with another pair of classmates, and find out in what ways the two pairs agree or disagree.

13-3

DIRECTIONS: Below are some sentences that define a term by giving a synonym. If the definition is acceptable, put an **A** on the line to the left of the number. If the definition is not acceptable, put an **N** next to the sentence. (Check a dictionary if you need help.)

Literature that some people find scatological—that is, obscene—at one period in history is often not viewed that way in another time.

Have students make the "not acceptable" definitions into acceptable ones.

A 1. Finks, or hired strikebreakers, played a big role in the emergence of unions in the United States.

A 2. Overbuilding endangers the aquifer, that important natural underground water supply.

N 3. A crackpot is somebody who uses both crack and pot.

N 4. Hibachi, the famous mountain in Japan, was once an active volcano.

A 5. Kudzu is a plant imported to the southern states to be helpful, but its rampant—that is, unchecked—spread killed many other kinds of vegetation.

N 6. Theologians, who are knowledgeable about theology, will help you understand that passage in the book.

N 7. A peptic drink is one that will give you pep.

N 8. Take the bypass, the road that will take you through the center of the city.

A 9. A constriction, a suddenly narrowed place, in the hose prevented water from running through it with enough force to wash the car.

N 10. At one time people thought that machines would eliminate workers, that is, make them more important than the machines they ran.

Topic Sentences for Extended Definitions

An extended definition obviously tells more about a word or phrase than a simple definition can. How much more to write depends on what information you think the audience wants or needs to know. The topic sentence for an extended definition will not always state the meaning of the term you are writing about. It will, however, give overall information about what the definition will cover.

EXAMPLE ▶ **Although many people think of a "heart attack" as fatal, the damage it does to a person's system is not always complete or immediate.**

Such a topic sentence suggests that the extended definition of a "heart attack" will tell about how it affects a person. Since the wording says damage is not always immediate, the extended definition might also be expected to tell about medical advancements that are saving lives.

Have students point out these elements in the extended definitions they write.

Although the topic sentence for any paragraph sets the overall content, when you write the rest of the paragraph you will enlarge on it. As in other kinds of paragraphs, the support or development may include many additional points such as one or more of the following:

- details of appearance
- information about background or development
- outstanding elements
- examples or illustrations
- characteristic features
- how something works

What to include in an extended definition depends on the information you believe will help make the term understandable to the audience.

Writers often decide to use an extended definition for an abstract term because doing so allows exploration of the term.

EXAMPLE ▶ **Courage can be shown as much by managing day-to-day living as by a single act of risking death.**

Stories or illustrations (narratives) of what are thought to be courageous behaviors in day-to-day living would help the understanding of anyone reading an extended definition following from such a topic sentence.

CAUTION: Some inexperienced writers are tempted to repeat a dictionary definition as either a topic sentence or as the opening statement in a paragraph of definition. *Nothing could be a worse course of action!*

Copying or paraphrasing a definition immediately tells the reader that you don't feel secure enough to do your own thinking and writing to be original. It suggests you don't really know what you're writing about.

Furthermore, dictionaries give you the "bare bones" of a definition, usually just enough to be helpful to readers who want to get a short understanding quickly.

Finally, the definitions in some dictionaries will send you thumbing through them to find the meanings of other words used. That is, they are sometimes circular or use words more difficult to understand than the one you are looking up.

In short, write your own definitions; don't depend on those someone has written for a dictionary.

Sharing

You may need to approve the word chosen before students begin working with abstractions to define.

1. Form a group of at least three people, and agree on a word representing an abstract idea that lends itself to an extended definition, and that you would be willing to define.
2. Agree on what sort of information and examples should be included in the extended definition.
3. As a group, write a paragraph of extended definition of the word you agreed upon.
4. Let each group share its extended definition with one other group, and accept comments about it from the group that reads it. Revise the paragraph if your group thinks it can be improved.

13-4

DIRECTIONS: Select a term you believe you could explain in an extended definition. It may be a term taken from *Activity 13-2*, one from your *Idea Journal*, or one you choose from another source.

I will define the term ________________________________

Fill in the spaces besow in order to show your preparatory work for this writing. Use your own paper if you need more space.

1. The basic elements of this term I want to include are:

   ____

   ____

   ____

2. The topic sentence for this paragraph of extended definition is:

   ____

   ____

   ____

3. I will support this topic sentence by including:

   ____

   ____

   ____

   Try to include at least one story, illustration, or example in your extended definition.

4. Write the extended definition on your own paper.

This reminds students of how they can incorporate narration, Chapter 10, into other kinds of writing.

RECAP—WRITING A DEFINITION

- Decide if your purpose for writing a definition will be best met by using a synonym, a short definition, or an extended definition.
- If the definition will be a synonym, find an appropriate word or short phrase.
- If the definition will be a short one, determine what the term includes and what it excludes.
- If you write an extended definition, write a topic sentence.
- Decide what support you will offer for the topic sentence that will lead to readers' understanding the definition.
- Write a paragraph of extended definition.

Chapter 14

Comparison and Contrast

In this chapter you will

- understand the differences between comparison and contrast
- see how audience and purpose affect writing
- practice finding something in common between items to be compared or contrasted
- find specific similarities and differences
- use point-by-point and item-by-item organizations
- choose connecting words to reinforce comparison or contrast writing
- practice writing comparison and contrast

You do more comparing and contrasting in daily life than you might think. Which kind of breakfast cereal to buy? Compare ingredients—and claims—on the boxes before making a selection. Which movie to see? Compare and contrast newspaper reviews of them and friends' comments before making a choice. Which course to enroll in? Compare and contrast hours they're available, personal importance or degree requirements, and reputation before making a choice. Which outfit to wear to the game? Compare and contrast comfort, appearance, impression you want to make on friends (or, maybe the three in reverse order) before deciding.

Many business decisions are also grounded in comparing and contrasting. Should the company add Site A or Site B to its holdings? Costs, importance, projected increase in business, availability and other factors will be compared—and all go into making the decision. Should we hire two new people in the department? Compare and contrast the advantages and disadvantages of doing so and not doing so.

Explanation

Comparison means finding likenesses among things, people, or ideas.

Contrast means finding differences among things, people, or ideas.

Comparisons and contrasts are usually made between two elements. It's possible to compare three or four elements, but working with two is easier, and for that reason both comparisons and contrasts in this book are limited to two.

Students should note here the usual linkage between comparison and contrast.

Although it's possible to compare without contrasting and contrast without comparing, **comparison and contrast are almost always linked.** Writing instructions, as in essays or tests, usually ask you to both compare and contrast. Often, when you choose your own writing topics, you will want to both compare and contrast them because by doing so you can establish fuller and more complete relationships.

Usually, people set out to compare and/or contrast what they already know to have something in common: a movie and the book it was based on (or vice versa), football players, recipes for lasagna, attitudes toward parenting, and so on. The book and movie share plot, characters, and main idea, but demands of the media make them differ. Because they play the same game, football players share many similarities of physique, stamina, and purposefulness, even though the two men being compared may play different positions on different teams. Recipes for the same food differ in amounts and kinds of ingredients. Even parents who agree on the basics of raising their children are bound to have differences from time to time. All these subjects, then, can be compared and/or contrasted in writing.

Audience and Purpose

Comparisons and contrasts are written to give information to readers. They also give insight into, or a new view of, the things, people, or ideas.

Sometimes the purpose of this sort of writing is to make clear or explain information. For example, a writer might use a comparison and contrast of the upkeep of salt water and fresh water aquariums to inform somebody considering which kind of tank to set up.

Another purpose for writing comparison and contrast is to analyze similarities and differences, as in looking at the qualities of different computer software programs to set up office procedures. Often, one known thing or idea is used to tell an audience about something that is similar, but unknown. Students familiar with high school rules and courses might learn more about the same elements of college if they were compared and contrasted. Finally, people are often persuaded to choose one product over another—for instance, one kind of car rather than another—when the elements involved in such a choice are compared and contrasted.

Just as in any kind of writing, the more the author knows about the audience, the more effective she or he can make the writing. For example, details or terms already known to a knowledgeable audience can be omitted or dealt with very quickly. Comparing type styles for a reader already familiar with such printing terms as "point" and "pica" means the author can skip the explanations; if the author wasn't sure the audience knew them, both would need to be defined.

Students ought to think about audience bias when they plan paragraphs.

Then, too, the author may be able to slant comparison and contrast writing by knowing special leanings or biases of the audience. If you were trying to raise money for a dog shelter, you might take advantage of working from a mailing list of known dog lovers. You could write a persuasive letter pointing out the advantages of contributing to a dog shelter versus contributing to a general shelter that takes in all sorts of other animals.

Comparison and contrast writing, like other forms, should be directed to a particular audience for a purpose you decide on in advance of starting to write.

Examples of Comparison and Contrast

COMPARISON

The Mississippi River is the longest river on the North American continent, and the Nile is the longest river on the African continent. Other river systems empty into each of these rivers, causing the Mississippi and the Nile to become wider and somewhat slower, until finally each forms wide deltas and each empties into a major body of water. Because the rivers are a convenient way of transporting people and their products, those who live along the rivers have been in communication with neighbors and have traded among themselves for a long time. Until dams controlled the two great rivers in very recent times, both flooded every year. Flooding meant people could not live right along the banks of each river. It also meant that the soil of the flooded area was constantly renewed, enabling the people to plant crops that would grow well. Agriculture, therefore, was a main source of income for people who could take advantage of the good soil.

This paragraph shows ways in which the Mississippi and the Nile are similar:

Listings such as these, rather than other kinds of prewriting visuals, will be most useful to students.

length	both are the longest rivers on their continents
formation	other river systems flow into both
endings	each forms a delta and empties into a large body of water
uses	both are used for transportation and trade
	flooding of both makes rich soil for crops

The italicized list in the left column tells what the two rivers have in common. Therefore, they can be compared.

CONTRAST

The two longest rivers on the North American and African contents flow in opposite directions. The Mississippi, which is 2,350 miles long, begins in Lake Itasca in Minnesota, and flows south through the United States until it empties into the Gulf of Mexico. In contrast, the Nile River, which is 3,405 miles long, flows north from its source in Lake Victoria, which borders three countries and touches the equator. It passes through two countries, the Sudan and Egypt, until it empties into the Mediterranean Sea. Along its length, the Mississippi is fed by many other rivers that are themselves very long. Among the better known of those rivers are the Missouri, the Ohio, the Arkansas, and the Red. The best known river joining the Nile is the Blue Nile. Along roughly its last half, the Nile flows through desert, so no other waters join it. Interestingly, each river has a city named Cairo located on it. In the United States, the city is in Illinois and it is pronounced Kar'o; its population is only about 6,000. Ki'ro, Egypt is the capital and largest city of that country, and is home to more than 5,000,000 people.

This paragraph of contrast gives the same kind of information for the Mississippi and the Nile rivers (direction, length, and so on). As in the example of the comparison paragraph, the following italicized list in the left column tells what the two rivers have in common. However, because it is a paragraph of contrast, it points out differences between the two rivers. Note that each statement about the Mississippi is followed by a statement on the same subject about the Nile.

	Mississippi	**Nile**
direction	flows south	flows north
length	2,350 miles	3,405 miles
source	Lake Itasca	Lake Victoria
location	in United States	Sudan & Egypt
feeders	several named	none named
city	pronounced Kar'o	pronounced Ki'ro
	about 6,000	over 5,000,000

Key #1 to Comparison and Contrast: Something in Common

You may want to have students practice finding common elements by having them call out names of places, things, perhaps people. These can be written on the board, then made into pairs, and commonality listed.

Before you can write either comparison or contrast, you must select subjects that have something in common. For instance, you would find it foolish to contrast a cup of coffee with a sheet of paper, because they have no relationship to each other (except, by a long stretch, that each holds something—coffee or writing). Only a little less far-fetched is a comparison of a kitten to a railroad car (both touch the ground at four or more points, both can move from one place to another)—but there's no reason for doing so.

What you compare and contrast—things that *do* have something in common—could be two versions of the same item or person or idea. The example paragraphs earlier in this chapter were both about the longest river on their continents. Below each paragraph you saw an italicized list of what the Mississippi River and the Nile River have in common.

Finding something in common between what you propose to compare and/or contrast is the key to this kind of writing. You might write about two athletic coaches: even if they were involved with different sports, they would provide enough to write about because they both had essentially the same jobs. Or you could compare and contrast notions of personal honor as it might be perceived in this country today, and as it was perceived in medieval times.

What you select to compare and contrast could also be quite different, provided you could find some elements in common between what you decide to write about. Therefore, either a comparison or a contrast, or both, could be written about "Nightline" and the "Oprah Winfrey Show." Both are popular television programs, which have the following in common:

- moderator
- format
- content

- timing
- popularity
- longevity

A list of this sort—that is, what the programs being compared have in common—is the beginning of writing about them, as it is about any other subjects.

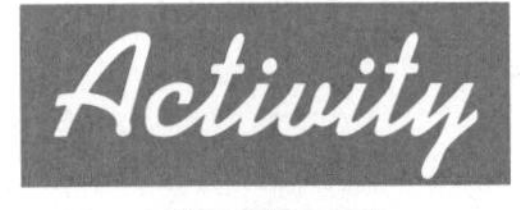

14-1

Have students add other pairs, perhaps from their *Idea Journals*, to extend this list.

DIRECTIONS: Make a list of as many elements in common as you can for each pair of words shown below.

EXAMPLE ▶ **This textbook and a Stephen King novel *have in common:***
printed pages, binding, contain ideas, author

1. Sandals and oxford shoes **have in common:**
footwear, protection from rough walking surface, both can be made of leather or canvas or synthetic materials

2. Whales and dolphins **have in common:**
mammals; live in salt water; travel great distances to find food

3. High school and college **have in common:**
students; teachers; grades; buildings; teaching and learning take place; administrators; places to eat; libraries; classrooms; sports teams; classes and courses

4. Apples and oranges **have in common:**
fruits; have seeds; grow on trees; juice made from them; have skins

5. A sailboat and a motorboat **have in common:**
travel on water; need some kind of propulsion; constructed of several kinds of material; need human to control them

6. My friends Harry and David **have in common:**
are men; like to fish; drive ; go to school ; behavior; attitudes on subjects; part time jobs

7. A(n) oak tree and a(n) maple tree **have in common:**
trunks; branches; leaves; roots; decorative uses

8. A vacation at ___the beach___ and a vacation at ___the mountains___ **have in common:**

costs money; away from work; lots of eating; meeting new people; time to get to; activities there

9. My ___psychology___ instructor and my ___math___ instructor **have in common:**

they are able to teach me; are strict about arriving on time; take time to help individuals; expect me to do the work; are hard graders, etc.

10. The movie ___________ and the movie ___________ **have in common:**

are action films; feature Mel Gibson; are set in far-away places; are available on VCR to rent

Key #2 to Comparison and Contrast: Finding Specifics

Mapping and brainstorming were covered in Chapter 4.

When you have identified the two people, things, or ideas that are going to be compared and/or contrasted, you must be sure that they really do have several characteristics that will make it possible for you to write about them in this way.

Developing a list of characteristics will give you ideas to work with in a convenient form. If you don't immediately think of what to put on such a list, try discussing the subjects with someone, try mapping, or try brainstorming.

Since an example of Key #1, finding something in common, was about "Nightline" and "The Oprah Winfrey Show," two very popular television shows, the example Key #2, finding specifics, will use the same subjects.

SPECIFIC SIMILARITIES

Begin by listing in the left column those qualities which both shows have in common. (They are in italics here, as they were in the examples earlier in this chapter.)

Next to each common quality, note ways in which the two shows are *similar*:

moderator	strong leader is always in control of show
format	has selected guests
	interviews guests
content	about people or ideas audience is interested in
timing	- - - - - - -
popularity	gets top ratings
longevity	broadcasting more than five years
audience	closed captioned for hearing impaired

Since the timing or length of the two shows differs, that item is left blank, although it could be crossed off. However, another point of similarity, the audience, was added because the programs have in common that they are closed captioned.

The following activities let you decide on similarities between pairs in items.

Activity 14-2

DIRECTIONS: Here are five pairs of items that can be **compared**. Some of what they have in common is listed in italics in the left column. If you think of others, add them. Next to each word in the left column, state briefly what is **similar** about the pair of items. Add more lines if you need them.

EXAMPLE ▶ **Compare cake and cookies**

uses *as snacks*
as desserts

how made *both are baked*
flour is main ingredient
often frosted

1. Compare football and basketball

equipment special shoes worn
special eyeglasses for some
played with balls
marked playing surface

players pros get big money
men or women
in good physical condition
can be played by all ages

spectators attract big crowds to games
popular to watch on TV
often bet on outcome of games

2. Compare two people you now work with on a job (or have worked with on an earlier job)

personality usually pleasant
helpful
sense of humor

experience more than three years

education high school graduation

3. Compare a bicycle and a motorcycle

structure	two wheels
	rubber tires
	metal frame
	handlebars

4. Compare where you live now and the last place you lived before moving there (if you have lived in more than one place)

location	same city
rooms	kitchen
	eating area
	living room
	bathroom
	bedrooms
heating	oil burner

5. Compare the singer (or musical group)____________________ and
(name)
the singer (or musical group)____________________
(name)

number of people	five
type music	rock
instruments	keyboard
	guitar
	drums

14-3

DIRECTIONS: Choose five of the subjects you responded to in *Activity 14-1* that you are willing to develop further. On your own paper, write the item number and topic of that previous activity. Make a column under "In Common" listing the items you wrote in the earlier activity. Next to each of them make another column listing specifics that they share.

EXAMPLE ▶

Items	This textbook and a Stephen King novel
In Common	
printed pages	both have more than 300 pages
binding	holds pages together
contains ideas	informative
	many new to me
author	one person

You now have information (from *Activities 14-2 and 14-3*) to write ten different paragraphs of comparison! In each paragraph, you could show the specifics of what the people, places, things, or ideas have in common.

Sharing

1. Form a group with two or three other people in the class.
2. Take turns reading aloud to each other one of the items you each did in *Activity 14-2*. Make additions or changes on your own work based on what others in the group have contributed.
3. Take turns reading aloud to each other one of the items each person did in *Activity 14-3*. Find items you did in common, if possible. Make additions or changes on your own work based on what others in the group have contributed.

SPECIFIC DIFFERENCES

In preparing to write a contrast showing ways in which "Nightline" and the "Oprah Winfrey Show" differ, first list the common qualities at the left. Then develop two lists showing specific ways in which the two shows *differ.*

Continuing with the example of the television shows being used to illustrate the various keys to comparison and contrast in this chapter, such a listing might look like this:

	"Nightline"	**"Oprah Winfrey"**
moderator	usually Ted Koppel	Oprah Winfrey
format	introduction gives background	interviews
	moderator questions guests	audience participation
	guests respond to each other	guests
content	newsworthy	about personalities
	sometimes well-known people	often about off-beat ideas
timing	½ hour	1 hour
	late night	daytime
longeivity	on air since 1980	national since 1985
audience	possibly college educated	probably mostly women
	people interested in news	

14-4

DIRECTIONS: In the left column are some suggestions about what the items to be **contrasted** have in common. Add others you can think of. Then there is a heading for each item to be contrasted. Under each heading, list the specific differences between them (based on what they have in common). Add lines if you need them to write on.

EXAMPLE ▶ **Contrast cakes and cookies**

You may want to help students by sharing some of the suggested responses in this *Activity.*

In Common	***Cakes***	***Cookies***
uses	serve on plate	eat from hand
	use spoon or fork	
	for celebrations	

how made	*in pan with sides*	*on flat pan*
	batter poured in	*can be dropped,*
		rolled and cut in
		shapes

1. Contrast camping in a tent and in a trailer (or motor home)

In Common	***Tent***	***Trailer (Motor Home)***
construction	nylon or canvas	metal & plastic
	has screening	on wheels
	metal poles	permanent
	user sets up	
where used	any flat ground	often campground
nice extras	lanterns	electric lights
	cook on campfire	gas or electric stove
	or portable stove	built in
	sleeping bags	regular beds

2. Contrast Thanksgiving and July 4

In Common	***Thanksgiving***	***July 4***
histroical reason	good crops of	signing Declaration
	early settlers	of Independence
how celebrated	turkey dinner	picnics
	with family	outdoors
time	4th Thurs. in Nov	on July 4

3. Contrast a bus and a train (or subway)

In Common	***Bus***	***Train***
size	one unit	several cars
power	diesel	electric
	gasoline	coal
		diesel
where used	on street	on tracks
cost	low + transfer	depends on distance
stopping places	almost anywhere	at stations

4. Contrast two movies you have seen recently

In Common	______________	______________
	write title	*write title*

main character	____________	____________
type	____________	____________
director	____________	____________
setting	____________	____________
	____________	____________

5. Contrast two people who are related to you in the same way (such as sons and/or daughters, parents, sisters and/or brothers, grandparents, cousins, aunts and/or uncles)

In Common	____________ *name*	____________ *name*
relationship	older son	younger son
appearance	blond	brown hair
	blue eyes	brown eyes
	6 ft. 2 in.	6 ft. 3 in.
personality	outgoing	reticent
	quick judgments	cautious
interests	outdoor sports	reading

Let students suggest additions to this *Activity* by adding pairs to contrast.

14-5

DIRECTIONS: Choose five pairs of items you have already worked with in *Activities 14-1, 14-2* or *14-3* from which to develop specific differences for this activity. On your own paper, write the activity and item number you will be working with and then name the two items. In the left column list what the items have in common. Make a heading for each of the two items and under them write the specific differences of the items.

EXAMPLE  **Items:**

This textbook and a Stephen King novel

[Name a specific novel if you can and use it for the heading]

In Common	***The Essentials of Basic Writing***	***Pet Sematary***
printed pages	498 pages	634 pages
binding	spiral	glued
		hard cover
purpose	instruction	entertainment
	non-fiction	fiction
author	Roth	King
publisher	Allyn and Bacon	Hall

You now have enough information (from *Activities 14-4 and 14-5*) to write ten different paragraphs of contrast. In each paragraph, you could show the specifics of how the people, places, things, or ideas you listed differ.

Sharing

1. Form a group with two or three other people in the class.
2. Take turns reading aloud to each other one of the items you each did in *Activity 14-4*. Make additions or changes on your own work based on what others in the group have contributed.
3. Take turns reading aloud to each other one of the items each person did in *Activity 14-5*. Find items you did in common, if possible. Make additions or changes on your own work based on what others in the group have contributed.

Key #3 to Comparison and Contrast: Organization

Students need to understand these two kinds of organization thoroughly so they can make informed choices.

Comparison and contrast have two formal organizations. If you follow one or the other, you will have a good paragraph. You may use either the **point-by-point** organization or the **item-by-item** organization.

If you think of what the subjects you are working with have in common and write them in order, you will have the point-by-point information and organization for the paragraph.

If you think of all the qualities one subject you are working with has, and then all the qualities of the second subject, and write them in order, you will have the item-by-item information and organization for the paragraph.

Suppose you had done some reading about two kinds of transportation devices, the hydrofoil and the hovercraft. Both rely on energy for their upward and forward motion. These craft have enough similarities and differences that you could write comparison and contrast paragraphs about them using either the point-by-point or item-by-item organization.

Here is a structural outline showing the **point-by-point organization**:

Hydrofoils and Hovercrafts

I. Where devices travel
 A. Hydrofoil
 B. Hovercraft
II. How devices controlled
 A. Hydrofoil
 B. Hovercraft
III. Uses
 A. Hydrofoil
 B. Hovercraft

Notice that it's important to follow the same order in each section of point-by-point writing; in this case, first it's information about the hydrofoil, then about the hovercraft. (A *content* outline would make evident if you were planning a comparison or a contrast paragraph.)

Here is a paragraph that **contrasts** the two devices **point-by-point.**

Contrast between Hydrofoils and Hovercraft
Both the hydrofoil and the hovercraft use energy for their upward and forward motion, but they differ in important ways. The hydrofoil, as the word *hydro* in its name says, is a craft that travels through and on water. On the other hand, the hovercraft, as its name suggests, *hovers* independently of the surface it goes over. Therefore, it can travel over water, but also over snow, marsh, sand, and above rails or roads if necessary. The hydrofoil is controlled by ladders or foils that emerge progressively from the water as the speed of the craft increases. The hovercraft rides on a bubble or cushion of air blown out through slots under or around the underside of its hull. The hydrofoil is already in common use as a passenger carrier in some parts of the world, and larger hydrofoils are being used for transporting goods over water. Hovercraft are not yet being used for great numbers of passengers, but their military and even industrial use is quickly increasing.

Here is a structural outline showing **item-by-item organization:**

Hydrofoils and Hovercrafts

I. Hydrofoils
   A. Where they travel
   B. How they're controlled
   C. What they're used for

II. Hovercrafts
   A. Where they travel
   B. How they're controlled
   C. What they're used for

Now here is the same information presented in an **item-by-item paragraph** organization.

Contrast between Hydrofoils and Hovercraft
Both the hydrofoil and the hovercraft use energy for their upward and forward motion, but they differ in important ways. The hydrofoil takes its name from the word *hydro*, meaning water, and it is a craft that travels through and on water. It is controlled by ladders or foils that emerge progressively from the water as the speed of the craft increases. The hydrofoil is already in common use as a passenger carrier in some parts of the world, and larger hydrofoils are being used for transporting goods over water. The hovercraft, on the other hand, *hovers* over the surface of water, snow, marsh, sand, and even above rails or roads if necessary. It rides on a bubble or cushion of air blown out through slots under or around the underside of its hull. Although hovercraft are not yet being used for great numbers of passengers, their military and even industrial use is quickly increasing.

Pointing out specific differences between these two paragraphs may be helpful to many students.

Topic Sentences in Comparing and Contrasting

Putting the topic sentence at the beginning of a comparison or contrast paragraph is a good idea, because it prepares the readers for what is to follow. In fact, you can often use the words "similar to" or "differ(ent) from" in the topic sentence so there is no question about what the readers should expect. If not those precise words, others that give readers some idea of what to expect are good.

Here are the topic sentences, which also are the first sentences, of the example paragraphs you have read so far in this chapter:

> The Mississippi River is the longest river on the North American continent, and the Nile is the longest river on the African continent.

(A comparison because both are described as the "longest river on the...continent.")

> The two longest rivers on the North American and African contents flow in opposite directions.

(A contrast because they "flow in opposite directions.")

> Both the hydrofoil and the hovercraft use energy for their upward and forward motion, but they differ in important ways.

(A contrast because "they differ in important ways.")

Students should get in the habit of developing topic sentence with content or substance.

Here is the topic sentence of a paragraph in the next section of this chapter.

> Some sea animals hunt for food while others must wait for food to come to them.

("While" is a clue word that sets up a contrast. Also, the sentence says "some...hunt...others...wait," which describes two different groups of sea animals.)

Try to include *content* in the topic sentence to prepare readers for what will follow. The sentence above about the hydrofoil and the hovercraft is the weakest of the topic sentences shown because it has the least content. "Differ in important ways" is vague writing, even though the sentence begins with something the two forms of transportation have in common.

TRANSITIONS

Transitions, including these, were presented in Chapter 7.

Words that signal connections among ideas—transitions—help tie thoughts together, and make reading easier and smoother for an audience. The particular words that are often used in writing comparison or contrast point the way toward the similarities or differences you are showing.

CONNECTING WORDS USED IN COMPARISON

also	and	as well as
both	each	equally
furthermore	have in common	in addition
in the same way	just as	like
similarly	the same	too

CONNECTING WORDS USED IN CONTRAST

although	but	conversely
different from	however	in contrast
instead of	neither	on the contrary
on the other hand	unlike	whereas
while	yet	

Read this paragraph without connecting words to make transitions:

> Some sea animals hunt for food. Others must wait for food to come to them. A barracuda will swim past a coral reef again and again, hunting for smaller fish to eat. The sea urchin doesn't look like a hunter. It moves around looking for its food. The conch, an animal living in a shell, hunts for its food. The coral polyps, which are animals, stretch their tiny tentacles to catch bits of food that drift by. Jellyfish drift through the ocean waiting for food passing close enough for them to take it in through their filters. Sea anemones are another kind of sea animal that can only eat food particles the water carries within their reach.

This paragraph is choppy and may be difficult to follow. You have no sense of what will follow from the first few sentences, unless you happened to catch the words "some" and "others" and put them together.

When transitions are added to the same material (and underlined so you can see them readily), see how the connections between ideas are clear and how the whole paragraph seems smoother. In the first sentence, the bolded and underlined word gives you the key to the sense of the paragraph: you can see that there will be a contrast. Midway through, when there is a shift from food hunters to animals that wait for their food, *another* boldface and underlined word emphasizes the contrasting information in the paragraph.

> Some sea animals hunt for food **<u>while</u>** others must wait for food to come to them. A barracuda will swim past a coral reef again and again, hunting for smaller fish to eat. <u>Although</u> the sea urchin doesn't look like a hunter, it actually moves around looking for its food. The conch, an animal living in a shell, is <u>also</u> one that hunts for its food. **<u>In contrast,</u>** the coral polyps, which are also animals, stretch their tiny tentacles to catch bits of food that drift by. Jellyfish drift through the ocean waiting for food passing close enough for them to take it in through their filters. Sea anemones are <u>still</u> another kind of sea animal that can only eat food particles the water carries within their reach.

Activity 14-6

This *Activity*, and the next one, take students through the whole process that culminates in writing a paragraph.

DIRECTIONS: Choose one of the pairs about which you have noted specifics to compare in *Activities 14-2* or *14-3* and which you believe you could write a paragraph about. OR, choose one of the pairs about which you have noted specifics to contrast in *Activities 14-4* or *14-5*. Then, do each of the following, in order, filling in the blanks as appropriate. Use your own paper if you need more space.

1. I am going to <u>compare contrast</u> these two items:
   (circle one above)
   ____________________ and ____________________
   taken from number _______ in *Activity 14-* ________
   which I wrote this way on page ________ of the text:
   (Use your own paper)
2. Next is an <u>item-by-item point-by-point</u> organization
   (circle one above)
   outline for the paragraph I will write.
3. On your own paper, write the paragraph. Use connecting words appropriate to the kind of paragraph you are writing.

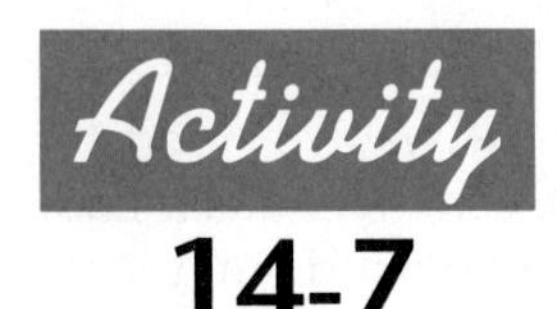

14-7

DIRECTIONS: Using the same sequence as in *Activity 14-6,* write the opposite kind of paragraph from the one you did above. That is, if you wrote a comparison paragraph, now write a contrast paragraph. If you used item-by-item organization, now use point-by-point organization. You may use the same two subjects or different ones taken from another number and another activity.

1. I am going to compare contrast these two items:
   (circle one above)
   ____________________ and ____________________
   taken from number _______ in *Activity 14-* ________
   which I wrote this way on page ________ of the text:
   (Use your own paper)
2. Next is an item-by-item point-by-point organization
   (circle one above)
   outline for the paragraph I will write.
3. On your own paper, write the paragraph. Use connecting words appropriate to the kind of paragraph you are writing.

RECAP—WRITING COMPARISON AND CONTRAST

- Choose two things, people, or ideas to compare or contrast (or both)
- Name the audience for which you will be writing
- Decide on a purpose for writing this piece
- Decide if you will compare or contrast these subjects
- List what the selected subjects have in common
- List specific similarities or differences (whichever you are working with)
- Select a method of organizing the information
- Write a topic sentence
- Use connecting words that show comparison or contrast

Chapter 15

Cause and Effect

In this chapter you will

- examine cause and effect writing as an if-then relationship of actions or ideas
- see two purposes for cause and effect writing
- learn the right questions to ask in moving from cause to effect or effect to cause
- be aware of four cautions in writing cause and effect
- apply critical thinking skills to writing about cause and effect
- develop paragraph organization based on placement of a topic sentence
- focus on connecting words to connect ideas

Critical thinking skills will be particularly evident in this chapter.

The phrasing is familiar:

> "What goes up must come down."
>
> "For every action there is a reaction."
>
> "Do that again and I'll punish you."

Or, consider some ordinary kinds of decisions we make:

> I'd like to wear jeans to work today, but if I don't follow the dress code of my office, which says "no jeans", I might get in trouble, and I like/need this job.

I really do want that car, so I'll try to get a loan with terms I can afford.

My friend probably ought to know about this, but if I tell what I know, I may lose a friendship I'd rather keep.

Whether we call these statements "cause and effect" or "problem and solution," all have to do with one happening leading to another. Often it is one action causing another to occur. But it may also be one way of thinking leading to another.

Explanation

Cause and effect writing **shows an "if-then" relationship**. When one thing happens, another follows, or may possibly follow.

If something goes up, ***then*** it must come down

If you do that, ***then*** I'll punish you

If I wear jeans to work, ***then*** I may get in trouble

If I tell my friend, ***then*** I may lose a friendship

Cause and effect writing has many uses, as the variety of statements above shows. That is, when you write about how people behave, you usually detail connections between what they did and why they did it, or what the results of that behavior are likely to be. If you write about events, you usually give reasons they occurred, or make judgments about what will follow as a result of the occurrence. In other words, it is the *relationship* or *connection* between the "if" and the "then" that is important in cause and effect writing.

Note the possible variations in terminology.

Sometimes the *"if"* elements are called "problems" rather than causes. The *"then"* elements may be called "results," or "solutions" almost as often as effects. The subject you write about will probably influence which of the words you want to use. For example, certain atmospheric conditions (cause) produce rain (effect). Or, poor study habits (cause) produce low grades (result). Or, a strike (problem) causes labor and management negotiation (solution).

There is also a chain effect at work in cause and effect. Very often the effect is the cause of something else, and the effect of *that* is a cause of still something more, and so on and on. As you begin examining cause and effect to write even one paragraph, you may find yourself in the middle of a series of interlocking relationships. You must then choose how much of the chain is best to include for the audience and purpose.

The terms "cause/problem" and "effect/result/solution" are almost interchangeable for our purposes now. The rest of this chapter, however, will use mostly the words "cause and effect."

These variations allow students flexibility. because they aren't limited to one cause to each effect, and vice versa.

Understand, also, that you are not limited to one cause for one effect. There may be several causes leading to one effect, or several effects that can be traced to one cause. Your paragraph should include as much of either as you decide is necessary.

Audience and Purpose

Cause and effect is often written **to inform an audience** because it deals with two different times: before and after—or now and future—or past and present. Even though there is a time element, it is different from narration or process writing. In both of those, the sequence of an event or a series of activities are important. The audience you write for in cause and effect is interested in both the events or activities as well as in their relationship to each other.

Another reason cause and effect writing is often used is **to persuade the audience** to think or act in a particular way. For instance, many organizations looking for contributions detail how $10 you send (the cause) can buy certain amounts of food (the effect) for a needy child. Besides, when you write persuasively, you know that you must give reasons that convince the audience. Therefore, establishing the connection between cause and effect can help you be convincing.

Suiting vocabulary to the audience was also pointed out in Chapter 2.

As with any other kind of writing, you must choose the wording understandable to the audience. If you are writing about the cause of volcanoes for people who know something about geology, you can refer to plate tectonics. But if you are writing for people who don't know the term, you need to explain it (that it is the movement of the geologic plates that form the crust of the earth) before you can go on to the matter of the volcanoes.

Example of Cause and Effect

The first sentence of the following paragraph is needed to establish the cause of weight gain. Then the audience can understand the reason for the statement in the second sentence. If the audience didn't need that information, the paragraph could begin with the second sentence.

> In normally healthy people, weight gain is caused by taking in more calories than the body needs. Therefore, if you want to lose weight, you either have to eat fewer calories or find ways to use up more calories than you take in. Dieting is probably the most popular way of losing weight, because then you are eating fewer calories. However, the body needs many elements in order to stay healthy, and "fad" or starvation diets are bad because they are not balanced. A better way of dieting is to keep track of everything you eat, either by your own careful choices or by buying, for a week at a time, the packaged meals sold by some diet companies. If you do not normally exercise, you should also begin sensible exercises for your age and life style to help your body use up calories. Together, watching the calories you eat and doing exercises that use more calories than usual should result in losing weight.

The topic sentence of this paragraph is the second one. It first states the **result**—to lose weight. Then it gives the **causes**—to eat fewer calories or to use more calories than you take in. The last sentence draws from the specifics mentioned in the paragraph and turns around the order. Therefore, it states the **cause** (watching calories and doing exercise) before the **effect** (losing weight).

At the beginning of this chapter you read a list of common sayings and situations representing if-then relationships: cause/effect or problem/solution. You also read a paragraph showing cause/effect; the information in it may even have been familiar to you. Now it is time to think about your own life and how often you see or hear or think about these same kinds of relationships and connections.

15-1

PART 1

DIRECTIONS: List here five cause/effect relationships you either say, hear people say, or are otherwise aware of. In spite of the single cause-single effect example, you may note more than one cause to a single effect or one cause with several effects. (Use additional paper if you run out of space here.)

EXAMPLE ▶

CAUSE	EFFECT
eat everything on your plate	*you will get dessert*

CAUSE	EFFECT
1. It rained	1. I got wet
	ruined my new shoes
	caught cold
2. "Wait until your father gets home"	2. "You'll get punished"
3. April showers	3. bring May flowers
4. If you touch the radio with wet hands	4. you could get a shock
5. If you stand under a tree during an electric storm	5. you are more likely to be hit by lightning

PART 2.

Note that in this *Activity* a distinction is made between cause/effect and problem/solution.

DIRECTIONS: List here five problem/solution relationships you are aware of or have experienced. That is, those that have already have occurred. You may note one problem with several solutions, or several problems that responded to one single solution. (Use additional paper if you run out of space here.)

EXAMPLE ▶

PROBLEM	SOLUTION
I have no clean shorts to wear	*Do my laundry*

PROBLEM	SOLUTION
1. didn't do homework that was due today	1. finish it in a hurry or ask for an extension
2. tire went flat	2. fix it or phone for someone who can
3. washing machine broke	3. have it fixed or go to laundromat or use another person's washing machine

4. am often late to work	4. get up earlier or leave home earlier or get another job
5. no change to make call from pay phone	5. call collect through operator or borrow money from someone

PART 3

You may want to have students provide support, add details, and write out one of these paragraphs.

DIRECTIONS: Choose three of the ten items above that you think you could write about in a paragraph. Write the topics (include both cause/effect and problem/solution) here:

Topic 1: ______________________________

Topic 2: ______________________________

Topic 3: ______________________________

Keys to Cause and Effect: "Why?" and "What If?"

EFFECT TO CAUSE

These are also key questions in developing critical thinking skills.

The child who keeps asking "Why?" is not being troublesome, but is trying to find the cause or connection between what is known and what is unknown. That is, if the effect is known, you ask "why" to find the cause that led to that effect.

Effect	Cause
Why do flowers grow?	They get nourishment from water, soil, and light.
Why do people get pellagra?	They don't get enough vitamins.
Why do airplanes fly?	Air lifts the wings.

Admittedly, these are fairly simple questions and the cause stated is also simple. You might, for example, continue asking "why" as a child often does, to get to more basic causes. Not getting enough vitamins is, itself, an effect that is caused by poor nutrition that is an effect of people not having the right food or enough food, which in turn is an effect of poverty that is caused by—well, take your choice.

While the simple answer that fits into a single paragraph might be adequate for one audience, another audience might need to have longer and more complex answers. Therefore, part of the decision about how much to write depends on the audience's need to know.

A Note About Asking Questions:

As the person who plans and writes, you have control over how much or how little information you want to include (given your audience and purpose). You may reach a stage where continually asking "Why?" and answering the question will take you so far back, or forward, that doing so is unproductive. You will go nowhere. The writer in you must decide when it's time to stop asking questions and start writing.

CAUSE TO EFFECT

When you move from something known in the present (the cause or causes), you can almost never know for sure what the effect (or effects) will be because it's in the future. If a cause (event or behavior) is known, you can ask "what if" to find a possible effect that will follow.

Cause	**Effect**
What if / the child scribbles on the wall of the house?	An adult will punish the child.
What if / you put this mold into a petrie dish under stated conditions?	You'll get penicillin .

Sometime you're sure of the answer to "what if", but mostly you are only guessing or making inferences. The effect may not yet have taken place, and you can only guess about the future.

Past actions, of course, can be written about with certainty. The history you studied in school or read about can be described as causes and effects with certainty, because we already know those relationships.

Perhaps the closest we can come to present "certainty" of cause and effect is in some principles in the natural sciences. For example, we know that if you put two objects of different weights into a vacuum and release them at exactly the same time (cause), they will fall at the same rate of speed (effect). But when you move into situations involving people or animals, or even many natural phenomena—including the weather—the "What if?" may be answered in different ways.

In the same way, when you know that a problem exists, you can ask, "What if I try Solution A?" Or, "What if I try Solution B?" You can never be sure that the solution you choose will really work as you expect it to; you can only make some good guesses backed up by experience and knowledge. For you are, after all, trying to foretell the future.

FOUR CAUTIONS IN WRITING CAUSE AND EFFECT

You may need to help students avoid these pitfalls in planning and writing their work.

1. Be careful about assigning a single cause to an effect, or a single effect to a cause. Here are two examples of how a single cause or a single effect are obviously wrong:

> World War I did not start just because the Archduke Otto of Austria was assassinated; there were many causes for the war and they went back over many years. (Multiple causes=one effect)
>
> Or, some food that was too badly burned to eat does not just have the effect of keeping the family waiting for dinner. It may also annoy or even anger the unfed people, and it will cost additional time and money to prepare something different. (One cause=multiple effects)

2. Be cautious about assigning the wrong cause to an effect, or the wrong effect to a cause.

> The history of science shows many examples of the wrong causes being given to an observable effect. Louis Pasteur discovered bacteria near the end of the 19th century and found that they were

responsible for meat spoiling under certain conditions. Until then, people believed (at various times in history) that angry gods caused spoiling, or that it was a spontaneous occurrence. (Real cause: bacteria, *not* gods or spontaneous happening=effect: spoiled meat)

Some children may like the taste of coffee and would rather drink it instead of more healthful beverages, such as milk, that might be available. In an effort to get them to drink something else, children have sometimes been told that drinking coffee will keep them from growing tall. We now know that although diet plays a part, genetics is the main determinant of height. (Cause: drinking coffee=unrelated effect on height.)

3. Try not to oversimplify. Oversimplification means reducing something complex by too much, or making it too easy. As soon as your reader thinks of reasons or alternatives you haven't considered, your writing loses believability.

For example, to suggest that someone is unemployed (an effect) because he or she doesn't try hard enough to find work (a cause) is to overlook many factors and, therefore, to oversimplify. There are many possibilities that can leave someone without a job. The unemployed person may not have the skills to qualify for available jobs, or the transportation to reach them. The person may have applied for jobs already filled or for those for which there were better candidates. Jobs the person could fill may be unavailable because bad economic conditions have forced many companies (and possible employers) out of business.

4. Be careful of overqualifying. When you "qualify" something, you put restrictions or limitations on it. To "*over*qualify" is to put so many exceptions on something that it is unusually narrow or limited. If you overqualify either causes or effects, you may make the audience decide that what you write is not believable, or is something it doesn't need to pay attention to.

For example, suppose you wanted to rent a car for a week. "Fine," says the car company. "All you have to do is qualify (cause) for this rental (effect). "And then you read the list of qualifications: you must be between 20 and 35, have an annual income of at least $35,000 a year, have a AAA credit rating with at least three recognized credit cards in active use, live in a Middle Atlantic state, drive at least 1,000 miles in the week (of which 800 are free and the rest are charged to you at 20¢ a mile). Obviously, such a list of qualifications is ridiculous! But your response is not. You'll rent a car from another company!

Activity 15-2

DIRECTIONS: Each effect stated below is followed by a list of possible causes. Circle the letter in front of those that seem possible and put an X through those that probably aren't related. Put a question mark in front of those you're not sure about. On the lines below the list, add other possible causes.

EFFECT:

The cake I baked was supposed to be high, but it collapsed in the pan.

POSSIBLE CAUSES:

(a.) Somebody stamped on the floor while cake was in the oven.

X b. Gremlins got into the cake batter.

? c. I was not experienced enough at baking.

(d.) I didn't follow the recipe accurately.

X e. Baking should have started earlier in the day

Other possible causes:

oven temperature not accurate

1. **Effect:** The traveler missed the plane.

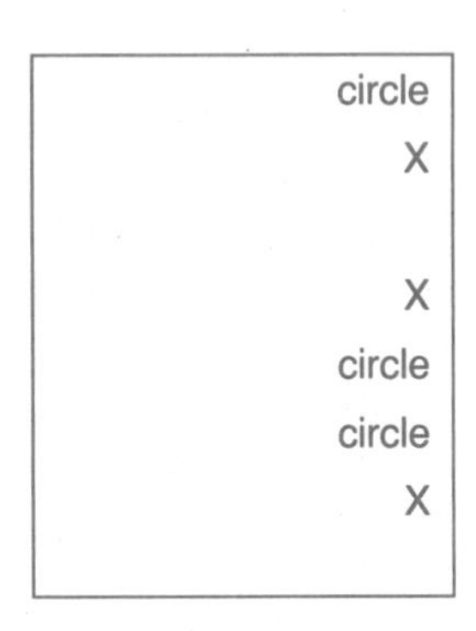

Possible Causes:

a. The traveler's watch was wrong.

b. The plane schedule didn't allow enough time to get to the airport.

c. Blue was the wrong color to wear that day.

d. Traffic heading to the airport was very heavy.

e. The traveler didn't realize departure time.

f. The flight schedule was changed without notice.

Other possible causes:

traveler didn't allow enough time

2. **Effect:** The store put all its merchandise on sale at very good discount prices.

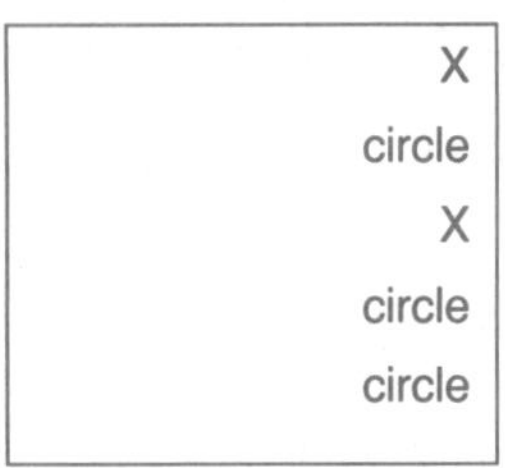

Possible Causes:

a. The landlord agreed to paint the building.

b. The store lost its lease.

c. It was doing the community a favor.

d. Bad management sent it into bankruptcy.

e. It didn't pay its suppliers' bills.

Other possible causes:

owner just decided to retire

3. **Effect:** The Greens are moving into a new apartment next month.

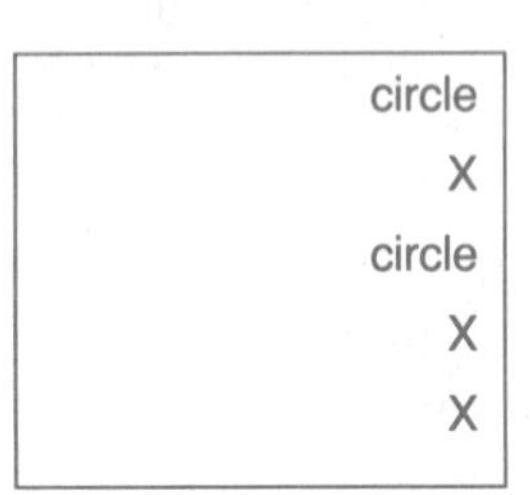

Possible Causes:

a. They want or need a bigger apartment.

b. A fortune teller said they should.

c. They can't pay the rent and needed a cheaper place.

d. The present place needs painting.

e. They are in the moving business and therefore move often.

Other possible causes:

their present one was sold to somebody who wants to live in it

4. **Effect:** My desk looks like a disaster area.

Possible Causes:

circle

a. I am lazy about getting the work on it done.

circle
circle
X

b. Somebody dumped a wastepaper basket on it.
c. I have more work than I can do.
d. My psychiatrist told me I have too neat and regular a life and should spice it up a little.

Other possible causes:

I am a sloppy person

5. **Effect:** A large box, full of fairly recent magazines with a variety of titles, was delivered to a local hospital.

Possible Causes:

X
circle
circle
circle
X
X

a. Somebody wants the patients to be better readers.
b. A kind-hearted person wants to give people in the various waiting rooms something to read.
c. A school collected them, along with newspapers, as a money-raising project, but discovered they weren't accepted by companies that bought waste paper and newsprint.
d. The box was delivered there by mistake; it was supposed to go to the local jail.
e. The magazines were all stolen from news dealers around town.
f. The hospital administrator mentioned the possibility of writing an article, so somebody thought the magazine articles would be good models to learn from.

Other possible causes:

the person was on the way to the dump with them but decided not to waste them

6. **Effect:** The student was selected for the school basketball team.

Possible Causes:

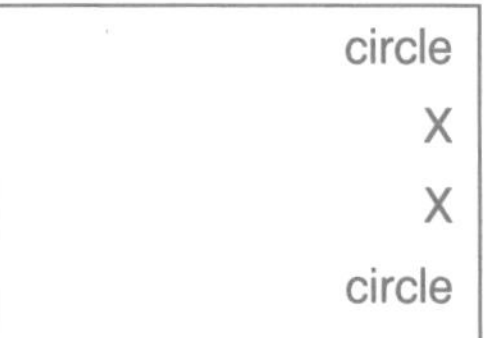

a. The student had practiced hard for years.
b. There were special springs in the student's shoes.
c. The school only had four others available for the team.
d. The student played basketball very well.

Other possible causes:

the coach was playing favorites

7. **Effect:** Tomatoes in the company's experimental agricultural area grew larger and faster than expected.

Possible Causes:

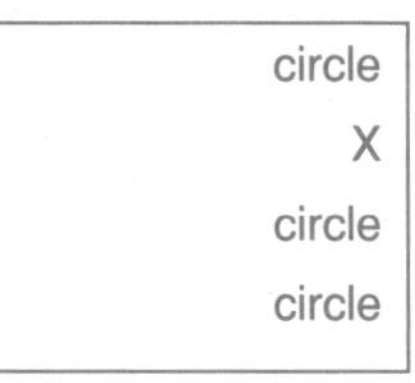

a. The new soil nutrients worked very well.
b. Outer-space aliens exchanged them nightly.
c. The experiment was working.
d. Someone was giving them special care.

Other possible causes:

the expectations weren't high enough

they were being grown hydroponically

8. **Effect:** The company office manager was promoted to vice president.

Possible Causes:

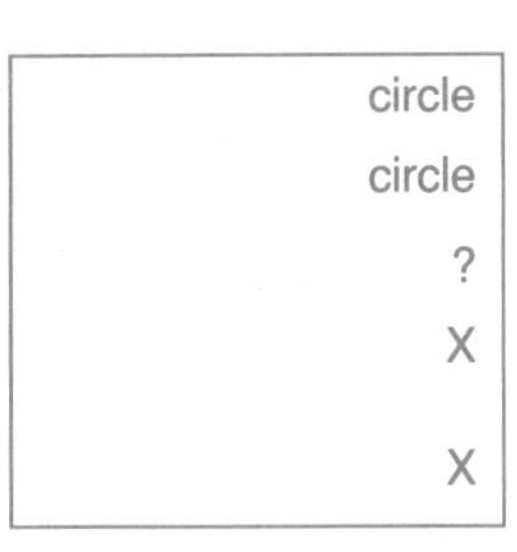

a. The manager had been doing a particularly good job.
b. The company was expanding and needed another vice president.
c. She married the president's son.
d. The company needed someone to move into a vacant office that had just been decorated.
e. The office manager was the only one who knew how to fix the computer.

Other possible causes:

the office manager was really the owner of the company

9. **Effect:** An "angel" donated money to sponsor the U. S. Olympic swimming team.

Possible Causes:

X
X
circle
circle
circle
circle

a. The donor didn't know what he or she was really doing.
b. The "angel" wanted his or her child to be chosen for the team.
c. The donation was a tax-saving device.
d. The "angel" was a frustrated Olympic swimmer.
e. The donor was glad to be able to support swimming in the U. S.
f. The donor hoped to encourage other wealthy people to support U. S. sports in this way.

Other possible causes:

the donation was in lieu of making a campaign contribution to someone

10. **Effect:** The book was on the best-seller list for six months.

Possible Causes:

circle
circle
X
circle

a. It's a very good book.
b. The book is getting good reviews.
c. The best-seller list was changed to include it.
d. The author has been appearing on lots of talk shows.

Other possible causes:

the book is being well promoted

DIRECTIONS: On your own paper, write three original statements, each telling an effect and then list one or more possible causes. You may be sure of both effect and cause because of your experience or knowledge of the effect. Or, you can know an effect and think up possible causes for it, as you had to do in *Activity 15-2*. (Use that *Activity* as your example, but don't put in the unrelated statements.)

Remind students to look in their *Idea Journals* for possibilities.

15-4

DIRECTIONS: Here are some causes from which will follow one or more effects. Write as many possible effects as you can think of for each stated cause. Remember that the question to ask in order to arrive at likely effects is "What if?" Do not limit your response to lines available on these pages.

EXAMPLE  **Cause:** You get on a self-service elevator at the street level and push the button for the third floor.
Possible Effects:
The elevator lifts you to the third floor. Nothing happens because the elevator is broken or the power has gone off. Somebody else is already on the elevator and has pushed the button for the second floor, so the elevator stops there first.

1. **Cause:** A state law does not allow smoking in any public building.
   Possible Effects:
   People who want to smoke have to go outside to do so. Some smokers will defy the law and smoke anyway.

2. **Cause:** You carry home an armload of books, intending to do homework assigned in them.
   Possible Effects:
   You do the homework. You do other things that are more interesting than the homework. You have a family or personal emergency that prevents you from doing homework in spite of good intentions.

3. **Cause:** Three men who lived in an inner city neighborhood and made good as college football players before turning pro spend a day in their old neighborhood giving football pointers to the children there.
   Possible Effects:
   The men feel they have accomplished good works. The children are impressed. The children decide to become pro football players. The news media pick up the story. The adult message about staying in school impresses the children. Other adults in the neighborhood are jealous of the apparently-successful men.

4. **Cause:** A rock slide blocks a mountain road.
   Possible Effects:
   People who need to drive on that road can't reach their destinations. Many schedules are demolished. Rock-and-debris moving machines are called in so the companies that own them and the people employed in those companies make money. The road has to be repaired.

5. **Cause:** An important baseball game between two rival schools must be cancelled because of rain.

   Possible Effects:

   The players and their families are very disappointed. The game has to be rescheduled. The players get more time to prepare for the game. The rivalry intensifies.

6. **Cause:** A television program you want very much to see is scheduled for the same time as your child's school play.

   Possible Effects:

   You videotape the program. You have a friend with a VCR tape it for you. You don't go to the school play but do watch the program. You decide you don't want to make a choice, so you do something different altogether.

7. **Cause:** Someone you once did a number of favors for dies and leaves you a piano and a violin.

   Possible Effects:

   You and/or members of your family take lessons on the instruments. You sell one and keep the other. You sell both instruments. You can't get the piano into your home, even though you'd like to have it there. You donate one or both of the instruments to an organization devoted to providing safe recreation for children. You refuse to accept the instruments.

8. **Cause:** A local DJ's program is cancelled by the radio station which carried it for several years, and it is replaced by a taped program sent in from another city.

   Possible Effects:

   Several people at the radio station lose their jobs. Some listeners don't care. Some listeners bombard the station with protests. Some listeners are so angry they won't tune in the station again. Some listeners like the new program. The new program attracts new listeners. Advertising revenues fall off because listeners fall off. The new program has no effect on the station's advertising income.

9. **Cause:** A British cricket player comes to your city, determined to introduce the game to all the elementary school children in town because he is convinced that by starting children at the game early they will come to view it as the important part of their sports life that people in his country do.

   Possible Effects:

   Many children take the to game and love it. Many children reject the game. Many children don't feel strongly one way or another about it. Some children are curious to learn the new game. Adults don't understand the game, so they don't care if their children play it or not. There is such sudden interest in cricket that there isn't enough equipment to meet the demand. The player and his game are the subject of ridicule and rejection. The player and his game are embraced by the community.

10. **Cause:** The car you are driving runs out of gas.

    Possible Effects:

    You can't get where you are heading. You have to find a way to get gas for the car. You ask passers-by for assistance. You kick yourself for not checking the gas gauge more carefully.

Students could write paragraphs after their discussion of *Activitiy 15-5.*

1. Form a group with two or three classmates.
2. Compare the *Possible Effects* you wrote in *Activity 15-5* with those written by the other people in your group.
3. Add to your own list any effects that other people thought of and that you find interesting.

Activity 15-5

In *Activities 15-2, 15-3,* and *15-4* there are a total of 23 stated causes or effects. Some of the information in those items you already know, and some of it you could guess about or make up. Any one of them could be a paragraph of cause and effect if you made up the information you didn't know for sure.

DIRECTIONS: Choose one of the items in the three *Activities* just noted that you could write a paragraph about. On your own paper, write the information you can put into such a paragraph, including what is printed in this book.

Problems are also both cause and effect. What we call a "problem" comes about as the result of one or more factors. In that sense, it is an effect. (Remember this interchangeability of terms early in the chapter.) But a problem needs to be solved, so it is also a cause.

If you know a problem exists and are looking for a solution (or solutions) to it, you have to do a lot of asking "What if?" before deciding. Remember, also, that if the solution has not yet occurred, neither you nor anybody else can know if it is the right one, that is, the one that will solve the problem.

Activity 15-6

DIRECTIONS: For each problem below, supply one or more possible solutions. Don't be concerned about whether or not your solutions are practical. Instead, be as creative as you wish and write your solutions in one or more sentences. (Use your own paper if you need more space.)

EXAMPLE ▶ **Problem:** A rich relative gives you an ordinary red building brick and says that if you can keep it in use in five different ways in the room, apartment, or house where you live for four weeks, you will receive $1000, tax free.

Solution:

I would use it as a door stopper, as a bookend for my books or CDs, put it in the toilet tank to save water when flushing the toilet, decorate it and stand it on a table as a conversation piece, and use it to prop up books when I read.

1. **Problem:** Two cousins you have never met in person, but whose parents you like a great deal, phone to say they are arriving the next day to stay with you for a week while they visit in your city.

   Solution:

   You could tell them you have been called out of town and can't allow them to stay at your place because you have a vicious dog that won't let anyone there when you aren't home. You could be pleasant and keep peace in the family by having them come and stay. You could say that you already have company and there simply isn't room for any more guests.

2. **Problem:** One of your close friends, someone you see every day, gave you a birthday present of a tee shirt you think is really ugly. (Never mind that nobody who knew you well would choose such a thing.) You don't know where it was bought, so you can't return it. You certainly won't wear it, so you keep it hidden in the bottom of your closet. About a month later, the friend asks you why you haven't been wearing the shirt.

   Solution:

   You could say that the laundry failed to return it, or that the dog ate it. Or you could tell the truth and say it's a wonderful tee shirt but just doesn't look good on you. Or you could say you loaned it to someone and it hasn't been returned yet.

3. **Problem:** Someone you know at work who has the same kind of job you do remarks that you hardly ever show any stress or strain. The person, who is feeling especially stressed out right now, asks you to design a program or course of action to follow and get to the point you are, that is, rarely showing any stress or strain.

   Solution:

   You could fulfill the request graciously. You could say you are too busy to design such a program. You could say that you are really under a lot of stress and strain but just don't show it.

4. **Problem:** You prepared a very nice dinner for two people: you and a guest you invited. When all the food is cooked just right and everything is ready, you sit down to enjoy the food and the time together. Just then, the doorbell rings and, when you get up to answer it, eight people you would rather not see just then come in without being invited and sit down or hang around you.

Solution:

You could tell the people you are just sitting down to dinner and there isn't enough, so they should leave. You could phone for pizza delivery to feed all of you and thus change plans for your own dinner. You could allow them to hang around until you finish the prepared dinner with your guest.

Have each student write out another problem, exchange the paper with a classmate, and write possible solutions to the problem.

5. **Problem:** You have been out riding a bicycle. It is starting to get dark and you have no lights or reflectors on the bicycle. You realize you are in a strange neighborhood, and you don't know where you are or how far from home. You don't see any cars passing or any people outside.

Solution:

You should try to find a main street and follow it, hoping that help will show up. You should always carry a map and not get into such a situation. You should carry a beeper or a portable phone when you go out alone like that. You should ride the bicycle earlier in the day so you won't get caught in the dark. You should always know where you're going when you go out riding on the bicycle.

Sharing

You may want to have each group share its selections with the entire class.

1. Form a group with two or three classmates.
2. Let each person select the problem she or he found *hardest* to find solutions for. Discuss with the others why it was hard.
3. Let each person select the problem he or she found it *easiest* to find solutions for. Discuss with the others why it was easy.
4. Let each person select what she or he believes is the best solution written for *Activity 15-6* and tell why it was selected.

Topic Sentences for Cause and Effect

Once you have established the if-then relationship of the cause and effect topic you are going to write about, put on paper a topic sentence for the paragraph you will write. Often, simply stating the cause and effect in the if-then form is enough to make the topic sentence.

The following examples of if-then topic sentences are based on *Activities* in this chapter.

- *If* you go out bicycle riding, *then* having a map—if not a portable telephone—with you may prove very helpful.
- *If* Jason is chosen for the school basketball team, *then* the coach thinks he can be relied on to play well.
- *If* the store marked all its merchandise for sale at discount prices, *then* it is because the store is going out of business.
- *If* you allow relatives to stay with you when they haven't been invited, *then* you are going to be constantly bothered by other relatives walking in and expecting to stay with you.

You do not need to use the words "if" and "then" in a topic sentence. Instead, you can arrange the information so that a reader can tell which part is the cause and which the effect.

EXAMPLES  **People who travel often *(cause)* will find it helpful to take a battery-operated clock with them. *(effect)***

Sunscreen products are selling very well *(effect)* because the public is recognizing how important it is to use them outdoors. *(cause)*

This returns to statements early in the chapter about the purposes of cause and effect writing almost always being to inform or persuade.

Both the topic sentences above are informational. However, earlier in this chapter you read that a second and frequent purpose for writing cause and effect is to persuade the reader. (see Chapter 16—Persuasion) For example, this topic sentence will result in a paragraph meant to persuade:

If you want to avoid skin cancer, you should put on sunscreen whenever you go outdoors for even a short time.

Activity
15-7

DIRECTIONS: Write four topic sentences for cause and effect and/or problem and solution paragraphs. At least two must be original and come from your *Idea Journal,* from discussions with classmates, or from ideas you get by talking with other people. The other two may come from ideas in any of the *Activities* in this chapter. Use your own paper.

ORGANIZING CAUSE AND EFFECT

Here are two possible topic sentences for a paragraph:

- The economy is starting to improve *(effect)* so the recession has bottomed out. *(cause)*
- The recession has bottomed out *(cause)*, and the economy is starting to improve. *(effect)*

Note: *"Bottomed out" is a phrase used by economists to mean that the lowest point—or bottom—has been reached.*

You can easily see that these are the same statements. Only the two parts are reversed. Now see how that topic sentence information can be used in different places within a paragraph. The cause part of the sentence is underlined and the **effect** part is in boldface and underlined.

These four versions demonstrate flexibility in organization. They are summarized in the chart immediately following.

VERSION 1

The economy is starting to improve, so the recession has bottomed out. What reports call the leading "economic indicators" point to this improvement. More home building is starting because loans to buy materials and pay the workers are easier to get. Fewer people are jobless, and that means they will have money to spend to make the economy better. Also, as more people are able to earn their way, fewer are applying for government assistance or state unemployment programs.

VERSION 2

What reports call the leading "economic indicators" show that more home building is starting because loans to buy materials and pay the workers are easier to get. Fewer people are jobless, and that means they will have money to spend to make the economy better. Also, as more people are able to earn their way, fewer are applying for government assistance or state unemployment programs. **The economy is starting to improve**, so the recession has bottomed out.

Because these are two-part topic sentences—the cause and then the effect—they can also be split and put in different places in the paragraph, as these next two versions of the same information show:

> **VERSION 3**
>
> **The economy is starting to improve.** What reports call the leading "economic indicators" point to this. More home building is starting because loans to buy materials and pay the workers are easier to get. Fewer people are jobless, and that means they will have money to spend to make the economy better. Also, as more people are able to earn their way, fewer are applying for government assistance or state unemployment programs. As a result, economic experts say that the recession has bottomed out.
>
> **VERSION 4**
>
> Economic experts say that the recession has bottomed out. What reports call the leading "economic indicators" point to this. More home building is starting because loans to buy materials and pay the workers are easier to get. Fewer people are jobless, and that means they will have money to spend to make the economy better. Also, as more people are able to earn their way, fewer are applying for government assistance or state unemployment programs. Therefore, there is evidence that **the economy is starting to improve.**

You *might* be convinced that you should always begin a paragraph with a topic sentence. But that would bore a reader because you would always be writing the same way! With cause and effect you can organize the paragraph in different ways, as these four versions with the same topic sentences and the same information show. Here are the possibilities of where to put the topic sentence in a paragraph:

Beginning		**Ending**
cause and effect		
effect and cause		
		cause and effect
		effect and cause
cause	- - - - - - - - - - - -	effect
effect	- - - - - - - - - - - -	cause

WORDS THAT SHOW CAUSE AND EFFECT RELATIONSHIP

At the beginning of this chapter you read that writing cause and effect is a matter of establishing an if-then relationship between actions and ideas. Here are some connecting words to help you establish that relationship:

accordingly	as a result
because	consequently
for this reason	hence
since	so
so that	then
therefore	thus

Notice that two of this list were used in Versions 3 and 4 above.

15-8

DIRECTIONS: Choose a topic sentence you developed for *Activity 15-6* and about which you are willing to write a paragraph. Write that sentence here:

____

____

Now write a cause-and-effect paragraph built around that topic sentence. Underline the topic sentence in the paragraph. Continue on your own paper if necessary.

____

____

____

____

____

____

____

____

____

____

____

RECAP—WRITING CAUSE AND EFFECT

- Decide on a subject you can write about. It must have if-then possibilities.
- Choose an audience and a purpose for writing.
- If you have not already determined both the cause/problem (or causes/problems) and effect/result/solution (or effects/results/ solutions) you will write about, do so by asking either "why" or "what if" questions.
- Keep in mind the four cautions about writing comparison and contrast.
- Develop a topic sentence.
- Decide on an organization for writing cause and effect.
- Use words that show relationships where they are needed.
- Write a paragraph of cause and effect.

Chapter 16

In this chapter you will

- learn why audience and purpose are especially important in writing persuasion
- relate claims to audience and purpose
- identify emotional and rational appeals
- practice four rational ways to support claims
- see how counterarguments can advance your claim
- examine the difference between a claim and a topic sentence
- learn to organize persuasion

You will probably want to encourage students to add their own examples which they can then draw from throughout the chapter.

"Persuasion" seems a less intimidating word to most students than does "argument."

Every time you watch an ad on television or read one in a magazine or newspaper, every time you write a letter of complaint or request, every time your job requires you to read spec sheets to choose a supplier for merchandise, every time you write a note asking that your child be excused early from school, you are dealing with persuasion. In fact, you are bombarded by persuasive spoken and written messages for most of every day. Almost every business in the country spends a great deal of time and money trying to persuade you to think or act one way or another. So do lots of people you know.

Sometimes you will find the word "argument" used instead of "persuasion," but the two words represent ideas so similar that they will be used interchangeably here. Actually, "argument" is the word used more often in academic writing because it has a long and scholarly history. This kind of argument has little to do with disagreements you have with parents or children about responsibilities at home, or the perhaps-heated words you exchange with friends (or enemies). Instead, it is the kind of argument a lawyer uses in presenting a case to a judge or jury, the kind of argument a scientist uses in presenting findings that will convince other scientists. It means a careful, reasoned way of presenting a point of view.

Explanation

Examples that students devise of how they are persuasive will be preparation for *Activity 16-1.*

Persuasion tries to get someone to think, believe, or act in a particular way. People you know and don't know, voices on radio and characters on television, articles and ads bombard you with persuasion. But then, you use your own persuasiveness on a lot of people, too.

If you have ever written a cover letter to go with your résumé, you tried to make that letter as persuasive as possible in order to get hired. If you have made application to attend a school, you probably had to write persuasively in the standard section that asks why you want to attend that particular school. Or, if you've filled out the "Why do you want this job?" section on an application, you've had to write persuasion. People who can make a good case for being hired or being admitted will not get what they want *only* on the basis of such mini-essays or letters—but being persuasive on paper often gives them the edge over other candidates.

Remind students of this when they have to make up their own claims.

Persuasive writing also has an important place in business and industry. There are business proposals one person (or a group of people) writes in order to get a contract to provide a service or a product to another company. There are letters of complaint and letters of praise, inquiries asking for information, and memos setting out policies some people have to be convinced to follow.

As simple a statement as, "This cake is delicious. Here—try a bite," is persuasive. You are being encouraged to act in a certain way. (Or, if you're on a diet, you are being encouraged to think, "If I take just a tiny bite, maybe I can try it.")

There is a school of thought that believes all writing of whatever kind, fiction or non-fiction, is persuasive. That is, underlying what someone writes is the author's desire to convince readers to believe, or think, or act in particular ways.

To this way of thinking, then, even a scientific report is not just informational, but is also meant to be persuasive. For example, there is a belief that dinosaurs died out because a giant meteorite fell to earth and blew so much dirt into the air that for years the sun was blocked off. The result was destruction of the plant life that was the food, or part of the food chain, of the dinosaurs. With no food, they died off. Informative? Yes. But the scientists who advance this theory keep gathering support for it (for example, where the meteorite landed, how much dust and dirt was blown up, and how far it spread). As additional information is published, those who write the information are trying to convince others to believe in this theory. Therefore, it is meant to be persuasive.

Audience and Purpose

As you set out to write persuasively, you need to know what will persuade the audience. Parents who go to PTA meetings are already convinced of the importance of the organization; they are willing to take the time and trouble to attend meetings, not just pay dues. On the other hand, you need to figure out what you can say to convince those parents who *don't* go to PTA meetings and, particularly, those who don't even join the group, that the organization is worth their time and money. So, while you could write one way about the importance of the PTA to those who belong, you would have to write in a different way to those who don't, and each piece of writing would stress different information,.

Students might be encouraged to discuss what it would take to get them to change their minds about something they disagree with.

Is the audience sympathetic to what you are writing about? Then it might not take much to persuade it to go along with your interpretation of the idea. But if the audience is unsympathetic or resistant, you will need to write more persuasively or offer more and better reasons before you can convince the audience to agree with your idea. For instance, despite brand loyalty, advertisers know they have a better chance of convincing soft drink users to try another brand than they have of convincing those who refuse to buy soft drinks to try any brand at all.

If you know that readers disagree with the view you are expressing, you may even be able to turn that to your advantage. That is, you can answer the objections that readers might have even before they are presented to you. The example of a persuasive paragraph in the next section shows one way to do that.

A reminder of this is usually helpful near the end of a persuasive paragraph because readers tend to remember best what they see last.

When you are writing mainly to inform people, you want them to receive and understand the information you are communicating. However, **when you are writing to persuade, you want a response.** That's your purpose. The response may be an action ("Pick up the phone and call me.") or a belief ("Yes, I agree with your suggestion.").

As you think back over writing you have done, both for school assignments and in your life outside of school, you will recall many instances in which you wanted to persuade one or more people to think or act in a particular way. The writing may have been anywhere from a few sentences to several pages. If you were successful in your persuasion, it was probably because you wrote for a particular audience and purpose, or because your timing was right, or because your writing was better than somebody else's.

16-1

DIRECTIONS: Fill in the blanks to respond to the questions and statements below that focus on persuasive writing you have done.

EXAMPLE ▶ **I wrote (what?):** *a cause and effect paragraph*

(when?) *last week*

mainly for (audience?)

others in my writing group and the teacher

to get this response: *a good grade*

How successful were you?

People in the writing group gave me help. Now I'm waiting for the teacher to read it

1. I wrote (what?) : an answer to a question on a job application
   (when?) last year
   mainly for (audience?) the shipping company employment manager
   to get this response: to get a job
   How successful were you? I got the job

2. I wrote (what?) : a note for the suggestion box at work
   (when?) three months ago
   mainly for (audience?) the bosses
   to get this response: to try out my suggestion
   How successful were you? They tried it and I got a $25 bonus.

3. I wrote (what?) : a letter
   (when?) last September
   mainly for (audience?) my friend away at school
   to get this response: an O.K. to go up there for a football weekend
   How successful were you? I went there.

4. I wrote (what?) : a letter
   (when?) a few weeks ago
   mainly for (audience?) the insurance company
   to get this response: to pay my claim
   How successful were you? don't know yet—no answer

5. I wrote (what?) : an essay
   (when?) about two weeks ago
   mainly for (audience?) my social science teacher
   to get this response: to get an A on the paper
   How successful were you? Not very. I got a C on the paper.

Example of Persuasion

This paragraph shows persuasion directed to a particular audience: parents of left-handed children. Its purpose is to encourage them to take an active part at school on behalf of their children.

> Parents of left-handed children ought to fight the way schools discriminate against their children. Left-handed children start to feel discrimination as soon as they begin school. They are given scissors designed for right-handed people. No wonder the left-handed children have trouble cutting out designs and can't do work as neatly as the other children. When they learn to write, they are taught to hold pencils in the right hand, and slant the writing the way right-handers do. Left-handers end up turning their wrists almost upside down and then being told their writing isn't slanted the proper way. When they get to higher grades, most of the chairs they use have the writing arms attached on the right side. That makes taking notes and writing tests very uncomfortable for the children because they don't have anything to rest their left arm on. Therefore, a parent should tell the school that a child is left-handed and that special accommodation is needed. There are left-handed scissors and writing chair-desks. If the school doesn't have them, it should buy them and make sure they are in every classroom the left-handed child goes to. The possible additional cost will be almost nothing compared to what will be achieved. The school principal should also remind teachers to be sensitive when there are left-handed children learning to write in their classes. Parents should keep tabs on how the school accommodates their children and complain if the school doesn't meet its obligation. Teachers should be made aware of the problems these children have, and help them deal with being left-handed in a right-handed world.

The purpose of this paragraph is expressed the first sentence. In fact, the words "ought to" are among those that make an obvious claim. They signal that the writer wants to persuade the reader to do, say, act, or believe something. In this case, it is to act.

The next seven sentences show ways in which left-handed children feel discrimination in school: through the kind of scissors they are given, the way they are taught to hold pencils, and the kind of chairs they must sit in. But then the paragraph gives examples of what a parent can do to fight each of these kinds of discrimination: by making sure scissors and writing chair-desks accommodate left-handed students and by alerting teachers to their problems. It concludes with the hoped-for response.

Four Keys to Writing Persuasion

Persuasion is more complex than other kinds of writing because you must incorporate in it several elements that you do not use, or always use together. Therefore, instead of just one principal key to persuasion, you must think of these:

- making a claim (which is not quite the same as writing a topic sentence)
- choosing an emotional or a rational appeal
- supporting the claim
- anticipating and responding to objections

KEY #1: MAKING CLAIMS

A claim is the position that you take on the subject you select to write about. It can't be a fact, but must be something that can be argued. For example, "The link between smoking and heart disease is well documented," is a fact. You can find many authoritative, written statements of this and a great deal of supporting information. But, "Uncle Clifford ought to stop smoking" is a claim. It is not a fact, but a statement that can be argued. You can provide support for such a claim, including the documentation that establishes the link between smoking and heart disease.

When you take a position and make a claim, you express your judgment on a matter, or offer a solution to a problem. The claim in the example paragraph, "Parents of left-handed children ought to fight the way schools discriminate against their children," is the author's judgmental statement. It is also the solution to a problem the author wants parents to address. Another person might feel that left-handed children ought to be taught to fit into a right-handed world, and so make a different claim with support for *that.*

Key words in a claim are those that show you are taking a position. For that reason, claims often, but not always, contain the words "ought to," "should," or "must"—or their negatives, "ought not," "should not," or "must not." Such qualifying words as "probably," "likely," or "apparently" may sometimes also be part of the claim.

Watch for claims that do *not* contain these key words but in which the author does take a position by expressing a judgment or offering the solution to a problem. "Milk prices are too high" is such a claim. You could restate it as "Milk prices ought to be lowered" if you are more comfortable with claims that contain a key word.

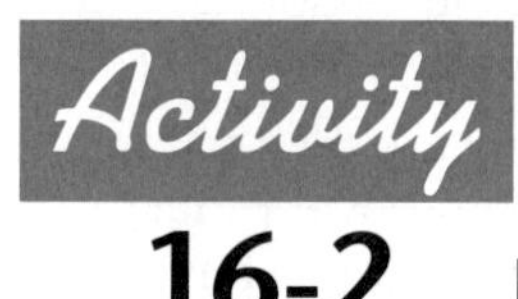

16-2

DIRECTIONS: In the space to the left of each statement, write an **F** if it is a fact and a **C** if it is a claim.

EXAMPLE ▶ __F__ **Human beings are mammals that live on land, yet some mammals live in water.**

__C__ **Private management of public schools will give children a better education than they are now getting.**

__C__ 1. Children should not go to school year-round.

__C__ 2. The cost of a stamp to mail a letter is one of the best buys around.

__F__ 3. Race-walking scholarships are available only at a few colleges and universities.

__C__ 4. You can almost assure yourself of a college scholarship if you practice to become an excellent race-walker.

__F__ 5. Yellow paper, much favored for note pads, is not recyclable.

__C__ 6. Drinking lots of water is probably an important factor in losing weight.

__F__ 7. People who do hard work on hot days must drink liquids if they don't want to get dehydrated.

__C__ 8. Studying will result in better grades.

__C__ 9. If you want to write quickly, you should learn to compose on a computer.

__F__ 10. Not all languages have the same sentence structure that English does.

When you decide on a claim, you ought to either choose one you know will appear reasonable to the audience, or be prepared for a particularly difficult time convincing your readers. Choose the first of these for now, because you will have an easier time writing a persuasive paragraph that you know has some chance of acceptance.

16-3

DIRECTIONS: Write a claim that you believe will seem reasonable to each audience and for the purpose stated in the items below. (Claim #1 will be more suitable for speaking than for writing.)

EXAMPLE 

Audience: Students in your class
Purpose: To prevent dissatisfaction with registration procedures for next term
Claim:

You should register for next term as soon as possible.

Student responses may differ from those shown here.

1. **Audience:** Children entering a kindergarten class
   Purpose: To start teaching them to get along with each other in a school setting
   Claim:
   You must each learn to share toys with other children in the class.

2. **Audience:** People applying for a fishing license
   Purpose: To prevent over-fishing in certain areas of the state river systems
   Claim:
   Limits should be put on the size and number of certain kinds of fish stocked in the rivers.

3. **Audience:** Attendees at a school soccer game that is being televised
   Purpose: To convince TV viewers of school spirit
   Claim:
   Everybody here should cheer as loudly and excitedly as possible.

4. **Audience:** Mid-management employees in a large, local manufacturing plant
   Purpose: To encourage them to enroll in business courses being offered by the local community college
   Claim:
   Taking business courses will help you move into better jobs.

5. **Audience:** Students at your school
   Purpose: To raise money for the school athletic program
   Claim:
   You should show school spirit by buying tickets to school athletic events.

16-4

DIRECTIONS: On your own paper, state three examples each of an audience, purpose, and claim that will seem reasonable to that audience. Use your *Idea Journal*, remembered conversations with friends, or your own thoughts as sources for the claims. You may want to write the claim first, then fit an audience and purpose to it.

Sharing

Form a group with three other people in the class and take turns discussing each other's responses to *Activity 16-4*. Offer whatever help you wish to others in the group.

KEY #2: EMOTIONAL AND RATIONAL APPEALS

Have students bring in ads that use emotional and rational appeals. Discuss them together.

Much of the persuasive writing you read, especially ads, urges you to do this, or buy that, or go somewhere. Instead of intellectual or moral or ethical reasons, the writers try to persuade you with a promise that something will make you look prettier or more handsome, because you will smell better (or not at all), because you will feel more self-assured, or because you will then fit in with a group you would like to belong to. In other words, the appeals are not to your reason, but to your **emotions.**

Business people don't decide to move an office location because the new one will have a better address (an emotional appeal to vanity). However, many move their offices because the new one is cheaper to rent or more accessible to suppliers. You may have changed a difficult class in high school for an easier one in hopes of being able to get a better grade and therefore a higher grade point average—which, in turn, would help you be accepted at a college you wanted to attend. Anyone writing to persuade another in favor of the office move or the class change would undoubtedly cite the rent or the better grade, and therefore appeal to the **reason** of the reader.

Both emotional and reasonable, or rational, appeals are used in writing persuasion. Sometimes you may use both in a single piece of writing. At other times, you will choose between them, depending on who you are trying to persuade (audience) and what you want to achieve (purpose).

16-5

DIRECTIONS: Put an **E** on the line to the left of each of the following statements that is an appeal to the audience's emotions, and an **R** on the line of each statement that is a rational appeal.

EXAMPLE ▶ _R_ **This refrigerator has a five-year warranty on the motor and a ten-year warranty on the exterior cabinet.**

_E_ 1. Use the same shampoo the stars use.

_R_ 2. This car gets 28 mpg in the city and 35 on the open road.

_E_ 3. Our baseball team is bound to win because we pay our players more than the other team does.

_R_ 4. We had an independent company perform a strength test on our product, and it exceeded the government standards.

_R_ 5. The electric razor was withdrawn from the market because many people reported permanent skin damage after using it.

_E_ 6. The perfume that will waft you away to gracious evenings.

R 7. Save the data on your home computer frequently, because even a far-away electric storm you're not aware of can cause the electricity to go off and you'll lose the work you've done.

E 8. "Super-Grow" is recommended by the people who grow prize-winning vegetables at county fair competitions all across the country.

R 9. On the basis of the high costs for entertainment in the last quarter, that item has been taken out of the projected budget for the next quarter.

R 10. Please take care of this matter for the company, since you will be going to the attorney's offices on other business.

Activity 16-6

DIRECTIONS: Look at the claims in *Activity 16-2, Activity 16-3,* and *Activity 16-4.* In the spaces below, copy five of those claims you think you could write paragraphs about. For each claim, note if you would use mainly an emotional or a rational appeal to the audience. Base your choice on the appeal you think the audience would most likely respond to.

EXAMPLE ▶ **Claim:**

You should register for next term as early as possible.

Main appeal:

Rational

Student responses will vary.

1. Claim:

   Everybody here should cheer as loudly and excitedly as possible.

   Main appeal: Emotional

2. Claim:

   Taking business courses will help you move into better jobs.

   Main appeal: Rational

3. Claim:

   Limits should be put on the size and number of certain kinds of fish stocked in the rivers.

   Main appeal: Rational

4. Claim: ______

   Main appeal: ______

5. Claim: ______

   Main appeal: ______

You may want to explore other kinds of emotional appeals in addition to those mentioned here. See also previous margin note.

KEY #3: FOUR RATIONAL WAYS TO SUPPORT CLAIMS

If you use emotional support for a claim, you appeal to qualities in the audience you believe will encourage them to respond to the claim: sympathy, desire to please, vanity, fear, pity, envy, desire for love, helpfulness, etc.

Rational appeals depend on evidence the reader's mind can accept. They are, therefore, intellectual, and include:

- Facts
- Statistics
- Examples
- Authorities

You may use all four kinds of support in an essay, but because a paragraph is so much shorter, you may decide to focus on one or, perhaps, two of these.

FACTS are statements that come from observation by one or more of the senses. Some facts you know by your own senses. You can look out the window and state the fact, "It's raining." Though it might be raining where you are, it isn't necessarily raining in other places, but the qualifier "here and now" is understood and the statement is accepted as fact. Or, you might observe the fact that Frank Sinatra is singing a song because you recognize the special sound of his voice.

Other facts you can't possibly observe, but accept anyway. "The Norman armies invaded England in the year 1066" is accepted as a fact because reliable sources *did* observe the event and their word has been handed down to us.

An audience you persuade by rational statements is bound to accept a claim supported by as many facts as you can present.

STATISTICS are facts presented in numerical form. Writing that the fish farm was able to increase production by 29% with the addition of a certain chemical to the water is a statement of fact that uses a number. Many business decisions are made on the basis of statistics: increases or decreases in production based on sales figures, salaries tied to productivity, loans made or refused on the basis of the company balance sheet, and so on.

Although there is an old saying that numbers don't lie, you probably also know that numbers (or statistics) can sometimes be manipulated to show what someone wants them to. "50% of the people who bought auto Brand X agree that their cars are lemons and always need repairs" sounds as if Brand X really makes terrible cars. However, if only four people were asked about Brand X cars, just two of them would account for the 50% negative response. That's very different from asking 4,000 purchasers and having 2,000 say the cars weren't made well, though the number is still 50%. Using statistics is often rather like having an eight-ounce glass holding four ounces of water. Some people would say "It's half full," and some would say "It's half empty."

So whenever you choose statistics to prove a claim, be sure they are accurate (if the reader can show they aren't, your whole argument collapses), relevant, and acceptable as support.

EXAMPLES in support of a claim are either about yourself or about other people and events. They must, of course, be tied closely to what you want to persuade the audience to believe, think, or do. Further, if you plan to rely on examples for support, they must be believable to the audience. The claim that UFOs are really alien space ships is hardly going to be accepted if the only example you can offer in support is that a couple in another state reported seeing one with "UFO" painted on the side.

Adequate support of a claim ought to rely on several examples. If some supporting examples are about yourself and some are about others, you have spread around the believability and can't be accused of offering a claim that depends only on your own experience. Furthermore, several examples are always better than just one.

AUTHORITIES that you turn to for support must also be believable to the audience. Reference books and other printed materials are usually accepted as authoritative because the compilers or authors have researched the topics they write about. The word of people whose business or profession is in the field of the claim is also usually accepted as believable. A geologist who supports a claim that oil can be extracted in large quantity from shale rock at a certain location is viewed as an authority. A real estate agent who says the same thing might be viewed more as an opportunist, even though the agent's knowledge of geology might be excellent.

If you choose to use as authority someone who does not seem to be expert in a field, you will be more likely to persuade the audience by telling why the person's statements ought to be accepted. Ms. Movie Personality may be a believable authority on makeup, but unless you mentioned that she had an engineering degree, she would not seem acceptable as an expert on vacuum cleaner motors. Many people *do* have much expert knowledge because of special interests apart from their jobs, but you must make the audience accept them as authorities, perhaps by stating their credentials, if you use their knowledge as support.

Audiences are also aware of the bias a person may bring to a subject, and you should be, too. For example, a person known to hold conservative political views will not be acceptable to many as an authority on liberal political matters. Nor should someone with known leanings in favor of extended city growth be offered as an authoritative voice on environmental preservation.

Quotations from authorities are often used to support claims. If you choose to use such quotations, be sure you give them accurately and that you use them in the way they were meant. The movie critic who wrote, "This is the most amazing film ever made," may have used the words to indicate what a bad film it was; to quote the words as if they were saying the film was good is to use them in a way they weren't meant.

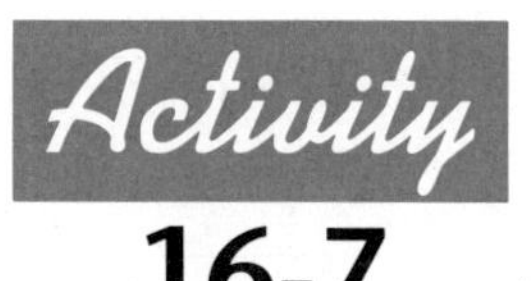

16-7

DIRECTIONS: Here are several claims and a supporting statement for each. In the blank space at the end of each statement, identify the support as fact, statistics, example, or authority.

EXAMPLE ▶ **Claim:** You should brush your teeth after every meal.
Support: I tried brushing after every meals seven years ago and haven't had a cavity since.

Example

1. **Claim:** Math should be removed as a college graduation requirement.

   Support: 70% of the graduates in the last five years who were not in science, engineering, or accounting reported no practical value in math courses they had taken.

   Statistics

2. **Claim:** Not winning the first time you try something doesn't mean you will never be a winner.

   Support: The current Miss America entered her state pageant six times before winning it and going on to the national Miss America pageant.

   Example

3. **Claim:** Worn-out tires should be put to good use instead of being burned.

   Support: Tires have been sunk and used to start new ocean reefs, or filled with soil and used to form walls for environmentally-sound homes.

   Fact

4. **Claim:** More men should be encouraged to become elementary school teachers.

   Support: Young children need male, as well as female, role models in their formative years.

   Fact

5. **Claim:** Use XYZ for headache relief.

   Support: The highly regarded independent laboratory, ABV, made studies that show XYZ cures headaches 75% faster than the next leading brand.

   Authority

6. **Claim:** Map makers have a responsibility to keep up with political changes in borders and with the names of countries.

   Support: Map maker X had all 1991 changes of the USSR and eastern Europe ready by February of 1992.

   Example

7. **Claim:** Ms. X should give up trying to be an actress.

   Support: "In her performance, Ms. X exhibited the entire range of emotions from A to B," wrote the respected film critic.

   Authority

8. **Claim:** The U.S. needs a uniform and mandatory inspection system for seafood.

   Support: Last year more than 1000 people died of food poisoning traced to contaminated seafood.

   Fact

16-8

PART A: DIRECTIONS: Choose five of the ten claims in *Activity 16-7* to work with here. Write the item number of each you choose next to each capital letter. Then add two rational supporting sentences to each of them, something you either know or make up, but which is not the same as the support in the previous *Activity*. Label the kind of support you write.

EXAMPLE ▶ **Claim number**

Example

Support 1:

An article in a dental magazine said that cavities decreased when people brushed after every meal. Authority

Support 2:

My wife has only had one cavity since she started brushing after each meal two years ago. Example

Student responses will vary. Those below are examples of possibilities.

A. Claim number 1

Support 1:

The math department at this school has a 40% failure rate because the courses are so difficult. Fact

Support 2:

The National Association of Mathematics Teachers says that increasing numbers of colleges are dropping their math requirements. Authority

B. Claim number 2

Support 1:

I entered the school Science Fair one year and didn't win anything, but the next year I won a first prize. Example

Support 2:

10% of winning race car drivers enter at least ten other races each year without placing among the top three. Statistics

C. Claim number 5

Support 1:

Olympic athletes Tom A, Dick B, and Mary C all heartily endorse brand XYZ. Authority

Support 2:

Sam Western gives it his seal of approval, because since taking XYZ for headaches, he hasn't missed a day of shooting on his films. Authority

D. Claim number 7

Support 1:

Her last two pictures bombed at the box office. Example

Support 2:

Her annual income from real estate, other investments, and a cosmetics business is six times that of her salary from a film. Statistics

E. Claim number 8

Support 1:

Now, some states have their own rules, but some have none at all. Fact

Support 2:

The government already has mandatory inspection systems for almost all other foods. Fact

PART B: DIRECTIONS: In *Activity 16-4* you wrote three original claims. On your own paper, record each of them. (You may change any that you no longer think you'd like to work with.) Write two statements of rational support for each claim.

Sharing

1. Form a group with two other people in the class.
2. Read aloud to others in the group the supports you believe are best in several responses to items in *Activity 16-8 A and B.*
3. Let others in the group evaluate the support you offer and suggest others.
4. Continue until each person in the group has heard from others.

KEY #4: MEETING OBJECTIONS

Students may need a warning against overplaying this aspect in writing persuasion.

No matter how carefully you tailor you claim and its supporting statements to the audience, thoughtful readers may have objections to either the claim or support. If you ignore such objections, you weaken your entire persuasion. Therefore, you can *strengthen* your case by anticipating—and responding to—possible objections before they are voiced.

In addition to the actual response you make, this part of your argument shows the audience that you are thoughtful enough to think through many possibilities, not just the one you voice. That, too, will make your argument more persuasive to those who might not immediately be on your side.

For example, suppose that you were writing about the claim in item 8 of *Activity 16-7:* The U.S. needs a uniform and mandatory inspection system for seafood. One objection might be that it would be very expensive to have such an inspection system. Then there is the problem of who would pay for such inspection: would it be the general public, the seafood processors and wholesalers, or the people who catch the seafood? Another objection might be that if only a very tiny percentage of the people who eat seafood meals get sick from them, no change in the present system is really necessary. Including responses to these objections when you write in support of the claim will make your claim stronger than if they were omitted.

Activity 16-9

DIRECTIONS: Write at least one objection to each of the following claims.

EXAMPLE ▶ **Claim:** Every high school student should be required to take a course on preserving the environment.
Objection:
People who are doing the most damage to the environment are past high school age.

1. **Claim:** News from a battle zone should be managed by the military so information doesn't get out that could help the enemy.
   Objection:
   Managing news interferes with the freedom of the press guaranteed by the Constitution.

2. **Claim:** Children under the age of eight should not be taught to swim at public expense unless they live near lakes, rivers, a gulf, or an ocean.
   Objection:
   They might visit or live near water when they get older.

3. **Claim:** Community problems such as crime and dirty streets should be solved by those who live in the particular community.
   Objection:
   People who live in any area can profit from outside advice given by those with knowledge or experience.

4. **Claim:** Businesses with five or more full-time employees should provide health care insurance coverage for all employees.
   Objection:
   Many small companies will be driven out of business because the additional cost will make it unprofitable to continue.

5. **Claim:** Golf and tennis tournaments should be either for amateurs or professionals, but both categories of players should not be allowed to compete in the same tournament.
   Objection:
   Amateurs these days are as good in these sports as the professionals are.

6. **Claim:** People who are eligible to vote but fail to do so in three successive elections should be fined.

   Objection:

   Voting is a privilege, not an obligation, so people are free to vote or not, as they choose.

7. **Claim:** In an effort to raise new generations that are good parents, high schools should require students to take at least one parenting course before they are allowed to drop out or graduate.

   Objection:

   Nobody who wants to drop out of high school will wait around to take a course.

8. **Claim:** No cigarette or alcohol ads should be permitted on large outdoor signs.

   Objection:

   Putting a ban on such ads would be undue restraint of trade.

9. **Claim:** Every person, male and female, should learn how to make simple home repairs.

   Objection:

   If too many people know how to do too much, those who make their living doing home repairs will have no customers.

10. **Claim:** Television programs should have a rating system similar to the one that movies have, so parents have a better idea of what is suitable for their children.

    Objection:

    Parents need to rely on their own judgment about what is or isn't suitable for their children, rather than rely on outsiders to give ratings to programs.

DIRECTIONS: In *Activity 16-4* you wrote three original claims that you worked with again in Part B of *Activity 16-8*. Using either the same claims, or others you make up, write one objection to each claim (on your own paper).

Sharing

1. Form a group with two or three other people in the class.
2. Let each person, in turn, real aloud to the others the claims and objections recorded for *Activity 16-10*.
3. Let others in the group note additional objections that readers of the claims might have.

Topic Sentences for Persuasion

Even though you may have done a considerable amount of planning before you are ready to write a paragraph of persuasion, you will still find it worthwhile to compose a topic sentence. Remember that a topic sentence gives an overall view of the main ideas you will include in a paragraph. However, in persuasion it will differ in one important way from the claim that is the basis of the paragraph: the topic sentence will refer to some of the support that will be included.

EXAMPLES  **Claim:** You should brush your teeth after every meal.
Topic sentence: Articles in dental journals and the experiences of ordinary people agree that for better dental health, you should brush your teeth after every meal.

Claim: Every high school student should be required to take a course on preserving the environment.

Topic sentence: Every high school student should be required to take a course on preserving the environment as a first step in preventing such deadly damage that future generations will have no idea of what earth was like in our time.

As these examples show, the topic sentence goes beyond the claim by giving more indication of what will be included in the writing built around it.

It isn't necessary to include all of the topic sentence in a persuasive paragraph. You need the topic sentence before you when you write, not to give away your whole argument at once to the reader.

16-11

DIRECTIONS: On the appropriate spaces below, write a claim that appeared in *Activities 16-2, 16-3, 16-7* and *16-9,* or one you decide on now. At least two claims must be those you originated, as for *Activities 16-6, 16-8B,* or *16-10.* Use each claim, with supporting material, to develop a topic sentence.

EXAMPLE  **Claim:**

Outdoor billboards should not be allowed to advertise cigarettes or alcohol.

Topic sentence:

Outdoor billboards should not be allowed to advertise cigarettes or alcohol because they reach too many impressionable children and adults who may turn to these two killer substances.

Student responses will vary. A few are given here as further examples.

1. Claim:

People who are eligible to vote but fail to do so in 3 successive elections should be fined.

Topic Sentence:

People who are eligible to vote but fail to do so in three successive elections should be fined because they may be responsible for bad government affecting all the rest of us.

2. Claim:

Businesses with five or more full-time employees should provide health care insurance coverage for all employees.

Topic Sentence:

Businesses with five or more full-time employees should provide health care insurance coverage for all employees as a way of reducing employee stress and absenteeism when employees are afraid to seek medical care for fear of high prices.

3. Claim:

Use XYZ for headache relief.

Topic Sentence:

Use XYZ for headache relief because it has been proved effective by top television and music stars for its safety and speed.

4. Claim:

____

Topic Sentence:

____

____

5. Claim:

____

Topic Sentence:

____

____

ORGANIZING TO WRITE PERSUASION

If you have done all the *Activities* in this chapter, you should by now have a considerable amount of material waiting to be incorporated into just one paragraph. But how to put that material into a piece of writing that will make somebody want or need to respond is a little more difficult than just accumulating information.

You will find it convenient to state your claim at the beginning of the paragraph, although you can do so at the end, instead. Offer support that will appeal to your reader's emotions and/or intellect. Usually, you do this by beginning with what is most important or most familiar to the reader. Don't be content with making just one-sentence statements of support, but develop each with as many details and explanations as you can. If you anticipate any objections, respond to them after you have stated your case for support of the claim. Remember that persuasion tries to get someone to respond, so you can always end a paragraph, or an essay, by telling the audience what kind of response you expect: more attention paid to something, a change in the way things are done, money allotted, etc.

16-12

These are examples. Student responses will vary.

Repeat this *Activity* as often as students need to write new persuasive paragraphs.

DIRECTIONS: Follow each direction in numerical order to plan and write a persuasive paragraph.

1. What subject will you write about?
   Little League baseball.
2. Write your claim here.
   Little League baseball should be abandoned.
3. Will you include emotional appeals? Yes? No?
   If "yes," note it here.
   It wasn't enough to bring out community fellowship.
4. What rational support will you offer?
   It is dangerous because team members don't usually wear sufficiently protective helmets. Studies show it encourages many parents to push their children too hard because they want to live their own fantasies through their children.
5. What objection(s) can you think of to your claim?
   Little League baseball is as American as apple pie.
6. Write a topic sentence for your persuasive paragraph.
   Little League baseball should be abandoned because it is physically and emotionally detrimental to children.
7. Write your persuasive paragraph on your own paper. At or near the end, be sure to include an indication of the response you want from the audience.

RECAP–WRITING PERSUASION

- Decide on an audience and a purpose for the persuasion you will write.
- Choose a subject to write about. It must be one on which you can take a stand.
- Make a claim about that subject that encourages the audience to think, believe, or act as you say.
- Decide on any emotional appeals you want to use and if they will be the main support for the claim.
- Decide on any rational appeals you want to use and if they will be the main support for the claim.
- Note objections the audience might have to your claim.
- Write a topic sentence.
- Plan the order in which you will present the information in the paragraph.
- At or near the end, include the response you want from the audience.
- Write a paragraph of persuasion.

Part III

Longer Forms of Writing

Chapter 17 Essays

In this chapter you will

- learn what an essay is
- note differences between paragraphs and essays
- apply paragraph ideas to essays
- learn how to expand ideas to develop essays
- choose thesis statements for essays
- plan the content of an essay
- learn and practice effective openings for essays
- use techniques for linking paragraphs
- learn and practice effective closings for essays
- see the differences revision can make
- proofread an essay for its mechanics

An essay is something like a conversation—a situation in which you can try out ideas for different people and occasions. Just as you may start a conversation with a particular idea in mind, listening to others and talking about your own idea may lead you through changing perceptions. Even if you end the conversation with the same viewpoint you started with, you will be richer for having heard other people.

An essay is a way of examining ideas on paper, of writing to discover what you think or feel or believe. The word "essay" comes from the French and means trying out or testing, in this case, of ideas.

This suggests writing as exploring and learning, not merely to repeat what a teacher already knows or expects.

To *think* about an idea is easy; sometimes the thoughts just flit around, vaguely, in your head. To *talk* about an idea takes more skill and organization. Still, many people enlarge their original notions when they are talking; they "think on their feet." But to *write* about an idea really forces you to consider and deal with it. For example, you may think you know in advance how you feel about a subject such as capital punishment, but when you start *writing* about it, the relative slowness of writing, and the thinking that must go into the ideas for each sentence, help you discover what you may not have considered before. Therefore, ideas often change and develop as you write an essay.

Students are reminded of the recursiveness of writing.

Essay writing has an long and interesting history. Only in rather recent times has much attention been paid in schools to instruction in writing a particular kind of essay: the academic essay. Rather than only exploring an idea on paper, the author of an academic essay is expected to do the exploring before or during writing various "drafts" of the piece. Research into how people write shows that good writers continue thinking about their ideas and changing what they put on paper (or on the computer screen) as they work. Only before showing the work to someone for final judgment does revision stop.

An academic essay is expected to be a tightly organized piece of writing on a subject the author has thought through. In this book, it will simply be called "an essay."

The chapter stresses that students should produce reasoned, not just "spilled out", writing.

The academic essay is not just something people write for teachers to grade in school. It is also the kind of article one might write in a local newspaper or, with slight alterations of organization, in business reports. It is, in fact, reasoned writing.

Differences Between Paragraphs and Essays

Have students compare one of their paragraphs and one of their essays according to the five points in this section.

1. Length. The most obvious difference between a paragraph and an essay is length. Even a "long" paragraph is shorter than an essay because the essay is a *series* of paragraphs. The exact number of paragraphs in an essay is variable, depending on how much you need to write on a particular subject for a particular audience. Some essays are two or three paragraphs long, while others are 50 or 60 paragraphs, or even more.

2. Focus. An essay, like a single paragraph, deals with a single idea. However, that idea can be written about in greater detail or looked at in more ways in the essay. The difference depends on what you want to accomplish.

Consider a tree as an object you want to focus your camera on, as a paragraph. You could turn the lens to a close-up and view varied sections of the trunk, leaves, and root system: an essay about a tree. Now, walk back or switch to a wide-angle lens. The single tree is still at the center of what you see, but you can also see that the tree is next to a house, there are people outside, a car in the driveway, and a dog chasing a squirrel up the tree. This new, wider view is what the essay can focus on: the tree as it fits into a suburban setting.

3. Flexibility. When you write a paragraph, you can present information in just one order: by time, by space, or by importance. Even the kind of paragraph you write is likely to fit just one category: description, narration, classification, cause and effect, persuasion, etc. In contrast, because the essay allows you to write a number of paragraphs, you don't have to organize each of them the same way and you don't have to limit your writing to one kind of paragraph.

4. Opening and Closing. Everything in a paragraph has to happen quickly. It must start immediately in order to make its point, and close quickly to end.

On the other hand, the added length of an essay allows you to take a whole paragraph (even longer, in some kinds of writing) to begin the essay, to get wound up slowly before you get to the central part, the *body*. The essay can also end with a paragraph, if you wish. (See "Effective Openings" on pages 271-273 and "Effective Closings" on pages 278-279.)

5. Thesis Statements and Topic Sentences. You already know that the main idea of a paragraph is expressed in a topic sentence. The main idea of an essay is expressed in a thesis statement. The thesis statement, then, can be a little more general than can a topic sentence.

AN EXAMPLE: PARAGRAPH AND ESSAY

Here is a paragraph that appears at the end of Chapter 24, "Nouns." The topic sentence is the third sentence: "One of the best things you can do [for the environment] is to plant a tree."

> If you're already separating newspapers from cans and bottles and sending all of them for recycling, maybe you feel that you can't do more to help the environment. That may not be true. One of the best things you can do is plant a tree. A program called Global ReLeaf is sponsored by a well-known organization, the American Forestry Association. It encourages people to improve the earth's environment by having more and better trees and forests. Of all the trees that die or disappear because they are cut down or removed by developers, only one in four is replaced. We need trees because they produce life-giving oxygen. They also filter air pollution, prevent soil from washing away, provide a place for wildlife to live, and reduce noise pollution. Properly planted trees can reduce air conditioning costs 10 to 50 percent and serve as windbreaks that cut heating costs. In cities, concrete and dark surfaces hold heat and are 6 to 10 degrees hotter than their surroundings. Planting trees in these places such as parking lots and along streets can make the city cooler.

This example shows how a single sentence can be expanded to an essay.

This paragraph gives a lot of information, but none of it is explained or explored. An essay that added all possible details would have to be rather long. For illustration here, then, look at the sentence about half-way through the paragraph that tells four specifics of what trees do: "They also filter air pollution, prevent soil from washing away, provide a place for wildlife to live, and reduce noise pollution."

The essay that follows is built around that sentence and still keeps the underlying notion of the main idea of the paragraph: helping the environment. Note how each of the phrases in that one sentence is expanded to a paragraph.

Every tree that is planted works in many ways to help improve the environment. A few of those ways are that trees act as a filter for air pollution, prevent soil from washing away, provide a place for wildlife to live, and reduce noise pollution.

Air pollution, especially that caused by carbon dioxide, is a big problem. Automobile exhausts and industrial wastes in the air are heavy with carbon dioxide, which is harmful to humans and other animals because it interferes with breathing. Trees combat this kind of air pollution because, through photosynthesis, the leaves produce oxygen. Increased oxygen in the air clears it and makes breathing easier.

Seeds that are planted by people or dropped by various natural methods need topsoil in which to anchor and grow. If that topsoil is washed away by rains or flooding, ground growth is impossible. Poor crops that cannot support farm families or add to the nation's food supply are one result of thin topsoil. Blowing dust and dirt that clog people's lungs and jam machinery are also results of thin topsoil. But tree roots spread out along and just under the ground, grabbing the soil and holding it in place.

The wildlife supported by just one tree is amazing. Everything from grubs and insects, life at the bottom of the food chain, live in trees. During nesting season, most birds choose trees as ideal nesting places; the leaves and height of branches give protection, and there is food nearby. Other animals, such as squirrels, make homes in tree trunks. Of course, all these animals contribute in their own ways to a healthy environment for people.

Finally, trees help reduce noise pollution. Research has shown that people's hearing can be damaged by too much noise. Tree trunks and branches act as buffers between noisy streets or highways and the people who live alongside them. The trees, therefore, fulfill still another role in helping to improve the environment.

The second sentence of this essay tells what will be included in the essay, although part of the first sentence also sets the stage for what follows. Together they form the **thesis statement** for this essay.

17-1

1. The first sentence of the essay contains its underlying idea. Write it here.

   Every tree that is planted works in many ways to improve the environment.

2. Write the last sentence of the essay here.

   The trees, therefore, fulfill still another role in improving the environment.

3. How are these two sentences related?

   Both are about trees helping the environment.

4. What does the author accomplish by using those first and last sentences?

   The essay is tied together.

5. Write here the thesis statement of the essay.

   Trees help improve the environment by acting as a filter for air pollution, preventing soil from washing away, providing a place for wildlife to live, and reducing noise pollution.

6. Underline the topic sentence of the second paragraph. Write it here.

   Trees combat air pollution because the leaves produce oxygen.

7. Underline the topic sentence of the third paragraph. Write it here.

   Tree roots spread out along and just under the ground, grabbing the soil and holding it in place.

8. Underline the topic sentence of the fourth paragraph and write it here.

   The wildlife supported by just one tree is amazing.

9. Underline the topic sentence of the last paragraph and write it here.

   Finally, trees help reduce noise pollution.

10. Look back at the topic sentences you wrote in items 6 through 9 and at the thesis statement you write in item 5. How are they related?

    Individual paragraphs are each about one part, in order, of the thesis statement.

11. What inference can you make about the relationship between the thesis statement of an essay and the topic sentences of paragraphs?

    The thesis statement includes the main ideas of all the topic sentences.

Sharing

1. Form a group with two or three other people in the class.
2. Look at the locations of the topic sentences you have underlined in each paragraph of *Activity 17-1*. Discuss different places within each paragraph where these sentences might be put.
3. The order of paragraphs in this essay follows the order of the four items in the topic sentence of the first paragraph. Try changing that order. Discuss the effects of making such changes on the essay and on its readers

You may also want to encourage students to use their *Idea Journals* throughout this chapter as starting places for writing ideas.

Applying Paragraph Ideas

Writing an essay follows the same process as writing a single paragraph, except that you will spend more time writing because you have many paragraphs rather than just one.

Begin to work on an essay by deciding who you are writing it for (audience) and why (purpose). See Chapter 2, "Getting Started." Then, pick your subject, if it hasn't already been given to you or if you haven't yet decided on it, by using some of the techniques detailed in Chapter 3, "Finding Subjects."

This section is a recap of Chapters 2 through 8.

Because you have more room and more freedom in the essay than in the paragraph, you may not have to narrow the subject so much (as in Chapter 4), but you still need to limit it to something you can handle well in the time and space available.

EXAMPLE ▶ **Audience: Classmates**
Purpose: To inform them
Possible subject: Operation Desert Shield

COMMENT: Much too big a subject! Thousands of pages have already been written on it, including many books. Those facts, by themselves, make the subject unsuitable. If other people have had to write books, what could you possibly say in a few pages?

If you reach this point, try some of the narrowing techniques to arrive at a limited topic:

- brainstorming
- clustering—a focus on one branch (or less) may give you a subject
- questioning
- a tree diagram
- a circle diagram

This is an important caution for students and they readily see the sense of it.

CAUTION: If there's even one book in the library or in a bookstore on the subject you're thinking of writing about, change your subject! If other people need several hundred thousand words, it's warning that you can't do a good job in the few hundred (or even few thousand) words you will write in your essay.

Essays are built around a *thesis statement* rather than a topic sentence. The idea of the thesis statement is the same as the idea of the topic sentence: to focus your thinking and that of the audience on what you will include in the essay. Like the topic sentence, the thesis statement is usually just one sentence (see Chapter 5, "Topic Sentences"). Deciding on a good thesis statement early in your planning will help lay out the content of the essay and save you a lot of time.

The order of presentation in an essay must be planned at least as well as for a paragraph (Chapter 6, "Planning Paragraphs"), if not more carefully. Because the essay gives you more time, space, and material to work with, there may be a temptation to just start writing from the thesis statement. Resist any such temptation! Make a plan, whether a formal outline or a series of notes, before you ever put pen to paper or hand to computer keyboard to begin writing.

After you write the essay from your plan (Chapter 7, "Drafting"), you still need to go over it several times and for different reasons (Chapter 8, "Revising"). Try moving ideas around. After you've written them down, you may discover that a slight change in order will help the audience to easier reading or better understanding. Or, you may see that you need to give more details in one place or another.

The emphasis here for students to trust themselves as writers is particularly important.

Knowing how to write different kinds of paragraphs (Chapters 9 through 16) gives you enormous writing possibilities because you can use any kind of paragraph you want or need. Rather than starting out by saying, "I'll write a paragraph of description and then two of comparison and contrast before finishing with a paragraph of persuasion," let the writing flow from your thinking. And *trust your own thinking*! You are, after all, the expert on your own writing. You may get help and support from other people, and you may improve everything from a word to the whole order of an essay. But in the end, writing is actually your creation and therefore must be what you want it to be.

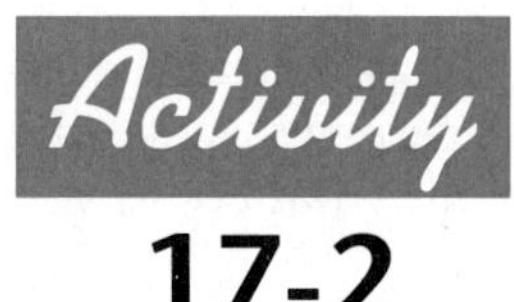

17-2

DIRECTIONS: Some of the writing ideas in the following list can probably be written about in a paragraph, and some probably require an essay. (An experienced writer might not want to tackle any of these ideas in less than an essay, but decide if you could write a paragraph about some of them.) The expected audience for either the paragraph or the essay is other students in your class and the purpose is to inform them. Put a **P** next to each idea that seems most suitable for a paragraph and an **E** next to each that would be better in an essay.

EXAMPLE ▶

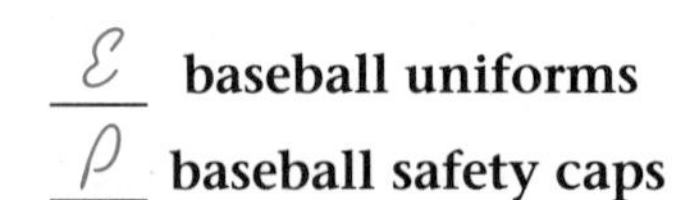

E **baseball uniforms**

P **baseball safety caps**

Students may expand those labeled "P" to essay ideas. Or, you could invite students to write essays based on items changed or listed here.

1. E rezoning for building in my neighborhood
2. P how to sharpen a knife
3. P a day-of-race diet for marathon runners
4. E safety of good street lighting
5. P parts of a business memo
6. E preparing a good science fair entry
7. E relocation of Japanese-ancestry citizens in the 1940s
8. E impact of the fax machine on business
9. P saving time by organizing tasks
10. E catching dolphins in tuna drift nets

Activity

17-3

Answers will vary.

1. List here the subjects of three paragraphs you have already written as *Activities* in this book.

1. ______________________
2. ______________________
3. ______________________

2. List here three ideas for paragraphs you haven't yet written but think you could do. They may be original, come from your *Idea Journal,* or have been suggested above or elsewhere in this book.

   1. ______
   2. ______
   3. ______

Note how slowly students are being led to writing paragraphs. Here, they only cite reasons for a choice. However, you might also want students to write an essay now on their selection.

3. If you had to choose one of the above six paragraph ideas to expand into an essay, which would it be?

   ______

   Why?

   ______

   ______

Expanding Ideas to Develop Essays

Once you have chosen a subject that's suitable for an essay—that is, one that doesn't try to cover too much ground—you will need to expand it, open it up, make it work for you. Only then can you actually plan out and write the essay. Four ways of expanding a starting idea to develop an essay are:

Activity 17-4 through *Activity 17-7* ask students to practice each of these methods, in order. You may want to ask students to do the appropriate *Activity* after each explanation rather than wait for them to occur in the text.

1. Using a paragraph you've written, either to develop one sentence further or as an idea-starter.
2. Turning around the narrowing techniques to make them into expanding techniques.
3. Making the purpose for writing very specific.
4. Asking yourself two more questions about the audience and using the essay as a way of answering them.

1. Using a paragraph you've written. The short essay earlier in this chapter is an example of how you can expand a single sentence from a paragraph into a complete essay. The sentence was "They [trees] also filter air pollution, prevent soil from washing away, provide a place for wildlife to live, and reduce noise pollution." It was already a "rich" sentence, meaning that it contained four different but related ideas. Expanding each of them gave plenty to include in the short essay.

If you don't have such an easy sentence to write from, use the paragraph as an idea-starter. Remember this: the subject you write the essay about doesn't have to be the same as the subject of the paragraph.

Here is a paragraph of narration that appeared in Chapter 10.

> Last Monday turned out to be a different and special day—the first time anybody gave me a surprise birthday party! It started out for me like any other day. When I first arrived at the office, the boss sent me to the post office to pick up a package. I worked at my desk from the time I returned until lunch, when I went to our usual

"hangout" to meet some friends. Instead of continuing the work on my desk when I got back, I was surprised to see my boss carrying a birthday cake with my name on it, and leading everybody into my office. Someone had told her that it was my birthday and they all arranged for a surprise party. Sending me to the post office was how she got me out of the way so the people could bring in the cake and party trimmings without me seeing anything. That birthday party is an event I know I will never forget because it was really so unexpected.

Some students may need help doing the analysis given here. You may find it helpful to practice, with them, similar analyses of passages.

Look, for a moment, behind the narrative or series of events that the paragraph tells. It's also the story of a boss who cares about people who work for her. It's also the story of how a pleasant and unexpected event makes someone feel special. It's also about spending time with friends (such as lunching at "our usual 'hangout'"). It's also a paragraph about a surprise party. There are, then, at least four ideas for essays in this one paragraph:

Bosses who care about people who work for them are smart to have such an attitude.

A happy, unexpected event will make a person feel special.

Spending a relaxing lunchtime with friends makes people feel refreshed and ready for an afternoon's work.

A surprise party is a good way to honor somebody.

Any one of those ideas could be the basic idea—or even a thesis statement—for an essay.

2. Turning around the narrowing techniques. Use an already narrow subject as a starting place to expand that idea. Begin with something as limited as any of these:

a current clothing fad

something you don't like about yourself

the car you wish you had

vegetables hard to find this week

a particular music or comedy performer

Use whichever limited subject you like as a starting place—perhaps something suitable for a paragraph. Then enlarge your view by applying some or all of the following methods:

These are explained in Chapter 4.

- freewriting
- brainstorming
- clustering
- questioning
- a circle diagram (start from the center and think of each successive ring as more general than the previous one)

Here are some examples of the sort of essay subject you might arrive at, using one or more of these techniques with the limited subjects noted above:

Group or class discussion about what might be included in each of these possible essay subjects will probably be useful to students who think they have nothing to write in an essay.

Limited	**Possible Essay Subjects**
a current clothing fad	place of fads in fashion marketing
don't like about yourself	what characteristics people like about you

Limited		Possible Essay Subjects
car you wish you had		advertising leading to false dreams
	or	passenger safety in new cars
vegetables hard to find		impact of quick transportation on fruit and vegetable business
	or	increasing difficulties for those with individual or small farms
music or comedy performer		effect of ticket prices on building audiences
	or	importance of laughter in improving health

All the possible essay subjects shown here can probably be written about adequately in a few pages—about the length of most student essays.

3. Making the purpose for writing very specific. Writing essays forces you to deal with basic notions of audience and purpose before making any definite writing plans. Deciding on your purpose for writing, in particular, is one place you can help yourself to expand ideas.

Don't be satisfied with the kind of generalized answer you might ordinarily be tempted to give to the question "What's my purpose in writing this essay?" Saying "to inform" or "to persuade" or "to entertain" won't help you much in expanding your ideas. Instead, try to be more specific. Consider these kinds of more specific purposes:

EXAMPLES ▶

To make my readers realize the influence of tennis "stars" on tennis clothing
To show readers how easy it is to make fun of what is unfamiliar
To make a case for increased pre-natal counseling
To encourage everyone who knows people who can't read to get the help that will make those citizens literate

Look carefully at these examples and think for a moment what could be said about them. You will then see that any one of them, besides being a purpose for writing an essay, can easily be the *subject* of an essay.

4. Ask yourself two more questions about the audience, and use the essay as a way of answering them.

These are the two questions:

1. What does my audience know about the subject?
2. What *else* do I want the audience to know?

Notice that the second question is *not* keyed to what the audience wants to know. Often, it doesn't know or care anything about your subject. Or else, it knows too little to ask any intelligent questions. So you depend on what *you want* the audience to know.

EXAMPLES ▶

Audience: my teacher.
Purpose: to let her know that motocross racing isn't a sport for dumbbells
What does she know about it? nothing
What do I want her to know? that it takes knowledge of the machine and think-ahead strategies to win

EXAMPLE ▶

Audience: readers of a local give-away paper
Purpose: to get people interested in collecting comic books so they will come into the comic book store where I work and start this hobby
What do they know about comic book collecting? most of them, probably nothing
What do I want them to know? the main reasons some comic books are more valuable than others

In each of the following four activities you will try one of the four ways of expanding ideas to arrive at a subject for an essay.

Activity 17-4

Answers to this *Activity* will vary.

DIRECTIONS: Developing ideas from paragraphs:

1. Select a paragraph you have already written. If it is stored on a computer disk, print out a fresh copy. If it is typed or hand-written, find a copy with as few marks as possible already on it.
2. Select one sentence from the paragraph that looks as if it could be expanded into an essay. Write that sentence here:

____

____

3. Select another sentence from the same paragraph that you can use as an idea starter, as explained in #1 above. Make a list of as many essay ideas as you can from that sentence:

____

____

____

17-5

Answers to this *Activity* will vary.

DIRECTIONS: Turning narrowing techniques into expanding techniques:

1. Select a narrowed idea for a paragraph you have thought about, one from your *Idea Journal,* or one suggested somewhere in this book. Write that narrow or limited idea here:

____

____

2. Expand that idea to essay length by using one or more of these techniques: freewriting, brainstorming, clustering, questioning, or a circle diagram. Use your own paper, but label everything you try so you can see the process.
3. Write here any possible essay subjects you can think of from using one of these expanding methods:

____

____

17-6

Answers to this *Activity* will vary.

DIRECTIONS: Making your purpose for writing more specific:

1. Select a subject to write an essay about. It may be one selected now, come from your *Idea Journal,* or have been suggested somewhere in this book. Write that subject here:

   ____

2. Choose an audience to write the essay for and note the audience here:

   ____

3. Write a very specific statement of purpose that tells what you want an essay for this audience and on this subject to accomplish:

   ____

   ____

17-7

Answers to this *Activity* will vary.

DIRECTIONS: Expanding an idea for an essay by asking questions about the audience:

Decide on at least two subjects you could write essays about and who the audience for each might be. Fill in a subject, purpose, and audience for each. Then answer both questions about the audience for **A** and **B**:

A. Subject: ______________________________

Purpose: ______________________________

____

____

Audience: ______________________________

1. What does my audience know about the subject?

   ____

   ____

2. What else do I want the audience to know about the subject?

   ____

   ____

   ____

B. Subject: ______________________________

Purpose: ______________________________

____

____

Audience: ______________________________

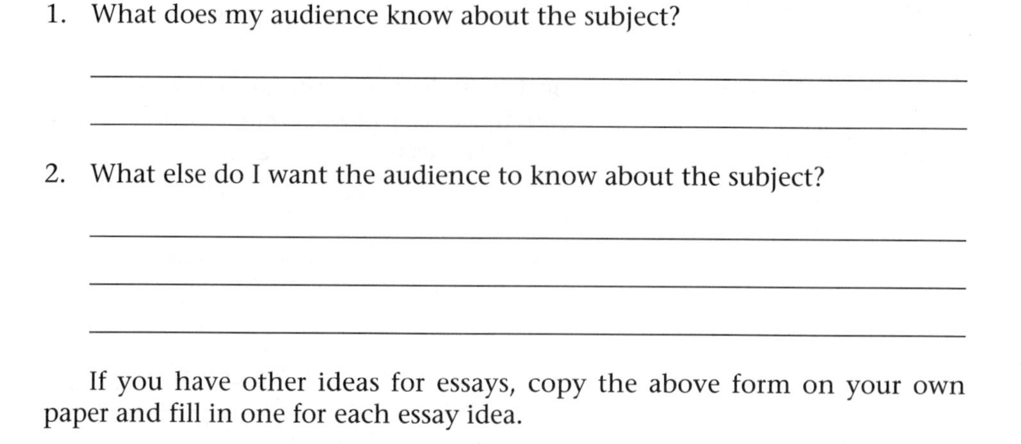

1. What does my audience know about the subject?

____

____

2. What else do I want the audience to know about the subject?

____

____

____

If you have other ideas for essays, copy the above form on your own paper and fill in one for each essay idea.

You can also *combine* any of these four ways of expanding ideas to focus on a subject for an essay:

1. getting ideas from a paragraph you've written,
2. turning around narrowing techniques,
3. making the writing purpose very specific, or
4. asking and answering questions about the audience.

Just because you have read about them separately and done an *Activity* to practice each doesn't mean you can only use one method. For instance, you may start brainstorming, then ask yourself questions about the audience as soon as you get a few ideas noted—and work from there to arrive at a thesis statement for an essay.

This *Activity* emphasizes the writing process by having students keep track of what they do and share the information.

17-8

DIRECTIONS: Working from item #3 of *Activity 17-3,* use at least two of the four methods for expanding ideas to arrive at a possible essay topic. Write on your own paper, but show the work you did so someone looking at the work sheet later can follow your thinking process.

Sharing

1. Form a group with two or three other people in the class.
2. Each person in the group should take a turn reading to the others the work done in *Activities 17-4* through *17-8* that seems promising as subjects for essays.
3. Discuss each person's possible essay topics. Let the individual know which you would like to read about, which you need more information about, etc.

Choosing Thesis Statements

You will have an easier time writing an essay if you decide in advance the main idea you want to get across to the reader (or readers). Although you could start writing with the hope that eventually you will land at a thesis statement, you will save time and trouble by deciding on one before you begin drafting an essay. There are two possible ways of deciding on a thesis statement for an essay. People choose whichever is more comfortable for them, depending on the way they usually think and solve problems.

If you are someone who thinks in terms of general ideas, you might decide first on the general idea of the thesis statement for an essay. Later, you would fill in the details to support it. Often, the thesis statement will help you decide on the details of support and the order in which to write information in the essay.

EXAMPLE  **Collectors value comic books for their art, their content, their rarity, and their condition.**

With this statement as a starting point, you can easily write details to make each part (art, content, rarity, condition) one or more paragraphs in the essay. You might use a first paragraph to introduce the idea of collecting comic books as a popular hobby. You could then end the essay with a paragraph about where to buy comic books to collect, or about the value of certain books. Either ending would relate to the purpose of writing as noted in the example under #4, above.

This method is often a comfortable way for students to work, even those who often write in generalities.

On the other hand, if you are a person who begins by thinking of specifics and details you want to include, you might first list what you want to include in the essay. Then when you look at the list, you could see how they are related and from there move to choosing a thesis statement.

Suppose you began with "a car I wish I had," one of the examples in #2, expanding ideas on page 259. There, it led to the more general notion of "advertising leading to false dreams." If your method of working is to go from the specific to the general, you would begin by making a list of what you want to say about that subject, a list that might look something like this:

Let students try to develop other examples from the same part of the chapter.

television ads

cars

everybody young, slim, healthy

3-4 ads every break

money easy to borrow

products: lots of food, local department stores, diamonds, furniture, refrigerators

always look easy to get

gives false impression of how people live

magazine ads

Not everything in this list fits together. However, suppose you put together the idea of ads appearing on prime time television, the appearance of those on the ads, and the merchandise advertised. You might arrive at a thesis statement something like this:

EXAMPLE  **The ads during prime time television can lead to individual frustration by giving the impression that you don't fit into society if you're not slim, healthy, and young, with money to buy cars, clothes, home appliances, and vacations.**

An essay for which this was the thesis statement might begin with commentary about what leads people to frustration, then move to a description of the models used to sell products on prime time television ads. The essay could then give descriptions of specific ads for cars, clothes, home appliances, and vacations, linking each to the idea of frustration.

Or, an essay with the same thesis statement could begin by describing a number of ads shown in one evening on one television station for the products mentioned. From there, the essay could give more details about the ads and their models, before concluding with material about the causes of frustration tied to inability to acquire products the ads try to make so desirable.

The most important reason for deciding on a thesis statement before you set out an order for presenting the content of an essay is to keep yourself on track. Once you start straying from what you've decided on as a thesis statement, you know that you either have to get back to what you decided on, or develop a different thesis statement to include your new thoughts. And then you need to stick to the new one you decided on.

Activity 17-9

Answers to this *Activity* will vary.

After students develop these thesis statements, you may want them either to start writing essays or continue directly to *Activity 17-11* for help in planning.

If you completed *Activities 17-4* through *17-8*, you will have at least seven essay ideas to work with. You may also have more than that number and, in doing the *Sharing* activity, your classmates may have made other suggestions you are willing to follow.

DIRECTIONS: Write a thesis statement for each of the essay subjects you arrived at by completing *Activities 17-4* through *17-8*. Or, if you developed other ideas for essays as you read this chapter, you should write them here. Use your own paper if you have additional essay ideas that don't fit in the space here.

1. Subject: ______________________

   Thesis statement for an essay: ______________________

   ____

   ____

2. Subject: ______________________

   Thesis statement for an essay: ______________________

   ____

   ____

3. Subject: ______________________

   Thesis statement for an essay: ______________________

   ____

   ____

4. Subject: ______________________

   Thesis statement for an essay: ______________________

   ____

   ____

5. Subject: ______________________________

 Thesis statement for an essay: ______________________________

 ____

 ____

6. Subject: ______________________________

 Thesis statement for an essay: ______________________________

 ____

 ____

7. Subject: ______________________________

 Thesis statement for an essay: ______________________________

 ____

 ____

Planning the Content of Essays

The content of an essay supports its thesis statement. It gives the specifics for the general statement that is the thesis of the essay. In addition to the supporting details, the essay may contain examples of the points being made and anecdotes (little stories that make a point related to the main ideas) or other illustrations of the support for the thesis. (See Chapter 7, pages 83-105.)

If you arrived at the thesis statement for an essay by working from details to the general statement, you already have the content of the essay. All you need to do is arrange those details in the order you will write about them.

Often, you will set up an order of content for the essay in the wording of a good thesis statement.

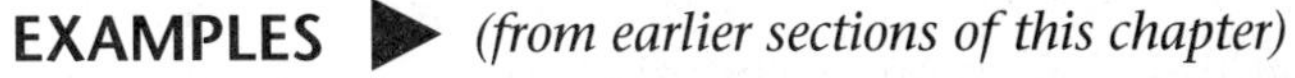

EXAMPLES ▶ *(from earlier sections of this chapter)*

Thesis #1: **The ads during prime time television can lead to individual frustration by giving the impression that you don't fit into society if you're not slim, healthy, and young, with money to buy cars, clothes, home appliances, and vacations.**

COMMENT: The content of an essay built from this thesis statement has to be:

1. Being slim
2. Being healthy
3. Being young
4. Having money
 a. To buy cars
 b. To buy clothes

c. To buy home appliances
d. To buy vacations

Thesis #2: **Collectors value comic books for their art, their content, their rarity, and their condition.**

COMMENT: The content of an essay built from this thesis statement has to be:

1. Art in comic books
2. Content of comic books
3. Rarity of comic books
4. Condition of comic books

Thesis #3: **They [that is, trees] also filter air pollution, prevent soil from washing away, provide a place for wildlife to live, and reduce noise pollution.**

COMMENT: An essay built around this thesis statement has to present the content in this order:

1. Filtering air pollution
2. Preventing soil from washing away
3. Providing place for wildlife to live
4. Reducing noise pollution.

Thesis #4: **Spending a relaxing lunchtime with friends makes people feel refreshed and ready for an afternoon's work.**

COMMENT: This thesis statement requires an explanation of how the relaxing lunchtime makes people

1. feel refreshed
2. ready for an afternoon's work

All the above arrangements of essay content illustrate the order of importance. Something had to be first and something had to be last. However, in some essays, depending on the subject, you will follow the order of presenting information in time or in space. (See Chapter 6, pages 65-82.) The order of content in an essay is arrived at by the same method as that of a paragraph, except that in the essay you have more time and space to achieve your goal of supporting the overall main idea of the piece.

OUTLINES FOR ORDER IN AN ESSAY

Some people firmly believe that you must have a formal outline of the content before you can start writing. That is, main ideas are designated by roman numerals, their most immediate supporting ideas by capital letters, *those* supporting ideas by arabic numerals, and—if you need to get very detailed—those supporting ideas by small letters. However, you do not need to use every level of symbol in an outline.

Since you can't divide anything into just one part, you must have at least two of every symbol. That is, if you have a I or a 1., you must have a II or a 2. If you have an A or an a, you must have a B or a b. Therefore, the symbols of an outline might look like this:

I.
    A.
        1.
        2.
    B.
II.

Note that you don't need to divide each symbol in the same way. If you write an outline, you can use either a sentence, ending with a period, or a phrase, with no end punctuation, after each symbol. Just don't mix both kinds in one outline.

Here is an example of a sentence outline based on the example of Thesis #1 earlier in this section. Notice how the words are indented to the right of the symbols so the symbols are easy to see when you look at the outline.

Note that the divisions here only go to two levels and are not equal for the roman numerals.

I. Ads show slim people, so they make you feel you should be slender.
II. Everybody in television ads seems healthy.
III. Older people are seldom shown in the television ads.
IV. Only people with money to buy the products advertised appear on the television ads.
    A. Cars are one of the products most often shown.
    B. People in the ads always wear nice clothes and many ads are for viewers to buy good clothes
    C. Home appliances are made very desirable to buy in the ads
    D.Vacations that people need a lot of money to take are also shown on television.

Most short essays don't go into enough detail to make a formal outline necessary. What works just as well for most people is a numbered list (as in the examples above). But do make a plan for the content and put it on paper. Don't depend on memory to put everything in an essay in the best place. Get it all written out!

17-10

DIRECTIONS: Here are several possible thesis statements; below each are topic sentences for paragraphs that support the thesis. Together, each could make up an essay. **Put a number next to each topic sentence to show what order makes the most sense to support the thesis statement.** At the end, write the order of the content: time, space, most important to least important, or least important to most important.

EXAMPLE ▶ **Thesis Statement:** Getting ready for a swimming race requires physical and mental preparations.

Topic sentences of supporting paragraphs:

___ Dry land exercises include running, aerobics, sit-ups and push-ups.

3 Swim practice takes place both morning and afternoon.

6 You can mentally view yourself swimming the race.

5 Meditation may help you prepare for the race.

2 Workouts with weights are good preparation.

4 Diet is also important in preparing your body for a race.

Order:

least to most important—first physical, then mental

A. **Thesis Statement:** A tour through our national parks in the eastern part of the country will show how varied our land is.

Topic sentences of supporting paragraphs:

2 Biscayne National Park is south of Miami, Florida.

6 Finally, you will reach Acadia National Park in Maine, our northernmost national park in the eastern states.

4 If you are willing to head a few hundred miles west from there, you could visit Mammoth Cave National Park in Kentucky.

1 Start at Everglades National Park on the southern end of the Florida mainland.

3 Great Smoky Mountains National Park is along the border where Tennessee and North Carolina meet.

5 Shenandoah National Park in Virginia is at the northern end of the Blue Ridge Parkway.

Order: space

B. **Thesis Statement:** Automated telephone dialing should be prohibited because it bothers people in their homes with sales pitches, giveaways that always seem to have strings attached, and requests for contributions from both legitimate and sleazy organizations.

Topic sentences of supporting paragraphs:

2 Don't believe the electronic telephone voice that offers you something for nothing, because there is always some string attached.

1 How annoying it is to sit down for dinner and be interrupted by somebody you don't know trying to sell you something you don't want or need.

4 Because there are no regulations about who may use automated telephone dialing, many sleazy organizations take up the phone lines asking you to send a contribution, usually one of money.

3 Some requests for contributions of money, clothing, or furniture are truly made by non-profit organizations.

Order: least to most important

C. **Thesis Statement:** The Chicago Bulls' 1991 win over the Los Angeles Lakers was their first National Basketball Association championship in the 25-year existence of its franchise.

Topic sentences of supporting paragraphs:

_4_ In other years, the Chicago Bulls kept losing to the Detroit Pistons in their league and couldn't even get to the final playoffs.

_1_ The L.A. Lakers had often reached the NBA finals with the help of such past stars as Kareem Abdul-Jabbar.

_3_ In 1991, Magic Johnson was a key player for the L.A. Lakers in helping the team reach the finals.

_2_ 1991 was the fifth time in the past eight years that the L.A. Lakers had been in the NBA finals.

_6_ Chicago won the fourth game of the finals in an exciting 97-82 victory.

_8_ The final game was almost a case of Michael Jordan vs. Magic Johnson.

_5_ Los Angeles won only the first game of the playoffs.

_7_ The Bulls had a 3-1 series lead going into the final championship game being played in Los Angeles.

Order: time

D. **Thesis Statement:** Many "polite" spoken and written phrases are used so often that neither speaker/writer nor listener/reader pays any attention to them.

Topic sentences of supporting paragraphs:

_1_ "How are you?" is a question to which the speaker almost never expects an answer.

_2_ "Have a nice day" is a throw-away line that is so much with us we hardly pay any attention to it when we hear it.

_3_ Writing "Dear" as the salutation in a business letter to somebody you don't even know seems silly.

_4_ Fortunately, "Yours truly" or "Very truly yours" are not in top fashion any more as ways to end business letters, because the writer certainly doesn't belong to the person receiving the letter.

Order: time or space

E. **Thesis Statement:** Living on a very strict budget requires careful food shopping.

Topic sentences of supporting paragraphs:

_4_ Take store discount coupons along, but don't use them unless they are for items on your shopping list and give you a real savings over other brands or similar products.

_1_ Before the next shopping trip, begin by making out menus for every meal that give everybody a balanced diet and nutritional snacks.

_3_ Make out a shopping list that you estimate is within your budget, and that uses lower cost ingredients or larger quantities available at savings for the menus instead of high-priced, pre-packaged foods.

5 The hardest part is sticking to your shopping list when you are in the store, and not letting a pretty package or a price that seems low lead you to buy what you don't really need.

2 Read grocery ads just before shopping and adjust your menu, if necessary, to take advantage of specials you can buy.

6 This kind of thinking ahead for careful shopping will help anyone stick to a budget.

Order: time

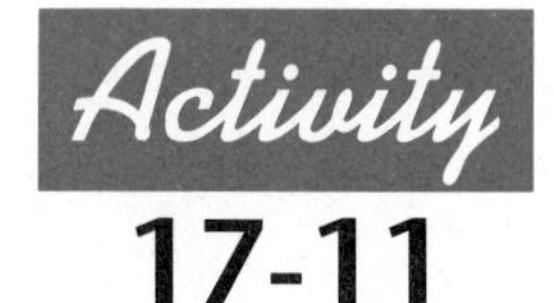

17-11

Responses will vary.

DIRECTIONS: Choose three of the thesis statements you wrote for *Activity 17-9* that you would be willing to write essays about. Write down each. Then make a plan—either an outline or a list—of the content for an essay based on each thesis statement.

1. Thesis Statement: ______________________

   Plan of Content: ______________________

2. Thesis Statement: ______________________

   Plan of Content: ______________________

3. Thesis Statement: ______________________

   Plan of Content: ______________________

Effective Openings for Essays

The first sentence of your essay may be your thesis statement—but it doesn't have to be. You will probably want to put the thesis statement in the first paragraph of an essay in order to help the audience know what is coming and therefore what to focus attention on. But even that isn't necessary, because you could use the thesis statement as a summary in the last paragraph.

This information often expedites a student's writing.

Furthermore, there's no rule that says you must write the opening paragraph of an essay first. Because some people find it hard to write the first paragraph, they start writing somewhere else in their plan. Starting with ideas or information you feel most comfortable with is a good way to get your draft going. Later, when you are moving along and have a good feel for what you are saying, you can go back and write the opening paragraph.

Knowing there is a range of possibilities for openings is reassuring to many students.

If you compose on a computer, putting the first paragraph at the beginning of your essay is easy, no matter when you write it; just indicate a block move for your word processing program. If you write in longhand or type your draft, draw insert arrows or use whatever method is comfortable (even to cutting and pasting) to put ideas in their proper order, including the opening paragraph.

Here are some ideas that you can use to write the first paragraphs for essays:

1. Make your subject clear for readers. This kind of opening will work if you are writing about something that the audience may not be familiar with.

EXAMPLE ▶

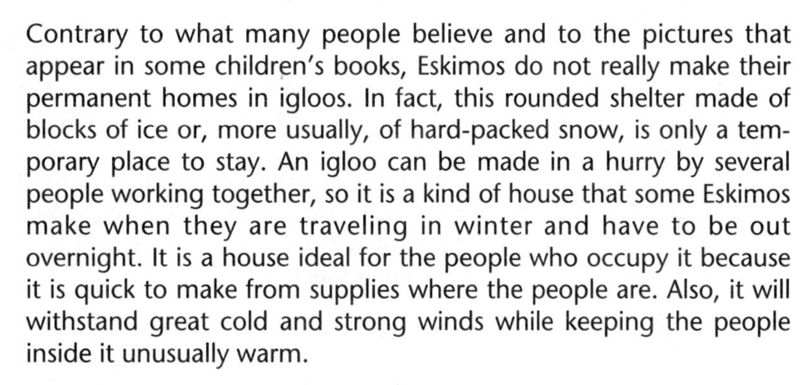
Contrary to what many people believe and to the pictures that appear in some children's books, Eskimos do not really make their permanent homes in igloos. In fact, this rounded shelter made of blocks of ice or, more usually, of hard-packed snow, is only a temporary place to stay. An igloo can be made in a hurry by several people working together, so it is a kind of house that some Eskimos make when they are traveling in winter and have to be out overnight. It is a house ideal for the people who occupy it because it is quick to make from supplies where the people are. Also, it will withstand great cold and strong winds while keeping the people inside it unusually warm.

The last two sentences could be the thesis statement about which an essay is written.

2. State your position on the subject you will be writing about. This sort of opening is particularly helpful to the audience if you are writing on a controversial subject or if your writing is meant to be persuasive. By stating your position, you help the reader follow your argument.

EXAMPLE 

Now is the time for citizens in the eastern half of this county to get together and keep building developers from ruining what little open space is left. The zoning board hasn't been willing to say "no" to people with money who want to put up shopping centers and industrial warehouses, town houses, and apartments. For the past seven years, these people have had their way, even though the business and living spaces are not completely sold or rented. Now there are only 50 acres of open space left to the east of County Road. An investment group is going before the zoning board on the 10th of this month to get permission to put up yet another shopping mall on that property. We citizens have to organize a program very quickly to save those 50 acres for park and wild land, and convince the zoning board to vote for us instead of for the builders.

This essay is certainly going to be about what citizens must do to organize and win against the builders' opposition in a zoning hearing. An essay directed to other citizens suggests that thesis in the first sentence and states it more specifically in the last sentence of what can be an opening paragraph for an essay.

3. Relate your topic to something current or well known. If you choose this kind of essay opening, you get readers to relate what you have to say by talking about something they are already familiar with.

EXAMPLE  We are horrified to hear about big and spectacular oil spills such as the one in Prince William Sound in Alaska when the tanker *Exxon Valdez* ran aground and spilled much of its cargo. We all think that Iraqi ruler Saddam Hussein did a terrible thing when he ordered oil spilled into the Persian Gulf just before the war called Desert Storm started. Even small oil spills take away a great deal from the clean water of the ocean and from the plants and animals that live in it. Yet oil spills from ocean-going vessels happen more often than any of us would like to think. Maybe they even happen more often than we would like to know about.

Many readers will remember the two big oil spills, so if you are writing about the results of even "small" oil spills, relating that subject to what is known might be a good way to start your essay.

4. A brief quotation directly related to your subject may be a good way for you to start an essay. The person quoted doesn't necessarily have to be well-known. But you must certainly be sure the quotation is directly related to your subject.

EXAMPLE ▶ "The hardest part about coming back from an injury is you always remember yourself at your best." So said Greg LeMond, the great American long distance bicycle racer that *Sports Illustrated* named "Sportsman of the Year" in 1990. I can easily relate to what LeMond meant. My injury was emotional, not physical, but I found that picking up the pieces of my life was hard because the good things I remembered couldn't be repeated.

As the opening of an essay, this paragraph sets the stage for the writer to share those aspects of rebuilding a life after an emotional injury.

5. State some striking fact or statistic in the opening paragraph. Again, however, remember that it must be directly related to the main ideas in the essay.

EXAMPLE ▶ If you ate a bowl of Cheerios for breakfast this morning, you probably had 400 individual Cheerios in the bowl. Each Cheerio weighed about .0025 of an ounce (without milk) and was 1/2 inch in diameter. And that's just one bowl of one kind of breakfast cereal. Think of the enormous need for grain created by Cheerios and all the other cereals that people eat daily. Yet if farmers can't make money by growing all these kinds of cereal grains because the market price gets lower and lower, they will change the crops they plant. Now is the time for Congress to pass new laws to help the farmers by buying their grain at prices that will allow them to make enough money to support themselves and their families.

The remaining paragraphs are obviously going to be an attempt to persuade the audience to urge congressional action to help farmers.

6. Placing the topic in time or giving some background will help readers draw upon their own knowledge as they start an essay. That means the reading will be easier and more pleasant.

EXAMPLE 

First there were heavy diving suits with metal helmets and air hoses so men could stay in the ocean longer than they could hold their breath. Then, during World War II, in 1943, Jacques Cousteau and Emile Gagnan developed an air-carrying tank and breathing controls for a man to wear while swimming. It was named SCUBA from the first letters of the words that described the gear: self-contained underwater breathing apparatus. Scuba gear began to be sold in this country after the war, but from then through most of the 1960s anybody who wanted to learn to use it had to be an excellent swimmer and go through very hard training. All that has now changed. Improved equipment and attractive underwater swim clothing plus much easier training make scuba diving a sport that appeals to more and more men, women, and children every year.

By setting the subject of scuba diving in time and giving a few sentences of background information, a reader who sees this first paragraph for an essay is set for what follows. The rest of the essay is going to be about modern equipment, clothing, and training.

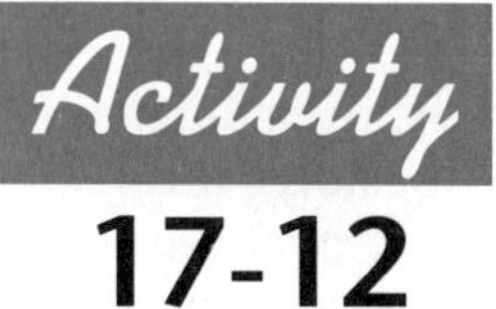

17-12

DIRECTIONS: In *Activity 17-11* you wrote three thesis statements for essays you could write, and a plan for the content of each statement.

On your own paper, write an opening paragraph for essays that would follow each thesis and plan for content. Try to select a different kind of opening for each thesis statement. Underline the thesis statement in the opening paragraph.

Sharing

Students will be asked to write a complete essay in *Activity 17-14*. You may want them to write one now and another in response to the later *Activity*.

1. Form a group with two or three classmates.
2. Let each group member read aloud the opening paragraphs written in response to *Activity 17-12*.
3. Members of the group should let each author know what they expect will follow each opening paragraph; the author should let group members know how accurate they are.
4. Members of the group should also comment on how good each opening paragraph seems to be as a starter for an essay.

Linking Paragraphs for the Body of an Essay

An essay is a series of connected—or linked—paragraphs. The first paragraph of a short essay is usually enough to introduce readers to the author's main idea (thesis statement), and an ending paragraph is usually enough space to bring all the ideas together. Between those, however, is the series of paragraphs called the "body" of the essay.

You must have at least one paragraph as the body, but there is no ideal number or upper limit on how many paragraphs the body can be. The number depends on how much you have to say on the subject, how complicated the subject is, and how much time you have for writing. Naturally, anyone limited to an hour of in-class writing can produce only a few paragraphs (especially if there is no prewriting in advance), while the same person will probably write many more paragraphs for the body of an essay prepared thoughtfully outside of class.

As you have already seen (in Chapter 7, on page 94), the sentences of a single paragraph read much more smoothly when they are connected by transitions rather than being plunked down on paper one after the other. Connecting the ideas of one paragraph with those of another is as important as connecting sentences. Because the essay is longer than one paragraph, the author has more to lead the reader through.

An essay should supply the reader with two kinds of links or connections:

1. The whole essay should be so linked that a paragraph can't be moved (or removed) without damaging the content.
2. One paragraph should be so linked to what comes before and after it that the reader cannot imagine any order of content other than the one on paper.

LINKING THE WHOLE ESSAY—COHESION

When everything in an essay fits together well—the words, the paragraphs, the ideas—it is called a "cohesive" essay. The word "cohesion" means to stick or hold together. It also means logically organized.

Your essays will be cohesive if you do everything you have been studying in this book and this chapter so far. That is, you should:

1. Select a subject narrow enough to be written about in the time available.*
2. Limit what you will say by writing a focused thesis statement.**
3. Make a plan for the content and stick to it. Even if you have a great deal of additional information, you may have to omit it for the sake of a cohesive essay.***

The payoff is an essay in which all the parts are linked—which a reader recognizes as cohesive.

---

* See Chapter 4, "Narrowing Subjects", pages 35-48

** See pages 262-264 in this chapter

***See pages 265-267 in this chapter

LINKING PARAGRAPHS IN AN ESSAY

Even though you write to a carefully organized plan of content, you must give readers connections from one idea to another, from one paragraph to another. That is, you need to link the beginning of one paragraph with the end of the one before it (and the beginning and ending paragraphs with the body of the essay).

Two kinds of links you can use are:

1. repetition
2. transitions

1. Repetition is a re-statement that ties ideas together by calling attention to them. Three kinds of repetitions are:

a) pronouns
b) same wording
c) synonyms

a) A **pronoun** is one kind of repetition because each time it is used, it reminds the reader of the noun it stands for. (In that sentence, the word "it" is used three times, each time reminding you of "a pronoun.")

b) Writing the **same word or phrase** in different paragraphs will link the paragraphs. Readers will relate the paragraphs to each other when they see the same wording.

c) Using a **synonym** is a variation of using the same word. In fact, it is sometimes a stronger kind of repetition because such a slight shift calls attention to the wording.

2. Transitions are the connecting words you use to show all kinds of relationships: addition, causality, summary, emphasis, and more. They were explained in detail in Chapter 7 on pages 94 and ff., and summarized on pages 101 and 102. Both the words and their uses are the same for paragraphs within an essay as they are for sentences within a paragraph.

In the following example of several paragraphs from an essay, repeated words, synonyms, or pronouns are underlined once and *transitions are in italics*. The thesis statement is in **bold type**.

EXAMPLE 

Businesses today, *more than ever before,* often depend on new forms of communication to be able to move great quantities of information quickly and accurately. **The fax machine, databases accessed through modems, the copying machine, improved telephone service, and personal television transmissions are devices that both small and large businesses depend on to communicate information.** If it is true that we really live in an "information society," it is *also* true that technology has provided the way for that information to be moved within a city or around the world in ways that would have surprised past generations.

The fax machine is probably the newest and most important business communication device. Fax is a shortened form of the word "facsimile",which means an exact copy of something. Any two businesses or people who have fax machines and phone numbers for them can now send such an exact copy of written or pictured information. The sender puts a document into a fax at one location and indicates it is to be transmitted to another location.

Special phone lines carry the "picture" of the document to the receiver's fax. *There,* it is turned back into a print document that rolls out of the receiver's fax. Instead of having to hire messengers to carry documents from one part of town to another or wait for mail services between cities or countries, information can now be communicated in minutes.

Another amazing development that helps businesses get information they need are the national databases accessed through computer modems. The databases collect and store mountains of information that are easily communicated to their business subscribers. Subscribers with a modem plugged into a computer and some written instructions about how to use it can request information from the database. Computers at the database company immediately search out what they have been instructed to find and send it back to the computer making the request. *Then* the information is either stored in the computer temporarily or immediately printed out so the business making the request can see the answer. Database information storage is not exactly "new" in the sense that it was just developed in the past two or three years, but it is something that many businesses depend on now to receive fast and accurate information.

Be sure students realize this is an unfinished example. You may want to assign them to finish the essay.

The copying machine is *still another* device that has been in offices for a number of years and that is used to communicate information. *Although,* it is so much a part of business that many people can't imagine working with having one handy,...

Activity 17-13

Answers to this *Activity* are in the Instructor's Section.

DIRECTIONS: Underline once the repeated words, synonyms, or pronouns that link the following paragraphs. Underline twice the transitional words and phrases that link the paragraphs.

Look at the development of job titles over the past 50 years and you will see a circular movement that changed unpleasant-sounding jobs into nice-sounding ones, formerly sexist job titles into gender-free titles, and now ordinary or unpleasant-sounding job titles into important or nice-sounding ones. The changes reflect the attitudes of workers and the society of the time. The jobs themselves haven't really changed, but calling them by other titles makes people feel better about themselves and their work.

Being called a "garbage collector" doesn't sound very nice, even if what you do is collect garbage. But if you are called a "waste management worker," you can feel better about the job. In the years that job titles changed, "janitors" turned into "building superintendents," and "undertakers" became "funeral directors."

In the 1960s and 1970s, as more women moved into the work force, everybody's consciousness was raised about who did what work. Jobs that were once only held by men, such as "policeman," "fireman," or "postman" began to go to women, also. Clearly, the job titles had to change. Now we have "police officers," "fire fighters," and "postal workers" or "mail carriers." Instead of attaching a person's gender to the job of serving food in a restaurant, "waiter" and "waitress" are being discarded in favor of "server."

In times of tight money, people can't always get the salary raises they want or deserve. But surveys show that they do want to be considered important on their jobs. As a result, employers are now giving people important-sounding job titles, which is very much like changing unpleasant-sounding job titles into nice-sounding ones. A college graduate who doesn't want to be a "secretary" will accept a job as "administrative assistant." In some businesses, a supply clerk is being called a "technician coordinator" and a "salesperson" is called a "sales consultant." These people are no longer hired by "personnel departments" but by "human resources consultants."

The matter of job titles seems to have come around again to making people feel good about who they are, even if the salary doesn't improve or the job itself get any better. At least a person can now hold an important-sounding job that doesn't hinge on gender.

17-14

DIRECTIONS: Look back at the three opening paragraphs you wrote for *Activity 17-12* and write an essay on your own paper that will follow any one of them. (Be sure to include the opening paragraph that contains the thesis statement.) As you write the essay and go over it before showing it to classmates, think about linking the entire essay and the paragraphs within it. When you are finished writing and revising, underline the repetitions once and the transitions twice.

Effective Closings for Essays

The worst thing to do in a closing paragraph is to bring up something new. The next worst thing to do is leave readers with questions, either about the previous paragraphs or about statements made in the closing paragraph.

The best thing to do in a closing paragraph is to let readers know you are ending the essay. A good final paragraph is a satisfying conclusion. A reader can look at one and know the end of the essay has arrived, that all questions have been answered, that there are no loose ends.

Contrary to some beliefs, rewriting the thesis statement in the final paragraph of an essay is not the most effective way of ending—unless the order of content has been from specifics to a generalized thesis statement which did not appear in the opening paragraph. Then, the thesis statement does tie together everything in the essay. But if it appeared in an earlier paragraph, the reader can easily look back to it. Also, it's unlikely you will be writing such a long essay (or one that goes so far off the track) that the reader could have forgotten what you said and need it repeated.

End an essay in a way that feels comfortable for you and that concludes what you are writing. In case you need some help, here are some ways to write effective closings for your essays.

You will recognize some of the thesis statements in the following examples because they have appeared earlier in this chapter, either alone or in sample opening paragraphs.

1. Make a comment on (but don't repeat) the thesis statement. Thesis statement: Getting ready for a swimming race requires physical and mental preparations.

EXAMPLE 

The more often you participate in swimming races, the more often you go through these physical and mental preparations. They help you be better prepared for each race you swim in. Also, doing all these kinds of exercises, including watching your diet, becomes part of your daily routine, so you expect to act and think in these ways. Everything is worth the time and work when you come in first in a race!

2. Remind the audience what action you want it to take. Thesis statement: Automated telephone dialing should be prohibited because it bothers people in their homes with sales pitches, giveaways that always seem to have strings attached, and requests for contributions from both legitimate and sleazy organizations.

EXAMPLE 

Do not be misled by the argument that automated telephone dialing is important because it creates jobs for the people who manufacture the equipment and the ones who sell and run it. Instead, think of yourself and the millions of others who are bothered when they are busy by the interruption of unnecessary telephone calls that only try to get you to pay out money. As already suggested, you should write complaints to your representatives and senators in Congress and join activist groups that will push for legislation to prohibit this kind of intrusion into your privacy.

3. Use a summarizing quotation. Thesis statement: Architects designing single and multi-family homes in cities and suburbs should incorporate patios with running water and plants whenever possible.

EXAMPLE 

Patios are a place where people can relax and, if they contain running water and plants, they are also environmentally desirable. As a result, architects who care about the needs of humans and the environment will feel better about themselves and their work when they try to include patios. As author Tor Eigeland wrote ("Escape from a Troubled World," *Aramco World*, Sept.-Oct. 1990: 5), a friend said to him, "The patio is the heart of the house; it is where friends come to talk. And it is also the lungs. The plants and the running water clean the air."

4. Link what you've written to something known or to a future possibility. Thesis statement: The Chicago Bulls' 1991 win over the Los Angeles Lakers was their first National Basketball Association championship in the 25-year existence of its franchise.

EXAMPLE 

The Bulls are not going to wait another 25 years for an NBA title. Now that they have tasted victory, the team is going to want a repeat. Michael Jordan and his teammates have gotten the winning combination and are really working as a team to help each other score. If there was a psychological barrier before, it is gone now. Basketball fans know that the Chicago Bulls are a team to watch in 1992 and beyond.

5. State a conclusion you've reached about your subject. Thesis statement: Collecting baseball, football, or basketball cards should not be considered a hobby just for young people, because it is followed by millions of adults.

EXAMPLE 

Collecting baseball, football, or basketball cards doesn't currently have the status of collecting coins or stamps. Maybe that is why few sports cards bring the prices that good coins and stamps do. It is also true that stamps have been printed for several hundred years and coins have been made for many thousands of years, so there are more rare stamps and coins to trade and sell. As the young people starting this hobby of sports card collecting may find when they become adults, there will be even greater opportunities for them to trade, buy, and sell cards. Maybe this hobby will some day have the same respectability as collecting coins or stamps.

In lieu of revising, you may invite students to write an alternate closing paragraph, then compare it to the one originally written.

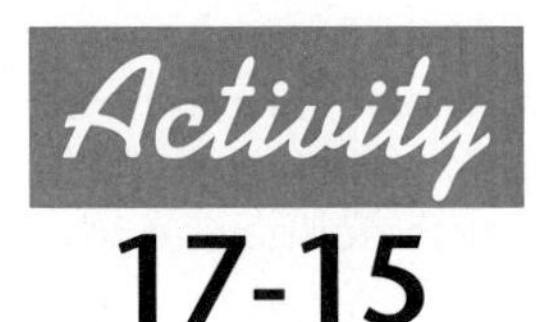

17-15

DIRECTIONS: Look back at the essay you wrote for *Activity 17-14*, and especially at the closing. Is it going to be satisfying to the reader? Does it bring the essay to a conclusion and not introduce new ideas? Unless you are completely satisfied with the ending, on the basis of what you now know about closing paragraphs, write a revised closing paragraph for your essay.

Revising an Essay

To revise an essay is to rethink it. Even if you have carefully constructed and followed a plan of content, when you finish writing an essay you should look at it carefully and think about where it can be improved.

Chapter 8 (pages 106-129) showed several ways you can revise a piece of written work. If you have really planned an essay carefully, you may not want to move parts of it around or remove sections of it. However, as you look at the final essay, you ought to think about:

- enlarging ideas, that is, adding more details or more examples to your draft*
- changing words to be more specific**
- changing sentence structures to make them more effective***
- making sure that voice and tense are consistent****

Here is an essay that shows how revision can improve a work. Marginal comments call your attention to some changes that were made.

BEFORE:

The headline on an ad showing some blocks, dolls, toy trains, a soccer ball, and some other toys says, "Imagine a child not knowing what these are for." The sentence is by a woman named Liv Ullman, who is vice president of the International Rescue Committee that sponsored the ad. It is too bad that there have to be children in the world that do not know anything about toys because they have never been able to have any.

The last sentence moves away from the ad to toys in general.

Too many children in all parts of the world, including our own country, need clothes and food so much that their parents do not have any money to buy extras, not even toys that can give the kids something to do with their time that is good and healthy for them.

The idea moves away from toys to other needs.

Toys teach children many things, such as how to take care of their possessions and how to play and have a good time and enjoy themselves. Sometimes when children play together with toys, you can see they are learning to share and these kids also get along with other people.

No exploration or details about what toys teach.

Some kinds of toys teach children to use their minds to figure things out, so they are educational. Other kinds of toys are just fun to use. There is a soccer ball in the picture of the ad and that is an example of a kind of toy which children use that keeps them healthy and gets them interested in sports.

A return to the ad, but without details. The essay just stops. It has no satisfying conclusion.

AFTER REVISION:

The headline on an ad showing some blocks, dolls, toy trains, a soccer ball, and some other toys says, "Imagine a child not knowing what these are for." The sentence is by a woman named Liv Ullman, who is vice president of the International Rescue Committee that sponsored the ad. The ad was meant to catch our attention and make us think. It really is too bad that there are children in the world who never had any toys because not having toys made them miss out on many things.

The third sentence is a transition between the ad and general statements about toys and children.

---

* See Chapter 24, "Nouns", pages 370-382, and Chapter 26, "Modifiers", pages 404-423

** See Chapter 31, "Word Choice", pages 469-482

*** See Chapter 20, "Varying Sentence Structure", pages 313-325

**** See Chapter 22, "Verb, Voice, Tense and Agreement", pages 339-350

The paragraph points out what children can learn from toys.

Toys teach children how to take care of what they own. If they don't use the toys for play, but make them into something to hit other kids with or pound at things, then the toys are ruined and can hardly be used. The child who owned the toy, but who didn't didn't take care of it, is the one who loses.

The essay continues with what toys teach.

Children who have toys to play with can have a good time and enjoy themselves. They can use their imaginations, bringing trucks and dolls to life. They can create, through imaginative play, a world and learn to get along in that world, just as they will some day have to do in the real world.

Here is the third aspect of what toys teach.

A third thing children learn when they have toys is that they can play with other children. That way, they have more toys and they also have people to be with. When children learn to play together, they also have to learn to share, and that is a very important lesson for life.

Now there is a fourth aspect of what toys teach.

Another thing toys teach children is to use their minds to figure things out. Not just the kind of toys called "educational," but all kinds of toys need to be figured out as kids get used to playing with them. Even something as ordinary as a ball is educational, because children can figure out why it rolls, where it's going to head if it's pushed or thrown, and other such things.

A fifth aspect of what toys teach. This is still more support for the thesis statement.

Finally, some toys lead children to get interested in sports and that will keep them healthy. Many sports are played outdoors and the fresh air helps make the body strong, so even children who stay indoors a lot in this country watching TV will be encouraged to be outside doing exercise.

The essay returns to the ad and comments about soccer, because it was mentioned in the first sentence.

The last sentence ties the essay together by referring to the content of the first paragraph.

The soccer ball pictured in the ad is an example of a sport that a person can play without much equipment except the ball. Maybe that is one reason soccer is so popular all over the world. Children who have this kind of toy might even learn to use it so well that they can get out of poverty by becoming soccer players when they are older. Whether in sports as adults, or in other ways, what children learn from toys about caring for property, using imagination, getting along with people, and using the mind are important lessons in life. It is sad for the future that too many children all over the world will miss out on all those things, and especially on the fun of having toys.

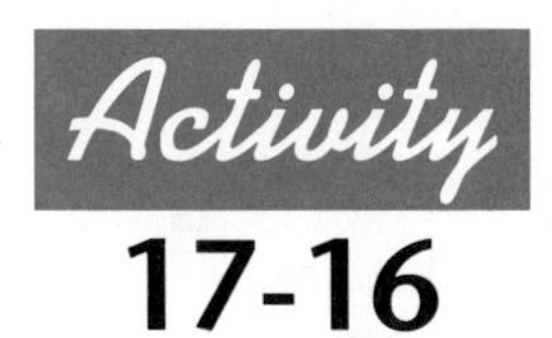

17-16

DIRECTIONS: On the basis of what you now know, revise the essay you wrote for *Activity 17-15*. Or, choose another essay you have written (or are close to finishing). Revise the selected essay.

Sharing

1. Team up with one or two classmates who have revised at least one essay.
2. Let each author read an essay aloud while the team member(s) listen carefully, but make no comments.

Encourage students to take the time to go through this entire process. They will find it worthwhile. (It will also help their listening skills.)

3. Then let the author read the essay through again, but this time each team member takes notes on what is good about the essay and what might be improved by further revision. Listeners should concentrate on the flow of ideas, the sound of sentences, and the choice of words. At the end of the essay, each person should share the notes with the author and other team members.
4. The author should make further revisions—if desired—on the basis of comments by the team members.

Proofreading

The final activity of preparing an essay is proofreading it. That is, checking over the work to make sure spelling*, punctuation**, and capitalization*** follow the customs of written English. This is done in the same way for essays as it is for paragraphs. (See Chapter 8, pages 106-129.)

Proofreaders use a standard set of symbols to show where changes and corrections are needed. Anyone reading the copy (or written text) of a newspaper, book, or magazine uses these symbols to show printers which changes to make. They are also used by people who read the copy of letters, legal documents, and other written materials so those who make corrections on a computer or a typewriter will know what to change. You should learn them, too, as a quick way of noting changes you want to make in writing.

These symbols are put in two places: at the point in the copy where the correction must be made and in the right margin next to the same line. (A slash mark separates two or more marks in the margin.) The double notation is a way of making sure that anybody who sees a page will not overlook any of the marks.

Many dictionaries show a page or so of proofreaders' marks. The following list gives you some that students most often need.

Mark	Meaning	Mark	Meaning
∧	Insert a letter or word here	¶	Start a new paragraph
#	Insert a space here	ℓ	Remove this
⊙	Put a period here	cap or ≡	Capitalize this letter
∧ with ,	Insert a comma	lc or /	Make this a small letter
∧ with :	Insert a colon	⁀	Close up the space
∧ with ;	Insert a semicolon	sp	Spell out or correct
∨ with "	Insert quotation marks	no ¶	No paragraph here
∨ with '	Insert an apostrophe	STET	Let original stand; disregard change
∿	Transpose these letters or words		

Here is a paragraph showing how the proofreader's marks are used on actual copy.

---

* See also Chapter 32, "Spelling," pages 482-498

** See also Chapter 28, "Commas," pages 431-444, and Chapter 29, "Punctuation," pages 445-460

*** See also Chapter 30, "Capitalization," pages 461-463

Whever you apply for credet to buy something, or to take out a
loan the companie you goto for this service will check on your
cerdit rating. There are both local a nd national credit rating and
reporting companys that collect information about you. Even if
you dont know you are bein investergated. Companies can getin-
formation about you from a bank, a card credit company, a store
wear you have a change acount, or any other place likely to no
anything about your finances. Many companys phone yur neigh
bors to ask questions aboutyou and your living habits. some even
visit your neighbors. In addition to all this Searching, which may
feel is an uncalled for invasion of privacy, if a cridit rating an
reporting compan y makes a mistake, you can loose your credit
and even your job.

Here is how the paragraph will look when all the corrections have been made.

> Whenever you apply for credit to buy something or to take out a loan, the company you go to for this service will check on your credit rating. There are both local and national credit rating and reporting companies that collect information about you, even if you don't know you are being investigated. Companies can get information about you from a bank, a credit card company, a store where you have a charge account, or any other place likely to know anything about your finances. Many companies phone your neighbors to ask questions about you and your living habits. Some even visit your neighbors. In addition to all this searching, which many feel is an uncalled for invasion of privacy, if a credit rating and reporting company makes a mistake, you can lose your credit and even your job.

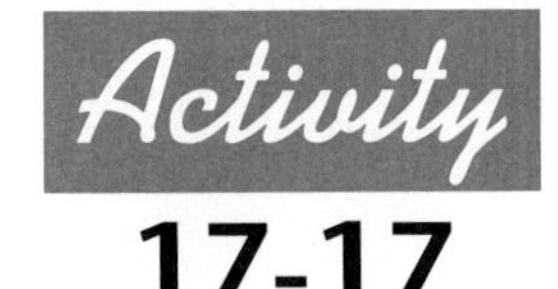

17-17

You may want to have students rewrite the essay with all the corrections made.

DIRECTIONS: Proofread the following short essay for spelling, punctuation, and capitalization. Use proofreaders' marks to show the corrections that should be made.

With the development of sensiitive scientific instrum ents and computers setup to analyse both present and past information, specialists are now beginnning to be able to warn poeple about the most scary natural disasters: hurricanes volcanoes tornadoes, and earthquakes. All are still dangerous but at least whether

Answers to this *Activity* are in the Instructor's Section

and other reports can tell people to get to safety, sometimes before they are hit by these disasters.

Hurricane forcasting is quite accurate now whereas in the not too distant past, people didn't know when a hurricane was going to start, There is now all kinds of evidnce gathered about these storms. When a hurricane forms forms, usally the U.S. Weather Service sends its planes to fly into the storm and threw the eye to collect information about winds and directions. Radio and televiision stations broadcast Details about the developement and progress of hurricanes now, and poeple who live in the path have time to get ready. They can take steps to save there property and they have time toget away from the hurricane if thats what they want to do

Scientists are increasingly able to tell when certain volcanoes are goeing to become active enough to blow. There are 540 volcanoes that have been active in the world. Three-fourths of them are in the so-called Ring of Fire" that stretches around the Pacific ocean. It run from islands north of Australa through Indonesia and Malaysia, through the Phillipines and Japan along all the Aleutian Islands of Alaska, down the West coast of the United States, and along the Pacific coast of south America. Sensitive Instruments and and computerized Information tell specialiststhat these volcanoes are likly to become active when one of the earths plates slides over another. the lower plate begins to melt and break through week parts of the earth's crust to come out through volcanoes that may not have been active for many hundrids of years.

Tornadoes are very unpredictable. Weather specialists now no enough to spot areaes were conditions are right for tornadoes to from. But they still don't know enuf to tell exactly wen and where the torndoes will take shape or if they will stay in the air. Or touch down. On of the scariest things about tornadoes is that come up very fast, so many people dont get any advance warning at all. Another is that most poeple just don't have any place to take shelter Also, there is no way to protect proprty from a tornado.

earthquakes are recorded constantly all over the world but nobody hasyet figured out how to predit them. Most of the small earthquakes or "tremors" don't cause any damage, but one strong quake, espesially in a populated aria, can wipe out buildings and kill thousands of people. In china, there is a whole network of rural farmers who watch their animals, specially the chickens, for unusual behavior; that methid hs turned out to be surprising accurate in determining if an earthquake was going to occurr. But in most of the world, and certinly in the United States, we depends on specialists with delicate scientific instrments to.moniter earth movements. Maybe soon they will be successsful infinding what they are looking for: a way to predict earthquakes.

With all the information now Available in advance about hurricanes volcanoes tornadoes and earthquakes, scientists continue trying to develope better instruments, and information to give people advance warning. Their is know way to save property or even the land in faceof these four kinds of natral disasters, but at least lives are being saved asmore is learened about them.

For *Activity 17-18* below, you may want to encourage students to show their work to people outside the classroom. They will often be willing to share the responses their writing evoked from others.

17-18

DIRECTIONS: Proofread the essay you wrote in response to *Activity 17-16:* Then make a clean copy of the work that you would be proud to show to someone whose evaluation you respect.

A WORD ABOUT GRAMMAR AND SPELL CHECKERS

Some people who use word processors for writing (or for keying in writing after it has been done in longhand) get a false sense of security. "I don't have to worry about grammar (or spelling) any more," people have been known to say. "I'll just let the grammar checker (or spell checker) go over my work and make it right."

It is true that there are many software programs to analyze grammar. However, you should realize that all that any of them can do is pick up what it has been programmed to spot. It cannot guess anything about what you want to say and the best way to say that. Nor can a grammar checker know what you know. For example, if it calls your attention to a passive voice construction, that construction is not necessarily wrong or "bad" as you have used it.

Spell checkers are wonderful to work with. Even if you are a good speller, they will pick up words you know how to spell but for which you hit a wrong key. If you truly don't know how to spell a word the checker "flags," you can often get a suggestion of the right spelling.

However, one thing the spell checker cannot do for you is decide whether or not you have written the correct word for the usage you need. "Their," "they're," and "there" are all correct spellings; only you can determine which one belongs where in a sentence such as "They're going to be there soon if their car doesn't break down." Both "form" and "from" are perfectly good words, so no spell checker will flag either as wrong—though you may have put the letters in wrong order when you typed. Only you can decide if "see" or "sea;" "write" or "right;" "buy," "by," or "bye" or any of the hundreds of other words that sound alike but have different meanings and spellings is correct.

The best advice: learn grammar and spelling customs. Then you can check the software instead of letting it check you!

RECAP—WRITING ESSAYS

- Understanding the difference between essays and paragraphs sets the stage for writing essays.
- The process of writing a paragraph can be applied to writing an essay.
- There are four ways of expanding ideas to develop essays.
- A good thesis statement sets the stage for writing an essay.
- Plan the content of an essay before writing it.
- Outlining is useful to make the plan of an essay clear.
- Write an effective opening for an essay.
- Link paragraphs in an essay by content, repetition, and transitions.
- Write an effective closing for an essay.
- Revise an essay for detail, wording, sentence structure, and consistency.
- Proofread an essay.

Chapter 18

Essay Tests

In this chapter you will

- learn how essay tests differ from other essay writing
- apply knowledge of audience and purpose to writing essay tests
- learn how to budget your time
- locate the information words in an essay question in order to write focused answers
- be guided by stated or unstated response words
- apply the writing process to essay tests

The introduction is intended to help students think beyond the classroom as the sole focus of essay tests. You may have other examples to share.

All through academic life you will be called upon to write essays, whether a quiz that can be answered with a paragraph, or a longer piece that serves as the final examination for a course. Classes from accounting to zoology are likely to give essay tests. You may have been asked to write an essay as part of the application for the school you now attend, or will be required to write one for a school you want to transfer to.

You may have written an essay for placement in this course, and you may need to write an essay to prove your work worthy of progress to another course after it. Some states require you to write an essay that assures the quality of your writing ability in order to enter upper division work. Increasing numbers of colleges require you to prove you can write well in your major field of study before you are awarded a degree.

All these come under the general heading of "essay tests." Mastering the art of writing them well under time pressure is a skill you will use throughout schooling, and be able to apply to most jobs. That is, being told 20 minutes before closing time to write a letter that will sooth an angry client is much like answering an essay test question on which your course grade depends—with a timer clicking in the background.

You are often asked to write essay tests because in doing so you demonstrate:

- your ability to think,
- your skill at selecting information and supporting your ideas,
- your memory and application of what you have learned.

What's Special About Essay Tests

If writing an essay quiz or test seems particularly hard, you aren't the only one who feels that way. Four reasons make answering an essay question different from (and probably harder than) other paragraph and essay writing you have studied in this book :

1. You have to work under the pressure of a time limit. Most tasks are easier when you can take all the time you want to do them. Essay tests don't allow you that luxury.
2. A lot may be riding on an essay test. Often, a course grade will be based completely, or in large part, on that single piece of writing.
3. You must search your own memory for the information; there are no guides to answers, as in multiple choice or completion questions.
4. You must put together two different skills. First, you must recall content information on the subject of the essay topic. Second, you must join that with all you have learned about the very complex process of writing good paragraphs and essays.

Audience and Purpose

Begin writing an essay test by deciding about audience and purpose, just as you do for any other kind of writing. Know who will read what you write. If it's your regular classroom teacher, who knows you by name, you may want to write more informally than if the reader will be a lecturer in a large class, or that person's assistant. If your essay will be read by outside evaluators (as in writing assessments given to hundreds, or even thousands, of students at the same time), or by other teachers in the school, you won't know the people, but you can certainly assume they will approach the reading in a businesslike way. Such readers will certainly appreciate your paper better if it is written clearly and directly. If they are going to read a great many papers in addition to yours, take special care to *make your handwriting legible:* you can be sure the readers will be pleased to find pages that are easy to read.

Students usually don't think of these differences and thus view all tests as the same.

Know how important a particular test essay (or part of it) is. Often, the essay test is scheduled to count for a certain portion of your course grade. For instance, in some courses, as much as a half the grade depends on a single essay. Or 60% of the grade on a test may come from the essay section in it. Put your time and energy into the essay accordingly. A quick quiz, given by a teacher who wants to make sure students are learning what they should from a class period, is writing you may want to treat lightly. But an essay test you must pass before you can pass the course is a lot more serious!

If you don't already know the answers to "Who will read and grade this essay?" and "Why am I writing this essay test?" or "How much does the essay test count?", make it your business to find out the answers before you begin writing.

Three Important DON'Ts

Students should really practice this admonition—even though it's tough to adhere to.

1. Don't start writing as soon as you get the test question or topic. Instead, take time to think about what you have to do, and how you will do it. Follow the sequence of activities in the rest of this chapter, from deciding on how to use your time, through the writing process, to proofreading.

If you have a choice of topics on which to write, first think about what you know of each one. Then, choose the topic or topics you know most about, *not* the one you think will impress the reader because it sounds hard or "intellectual."

Help students to understand the futility of trying to outguess someone they don't know.

2. Don't plan on recopying for neatness once you've written an essay test. Make whatever changes you think necessary as you write or revise during the test time. Anybody who reads a timed test knows that with a longer time to write, the student would have made improvements. Readers are looking for information and for writing ability, not for a pretty paper.

3. Don't sacrifice quality for quantity when you answer an essay question. A shorter answer that is direct and complete is preferable to a longer one that wanders around and indicates the writer doesn't have a grasp of the ideas required to respond to the question or the control needed to express them in writing. A long response, by itself, is not impressive. As a matter of fact, if you find yourself with time remaining after you've written a good essay, *don't* tack on wording just to make the answer look longer. Instead, in order to improve the quality of your writing, spend the extra time on proofreading and revising the wording of what you've already written.

Three Important DOs—Before You Write

1. Read the entire test or exercise through before doing anything. That is, try to get a sense of what you are expected to do before actually starting work. A test may be a mixture of essay and multiple choice or fill-in questions. Or you may have to write both short and long answers. Find out, by reading the entire test, which parts are likely to be easier for you than others—and how much time you are allowed for each response.

Emphasizing good time use in test taking can't be done too often.

2. Use your time wisely. Generally, put more time into answering questions that count for more of your grade. You can budget essay test-writing time by knowing time limits, and points or percentage of a total score. Essay tests tell you one or both of these:

a) An actual time limit may be part of the instructions.

EXAMPLE ▶ **You will have 20 minutes to answer this question.**

b) How much of the grade a particular question will count. The test instructions may tell you.

EXAMPLES ▶ **This question will count as ½ of your grade.**
or
This question is worth 45 points.

COMMENT: Add up all the percentages or points on all the parts of a test. This will tell you which one carries the most weight, and, therefore, which you should spend the most time on.

Remember to include thinking and planning as well as revision and proofreading as part of the writing time.

EXAMPLE ▶ **You have 15 minutes to answer this part of the test; your response will be ⅓ of your grade.**

COMMENT: ⅔ of the test grade will depend on other questions, so you don't have too much riding on this essay. You should spend more of the 15 minutes for planning and deciding on content for the essay than for revising or proofreading, perhaps allowing just two or three minutes for the final going-over.

EXAMPLE ▶ **Answer three of the six questions below. You have ½ hour to write a response that will count 50% of the grade.**

COMMENT: First, decide on the three questions you can answer most easily. Then, allot ten minutes (one-third of the half-hour) to writing on each of them (including the planning, revising, and proofreading). The 50% of the grade you can earn by doing this section of an essay test will be very important toward the total score.

3. Read each question or topic carefully enough to find out what's expected in your answer. Are you to recall information and repeat it? Are you to refer to other material (such as films, books, theories, experiences, etc.)? Are you to use a quotation as a springboard to developing your own ideas? Read the question or topic so that you understand exactly what you are to do.

Every essay question or topic will include, either stated or implied, two kinds of instructions to guide you to the expected response:

> Explanations of these two kinds of words follow. They are the keys to good essay test answers.

1) **Information words** that tell you the topic or limitations of the essay you are expected to write.
2) **Response words** that tell you what kind of essay you should write.

As soon as you receive an essay test topic, read it slowly to figure out what information words it contains. If you can write on the test paper, underline those words once. If you can't underline them, put them on your writing or scratch paper.

Then find the response words, and either underline them twice or put them on your own paper. Doing so will help you move quickly in planning your response, because you will know what kind of information to write and, in some cases, how to organize it.

In a moment you will have the chance to work with both Information Words and Response Words.

INFORMATION WORDS

Look for **nouns and modifiers** as your information words. That is, look for people, places, objects, events, or ideas—the nouns—as indicators of what you should write about in your response. Also, see if you spot modifiers—adjectives or other nouns—that limit the noun so you don't expect to be writing about the whole world in an answer you have 15 minutes to put down on paper.

EXAMPLE ▶ **Account for Senator Eugene McCarthy's popularity as a possible presidential candidate.**

Interpretation: The topic is Senator Eugene McCarthy. You can see, also, that you are to write about his popularity. McCarthy was a U.S. senator, so obviously he was popular enough to be elected to that office. He may also have been popular with women or with environmentalists or with joggers in his home town. But the essay test is asking you to write only about his popularity as a possible presidential candidate, which is a helpful limitation for you.

EXAMPLE ▶ **How did the loss of the *Titanic* contribute to safety measures in nautical design?**

Interpretation: The topic is the steamship *Titanic*, which sank when it ran into an iceberg on its first voyage. Although believed to be a safe ship because of design features, there were obvious failures in that design. The loss of this ship and most of the people aboard led to safety measures in the design of other ships.

18-1

Answers to this *Activity* appear in the Instructor's Section.

The *Sharing* section at the end of this chapter invites students to contribute their own, recalled essay test questions. However, you may wish to have students do so in conjunction with this exercise. Or, they may do so now and, again, later.

DIRECTIONS: Each of the following statements or questions are typical of those you might encounter in essay tests for college courses. Underline the **Information Words** in each of them—that is, the words that tell you how to limit your essay response. Use the examples above as guides.

1. Describe and discuss the effect of the roof overhangs for the building design shown at the beginning of this exam paper.
2. Compare the methods and events used by Cavour in uniting Italy to those of Bismarck in uniting Germany.
3. Contrast the characteristics of alcohol addiction with those of heavy drinking.
4. Was Napoleon a Corsican monster, a French Emperor, a tyrant, a lawgiver, a sawed-off egomaniac, a great man, a military genius, or a butcher? Defend your answer with specific references.
5. Under what circumstances do we on earth see a total eclipse of the sun?
6. Look at this famous photo of a Chinese man standing in front of an advancing tank in Tiananmen Square, Beijing. Account for its impact on people around the world who see it.
7. Studies show that the greatest number of trauma cases occur between 6 p.m. and midnight. Can you account for this finding?

8. Enumerate and discuss the ways in which community service could help high school students feel more civic responsibility.
9. A proposal was made to the local school board that children should be taught by teachers of their own race and ethnicity. Do you agree or disagree with the proposal? Defend your position.
10. Compare the behavior of social insects, such as honeybees, with the social structure found among higher animals, such as baboons.
11. Explain how the invention of Hadley's sextant made ocean exploration safer and more successful.
12. List the factors which led to the rapid growth of the textile industry in New England. Discuss both natural resources and sociological factors.
13. While most people agree that science and technology have enriched our lives, others believe the problems they bring outweigh the benefits. Give at least three examples of inventions which have brought both good and bad into our lives.
14. Imagine that you have been asked by a manufacturer to write directions for using an abacus. What would you write to explain how to use the abacus to add?
15. Briefly trace the history of the Hate Crime Statistics Act signed by President Bush.
16. Analyze the use of Native American rhythms in the music of Aaron Copland.
17. While Impressionism is thought of as a movement in painting, its influence extended into music, literature, and architecture. Describe examples in each of these fields and identify their common elements.
18. Summarize post World War I events which led to the 1929 stock market crash.
19. Use examples to prove that introduction of exotic species of plants harmed the ecological balance of South Florida.
20. Argue for or against calling up for active duty the mothers who are in the military reserves and who have young children.

RESPONSE WORDS

"Response words" in an essay assignment are those that tell what kind of answer you should write. Look for **verbs** that instruct you to perform a particular action, such as "discuss," "summarize," or "enumerate."

EXAMPLES  **Discuss possible causes of the stunted growth of the plants described in Laboratory Study #9.**

Compare and contrast the writing styles of Hemingway and Faulkner on the basis of their short stories you were assigned.

What follows is a long list, but it shows the variety of expectations about writing. Memorizing such a list isn't useful, but using it as reference is.

The following list shows some of the response words you are likely to find on essay tests, and what each one asks you to do in writing an essay test or exam. After each explanation is an example of how the response word might appear in an essay topic or question. In each example, the response word is in color and boldface, and the information words are italicized.

Response Word	What's Expected
Analyze	Break apart the object or information into its separate parts and show how they fit together.

EXAMPLE ▶ Analyze the *"Statue of Liberty" play.*

Argue	Use logic and reasoning power to persuade your reader(s) to agree with the point of view you represent.

EXAMPLE ▶ Argue for *stiffer handgun laws* in *your state.*

Compare	Show likeness of two (or more) things, people, events, or ideas.

EXAMPLE ▶ Compare the *short story* "Soldier's Home" and its *film version.*

Contrast	Write about the differences among objects, events, people, or ideas that have some elements in common. (Often paired with "compare".)

EXAMPLE ▶ Contrast the *picture quality* of films on *videotape* to those on *videodisc.*

Criticize	Evaluate the positive and negative elements of the subject or topic. (Contrary to popular belief, criticism is not just fault-finding.)

EXAMPLE ▶ Write a criticism of the *student art show* that might be published in the campus newspaper.

Define	Tell what the terms mean by placing each in a category and then telling how they differ from other items in that category.

EXAMPLE ▶ Define *inductive* and *deductive reasoning.*

Describe	Present in an orderly way as many details as possible to help the reader visualize the subject.

EXAMPLE ▶ Describe how you would *decorate* a *12 x 12 bedroom* for a *teen* living at home on a *strict budget,* and willing to *do some of the work* with help from family members.

Discuss	Consider the subject from all angles and present them as clearly and unemotionally as possible.

EXAMPLE ▶ Discuss the *need, or lack of it,* for *stricter zoning* rules in *your neighborhood.*

Response Word	What's Expected
Enumerate	List all the items you will be writing about, briefly mentioning something about each as you proceed.

EXAMPLE ▶ **Enumerate** the most *recent contributions* to practical *science* from *manned spaceship* exploration.

Evaluate	Judge the quality of an issue, idea, event, or object by weighing its characteristics and their values or lack of them.

EXAMPLE ▶ **Evaluate** the *suitability of this film* for viewing by *children under 10* years old.

Explain	Provide information and details (and, perhaps, statistics) that make the topic clear, or interpret it, or tell why or how something is.

EXAMPLE ▶ **Explain** how library *books* are *organized* according to the *Library of Congress system.*

Illustrate	Show how or why something *is* by giving examples to make it clear and understandable.

EXAMPLE ▶ **Illustrate** why some people feel that the *lyrics of rock songs* are *harmful to children.*

Interpret	Point out how an object, idea, or event fits into or relates to larger groups or other categories.

EXAMPLE ▶ **Interpret** the *role of the United States* in sending *observers* to *elections* in such countries as *Nicaragua and Haiti.*

Justify	Give reasons for a point of view or for a position by supplying evidence or facts to support it.

EXAMPLE ▶ **Justify** *reducing* the number of *travelers on the Colorado River by 3%* for each of the *next five years.*

Prove	Support a position by using logical reasoning and factual information.

EXAMPLE ▶ **Prove** that *changing the registration cut-off date* at your school would *not affect enrollment* seriously.

Response Word	What's Expected
Summarize	Present information in a condensed form by stating only the main ideas and writing from the original author's point of view.

EXAMPLE ▶ Summarize the *explanation of Newspeak* that Orwell gives in his book, *1984*.

Response Word	What's Expected
Trace	Follow the development of an idea, a process, or an event over a period of time.

EXAMPLE ▶ Trace the major events leading to the beginning of the *Revolutionary War.*

You can readily spot one of the above verbs in an essay test assignment. Ideally one or another of these **response words** will appear.

WHEN INSTRUCTIONS DON'T HAVE RESPONSE WORDS

Often, instructions for writing are not stated as clearly as those above; the response words are suggested, but they don't actually appear. Instead, you must interpret the instructions for an essay test to find which of the response words will fit what you are asked to write.

EXAMPLE ▶ **What are the chief causes of homelessness in this city?**

Interpretation: You are being asked to tell the chief causes—or, more specifically, to *identify* them

Therefore, **substitute a response word** for the opening words of the question, and you will know what you are expected to write: "*Identify* the chief causes of homelessness in this city."

This section heads off the possible complaint from students that they get questions without response words and therefore don't know what to do about answering them.

18-2

DIRECTIONS: None of the following essay exam topics or questions below uses the response words you have learned in this chapter, but such words can be substituted for those that do appear. On the line under each topic or question, write an appropriate response word. Use the listing just before this section as a guide.

EXAMPLE  **What are the ethical implications of one real estate broker giving another the keys to to a client's house without the client's permission or knowledge?**

Response Word:

Discuss

1. Choose two characters from the Joyce Carol Oates stories you read this term and show how they are similar.
   Response Word:
   Compare

2. What does the article say about Rosalind Franklin's contribution to the discovery of DNA by Watson and Crick?
   Response Word:
   Summarize

3. Why are the Pilgrims considered the first Europeans in American in spite of ample evidence that there were earlier settlers?
   Response Word:
   Explain or Justify

4. Why did the use of Roman numerals decline after development of the 10-based positional notation system?
   Response Word:
   Discuss or Explain

5. What are the common goals of the various methods of bilingual education?
   Response Word:
   Explain or Analyze

6. Have the lives of Haitians improved since the departure of the Duvaliers?
   Response Word:
   Analyze or Describe

7. What were the main accomplishments of Simon Bolivar for his country?
   Response Word:
   Identify and discuss

8. Why are most leaves green?
   Response Word:
   Explain

When you have identified the kind of response expected of you, and the information you must work with, you will know what you need to write.

This section is a summary of the writing process (in Chapters 1 through 8) applied to answering essay questions.

Five Steps To Writing Effective Test Answers

1. Think about what to include in your answer. Some essay questions suggest the information you must write about, but others leave much of the content up to you. For instance, when you are asked to relate a quotation to what you know, no real limits are given to you. Or, if the essay test only gives you a sentence or subject to respond to, you must first decide what you want to say.

Sketch out your possible answers by taking a few minutes for such activities, just as you do in narrowing a subject for any kind of writing (see Chapter 4). However, because you are working under a time limit, these methods are usually the most productive:

- jotting down notes
- listing possibilities
- clustering

Get as much down about the subject as you can. Don't worry about what you have time to include, and don't think about putting the information in order until after you have gotten some ideas noted on a scratch paper.

2. Decide exactly what to include in your essay, and write a sharply-focused thesis statement. The time limit of an essay test means you must decide on the main point to make in your answer *before* you start writing. There is no time to do exploratory writing and work your way into a focal point. Decide on the principal point you want to make, and phrase it as a thesis statement that can begin your response.

Many instructors in test-taking recommend this highly.

Some students find it convenient to repeat the response information words of the question in the thesis statement as a way of being sure to stick to the point of the essay topic. However, be sure to make the rest of the thesis statement specific, just as you would for any kind of non-test situational writing.

EXAMPLE OF ESSAY TOPIC:

Explain the *function* of the part of the brain which makes us uniquely human.

Note how the underlined words of the essay test topic are repeated in the thesis statement as a guide to writing the essay.

The word "function" in the essay topic, which is in italics, is extended in the thesis statement by telling what the functions are.

POSSIBLE THESIS STATEMENT:

The cortex of the cerebrum makes us human because it is the part of the brain that enables us to *organize, remember, communicate, understand,* and *create.*

Stick to writing what you plan in the thesis statement! Don't take a chance of going over the time limit by suddenly deciding it would be nice to include this or that in your response.

Three more steps follow this *Activity.* Either assign them now and hold this *Activity* until afterwards, or follow the order of the text.

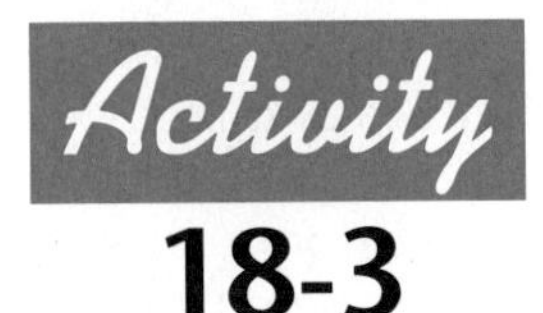

18-3

DIRECTIONS: Write a possible thesis statement for each of the following essay topics. Make your thesis as specific as possible, even though you may not feel familiar enough with the essay topic to actually write about it. Try using the response information words in the thesis statements.

1. **Topic:** Are organized sports beneficial to grade-school age children?

   Possible Thesis Statement:

   Organized sports are beneficial to grade-school children because they offer children at least 10 valuable lessons in cooperation and coordination.

2. **Topic:** Is our government making progress in its "war against drugs"?

   Possible Thesis Statement:

   The government will not make any real progress in its "war against drugs" until education succeeds in cutting down the demand for drugs.

3. **Topic:** Compare and contrast the Japanese system of education with that of the United States.

   Possible Thesis Statement:

   Both Japan and the United States have extensive systems of required education because both believe the futures of their countries depend on educated citizens. However, uniformity and cooperation are valued in Japan while creativity and individuality are stressed in U.S. schools.

4. What are the chief characteristics of a good sportscaster?

   Possible Thesis Statement:

   A good sportscaster should have such characteristics as knowledge about a variety of sports, a good speaking voice, the ability to think and speak quickly in front of an audience, not get angry or flustered while on the air, and have a personality that comes across as pleasant and trusting.

5. Account for the fact that collecting football and baseball cards are two of the fastest growing hobbies.

   Possible Thesis Statement:

   Collecting football and baseball cards are fast-growing hobbies because they don't require much money to get started, they fit in with the American interest in those sports, and they don't require a lot of room.

Although the thesis statement of an essay can be stated anywhere in the piece—or remain unstated— you will help yourself and your readers by writing it within the first paragraph of an essay test response. In a short response, you should make it the first sentence. That way, you have something on paper to keep you on track as you write the essay, and your reader knows what to be watching for as a shaping idea for the response.

3. Plan on an order for the essay. The response words—such as "discuss," "enumerate," "trace," "compare," and so on telling you what kind of answer is expected on the essay test—will often help you decide on the order for presenting information. Remember that anyone reading an essay test wants to be sure you know the information requested, so present it as directly as you can, and in an orderly way.

If you work from a thesis statement and follow a plan, you should include everything you want to say as you write. If a great new thought comes to you after you've started writing, check your time limit before including it. Sometimes you're better off leaving out those great thoughts if including them will push you too much. If you *do* want to include a phrase or some wording that comes to you after you've written the sentence where it belongs, use a caret (^) to insert the information neatly.

Basically, though, you are better off sticking to a plan for your essay response, rather than making changes that will distract you from writing against the clock.

4. Choose words you are comfortable with, and know you are using them correctly. The only words that will impress the person (or people) reading your essay test are those that communicate accurately and quickly. Essay test responses are no place to try out words you're not sure of.

Whenever possible, use words special to the course for which you're are writing the essay test, as long as they're appropriate to your response. Such "special" or "technical" words show you understand the material well enough to write in the "language" of what you have been learning. They are also, often, "shortcut" words (such as *austral, fractal, nihilism, tectonics,* and so on) that carry a lot of information for people who know them, as the reader of your essay test certain will.

Again, the issue of timing is brought forth.

5. Proofread what you've written. Leave enough time to look over the essay you've written, whether it's ten lines or ten pages (which you might write in a two-hour final exam). Give what you've written a quick reading to be sure that:

- you haven't left out words that need to be in a sentence for sense
- you have written complete sentences
- words are spelled conventionally
- pronouns have clear antecedents (if not, cross off the pronoun and substitute its antecedent)
- capitals and punctuation marks, especially commas, follow the conventions of their usage

Sharing

1. On your own paper, write one or more essay test questions or topics you recall having been given in any of the courses you are now taking (or any you recall from previous courses).
2. Form a group with two or three other people in your class. Share the essay test questions the people in your group have written.
3. Let the group discuss how they did—or should have—answered the questions. Focus your discussion on the RESPONSE words and the information words that directed (or should have directed) your response.

RECAP—ANSWERING ESSAY QUESTIONS

- Take a time limit seriously and work within it.
- Know what is expected of you in the test.
- Determine the information words.
- Find the actual or suggested reponse words.
- Write a sharply focused thesis statement, and stick to it.
- Write the essay response as clearly as possible, using easy-to-understand words.
- Use the language (that is, special wording) of the course or subject you are writing the test for.
- Allow time for proofreading an answer.

Part IV

Sentence Grammar

Chapter 19 Subjects and Verbs

In this chapter you will

- define and identify the subjects of sentences
- be able to spot and use verb forms as subjects
- recognize compound subjects
- define and identify action and linking verbs in sentences
- write sentences in which subject and verb agree
- determine the direct and indirect objects of verbs

People speak and write in sentences in order to communicate with each other. A sentence tells someone (the audience or reader) about:

- a person
- a place
- a thing
- an idea
- an activity
- an emotion ***or***
- a feeling

Sentences have two parts: a subject and a verb. Either part may also have additional wording that tells more about them, but if either the subject or the verb is missing, there can't be a complete sentence.

Full sentences—that is, statements containing both a subject and a verb—are particularly important in writing, because the author seldom comes face-to-face with the reader. If something as basic as the subject or verb is missing, the reader will certainly have questions about the meaning of the writing. However, the author will never know what they are. Therefore, a missing subject or verb can cause missed communication.

Subjects

The subject of a sentence tells who or what the sentence is about. It may be a person, place, thing, idea, and so on.

You can identify the subject of a sentence by answering the question, "Who or what is this sentence about?"

EXAMPLES 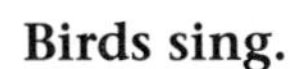

Birds sing.
(The sentence is about birds.)
Dick Tracy solved the mystery.
(The sentence is about Dick Tracy.)
Honesty is a virtue.
(The sentence is about honesty.)

19-1

DIRECTIONS: Underline the subject in each of the following sentences.

EXAMPLE ▶ **Bolivia is in South America.**

1. My terribly fat cat won a prize in a local contest.
2. This map will help you get to the Land of Oz.
3. Disneyworld is a popular vacation spot.
4. Children sometimes disobey their parents.
5. Moose are not very attractive animals.
6. Computers have changed the way many offices operate.
7. Anger should not prevent you from dealing with a problem.
8. I am going fishing this weekend.
9. Castles had thick walls for protection from both weather and enemies.
10. Happiness was evident among all the wedding guests.
11. Economics is a required subject for a business degree.
12. The driver stopped the car because Ramon wanted to get some ice cream.
13. Colorado is a beautiful state.
14. As soon as the sun went down, the bright lights of the hotels made the city look like fairyland.
15. Equality under the law is promised for all citizens.

cat
map
Disneyworld
Children
Moose
Computers
Anger
I
Castles
Happiness
Economics
driver
Colorado
lights
Equality

The subject of a sentence may be an action. The word showing action will have an "-ing" ending or the word "to" before it.

EXAMPLES  **Running is good exercise.**
(The sentence is about running.)

To fly was his chief goal in life.
(To fly is what the sentence is about.)

EXPLANATION: *Running* is the verb "run" with an "-ing" ending; it is the subject of the sentence. *To fly* is the verb "fly" with "to" in front of it; it is the subject of the sentence. Both these verb forms show action, and are the subjects of sentences.

19-2

DIRECTIONS: Underline the subjects in the following sentences.

EXAMPLE ▶ **Riding a bicycle requires good balance.**

Learning
Betting
Framing
To apply
swimming
Leaving
To take
Playing

1. Learning can be a pleasure.
2. Betting on horses is a sure way to lose money.
3. Framing the picture yourself is cheaper than having someone else do it.
4. To apply for an athletic scholarship is a commitment to play.
5. In the summer, swimming is a popular pastime.
6. Leaving the scuba tanks on shore was not a smart thing to do.
7. To take a test without studying is foolish.
8. Playing soccer in high school may lead to a college scholarship.

Two or more words that tell who or what a sentence is about are called a *compound subject.*

EXAMPLES  **Gabriel, Will, and Francis rode their motorcycles to San Diego.**
(The sentence is about Gabriel, Will, and Francis.)

Drums and guitars are in all the bands I've ever heard
(The sentence is about both drums and guitars.)

Reading and writing are necessary skills.
(The sentence is about both reading and writing.)

19-3

DIRECTIONS: Underline the compound subject in each of the following sentences.

EXAMPLE ▶ **Cooking and cleaning are jobs I hate.**

1. Mary and Henry are the best spellers in the third grade.
2. Daydreaming and wishing for miracles can take up a lot of time.
3. To forgive and forget are good rules for happiness.
4. Black and white are the only colors that babies less than three months old can see.
5. Both Jane and Sam fly on business frequently for their companies.
6. In the early morning in the country, the robins and finches wake me up.
7. On the menu were snapper from the ocean and trout from fresh water streams.
8. Where are the records and tapes I ordered for the party?

Mary and Henry
Daydreaming and wishing
To forgive and forget
Black and white
Jane and Sam
robins and finches
snapper and trout
records and tapes

Subjects are fairly easy to identify in sentences that make statements (also called **declarative sentences**). They often appear near the beginning of the sentence, and, of course, they always tell who or what the sentence is about.

Subjects may not be quite so easy to spot in sentences that ask questions (also called **interrogative sentences**). Rephrasing the question or answering it with a statement will help you discover the who or what the sentence is about. That way, you can identify the subject of the sentence.

EXAMPLES  **How much is that doggie in the window?**

***Rephrased:* The doggie in the window is how much?**

***Answered:* The doggie in the window is $200. (What is the sentence about? The doggie. It is the subject.)**

What is the current rate of interest on a savings account?

***Rephrased:* The current rate of interest on a savings account is what?**

***Answered:* The current rate of interest on a savings account is 7.7%. (What is the sentence about? The rate of interest. It is the subject.)**

19-4

DIRECTIONS: Underline the subjects in the following sentences.

EXAMPLE ▶ **What is the <u>homework</u> for tomorrow?**

girl
trombonist drummer
To read
Mr. Rodriguez
Studying
Gone
Joe
You

1. The little girl put her doll to sleep under the tree.
2. The trombonist and the drummer signed "run-of-the-tour" contracts.
3. To read is Marco's favorite pastime.
4. Mr. Rodriguez experimented with a new crop on part of his farm.
5. Studying German makes my brain tired.
6. Gone was every piece of evidence from the courtroom.
7. Does Joe intend to return to the classroom next week?
8. You put down that rock!

19-5

DIRECTIONS: Fill in your own subjects to make the following sentences complete.

EXAMPLE ▶ **Fortunately, ___*cars*___ slowed down at the dangerous curve.**

Answers will vary.
These are possibilities.

1. The ___bus___ carried a full load of passengers.
2. A(n) ___gymnast___ seemed about to set a new record.
3. ___Mitchell___ buttoned the heavy coat as protection from the blowing snow.
4. Because of the sunny, warm weather, ___we___ decided to stay on the beach until it was almost dark.
5. For months, ___families___ filmed holiday messages to send the American forces stationed in Saudi Arabia.
6. The ___noise___ startled everyone in the house.
7. ___Papers___ and ___cans___ made the park one of the messiest you could ever see.
8. Changing the costume quickly, the ___jugglers___ then gave a most amazing performance.

Verbs

A complete sentence requires both a subject and a verb. The verb tells either what the subject does or describes its state of being.

Here are some of the examples you just read in this chapter that identified the subject. They are printed again to help you identify the **verbs** in the sentences. See how the verb in each tells something about the subject.

EXAMPLES ▶

Birds sing.
(What about the birds? They sing. The subject does something.)

Honesty is a virtue.
(What about honesty? It is something: a virtue. It describes the subject's state of being.)

Jealousy ruins many marriages.
(What about jealousy? It ruins marriages. The subject does something.)

Gabriel, Will, and Francis rode their motorcycles to San Diego.
(What did Gabriel, Will, and Francis do? They rode their motorcycles. The subjects do something.)

19-6

DIRECTIONS: Underline the verbs in the following sentences that show what the subject does or is.

EXAMPLE ▶ **The wind blew and howled all night.**

1. Manufacturing increased when more people were hired at the computer plant.
2. The wind blew and shook all the pears off the trees.
3. Marilyn borrowed my car yesterday to visit her sister.
4. Neither Marilyn nor Jose returned the car last night.
5. I bought the car last summer with hard-earned money.
6. My dog ripped all the seat covers off last summer.
7. Just before Thanksgiving, my friend's pet monkey chewed up the side panels and floor mats.
8. Can you keep a secret from Marilyn?

increased
blew and shook
borrowed
returned
bought
ripped
chewed up
Can keep

Verbs that tell what the subject does are called "action verbs."

EXAMPLES ▶ **Lou answers 911 calls.**
(What does Lou do? <u>Answers</u> 911 calls.)
Willa and William often fish for their supper.
(What do Willa and William do? They <u>fish</u>.)

19-7

Answerw will vary.
Jose *hugged*
computer *runs*
Mother *baked*
players *run*
Miranda *reads*
Watering *makes*
artist *sold*
Horns *blow*

DIRECTIONS: Underline the subject of each sentence. Then, fill in each blank with an action verb.

EXAMPLE ▶ **<u>Jason and Chris</u>** *walked* **to the baseball card show.**

1. Jose ________ his dog when it won first prize in the show.
2. This new computer ________ faster than the old one.
3. Mother always ________ a cake or cookies for after-school snacks.
4. Basketball players ________ from one end of the court to the other.
5. Miranda ________ books so quickly I can hardly keep count of them all.
6. Watering flowers ________ them grow.
7. One artist whose work I like ________ several paintings at the art show this week.
8. Horns ________ loudly every time there is a traffic jam on Route 56.

Linking Verbs

Verbs that link or connect the subject with other words in the sentence that identify or describe it (or them) are called "linking verbs."

EXAMPLES  **Bill is a registered nurse.**
(The linking verb <u>is</u> identifies Bill as a registered nurse. The sentence might also state: <u>A registered nurse is Bill.</u>)
Cathy seems courageous.
(The linking verb <u>seems</u> describes a quality Cathy has.)

The linking verbs are:

appear	**become**	**seem**	**feel**
look	**smell**	**taste**	**sound**

and the many forms of *be:*

am	**is**	**are**	**was**
were	**has been**	**have been**	**had been**

19-8

DIRECTIONS: Underline the linking verb in each of the following sentences.

EXAMPLE ▶ The milk smelled sour.

was
is
were
smells
looks
was
taste
seemed
appears
has been

1. Donna was often ill during her childhood.
2. The price of a ticket is fifty dollars.
3. Good food and good music were the prescribed remedy.
4. The dumpster behind the cafeteria smells putrid.
5. The Ovation guitar looks both unusual and expensive.
6. Bob Fernandez was the engineer on board the *Norway*.
7. In June, the mangoes taste very sweet.
8. The car seemed a lemon, even to Mr. Goodwrench.
9. Thunder Mountain appears dangerous to me.
10. David Letterman has been a popular late-night host since 1983.

19-9

Answers to this *Activity* appear in the Instructor's Section.

DIRECTIONS: For each sentence in the following paragraph, underline the subject once and the verb twice.

Armadillos are small American mammals with rough, bony shells. Several kinds of armadillos exist in Texas, Louisiana, and along the southern Atlantic coast. Armadillos have long, sharp claws to dig tunnels in the ground. The armadillo may decide to live in it. Insects, earthworms, snails, and spiders are their chief foods. Their hard shells, which look like suits of armor, are a protection for these little animals to hide inside of. The armadillo cannot bite in self-defense. Armadillos' mouths are equipped with only small back teeth.

Subject and Verb Agreement

The subject and verb of a sentence must always agree with each other in number.

Singular means there is just one of something.
Plural means there are two or more of something.

If the subject of a sentence is singular, the verb must also be singular. If the subject of a sentence is plural, the verb must be plural.

EXAMPLES ▶ The puppy was in the yard.
(Puppy is singular; so is the verb was.)

The puppies were in the yard.
(Puppies means two or more of the animals, so it is a plural. The verb were is plural.)

The ostrich seems playful.
(Ostrich is a singular, so it requires the singular verb form, seems.)

Ms. Jones runs the business efficiently.
(Ms. Jones is a singular form, even though it ends in "s" as most plurals do. It takes the singular verb, runs.)

> **Compound subjects take a plural verb if they are connected by the word "and."**

EXAMPLES  Frankie and Johnnie were eating a picnic dinner.
(Frankie and Johnnie are the compound subject, so the verb is in the plural.)

Eating healthy foods and getting plenty of exercise are the keys to good health.
(Eating healthy foods and getting exercise form the subject, so the verb is a plural.)

> **The verb agrees with the nearest subject word in the sentence if the compound subjects are connected by the word "or," or "nor."**

EXAMPLES  Either Julia or her brothers have the ball
("Julia or brothers" is the compound subject, and since "brothers" is closest to the verb, the plural form have is correct.)

Neither the students nor the teacher seems to mind working in a cold room.
("Teacher," a singular word, is the second part of the compound subject joined by "nor," so the verb is singular.)

Activity 19-10

DIRECTIONS: If the subject (or compound subject) and verb in the following sentences agree, put a letter A on the line to the left of the sentence. If the subject and verb do *not* agree, put an N next to the number and revise the sentence on the lines provided to make the subject and verb agree in number. Underline the wording you have changed. One is done for you as an example.

N **The gambler and the lady is in Las Vegas to try their luck.**

The gambler and the lady are in Las Vegas to try their luck.

N 1. Neither the apple tree nor the lilac bush are in bloom.

Neither the apple tree nor the lilac bush is in bloom.

A 2. There rush three of the fastest line-backers I've ever seen!

N 3. The hungry mice is in the cupboard.

The hungry mice are in the cupboard.

A 4. Either we with our listening problem or Joe with his hearing problem has to find peace somewhere.

A 5. Clark was the man in the race on whom we bet.

N 6. Every boy and every girl who took the training have made the team.

Every boy and every girl who took the training has made the team.

N 7. Each of the English classes subscribe to *Time.*

Each of the English classes subscribes to *Time.*

A 8. The band's favorite music is James Taylor's ballads.

Activity 19-11

DIRECTIONS: Underline the correct form of the verb or verbs in each of the following sentences.

EXAMPLE ▶ The Christmas ornaments (is, are) stored until next year.

1. If neither Mother nor you (object, objects), I would like to use the car tomorrow. — objects
2. There (is, are) a piece of cake and a glass of milk on the table. — are
3. Neither of these roads (leads, lead) to Seattle. — leads
4. The winner, as well as the other contestants, (has, have) received offers for television appearances. — has
5. Fifty dollars (was, were) the specialist's fee for the consultation. — was
6. It is one of the most amazing discoveries that (has, have) come out of the university medical research laboratories! — has

| have |
| is |

7. There (has, have) been a number of burglaries in the neighborhood recently.
8. My favorite dessert (is, are) raspberries and cream.

Activity 19-12

DIRECTIONS: On the lines below, write a series of related sentences on one of the topics listed here. Be sure you write complete sentences, and that the subject and verb in each sentence agree in number.

school	a hobby	a wish	the environment
someone you know	courage	heroes	
patriotism	[any other subject of your choice]		

Answers will vary.

____

____

____

____

____

____

____

____

____

Activity 19-13

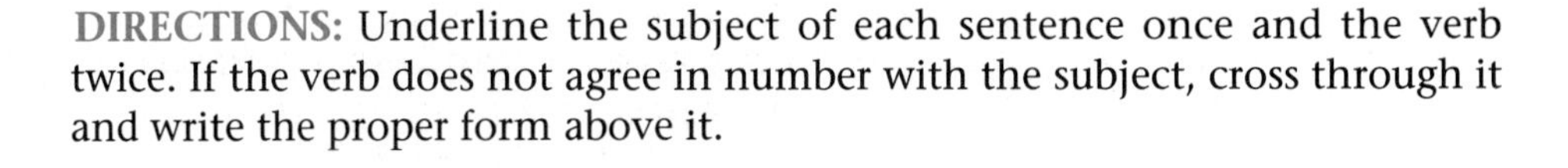

DIRECTIONS: Underline the subject of each sentence once and the verb twice. If the verb does not agree in number with the subject, cross through it and write the proper form above it.

EXAMPLE ▶ **In football, a "bomb" ~~are~~ *is* a very long and fast pass.**

Answers to this *Activity* are in the Instructor's Section.

Are you choosing a career for the first time or think of changing one? You should look for help. Couselors in schools and colleges has a lot of information available to you. Computer programs print out suggestions based on answers you give to many are questions. People who have jobs you are considering is also good sources of information. Most of them happily talk about and shares their interest in their jobs.

Direct and Indirect Objects

A word that completes the meaning of an action verb by answering *what?* or *whom?* is called a "direct object."

EXAMPLES ▶ **Jonathan caught a shark.**
(*What* did Jonathan catch? A shark. It is the direct object of the verb "caught.")
The city bus company hired conductors.
***Whom* did the bus company hire? Conductors. It is the direct object of the verb "hired.")**

A word that completes the meaning of some action verbs by answering *to whom?, for whom?, to what?* and *for what?* is called an "indirect object."

EXAMPLES ▶ **Millie gave me a present.**
(*To whom* did Millie give a present? To me. It is the indirect object of the verb.)
I owe music my thanks.
(*To what* do I owe thanks? To music. It is the indirect object of the verb "owe."

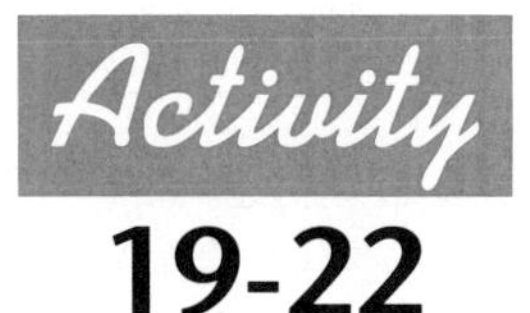

19-22

DIRECTIONS: In the following sentences, underline the indirect object once and write the letters ***IO***, for indirect object, above it. Underline the direct object twice and write ***DO***, for direct object, above it.

EXAMPLE ▶ **Please hand me the computer disk.** (IO above "me"; DO above "computer")

Answers to this *Activity* are in the Instructor's Section.

1. A change in Soviet power gave citizens a taste of democracy.
2. Reading has always given me great pleasure.
3. The winning runner always breaks the tape first.
4. Please give me the keys before you leave.
5. If you take a course in psychology, you will learn about human behavior.
6. The intended receiver snagged the ball and scored a touchdown.
7. The suspect offered a confession in exchange for a plea bargain.
8. Electronics repair courses teach students marketable skills.

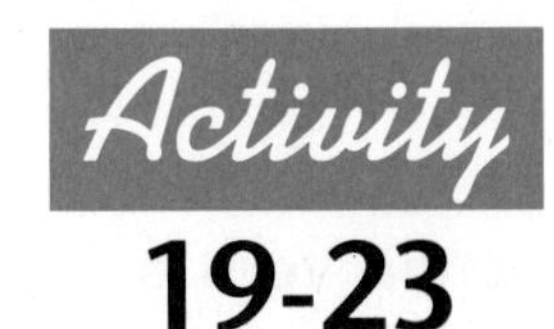

19-23

DIRECTIONS: Identify the subject, verb, direct object, and indirect object in the sentences of the following paragraph by writing ***S*** (for subject), ***V*** (for verb), ***DO*** (for direct object), and ***IO*** for (indirect object) above the appropriate words.

S V IO DO
Political cartoons tell you how an artist feels about current
S V
events. Being able to read them is almost an art in itself. These
S V DO
drawings sometime use symbols, such as a donkey to represent
the Democratic party and an elephant for the Republican party.
S V
Another device a political cartoonist uses is caricatures. That is,
S V DO
by exaggerating size, the artist caricatures dominance of one
person or country over another. Or, by exaggerating a person's
physical features, such as wrinkles, big ears, or a pointed nose,
S V DO
the political cartoonist pokes fun at the person.

Chapter 20

Varying Sentence Structures

In this chapter you will

- be able to identify phrases and spot prepositional phrases
- see how independent and dependent clauses are used
- use coordinating and subordinating conjunctions properly
- study the four types of sentences
- combine sentences to vary structures

How boring it is to read a series of sentences that all have the same structure! "See Spot. See Spot run. Jane sees Spot run. Dick sees Spot run." Beginning reading books used to have page after page of sentences that simple and that repetitive.

Writers who can deal with simple subject and verb sentences often don't trust themselves to write sentences of more variety and complexity, even though they speak such sentences with ease. Understanding the "building blocks" of sentences—phrases, clauses, and conjunctions—will show you how to vary sentence structures and therefore give you security about writing them. Such variety of sentence structures will also make anybody's writing more interesting to read.

Phrases

A phrase is a group of related words that *does not* have a subject and a predicate.

EXAMPLES  **The girl with the red sweater is my sister.**
The best time to study is in the morning.

The most common kind of phrase is a **prepositional phrase.** A prepositional phrase **begins with a preposition,** and has a **noun or pronoun as its object**. The object identifies who or what the preposition is pointing to. The preposition, its object, and related words make a prepositional phrase.

preposition *object*
The girl with the red sweater is my sister.

preposition object
The best time to study is in the morning.

Here are some of the most often-used prepositions:
(read across and you will see relationships among many words)

above	below	beside
in	out	inside
before	during	after
among	between	
under	over	on
up	down	upon
behind	beside	
with	for	of
across	near	
into	through	from

Activity 20-1

DIRECTIONS: Circle the prepositions and underline their objects in each of the following sentences. Some sentences will have more than one prepositional phrase.

Answers for this *Activity* are in the Instructor's Section.

 **The main headline in the newspaper today was about an explosion downtown.**

1. The parade down Main Street ended near the post office.
2. Did Juan put water in the radiator when he went to the gas station yesterday?
3. The crackling of the fire brought back memories that made my mouth water for roasted marshmallows.
4. The flight does not leave today, but it will depart early in the morning tomorrow.
5. Is that a police cruiser behind our car?

6. This room is excellent for our needs, which are to practice in the mornings and evenings and to sleep in the afternoons.
7. Hillary crawled slowly from the sleeping bag and began to hunt for firewood.
8. In the winter when ice is on the lake, I like to sail my ice boat across the lake and along the shore.

20-2

DIRECTIONS: To make meanings clear in the following sentences, supply a preposition for the blanks.

EXAMPLE ▶ Ship propellers work *under* **the water.**

on on
through
among on
to
with
off into
on
at

1. More information is stored ________ the hard disk than ____________ a single floppy disk.
2. Do not go ______________________ the museum too quickly or you will miss seeing a great deal.
3. I always find it hard to choose ____________ the many dishes _______ a restaurant menu.
4. My digital watch is identical ________________ the one you are wearing.
5. The rooms ____________________ a view are much more expensive than those without one.
6. The stunt man jumped________ the wagon and swung up _________the saddle.
7. Students often find it difficult to concentrate __________________ their homework when the radio or television is playing.
8. Will the football player stay _________________ home while his broken ankle is mending?

Clauses

A clause is a group of related words that *has a subject and a predicate.*

The subject of each clause below is underlined once and the predicate is in italics. (Remember that the predicate of a sentence is the verb and its related wording.)

EXAMPLES ▶ **The manufacturer *shipped the stereo components early last month.***

The Iditerod *is a famous dog-sled race in Alaska.*

When the curtain *was closed*, the cast *congratulated each other for the wonderful performance.*

The first two sentences each contain one clause; the third sentence contains two clauses.

Two kinds of clauses are:

- independent clauses
- dependent clauses

An *independent clause* is one that *can stand by itself* and states a complete idea.

Here are the first two examples from those above:

The manufacturer shipped the stereo components early last month.

The Iditerod is a famous dog-sled race in Alaska.

You can see that these are also sentences. Therefore, a single, independent clause is a sentence.

A *dependent clause* must be incorporated into a *sentence with at least one independent clause.* That is, a dependent clause cannot stand alone, because it states an idea that, to be complete, needs an independent clause.

Here is the third example of those you saw above:

When the curtain was closed, the cast congratulated each other for the wonderful performance.

"When the curtain was closed" is not a clause that makes sense by itself. It is a dependent clause, and you wait for the rest of a statement before it can be complete. (You will also recognize it as a sentence fragment.)

A dependent clause is sometimes called a "subordinate" clause. (The terms may be used interchangeably.) It begins with a subordinate conjunction. See the list on page 319 for a listing of the most often-used words to begin dependent clauses.

20-3

DIRECTIONS: On the line to the left of each number, write an **I** if the clause is independent and a **D** if it is dependent.

EXAMPLE ▶ __I__ **World Cup soccer matches attract international attention.**

__I__ 1. Gang rape of women is increasing on college campuses nationwide.

__D__ 2. Because cracks were found in a vital part of the rocket.

__I__ 3. The geologist took samples of the rock.

__I__ 4. The stolen jewelry was never recovered.

__I__ 5. Thousands of people watch *Lifestyles of the Rich and Famous* every week.

__D__ 6. Although the weather forecast is usually accurate.

__I__ 7. The Micosukee have an effective educational system.

__I__ 8. Carved houseposts are often given at potlatches.

A dependent clause may substitute for a noun or a pronoun and may, therefore, be used as
- **the subject of a sentence**
- **the object of a verb**
- **the object of a preposition**

In the following examples, the dependent clauses are underlined.

EXAMPLES ▶ **What he said to the coach shocked the rest of the team.**
Subject of the sentence

Julio thought that he would not be recognized.
Object of the verb

The cost of the barbeque depends on how many people will be attending.
Object of the preposition "on"

20-4

DIRECTIONS: Find and underline the dependent clauses in each of the following sentences. Over each, write the part of the sentence the clause is substituting for: An ***S*** for the subject, an ***OV*** for the object of the verb, an ***OP*** for the object of a prepation

EXAMPLE ▶ OV
Police located the stolen car when the thief answered the car phone.

1. OP
Cover the plants with whatever is available, or they will freeze.

2. S
What these people have left behind is unbelievable.

3. S
Where I live is really the cause of my problem.

4. OV
The director of the museum announced quietly that she was resigning from her post.

5. OP
Hugo was frightened by what he saw in that room.

6. OV
The thin, brown dog greedily ate whatever was in the dish.

7. OV
I am going into town to shop, and will pick up whatever you left at the cleaners.

8. OP
Mr. Sullivan wrote out the directions to the meeting place and gave
OP
them to whomever was going to be driving there.

Conjunctions

A conjunction joins elements within a sentence. Sometimes a phrase or clause joins one part of a sentence to another. But ordinarily a single word does the joining. Two kinds of conjunctions that will help you to vary sentence structures because they work with clauses are:

1. coordinating conjunctions
2. subordinating conjunctions

1. Coordinating Conjunctions

***Coordinating* conjunctions *join independent clauses* that express ideas of equal value or importance in a sentence.**

The coordinating conjunctions are *and, but, or, nor, for, yet,* and *so.* Usually, put a comma before these conjunctions when they join two long independent clauses.

EXAMPLES ▶ **Either I will go to the store or you will have to go.**

Every door was locked, but we found an unlocked window.

COMMENT: No comma appears in the first sentence because each clause is so short.

20-5

DIRECTIONS: If the independent clauses below express ideas of equal value or importance, write the most appropriate coordinating conjunction between them. If the clauses are not of equal value, leave the space blank. Use commas as needed.

EXAMPLE ▶ **The book was due three days ago ___, but___ I returned it today.**

,so

, and

, yet

and

, but

and

1. Downhill racing skiers use both edges of each ski ______ each edge must be carefully prepared before a race.
2. The new home bread-baking machines are expensive but easy to use ______the bread is delicious.
3. It has finally stopped raining _______ the roads are still muddy.
4. The Indy 500 race driver pulled into the lead, ______ his race team got ready to celebrate.
5. Majoring in marine biology was the smartest decision I ever made _______ courses are tough.
6. I trumped my partner's ace ________ we won the bridge game after all.
7. Woodshop is a popular non-credit course at the college, _______ people start registering for it very early.
8. I know who won the election _______ do not want to make such information public.

2. Subordinating Conjunctions

***Subordinating* conjunctions *connect dependent* clauses *with independent* clauses.**

Common subordinating conjunctions are

after	although	as
as if	as though	because
before	ever since	if
rather than	since	so that
that	unless	until
when	whenever	where
whereas	while	

EXAMPLES ▶ **When I eat popcorn, it always gets stuck between my teeth.**

If the chair is worth repairing, I won't get a new one.

I would like to go to the party now, although it started four hours ago.

20-6

DIRECTIONS: Supply the most appropriate subordinating conjunction in each of the following sentences.

EXAMPLE ▶ **Alec refuses to play the piano before an audience *unless* his parents force him to.**

until

Because

when

although

Unless

while

because

so that

1. I didn't know there were so many different kinds of bamboo __________ I read an article in the *National Geographic*.
2. __________________ so many students showed up for football tryouts, the coach had to schedule several tryout days and assign people to them alphabetically.
3. Marta could paint beautiful pictures ____________________ she felt in the mood to do so.
4. Horror movies are good box office money-makers _______________ many parents won't let their children see such films.
5. __________________ you wear cool clothing, you could get heat stroke in the tropics.
6. The elderly carnival worker had a heart attack _____________ controlling the ferris wheel.
7. Be sure to study the section of the book on how air lifts glider wings ____________ you never know when you might need that information.
8. Hilda always goes grocery shopping on Saturday __________________ she will not run out of food.

Coordinating and Subordinating Conjunctions in Sentences

20-7

DIRECTIONS: Supply either a coordinating or a subordinating conjunction as seems most appropriate to the sense of each of the following sentences.

EXAMPLE ▶ **I wanted to go swimming, *but* I forgot to bring my swim suit.**

Answers
When
While
if
that
Because
since *or* because
when
as if

1. ________ Elmo finished practicing the drums, he went out to shoot baskets.
2. ________ the sun was setting, I watched the last day of my vacation also disappear.
3. It is impossible to know ________ the party will be a success.
4. In the morning, I did not know ________ I would be leaving Michigan that same afternoon.
5. ________ she has a new motorcycle, Bess plans to ride in the next club trip.
6. I waited for the bus, which was silly ________ I was in a hurry.
7. Mitchell enjoyed being carried around ________ he was a little baby.
8. It looks________ the sun will come out.

Activity

20-8

DIRECTIONS: Decide if the italicized conjunction in each sentence suits the meaning or intent of that sentence. If it *does*, write a C on the line to the left of that sentence. If it *does not* seem appropriate, write a more suitable conjunction on the line.

EXAMPLE ▶ *when* **The playgoers had just taken their seats in the theater *than* the play began.**

C 1. *While* I was in the office, my husband called me on my beeper.

unless 2. The bank refused to cash the check *except* Mr. Guedes had two forms of identification.

unless 3. There isn't much chance of winning the lottery *without* you are very lucky.

When 4. *Where* any well-known person reaches the age of ninety, everyone wants to know his or her secret for a long life.

When 5. *Immediately* she looked at the tennis racket, she knew that it was the one she wanted.

C 6. *Since* I have no real interest in numbers, I find mathematics very uninteresting.

___if___ 7. The accounting instructor asked the students *when* they would need more time to prepare their reports.

___when___ 8. Everyone stopped talking *directly* the police arrived on the scene.

Four Types of Sentences

A sentence must contain at least one independent clause (that is, one that contains a subject and a verb) so that it communicates a complete thought. A sentence may, however, contain additional clauses, either dependent or independent. These various combinations are described as:

- simple sentences
- compound sentences
- complex sentences
- compound-complex sentences.

A *simple sentence* contains only *one independent clause.*

In the examples below, the subject of the clause is underlined once and the verb is in italics.

EXAMPLES  **Jolie *baked* a cake for the school carnival.**

Howard and his sister now *own* the restaurant.

The crowd *laughed and shouted* at the beach.

COMMENT: The first example has just one subject and one verb. The second sentence has a compound subject; the third sentence has a compound verb. Each sentence, however, contains a subject and verb and it can stand alone, so each is an independent clause.

A *compound* sentence contains *two or more independent clauses.*

The independent clauses are usually joined by a comma and a coordinate conjunction: *and, but, or, nor, for, yet,* or *so.*

Sometimes the independent clauses are joined by a semi-colon.

In the examples below, the subject of each of the independent clauses is underlined, and the verb of each is in italics.

EXAMPLES  **Chess *is* a difficult game to learn to play, but dominoes *is* a much easier game to learn.**

Professor Bobich *enjoys* fishing, and her husband often *accompanies* her on fishing trips.

The sun *beat* down on the campers all day; they finally *left* for home late in the afternoon, but they *agreed* to return soon.

A *complex* sentence contains *one independent clause* and *at least one dependent clause.*

In the examples that follow, the independent clause is in regular type and the dependent clause is in italics. In each clause, the subject is underlined once and the verb is in boldface.

EXAMPLES  Dr. Weymouth **gave** me some medicine *which I **did not like.***

*If you **are going** to the movies,* I **would like** to go with you.

*Although the winter **promises** to be cold* and *although snow **has** already **started** falling,* the agency **will not increase** your heating fuel allowance.

A *compound-complex* sentence contains *at least two independent clauses* and *at least one dependent clause.*

In the following examples, the independent clauses are in regular type and the dependent clauses are in italics. The subject of each clause is underlined once and the verb is in boldface.

EXAMPLES  The mayor **spoke** eloquently of the new museum, but he **did not mention** the fact *that the money for it **would be raised** by new city taxes.*

The world **appears** to be growing smaller *because world travel **is** so common,* and many foreign customs *which we once **considered** strange* **have become** familiar to us today.

COMMENT: Notice that a dependent clause may come inside of an independent clause, as it does in the sentence immediately above.

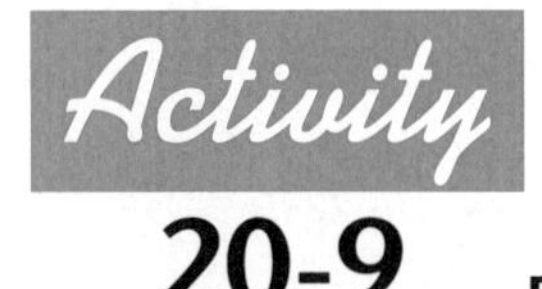

20-9

DIRECTIONS: Underline the independent clauses and draw a circle around the dependent clauses in each sentence below. Below each sentence, write if it is a simple, compound, complex, or compound-complex sentence.

EXAMPLE 

People (who know shorthand and typing) can easily get work, and (if they are also computer literate,) the job search will be even easier.

compound-complex

Answers for this Activity are in the Instructor's Section.

1. My father served in the Navy for twenty years, and his knowledge of the sea is amazing.

____

2. Because the Wisconsin team has not lost a game in three years, it has been chosen for the post-season championship play-off.

____

3. Helmut worked in the post office every Christmas season for fifteen years and knows every zip code in the state.

____

4. If you want to mail a package and have it arrive at any time in the near future, you have to sent it by Priority Mail.

____

5. Either I am going to watch television all evening and enjoy being a couch potato, or I am going to the jazz concert with my cousin.

____

6. Tonight I have to wash my hair and wash the cat, too.

____

7. Because no one else volunteered, Jason drove the car to the airport.

____

8. It is very strange that the phone did not ring all day, but tonight I can get nothing accomplished because it rings every five minutes.

____

20-10

DIRECTIONS: In brackets after each number are instructions telling you which kind of sentence to create. You are also given either an independent or a dependent clause to include in the sentence you develop. Circle each clause you add and write above it an **I** if you added an independent clause or a **D** if you added a dependent clause.

EXAMPLE  [**create** a complex sentence]
Use this clause: a new show opened last Sunday at the planetarium
Sentence:

Because some special equipment was finally installed a new show opened last Sunday at the planetarium.

1. [**create** a simple sentence]
   Use this clause: the weather report predicted rain and high winds
   Sentence:

   retain and punctuate as a sentence

   The weather report predicted rain and high winds.

2. [**create** a compound-complex sentence]
   Use this clause: because the playing field remained wet
   Sentence:

   add at least two independent clauses—other dependent clauses may also be added

   Because the playing field remained wet, the umpires cancelled the game, and both teams went home.

3. [**create** a complex sentence]
   Use this clause: although the amateur carpenter tried hard
   Sentence:

   add at least one independent clause

   other dependent clauses may be added

   Although the amateur carpenter tried hard, the table legs were uneven.

4. [**create** a compound sentence]
   Use these clauses: according to its aerodynamics, the bumblebee should not be able to fly
   Sentence:

   add at least one other independent clause

   According to its aerodynamics, the bumblebee should not be able to fly, but nobody seems to have told that to the bumblebees.

5. [**create** a complex sentence]
   Use this clause: cold weather caused the pipes to freeze
   Sentence:

   add one or more dependent clauses

   Because they were outdoors and unprotected, cold weather caused the pipes to freeze.

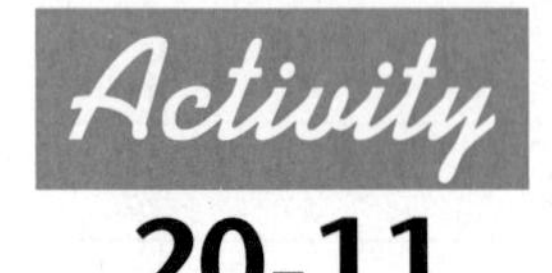

20-11

DIRECTIONS: Each group of sentences above the writing lines may be combined to create sentences of independent and dependent clauses. Write the individual sentences, and then write them as a paragraph. Supply connecting words and punctuation. You may also make slight changes so the ideas read better, but *be sure to keep the original idea* expressed by the sentences.

There is a village.
It is a little village.
About 250 live in the village.

There is a little village of about 250 people.

The houses are in a cluster.
The houses are beside the river.

Their houses are clustered beside the river.

There is a church.
The church is white.
The church is on a green hill.
The church is near the river.
A bridge spans the river.

There is a white church on a green hill near the river, and close to where a bridge spans the river.

The village has a baseball field.
The village has a general store.
The baseball field and the general store are on the street.
The street they are on is around the corner from the church.

The village has a baseball field and a general store on the street around the corner from the church.

A salmon hatchery is on the river.
It is downstream from the city.
It straddles the river.
The hatchery is old.
It is one of the oldest in the country.

Downstream from the city, an old salmon hatchery, one of the oldest in the country, straddles the river.

Write the paragraph here:

Answers will vary. The following sentences combining all the above elements represents just one possibility for a student response.

There is a little village of about 250 people who live in houses clustered beside the river. There is a white church on a green hill near the river, and close to where a bridge spans the river. The village has a baseball field and a general store on the street around the corner from the church, Downstream from the city, an old salmon hatchery, one of the oldest in the country, straddles the river.

Chapter 21

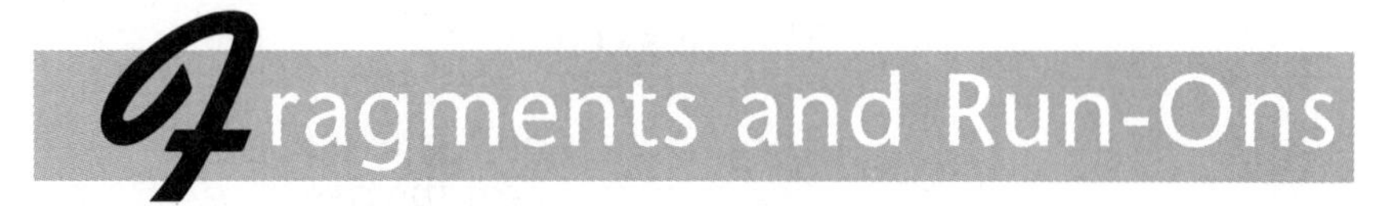

Fragments and Run-Ons

In this chapter you will

- learn to identify four kinds of sentence fragments
- correct sentence fragments
- recognize run-on sentences (comma splices and fused sentences)
- practice four ways of changing run-ons into complete sentences

Much of the sense a reader gets from a piece of writing depends on the reader's expectations: that words be spelled conventionally, that they appear in a familiar order, and that the words be organized into sentences.

A sentence communicates a single, complete thought. Sometimes writers leave out part of what is needed for a complete thought. Or, sometimes more than one thought is presented on paper as if it were only one. In either of these cases, the reader is left confused because the expectation of what a sentence is hasn't been met. Left to figure out what the single, complete thought was *supposed* to be, the reader misses what the writer intended to communicate.

Therefore, a writer helps readers to understand content by meeting the expectation of complete sentences. That is, a sentence must contain at least one complete subject and a complete predicate; it begins with a capital letter and ends with one of three end-punctuation marks, usually with a period.

Anything less—or more—interferes with the writer communicating to the reader.

Sentence Fragments

A sentence is a complete idea that can stand alone. That is, it contains just one complete subject and one complete predicate (that includes the verb). In order to identify a sentence, find the subject (that tells who or what the sentence is about) and the verb that works with it (and tells what the subject does or is).

A fragment is *part of a sentence* punctuated as if it were a complete sentence. The group of words does *not* make a complete sentence and *cannot* stand alone for one of these reasons:

- **the subject is missing**
- **the verb is missing**
- **the words are a phrase (so both subject and predicate are missing)**
- **the words are actually a dependent clause.**

EXAMPLES ▶ **Sat down on the sidewalk and began to cry.**

***COMMENT:* Who or what** sat down? Although punctuated as a complete sentence, it is a fragment because the subject is missing.

The child in the red hat pulling the sled down the street.

***COMMENT:* What** did the child do, think, say, or believe? Although punctuated as a complete sentence, it is a fragment because the verb is missing.

On the horizon.

COMMENT: These words are a phrase. Therefore, although they are punctuated as a complete sentence, it is a fragment because both the subject and the verb are missing.

After I picked a big bucket of blueberries.

***COMMENT:* What** happened after the bucket of blueberries was picked? Although punctuated as a complete sentence, this wording is a fragment because it is actually a dependent clause. The clue word, "after," is one that often begins a dependent clause. At least one *independent* clause is required to work with a dependent clause in order for there to be a complete sentence. (See Chapter 20, pages 313-325, for more about dependent clauses.)

Some words that ordinarily begin a dependent clause are

after	although	as
as if	as though	because
before	ever since	if
rather than	since	so that
that	unless	until
when	whenever	where
whereas	while	

21-1

DIRECTIONS: In the space to the left of each number, write an **F** if the words that follow are a fragment and a **C** if they are a complete sentence.

EXAMPLE ▶ _F_ **While I was standing in the kitchen waiting for dinner.**

_F_ 1. Every day as he was riding the bus.
_F_ 2. An only child.
_F_ 3. Is to preserve wildlife.
_C_ 4. The injured bird was returned to the nest after treatment.
_F_ 5. At the point where the two paths joined, in the intersection where the wild flowers were blooming.
_F_ 6. Whenever he was sleepy.
_C_ 7. Do whatever you like.
_F_ 8. Declared a disaster area because the tornado destroyed 300 homes.

Make a fragment into a complete sentence, one that will communicate a whole idea to a reader, by providing the missing element: a subject or a verb or an independent clause.

The examples of four different kinds of fragments, shown on page 327, can be made into complete sentences by supplying the missing parts.

EXAMPLES  **Fragment: Sat down on the sidewalk and began to cry.**

Add a subject: The <u>child</u> sat down on the sidewalk and began to cry.

Fragment: The child in the red hat pulling the sled down the street.

Add a verb: The child in the red hat pulling the sled down the street <u>looked</u> happy but cold.

Fragment: On the horizon

Add a subject and verb: The <u>sailboat</u> *came* into view on the horizon.

Fragment: After I picked a big bucket of blueberries.

Add an independent clause: After I picked a big bucket of blueberries, <u>I had enough berries to make a pie and several jars of preserves</u>.

Activity 21-2

DIRECTIONS: Some of the following groups of words are complete sentences and some are fragments.

Put a **C** on the line to the left of each number marking a complete sentence.

Put an **S** on the line if you need to add a subject to a fragment in order to make a complete sentence. Write the sentence, using proper capitalization and punctuation, on the lines provided.

Put a **V** on the line if you need to add a verb to a fragment in order to make a complete sentence. Write the sentence, using proper capitalization and punctuation, on the lines provided.

Put **SV** on the line if you need to add a subject and a verb to a fragment in order to make a complete sentence. Write the sentence, using proper capitalization and punctuation, on the lines provided.

EXAMPLE ▶ *S* **Willing to referee the basketball game.**

Revision:

Ms. Kiefer, the coach at my school, was willing to referee the basketball game.

Revisions of fragments in this exercise will vary. What appears here are suggestions.

C 1. As soon as the contest ended, the school found out its science entry had won.

Revision:

SV 2. Harder and harder.

Revision:

The crew rowed harder and harder.

S 3. Seems a very strange thing to do.

Revision:

Skiing in summer seems a very strange thing to do.

V 4. The brown and white spotted dog.

Revision:

The brown and white spotted dog listened carefully and followed directions. (compound verb)

V 5. "Once upon a time," which is the way all good fairy tales begin, a ten-foot-tall dragon.

Revision:

"Once upon a time," which is the way all good fairy tales begin, a ten-foot-tall dragon climbed out of the cave where he had lived for a thousand years.

C 6. The news camera operator suddenly became uncomfortably aware that the water in the street was rising quickly.

Revision:

V 7. Through the open window, I.

Revision:

Through the open window, I heard a band sent to serenade the lovely lady who lived next door.

S 8. Tumbled over and over after falling down the steep cliff.

Revision:

Jack and Jill tumbled over and over after falling down the steep cliff. (compound subject)

V 9. Ilia, the main character in the newly-released and award-winning film.

Revision:

Ilia, the main character in the newly-released and award-winning film, was really out for all she could get.

S 10. Ran the last play and therefore won the Bowl game.

Revision:

The Dolphin quarterback ran the last play and therefore won the bowl game.

21-3

DIRECTIONS: If there is a fragment in any of the following pairs of word groups, underline it. Then join the two word groups together by writing them as a complete sentence with proper capitalization and punctuation.

If there is no fragment in any of the following pairs of word groups, write the letter C to the left of the number of that pair.

EXAMPLE ▶ **The fire truck was not speeding to the nearby warehouse. Although it turned the corner too sharply and almost tipped over.**

Revision:

The fire truck was not speeding to the nearby warehouse, although it turned the corner too sharply and almost tipped over.

1. A. The magazine editor wanted to increase her sales.
   B. By increasing public awareness of the issues involved.

   Revision:

   The magazine editor wanted to increase her sales by increasing public awareness of the issues involved.

Sentence B is a fragment.

Sentence B is a fragment.

2. A. Although the painting was not complete, it was obviously a bowl of fruit.
   B. Juicy, ripe, and ready to eat.
   Revision:
   Although the painting was not complete, it was obviously a bowl of juicy, ripe, and ready-to-eat fruit.

Sentence A is a fragment.

3. A. A long time to sit and wait.
   B. The wreck that took place on the busy freeway slowed traffic to a crawl for over three hours.
   Revision:
   The wreck that took place on the busy freeway slowed traffic to a crawl for over three hours, a long time to sit and wait.

Both sentences are correct, no fragments.

4. A. Whichever choice you make, be sure to register in time for your name to be added to the list.
   B. Don't be late.
   Revision:

Sentence A is a fragment.

5. A. Although the club decided to change its by-laws.
   B. Members agreed that dues should not be raised.
   Revision:
   Although the club decided to change its by-laws, members agreed that dues should not be raised.

Sentence A is a fragment.

6. A. Never giving the problem a second thought.
   B. I decided to give the stray dog to an animal shelter.
   Revision:
   Never giving the problem a second thought, I decided to give the stray dog to an animal shelter.

Sentence A is a fragment.

7. A. Before shutting the garage door.
   B. Put the mower in the garage.
   Revision:
   Put the mower in the garage before shutting the garage door.

Sentence B is a fragment.

8. A. Hermione is one of those people who always seems to know exactly what to do.
   B. Unlike me, because I never seem to know.

   Revision:

   Hermione is one of those people who always seems to know exactly what to do, unlike me, because I never seem to know.

21-4

DIRECTIONS: Revise the fragments in *Activity 21-1* into complete sentences. Write on your own paper and be sure to number the sentences accurately.

Find a partner with whom to exchange the sentences you wrote in fulfilling *Activity 21-4*. Be sure you each added the proper elements to the fragments so that they were turned into complete sentences. Discuss ways in which you each varied what you added.

Activity

21-5

DIRECTIONS: Correct all the fragments in the following paragraphThen write the corrected version of the paragraph on your own paper. Underline the main subject of each revised sentence (or independent coause) once and the main verb twice.

EXAMPLE  **Although he looked everywhere. Robert could not find his wallet.**

Corrected Version:

Although he looked everywhere, Robert could not find his wallet.

The answers to *Activities 21-4* and *21-5* are in the Instructor's Section.

Cats make perfect pets. Because they are very quiet and clean. They do not chew up your shoes. And they are easier to take care of than dogs. Who need more attention and special treatment. If you ever wondered how the expression "cat nap" came about. It is probably because cats take an average of sixty-five naps a day. Furthermore, cats only need about twenty minutes of petting each day. Unlike dogs. Who require a great deal more attention and exercise. Recent studies show that cats are increasing in popularity as pets. Since more people live in apartments today and lack space. It is nice to have a cat sleeping around your house. In odd places and coming to you to be petted. Now and then while never demanding very much.

Run-On Sentences: Comma Splices and Fused Sentences

Wording punctuated as a single sentence but that is actually two or more sentences is called a **run-on sentence.** Think of it as a thought that runs on and on. "Run-on" is a general term. Actually, there are two kinds of run-ons:

- a comma splice
- a fused sentence.

A *comma splice* is two or more sentences with a comma separating them. (A "splice" is a joining; we speak of "splicing" rope or film to put pieces together and make a single length.)

EXAMPLES  **The Academy Awards are given annually, they honor people in the motion picture business.**

COMMENT: The wording before the comma is a complete sentence; so is the wording after the comma. Because these two sentences are joined by a comma, the statement is described as a *comma splice*. Sometimes it is called a "run-on sentence."

Sylvia went to Japan to study the educational system that has produced so many high-achieving students, she said she learned a great deal as a result of the trip.

COMMENT: Both the wording before the comma and after it are independent clauses. These clauses should be separated by some sort of punctuation mark to show a reader that each is a complete sentence and can stand alone.

A *fused sentence* is two or more sentences without end punctuation between them. ("Fusing" mixes or melts together elements so they are blended, as a glassblower joins parts of a figure so there is no seam to mark the joining.)

EXAMPLES  **The Grammy Awards are given annually they honor people in the music business.**

COMMENT: "The Grammy Awards are given annually" is a complete sentence. "They honor people in the music business" is also a complete sentence. When they appear together, without punctuation marking the end of one sentence and the beginning of another, they are called a *fused sentence*. Sometimes it, too, is called a "run-on sentence."

The weather forecast said "Snow today" you better wear warm clothes.

COMMENT: The quotation of the weather forecast ends one sentence and the word "you" begins another sentence. Written together without punctuation, they parts are called a *fused sentence* or a "run-on."

21-6

DIRECTIONS: Put an **R** to the left of the number of each run-on sentence and a C to the left of the number of each correct sentence in the following list.

EXAMPLE ▶ R **The ferryboat capsized many people were drowned before rescue boats arrived.**

R 1. Many countries besides the United States have had civil wars Spain had such a war in the 1930s.

R 2. The apple trees are flowering now, I know the fruit will soon begin to form.

C 3. When few student athletes graduate from a college, many people suspect something is wrong with the athletic scholarship program at that school.

R 4. Simon Bolivar is a central figure in South American independence, he is sometimes called the "Great Liberator."

C 5. The waterway is now clear, yet no ships will start through it until next Tuesday.

R 6. The matter of ethics in business continues to be a great interest to most people, however, some in the business community seem not to pay much attention to ethics.

R 7. The barriers to jobs formerly thought to be for only men or for women have come down in the past ten years many men are now telephone operators and nurses, many women are now mechanics and fire fighters.

R 8. The Baths of Caracalla were built during the days of the Roman empire they are now a great tourist attraction in Rome.

A run-on (comma splice or fused sentence) must be separated into individual units by using one of these four methods:

- **Begin each sentence with a capital letter and end each sentence with a period (or other end punctuation mark).**
- **Put a semicolon between independent clauses if they express closely-related ideas.**
- **End the first with a comma, and begin the second one with a coordinate conjunction (that is, begin with *and, but, or, for, nor, so,* or *yet*).**
- **Change one sentence into a dependent clause that will work with the other sentence (which is already an independent clause).**

EXAMPLES 

Run-on: The human heart has four chambers blood runs through all of them for a single heartbeat.

Sentences separated by periods:
The human heart has four chambers. Blood runs through all of them for a single heartbeat.

A sentence containing a semicolon:
The human heart has four chambers; blood runs through all of them for a single heartbeat.

A sentence containing a comma and a coordinate conjunction:
The human heart has four chambers, and blood runs through all of them for a single heartbeat.

A sentence containing an independent and a dependent clause:
Because the human heart has four chambers, blood must run through all of them for a single heartbeat.

Transitional words such as *however, nevertheless, instead, otherwise, indeed, moreover,* and *also* are sometimes used after a semicolon to make the connection between the two independent clauses smoother. When they are used this way, put a comma after the transitional word.

EXAMPLES 

I tried to learn to paddle a canoe during vacation; however, I often tipped over.

You may not make the team the first time you try out for it; nevertheless, you should keep trying.

Activity 21-7

DIRECTIONS: Correct the following run-on sentences by using each of the four methods at least twice during this *Activity*. State the method used on the line after the correction you make.

EXAMPLE ▶ The little boy begged his mother for candy, she refused to buy any for him.

Correction:

The little boy begged his mother for candy, but she refused to buy any for him.

Method used:

comma and coordinate conjunction

1. Technology is growing so rapidly that it is very difficult to keep up, indeed, many new products appear each day.

   Correction:

   Technology is growing so rapidly that it is very difficult to keep up. Indeed, many new products appear each day.

   Method used:

   Sentences separated by period.

2. It is always a good idea to keep a flashlight in your car, although chances are good that you will never need to use one, it can be a real benefit if you have a flat tire at night.

   Correction:

   It is always a good idea to keep a flashlight in your car. Although chances are good that you will never need to use one, it can be a real benefit if you have a flat tire at night.

   Method used:

   Sentences separated by a period.

3. I decided to sign up for an astronomy class the stars have always held great mystery I would like to know more about them.

   Correction:

   I decided to sign up for an astronomy class. The stars have always held great mystery; I would like to know more about them.

   Method used:

   Sentence containing a semicolon

4. One of the greatest athletes of the 1980s was Bo Jackson probably no other athlete of the day excelled in such a variety of sports.

   Correction:

   One of the greatest athletes of the 1980s was Bo Jackson; probably no other athlete of the day excelled in such a variety of sports.

   Method used:

   Sentence containing a semicolon

5. In college it seemed that lunch was a luxury, bus fare was far more important than anything else.

   Correction:

   In college it seemed that lunch was a luxury, for bus far was far more important than anything else.

   Method used:

   Comma and a coordinate conjunction

6. The Sugar Maple is one of the most brilliantly-colored trees in fall the Japanese Maple is unsurpassed for its electrifying color display.

   Correction:

   Although the Sugar Maple is one of the most brilliantly colored trees in fall, the Japanese Maple is unsurpassed for its electrifying color display.

   Method used:

   Independent and dependent clauses

7. Planning for retirement is important at every stage of life depending on Social Security for support in retirement is unrealistic.

   Correction:

   Planning for retirement is important at every stage of life, for depending on Social Security for support in retirement is unrealistic.

   Method used:

   Comma with a coordinate conjunction

8. Suddenly the wind stopped the eye of the hurricane was passing over.

   Correction:

   When the wind stopped, we knew the eye of the hurricane was passing over.

   Method used:

   Independent and dependent clauses

Sharing

1. Exchange *Activity 21-7* with a partner.
2. Be sure your partner has used each method of correction at least twice.
3. Compare differences between your corrections and your partner's, with each person giving reasons for the choice of correction method used.

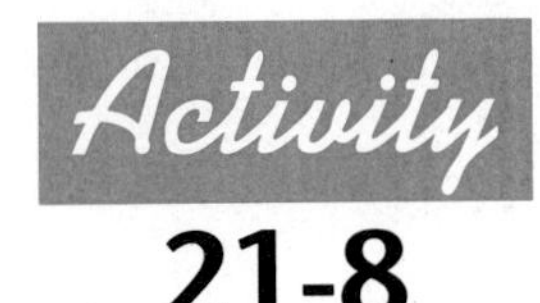

21-8

DIRECTIONS: The following paragraphs contain sentence fragments and run-ons. In order to correct them, do the following:

Draw a circle around every comma that should be a period.

Underline every fragment.

Insert the omission symbol (^) where commas or semicolons are needed and make the correction.

Insert the omission symbol (^) if any subject or verb is missing and write the missing word above the line.

Put three short lines below any letters that should be capitalized and write the capital letter above.

Put a slash mark through any letter that should not be capitalized.

Answers to this *Activity* are in the Instructor's Section.

PARAGRAPH 1:

Landscaping your lawn can do more for the environment than just adding beauty, in fact, a new type of landscaping, called xeroscaping, can conserve water and require less maintenance than traditional methods. Xeroscaping requires rock or bark, not grass, with this method less water is wasted in summer. Which is especially important in areas where there is little rainfall.

PARAGRAPH 2:

Living in a climate where winters are cold and snowy presents problems that require special advance planning, for example, buying snow tires sealing up windows, and cleaning the furnace are just a few of the things that should be done before winter actually begins. Waiting until needed items are no longer available Can make winter unpleasant, buying in advance can make a cold winter easier, Indeed preparing for winter can make it a pleasant time. An opportunity to spend time indoors with your family getting to know one another better.

Chapter 22

Verb, Voice, Tense, and Agreement

In this chapter you will

- identify active and passive voice
- determine when to use active or passive voice
- relate the verb tenses to the time elements they express
- learn how the principal parts of regular verbs are formed
- practice choosing regular present, past, and future tense verbs that agree with their subjects.

The verb is the most important part of a sentence. The subject, or a noun, cannot communicate a complete thought:

lipstick ships pogo stick

Even a noun with modifiers cannot communicate a complete thought:

bright red lipstick in a plastic case

cruise ships that each hold a thousand people

4-foot-tall pogo stick painted purple and turquoise

But a one-word verb can be a sentence because it communicates a complete thought:

Run. Stop. Listen. Sit.

A sentence, as you know, must have a subject as well as a verb. The subject in each of the four sentences above is the word "you." However, it is understood, rather than being stated. The complete sentences, then, are actually:

You run.

You stop.

You listen.

You sit.

All verbs have voice and tense. The "voice" of a verb tells whether its subject is acting, or is being acted upon. The "tense" of a verb indicates time. Both regular and irregular verbs change their forms depending on voice and tense.

Active and Passive Voice

The verb in a sentence tells the action or state of being of the subject. (The subject is who or what the sentence is about.) The voice of a verb tells whether the subject is performing an action, or is being acted upon.

If the subject of a sentence performs the action, a verb is in the active voice.

EXAMPLES ▶ **The boy threw the ball over the fence.**
The history class learned about the Civil War from the textbook.
Experienced life guards teach the advanced swimming class.
Everyone in Mexico celebrates the Cinco de Mayo.

Notice that in each of these sentence someone, the subject, is doing or did something:

boy	threw
class	learned
life guards	teach
everyone	celebrates

If the subject of a sentence is acted upon, a verb is in the passive voice.

EXAMPLES  **The ball was thrown over the fence by the boy.**
The Civil War was learned about by the history class from the textbook.
or
The Civil War was taught to the history class from the textbook.
The advanced swimming class was taught by experienced life guards.
Cinco de Mayo is celebrated by everyone in Mexico.

Now the subjects of the sentences change and instead of performing an action, each ***is acted upon:***

ball	was thrown
Civil War	was learned
or	was taught
class	was taught
Cinco de Mayo	is celebrated

Look closely at these examples of verbs in the passive voice and you will see that each of them is actually two words: some form of *to be* plus another verb, one that is called the **past participle** of a verb. If it is a regular verb (see pages 345-350 for an explanation of the term), as are all those above, it *ends in -d or -ed or -t*, the same as its past tense. However, if the verb is irregular (see Chapter 23 for an explanation), it will have another form (see the chart on pages 357-359).

Passive voice verbs are formed by combining some form of *to be* (such as *am, is, are, was, were, has been, have been,* or *had been*) with the past participle of a verb.

To see the difference between active and passive voice in writing, read the following two passages:

Accurate and effective proofreading is a skill anyone can learn. You may need time and a little patience to learn the symbols to use, but that should not take long. You will need a dictionary, a grammar handbook, a ruler, some sharp pencils, and a pad of post-it notes or a box of paper clips before you start proofreading. Then, start reading slowly. Check spelling, punctuation, and grammar, and mark places you decide are incorrect.

A skill that can be learned by anyone is accurate and effective proofreading. A little time and patience are needed to learn the symbols to use, but that should not take long. A dictionary, a grammar handbook, a ruler, some sharp pencils, and a pad of post-it notes or a box of paper clips are needed. Then, reading should start slowly. Spelling, punctuation, and grammar should be checked and places that are believed to be incorrect should be marked.

The left column—the active voice—seems to move forward more quickly. It addresses the reader more directly (by using second person) than does the second column (which is in the third person). The left column has a sense of action, of something happening or something to do, that is lacking in the passive voice constructions of the right column.

Mostly then, choose to use the active voice if you want to make your writing lively.

NOTE: When you are thinking about active and passive voice, apply the test of whether the subject is acting or is acted upon *only to the verb of the main (or independent) clause in a sentence.* If you write a compound sentence, which has two independent clauses, try to keep the verbs of both in the same voice.

Activity 22-1

DIRECTIONS: Write an **A** on the line to the left of a sentence that is in the active voice, and a **P** if the sentence is in the passive voice.

EXAMPLE ▶ __P__ **Dr. Lee was chosen by the hospital committee to head the research on heart disease.**

A 1. Rock climbers often try to reach the top of Half Dome in Zion National Park.

A 2. Strong winds blew down the trees.

P 3. While hiking through the woods, I was sprayed by a skunk hiding in the bushes.

A 4. President Theodore Roosevelt started the National Park System.

P 5. The movie that won the Academy Award this year has never been seen by us.

A 6. Hans lowered his voice to a whisper during the concert.

A 7. Everyone was asked to contribute to sending the diving team to the Pan American games, but not everyone sent a contribution.

A 8. Waves crashed on the shore, and the wind blew boats from the water onto land during the hurricane.

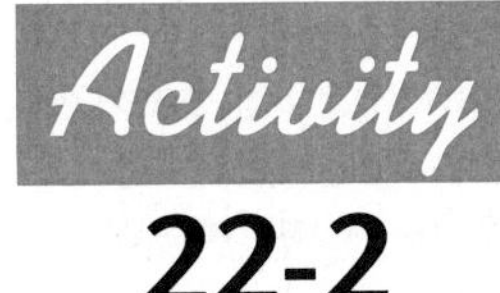

22-2

DIRECTIONS: Write an **A** on the line to the left of a sentence that is in the active voice, and a **P** if the sentence is in the passive voice. On the lines below each sentence, **change the active voice sentences into the passive voice and the passive voice sentences into the active voice.** Remember that you form the passive voice by joining some form of the verb "to be" with the past participle of a verb. You may have to vary the wording when you change the voice, but keep the idea of each sentence.

EXAMPLE  *A* **The office manager ordered executive desks for everyone in the department.**

Executive desks were ordered by the office manager for everyone in the department.

P 1. Trees were planted along the parkway by the civic group to which I belong.

The civic group to which I belong planted trees along the parkway

A 2. Burglars broke into the jewelry store during the night.

The jewelry store was broken into during the night by burglars.

A 3. A construction crew is repaving the highway near my house this week.

The highway near my house is being repaved this week by a construction crew.

A 4. Sponsors of the state lottery invited the winners to a party.

Winners of the state lottery were invited to a party by the lottery sponsors.

A 5. Two police officers routed traffic away from the scene of the serious accident.

Traffic was routed away from the scene of the serious accident by two police officers.

P 6. The lawn mower was broken by someone who was careless.

Someone who was careless broke the mower.

P 7. All the change from her coin purse was used up by the parking meters.

She used up all the change in her coin purse for the parking meters .

P 8. Individual copies of the exam were distributed to each student by the teacher.

The teacher distributed individual copies of the exam to each student.

22-3

Answers to this *Activity* are in the Instructor's Section.

DIRECTIONS: The following paragraph is written mostly in the passive voice. On your own paper, rewrite it in the active voice.

> In the early days of Arizona, many city jails were built of adobe by the townspeople. Such jails were dug out of by inmates. Escapes were made by them often and easily. A miner named Margarito Verala was hired by the town of Clifton to build an escape-proof jail. The jail was carved out of solid rock by Verala. The job was finished by Verala and his pay was taken to a saloon. He wanted a toast drunk to himself for what he did. The other drinkers didn't want to do that, so a hole was shot in the ceiling by Verala. For doing that, the jail he built was tried out by Verala as its first inmate.
>
> (Adapted from *Arizona Highways,* June 1991: 47)

When Passive Voice Might be Preferable

Although writing in the active voice is almost always preferred to that in the passive voice, three writing situations for which you might deliberately choose to use the passive voice are:

- **If the person (or animal) performing the action is unknown.**

  Mario's home was burglarized while he was on vacation.

- **If the object of the action is more important than the one who performed it.**

  First prize in the junior science fair was awarded to Hilary.

- **If the writer, or another person, doesn't want to take responsibility for something.**

  The budget cuts were passed, despite a plea from parents that less money would surely result in less education for their children.

This last reason is why many government documents are written in the passive voice; if something goes wrong or turns out to be unpopular, there's nobody to blame!

Tense and Time: An Overview

The tense of a verb tells about the time that an action by or about the subject takes place: in the past, the present, or the future. The **simple tenses** are, therefore, called by those names:

- **Present Tense**—an action is now happening:

  The children **study** their books.

- **Past Tense**—an action has already happened:

  The children **studied** their books.

- **Future Tense**—an action will happen:

  The children **will study** their books.

All these become the building blocks for the **perfect tenses.** "Perfect" means "completed." That is, an action begun by one verb (either stated or implied) is completed by another verb. The perfect tenses give a writer flexibility to express other kinds of time:

- **Present Perfect Tense**—action begun earlier has just ended:

  The children **have studied** their books.

- **Past Perfect Tense**—action completed before another took place:

  The children **had studied** their books.

- **Future Perfect Tense**—action begun that will be completed at a stated time in the future:

  The children **will have studied** their books.

There are also **progressive tenses** of verbs. They show that an action is going on during the time that the verb in the sentence indicates. So, there are **Present Progressive** (The children *are studying.)*, **Past Progressive** (The children *were studying.*), and **Future Progressive** (The children *will be studying.*) tenses.

The important point about all these tenses for you as a writer is to know that English gives you words to express time *very exactly.* If you choose the right tense, the verbs of a sentence will tell your readers just what you want them to know about time.

To form the tense you need for a verb, you must know its principal parts. Every verb has four principal parts:

Present **Past** **Present Participle** **Past Participle**

You must also know that there are both **regular verbs** and **irregular verbs.** The principal parts of all regular verbs are formed in the same way. Fortunately, most verbs are regular, and once you learn how to form those parts for one verb, you can apply the same rule to other regular verbs.

Irregular verbs are so called because, except for the present participle, their principal parts are formed by changes *within* the word itself.

The present participle for both regular and irregular verbs is formed by adding *–ing* to the simple present of the verb. Therefore, the present participle is often omitted from charts showing the principal parts of verbs. (Sometimes, it is not even mentioned in books as a principal part.)

Probably the main use of the present participle is in the Progressive Tenses. There, it is used with a helping verb that is some form of "to be."

Regular Verbs

Consider the **infinitive** form of a verb—**"to" + a verb**—as a starting point: Examples:

to walk

to shop

to play

to copy

to dance

Take away the "to," and what remains is the **verb stem**. From the verb stem will be created the various forms of a verb as it appears within a sentence.

Principal Parts of Regular Verbs

Present	*Past*	*Past Participle*
walk	**walked**	**walked**
shop	**shopped**	**shopped**
play	**played**	**played**
copy	**copied**	**copied**
dance	**danced**	**danced**

As you can see from this short sample of regular verbs, the Past Participle form is the same as the simple Past Tense. It is always shown and spoken of as a separate part, however, because it is used in some special ways, as when it is joined with some form of "to be" to form the passive voice. (See page 352.)

If you are not sure of the principal parts of a verb, check a dictionary. Many dictionaries show them either immediately after the verb stem, at the beginning of an entry, or at the end of an entry.

Verb forms show number and person. **Number**, of course, means that the verb will be either **singular or plural**, depending on the subject of the sentence. **Person** means how the writer addresses the reader. For convenience, charts such as the one on the next page show the pronoun to illustrate person.

	Singular	*Plural*
1st Person (writer speaks)	**I**	**we**
2nd Person (writer speaks to reader)	**you**	**you**
3rd Person (writer speaks about someone or something)	**he** **she** **it**	**they**

Knowing the verb forms is necessary for writing so that you can make the verb agree with the subject in a sentence, as Chapter 21 pointed out.

The verb of a sentence must agree in number and person with the subject of the sentence.

PRESENT TENSE ENDINGS AND AGREEMENT

In order to make the subject and verb of a sentence agree in the Present Tense, you will need to use the correct form of the verb.

Add *–s* or *–es* to the Present Tense of a regular verb if the subject is a single person, animal, or thing, or a third-person pronoun.

The Present Tense of a regular verb remains the same in first and second person singular, and in all plurals.

EXAMPLES ▶ **My cat plays with my dog.**
Judy washes her car every Sunday.
One gear engages another to make the clock run.
He launders the clothes almost daily.
It proves we are right!
I clean my closet every season.
They study together.

22-4

DIRECTIONS: Underline the proper Present Tense verb form from those in parentheses in each of the following sentences.

EXAMPLE ▶ **A pasta diet (contain / <u>contains</u>) very little Vitamin B.**

lives
ride
causes
work
looks

1. Casandra now (live / lives) in a new house.
2. I (ride / rides) the subway to work.
3. Too much coffee (cause / causes) insomnia and nervousness.
4. Ellen and Terry (work / works) in the bookstore at school.
5. Superman (look / looks) down on the city as he flies.

jumps

uses

scrapes

6. Because Bill practices, he now (jump / jumps) further than anyone who goes to the health club.
7. Swimming (use / uses) more calories than walking does.
8. Tom (scrapes/ scraped) off the old paint before sanding the walls.

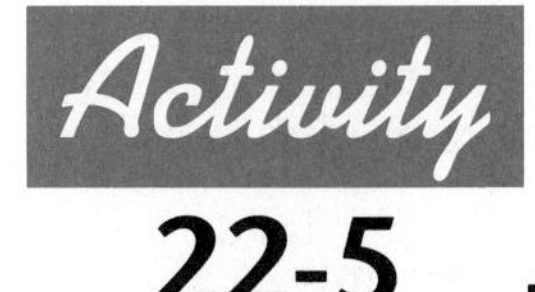

22-5

DIRECTIONS: To the left of each sentence is a verb in bold type. On the blank line in the sentence, write the form of that verb in the Present Tense so it agrees with the subject.

EXAMPLE  **engage** **He** ___*engages*___ **me in conversation near the water cooler every day.**

make
holds
run
helps
seems
beats
relaxes
focuses

1. **make** Eating too much can __________________ people fat.
2. **hold** The suitcase ______________ all my clothes for the trip.
3. **run** Every morning the joggers ______________ through the park.
4. **help** On Thanksgiving my club usually __________ serve dinner to hundreds of needy people.
5. **seem** The flea market in town _______ more crowded than usual.
6. **beat** Your pulse ______________ regularly when you are healthy.
7. **relax** An ocean cruise __________ almost everybody who takes one.
8. **focus** Steve _______ the camera carefully before snapping a picture.

PAST TENSE ENDINGS AND AGREEMENT

In order to make the subject and verb of a sentence agree in the Past Tense, you will have to use the correct form of the verb.

My cat played with my dog.
Judy washed her car every Sunday.

Form the Past Tense of a regular verb by adding *–d* or *–ed* to a verb stem

EXAMPLES ▶ **One gear engaged another to make the clock run.**
He laundered the clothes almost daily.
It proved we are right!
I cleaned my closet every season.
They studied together.

22-6

DIRECTIONS: Underline the correct form of the simple Past Tense verb in each of the following sentences.

EXAMPLE ▶ I (vote / voted) in every election.

heard
started
refused
opened
buttoned
filmed
cleared
exercised

1. The dog (hear / heard) a whistle that a human cannot.
2. The car (starts/ started) easily, even in cold weather.
3. She (refused / refuse) to be put on welfare because she would rather earn her own way.
4. The bomb squad (opening /opened) the package very carefully.
5. A woman living in my apartment house (buttoned / button) a fur-trimmed coat on her pet dog.
6. During Operation Desert Shield, many local television stations (film / filmed) messages from folks at home to service people.
7. The smoke finally (clearing / cleared) and everyone could see how badly the building was damaged.
8. They (exercised / exercise / exercises) daily to stay in good health.

22-7

DIRECTIONS: Some of the Past Tense verbs are correct in the following sentences, but some are not. If the verb is correct, put a C on the line after the sentence. If the verb is *not* correct, put an X through the wrong verb form and write the correct one on the line after the sentence.

EXAMPLE  **The old office computer ~~work~~ too slowly to keep up with everything in this office.**

worked

1. Addy ~~carry~~ a full briefcase with her to work every day.

   carried

2. The college registrar added classes to accommodate students.

   C

3. Mother always ~~bake~~ a cake or cookies for after-school snacks.

   baked

4. In the last basketball game, players ~~bounce~~ the ball from one end of the court to the other.

   bounced

5. After the picnic, everyone ~~rest~~ under the shady trees.

   rested

6. Hugo ~~look~~ tired after he won second place in the 10K race.

   looked

7. I tried to get a ticket for the football game but none was available.

   C

8. Arturo always ~~dream~~ of being on a pro baseball team.

   dreamed

22-8

The answers to this *Activity* are in the Instructor's Section.

DIRECTIONS: On your own paper, rewrite the paragraph below so that all the verbs not already in the Past Tense are put into the Past Tense. Then, circle the verbs you changed.

Helmut was surprised that his geology course turn out to be so interesting. The teacher lecture, show slides and movies, and test the class fairly and often. The section of the course about how great land plates move and therefore change the appearance of the earth's surface was new information to him. Helmut learn about how large land masses lift to form mountains and plateaus. Other land masses press together until they buckle and became mountains. As glaciers move slowly toward the sea and rivers cut through mountains, the surface of the earth also change. Helmut also discover that rocks, coal, and minerals develop because of great heat and pressure within the earth.

REMINDER: The **four principal parts of a verb are the Present, the Present Participle, the Past, and the Past Participle.** The verb stem is the Present of a regular verb. All regular verbs form the Present Participle by adding *-ing* to the verb stem. All regular verbs form the Past Participle in the same way as they form the Past Tense: by adding *-d* or *ed* to the Present Tense.

Activity

22-9

DIRECTIONS: Fill in the blanks to make a complete chart showing the principal parts of the regular verbs on each line.

Present	Present Participle	Past	Past Participle
1. skip	skipping	skipped	skipped
2. hop	hopping	hopped	hopped
3. scream	screaming	screamed	screamed
4. help	helping	helped	helped
5. ask	asking	asked	asked
6. paint	painting	painted	painted
7. dismiss	dismissing	dismissed	dismissed
8. correct	correcting	corrected	corrected
9. watch	watching	watched	watched
10. change	changing	changed	changed

USING THE FUTURE TENSE

The simple Future Tense is the easiest one to write because the verb stem does not change. Instead, the word "shall" is combined with the word stem (Present Tense) for the first person, and the word "will" for second and third person. Both singular and plural are the same.

	Singular	**Plural**
1st Person	I shall call	we shall call
2nd Person	you will call	you will call
3rd Person	he, she, it will call	they will call

Even this simple form is changing. When was the last time you ever heard a person on the phone say, "I shall call you back"? Probably never. Nor are you likely to. Nowadays, "will" is so often substituted for "shall" that it is surprising to many people to read the word, and even more surprising to have to use it.

22-10

DIRECTIONS: After each number is a regular verb stem and a simple tense. Write the correct verb form in the blank space in the sentence that follows.

EXAMPLE ▶ **help - past tense**
Impala received a community service award because she *helped* **so many people.**

1. **braid - present tense**
   The hairdresser ______________ so many people's hair daily she could almost do it in her sleep.
2. **print - future tense**
   This new printer ______________ a thousand pages in half the time the old printer took to do the job.
3. **fix - present tense**
   My mechanic ______________ cars for a very fair price.
4. **call - future tense**
   "Mr. Lee ______________ you by 10 a.m."
5. **collect - past tense**
   Ray ______________ more than $300 for the Heart Association.
6. **acknowledge - past tense**
   I ______________ that letter the day after it arrived.
7. **bill - present tense**
   The telephone company ______________ my number on the tenth of each month.
8. **work - future tense**
   My son ______________ on the lawn next Saturday for sure.

Answers: braids; will print; fixes; will call; collected; acknowledged; bills; will work

Chapter 23

Irregular Verbs and Verb Agreement in Special Uses

In this chapter you will

- learn the special forms of *to be, to do,* and *to have*
- practice using these verbs alone and as helpers to other verbs
- see how the perfect tenses help you express time in writing
- study and use the principal parts of irregular verbs
- use the past participle and the perfect tenses
- practice subject-verb agreement in the special cases of sentences that
  - begin with "here" or "there"
  - have phrases between the subject and the verb
  - have compound subjects
  - are questions

Three Special Verbs

Three of the shortest verbs are also probably three of the most-used verbs: **to be**, **to do**, and **to have**. They also seem to be troublesome to some writers when they are used by themselves in sentences, and as helpers with other verbs.

Here is listed information for their varied tenses that you read about in Chapter 22.

For the Verb "To Be"

PRESENT TENSE

	Singular		*Plural*	
	Subject	**Verb**	**Subject**	**Verb**
1st Person	I	am	we	are
2nd Person	you	are	you	are
3rd Person	he, she, it	is	they	are

PAST TENSE

	Singular		*Plural*	
	Subject	**Verb**	**Subject**	**Verb**
1st Person	I	was	we	were
2nd Person	you	were	you	were
3rd Person	he, she, it	was	they	were

PRESENT PERFECT TENSE

	Singular		*Plural*	
	Subject	**Verb**	**Subject**	**Verb**
1st Person	I	have been	we	have been
2nd Person	you	have been	you	have been
3rd Person	he, she, it	has been	they	have been

The **Past Perfect Tense** is *"had been"* in each person and in both singular and plural.

The **Future Tense** is *"shall be"* in the first person singular and plural, and *"will be"* in the second and third person singular and plural.

The **Future Perfect Tense** is *"shall have been"* in the first person singular and plural, and *"will have been"* in the second and third person singular and plural.

For the Verb "To Do"

PRESENT TENSE

	Singular		*Plural*	
	Subject	**Verb**	**Subject**	**Verb**
1st Person	I	do	we	do
2nd Person	you	do	you	do
3rd Person	he, she, it	does	they	do

PAST TENSE

	Singular		*Plural*	
	Subject	**Verb**	**Subject**	**Verb**
1st Person	I	did	we	did
2nd Person	you	did	you	did
3rd Person	he, she, it	did	they	did

PRESENT PERFECT TENSE

	Singular		*Plural*	
	Subject	**Verb**	**Subject**	**Verb**
1st Person	I	have done	we	have done
2nd Person	you	have done	you	have done
3rd Person	he, she, it	has done	they	have done

The **Past Perfect Tense** is *"had done"* in each person and in both singular and plural.

The **Future Tense** is *"shall do"* in the first person singular and plural, and *"will do"* in the second and third person singular and plural.

The **Future Perfect Tense** is *"shall have done"* in the first person singular and plural, and *"will have done"* in the second and third person singular and plural.

For the Verb "To Have"

PRESENT TENSE

	Singular		*Plural*	
	Subject	**Verb**	**Subject**	**Verb**
1st Person	I	have	we	have
2nd Person	you	have	you	have
3rd Person	he, she, it	has	they	have

PAST TENSE

	Singular		*Plural*	
	Subject	**Verb**	**Subject**	**Verb**
1st Person	I	had	we	had
2nd Person	you	had	you	had
3rd Person	he, she, it	had	they	had

PRESENT PERFECT TENSE

	Singular		*Plural*	
	Subject	**Verb**	**Subject**	**Verb**
1st Person	I	have had	we	have had
2nd Person	you	have had	you	have had
3rd Person	he, she, it	has had	they	have had

The **Past Perfect Tense** is *"had had"* in each person and in both singular and plural.

The **Future Tense** is *"shall have"* in the first person singular and plural, and *"will have"* in the second and third person singular and plural.

The **Future Perfect Tense** is *"shall have had"* in the first person singular and plural, and *"will have had"* in the second and third person singular and plural.

REMINDER: The subject and verb in every sentence must agree in person and number.

23-1

DIRECTIONS: Underline the correct **present tense** form of the verb "to be," "to do," or "to have" in each sentence.

EXAMPLE ▶ **The male cardinal bird (have / <u>has</u> / had) bright red feathers.**

is
is
are
are
does
do
have
has

1. Zoyla (is / are / were / was) in Spain visiting her relatives.
2. Psychology (be / has been / were / is) the study of mental processes and behavior.
3. You (are / is / have been) right to get a protractor so you can do your math homework.
4. Great underground pressures (have been / are / is / been) responsible for creating oil and natural gas.
5. A painter in our neighborhood (done / does / do) an art demonstration for the public school children every year.
6. If you (to do / does / do / done) this favor for me, I will always be grateful.
7. The coaches of the basketball team (have / has / had) the trophy the team won last year.
8. Michiko (had / to have/ have had / has) some knowledge of Japanese, so she can speak with her grandparents when she visits them.

23-2

DIRECTIONS: Underline the correct **past tense** form of the verb "to be," "to do," or "to have" in each sentence.

EXAMPLE ▶ **We (have /<u>had</u>/ will have had) to run for cover when the rain began.**

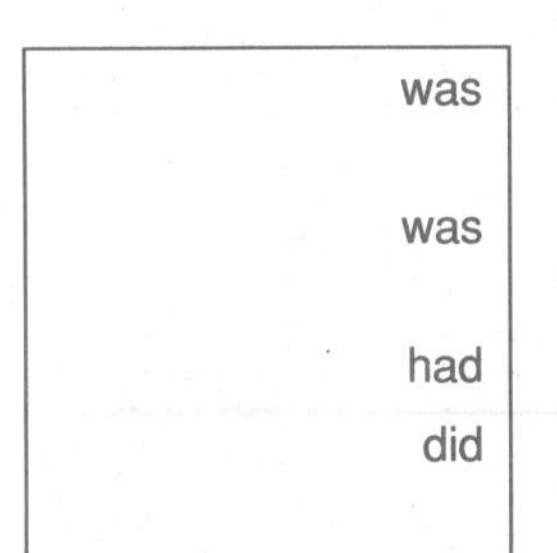

1. Ciro (were / have been / was / is) behind the goal post when the winning point for the kick after a touchdown sailed through the uprights.
2. Accounting (was / be / were / is) not a course required for business majors when I was in college.
3. So you finally (have / had / will have had) enough pizza!
4. They (do / did / have done) not honor our movie passes because a special film was playing.

did
had
were
had

5. Millie and I (do / did / have done) the only possible thing; we left.
6. Even my dog (had / have / done had) too much to eat at the family reunion picnic.
7. Dick and Rick (was / were / be / are) balloon masters for the sunrise races last weekend.
8. If I (had / have / done / shall have had) received your message, I would have called back.

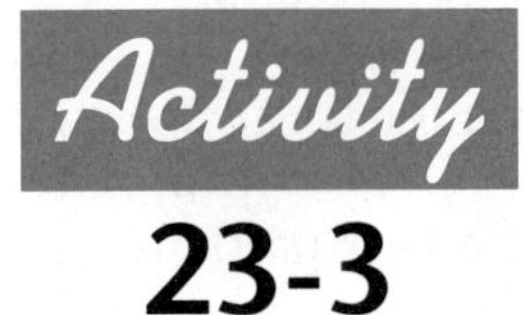

23-3

DIRECTIONS: On the basis of clues in the wording and content of each sentence, decide if the verb should be in the present tense or the past tense. Then, write the correct form of *to be, to do,* or *to have* on the line to complete each sentence.

EXAMPLE ▶ **After the tree was cut down, the birds** *did* **not have their nest any more.**

have
were
is
do
had
did
are
Did

1. I ______________ to go to the grocery store in ten minutes.
2. William and Mary ______________ joint British rulers from 1689 to 1702.
3. The yacht belonging to Queen Elizabeth II of Great Britain ____ one of the largest private ships now afloat.
4. "Two wrongs ____________ not make a right," is an old saying.
5. My family ______________ season football tickets last year.
6. The Smiths ______________ not realize they had parked in front of a fire hydrant until they saw a ticket on the car.
7. I often hear someone in my family say to me, "You __________ now the first in the family to go to college."
8. ______________ Sybil wash the dishes last night?

23-4

The answer to this *Activity* is in the Instructor's Section.

DIRECTIONS: This paragraph is in the present tense. On your own paper, rewrite it in the past tense.

Monument Valley, Utah, is an almost unheard-of place in the 1930s when the film director John Ford learns about it. Ford decides he has to set some of his westerns in that beautiful place. So he does what any other film director would do: he has scripts write that take place in Monument Valley. Then there is only one location on which to shoot them: in Monument Valley itself. So he does that. However, first he has to arrange for the Navajo nation to give permission to shoot film on their land. Ford also finds he needs many Native Americans for the big scenes that show off the valley landscape so well. So that the scenes are accurate, Ford hires many of the Navajo people for his films.

Sharing

Form a group with at least two other people in the class. Share your version of *Activity 23-4* and see where your work is the same as and different from the past tense paragraph of others in the group.

Using The Perfect Tenses

Look at back at the three special verb charts—as well as the overview of tense and time on page 344—and you will see that all the perfect tenses use some form of "to have" as helpers with a past participle of a verb. The past tense and the past participle of regular verbs are all formed by adding ***–d*** or ***–ed*** to the present tense. The following activity will let you try expressing ideas in some of the perfect tenses.

23-5

DIRECTIONS: Each of the following statements can be expressed in fewer words than appear here if you use the appropriate perfect tense. The verb stem to use as the main verb in the sentence is in capital letters at the end of the descriptive sentence. Rewrite each sentence using the appropriate perfect tense (that is, the correct form of "to have" + the past participle of the main verb).

EXAMPLE  **Marilyn began sewing a new dress last week and just completed it. SEW**

Marilyn has sewed a new dress.

1. The botany class began a field trip this morning and will be back at school at a stated time in the future: the time of normal dismissal. COMPLETE

   The botany class will have completed its field trip at the normal school dismissal time.

   —future perfect

2. I began baking some cookies this morning and they were finished in time for the charity bake sale. BAKE

   I have baked some cookies for the charity bake sale.*—present perfect*

3. The orchestra performed at twelve wedding receptions before it went on to its next booking. PLAY

   The orchestra had played at twelve other wedding receptions. *—past perfect*

4. Mitchell's Drug Store began a redecorating project six weeks ago and now that it is completed, the store is ready for customers again. OPEN

   Mitchell's Drug Store has opened its redecorated store. *—present perfect*

5. The tires on the car take a while to rotate, so I began doing the job earlier in the day and now will be finished with that job by the time I want to use the car. ROTATE

   I will have rotated the tires before I use the car again. *—future perfect*

Irregular Verbs

Earlier you learned that verbs may be classified as regular or irregular. Regular verbs follow the same patterns for their present tense third person forms and references to singular people, animals, or things. Both the past tense and past participle of regular verbs are made by adding ***–d*** or ***–ed*** to the verb stem.

About the only thing regular and irregular verbs have in common is that both form the present participle by adding *-ing* to the present tense. Therefore, the present participle is usually omitted from lists of the principal parts of verbs.

Irregular verbs do not follow a particular pattern of change from one principal part to another. Instead, changes are internal. The past tense and past participle may be identical to or different from each other. Or, the three principal parts may all be the same.

There are so many irregular verbs that the following list can show only a few of them. If you need to find the past tense or past participle of a verb not shown here, check a dictionary.

Three Principal Parts Of Irregular Verbs

PRESENT	PAST	PAST PARTICIPLE
arise	arose	arisen
beat	beat	beaten
become	became	become
begin	began	begun
bid	bid	bid
bid	bade	bidden
bind	bound	bound
bite	bit	bitten
blow	blew	blown
break	broke	broken
bring	brought	brought
burst	burst	burst
buy	bought	bought
catch	caught	caught
choose	chose	chosen
cling	clung	clung
come	came	come
cost	cost	cost
deal	dealt	dealt
dig	dug	dug
dive	dived	dived
do	did	done
draw	drew	drawn
drive	drove	driven
drown	drowned	drowned
eat	ate	eaten
fall	fell	fallen
feed	fed	fed
fight	fought	fought
find	found	found
fly	flew	flown

PRESENT	PAST	PAST PARTICIPLE
forget	forgot	forgotten
forsake	forsook	forsaken
freeze	froze	frozen
get	got	gotten
give	gave	given
go	went	gone
grow	grew	grown
hear	heard	heard
hide	hid	hidden
hold	held	held
keep	kept	kept
know	knew	known
lay	laid	lain
lead	led	led
leave	left	left
lend	lent	lent
lie	lay	lain
light	lit	lit
lose	lost	lost
make	made	made
mean	meant	meant
pay	paid	paid
put	put	put
raise	raised	raised
read	read	read
rid	rid	rid
ride	rode	ridden
ring	rang	rung
rise	rose	risen
run	ran	run
say	said	said
see	saw	seen
sell	sold	sold
send	sent	sent
shake	shook	shaken
shine	shone (shined)	shone (shined)
shoot	shot	shot
show	showed	shown
shrink	shrank	shrunk
sing	sang	sung
sink	sank	sunk
sit	sat	sat
speak	spoke	spoken
spring	sprang	sprung
stand	stood	stood
steal	stole	stolen
stride	strode	strode
strike	struck	struck
strive	strove	striven
swear	swore	sworn
swim	swam	swum
swing	swung	swung

PRESENT	PAST	PAST PARTICIPLE
take	took	taken
teach	taught	taught
tear	tore	torn
tell	told	told
think	thought	thought
throw	threw	thrown
wake	woke, waked	waked,wakened
wear	wore	worn
win	won	won
write	wrote	written

23-6

DIRECTIONS: Circle the correct past tense verb in each of the following sentences. Most of them are irregular verbs, but a few are regular verbs.

EXAMPLE ▶ The president (flied / <u>flew</u>) overseas to the meeting in "Air Force One."

1. A school child (blew / blowed) the detective's cover.
2. In the living room was a Chinese teapot which she (buyed / bought) on a recent visit to the flea market.
3. Students are now (teached / taught) basic statistical terms in middle school.
4. Voters (went / goed) to the polls in decreasing percentages over the past five years.
5. Last month the stockholders (chose / choosed) a new president.
6. What (came / come) out at the investigation led to a complete replacement of all the top managers at the agency.
7. Tutors (helped / help) students who were having trouble in social studies class.
8. Yesterday the School Board (decided / decide) there would be a six-period school day beginning in September.
9. If Marietha (lose / lost) the earrings I let her wear, she will have to replace them.
10. Jonathon (kept / keep) the secret just as he said he would do.

blew
bought
taught
went
chose
came
helped
decided
lost
kept

23-7

DIRECTIONS: All the main verbs in the following sentences should be in the past tense. Draw a line through any that is not and write the correct form above the word. If there is no error in the sentence, write a *C* on the line to the left of the sentence number.

EXAMPLE ▶ Hard-working police ~~catched~~ *caught* the thief easily.

____ 1. Volunteers ~~feeded~~ fed more than 200 homeless people last night in this city.

__C__ 2. Street lights lit up the neighborhood, making us all feel safe.

rose

____ 3. Balloons ~~rised~~ slowly over the city after thousands of them were released during halftime of the football game.

led

____ 4. Michael Jordan ~~leaded~~ the scoring for his team almost every year.

sold

____ 5. LLP Realty Company ~~selled~~ the house down the street from me, so I will let them try to sell my house, too.

sprang

____ 6. Hundreds of volunteers ~~springed~~ into action to keep flood waters from doing too much damage in the city.

__C__ 7. The abacus, a counting frame of beads on wires, used at the nursery school was a gift from a math teacher.

____ 8. The great scientist Charles Darwin, born in England in 1809, was ~~bringed~~ up in a family that did little to encourage inquiry.

brought

Activity 23-8

DIRECTIONS: Next to each sentence number is the present tense of a word. Use the sense of the sentence as a guide and fill in the blank with either the present tense or the past tense of that word.

EXAMPLE ▶ find **Robert finally** *found* **the missing card after rummaging through every drawer in his desk.**

built

have won

breaks

bound

burst

wore

choose

shot

1. **build** It is remarkable that the ancient Romans ____________ the roads and aqueducts they did all over present day Europe.
2. **win** Ecology projects ______________ first prizes at the science fair for the past three years.
3. **break** If the measuring equipment ____________ one more time we will have to replace it.
4. **bind** The robber entered the house, ________ and gagged two members of the family who were home, and got away with money and jewels.
5. **burst** That the dam did not ____________ seemed a miracle to the engineers monitoring it.
6. **wear** The bride broke with tradition when she _____________ a green velvet wedding gown.
7. **choose** Please _____________ the team members now, because the rest of us may want to go home.
8. **shoot** In the early days of the movie industry, all films were _________ outdoors because the natural light was necessary.

23-9

DIRECTIONS: Edit this paragraph from the present tense to the past tense by putting a line through each verb that should be in the past tense and writing the correct form above it. (Some verbs are regular and some are irregular.)

thought ran
I never ~~think~~ much about seeds until I ~~run~~ across a

learned
book on the subject at the library. Then I ~~learn~~ some

found
surprising information. Some seeds of grain were ~~find~~

were
thousands of years after they ~~are~~ put in Egyptian tombs, yet

sprouted
they have ~~sprout~~ before the watchful eyes of scientists today.

built-in
The seeds of some desert plants have ~~build-in~~ rain gauges and

will sprout when enough moisture reaches them. The book

showed looked had saw
~~shows~~ seeds that ~~look~~ as if they ~~have~~ wings. I also ~~see~~

were shot
pictures of seeds that ~~are shoot~~ from their plants and others

had helped
that ~~have~~ parachutes that ~~help~~ them move over great

learned
distances. I ~~learn~~ that birds, other animals, and the wind

transported
~~transport~~ still other seeds.

Sharing

Form a group with two other people in the class who have done *Activity 23-9* and share your rewriting with them. Be sure all the verbs are in the past tense. Discuss any differences among the paragraphs.

Using Past Participles of Irregular Verbs

To write about an action begun by one verb and completed by another, you must use some form of the verb *"to have"* + the past participle of a verb. The form of the helping verb *"to have"* depends on whether the action is in the present, past, or future, if the subject is singular or plural. These are called the perfect tenses, in the sense that "perfect" means "completed."

- **Present Perfect Tense:**

  action begun earlier is continuing

  The final testing of the rocket **has begun**.

- **Past Perfect Tense:**

  action completed before another took place

  The final testing of the rocket **had begun** before the contract was signed.

- **Future Perfect Tense:**

  action begun that will be completed at a stated time in the future

  The final testing of the rocket **will have begun** by the time Congress considers a budget for its further development.

Words such as "not," "never," "only," "just" and similar words are never part of a verb, even though they may come between other verb parts in a sentence.

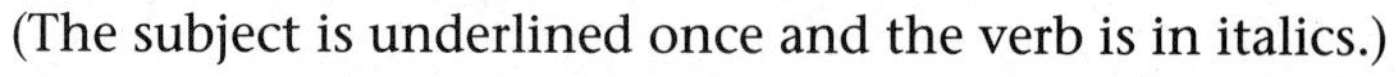

EXAMPLES ▶ (The subject is underlined once and the verb is in italics.)

The final testing of the rocket *will* not *have begun* by the time Congress considers a budget for its further development.

The final testing of the rocket *had* just *begun* when the contract was signed.

23-10

DIRECTIONS: Circle the present perfect tense verb (that is, a helping verb + a past participle) in each of the following sentences. Underline the subject of the sentence and draw an arrow pointing from the verb back to the subject of the sentence. Be sure the helping part of the verb agrees in number with the subject.

EXAMPLE ▶ **The zoning board has broken every promise it made to the people about land use.**

1. Passengers on the rented fishing boat have caught a record number of fish so far today.
2. Josh has written such a good poem for class that the rest of us will have to try to improve our own.
3. The antenna has broken, but I am putting it back on.
4. Half the plants have grown taller than expected and they continue to grow.
5. The guests had not left by midnight, so they were probably having a good time.
6. Herbert has not made that dessert in such a long time that he is in the kitchen now looking up the recipe.
7. Miranda has shaken the little bank as hard as she could to get the money out, but coins still seem to be in it.
8. Many birds have already flown back here and others continue to arrive daily.

23-11

(The regular past tense verb is underlined, the past perfect tense verb is shown in bold face.)

phoned	**had left**
blew	**had taken**
had found	meant
went	**had written**
were	
had broken	
met	**had driven**
thought	**had gotten**
had known	was

The past perfect tense indicates that one action was completed before another took place. Therefore, there will be two verbs in a sentence containing the past perfect tense; one in the regular past tense and the other, the one in the past perfect tense, "had" plus the past participle.

DIRECTIONS: In each sentence, underline the regular past tense verb once and the past perfect tense verb twice.

EXAMPLE ▶ **After we had sat in the waiting room for half an hour, we discovered the doctor had already left the office.**

1. Dale phoned after David had left for work.
2. The live oak seed blew into our yard and by the following year had taken root, so we now have a tree in an unexpected place.
3. I had found my bank account short, although I meant to pay the bill last week.
4. Magaly went to the office at 7 a.m. and had written all her memos by nine o'clock.
5. Surprisingly, the swimmers who were the youngest in their age groups had broken every club timing record by the end of the day.
6. After Harry met Sally through a computer match, they had driven across the country.
7. Six patients in the experiment thought they had gotten the real medicine instead of the useless look-alike.
8. If only the pirates had known the treasure was under a false deck.

23-12

DIRECTIONS: The present tense of an irregular verb appears directly after the number of each sentence. Complete the sentence by writing in the blank space the indicated perfect tense of that verb.

EXAMPLE ▶ **make** **The charity's leaders are certain that by the end of the day they will** *have made* **enough on the raffle to keep the shelter home open for another six months.**

had brought
bought
had taken
have been bound
had heard
have heard
had eaten
have decorated

1. **bring** When the tennis players saw that someone _______________ new balls, they resumed playing the match.
2. **buy** Ice hockey is such an exciting sport that Randy has __________ season tickets to see the local team.
3. **take** The nurse _____________my temperature before I saw the doctor.
4. **bind** The book will ________________ in leather by the time the company presents it to you.
5. **hear** Everyone in town probably ______________ the rumor before I did.
6. **hear** If you ______________________ it, I don't want to know.
7. **eat** Juan didn't know if food would be served at the board meeting, so he _______________________ before he went to it.
8. **light** In an effort to make a traditional Scandinavian Christmas, Helga and Sven _____________________ their tree with real candles.

Subject–Verb Agreement in Special Uses

You already know that subjects and verbs in a sentence must agree in number. The subject tells who or what the sentence is about and the verb tells who or what does what. Ordinarily, in English sentences the subject appears first and the verb follows right behind. Therefore, as soon as you decide whether the subject is singular or plural, you will know if you must make the verb singular or plural.

However, we also use a number of sentence constructions that may be confusing to writers. They are sentences that:

- begin with "Here" or "There" followed by a verb (before the subject)
- have phrases between the subject and verb
- have a compound subject
- are questions

SENTENCES THAT BEGIN WITH "HERE" OR "THERE"

Here are some sentences that begin with words (in bold type) that cannot be their subjects:

Here are the reports you wanted.

Here stood the blacksmith's shop.

There is a fly in my soup!

There go two iguanas crawling along the telephone wire.

Use the test of asking who or what each sentence is about and you will find the subject of each sentence above; it is underlined once, below. If you then ask what the subject does or is, you will find the verb in each of the sentences; it is in italics. Notice that a singular subject has a singular verb and a plural subject has a plural verb.

Here *are* the reports you wanted.

Here *stood* the blacksmith's shop.

There *is* a fly in my soup.

There *go* two iguanas *crawling* along the telephone wire.

The verb always appears before the subject in sentences that begin with "here" or "there."

The subjects and verbs of sentences that begin with "Here" or "There" still agree in number. You can easily turn the sentences around to a more usual construction by moving the first word to another place in the sentence. Examples are: "The reports you wanted *are* here," or "Two iguanas *are crawling* along the telephone wire there."

23-13

DIRECTIONS: Underline the subject once and the verb twice in each sentence below.

EXAMPLE ▶ There is a shortage of male teachers in elementary schools.

(The verb is shown in bold face).

is	example
comes	bride
goes	groom
is	marker
is	photo
stampeded	herd
are	thousands
comes	sun

1. Here is an example of a report you can write on the computer.
2. Here comes the bride.
3. There goes the groom.
4. Here is the newest marker on the "Walk of the Stars."
5. There is a photo of my mother as a child.
6. Here stampeded a herd of buffalo when Jose was a child.
7. There are thousands of cans to be taken to the recycling station.
8. Here comes the sun out again from behind the clouds.

23-14

DIRECTIONS: Fill in a singular or plural verb so it will agree with the subject of each sentence. Try to choose verbs other than variations of "to be" for some of the sentences.

EXAMPLE ▶ Here *is* the drawing pencil you asked for.

are
are
is
are
are
come
go
was

1. Here are cooks preparing a barbecue for 300 people.
2. There are pastry chefs decorating cakes and cookies for the banquet.
3. There is an early flight that will get you to the state capital in time for a full business day.
4. Here are the plans for a new community center.
5. There are always foods that are strange to me when I travel to other countries.
6. Here come the hot air balloons for the annual Memorial Day race.
7. There go the marathon racers past my window.
8. There was a ship aground here, but it was finally pulled off the sand bar.

SENTENCES WITH PHRASES BETWEEN THE SUBJECT AND VERB

When the subject and verb of a sentence are separated by other words, sometimes there is concern over the verb. Should it be singular or plural? The problem is particularly troubling if the subject is a singular and the separating words conclude with a noun ending in *–s*; unwary writers may become confused and think the verb should agree with a plural. It shouldn't.

The verb should agree with the subject of a sentence in number, even if the two are separated in the sentence.

In the following examples, the subject of the sentence is underlined once and the verb is in italic. Notice that they agree in number.

The alarm clock which is next to my radio on the night table *wakes* me at 7 every morning.

A large box on the shelves next to the books *is* red and blue.

None of the airplane models *flies*.

23-15

DIRECTIONS: Underline the subject once in each sentence and circle the correct verb.

EXAMPLE ▶ **Scientific methods of inquiry (use / uses) techniques developed long ago.**

(The subject is underlined, the correct verb is shown in bold face.)

birds	**demonstrate**
Whales porpoises	**are**
Swimming diving	**give**
machines	**have**
Commissioners	**vote**
Crafts food	**are**
Part	**is**
Tickets	**are**

1. Birds flying through the sky (demonstrate/ demonstrates) aerodynamics.
2. Whales and porpoises, although living in the sea, (is / are) mammals because they breathe air.
3. Swimming and diving in the cool water (gives / give) a relaxing feeling.
4. FAX machines in the home (has / have) revolutionized the way people work outside an office.
5. The Commissioners of our county (vote / votes) on hundreds of applications for zoning changes every month.
6. Crafts and food from each country represented by a student at this school (is / are) on display.
7. Part of the holdings of the museum (is / are) on display, but the rest is in storage.
8. Tickets for the Indy 500, a goal of every racing fan, (is / are) already sold out.

AGREEMENT IN SENTENCES WITH COMPOUND SUBJECTS JOINED BY "AND," "OR," AND "NOR"

A compound subject has two parts that answer the question "Who or what is this sentence about?"

bread and butter (both singular words)

cats and dogs (both plural words)

a frog and three princesses
(one singular word and one plural word)

three bees and a bonnet
(one plural word and one singular word)

That the compound subject has singular or plural words in any combination does not determine whether the verb is singular or plural. Only the connector *"and"* does, because that signifies two parts and therefore a plural subject.

Use a plural verb with a compound subject joined by "and."

EXAMPLES ▶

A cat **and** a dog **are** my constant companions.

Marine life **and** birds **were** affected by the oil that the Iraqis dumped into the Persian Gulf.

Use a singular verb when two singular subjects are joined by "or" or "nor."

EXAMPLES ▶

Either Frank **or** Jerry **drives** carpool this week.

Neither the house **nor** the apartment **was** ready to be painted, so the painters remained idle.

Use a plural verb when two plural subjects are joined by "or" or "nor."

EXAMPLES ▶

Neither the rings **nor** the watches **sell** well at the flea market.

Either the cupcakes **or** the cookies **attract** buyers at the bake sale.

When "or" or "nor" join both a singular and a plural for a subject, the verb agrees with the number of the word nearest to it.

EXAMPLES 

Crayons **or** a drawing pen **produces** reproduction-quality art work.

A drawing pen **or** crayons **produce** reproduction-quality art work.

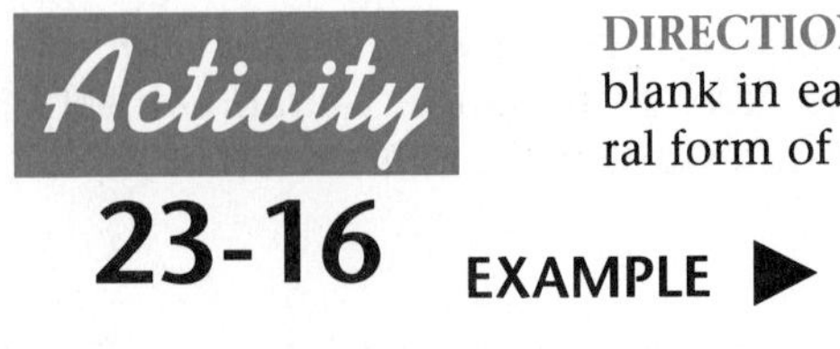

23-16

DIRECTIONS: The infinitive form of a verb is in parentheses just before a blank in each sentence. On the space, write the appropriate singular or plural form of that verb in the present tense to complete the sentence correctly.

EXAMPLE ▶ **A salesperson and a teller (to be) ___*are*___ employees of the month.**

is
win
was
park
enters
bring
makes
make

1. Either carrots or cauliflower (to be) _____ on the special dinner this week.
2. Either a sword or matched pistols always (to win) ________ the prize for most ancient entry in the show.
3. Neither the photographs nor the painting (to be) ________ accepted for the art show last month.
4. A Ford and a Chevrolet (to park) __________ in front of my neighbor's house every evening.
5. By custom, the flight attendants or the pilot (to enter) ____________ the plane first.
6. Swimming and playing baseball (to bring) ____________ children to the park during the summer.
7. Apples or a pineapple (to make) _________ a refreshing summer dessert.
8. Reading and writing (to make) ____________ a literate person.

SUBJECT–VERB AGREEMENT IN QUESTIONS

The subject usually follows the verb in a question. When you write questions, you must decide on the subject of the sentence before you write it so you can get agreement in number between the verb, which you write first, and the subject. Otherwise, you should look for subject-verb agreement when you edit questions you have written.

One way to be sure you have agreement is to turn a question into its own answer. Another is to turn the question into another question, but not one that begins with the same word. The subjects are underlined once and the verbs are in italics in these examples.

EXAMPLES  ***Question:*** **What is the current interest rate on auto loans at this bank?**

Answer: **The current interest rate *is* what on auto loans at this bank?**

Notice that sometimes the verb is more than one word

***Question*:** **Will it rain again tomorrow?**

Answer. **It *will rain* again tomorrow.**

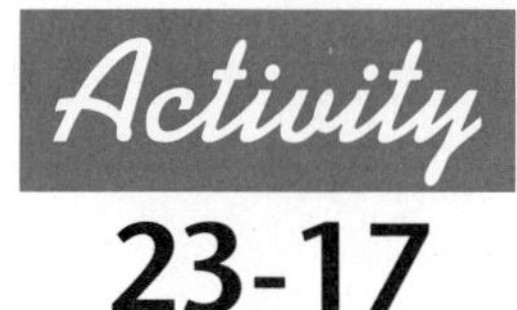

23-17

DIRECTIONS: Change each question into a statement that you write on the lines below. Then underline the subject once and the verb twice for both question and statement. (They should be the same words, of course.)

EXAMPLE ▶ **Who do you think will win the next Super Bowl?**

You do think who will win the next Super Bowl?

Verbs that students are asked to underline twice are shown in bold face.

1. What courses should high school students take in order to be well prepared for college?

   High school students **should take** what courses in order to be prepared well for college?

2. Where did you hide the cookies?

   You **did hide** the cookies where?

3. When do you expect Carla home from shopping?

   You **do expect** Carla home from shopping when?

4. Why are all the flags and pennants hanging across the streets today?

   All the flags and pennants **are hanging** across the streets today for what reason?

6. How did Malcolm get this television set running again?

   Malcolm **did get** this television set running again, how?

7. Do you believe that setting limits on water usage is really doing any good?

   You **do believe** that setting limits on water usage is really doing good.

8. What color scheme would be good for this room?

   A color scheme **would be** good for this room.

Chapter 24

Nouns

In this chapter you will:

- examine how nouns are used in sentences
- identify and use common nouns
- learn about capitalizing proper nouns
- know what a collective noun is and when it agrees with a singular or a plural verb
- form noun plurals
- identify compound nouns and learn how to make them plural
- learn how to make the possessives of nouns

Nouns may have been the first words that people used for communication—words to identify people and things around them. The first words that toddlers learn to say—usually "Mama" and "Dada," or their equivalents in other languages—are nouns. Only after security in naming familiar people and things does a child begin to talk about actions.

Nouns are words that name people, places, or things. Nouns also name ideas and beliefs.

EXAMPLES ▶ **nurse** **city** **toy**
democracy **religion** **people**

One way to find out if a word is a noun is to put "a," "an," or "the" in front of it. (You may have learned that these three words are called "articles.") Try this trick with the six words above that are examples of nouns. At least one of the articles goes with each of them and sounds right. But try the articles with these next words:

happy waltzing courageous sad

Obviously "a happy" and "the sad" don't make sense, so those words cannot be nouns.

CAUTION: Some words can be either nouns or verbs, depending on how they are used in a sentence.

EXAMPLES ▶

The championship fight went 15 rounds.

Fight is a noun and the subject of that sentence.

I will fight for my right to overtime pay.

Fight (together with the helper "will") is a verb and describes an action.

The new doctor in town has a big practice.

Practice is a noun, a naming word in that sentence.

If you practice basketball, you may make the team.

Practice is a verb and tells an action.

How Nouns Work in Sentences

Look at these seven sentences. Each contains the noun "students", but it appears in a different place in each sentence and it works differently in each sentence.

1. The students left without knowing their grades on the test.
2. An increase in tuition shocked the students.
3. The number of students enrolling early has increased recently.
4. The school registrants quickly became students once they began classes.
5. The faculty sent the students a petition.
6. Students, you all earned As.
7. The most powerful people on campus, the students, decided to declare a school holiday next Tuesday.

"Students" is the subject of the sentence in #1. It tells who the sentence is about and the verb "left" tells what the students did. In sentence #2, "students" received the action of the verb, the shock. Technically, that is called a direct object. In sentence #3, "students" is the object of the preposition "of." In sentence #4, "students" renames the subject, which is "registrants." "Students" is an indirect object in sentence #5. In sentence #6 the word "students" is used in direct address, and in sentence #7, the same noun further identifies who the most powerful people on campus are.

These sentences illustrate that although the word "students" appears in sentences in different places and serves different functions (that is, works in different ways), the fact that "students" is a noun doesn't change.

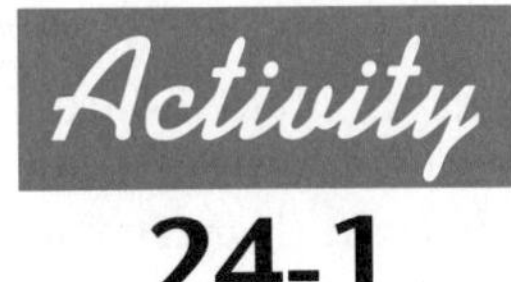

24-1

The answers to this *Activity* are in the Instructor's Section.

DIRECTIONS: Underline all the nouns in this paragraph.

Many people identify with cartoon characters. Surprisingly, the characters that are special favorites are usually losers, not winners. Mickey Mouse was a big hit from his first animated cartoons created by Walt Disney in the 1920s. Even today, he continues to chased by characters bigger and stronger than he is, and he is often on the losing end. Having a girlfriend, Minnie Mouse, is one of the few ways in which he is more fortunate than some other characters in his films. Fred Flintstone, supposedly living in the Stone Age, usually ends up doing what his wife, Wilma, and the children want. That suggests that he, too, is a loser. His counterpart of the future, George Jetson, is always having run-ins with his boss that make him seem like a loser. Charlie Brown, who began life as a character in a comic strip, had a stage musical written about him, and is now featured in film specials, is also a loser. In fact, psychologists and philosophers have written about Charlie Brown. They have tried to analyze his appeal to people of all ages. The latest in this long line of cartoon characters the public has made a big favorite is the Simpson family. Bart Simpson often gets in trouble with his father, but he may be popular because he says things many people think but don't say out loud.

Common and Proper Nouns

A *common* noun names one or more members of a class or group of people or things.

EXAMPLES ▶

hat	**book**	**sister**
college	**boxes**	**women**
months	**tires**	**eye**

Most of the nouns you are likely to use in writing are common nouns. Unless a common noun begins a sentence (and therefore the first letter of the first word is capitalized), it is not capitalized.

A *proper* noun names a particular person, place, or thing. It is always capitalized.

EXAMPLES ▶

Chicago	**Elena**	**France**
Central Park	**English**	**Mickey Mouse**

Many sentences contain one or more common nouns, one or more proper nouns, or a mix of both common and proper nouns.

EXAMPLES ▶ My sister Elena gave me a hat from France.

COMMENT: The common noun is "sister" but Elena is the name of a particular person who is also a sister; it is a proper noun.

Rudolph registered for German, Biology 101, and economics.

COMMENT: "Rudolph" is a particular person and "Biology 101" is a particular course. As the name of a particular language, "German" is always capitalized. The word "economics" in the sentence is not capitalized because it names an area of study but not a particular course.

24-2

DIRECTIONS: In the following sentences, underline each common noun once and each proper noun twice.

EXAMPLE ▶ A girl named Esmeralda asked her mother to buy her a new baseball bat.

Answers to this *Activity* are in the Instructor's Section.

1. By studying hard, the engineering student passed all the exams by a small margin.
2. The growth of home businesses is possibly a result of the weak economy and the fact that many people are tired of commuting.
3. The flowers that bloom in May after a long cold winter uplift the spirits after the long, dreary grey days.
4. "In-line skates," a type of roller skate but with the wheels all in a single row, are rapidly replacing traditional skates in popularity.
5. Alphonse was surprised to meet his high school friends Ricardo and Beatrix in the cafeteria of the college.
6. Wallpaper is not so difficult to hang, and the look it can add to a small bedroom or kitchen makes the effort worthwhile.
7. Vandals drove around the streets last night breaking car windows and knocking down mailboxes.
8. When fighting began, the name Operation Desert Shield was changed to Operation Desert Storm.

Some proper nouns are a combination of several words:

New York

Oakland Raiders

Federal Bureau of Investigation

Department of the Interior

All the principal words in such combinations are capitalized; others are not. You can see that "of" and "the" in the above examples are not capitalized.

24-3

DIRECTIONS: Some nouns in the following sentences should be capitalized because they are proper nouns. Use the proofreader's mark of three short lines under each letter that should be capitalized.

EXAMPLE ▶ **The 1995 superbowl game will be played in miami, florida.**

Answers	Sentences
Mason John L. Mason	1. The mason jar, a wide-mouthed jar used for preserving foods at home, was invented by john l. mason.
Frances Easter	2. My sister, frances, is coming home for the weekend of easter vacation.
National Basketball Association	3. The national basketball association regulates all professional basketball games.
Department Transportation	4. The department of transportation employs engineers who specialize in planning highway projects.
England	5. In england schools are operated year-round, and students choose one session for vacation.
English Institute Spanish, Vietnamese, Russian, Tagalog, Hopi	6. In a single class of our english institute, a listener might hear students speaking their native languages of spanish, vietnamese, russian, tagalog, and hopi.
Lillian Christmas, Valentine's Day, Mother's Day	7. When lillian worked at a florist's shop, she told me that more orders came in for christmas, valentine's day, and mother's day that for any other holidays during the year.
Isaac Newton's	8. Students in science classes like to hear the story about an apple falling on isaac newton's head and leading to his theories about gravity, though they know it probably isn't true.

Collective Nouns

A *collective* noun names a group of people or objects that is viewed as or acts as a single unit.

EXAMPLES ▶

chorus	**Navy**	**jury**
family	**committee**	**class**
audience	**crowd**	**faculty**
government	**orchestra**	**team**

Activity 24-4

DIRECTIONS: Underline the collective nouns in the following sentences.

EXAMPLE ▶ **Our <u>family</u> is going to have a July 4th reunion this year.**

Answers
collection
class
chorus
crowd
public
audience group
committee
company

1. A baseball card collection can be valuable, as well as entertaining for the collector.
2. The class gave the teacher a standing ovation for her lecture on equal rights.
3. The "Star Spangled Banner" was sung by a chorus of fifty young children from Japan who learned the words phonetically.
4. In front of the store an angry crowd protested the hiring practices of the new management.
5. Television has great impact on the public in forming its views and opinions.
6. The audience gave the local choral group a standing ovation after the concert.
7. The committee decided to study the test results further before making a decision.
8. If a small company does not have a good business plan, it will certainly have problems getting started.

VERB AGREEMENT WITH COLLECTIVE NOUNS

Because a collective noun names individuals that act as a single unit, sometimes the question arises of whether to use a singular or a plural verb with it. Remember that a noun and verb acting together must agree in number. A singular word is about one, a plural is about two or more.

If a collective noun is treated in a sentence as a single unit, use a singular verb.

EXAMPLES  The subject is underlined once and the verb is in italics.

The Jones <u>family</u> *feels* that its safety is threatened by living so near a juvenile detention center.

The church <u>choir</u> *wants* its leader to be rehired.

COMMENT: The singular pronoun "its" in each sentence is a clue that the subject of the sentence, the collective noun, is behaving as a unit. Therefore, the sentences use verbs that agree with the singular.

If a collective noun is viewed as the parts that make it up, use a plural verb.

NOTE: The word *"number"* may help you decide if the verb that goes with a collective noun should be singular or plural. If the word before it is "the," treat the collective noun as a singular and use a singular verb. If the word before it is "a," consider the collective noun a plural and use a plural verb.

EXAMPLES ▶ **The number of farms facing foreclosure *is* increasing**
A number of voters *are* showing up late at the polls.

24-5

DIRECTIONS: Determine if the collective nouns in the following sentences are used as singulars or plurals. Then underline the correct verb for each.

EXAMPLE ▶ **The band (packs / pack) their instruments hurriedly and leave by separate entrances to escape fans.**

raise
have quit
are
resume
was
seems
disagree
has

1. I watched the school committee (raise / raises) their hands in a show of support for the school's building project.
2. A number of cars (has quit / have quit) speeding in front of the school since fines have gotten higher.
3. Representatives of the public (is / are) acting as watchdogs and singling out corrupt officials in increasing numbers.
4. The faculty (resume / resumes) office hours on an individual basis next week.
5. In front of the theater, the angry mob (was / were) protesting the previewing of a movie about Adolf Hitler.
6. The committee (seem / seems) unable to come to a decision.
7. If jury members (disagree / disagrees) among themselves about the evidence, the judge will declare a mistrial.
8. The number of people waiting in line (has / have) increased in the last five minutes.

Compound Nouns

A compound noun is two or more words that always operate together.

Sometimes they are two separate words that are joined: headache, armchair, or notebook.

Some compound words are always written as two separate words, because neither one makes the same sense without the other: ice cream, money order, or common sense. There are even a few three and four-word compounds: assistant comptroller general, deputy chief of staff, chief executive officer.

Still other compound words are hyphenated: brother-in-law, cure-all, or go-between. Nouns that go with *ex, vice* or *elect* are also hyphenated: ex-president, vice-president, or president-elect.

Some compound nouns form their plurals the same way as other nouns, but there is a slight difference for others. The explanation is in the following section on plurals.

Forming Plurals

REMINDER: A singular noun names one person, place, thing, idea, or belief. A plural noun names two or more persons, places, things, ideas, or beliefs.

Although most plurals are formed in a regular way, some are not. Either the ending of the singular changes to accommodate the plural, or the word changes internally and completely.

Here is a summary and a few examples of how to form plurals from singular nouns. For a more complete explanation with examples, see the section in Chapter 32—Spelling, titled "Forming Plurals of Nouns", on pages 482-498.

1. Add an *–s* to the end of the singular. This applies also to words ending in *–o* or in a *vowel + y.*
   pencil – pencils   book – books
   piano – pianos   holiday – holidays

2. Add an *–es* to the end of a singular ending in *s, ss, x, ch* or *sh.*
   box – boxes   dress – dresses
   sandwich – sandwiches   consensus – consensuses

3. If the singular ends in a *consonant + y,* change the *y* to an *i* and add *–es.*
   century – centuries   study – studies

4. Some singulars that end in *–o* add an *–es.*
   tomato – tomatoes   mango – mangoes

5. Singulars that end in *f* or *fe* change the *f* to a *v* and add *–es.*
   leaf – leaves   half – halves

6. The internal changes that some plurals undergo just have to be memorized.
   foot – feet   mouse – mice

PLURALS OF COMPOUND WORDS

A one-word compound forms the plural by adding *-s* or *-es* to the end of the word, just as if it were not a compound word.

EXAMPLES ▶ **cookbook–cookbooks** **courthouse–courthouses**

A two- (or more) word compound or a hyphenated compound forms the plural by making the chief element plural.

EXAMPLES ▶

copy writer	copy writers
cross reference	cross references
notary public	notaries public
mother-in-law	mothers-in-law
grant-in-aid	grants-in-aid

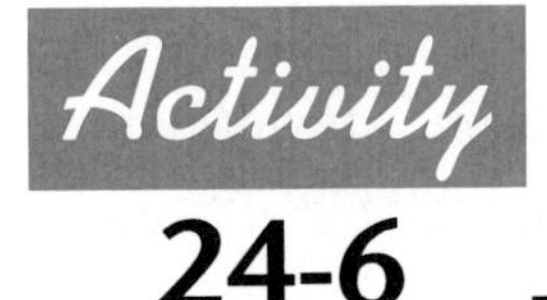

24-6

DIRECTIONS: Write the plural below to each singular compound.

EXAMPLE ▶ **basketmaker**

basketmakers

1. lady-in-waiting

   ladies-in-waiting

2. withdrawal

   withdrawals

3. last-minute rush

   last-minute rushes

4. editor-in-chief

   editors-in-chief

5. assistant corporate counsel

   assistant corporate counsels

6. trade union

   trade unions

7. brother-in-law

   brothers-in-law

8. man-of-war

   men-of-war

24-7

DIRECTIONS: To practice your skill with nouns, follow the directions below and write a sentence using the kind of noun specified. Underline the noun or nouns you write in the sentence. Check all spelling, make sure all subjects and verbs agree, and edit for capitals and punctuation. Use your own paper if you need more space.

EXAMPLE ▶ A common noun, singular:

My aunt is coming to visit next week.

Answers will vary. Possibilities are shown here.

1. a collective noun, singular

   The jury met in secret.

2. a proper noun, singular

   Give the list of addresses to Milton so he can sent out invitations.

3. a compound noun, plural

   After many hardships, the Pilgrims landed.

4. a compound noun, singular

   My sister-in-law is giving a party.

5. a common noun, singular

   Please put the box on the table.

6. a collective noun, plural

   The chorus go their way after every rehearsal.

7. a proper noun, plural

   My son was in a classroom with four Davids.

8. the plural of "baby"

   The two babies in the photo are smiling.

Activity 24-8

DIRECTIONS: Some of the singular or plural nouns in the following sentences are correct and some are not. Draw a line through each incorrect word and write the correct one above it.

EXAMPLE ▶ The ~~bug~~ *bugs* are finally caught and now the exterminator can identify them.

1. International Business Machines are a company that employs person all over the world.

2. Statistics is a course I just can't seem to pass.

3. Millie's three brother-in-laws are planning a surprise party for her husband.

4. The Joneses family feel that they are not safe because they live so close to a juvenile detention center.

5. The Grand Juries is meeting in closed sessions in order to fulfill its public duty.

6. Allyn and Bacon is a well-established book publisher.

7. People who have homes in the northern part of the United States have to rake up the leafes that fall from their trees in the autumn.

8. The manager says that there are no vacancys in this office

---

Possessive Forms of Nouns

The possessive form of a word shows ownership. It consists of a word or phrase such a "of," "owned by," or "belongs to" or an apostrophe in some combination with the letter "s". The second of these—the apostrophe—is used in so much writing that it is the one you will concentrate on in this chapter. For a more complete explanation of forming possessives, with examples and *Activities*, see the section in Chapter 29—Punctuation, titled "Apostrophes" on pages 445-460.

Purists say that an inanimate object cannot "own" anything; therefore, there can't be possessives for such nouns. That is, you can't properly say or write "the book's cover" or "the table's legs." In practice, however, most people do use possessive nouns for inanimate objects as well as for animate ones.

Here, however, is a summary and a few examples of how to form possessives for both singular and plural nouns.

1. Add an apostrophe and an s ('s) to singular nouns and to plurals that do not end in "s."
   child's [hat] cat's [tail] children's [story]

2. Add only an apostrophe to regular plural words that end in "s."
   guests' [gift] attorneys' [cases] players' [awards]

3. Show joint possession of a single item by using the apostrophe only with the last word.
   Susie and Sam's chicken salad
   Will and Ted's adventure

4. A possessive is added to the ending of a compound noun
   secretary-treasurer's [report]
   co-workers' [contributions]

24-9

DIRECTIONS: Correct the possessives of nouns in each of the following sentences by circling the error in the sentence and writing the proper word or words on the line at the end of the sentence.

EXAMPLE ▶ **The sheriff deputies who beat an unarmed motorist were all reprimanded.**

sheriff's

1. The plants blossoms shaded from pale pink to deep red.

   plant's

2. The freshman's report was almost as good as the seniors.

   senior's

3. It's somebody elses' problem now.

   else's

4. The Smith's trailer was parked next to us during vacation.

   Smiths'

5. Mary's daughters'-in-law gifts to her on Mother's Day made her feel very happy.

   daughter-in-laws'

6. When two girls were accepted for what began as the boys' basketball team, it became the boys' and girl's basketball team.

   boys and girls'

7. Denny's job at the boatyard was restitching boat's sails.

   boats'

8. Each person in the band lined up an arms' length away from the other.

   arm's

In this chapter you have worked with four different kinds of nouns: common, proper, collective, and compound. *Activities* have given you practice in making subjects and verbs in a sentence agree. You have also practiced how to make singular nouns into plurals and how to form the possessives of both kinds. Now it is time to apply all that knowledge about nouns to an editing task.

24-10

The answer to this *Activity* is in the Instructor's Section

DIRECTIONS: Circle each noun error in this paragraph. Then rewrite the paragraph on your own paper and circle each correction.

If you're already separating newspaper from can and bottles and sending all of them for recycling, maybe you feels that you can't do more to help the environment. That may not be true. One of the best thing you can do is plant a tree. A program called Global ReLeaf is sponsored by a well-known organization, the american forestry association. It encourage people to improve the earth environment by having more and better tree's and forest's. Of all the trees that die or disappear because they are cut down or removed by developer, only one in four is replaced. We need trees because they produce life-give oxygen. They also filter air pollution, prevent soil from washing away, provide a place for wildlife to live, and reduce noise pollution. Properly planted trees can reduce air conditioning cost 10 to 50 percent and serve as windbreak that cut heating costs. In cityies, concrete and dark surfaces hold heat and are 6 to 10 degrees hotter than their surroundings. Planting tree in places such as parking lot and along street can makes the city cooler.

Chapter 25

Pronouns

In this chapter you will

- identify pronouns and their antecedents
- revise for pronoun-antecedent agreement in number
- write gender-fair sentences
- have pronouns agree with the case of their antecedents
- practice consistent point of view
- choose verbs that agree with indefinite pronouns
- know and use correctly the reflexive, intensive, relative, and demonstrative pronouns

Because nouns and noun phrases are so important in speaking and writing, the ideas they represent sometimes must be repeated in a single sentence. Yet such repetition is tiresome and seems awkward.

Consider this sentence with the repeated word underlined.

> Bananas are healthy to eat because bananas contain potassium.

Sound strange? To most people it does. A more usual way of expressing that idea would be to say (or write):

> Bananas are healthy to eat because **they** contain potassium.

In the second sentence, the word "they" is a pronoun that takes the place of the noun "bananas."

Here is another sentence few of us are likely ever to use:

> Learning to fly an airplane was the high point of Elaine's life because learning to fly an airplane was something Elaine had always wanted to do.

However, written as it is below, the repetition and awkwardness are eliminated by using pronouns.

> Learning to fly an airplane was the high point of Elaine's life because **it** was something **she** had always wanted to do.

Pronouns are words that take the place of nouns or phrases that serve as nouns in a sentence.

Here are some other sentences showing how pronouns are used. The pronouns are in bold face type and the nouns or noun phrases they replace in the sentence are underlined. You can substitute any of the underlined wording for the bold face pronouns.

EXAMPLES 

Humanities courses are required because **they** give people insight into the arts of various cultures.

Melinda continued to study the violin because **she** kept learning enough to play in the orchestra.

After all the students conducted interviews for the sociology questionnaire, **we** met in the classroom to examine **our** findings.

Pronouns are easy to recognize because there are only a few hundred of them. Some of those you use often are:

I	we	he	she
it	they	me	us
him	her	them	my
our	your	his	her
this	these	those	

Later in this chapter you will see lists of particular kinds of pronouns to help you use them accurately in your writing. For now, the pronouns shown here are enough to get you started recognizing them.

Pronouns and Antecedents

Pronouns have no meaning by themselves; they take meaning from the words they take the place of. In the example sentences above, you can see how pronouns substitute for words.

Pronoun	*Takes the place of*
they	humanities courses
she	Melinda
we	students
our	students'

Notice that the pronoun "our" is in a special form—the possessive form—because the noun it replaces has the possessive form "students'" in the third example sentence.

All the examples of pronouns so far have come *after* the nouns or noun phrases they replace. That is because nothing can substitute for, or take the place of, what is unknown, for something yet to come.

EXAMPLE ▶ **It** was hot and sunny the day of the game.

What does "it" mean? Because the sentence appears alone, with nothing before, the meaning of the word remains unknown until the end of the sentence. Then, you discover that the word really means "the day of the game."

The sentence would be better *without* a pronoun:

The day of the game was hot and sunny.

To read and constantly be left in doubt about meaning is difficult. Therefore, the custom in English is that the words a pronoun replaces appear before the pronoun.

The words that pronouns replace, and which give them meaning, are called their *antecedents*. They usually appear *before* the pronouns.

EXAMPLES ▶ (Pronouns are in **bold type**; antecedents are underlined.)

Urban anthropology is becoming a popular course because **it** allows people to work close to home.

Nursing homes say **they** need many more caring people to train for jobs with **them.**

Activity 25-1

DIRECTIONS: Circle the pronoun (or pronouns) in each of the following sentences. Underline its antecedent. Draw an arrow pointing from the pronoun back to its antecedent. There may be more than one pronoun in a sentence, and the antecedents may be more than one word.

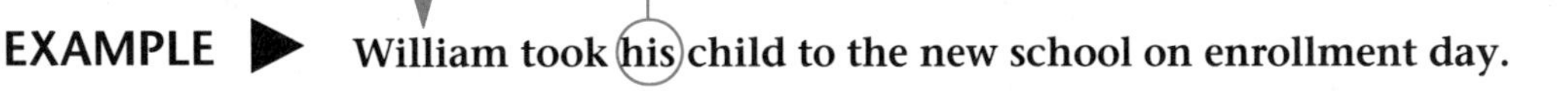

EXAMPLE ▶ **William took his child to the new school on enrollment day.**

1. Bungee jumping may be an exciting sport, but it seems very dangerous.
2. Many minor auto accidents don't appear in statistical studies because they are never reported.
3. Even though David didn't like the job, he learned a lot from it.
4. Flour milling and grinding must be repeated several times, but they can be done rather quickly with modern machinery.
5. Horror movies are so scary to young children that they shouldn't be allowed on television.
6. As AIDS spreads, it affects more women and children than ever before.
7. Statistics is considered such a basic course that it is now required in more than half the degree programs at this college.

A real problem in speaking and writing is that sometimes people forget to supply an antecedent for a pronoun.

EXAMPLE ▶ **They** really ought to put a traffic light on the corner of Main and Oak Streets.

COMMENT: Who should put up a traffic light? If such a sentence occurs during a dialog, the listener can ask the speaker, and the missing antecedent can be supplied.

REVISION:

The Department of Transportation ought to put a traffic light on the corner of Main and Oak Streets.

Writers who leave out the antecedents of pronouns put their readers in a much more difficult position, because the reader can't ask for the same sort of help. Writers, therefore, have to be especially careful to be sure each pronoun has a clear antecedent.

EXAMPLE ▶ Joy loved working in the chemistry lab, but **it** was a subject that she had to study very hard in order to pass.

COMMENT: What is the antecedent of "it"? Not "chemistry lab." The sentence, then, must be rewritten so it makes sense to a reader.

REVISION:

Joy loved working in the chemistry lab, but chemistry was a subject that she had to study very hard in order to pass.

Or, consider the confusion of this sentence, because "her" appears three times and nowhere are the antecedents made clear:

EXAMPLE ▶ Jane told **her** mother that **her** cat had turned over **her** bowl.

COMMENT: Whose cat turned over whose bowl? Was it Jane's or her mother's? Did the bowl belong to the cat, to Jane, or to her mother? A sentence with complications between pronouns and their antecedents must be completely rewritten.

POSSIBLE REVISION–1:

Jane told her mother that the Siamese cat she bought Jane as a birthday gift had just made a mess on the floor at feeding time by turning over its food bowl.

POSSIBLE REVISION–2:

Jane told her mother that her mother's Siamese cat, which Jane had bought her as a birthday gift, had turned over the bowl that mother had just made in ceramics class.

COMMENT: Longer? Yes. But clearer? Absolutely. Remember that some sentences must be completely rewritten in order to have clear antecedents for the pronouns.

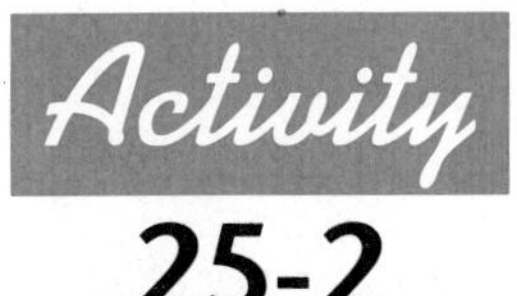

25-2

DIRECTIONS: Circle the pronouns in each of the following sentences. Rewrite the sentence(s) on the lines below so pronouns and their antecedents are clear. Supply antecedents if you must.

EXAMPLE ▶ **Maria and Jolanda accidentally broke her favorite ceramic doll while playing catch in her den.**

Revision:

Maria and Jolanda accidentally broke Maria's favorite ceramic doll while playing catch in Maria's den.

1. Kwan Lo loved to read about orchid-raising, although she had never grown one herself.
   Revision:
   Kwan Lo loved to read about orchid-raising, although she had never grown an orchid herself.

2. When Fred talked to Jim on the phone, he did not think that his boss would get angry because he had talked so long.
   Revision:
   When Fred talked to Jim on the Phone, Fred did not think that his boss would get angry because he had talked to Jim for so long.

3. I put the book on the table and opened it, but it was too dark to read.
   Revision:
   I put the book on the table and opened it, but I couldn't read because of the darkness.

4. All arrivals are searched for contraband, but it doesn't always reveal what people manage to conceal among personal items.
   Revision:
   All arrivals are searched for contraband, but the search doesn't always reveal what people manage to conceal among personal items.

5. While smelly garbage dumps are unsightly, it is a source of energy that should be utilized.
   Revision:
   While smelly garbage dumps are unsightly, the dump is a source of energy that should be utilized.

6. The sociology text said that watching violent cartoons is reported to strongly affect young children, and it can cause aggressive behavior.
   Revision:
   The sociology text said that watching violent cartoons is reported to strongly affect young children, and watching such cartoons can cause aggressive behavior.

7. After hearing how angry Jorge was with the supervisor, Bob suspected that he would not go to the company dinner.
   Revision:
   After hearing how angry Jorge was with the supervisor, Bob suspected that Jorge would not go to the company dinner.

8. The movie had murder, romance, and mystery, and I especially like this.
   Revision:
   I especially liked the murder, romance, and mystery in the movie.

Pronoun-Antecedent Agreement: Number

A pronoun must agree in number with its antecedent

"Number" means either singular or plural. That is, the pronoun and its antecedent must **both** be either singular or plural. In the following examples, the pronouns are in bold type and their antecedents are underlined.

EXAMPLES ▶

Lacks Agreement

Since a soccer <u>player</u> must be in peak physical condition, **they** must stay in training most of the year.

The pronoun in this sentence is "they," a plural word. Its antecedent is "soccer player," a singular. Therefore, either the pronoun or its antecedent must be changed so that the two can agree in number.

AGREEMENT - Plural Pronoun And Antecedent
(wording change is in italics)

Since soccer *players* must be in peak physical condition, **they** must stay in training most of the year.

COMMENT: The pronoun "they" can mean both men and women who play soccer. Changing the word "player" to "players" makes the sentence refer to *all pe*ople who play the game.

Another way to handle the problem of making pronoun and antecedent agree is to use "he or she" instead of "they." Such wording is unfamiliar to many people, so they think it is awkward. However, with continued use, it will become more familiar. Also, some people may object, unnecessarily, to using three words instead of just one. But it is a good solution to making your writing **gender-fair.**

If you kept the first part of the sentence as it is—that is, in the singular—and used a singular pronoun (either "she" or "he") after the comma, you would be guilty of gender bias.

In order to be gender-fair in your writing, you should use masculine pronouns (such as *he, his, him*) only if you are specifically referring to males. Use feminine pronouns (such as *she, her, hers*) only if you are specifically referring to women. If you refer to both men and women, you must use pronouns that include both genders, or shift wording to avoid pronouns altogether.

AGREEMENT Not Recommended:

Since a soccer player must be in peak physical condition, **he** must stay in training most of the year.

or

Since a soccer player must be in peak physical condition, **she** must stay in training most of the year.

COMMENT: Neither of these forms is recommended, because each leaves out many soccer players only on the basis of their gender.

AGREEMENT: Singular Pronouns and Antecedent
(wording change is in italic)

Since a soccer player must be in peak physical condition, ***she or he*** must stay in training most of the year.

AGREEMENT: Other Possibilities

If the sentence referred only to male or only to female players, other possibilities for revisions that do show agreement are:

Since a female soccer player must be in peak physical condition, **she** must stay in training most of the year.

or

Since a male soccer player must be in peak physical condition, **he** must stay in training most of the year.

25-3

DIRECTIONS: Correct the following sentences so the pronouns and their antecedents agree in number and without confusion. Cross out any word you are changing and write the correct word (or words) directly above it. Remember to be sure that each sentence is gender-fair.

Any zoo society ~~member~~ members who ~~wants~~ want to bring a guest should remember to bring their membership cards to the front gate.

1. A student wanting to use the card catalog or to check out books must have ~~their~~ her or his library card.

2. When Professor Jackson asked questions about radon, his students replied to ~~them~~ the questions with answers about radar, probably, because ~~he~~ Professor Jackson spoke in such a soft voice that ~~they~~ the students didn't hear him properly.

3. A patient who is given specific directions by a doctor seldom follows ~~their~~ the doctor's directions carefully.

4. The word processing class was taught every Saturday, but ~~it~~ the class was not always taught by someone who knew the computer program thoroughly.

5. Experts agree that a young child should not participate in hard contact sports because ~~their~~ the child's bones and muscles are not yet fully developed.

6. Environmentalists who work to control destruction of the Brazilian rain forest are saving ~~them~~ it for the people of the world.

7. In order to teach children how to think for ~~himself~~ themselves, a parent must let them make a few mistakes, which can be painful experiences for ~~them~~ the children.

8. Experiments have proven that a dolphin can communicate in a manner that only ~~they~~ the dolphins understand.

Collective Nouns and Pronoun Agreement

Collective nouns are those that represent a group of individuals or things considered as a single unit. A sports team, for example, consists of individual players. However, when they are playing together, they are thought of as a single unit, the team.

Other examples of collective nouns are:

band	group	jury
government	class	choir
family	committee	school
company	panel	tribe

The decision to use a singular or plural pronoun with a collective noun depends on its use in the sentence.

A collective noun is usually considered a single unit, so a singular pronoun is used with it. If the individual people or objects that make up the collective noun are to be considered separately, the pronoun must be a plural.

A pronoun whose antecedent is a collective noun will be singular or plural, depending on the way the noun is used in a sentence.

EXAMPLES ▶ (Pronouns are in **bold** type; antecedents are underlined.)

The Board of Directors had **their** photographs made in individual poses before taking the group picture.

COMMENT: Because the sentence refers to "individual poses," the directors are considered separate people. The plural pronoun "their" is evidence of their individuality.

The Board of Directors held **its** quarterly meeting last week.

COMMENT: The Board of Directors met as a unit, so the singular pronoun "its" is appropriate in the sentence.

25-4

DIRECTIONS: Underline the correct form of the pronoun in each sentence by deciding if its antecedent is singular or plural. That is, decide if the group described by the collective noun is acting as a unit (singular) or as individuals (plural).

EXAMPLE  **The class had (their / its) annual picnic planned for the weekend, but no one came due to the bad weather.**

1. The jury sent back (their/its) decision in less than an hour.
2. The rock group was unhappy with (their/its) last album.
3. Never expect to understand the inner workings of the government and (their/its) manner of making decisions.
4. The members of the band didn't want (their/its) autograph session to last all afternoon.
5. After the orchestra returned to (their/its) seats, the players had to hunt for the right music because the conductor announced a selection they didn't expect to play next.
6. The passengers were followed into the plane by the aircraft's crew carrying (their/its) equipment, which included pillows for the long overnight trip.
7. The other team's high score made it obvious that my home town team has lost (their/its) best kicker.
8. The choir performed an arrangement that featured (their/its) best alto singer.

Answers: 1. its 2. its 3. its 4. their 5. their 6. their 7. its 8. its

Compound Antecedents, Pronoun Agreement, and Gender-fairness

If the words of a compound subject are joined by the words ***or*** or ***nor***, the subject is considered singular, and will ordinarily take a singular pronoun for agreement.

However, consider the problem of the following sentence:

> ***PROBLEM:***
> The manager or the assistant manager will request that (**his? her?**) employees ask for vacation time one month in advance.

If both the manager and the assistant manager are male, the pronoun "his" would be accurate. If both people were female, "her" should be used. However, if the manager were female and the assistant manager male (or vice versa), the singular pronoun would not be gender-fair. To use the pronoun "their," a plural, would not follow the custom of a pronoun agreeing with its antecedent in number.

A good solution for this particular situation is to omit the pronoun entirely. It isn't necessary for the sense of the sentence.

> ***SOLUTION:***
> The manager or the assistant manager will request that employees ask for vacation time one month in advance.

If a compound subject using *or, nor, either/or* or *neither/nor* is the antecedent of a pronoun, the pronoun should agree in number with the second part of the subject.

However, sometimes the pronoun can be omitted without loss to the sentence.

Custom dictates that if the second word of a compound subject is plural, the entire subject be treated as a plural. As antecedent, it would therefore have a plural pronoun.

EXAMPLES  The doctor or the nurses will make every effort to ensure the comfort of **their** patient who had suffered a broken hip.

Suppose the two parts of the compound subject were reversed. Then the singular verb would be correct. However, the gender of the doctor and the nurses would govern the choice of pronoun.

> The nurses or the doctor will make every effort to ensure the comfort of **her** patient who had suffered a broken hip.

Again, the alternate of omitting the pronoun is possible for this sentence.

> The doctor or the nurses will make every effort to ensure the comfort of the patient who had suffered a broken hip.

25-5

DIRECTIONS: Draw a line under the correct choice of pronoun in parentheses for each compound antecedent in these sentences. If gender is not evident in the sentence, choose an appropriate pronoun to underline. In sentences where there is a choice of verbs, circle the correct choice.

EXAMPLE  **After walking all over the zoo, neither the students nor the teacher could find (his / his or her / her / their) way back to the information booth.**

Note: Multiple answers show any one is acceptable.

1. Neither the flight attendants nor the pilot wanted (his / her / his or her / their) plane delayed for another three hours. — his/her/his or her
2. Neither the birthday guests nor the host, who was sitting patiently waiting for the entertainment to begin, wanted (his / his or her / her / their) ice cream to melt. — his
3. The researcher and the writer will want to include (her / his / her or his / their) notes in the folder of background information on the news article. — their
4. Either poor study habits or a short attention span will take (its / their) toll on a student's grades. — its
5. Neither the agent nor the clients had made (his / her / her or his / their) reservations for the awards' banquet. — their
6. Either the leader or the group members misunderstood (her / his / her or his / their) instructions on how to arrange the exhibit of rare roses. — their
7. Neither the jury members nor the judge understood what (he / she / she or he / they) (was/were) hearing due to the rapid speech of the defendant. — she or he was
8. The coach for either women's softball or volleyball will wait a few more days before (she / he / it / he or she / they) (make / makes) a request for a salary increase. — she/he/he or she/they make/makes

---

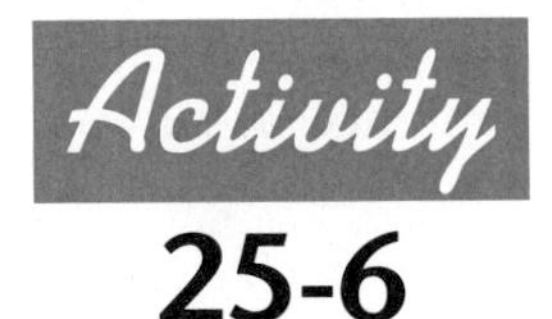

25-6

DIRECTIONS: Select three of the sentences in *Activity 25-5* that can be revised by being rewritten. Write the number of the item in the space provided, and revise the sentence to keep the same sense as the original, but eliminate the pronoun problem.

EXAMPLE  (The example sentence is reprinted here.)
After walking all over the zoo, neither the students nor the teacher could find (his / his or her / her / their) way back to the information booth.
Revision:
The students and their teacher walked all over the zoo but couldn't find the way back to the information booth.

Answers will vary.

(Write in the number from Activity 25-5 in the blank.)

1. Another way to write sentence number _____ is this.
   Revision:

   ____

2. Another way to write sentence number _____ is this.
   Revision:

   ____

3. Another way to write sentence number _____ is this.
   Revision:

   ____

Sharing

1. Form a group with two or three colleagues.
2. Compare responses to *Activities 25-5* and *25-6*.
3. On the basis of the sentences you compared, what did group members do in common? What did they do differently from each other?
4. Discuss what the group believes are the most effective choices and revisions.

Pronoun–Antecedent Agreement: Case

You already know that pronouns change forms to agree with their antecedents according to number (singular or plural) and gender (masculine, feminine, neuter, or without gender indication). Pronouns also have different forms according to case, or how they are used in a sentence: as subject, as object, or as possessive.

The case of a pronoun is determined by how it is used in a sentence. The case may be subjective (as a subject), objective (as an object), or possessive (to show ownership). The pronoun changes according to its case.

The case of a pronoun is also tied closely to the **person** it represents. That is, a pronoun shows if

someone speaks	first person
someone or something is spoken to	second person
someone or something is spoken about	third person

The chart below shows the forms of the personal pronouns. Notice how they differ on the basis of case (how they are used), number (singular or plural), gender, and person.

CASES OF PRONOUNS

Singular

Subjective	Objective	Possessive	Person
I	me	my; mine	1st
you	you	your; yours	2nd
he	him	his	
she	her	her; hers	
it	it	its	3rd
who	whom	whose	
whoever	whomever		

Plural

Subjective	Objective	Possessive	Person
we	us	our; ours	1st
you	you	your; yours	2nd
they	them	their; theirs	3rd

In order to choose the correct pronoun for a sentence, decide how it is being used: as a subject, as an object, or as a possessive. Even if there is a compound subject or object—that is, one that has two words—the choice of pronoun still depends on how it is used in the sentence. Refer to the chart, "Cases of Pronouns," if you have doubts about the word to use.

EXAMPLES  **Pronouns as subjects:**

I plan to study archaeology.

You and (**I**/me) should go to the boat races next week.

You should choose "I" because it is part of the subject.

Pronouns as objects:

Between (she/**her**) and (I/**me**) there are few secrets.

You should choose "her" and "me" because they are objects of the preposition "between."

Pronouns showing possession:

Lisa said that it was not clear **whose** decision it was to cancel the dinner party, but that the decision was not **hers**.

"Whose" in the first line shows ownership of the decision. "Hers" in the last line shows that Lisa owned (or made) the decision.

25-7

Pronouns that students are asked to circle are shown in bold face.

DIRECTIONS: Circle the correct pronoun from those in parentheses in each of the following sentences. If there are other pronouns in any sentence, underline them.

EXAMPLE ▶ **The teacher chose Sebastian and (I / me) to represent the class at the meeting.**

1. To (who/whom) should I give the keys to the office? — **whom**
2. Liana always sounds better than (I/me) when she answers the phone. — **I** she
3. Even though both boys tried to clean up the room, Kyle always did a more thorough job than (he/him). — **he**
4. Who was yelling at (who/whom)? — Who **whom**
5. I think the president of the club was better informed than (they/them) about what should be included on the petition. — I **they**
6. The president is (her/she). — **she**
7. Enrico and (I/me) decided to take the blame for (whoever/whomever) was guilty. — **I** **whomever**
8. The person (who/whom) we believed to be hurt was later discovered to have survived the accident without injury. — **who** we

25-8

The answers to this *Activity* are in the Instructor's Section.

DIRECTIONS: Write in the correct pronouns on the lines provided.

When Pat and ______ decided to take a vacation together, ______ children objected. _________ said that _________ would be away from home too long, and that _____ would cost more money than we should spend. However, ______ said that ______ was for ______ to decide, because _______ would be spending ________ time and ___________ money. Besides, __________ told ___________ that would bring home presents for each of _________ .

Consistent Person (Point of View)

"Consistent" means to agree or go together. For example, tennis shoes are not usually worn with formal clothing; to dress that way means a person's outfit is not consistent. Consistency in dress means sports clothes worn with the tennis shoes, or dress shoes with the formal clothing.

"Point of view" is a term applied to the way in which the writer (the person) looks at the subject. In order to keep writing clear, an author should be as consistent as possible in using first, second, or third person within sentences, paragraphs, and whole pieces of writing.

Inconsistent person or point of view is called a "shift." It should be avoided because it is confusing to the reader.

As the chart on pages 394-395 showed, the term "person" tells how a writer views the subject. A slight variation of the diagram is reproduced here, together with a reminder of the pronouns used for each person:

the writer speaks — first person
Use the pronouns "I" or "we"

the writer speaks to the reader — second person
Use the pronoun "you"

the writer speaks about someone or something — third person
Use the pronouns "he," "she," "it," or "they." Or, let the pronouns agree with their antecedents.

Pronouns throughout writing of any length should be as consistent as possible with the point of view a writer selects.

In the following examples, the writer's point of view is in italics in parentheses and pronouns showing point of view are in bold type.

EXAMPLES ▶

1. **Shift in point of view**

   Drivers (third person) who are required to wear glasses to drive should always wear them. If **you** (second person) drive without them, **you** (second person) are taking a chance that an accident might occur.

   Consistent point of view

   Drivers (third person) who are required to wear glasses to drive should always wear them. If **they** (third person) drive without them, **they** (third person) are taking a chance that an accident might occur.

2. **Shift in point of view**

   Having long range goals is important (third person), because planning increases the chances of **your** (second person) success.

   Consistent point of view

   Having long range goals is important (third person), because planning increases the chances of success (third person).

REMINDER: Not all sentences need to have a pronoun; in some revisions earlier in this chapter you were able to eliminate a pronoun.

25-9

DIRECTIONS: Each item that follows lacks consistent person or point of view. Circle what ought to be changed. Then name the point of view or person that you selected for the revised passage, and rewrite the item to make it consistent. .

EXAMPLE  **After the Civil War must have been an exciting time because many things began to happen. I think it was good that the government bought Alaska and took over Midway Island. You could also say that The Age of Imperialism begins.**

Consistent point of view:

Third Person — After the Civil War must have been an exciting time because many things began to happen. Among them was that the government bought Alaska and took over Midway Island. The Age of Imperialism is said to have begun then.

Responses will vary, based on student selection of point of view.

1. If I had the money, you can build up a great video collection. Many classic films ought to be in such a collection. Or, you could decide to specialize in certain kinds of films. Mysteries, musicals, comedies, horror, adventure, and war stories are some of the kinds of video films that I know people collect.

   Consistent point of view:

   ____

   ____

   ____

   ____

2. The 1950s brought a new kind of popular music in the United States: rock 'n' roll. You could say that it was a combination of country music and the rhythm and blues popular among many black people. I heard that Chuck Berry and Little Richard wrote and performed many rock 'n roll songs. The most famous rock 'n' roll singer was certainly Elvis Presley.

   Consistent point of view:

   ____

   ____

   ____

   ____

3. For a class assignment, we had to write about our ideal vacation. I said that I would want to go around the world because you can see so many different things in different countries. I would like to take that kind of vacation, although it would not be like the Jules Verne book, *Around the World in 80 Days*. You could do it faster now. The astronauts can go

around the world is something like 80 minutes or maybe even less, but they aren't on a vacation and they don't get to see very much from where they are. Nevertheless, teachers say that many students who write about an ideal vacation say they would like to go around the world.

Consistent point of view:

____

____

____

____

25-10

The rewriting of this *Activity* is in the Instructor's Section.

DIRECTIONS: Circle all the pronouns in the following paragraph. Then rewrite the paragraph in the third person point of view. Use your own paper to write the paragraph.

The study of ancient people can reveal to us an understanding of the problems of modern cities. If you look at the way ancient people progressed from separate groups of nomadic tribes to living together in cities among other family units, we see why modern cities have different kinds of problems from those of ancient cities. The most important difference that you see between ancient and modern cities is that cities no longer have unity in a centralized local government which, ideally, addresses our problems on a local level. Lack of a strong local government in which we all participate could be the single factor responsible for the increase in crime, the feeling of isolation, and the lack of safety you feel in large cities.

Sharing

1. Form a group with two other people in the class.
2. Exchange the revisions you made for *Activity 25-9* and *Activity 25-10.*
3. Discuss which response to each activity from within the group you believe is most effective, and tell the author why you believe it is a good response. If there were differences of opinion about how to revise these works, share them with the group.

Indefinite Pronouns and Verb Agreement

Indefinite pronouns got that name because they don't necessarily require an antecedent noun or pronoun.

EXAMPLES ▶ **Everybody** made fun of me.
Someone is knocking on the door.
Nothing moved!

However, indefinite pronouns may refer to a noun or pronoun that comes after it in the sentence, or even in the paragraph.

EXAMPLES ▶ **Everybody** may collect his or her pay later.
Few playwrights see their work produced on Broadway.

Verbs must agree in number with indefinite pronouns that are the subjects of sentences. Singular indefinite pronouns take singular verbs.

Plural indefinite pronouns require plural verbs. Some indefinite pronouns are considered either singular or plural, depending on their meaning in a particular sentence.

The charts below show singular, plural, and either singular or plural indefinite pronouns. Compound words ending in *–body,–one,* or *–thing* make up most of the list of singular indefinite pronouns. However, there are others, as this chart shows:

SINGULAR INDEFINITE PRONOUNS

–body	–one	–thing	Other
anybody	anyone	anything	any
everybody	everyone	everything	another
nobody	no one	nothing	each
somebody	someone	something	either
			every
			much
			neither
			none
			one

OTHER INDEFINITE PRONOUNS

Singular or Plural	Plural
all	both
any	few
more	many
most	several
none (occasionally)	
some	

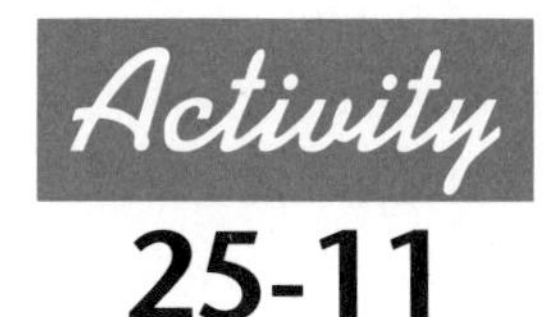

25-11

DIRECTIONS: Circle the correct pronoun and verb in the following sentences that offer a choice of words in parentheses. Refer to the chart if necessary, but more importantly, look at the other words in the sentence to see if the pronoun refers to more than one person or thing.

EXAMPLE ▶ **None of the hospitals in that area has (~~its~~/ their) emergency room open twenty-four hours a day.**

he or she is
he or she
their
her or his
their
her or his
his
his or her

1. Anybody can ride a bicycle if (they are/he or she is/ he is) coordinated.
2. Tawanda was grateful that somebody told her that (he/ she/he or she/they) could not hear her from the back of the room when she practiced her speech.
3. Several of the protesters marched with (his or her/their/his/her) eyes blindfolded in protest of the company's refusal to agree to a meeting.
4. Not everyone is willing to help (his/her/her or his/their) neighbor.
5. All of the graduates threw (his or her/their/its/her/his) hats into the air after graduation.
6. No one should neglect (her or his/he/she/their) opportunity for an education.
7. None of the men is hesitant to speak (his/their) mind.
8. Any of the students who spoke at the rally received a special invitation to visit (his/her/his or her/their) representative's office in Washington, D.C.

Other Pronouns: Reflexive, Intensive, Relative, and Demonstrative

Reflexive and Intensive Pronouns are both formed in the same way: by adding *–self* or *–selves* to a personal pronoun.

REFLEXIVE AND INTENSIVE PRONOUNS

	Singular	Plural
1st Person	myself	ourselves
	oneself	
2nd Person	yourself	yourselves
	herself	
3rd Person	himself	themselves
	itself	

"Reflexive" means to turn back upon itself. Therefore, a **reflexive pronoun** is one that turns back to another word in a sentence: the subject.

Reflexive pronouns **refer to the noun or pronoun that is the subject of the sentence. They are necessary to make the sentence clear.**

EXAMPLES  The roofers allowed **themselves** no breaks because they wanted to complete the job before another rainstorm came.

Jason wrote the letters **himself** asking for the autographs of the basketball players.

I designed the poster **myself** and won a prize for doing it.

A reflexive pronoun is not a substitute for the pronouns "I," or "me," that some writers don't want to use because they are fearful of using it in the wrong way, or of sounding egotistical.

WRONG: Tim and **myself** will be glad to move the piano for you.

RIGHT: Tim and **I** will be glad to move the piano for you.

WRONG: The argument is between Ralph and **myself.**

RIGHT: The argument is between Ralph and **me.**

Something that is "intensive" has concentrated power or force. Therefore, an **intensive pronoun** is one that makes writing more forceful.

***Intensive pronouns* add special emphasis to nouns or other pronouns. They *are not necessary* to the sense of the sentence.**

EXAMPLES  I **myself** turned in the report when it was due, so I know the work was completed.

The silver was, by **itself**, an unexpected gift.

The silver **itself** was an unexpected gift.

Relative pronouns show the relationship of a noun or pronoun to a group of words containing a subject and a verb. These pronouns have specific kinds of words they refer to, as this chart shows.

RELATIVE PRONOUNS

that	*refers to*	**things, animals, sometimes people**
which whichever	*refers to*	**things, animals**
who, whom, whose, whoever whomever	*refers to*	**people**

EXAMPLES  Sharpshooters managed to kill the tiger **that** had already injured people and destroyed property in the village.

The plumber finally located the pipe **which** broke and caused flooding in the basement.

Please let me know **who** will be responsible for handling the Community Chest collection in this company.

Demonstrative pronouns point out nouns or other pronouns that come after them. The differ in the singular and plural forms, and also in whether they are referring to things close or far away.

DEMONSTRATIVE PRONOUNS

Singular		Plural
this	what is *close*	**these**
that	what is *far*	**those**

EXAMPLES ▶ We will reach **those** mountains by this afternoon if we keep driving at a steady pace.

This book in the display case is a favorite of many children who come to the library.

25-12

DIRECTIONS: Fill in the blanks in the following sentences with the appropriate reflexive, intensive, relative, or demonstrative pronoun.

EXAMPLE ▶ *This* **fossil I am holding in my hand was once a living sea creature.**

1. The circus strong man lifted the stalled car by ______________ and put it back on the road.
2. "I really did write this report by ____________," said the angry student.
3. The third-grade children planned the party ______________, and even put up their own decorations.
4. The doctor ___________________________ could not have stitched the wound any better than the emergency technician did.
5. The fashion show _________________ students in the clothing design course put on was of professional quality.
6. In the final days of the short Desert Storm war, Iraqi soldiers were surrendering to ______________ Coalition Forces they could find.
7. Training astronomers _______________ can unlock even more secrets of the universe is a science priority.
8. ______________ problem of better recycling methods is not going to be solved immediately.

himself

myself

themselves

herself or himself

that

whichever

who

This *or* That

Chapter 26

Modifiers

In this chapter you will

- identify modifiers in sentences
- see how adjectives and adverbs are used
- spot and correct dangling modifiers
- spot and correct misplaced modifiers
- learn when to use *good* or *well, bad* or *badly*
- use comparatives and superlatives

To modify something is to make a change in it. Car engines are often modified for racing or for better gas mileage. Modify the blueprints of a building and you specify changes. Modify your position on a subject—say, on a seven-period day for school children—and you change your belief or the stand you take.

In writing, every time you add to the essential words in a sentence—the subject and verb (and sometimes the completers)—you change the meaning slightly. The words that make such changes are called **modifiers.** When you use modifiers in sentences, you make your meaning more exact for readers.

Begin with the essential words (underlined once) in a sentence, a simple subject and verb:

The ball bounced.

Add a modifier (in italics) to tell more about the ball (subject):

The *blue* ball bounced.

Add another modifier (in italics) to tell more about the bounce (verb):

The *blue* ball bounced *high*.

Now add a few more modifiers:

The *blue* ball *with white stars on it* bounced *high over the fence.*

More modifiers = more details = more exact meaning for readers.
Here is another sentence showing just the essential words (underlined once), a subject, a verb, and a direct object:

The manager fired people.

Add modifiers (in italics) to tell more about the subject:

The *very fair, long-suffering* manager fired people.

Add a modifier (in italics) to the verb:

The *very fair, long-suffering* manager *regretfully* fired people.

Add modifiers(in italics) to tell more about the completing word (direct object):

The *very fair, long-suffering* manager *regretfully* fired *three* people *caught stealing merchandise from the store.*

More modifiers = more details = more exact meaning for readers.

A REMINDER OF TERMS

A **phrase** is a group of words that go together because they have some relationship to each other.

EXAMPLES  **in the house**

carrying the package

to handle it carefully

A clause is a group of words that has its own subject (underlined once in these examples) and verb (in italics in these examples). At least one independent clause is required for a sentence.

EXAMPLES  **The rain *stopped.* (independent clause)**

Willard drove fast because the store *was closing.* (dependent clause)

The boy *ate* the candy. (independent clause)

If we *run,* we can catch the next bus to the mall. (dependent clause)

Modifiers may be words, phrases, or clauses.

EXAMPLES  (underlined words are the essentials of the sentence; words in **bold** face type are modifiers)

The **quick, brown** fox jumped over the **lazy** dog.

The house **around the corner** was painted **yellow.**

He is the senator **who voted for the tax.**

The pot **on the stove** began to boil **rapidly.**

After the teacher called on him, the boy mumbled the answer.

26-1

DIRECTIONS: Underline once the essential words in each sentence. (Remember that the essential words in a sentence are the subject and verb; some sentences also require completing words in order to make sense.) Underline twice the modifiers in each sentence.

EXAMPLE ▶ **Good teachers inspire students to do their best.**

The answers to this *Activity* are in the Instructor's Section.

1. Most parents insist on good manners.
2. The school bus had a flat tire.
3. Male birds are often the most colorful.
4. A rainy day can be a good time for reading.
5. Fishing is a healthy outdoor hobby.
6. The 12-car passenger train was late.
7. Electronic home games have improved in recent years.
8. Wash-and-wear clothes make ironing unnecessary.

In the next activity, you will have a chance to work with more complex groups of words, phrases and clauses.

26-2

DIRECTIONS: Underline once the essential words in each sentence. Underline twice the modifiers in each sentence.

EXAMPLE ▶ **Many well-informed voters favor a slight tax to cover the cost of political campaigns.**

The answers to this *Activity* are in the Instructor's Section.

1. Snorkeling is a safe and inexpensive hobby for all ages.
2. Some young parents take parenting classes to learn how to take better care of their children.
3. College students should learn the basics of note taking and study skills.
4. Old quilts have become popular collectors' items.
5. Car maintenance often prevents expensive problems.
6. Air travel is safer and quicker than travel by car.
7. Fresh-water fish do not taste like salt-water fish.
8. Professional basketball players seem taller each year.

26-3

DIRECTIONS: In each blank, write as many modifiers as you wish to make the sentences more specific. Do not feel limited by the lengths of the lines. Some sentences already have one or more modifiers printed.

EXAMPLE ▶ **The** *gold* **mine no longer produced, but the owners made it** *into a tourist attraction.*

The answers to this *Activity* are in the Instructor's Section.

1. My ______________ usually runs ______________________.
2. At ______________ camp we sometimes played ______________ that were ______________.
3. The ______________ garden contained many ______________ that made the neighborhood attractive.
4. If you visit ______________, be sure to see the ______________, because ______________.
5. A ______________ book that I read ______________ is about ______________.
6. ______________ motors need ______________ maintenance if they are ______________.
7. Vacationing is ______________, especially when ______________.
8. ________________________ floors may be better to have than floors, depending on ______________.

Adjectives and Adverbs

Modifiers are classified as either adjectives or adverbs. The difference between them depends on what they modify.

Adjectives modify nouns or pronouns. Adjectives in a sentence usually appear before the words they modify.

EXAMPLES ▶ (adjectives are underlined)

The quaint ferry boat chugged across the bay.

The melting butter dripped off the sides of the waffle.

Ivy's smile is beautiful and bright.

Ricardo is happy to help everyone.

Activity 26-4

DIRECTIONS: Circle each adjective in the following sentences and draw an arrow pointing to the word each modifies.

EXAMPLE ▶ 

The answers to this *Activity* are in the Instructor's Section.

1. We had ham sandwiches for lunch today.
2. In fall the beautiful maple trees show flashy colors.
3. Some drivers fail to obey stop signs.
4. Young children at play are very imaginative.
5. A good basketball player shows speed and agility.
6. Better income-tax laws might benefit everyone.
7. She is the girl with the nice smile.
8. The salt-water crocodile is smaller than its cousin, the fresh-water crocodile.

Adverbs modify verbs, adjectives, or other adverbs. Adverbs answer such questions as "how?" "how much?" "when?" "where?" "why?" "how often?"

EXAMPLES ▶ (adverbs are underlined)

The ball rolled <u>away</u>.

I decided <u>recently</u> to make a will.

She was looking <u>hurriedly</u> through her purse for her house keys.

I <u>just</u> finished my homework.

26-5

DIRECTIONS: Circle each adverb in the following sentences and draw an arrow pointing to the word each modifies.

EXAMPLE ▶ Everyone stayed indoors because it snowed (hard.)

1. The graduation ceremony was (very) long.
2. I think that I can (quickly) finish painting the room with some help from friends.
3. The concert went (smoothly.)
4. (Always) take a raincoat when you go on vacation.
5. Grace has (extremely) serious problems.
6. Jake yelled (angrily) at the carpenter.
7. Crocus bloom (early) in the spring.
8. An angry bluejay will attack (viciously) if the nest is in danger.

Sometimes an adjective can become an adverb by the addition of *-ly* at the end of the word. Here are some examples:

Adjective	Adverb	Adjective	Adverb
beautiful	beautifully	easy	easily
effortless	effortlessly	happy	happily
heavy	heavily	honest	honestly
intense	intensely	light	lightly
loud	loudly	mere	merely
narrow	narrowly	poor	poorly
quick	quickly	rich	richly
silent	silently	similar	similarly
strong	strongly	thick	thickly
true	truly	usual	usually

Of course, when a word shifts to become an adverb, it functions a little differently in a sentence.

EXAMPLES ▶ **He was quick to understand the problem.** ***(adjective)***
He was quickly reminded of his duties. ***(adverb)***

Other words are simply adverbs; they are not formed by the addition of *–ly*. Some of them are listed below. However, the ones marked with an asterisk (*) in the list, can also act as other parts of speech.

Adverbs		
after*	ahead	before*
behind*	beyond*	during
just	less	more
never	now	often
only	seldom	sometimes
somewhere*	than	then*
there	well	when*
where		

EXAMPLES ▶ **Oswaldo left after the first half of the ball game.** *(adverb - modifies "left")*

In many languages the modifier is placed after the noun it modifies, not before it. *(preposition—"noun" is its object)*

Certain words keep the same form as both an adjective and an adverb. You can tell the difference because of what the word modifies.

EXAMPLES ▶ **James drives fast.** *(adverb- modifies "drives")*
He usually drives in the fast lane. *(adjective—modifies "lane")*

26-6

DIRECTIONS: Circle the correct word of the choices offered in each sentence. In the blank at the end of the sentence, identify the word you circled as either an adjective or an adverb.

EXAMPLE ▶ **Everyone left the stadium (hurried, hurriedly) as soon as the game was over.**

adverb

Answer key	Exercise
heavily	1. The gambler paid (heavy, heavily) for the mistake. adverb
rapid	2. After the storm, everyone made a (rapid, rapidly) exit from the shelter. adjective
softly	3. A former U.S. president, Theodore Roosevelt, is credited with saying, "Speak (soft, softly) and carry a big stick." adverb
thick	4. The milkshake clung in (thick, thickly) blobs on the side of the glass. adjective
thickly	5. The airport was fogged in so (thick, thickly) that the flight was cancelled. adverb
hurried	6. Never rush out in such a (hurried, hurriedly) way that you forget your driver's license. adjective
intense	7. Joel is (intense, intensely) about his work. adjective
slowly	8. Walking (slow, slowly) and in the center of the spotlight, the singer left the stage. adverb

Phrases that act as modifiers in a sentence may begin with a preposition, an infinitive, a past participle, an *-ing* word, or sometimes even with a noun.

Because it is a single unit, a modifying phrase usually functions as if it were a single adjective or an adverb.

EXAMPLES  (modifying phrases are underlined)

Modifying phrase beginning with a *preposition:*
That dog with the glossy brown coat is my pet.

Modifying phrase beginning with an *infinitive:*
To give her credit, Molly always came to work on time.

Modifying phrase beginning with a *past participle:*
Rusted beyond recognition, the old statue was going to be restored.

Modifying phrase beginning with an *–ing* word:
Copying rapidly from his notes, the secretary made a list of bidders for office supplies.

Modifying phrase beginning with a *noun:*
My uncle's clock, a piece from the Victorian era, is one of the most beautiful on loan to the museum for the exhibit.

26-7

DIRECTIONS: Circle the modifying phrases in each of the following sentences. There may be more than one phrase in some sentences.

EXAMPLE ▶ **The coach planned the baseball game (to finish by 6 p.m.)**

Answers	Sentences
to work at night	1. I never want to work at night because I am not a night-owl.
Dragging heavy sacks behind them	2. Dragging heavy sacks behind them, cotton pickers used to work in the fields all day.
to leave a fire unattended	3. Safety-conscious people know it is never a good idea to leave a fire unattended.
Bored to tears	4. Bored to tears, the audience appeared to be sleeping.
Taking courses to learn new skills	5. Taking courses to learn new skills is a good employment strategy.
to take insect repellent.	6. If you go camping, remember to take insect repellent.
After the dance to a nice restaurant.	7. After the dance, we went to a nice restaurant.
to miss important information they might otherwise hear.	8. People who do a lot of talking are likely to miss important information they might otherwise hear.

26-8

DIRECTIONS: Below each modifying phrase, write an original sentence that includes that phrase.

EXAMPLE  **after the rain**

The rivers flowed faster after the rain.

1. to keep flowers fresh

   To keep cut flowers fresh, you should change the water daily.

Student sentences may vary. These are possibilities.

2. followed him home
   Our nephew said his new dog followed him home.
3. resting on the couch
   When I go to see my grandmother, she is always resting on the couch.
4. under a tree
   If you are caught outdoors in a storm, never stand under a tree.
5. covered with spots
   The sofa I had is covered with spots and needs cleaning.
6. hanging clothes out to dry
   The next-door neighbor is hanging clothes out to dry and saving electricity
7. to gain success
   Hard work is the best way to gain success.
8. covering the wall
   While I was at my aunt's house, I found my young cousin covering the wall with crayon marks.

Clauses that act as modifiers may function as adjectives or adverbs.

Adjectival clauses usually begin with one of these words: *who, whom, that, which,* or *whose.*

Adverbial clauses usually begin with one of these words: *because, while, unless, as, if, although,* or *after.*

EXAMPLES ▶ (modifying clauses are underlined)

If you want to save money, try to stay away from shopping malls. *(adverbial)*

Mr. Fonz is the teacher who always gives low grades. *(adjectival)*

26-9

DIRECTIONS: Draw a line under each modifying clause in the following sentences.

EXAMPLE  **The neighbor whose van was stolen last week decided to move out of town.**

if you want to catch the elevator
who said he wanted to help needy children

1. You had better walk quickly if you want to catch the elevator.
2. A boy who said he wanted to help needy children pledged half of his allowance for a year.

While you are waiting to catch a bus who are waiting

that I bought last week

because they want their children to feel good about their schoolwork

whose idea of work centers around filing—mostly, her nails

although she took a class to review it and studied very hard

that she reacted with anger

3. While you are waiting to catch a bus, it is interesting to watch all the others who are waiting.
4. The new suitcase that I bought last week has a broken strap already.
5. Most parents want their children to make good grades because they want their children to feel good about their schoolwork.
6. Maurina is a person whose idea of work centers around filing—mostly, her nails.
7. Felicia failed to pass her driving test, although she took a class to review it and studied very hard.
8. The reason that she reacted with anger is not easy to understand.

26-10

DIRECTIONS: The proofreading symbol for inserting words in a sentence is called a "caret" and it looks like this: "^." Indicate the place where each clause can best be inserted in the sentence following it. Then mark the place of insertion with a caret and a line extending from the top of it and circling the modifying clause.

EXAMPLE ▶ **who was catcher in the trapeze act**

The man ^ wanted to take a vacation.

Caret shows where clause above it should be inserted.

1. which one I don't know,

   One of the brothers, ^ gave me his car phone number.

2. who does an extra research project

   The student ^ will get extra credit.

3. that have no scent

   I don't care for flowers ^.

4. which was built last fall,

   The new mall, ^ has a number of specialty shops.

5. who will do anything he can to help others

   Diego is a friend ^.

6. who is my best friend,

   I can't tell Gloria, ^ that her new hair style looks terrible.

7. unless you want to take the course again

   You had better study hard ^.

8. although he has little free time

   Allan makes beautiful stained glass window ^.

From all the examples above and all the work you have been doing with modifiers so far in this chapter, you may already have figured out the best place for modifiers within a sentence.

Modifiers should be next to, or as close as possible to, the words they modify.

Unfortunately, sometimes people write sentences with modifiers—usually phrases—that don't follow this principle. The error may be one of two kinds, either a dangling modifier or a misplaced modifier.

Dangling Modifiers

A group of words—usually a phrase—that seems to modify something in a sentence but really doesn't describe anything in that sentence is called a dangling modifier. It dangles—just hangs on the page by itself. Often, the resulting sentence is either funny or confusing.

(dangling modifiers are underlined)

EXAMPLES ▶ **Washed overboard, I saw the life preserver float away from the boat.**

COMMENT: Was it the speaker or the life preserver that was washed overboard?

Running down the hill, I saw a large poster of Elvis Presley.

COMMENT: Was the poster running down the hill? Or just the speaker?

Dangling modifiers can't be "repaired" just by moving them to another place in the sentence because they really don't modify anything in that sentence. Therefore, the only ways to deal with them are to:

1. Throw out the dangling modifier

   or

2. Revise the sentence and perhaps include something of the idea of the modifier.

Here is how those two methods might work with the example sentences above:

EXAMPLES 

1. **I saw the life preserver float away from the boat.**
2. **I saw the life preserver that had washed overboard start to float away from the boat.**

1. **I saw a large poster of Elvis Presley.**
2. **As I was running down the street, I saw a large poster of Elvis Presley.**

26-11

DIRECTIONS: Some of the following sentences have dangling modifiers and some don't. If there *is* a dangling modifier, put a **D** on the line next to the sentence number and revise the sentence by trying to include something of the idea of the dangling modifier into the sentence.

EXAMPLE ▶ D **Driving to the grocery store, the family dog jumped out of the car.**

Revision:

As we were driving to the grocery store, the family dog jumped out of the car.

D 1. Carrying the feed bucket, the neighbor's duck pecked at me.

Revision:

As I was carrying the feed bucket, the neighbor's duck pecked at me.

____ 2. Whistling and howling, the wind blew the window open.

Revision:

D 3. Wearing a new dress, I saw my sister come into the room.

Revision:

I saw my sister, who was wearing a new dress, come into the room.

____ 4. Before we left, the teacher gave us our last assignment.

Revision:

D 5. Afraid of the loud noise coming from the drill, his eyes began to get larger.

Revision:

The little boy's eyes began to get larger as he grew more and more afraid of the loud noise coming from the drill.

D 6. Unable to stand the hot climate, moving further north seemed a good idea.

Revision:

Because the family could not stand the hot climate, they decided that moving north seemed to be a good idea.

___ 7. The top, spinning wildly, fascinated the young child.

Revision:

___

___

D 8. Running and looking backward, Jane's feet got tangled up and she fell.

Revision:

Because she was running forward but looking backward, Jane's feet got tangled up and she fell.

Misplaced Modifiers

A modifier that is written in the wrong place—that is, not next to what it modifies or close enough so any reader can understand what it modifies—is called a misplaced modifier. That's because the writer actually misplaced a part of the sentence, put it in the wrong location and one that's hard to find, at that. Most such misplaced modifiers are phrases.

(misplaced modifiers are underlined)

EXAMPLES ▶ **My mother wired me money so I could come home <u>by Western Union.</u>**

I saw a thin man holding a door open <u>with a big smile.</u>

Sometimes misplaced modifiers are funny because the sense or meaning of the sentence is twisted out of shape. Mostly, however, a misplaced modifier makes reading difficult for the audience which has to stop and figure out what the writer probably meant.

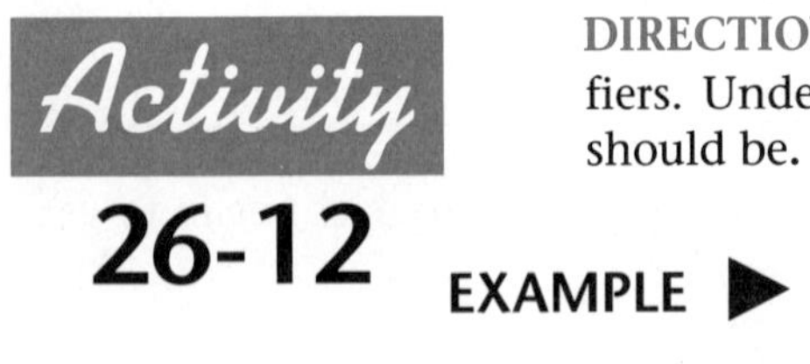

DIRECTIONS: **Some** of the sentences that follow contain misplaced modifiers. Underline any you find. On the lines below, write the sentence as it should be.

EXAMPLE ▶ **Joe described how he fell and broke his leg (after the rescue.)**

Revision:

After the rescue, Joe described how he had fallen and broken his leg.

1. The librarian listed only four books on gardening.

Revision:

___

___

Riding a tricycle

2. Riding a tricycle, I saw a little girl bump into a tree.
Revision:
I saw a little girl riding a tricycle bump into a tree.

Jumping from the lake

3. Jumping from the lake, a very large fish landed in our boat.
Revision:
A very large fish jumped from the lake and landed in our boat.

4. Never one to give up, my son worked for two days on a math problem.
Revision:

Waving wildly

5. Waving wildly, I saw the ship's flag.
Revision:
I saw the ship's flag waving wildly.

at night

6. He works two jobs so that he can pay his bills at night.
Revision:
He works two jobs at night so that he can pay his bills.

7. After looking both ways, I dashed across the street.
Revision:

peering through the bars of the cage

8. John waved peering through the bars of the cage at the animals.
Revision:
John waved at the animals peering through the bars of the cage.

26-13

The answers to this *Activity* are in the Instructor's Section.

DIRECTIONS: Underline the dangling and misplaced modifiers in the paragraph below. Then, on your own paper, revise the paragraph to solve the problems.

I saw a deer driving down the highway on my way for the job interview as reporter for the local newspaper. Right away I knew I was going to like this small city! I got the job and have been happy ever since because I get to meet such interesting people. For instance, Harriett Sullivan's business is painting houses with her three assistants. She is the first female house painter I have ever met. Then there is Mike Wilson who, I think, is a very fair person. He is the owner of the condemned building who discussed the plan to demolish it with the tenants. The only thing I haven't liked since moving here happened three days ago. Walking through the park after the rock concert, the trash people left behind was amazing.

Good/Well; Bad/Badly; Real/Really

These pairs of words—the first an adjective, the second an adverb—are often confused by writers.

Use the adjectives *good, bad,* or *real* after linking verbs. Use the adverbs *well, badly,* or *really* to modify action verbs.

EXAMPLES ▶ ***Wrong:*** I played real good today.

COMMENT: *How* did you play? The word that answers that question must be an adverb, so it has to be "well." *How* well? The modifier that answers that question, must be another adverb: really

Right: I played really well today.

Wrong: I feel badly today.

COMMENT: "Feel" is a linking verb, so it must be followed by an adjective: bad.

Right: I feel bad today.

REMINDER: Linking verbs are any form of these verbs: ***be, appear, seem, become, grow, turn, remain, prove, look, sound, taste, feel, smell.*** They express a link of identity or description to the subject of the sentence (before them) and any modifiers (after them).

Activity 26-14

DIRECTIONS: Underline the correct word in parentheses within each of the following sentences.

EXAMPLE ▶ **Willa decided her feet smelled (bad, badly) after the hike, so she hurried to take a shower.**

1. The little girl felt (bad, badly), and when her mother took her temperature, it was (real, really) high.
2. If you feel very (strong, strongly) on the subject, you should write a letter to the office manager protesting the dress code.
3. Luz says that she thinks cigarettes smell (bad, badly), so she doesn't allow smoking in her home.
4. After the marathon race, Ian felt (good, well) even though he had run (bad, badly).
5. Most children are (real, really) happy at the end of the school year.
6. Confident that he did (good, well) on the test, Lorenzo turned in his paper before the time limit was called.
7. Jean did understand the homework assignment and so felt (bad, badly) about not doing (good, well) on it.
8. The hockey team played (good, well) but lost the match.

Answers:
1. bad, really
2. strongly
3. bad
4. good, badly
5. really
6. well
7. bad, well
8. well

Words That Make Comparisons

You have a choice of many single words to modify a person, thing, or action.

EXAMPLES ▶ **The boat with tall masts won the race.**

Jason did his homework hurriedly.

Wintergreen desperately wanted to be president.

Gordo got his nickname because he is fat.

The underlined words are called the positive forms. However, if you wanted to compare two things, such as the height of the masts on one boat with the height of the masts on another, use the comparative form. To compare three things, use the superlative form.

EXAMPLES  **The boat with the tall masts did well, but the boat with the taller masts did better, and the boat with the tallest masts won the race.**

COMMENT: If you chose not to write such a long sentence, you could write, "The boat with the tallest masts won the race," and a reader would understand that there had to be at least two other boats in competition with the winner.

Jason did his homework more hurriedly than Gabe did.

COMMENT: The comparison here is with the speed Gabe used, not with the person, so the word "did" must appear in the sentence. If you were to write out the comparison that is implied, it would be ". . . than Gabe did his homework." Use the word "than" after comparatives to make meanings clear if there is any possibility of misinterpretation.

Make the comparative form of one-syllable words by adding *–er* to the word. If the positive form ends in a single consonant, double that letter before adding the *–er.*

Make the superlative form of one-syllable words by adding *–est* to the word.

Positive	Comparative	Superlative
small	smaller	smallest
long	longer	longest
fat	fatter	fattest
cold	colder	coldest
thin	thinner	thinnest

Make the comparative and superlative forms of two-syllable words that end in *–y* by changing the *–y* to an *–i* before adding the *–er* or *–est.*

Positive	Comparative	Superlative
happy	happier	happiest
pretty	prettier	prettiest

Make the *comparative* form of most other *two-syllable words* and *all three- or more syllable words* by putting *more* before them.

Make the superlative form of *most other two-syllable words* and *all three-or more syllable words* by putting *most* before them.

Positive	Comparative	Superlative
hurriedly	more hurriedly	most hurriedly
interesting	more interesting	most interesting
careful	more careful	most careful

OTHER FORMS OF COMPARATIVES AND SUPERLATIVES

A few words are called irregular modifiers because their comparative and superlative forms are made in different ways:

Positive	Comparative	Superlative
good	better	best
well	better	best
bad	worse	worst
badly	worse	worst
many	more	most
much	more	most
little	less	least

As you can see from this list, "more" and "most" as well as "less" and "least" are among the group.

EXAMPLES  **Sybil's report was <u>less interesting</u> than Manuel's was.**
Sybil's report was <u>more interesting</u> than Manuel's was.
This is the <u>least roomy</u> car I've ever ridden in.
This is the <u>most roomy</u> car I've ever ridden in.

NOTE: "Unique" is an adjective that means something is the only one of its kind or without equal. Therefore, you *can't* use comparatives or superlatives with it.

"Perfect" is another such word. It means what is complete and flawless of its kind. Obviously then, if something is already "perfect," it cannot be more than that. (You might, however, write about a person, place, or thing that is "less than perfect" or "almost perfect."

Some words allow you a *choice* between how you show the comparative and superlative:

Positive	Comparative	Superlative
yellow	yellower	yellowest
	or more yellow	most yellow
roomy	roomier	roomiest
	or more roomy	most roomy

NEVER use two comparative or two superlative forms for the same word in one sentence.

EXAMPLES ▶ ***Wrong:*** John feels more better today.

Right: John feels better today.

Wrong: Patricia's dress is the most fashionablest in the show.

Right: Patricia's dress is the most fashionable one in the show.

Activity 26-15

DIRECTIONS: Underline the correct comparative or superlative form in each of the following sentences.

EXAMPLE ▶ **Gilda ate the (more, most) dessert at the party, but didn't use sugar in her coffee because she said she was dieting.**

1. Jasper is tall, but he is not as tall as Hernando, who is the (taller, tallest) in the class.
2. Of the twins in my family, Yolanda is (more, most) talkative, and of the two sets of twins in my class, Pat is the (more, most) outgoing.
3. Painting a room white will make it look (bigger, biggest).
4. Of the hobbies wood-working and plastic-working, wood-working probably has (more, most) classes available.
5. When the Simmons family won the grand prize on the game show, it received the (more, most) expensive trip the show had ever given away.
6. You may find that you need a (large, larger) ring size than usual when weather gets hot and humid.
7. Herbert's newly-trimmed beard makes him look (young, younger) than when he wore it long.
8. I think the Boeing 747 is the (more, most) comfortable airplane in service today.

tallest
more
most
bigger
more
most
larger
younger
most

DIRECTIONS: Complete the following chart by writing in the missing positive, comparative, or superlative forms of the words on the lines.

	Positive	Comparative	Superlative
1.	round	rounder	roundest
2.	high	higher	highest
3.	debatable	more debatable	most debatable
4.	good	better	best
5.	hot	hotter	hottest
6.	corrupt	more corrupt	most corrupt
7.	simple	simpler	simplest
8.	terrible	more terrible	most terrible
9.	happy	happier	happiest
10.	zestful	more zestful	most zestful

DIRECTIONS: On the lines below, write five original sentences using one or more of the words in the above chart in each sentence. Underline each word from the chart as it appears in your sentence.

EXAMPLE  *My kite flew higher than the school building, but Kit's kite flew higher than that.*

1. South Florida has hotter year-round temperatures than North Florida, yet North Florida is much hotter in the summer.
2. My poodle is one of the happiest dogs on the block.
3. Public officials who are currupt seldom get re-elected.
4. It is good that many homeless in America are being helped, but it will be better when more can be done about the situation.
5. Paul is happier than Ramon, but Justin is the happiest of the three.

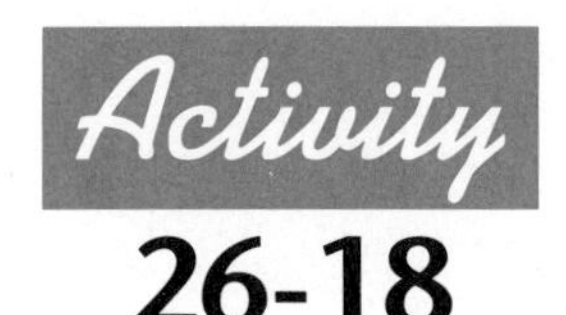

26-18

DIRECTIONS: Proofread the following paragraph by crossing out any errors. Write corrections above words that need them.

Even if you feel you are doing good in your job now and don't need to know anything new, you should think about learning a new skill that is in demand. Technology is growing more faster than almost any other industry today, so taking computer courses is a real wise decision. In our changing economy, it's also a gooder idea to upgrade your job skills so that if your current employer begins to reduce the work force, you will not suffer so bad. You will be ready to look for a job in a field that is growing more bigger every day. The most computer classes you can take, the best you will be prepared to stay a worker. You may be surprised at how easy you can learn to operate or repair a computer. Don't be afraid you won't do good, because you will. You may even do so good that you choose to make a job change. The worse that can happen is that you will have a more better understanding of computers and technology.

Even if you feel you are doing ~~good~~ well in your job now and don't need to know anything new, you should think about learning a new skill that is in demand. Technology is growing ~~more~~ faster than almost any other industry today, so taking computer courses is a ~~real~~ really wise decision. In our changing economy, it's also a ~~gooder~~ good idea to upgrade your job skills so that if your current employer begins to reduce the work force, you will not suffer so ~~bad~~ badly. You will be ready to look for a job in a field that is growing ~~more~~ bigger every day. The ~~most~~ more computer classes you can take, the ~~best~~ better you will be prepared to stay a worker. You may be surprised at how ~~easy~~ easily you can learn to operate or repair a computer. Don't be afraid you won't do ~~good~~ well, because you will. You may even do so ~~good~~ well that you choose to make a job change. The ~~worse~~ worst that can happen is that you will have a ~~more~~ better understanding of computers and technology.

Chapter 27

Parallelism in Sentence Structure

In this chapter you will

- see how parallel structures give force to writing
- practice comparison and contrast with parallel structures
- use parallelism to emphasize coordination
- try parallelism with words, phrases, and clauses

"I came; I saw; I conquered." ***Julius Caesar***

"...that the government of the people, by the people, and for the people shall not perish from the earth." ***Abraham Lincoln***

"Ask not what your country can do for you; ask what you can do for your country." ***John F. Kennedy***

"Give me your tired, your poor,/Your huddled masses yearning to breathe free... ***Emma Lazarus***

There is a rhythm and a power to these words by those whose names you recognize. The words stick in people's minds because of their rhythm. They also have force because of the repetition of grammatical structures. Caesar's boast is three independent clauses or sentences. Lincoln's is three prepositional phrases, and Kennedy's sentence is in two parts that mirror each other while shifting two of the words. The lines from the Emma Lazarus poem inscribed on the base of the Statue of Liberty are three modifiers of the noun "masses." All these are examples of parallel structures.

Parallelism in your own writing is a way of joining similar ideas and information—often of equal importance—and of giving them emphasis through repetition.

Parallelism is a repetition of grammatical structure that gives equal emphasis to two or more elements.

EXAMPLES ▶ Linda has a collection of **maps, globes,** and **guide books.** *(nouns of equal content)*

Humberto likes **to run, to jump,** and **to play.** *(verb forms repeated)*

Maria raises **chickens to eat** and **hamsters to sell.** *(phrases are parallel)*

Marilyn couldn't decide whether **to go on to college** or **to pursue her modeling career.** *(clauses are parallel)*

You can see from the examples that the repeated structures can be almost any part of a sentence. That is, what is parallel may be

- Nouns
- Verbs
- Modifiers
- Phrases
- Clauses

The repeated structures may also be full sentences (independent clauses) that are next to each other, as in

First, wash the car. Then, scrub the porch.

27-1

DIRECTIONS: Some of the following groups of words are in parallel structure and some are not. Put a **P** on the line next to the number of each group that shows parallelism. Leave the line blank if the group is *not* in parallel structure.

Then, on the line below each group write the reason you decided the group was parallel or not.

EXAMPLE ▶ ____ **books, records, pen**

two are plural but the third is not

P **coming and going**

both are verbs ending in -ing

P 1. at school, at home, at work

all are prepositional phrases

___ 2. to read, writing, and geography

the first is an infinitive, the second a verb form, the third is a noun

P 3. a good book, a cozy fire, and a cup of tea

all are nouns with modifiers

___ 4. is devoted to the children and they are described

verb forms "is devoted" and "are" differ

___ 5. bought an old house and it was remodeled

verbs "bought" and "was remodeled" differ

P 6. neither saw nor heard

both verbs are past tense

P 7. was pretty...was prettier

linking verb is followed by comparative form of same word

P 8. we examined ...we found

same pronoun is followed in each case by past tense verb

The choice of whether or not to make structures parallel is often up to you when you are writing or revising. Remember that the rhythm and power of parallelism helps the quality of your writing.

However, some grammatical structures *require* that you use parallelism: paired wording and the coordinate conjunctions which, because of how they control the sentence, indicate equal elements.

Always use parallel wording with these pairs:

either	**or**
neither	**nor**
not only	**but also**
both	**and**
whether	**or**

(parallel wording is underlined)

EXAMPLES ▶ Jack was **neither** tall **nor** handsome.

Scientists are not sure **whether** our weather is changing from the greenhouse effect **or** from a cycle of nature.

Not only is St. Augustine the oldest city in Florida **but** it is **also** the most beautiful city in the state.

Always use parallel wording on both sides of the coordinate conjunctions *and, but, or, nor,* and *yet.*

(parallel wording is underlined)

EXAMPLES ▶ Sam will go to the movies **and** to the grocery.

The professional wrestler was short, stocky, and muscular **but** the gymnast was small, thin, and muscular.

Hurricanes are often considered our most destructive storms **yet** tornadoes may be just as destructive.

27-2

DIRECTIONS: Some of the following sentences have parallel structures and some do not. Put a **P** on the line to left of each sentence which shows parallelism and an **N** if it does not have parallelism. If a sentence is not parallel, underline the wording which violates parallelism and revise it so the wording is parallel.

EXAMPLE ▶ _N_ **On the television news tonight people were shown burning buildings and many stores were looted.**

On the television news tonight people were shown burning buildings and looting of stores.

_P_ 1. T. S. Eliot was a distinguished poet, a noted playwright, and a dedicated cat lover.

_P_ 2. Either you are seriously mistaken or I am.

for warning merchant ships of their presence.

_N_ 3. Governments of the United States and Canada often collaborate in maintaining a sea patrol to destroy icebergs and for warning merchant ships of their presence.

Governments of the United States and Canada often collaborate in maintaining a sea patrol to destroy icebergs and to warn merchant ships of their presence

students will better understand the discussion if they can hear everything that is being said.

_N_ 4. A clear, strong voice not only helps a teacher to hold the attention of the class, but students will better understand the discussion if they can hear everything that is being said.

A clear, strong voice not only helps a teacher to hold the attention of the class, but helps students to better understand the discussion.

_P_ 5. Our guide was undecided about whether to continue on to the difficult trail or to return in safety to camp.

drinking

_N_ 6. A person who gets plenty of rest and drinking lots of fresh orange juice may ward off a common cold.

A person who gets plenty of rest and drinks lots of fresh orange juice may ward off a common cold.

and then he was thinking about sell it. But he made the decision

_N_ 7. He inherited the farm from his grandfather, and then he was thinking about sell it. But he made the decision not part with it.

He inherited the farm from his grandfather, thought about selling it, but decided not to part with it.

___ 8. The van ahead of us was either being driven by an intoxicated person or by an inexperienced driver.

____

____

27-3

DIRECTIONS: Each group of sentences below can be combined to make a single sentence with parallel grammatical structure. Write such a sentence below the sentence group.

EXAMPLE ▶ **Lin usually gets As in history.**
Lin usually gets As in economics.
Lin usually gets As in sociology.
Lin usually gets Bs in the natural sciences.

Lin usually gets As in history, economics, and sociology, but she usually gets Bs in the natural sciences.

1. The Kentucky Derby is a famous race that horses run every year.
   The Belmont is another famous yearly race.
   The Preakness is a third famous yearly race.

   The Kentucky Derby, the Belmont, and the Preakness are three famous annual horse races.

2. The Alamo is in San Antonio, Texas
   It was built as a Spanish mission.
   It became a fort.
   It is now a museum.

   The Alamo in San Antonio, Texas, was built as a Spanish mission, became a fort, and is now a museum.

3. Henry loves spaghetti.
   Henry loves spinach.
   Henry loves apple pie.
   Martine loves steak.
   Martine loves green beans.
   Martine loves chocolate cake.

   Henry loves spaghetti, spinach, and apple pie, but Martine loves steak, green beans, and chocolate cake.

4. The continental United States is divided into four time zones.
   There are 22 states and the District of Columbia in the Eastern time zone.
   There are 19 states in the Central time zone.
   There are 13 states in the Mountain time zone.
   There are only five states in the Pacific time zone.

   The continental United States is divided into four time zones with 22 states plus the District of Columbia in the Eastern zone, 19 states in the Central zone, 13 states in the Mountain zone, and five states in the Pacific zone.

5. Brian Wildsmith's *Birds* may be my favorite children's picture-story book. Maurice Sendak's *Where the Wild Things Are* may be my favorite children's picture-story book.

   Either Brian Wildsmith's *Birds* or Maurice Sendak's *Where the Wild Things Are* is my favorite children's picture-story book.

6. Dogs are not the most popular pets in the U.S. today.
   More cats are kept as pets in the U. S. today.
   Birds are also common pets.
   Rabbits are also common pets.
   Pigs are also common pets.

   More cats than dogs are kept as pets in the U. S. today, but birds, rabbits, and pigs are also common pets.

7. I may go to California this summer to visit a cousin.
   I may go to Texas this summer to visit a cousin.
   I may go to Colorado this summer to visit a cousin.
   I may stay home this summer and look for a job.

   I may go to California, Texas, or Colorado this summer to visit cousins, or I may stay home this summer and look for a job,

8. We may cook hamburgers Sunday at the picnic.
   We may cook hot dogs Sunday at the picnic.
   We may order in pizzas Sunday at the picnic.
   We may order in fried chicken Sunday at the picnic.

   Either we will cook hamburgers and hot dogs Sunday at the picnic, or we will order in pizzas and fried chicken.

Sharing

1. Form a group with two or three other people in the class. Let each person bring to the group meeting one piece of writing done during this term.
2. Read the work of others in the group, watching only for places where the author has written sentence structures that contain parallel elements or a series of sentences with parallel structure. Mark such passages in the margin.
3. Then reread the work of others in the group, this time pointing out places where the author could make the writing better by using parallel structures.

27-4

DIRECTIONS: The following paragraph would be better if the wording were parallel. Revise the paragraph for parallel wording and rewite the entire paragraph.

Sometimes when I have a weekday off during the summer, my family and I like to go to the zoo in our city. It is one of the finest and most large zoos in the country. It has animals from Africa and there are some from Asia, and it contains animals that come from Australia. The kids watch the animals and learning takes place about them. Informational signs are all over and there are also booklets about the animals all over. After a busy day at the zoo, we head to a special place nearby that we know about to swim and for picknicking. The reason we like to do these things on a weekday is that on weekends the zoo and also our special place nearby are full of people who are sloppy and they make a lot of noise.

Sometimes when I have a weekday off during the summer, my family and I like to go to the zoo in our city. It is one of the finest and largest zoos in the country. It has animals from Africa, Asia, and Australia. The kids watch the animals and learn about them. Informational signs and booklets about the animals are all over. After a busy day at the zoo, we head to a special place nearby that we know for swimming and picknicking. The reason we like to do these things on a weekday is that on weekends the zoo and our special place nearby are full of people who are sloppy and noisy.

Part V

Mechanics

Chapter 28 Commas

In this chapter you will

- review using a comma or commas
  - to separate items in a series
  - to separate modifiers
  - after introductory units
  - with conjunctions between independent clauses
  - around non-essential phrases
  - to set off appositives
  - for other purposes
- practice using commas in sentences and paragraphs

Reading long passages without commas would be very difficult. You wouldn't know where the author intended you to pause or how sentence elements are related to one another. Therefore, as a writer, you use commas as signals that make clear the meanings of many sentences.

Commas have so many different customs of use that many people believe they are the most difficult punctuation mark to master. They work with words, as well as with phrases and clauses. Also, commas are used in a number of other ways, from noting dates to the closings of letters. In this chapter you will review and practice the customs for using commas to set off:

- a series of items or of modifiers
- introductory words, and dependent phrases and clauses
- independent clauses joined by coordinate conjunctions

- phrases or clauses in a sentence that are not required for meaning to be clear
- nouns or noun phrases which identify or explain another noun or nouns
- interrupters or secondary information
- a variety of other uses

Commas to Separate a Series of Items

Use commas to *separate items in a series.* Also, use a comma if there is an "and" before the last item, unless the two are closely connected in meaning.

EXAMPLE  **The archaeologists working at the burial mound uncovered weapons, pottery, ceremonial beads, and ornaments.**

COMMENT: By putting the comma before the "and," the writer indicates that the ceremonial beads were a category different from the category of ornaments. If the comma were not there, the reader would understand that both the beads and the ornaments were ceremonial.

28-1

DIRECTIONS: Put commas where they are needed to make meaning clear in the following sentences. Be sure to make the commas dark enough to be seen easily.

EXAMPLE  **Many students at this school come from South America, Central America, Africa, and Asia.**

1. François sent his daughter to the grocery store to buy oranges apples potatoes cereal and milk.
2. She studied at night worked all day and went to the library whenever she had a free moment.
3. Accounting history English and statistics require a great deal of homework.
4. Many cities have streets named for John F. Kennedy Martin Luther King Jr. Jimmy Carter and George Washington.
5. The destructive forces of nature include tornadoes floods lightning and hurricanes.
6. Farmers who plant food crops have to deal with the problems of insects bad weather plant diseases and the high cost of labor to harvest a crop.
7. Coffee is grown in Brazil Jamaica El Salvador and many other countries.
8. Snakes crocodiles alligators and lizards all belong to the reptile family.

oranges, apples, potatoes, cereal,

night, worked all day,

Accounting, history, English, and statistics

John F. Kennedy, Martin Luther King, Jr., Jimmy Carter, and George Washington.

tornadoes, floods, lightning,

insects, bad weather, plant diseases,

Brazil, Jamaica, El Salvador,

Snakes, crocodiles, alligators,

Commas to Separate Modifiers (Adjectives)

Use commas to separate two or more adjectives (modifiers) of equal importance. (Adjectives are of equal importance if "and" or "or" could separate them.) **That is, "and" or "or" could separate the adjectives.**

EXAMPLES  **Tall, stately trees were growing near the wall.**
Rude, obscene, or loud comments will not be tolerated.
BUT: Old oak trees bordered the driveway.
(No comma because "old" [age] and "oak" [species] are not of equal importance.)

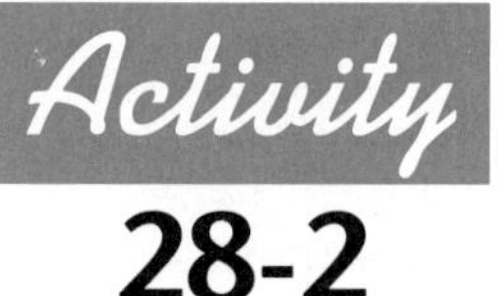

28-2

DIRECTIONS: Put commas where they are appropriate in the following sentences. Be sure to make them dark enough to be seen easily. Not all sentences will require commas.

EXAMPLE  **The well-dressed man was thin, tall, and dark.**

Answers
long, rolling
Red, green, yellow,
young, spirited
enameled, ornately-decorated
vain, proud,
Bright red, delicious-looking

1. The long rolling waves were perfect for surfing.
2. Red green yellow and blue ribbons were tied to the balloons.
3. The young spirited horses were ready to begin the race.
4. The enameled ornately-decorated vase was on top of the highly-polished table.
5. The two laughing sisters hopped up and down on the porch while clapping their hands.
6. Birds with brilliant feathers are often described as vain proud and haughty.
7. The small child had sad blue eyes that gave him a look of great wisdom.
8. Bright red delicious-looking fruit was piled in a huge plastic bowl in the center of the table.

28-3

DIRECTIONS: Sometimes the information in several short sentences can be combined to achieve better sentence structure. If so, such information could become a series of items or modifiers separated by commas. Using the content of each group of sentences, rewrite the information as a single sentence. Use your own paper if you need more space.

EXAMPLE  **The day was windy.**
The day was cloudy.
The day was cold.

The day was windy, cloudy, and cold.

1. Michael found fresh yellow peppers at the grocery store.
   Michael found fresh red peppers at the grocery store.
   Michael found fresh green peppers at the grocery store.
   He wanted them for his dinner salad.

   Michael found fresh yellow, red, and green peppers at the grocery store for his dinner salad.

2. I have a favorite CD store.
   The store features a large stock of CDs.
   The store features a stock of current CDs.

   My favorite CD store features a large, current stock of CDs.

3. Ruth has a final in English on Monday.
   Ruth has a final in math on Monday.
   Ruth has a final in geology on Monday.

   Ruth has finals in English, math, and geology on Monday.

4. Acid rain is harming the environment.
   Destruction of the rain forest is harming the environment.
   Deliberate and accidental oil spills are harming the environment.
   The dumping of toxic waste is harming the environment.

   Acid rain, the destruction of the rain forest, deliberate and accidental oil spills, and the dumping of toxic waste are harming the environment.

5. All the friends at the wedding had a wonderful time.
   All the aunts at the wedding had a wonderful time.
   All the uncles at the wedding had a wonderful time.
   All the cousins at the wedding had a wonderful time.

   All the aunts, uncles, cousins, and friends had a wonderful time at the wedding.

Commas After Introductory Words, Phrases, and Clauses

Use a comma to set off an *introductory word* at the beginning of a sentence.

EXAMPLES 

However, everyone must be concerned about the environment.

Yes, it is true that salesman said the product would not stain the carpet.

Use a comma after an *introductory phrase* at the beginning of a sentence.

EXAMPLES ▶ **In deciding to finish school, Juanita showed good judgment.**

To demonstrate the principle of gravity, the teacher dropped a pencil and a book on the floor.

Behind the house, at the back near the garage, the rake leaned against a tall pile of leaves.

Activity 28-4

DIRECTIONS: Put commas where they are needed after introductory words or phrases in the sentences that follow .

EXAMPLE ▶ **No, you should not go to the play alone.**

Well,
skin-diving,
Incidentally,
other hand,
outdone,
Yes,
the truth,
Startled,

1. Well I'll have to take that into consideration.
2. Keeping in mind the danger of skin-diving it is important to dive with a partner.
3. Incidentally did you remember to take out the garbage?
4. On the other hand most students study less than they should.
5. Not to be outdone the gymnast did a triple flip from the bar.
6. Yes it is true that young children need a regular bedtime.
7. To tell the truth the parrot is quite a noisy pet.
8. Startled I dropped the cup on my foot.

Use a comma *after a dependent clause* that begins a sentence.

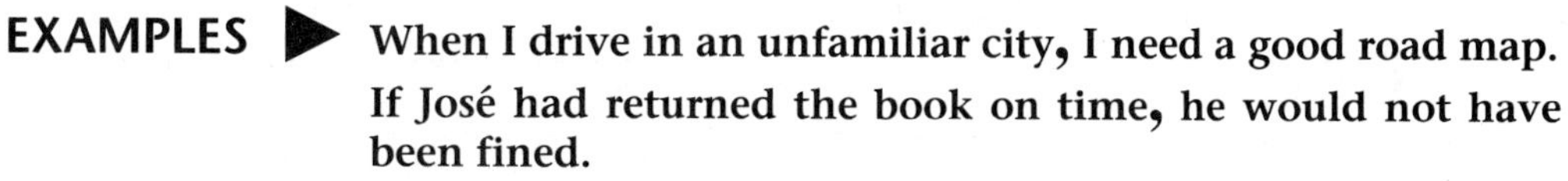

EXAMPLES ▶ **When I drive in an unfamiliar city, I need a good road map.**

If José had returned the book on time, he would not have been fined.

COMMENT: A subordinate (dependent) clause is a group of words containing a subject and verb, but it cannot stand alone. It begins with a subordinating word (see Chapter 21):

after	although	as
as if	as though	because
before	ever since	if
rather than	since	so that
that	unless	until
when	whenever	where
whereas	while	

Activity 28-5

DIRECTIONS: If commas are needed in any of the following sentences, insert them as appropriate.

EXAMPLE ▶ **If you want the best results, it is important to follow directions carefully when you assemble a toy from a kit.**

Answers
movie,
the car,
plan ahead,
bookshelf,
specializes,
window,
highway,

1. So that you are sure to get into the movie get your tickets before you wander around the mall.
2. When the mechanic looked at the car the problem with the radiator was corrected almost immediately.
3. Several students stayed to ask questions after the class was over.
4. Although it is better to plan ahead always be willing to change plans.
5. After Nguen finished building the bookshelf he decided to make a table.
6. When a doctor specializes at least three years of additional study are required beyond medical school.
7. As I was looking out the window I felt a chill from just seeing the heavy snowfall.
8. When you reach the highway turn right.

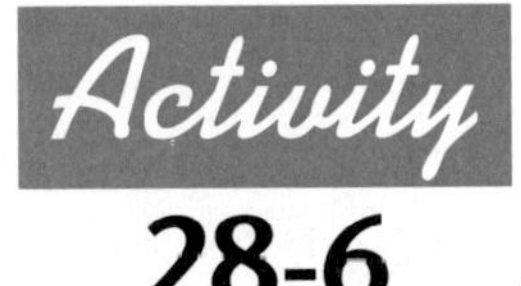

28-6

DIRECTIONS: Combine the following short sentences in each group to make one sentence that begins with a dependent clause

EXAMPLE ▶ **The clock kept losing time.**
We had to have the clock fixed.

Because the clock kept losing time, we had to have it fixed.

1. This computer will not perform the way I expected it to.
   This computer is frustrating me.

   Because it will not perform the way I expected it to, this computer is frustrating me.

2. We got to the concert.
   We found out something.
   Some other people had taken our seats.

   When we got to the concert, we found some other people had taken our seats.

3. The Persian Gulf War was short.
   The Coalition forces lost people.
   The Coalition forces lost equipment.

   Although the Persian Gulf War was short, the Coalition forces lost people and equipment.

4. The basketball game may be on TV tonight.
   Be sure to let me know what is on.
   I want to watch the basketball game on TV.

   If the basketball game is on TV tonight, be sure to let me know so I can watch it.

5. The family next door was at work.
   Thieves broke into a house.
   The house broken into was the one belonging to the family next door.

   While the family next door was at work, thieves broke into their house.

Commas with a Conjunction Between Independent Clauses

Use a comma between two independent clauses joined by a coordinate conjunction. The coordinate conjunctions are *and, but, for, or, nor, so,* and *yet.*

EXAMPLES ▶ ***Batman*** **was my favorite movie for a long time, but I recently saw a rerun of *Rocky*, and now have a new favorite.**

I do not like seafood, yet I love to smell clam chowder as it is cooking.

COMMENT: See Chapter 20, pages 313-325, for more information about independent clauses and coordinating conjunctions.

28-7

DIRECTIONS: The proofreading mark for a comma is an inverted ^ (that is, the V points up), with a comma under it. Using this proofreading mark, put a comma in each of the following sentences where one is needed.

EXAMPLE ▶ **Jolanda and Darlene decided that they wanted to study nursing ^, so both women enrolled for classes.**

careers^,
collapse^,
building^,
mountains^,
bonuses^,
day^,
events^,
winter^,

1. It is never too late to change careers but it helps if you plan ahead by studying and setting goals.
2. The bank seemed ready to collapse but my money was insured by the federal government.
3. The head of the environmental committee led the parade of people in front of the building and the group succeeded in making its point about litter.
4. Hiking on the Appalachian Trail is a wonderful way to see the mountains and the mountains certainly give you a view of what America must have been like when it was first settled.
5. Many businesses do not have employee bonuses yet having them would seem the perfect way to increase productivity.
6. Eric and Joachim play "Nintendo" for many hours each day so their parents are considering restricting them to one hour a day
7. Reading *Newsweek* magazine regularly is a good way to keep up with current events so anyone who feels uninformed should get a subscription.
8. Many birds who migrate fly hundreds of miles each winter yet they arrive at the same location every year.

Commas for Phrases or Clauses that are NOT Needed for Meaning in a Sentence

Use commas to set off phrases or clauses that are *not needed for meaning in the sentence.* Such a phrase or clause at the beginning or end of a sentence will require just one comma; in the middle of a sentence it will need a comma before and one after.

Do *not* use commas to enclose a phrase or clause that is necessary for the full meaning of the sentence.

EXAMPLES ▶ **Anna, who lives down the street, always walks her dog early in the morning.**

COMMENT: The clause "who lives down the street" could be removed without the sentence changing its principal idea, that it is Anna who walks her dog. The fact that Anna lives down the street is extra information and is *not* needed for the sentence to make sense. That is, the clause is *not* needed for meaning, so it is enclosed in commas.

The cave, hidden by bushes, was a perfect place for the children to play.

COMMENT: The phrase "hidden by bushes" adds to a reader's understanding of the sentence, but the sense of the sentence would not be changed in any great way if the words were omitted. Therefore, commas enclose the phrase.

BUT: The girl who lives down the street always walks her dog early in the morning.

COMMENT: The clause "who lives down the street" is necessary for meaning. That is, it tells exactly which girl walks her dog every morning. If you took the clause out of the sentence, the meaning would change. Therefore, there are no commas enclosing the descriptive words "who lives down the street" that tell about the girl who walks her dog.

OR: The cave that was hidden by bushes was a perfect place for the children to play.

COMMENT: The phrase "that was hidden by bushes" identifies this particular cave; others might not have been such a perfect playing place. The phrase is necessary for the sense of the sentence and therefore commas do not enclose it.

CAUTION: As a writer, you must consider the intent of a sentence before deciding whether or not a phrase or clause requires commas to set it off.

EXAMPLE ▶ **The marathon runner feeling ill decided to drop out of the race.**

or

The marathon runner, feeling ill, decided to drop out of the race.

COMMENT: The first sentence focuses on a particular runner from among all those in the race: the one who felt ill. The second sentence is about a decision the runner made. Whether it was because of feeling ill or being too warm doesn't really matter within the context of the sentence.

28-8

DIRECTIONS: In each of the following sentences, underline the clause that is **not** necessary to the meaning. On the line below, write the sentence and insert commas where they are required.

EXAMPLE ▶ **Madame Curie <u>who discovered radium</u> was born in Poland.**

Madame Curie, who discovered radium, was born in Poland.

1. The animal we call "coral" which builds a covering of limestone leaves behind its skeleton when it dies.

   The animals we call "coral," which builds a covering of limestone, leaves behind its skeleton when it dies.

2. Comets which are related to asteroids sometimes have tails that are thousands of miles long.

   Comets, which are related to asteroids, sometimes have tails that are thousands of miles long.

3. I just finished my homework which required me to use the dictionary.

   I just finished my homework, which required me to use the dictionary.

4. Mr. Parker who runs the local dairy has been raising cattle on his farm for forty years.

   Mr. Parker, who runs the local dairy, has been raising cattle on his farm for forty years.

5. The Manatee an endangered species lives in the coastal waters of Florida.

   The Manatee, an endangered species, lives in the coastal waters of Florida.

6. The little puppy who seemed not to care where he was sat near his water bowl and barked.

The little puppy, who seemed not to care where he was, sat near his water bowl and barked.

7. The computer which is becoming more complex each day is no longer the newest addition to the technological age.

The computer, which is becoming more complex each day, is no longer the newest addition to the technological age.

8. The Statue of Liberty which attracts thousands of tourists weekly was completely restored with funds raised by small groups.

The Statue of Liberty, which attracts thousands of tourists weekly, was completely restored with funds raised by small groups.

Activity 28-9

DIRECTIONS: Put commas in those sentences that need them, and write a C on the line to the left of the number to show it is a sentence to which you have added a comma. Leave the other sentences as they are

EXAMPLE ▶ ___ **The man wearing black is Jack's cousin.**
 **Mr. Morris, wearing black, is Jack's cousin.**

2. C Jack, looking around the room,
3. C room, sporting the Bart Simpson poster,
4. C Mr. Stakowski, wearing a red sweater,

6. C The bus, looking sadly in need of repair,

8. C The tree, waving leaves in the breeze,
NOTE: 6 and 8 could also be without commas.

___ 1. The soccer team that had big smiles was certainly the one that won.
___ 2. My cousin Jack looking around the room noticed the new picture that I bought last week.
___ 3. The door to my room sporting the Bart Simpson poster is never closed to my friends.
___ 4. Mr. Stakowski wearing a red sweater was the leader of the group on the last nature hike.
___ 5. Esmerelda leaned over the railing and shouted to her friends in the hallway below.
___ 6. The bus looking sadly in need of repair wobbled slowly down the street.
___ 7. The hermit crab wears a borrowed house and changes it often..
___ 8. The tree waving leaves in the breeze was ablaze with color.

Appositives

Use commas to set off a word or group of words that rename or identify a noun or pronoun in the sentence.

EXAMPLES  **Beethoven, the deaf composer, had to quit school at thirteen, and by age eighteen supported his mother and brothers.**

We spent three days in Atlanta, the capital of Georgia, studying Civil War history.

Snooker and carom are the English and French versions of billiards, a game played around the world.

COMMENT: In the first sentence, "the deaf composer," identifies Beethoven and is at the beginning of the sentence. In the second sentence, the appositive identifying Atlanta is in the middle of the sentence. In the last sentence, the words describing billiards are at the end. Therefore, an appositive can appear anywhere in a sentence, as long as it is next to the word or group of words it renames or identifies.

28-10

DIRECTIONS: Underline the appositives in the following sentences and circle the word or group of words they rename or identify. Add commas to set off the appositive.

  **The (queen bee), <u>the mother of all the bees in a hive</u>, is fed and waited upon by the worker bees.**

Words that students are asked to circle are shown in italics.

Salvador Dali, <u>a painter whose work is surrealistic</u>,

<u>Ford Mustang</u>, *a relatively inexpensive car.*

<u>a solution for our waste problems</u>, *recycling*,

Bioluminescence, <u>light that has little or no heat</u>,

Mr. Penagos, <u>my Spanish teacher</u>,

Stephen King, <u>the famous author</u>,

Widget, <u>the popular, all-purpose mechanical device</u>,

Oscar, <u>the Academy Award statuette</u>,

1. Salvador Dali a painter whose work is surrealistic is one of the few artists who became famous in his lifetime.
2. A car that has been popular since the 1950s is the Ford Mustang a relatively inexpensive car.
3. One beginning toward a solution for our waste problems, recycling is becoming more widely practiced.
4. Bioluminescence light that has little or no heat can be seen in many forms of insect and animal life.
5. Mr. Penagos my Spanish teacher told us a funny story about the time he went to Mexico on vacation.
6. Though he writes horror stories Stephen King the famous author lives in a small New England town and leads a fairly ordinary life.
7. I expect to buy a Widget the popular all-purpose mechanical device as soon as the price comes down.
8. Receiving an Oscar the Academy Award statuette is the highest point in the professional lives of most people in the movie industry.

Other Uses of the Comma

Use commas to set off interrupters or secondary information within a sentence.

EXAMPLES ▶ **It is unheard of, to be sure.**

We may, perhaps, have been wrong to plan the picnic for next week.

John, not Freddy, played the drum solo at the concert.

Use a comma between the day of the month and the year.

EXAMPLES ▶ **Jason was born February 3, 1977.**

BUT: Do not use a comma after the day if you invert the day and month (as in "military style" dates).

Jason was born 3 February 1977.

AND: Do not use a comma between a month and a year, or a season and a year.

Jason was born in February 1977.

Jason was born in Winter 1977.

AND: Put a comma after the year, if the date does not end the sentence.

Jason was born February 3, 1977, in County Hospital.

Use a comma between the city and state in an address, and between units of an address written as text (not set vertically).

EXAMPLES ▶ **Howard lives in Boston, Massachusetts.**

Joachin's address is 490 Elm Street, San Francisco, California 99123.

COMMENT: Note that there is *never* a comma between a state (abbreviated or not) and a zip code number.

Use a comma to set off the name or title of a person or persons addressed.

EXAMPLES ▶ **Mary, it is your turn to sit in the back seat.**

What are you doing, Joshua?

Server, please bring the check.

Come here, Lynn, and sit next to me.

Use a comma to set off a mild interjection—that is, one without strong feeling or emotion.

EXAMPLES ▶ **Well, I think it is time to go home now.**
Oh, the answer should be obvious.

Use a comma after the greeting in an informal letter, and after the closing in both informal and business letters.

EXAMPLES ▶ **Dear Wilma,**
Sincerely,
Yours truly,

28-11

DIRECTIONS: Put commas where they are needed in the following sentences.

EXAMPLE ▶ **Today is July 4, 1776, and the Continental Congress is about to meet in Philadelphia, Pennsylvania.**

1. Goodness it takes a long time to make bread from flour yeast and water.
2. Ivan graduated from college on April 29 1985 and he joined the Air Force the next year.
3. Is it true that you are going back to El Salvador when you finish this project Ricardo?
4. The entire movie furthermore lacked any excitement.
5. Susan's parents are moving to Salt Lake City Utah.
6. Well we never know how strong we are until the need for strength arises.
7. On August 22 1951 the Harlem Globetrotters performed before 75,052 spectators in the Olympic Stadium in Berlin.
8. Remember to take out the garbage Francis before you turn on the television.

Goodness, flour, yeast,
April 29, 1985,
project, Ricardo
movie, furthermore,
Salt Lake City, Utah
Well,
August 22, 1951,
garbage, Francis,

Activity

28-12

DIRECTIONS: Add commas where needed in the following paragraph, and mark with an X those commas which should not be in the paragraph.

After my school team won the last, football game of my senior year we decided, my three friends, and I, to join another group of friends to go to a victory dance, at the gym. Inside, the gym was decorated, with balloons banners colored lights and streamers. On the stage next to the band the principal was making an announcement. He said "Rude offensive, behavior will not be tolerated and no one wearing shoes, will be allowed on the dance floor." I guess that he said this, because the floor might be damaged, but I saw several couples dancing with their shoes on anyway. The band a local one wasn't very good but it was trying I suppose. In addition the band was so loud that I had to try to read lips to understand what anyone was saying which added to the confusion. However going to the dance seemed a good choice at the time since all our friends were there. We planned to leave soon and go to the annual Harvest Festival which takes place every year on November, 21. Right after, thinking about leaving I saw my best friend, Charles who was wearing bright pink socks pull off his shoes. As I watched him dance a small crowd gathered so I pulled off my shoes, and, joined him in the fun. I learned a valuable lesson. If you are patient what starts out as a disaster just might turn out to be fun.

After my school team won the last football game of my senior year, we decided, my three friends and I, to join another group of friends to go to a victory dance at the gym. Inside, the gym was decorated with balloons, banners, colored lights, and streamers. On the stage, next to the band, the principal was making an announcement. He said, "Rude, offensive behavior will not be tolerated, and no one wearing shoes will be allowed on the dance floor." I guess that he said this because the floor might be damaged, but I saw several couples dancing with their shoes on anyway. The band, a local one, wasn't very good, but it was trying, I suppose. In addition, the band was so loud that I had to try to read lips to understand what anyone was saying, which added to the confusion. However, going to the dance seemed a good choice at the time, since all our friends were there. We planned to leave soon and go to the annual Harvest Festival, which takes place every year on November 21. Right after thinking about leaving I saw my best friend, Charles, who was wearing bright pink socks, pull off his shoes. As I watched him dance, a small crowd gathered, so I pulled off my shoes and joined him in the fun. I learned a valuable lesson. If you are patient, what starts out as a disaster just might turn out to be fun.

Chapter 29

In this chapter you will

- use apostrophes for possessives and contractions
- use quotation marks for quotations and titles
- review end-of-sentence punctuation marks
- use other punctuation marks conventionally

Punctuation marks are the signposts that you, as a writer, give to your readers. They tell readers how to interpret a series of words, when to pause in reading, when a listing or omission will follow, or when a person owns something. In short, you direct how someone will read, and get meaning from, your writing by putting the punctuation marks or symbols at the appropriate places.

Each section in this chapter is about one kind of punctuation symbol, in addition to Commas (in Chapter 28), you use to signal readers:

- apostrophes
- quotation marks
- colons
- parentheses
- periods
- question marks
- exclamation marks
- dashes

Apostrophes

Apostrophes have two main uses:

1. **to show possession** or ownership, and
2. **to show a contraction**—that is, one or more letters are omitted.

APOSTROPHES FOR POSSESSION

One way to show possession is to use such wording as "owned by," "belongs to," or "of."

The apostrophe is a shorter way to show possession.

	(shows possession	*(shorter form)*
EXAMPLES ▶	**the dog owned by Jane**	**Jane's dog**
	the car that belongs to my cousin	**my cousin's car**
	the smile of the child	**the child's smile**

Show possession by adding an apostrophe and an *s* ('s) to words that do not end in "s."

EXAMPLES ▶ **the teacher's book**
the men's ideas
Roberto's money

29-1

DIRECTIONS: Either the long form or the short form (using the apostrophe and "s") of the phrase is missing from each pair in the following list. Fill in the omitted form so that each column will be complete.

EXAMPLE ▶ *(long form)* **the baseball owned by my brother** *(short form)* *my brother's baseball*

	(long form)	*(short form)*
1.	the records possessed by Mark	Mark's records
2.	the secretary of the lawyer	the lawyer's secretary
3.	the collar of the dog	the dog's collar
4.	the nest of the bird	the bird's nest
5.	the voice of a singer	a singer's voice
6.	the uniforms owned by the team	the team's uniforms
7.	the towel belonging to Cliff	Cliff's towel
8.	the camera owned by Felicia	Felicia's camera

29-2

DIRECTIONS: Rewrite each of the following sentences using apostrophes to show ownership.

EXAMPLE ▶ **I tried to find the homework belonging to Jean.**

I tried to find Jean's homework.

1. We must all work to protect the environment of the earth.

   We must all work to protect the earth's environment.

2. The battery of the car died, leaving me stranded.

   The car's battery died, leaving me stranded.

3. The lost coat belonging to Jeremy turned up in the cloakroom.

   Jeremy's lost coat turned up in the cloakroom.

4. The fast ball possessed by the pitcher was clocked at 95 mph.

   The pitcher's fast ball was clocked at 95 mph.

5. The computer of Willamae is not as new as the computer of Wilhelmena.

   Willamae's computer is not as new as Wilhelmena's.

6. The cut on the front paw of the dog belonging to Antonio required stitches.

   The cut on Antonio's dog's front paw required stitches.

7. The record collection of Bob is larger than the collection of Bill.

   Bob's record collection is larger than Bill's.

8. The return address of the letter was smeared, so I couldn't read it.

   The letter's return address was smeared, so I couldn't read it.

Show *joint possession* of a single item by using the apostrophe only for the last owner noted.

EXAMPLES ▶ **We saw photos of mother and dad's vacation.**
Glenn and Steven's friendship began in first grade.
Judy and Tim's grandchildren are adorable!

Show possession by adding *only* an apostrophe to words that end in "s."

EXAMPLES ▶ **Ross' weekend plans**
the girls' boyfriends
the police officers' cars

29-3

DIRECTIONS: Fill in the blanks on the right column by writing the short possessive form for each phrase in the left column.

EXAMPLE ▶ *(long form)* *(short form)*
the departure of the airplanes *the airplanes' departure*

	(long form)	*(short form)*
1.	the sounds of the horns	the horns' sounds
2.	the leaves of the trees	the trees' leaves
3.	the grades of the classes	the classes' grades
4.	the presidents of the clubs	the clubs' presidents
5.	the prices of the stores	the stores' prices
6.	the applause of the fans	the fans' applause
7.	the assets of the companies	the companies' assets
8.	the anchors of the boats	the boats' anchors

29-4

DIRECTIONS: Rewrite the following sentences using apostrophes to show ownership.

EXAMPLE ▶ **The banks of the rivers are eroding.**
The rivers' banks are eroding.

1. The lead singers of the two bands sang a song together.

   The two bands' lead singers sang a song together.

2. The designs of the dresses are similar to those worn in the 1920s.

   The dresses' designs are similar to those worn in the 1920s.

3. The motor home of the Joneses was parked in the driveway.

   The Joneses' motor home was parked in the driveway.

4. I will check the schedule of the bus to see what time it leaves.

   I will check the bus' schedule to see what time it leaves.

5. The dog belonging to Douglas ran away.

   Douglas' dog ran away.

6. The parents of the twins bought them identical clothes.

   The twins' parents bought them identical clothes.

7. The stories of the two reporters had several differences.
   The two reporters' stories had several differences.

8. The rates of most hotels are higher during peak tourist times.
   Most hotels' rates are higher during peak tourist times.

A Note About Possessives

"Purists" say that inanimate objects—chairs, pens, hotels, etc.—cannot have possessive forms because they cannot own anything. Therefore, to refer to parts of them—the seat of the chair, the tip of the pen, the rooms of the hotel—the longer, phrase form is accurate. However, in ordinary conversation and in informal writing, we do use "the chair's seat," "the pen's tip," and the "hotel's rooms."

SHOWING POSSESSION WITHOUT AN APOSTROPHE: POSSESSIVE PRONOUNS

> **The *possessive pronouns* already show ownership and *never* contain an apostrophe.**

These are the possessive pronouns:

my mine our ours your yours their
his her hers its their theirs

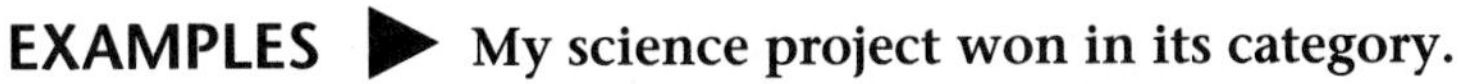

EXAMPLES ▶ **My science project won in its category.**
(Note that "its" is a possessive pronoun and quite different from the contraction "it's or "it is.")
Her feeling is that your homework wasn't done carefully.
Where is his home?

APOSTROPHES FOR CONTRACTIONS

A **contraction is two words combined** to form one word. In the combining, some letters are omitted.

> **An apostrophe indicates a contraction by showing where letters have been omitted in combining the words.**

EXAMPLES ▶ it + is = **it's** (the letter "i" is omitted)
(This contraction is quite different from the possessive word "its," which has no apostrophe.)
I + will = **I'll** (the letters "wi" are omitted)
you + have = **you've** (the letters "ha" are omitted)
did + not = **didn't** (the letter "o" is omitted)
can + not = **can't** (the letters "no" are omitted)
he + is = **he's** (the letter "i" is omitted)

29-5

DIRECTIONS: Write the contraction next to each of the following word groups.

EXAMPLE ▶ can not *can't*

1. you are *you're*
2. will not *won't*
3. could not *couldn't*
4. you have *you've*
5. does not *doesn't*
6. you will *you'll*
7. let us *let's*
8. we are *we're*
9. should not *shouldn't*
10. I am *I'm*
11. he is *he's*
12. they will *they'll*
13. they had *they'd*
14. has not *hasn't*
15. were not *weren't*

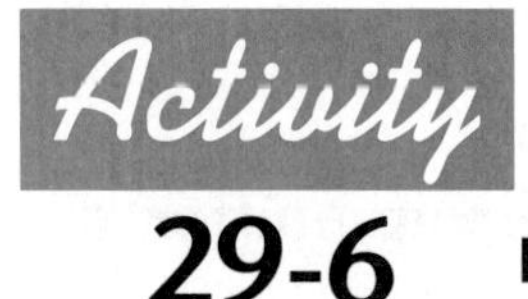

29-6

DIRECTIONS: Rewrite the following sentences, using contractions instead of the longer forms that now appear. Circle the contraction you write.

EXAMPLE ▶ **You will never guess who I saw today!**

(You'll) never guess who I saw today!

Contractions are shown in italics.

1. He is one of the nicest people I have ever met.
   He's one of the nicest people *I've* ever met.

2. They will have to stay home Saturday night if they do not do well on their exams.
   They'll have to stay home Saturday night if they *don't* do well on their exams.

3. They have not been to Colorado before.
   They *haven't* been to Colorado before.

4. Let us go to the movies tonight if you are feeling better.
   Let's go to the movies tonight if *you're* feeling better.

5. They had better be quiet, or I will throw them out of the library.
   They'd better be quiet or *I'll* throw them out of the library.

A NOTE ABOUT CONTRACTIONS

Because we usually use contractions in speaking, they are acceptable for personal writing, business memos, and other informal purposes. They are also used increasingly in business letters. However, contractions are often considered unsuitable for formal writing or for academic work. Ask your instructor if there is a policy or a preference about using or not using contractions. Generally, let your choice of audience and the purpose for which you are writing be guides to the appropriateness of contractions.

Quotation Marks

Quotation marks must appear in pairs, one at the beginning of the quoted material and one at the end.

Enclose the *exact words* of another person (a speaker or writer) in quotation marks.

EXAMPLES ▶ **Francisco told Millie, "I'd love to stay and talk, but I don't have the time today."**

"We better go to the theater early," warned Tillie.

Shakespeare wrote, "Neither a borrower nor a lender be."

Do not confuse a direct quotation with an indirect one.

DIRECT: Jimmy said, "I've never been to Canada."

INDIRECT: Jimmy said that he'd never been to Canada.

COMMENT: In the direct quotation, Jimmy is making the statement. The indirect quotation *reports* that Jimmy said something.

Begin the first word of a quotation with a capital letter. If the quotation is interrupted by a comment, begin the second part of the quotation with a small letter.

EXAMPLES ▶ **"I never knew you like sailing," he said.**

She replied, "No, I didn't expect to be here so early."

COMMENT: Note where commas and period are placed when there is a quotation.

EXAMPLES ▶ *(with interrupter)*

"I haven't eaten all day," he said, "but I'm not hungry."

"I have so much homework," Pat complained, "that I don't know if I can get it all done."

Enclose in quotation marks the titles of short written works, including poems, short stories, book chapters, essays, newspaper headlines, magazine articles, and songs.

EXAMPLES ▶ **Professor Crabbe assigned us to read a newspaper article titled "The Future of the Space Program."**

"Hey, Jude" is my favorite Beatles' song.

We read "The Open Door" in English class.

Did you ever read the Edgar Allan Poe poem called "The Raven"?

CAUTION: Titles of longer written works—books, newspapers, plays—as well as movies and television series are underlined or printed in *italics*.

***CAUTION:* *Never* enclose the titles of your own essays or other class work in quotation marks and *never* underline them.**

29-7

DIRECTIONS: Some of these sentences have quotation marks where they don't belong, and some of them do *not* have quotation marks where they should be. Some of the capitalization with quotation marks will also need to be corrected. Write the *correct* forms of the sentences on the lines below each. Be sure to make all the punctuation marks clear and easy to read.

EXAMPLE ▶ The witness told the jury, I know exactly who shot the man.

The witness told the jury, "I know exactly who shot the man."

1. Wilma sang Over the Rainbow as her audition piece for the school production of The Wizard of Oz.

   Wilma sang "Over the Rainbow" as her audition piece for the school production of The Wizard of Oz.

2. The surprised shopper said, I wouldn't have believed a person really spent so much money on a camera!

   The surprised shopper said, "I wouldn't have believed a person really spent so much money on a camera!"

3. "Just because I run five miles a day, Jerry said," "Doesn't mean" I could "run a marathon."

   "Just because I run five miles a day," Jerry said, "doesn't mean I could run a marathon."

4. I submitted an article called Changes in America's Small Towns to Around the U.S.A. magazine.

   I submitted an article called "Changes in America's Small Towns" to Around the U.S.A. magazine.

5. Herbert said to me, "if I'd known you like apple pie so much," i would have baked you "two."

   Herbert said to me, "If I'd known you like apple pie so much, I would have baked you two."

6. The opening chapter, Why We Study the Stars, gave beginning astronomy students an introduction to the course.

   The opening chapter, "Why We Study the Stars," gave beginning astronomy students an introduction to the course.

7. "I want to know who did this, fumed the teacher, "And I want to know right now!

   "I want to know who did this," fumed the teacher, "and I want to know right now!"

8. Jim told everyone, I could have arrived earlier "if it were not for car problems."

   Jim told everyone, "I could have arrived earlier if it were not for car problems."

29-8

DIRECTIONS: In the space to the left of each statement, write an **I** if it is an indirect quotation, and a **D** if it is a direct quotation. On the lines below each sentence, change the indirect quotation to a direct quotation and the direct quotation statement to an indirect quotation.

EXAMPLE ▶ _D_ **"Let's stay home tonight and watch a movie on the VCR,"said Brenda to Elena.**

Brenda suggested to Elena that they stay home tonight and watch a movie on the VCR.

_D_ 1. Announcing that the flight had been overbooked, the flight attendant asked, "Would anyone like to give up a seat on this flight in exchange for a ticket to any U.S. city on our routes?"

Announcing that the flight had been overbooked, the flight attendant asked if anyone would like to give up a seat on this flight in exchange for a ticket to any U.S. city on the company's flight routes.

_D_ 2. All of Oliver Twist's problems began at dinnertime at the orphanage when he said, "Please sir, I want some more."

All of Oliver Twist's problems began at dinnertime at the orphanage when he said that he wanted some more.

_I_ 3. The famous actor told the talk show host that all he'd ever wanted was a nice family, a little house, and a dog.

The famous actor told the talk show host, "All I ever wanted was a nice family, a little house, and a dog."

_D_ 4. "Do you have any idea how fast you were going?" the police officer asked.

The police officer asked if you had any idea how fast you were going.

_I_ 5. He told the gas station attendant to fill it up with unleaded.

He told the gas station attendant, "Fill it up with unleaded."

_I_ 6. The waiter recommended that we try the clam chowder.

The waiter recommended to us, "Try the clam chowder."

_D_ 7. "For an A student," I told Carol, "you sure don't spend much time studying."

I told Carol that for an A student, she sure didn't spend much time studying.

_D_ 8. "I'll stop by after I finish my laundry," Hugo said.

Hugo said that he would stop by after he finished his laundry.

End Punctuation Marks

The end of a sentence is shown by one of three punctuation marks:

- a period *or*
- a question mark *or*
- an exclamation mark

Use a *period* at the end of a sentence that makes a statement.

EXAMPLES ▶ The reporter asked the rookie what the biggest difference was between college and pro basketball.

I often wonder how birds know to fly south for the winter.

CAUTION: Use only *one period* if the sentence ends with an abbreviation.

I was awakened from a sound sleep at 4 a.m.

Use a *period* at the end of a sentence that makes a polite command or a mild exclamation.

EXAMPLES ▶ Mom said to be home before dark.

What a shame that we missed you when you were in town.

Use a *question mark* at the end of a sentence that asks a direct question.

EXAMPLES ▶ What time is it?

Who won the ball game last night?

Use an *exclamation mark* at the end of a sentence or statement that expresses a strong emotion.

You're driving me crazy!

That's terrific!

Ouch!

Remember two important things about exclamation marks:

1. **Don't use exclamation marks very often.**
2. **Don't confuse a strong, emotional command with a polite command or mild exclamation that requires only a period at the end.**

Activity 29-9

DIRECTIONS: Put the appropriate punctuation mark at the end of each of the following statements. Make the mark dark enough to be read easily.

EXAMPLES ▶ **Great Scott! How can we collect our winnings?**
Enrique asked Maryann if he could borrow $5 .

1. Marge cleans out the bird cage weekly (.)
2. The newborn child weighs 9 lbs., 4 oz (.)
3. Abandon ship (!)
4. What is today's date (?)
5. I can't believe how wonderful the weather has been this winter (.)
6. Does this sweater go with those pants (?)
7. Wow (!)
8. If you're looking for good gas mileage, don't buy that car (.)
9. I asked Red how he got his nickname (.)
10. Give me my money back (!)

End Punctuation with Quotation Marks

Put a period inside the closing quotation marks to show the end of the quotation and the end of the sentence.

EXAMPLE ▶ **Just as we were leaving for the beach, we heard the weather reporter say, "There's an 80 percent chance of rain this afternoon."**

Put a comma at the end of a quotation inside the closing quotation marks, and then continue the sentence.

EXAMPLE ▶ **The sign read, "No fishing, swimming, or loitering," but we paid no attention to it.**

Put a colon or a semicolon outside the closing quotation marks in a sentence

EXAMPLES ▶ **The final section of the questionnaire was called "Comments"; it gave us a lot of information.**
Helga arranged for us to pick up several passes stamped "Special Press Section": one for Manny, two for Suanne, one for Lily.

If a quotation ends with a question mark, put it inside the quotation marks.

If an entire sentence is a question and quoted words appear at the end of the sentence, put the question mark after the quotation marks.

EXAMPLES ▶ **"Where are my glasses?" is heard constantly around our house.**

Have you read "The Lady or the Tiger"?

If a quotation ends with an exclamation mark, put it inside the quotation marks.

If an entire sentence ends with an exclamation mark and quoted words appear at the end of the sentence, put the exclamation mark outside the quotation marks.

EXAMPLES ▶ **Janice yelled, "I smell something burning!"**

It sounds so familiar to hear somebody in the house say, "Jennifer did it"!

Activity 29-10

DIRECTIONS: Punctuate correctly each of the following sentences that contain quotation marks. Please write dark enough so your marks can be seen easily.

EXAMPLE ▶ **Vivian said , "I have the solution to the problem . "**

1. Yogi Berra, the famous baseball player, said , "It ain't over 'til it's over ."
2. The police officer shouted , " Put your hands up !" while chasing the suspected criminal.
3. The chef asked , " Is the soup too cold ?"
4. The movers labeled my CDs , " Handle with care ."
5. Have you read " The Story of an Hour " ?
6. All I could hear was a loud " Wow !"
7. In the War of 1812, Andrew Jackson was called "Old Rough and Ready" ; he was never called that in person after he became president of the United States.
8. " You need to have credit in a language in order to transfer ," my advisor told me last week.
9. Japan honors many of its crafts people by calling them " National Treasures " : ceramists, weavers, bell makers, basket makers.
10. The art instructor stated emphatically , " I have seen enough unusual designs to last me all year ! "

Colons

Use a colon at the end of a complete statement to show it will be followed by a list of specifics within the sentence.

EXAMPLES ▶ **I enjoyed all the books I read last summer, but three stand out particularly in my memory: The Shining, David Copperfield, and All Quiet on the Western Front.**

The course taught several kinds of dance: square dancing, clogging, modern jazz, and tap.

CAUTION: Do *not* use a colon after any form of the verb "to be", such as "is", "are", or "were", that is the verb in a sentence.

Improper use of colon:

The American flag is: red, white, and blue.

Correct forms:

The American flag is red, white, and blue.

or **The American flag has three colors: red, white, and blue.**

NOTE: A colon is also used to introduce a list that is not considered part of a sentence, as in the following box.

Use a colon to:

- **separate hour and minute in time**
- **separate chapter and verse in biblical references**
- **end the salutation in a formal or business letter**

EXAMPLES ▶ **The meeting will begin at 7:30 sharp.**

My plane arrives at 5:17 p.m.

The quotation comes from John 3:16.

Dear Purchasing Agent:

Dear Ms. Phillips:

29-11

DIRECTIONS: Insert colons in any of the following sentences where they should be. Be sure to make the colon dark enough to be seen easily.

EXAMPLE ▶ **We will give the new puppy one of three names : Fido, Spot, or Ted.**

1. Brian called at about 11:15 this morning.
2. Read the passage in Genesis from 4:2 to 4:5.
3. My favorite ice cream flavors are vanilla, chocolate, and strawberry.
4. I can't go for two reasons: I don't have the time and I don't have the money.
5. The party was pushed back an hour, so it will start at 8:30.
6. The visiting team had characteristics we didn't : speed, strength, and better preparation.

7. The letter began, " Dear Dr. Winslow :" although it was not very friendly from then on.
8. The family planned stops in several countries during our South American trip : Peru, Chile, Argentina, and Brazil.

Parentheses and Dashes

Both parentheses and dashes set off a comment or explanation that isn't necessary to what you are writing, but is helpful for the reader to know.

Parentheses enclose non-essential or incidental information but *de-emphasize* the interruption of that material to a sentence. Parentheses are always used as a pair.

EXAMPLES ▶ **The day I was born (December 7, 1941) is an important day in United States history.**

My favorite Kevin Costner movies (*Dances with Wolves* and *Field of Dreams*) are available on videotape.

COMMENT: The parentheses set information apart in these sentences just as commas might, but they give it a bit more importance.

Dashes emphasize or dramatize information that is incidental to a sentence. Dashes are used in pairs within a sentence or singly just before the final words of a sentence.

A dash is made on a typewriter or computer by two hyphens together. It is handwritten by extending a line approximately the length of two letters. There are no spaces between the dash and the word they follow or lead to.

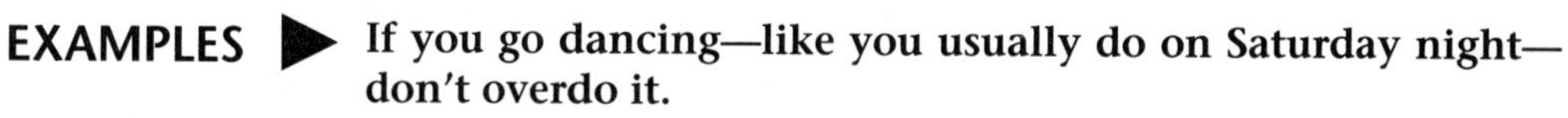

EXAMPLES ▶ **If you go dancing—like you usually do on Saturday night—don't overdo it.**

I'm leaving if Uncle Raul brings his guitar—as he often does.

Remember two important things about these marks:
1. **Don't use parentheses and dashes very often.**
2. **Don't let the words enclosed in parentheses or dashes interrupt the flow of what you are writing.**

29-12

DIRECTIONS: On the line to the left of each sentence, write a **C** if parentheses or dashes are used correctly in the sentence, and an **I** if they are incorrect. If you write an I in the space, make the proper corrections in the sentence.

EXAMPLE ▶ __I__ **The designer's newest line (spring sportswear) was in the catalog.**

Answers
I done—not
C
I 30 years—is retiring
I (Shops at the Sea)
C
I (Richard Nixon)
I inside—Dutchman's
C

___ 1. Parents' jobs are never done not even when their children have children of their own.

___ 2. My birthplace (Chicago) is known for its very severe winter weather.

___ 3. Our family doctor—the one who we've used for the past 30 years is retiring in March.

___ 4 The most popular mall in the city Shops at the Sea is going out of business.

___ 5. Only one player—Hank Aaron—has hit more lifetime home runs than Babe Ruth.

___ 6. Only one U.S. president Richard Nixon has resigned.

___ 7. I predict the winner will be the horse starting on the inside Dutchman's Calling Card.

___ 8. If you get to work late again as you have the last six days—you will be fired.

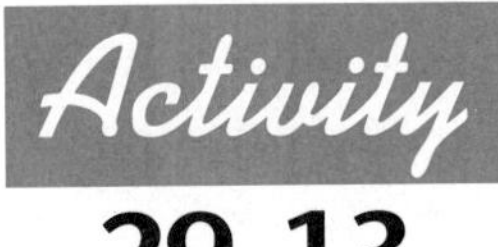

29-13

DIRECTIONS: Write a paragraph, on your own paper, on any *one* of the following topics:

My favorite songs and music

Newspaper articles I've read on topics of interest

Books, stories, and poems I enjoyed reading

Write the paragraph for other students in your class to let them know something about you. Pay particular attention to what you have learned in this chapter about using apostrophes, quotation marks, end punctuation marks, quotation marks, colons, and parentheses or dashes.

Sharing

Share the paragraph you wrote for *Activity 29-13* with at least one other person in the class. Help the author of the paper you read by editing it for the punctuation marks listed in the *Activity* directions.

29-14

DIRECTIONS: Put quotation marks and end punctuation in the following dialogue where they are needed.

I overheard the most frightening conversation today while I was riding on the subway. A woman said to a man, I'm really worried about Eva The police found the gun in her house

The answers to this *Activity* are in the Instructor's Section.

Startled, the man replied But they still haven't found the body, have they?

"Well, that's just the thing the woman said as she squirmed in her seat Victoria knows where they dumped it, and I think she's going to go to the cops

We all know what will happen to her if she does that the man said. She'll get rubbed out the same way Naomi did after she went to the police

Well the woman said with a hint of doubt, can Eva risk killing someone else at this point

"Maybe you're right her male friend said If she asked me, I'd tell Eva to quit while she's ahead.

Eva's not looking for anyone's advice right now" the woman responded not yours, mine, or anyone's

The man responded You're right But I'm beginning to worry because there's too much evidence that looks pretty bad I wouldn't be surprised if all of our friends are in for some time in prison What do you think

I have no idea what's going to happen,the woman said "I can't wait to see tomorrow's episode on TV of Life Goes On

---

Activity 29-15

The answers to this *Activity* are in the Instructor's Section.

DIRECTIONS: Edit the following paragraph by putting apostrophes in the appropriate places.

Ive got many hobbies, but my favorite is traveling. In the past ten years, Ive been to Europe, Japan, the Middle East, the Soviet Union, and across the United States. Its difficult for many people to believe, but Id say that my favorite trips werent the ones I took across the sea. They're the ones I took to see different parts of the United States Id never seen before. New Hampshire and Vermont foliage in the autumn are something you shouldnt miss! As for history, Philadelphias Independence Hall and Liberty Bell are "must-sees." So are many of Bostons sights. My brother-in-laws apartment in New York City overlooks one of the worlds greatest cities. Floridas and Californias beaches provide year-round fun in the sun. Mountain lovers desires can be met in both the east and the far west. There are even deserts in the United States! So, if you plan any trips across the United States, Im sure yours will be as fascinating as mine were.

Chapter 30

Capitalization

In this chapter you will

- review the use of capital letters
- practice using capital letters in sentences and paragraphs

You have always used both capital and small letters in all your writing. In your earlier school days, you learned the customs about which words should be capitalized and which shouldn't. However, there are many customs, so they are sometimes hard to recall. In this chapter you will review several uses of capital letters. In order to help in your recall, they will be grouped according to these four uses:

- Capitals for first words
- Capitals for naming people and their titles
- Capitals for geographic locations, their people, and their languages
- Capitals for naming times, groups, events, and documents

Capitals for First Words

Capitalize the first word in a sentence.

EXAMPLES ▶ **We moved our picnic inside when it began to rain.**
Our teacher warned that the test would be hard.

Capitalize the first word in a direct quotation.

EXAMPLES ▶ **Patrick Henry said, "Give me liberty, or give me death."**

The salesperson told me, "This car is exactly what you want."

CAUTION: Do *not* capitalize an indirect quotation.

The doctor said that my friend needed glasses.

Explanation: The doctor is not being quoted. Instead, what was said is only being reported. (See Chapter 29, "Quotation Marks".)

30-1

DIRECTIONS: In the following sentences, underline each letter which should be capitalized and write the capital above it.

EXAMPLE ▶ **dave asked me, "have you eaten yet?"** (D, H)

1. many people enjoy playing baseball. (M)
2. the food was cold when it was brought to our table. (T)
3. the lawyer shouted, "my client is not guilty." (T, M)
4. The nurse told the child, "you're going to be fine." (Y)
5. the governor said he wasn't going to raise taxes. (T)
6. a helpful boy climbed the tree to rescue the kitten. (A)
7. After the lecture, the professor said, "does anyone have any questions?" (D)
8. boating and stamp collecting are her favorite hobbies. (B)

Capitals for Naming People and their Titles

Always capitalize the word "I."

EXAMPLES ▶ **My friend Tony and I are going out for dinner.**

Later, I realized that the first person I saw at the party was Miguel.

CAUTION: Do *not* capitalize the other pronouns. (That is, do not capitalize *he, she, we, you, they* and so on ***unless*** they begin a sentence or a direct quotation.)

Because she was running late, Jane phoned and told me not to wait for her.

She phoned and said, "We are running late, so don't wait for us. "

Explanation: In the second sentence, the pronouns "she" and "we" are both in positions where words are normally capitalized.

Capitalize people's names and nicknames.

EXAMPLES ▶ Between you and me, I think Maria is prettier than Sarah.

Pee Wee Reese was one of baseball's greatest shortstops.

30-2

DIRECTIONS: In the following sentences, underline each letter that should be capitalized and write the capital letter above it.

EXAMPLE ▶ If you and mark go, i think you should take an umbrella. (M, I)

1. My neighbor bill asked what i wanted for my birthday. (B, I)
2. Rushing to the window, randy asked if i had heard the noise. (R, I)
3. We called ted "lefty" because he was the only left-hander on the team. (T, L)
4. My date with rebecca did not go as well as i would have liked. (R, I)
5. If josé, you, and i go to the store, I think we should wait for jennifer. (J, I, J)
6. you told me that you do not have junior's telephone number. (Y, J)
7. you have enough paint to do both the kitchen and eric's room. (Y, E)
8. she likes reading mysteries, but i prefer biographies. (S, I)

Capitalize people's titles only when they are used with their names.

EXAMPLES ▶ My report is about President Abraham Lincoln.

***BUT:* The president met with his advisors today.**

Coach Don Shula guided the Miami Dolphins to a 17-0 record in 1972.

***BUT:* The coach cancelled practice because of the rain.**

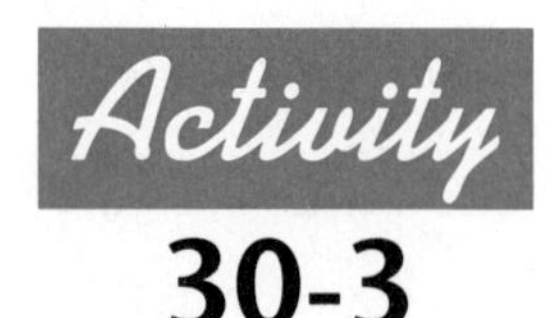

30-3

DIRECTIONS: A proofreading symbol to have small letters printed as capitals is a triple underlining (This is an example.) Put this proofreading symbol under all small letters that should be capitalized.

Military heroes like general george patton hold a special place in history.

1. Our pilot, captain miller, said we would arrive in twenty minutes.
2. My tennis coach helped me to improve my serve.
3. The high school principal spoke to the faculty about his plans to invite senator philabuster to an assembly program.
4. the case was heard by judge dixon .
5. Christopher Columbus' journey to the new world was funded by King ferdinand and queen isabella.
6. the crowd was silent throughout the senator's long speech.
7. The doctor i met specialized in orthopedics.
8. i enjoyed listening to rabbi Lopez's sermon.

Capitals for Geographic Locations, their People, and their Languages

Capitalize the names of geographic locations:

- continents
- countries
- states
- counties
- cities
- rivers
- mountains
- planets
- areas or regions
- specific streets

EXAMPLES ▶ **Last summer we traveled to Europe, spending time in Spain, Italy, France, and Germany.**

This mission should give researchers new information about conditions on the planets Mars and Mercury.

The Cumberland River runs through Nashville, the capital of Tennessee.

CAUTION: *DO NOT* capitalize ordinary *compass directions* unless they refer to a specific area or region.

Head east on Main Street to reach the gas station.

BUT: **Some of the best snow skiing in the East is in Vermont.**

30-4

DIRECTIONS: In the following sentences, underline *all* the letters which should be capitalized and write the capital above each.

EXAMPLE ▶ **More people live in new york than in any other city in the united states.**

N Y U S

1. The southern-most point in the continental united states is key west, florida.
   U S K W F
2. The farther north we drive, the cooler the temperature gets.
3. The south is known for its hospitality.
   S
4. the street just west of elm street is prairie avenue.
   T E S P A
5. The pacific ocean is the largest body of water on earth.
   P O
6. a lot has been written about possible life on the planet mars.
   A M
7. I hope to climb mt. everest, the world's tallest mountain.
   M E
8. Many universities offer study abroad programs in europe, especially in spain and france.
   E S F

Capitalize the names of nationalities, ethnic groups, and languages.

EXAMPLES ▶ **The Swiss ski instructor said he grew up on the slopes.** *(nationality)*

Doris felt it was more practical to learn Spanish than Swahili or Latin. *(languages)*

Many Native Americans live by the customs of their ancestors. *(ethnic group)*

Many elected political officials in the U.S. are African-Americans. *(ethnic group)*

30-5

DIRECTIONS: Put the proofreader's symbol for a capital letter—three lines under a small letter that should be capitalized—under the appropriate letters in the following sentences.

EXAMPLE ▶ **Every Saturday night, we order chinese food.**

1. I learned to polka at a polish club in chicago, a city where there is a large polish population.

2. After studying french for three years, we were prepared for our trip to paris.
3. There is great diversity in the city because of its large latin and oriental populations.
4. Just as american children grow up playing baseball and football, canadians grow up playing ice hockey.
5. In halting english, the italian man told the american official he had lost his passport.
6. The pianist played to large audiences during her tour through navaho, zuni, and hopi areas, and she was well received in many small cities in the Western states.
7. The movie *Glory* told the story of an african-american regiment which fought in south carolina during the Civil War.
8. My uncle went to acapulco and brought me back a real mexican sombrero.

Capitals for the Names of Particular Times, Groups, Events, and Documents

Capitalize the names of days, months, and holidays.

EXAMPLES ▶ The math class meets on Tuesdays and Thursdays.
Hubert was born on Flag Day, which is June 14.

Capitalize the names of organized groups, including:

- clubs
- religions
- political groups
- associations
- unions
- companies

EXAMPLES ▶ The American Medical Association holds an annual meeting, usually in March.

The Democratic and Republican candidates met in a debate before members of the Airline Pilots Association and the International Association of Machinists.

Roman Catholic, Jewish, Lutheran, Baha'i, and Buddhist students were on the planning committee for Campus Interfaith Week.

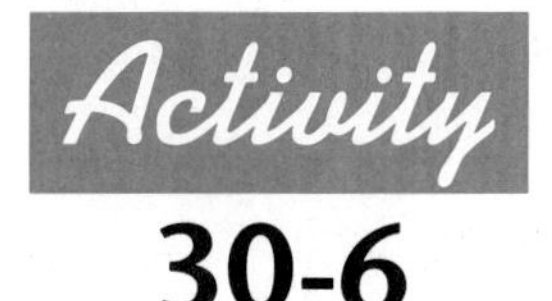

30-6

DIRECTIONS: Use the proofreader's triple underlining to show letters in the following sentences which should be capitalized. However, use the proofreader's symbol of a slash mark through a capital which should be a small letter.

EXAMPLES ▶ **Watching football games on weekends and on monday nights seems to be an American pastime.**

The National honor society meets after School on tuesdays.

1. The city puts on a fireworks display each year on independence day.
2. Six inches of snow on a friday last january brought out all the neighborhood children with their Sleds on saturday And sunday.
3. Employees of general electric receive many Retirement Benefits.
4. members of the American civil liberties union supported the striking Union workers from Thanksgiving day until the end of november.
5. The league of women voters holds periodic voter registration drives for both Democrats and republicans.
6. On easter sunday, Chris' family is having an easter egg hunt.
7. The baptist church is on the same block as the greek orthodox church.
8. The xerox stockholders' meeting is next monday at Noon.

Independence Day

Friday January
sleds Saturday and Sunday

General Electric
retirement benefits
Members Civil Liberties Union
union Day November

League Women Voters
Republicans

Easter Sunday Easter

Baptist Greek Orthodox

Xerox Monday noon

Capitalize the names of historical periods, events, and documents.

EXAMPLES ▶ **Many people view the Spanish Civil War as a rehearsal for weapons used in World War II.**

The Roaring Twenties came to an end with the start of the Great Depression.

Capitalize the names of specific school courses.

EXAMPLE ▶ **Ms. Gonzalez teaches Honors Calculus.**

CAUTION: Do *not* capitalize general areas of study.

I've taken many psychology classes, but my favorite was Child Psychology.

EXPLANATION: The general area of study is "psychology." "Child Psychology" is a specific course taken in that academic area.

Capitalize the *first letter of all words* in the *titles* of books, chapters, magazines, articles, short stories, essays, poems, plays, movies, and television programs.

***Except,* do not capitalize articles, conjunctions, and most prepositions (unless they begin the title).**

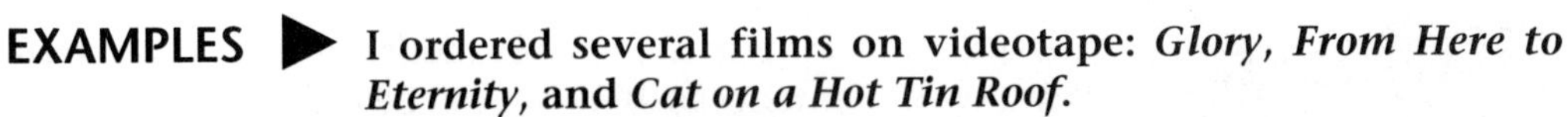

EXAMPLES ▶ **I ordered several films on videotape: *Glory*, *From Here to Eternity*, and *Cat on a Hot Tin Roof*.**

Included in my textbook are the story "The Tell-Tale Heart" and the essay "Politics and the English Language."

Activity 30-7

DIRECTIONS: Circle each small letter which should be capitalized in the following sentences. Put a slash mark through any capital letter which should be a small letter.

1. The hardest course I take is european history.
2. the first amendment of the bill of rights guarantees Freedom of Speech.
3. The Governor lectured today to my History class.
4. When i was stationed in the Middle East, I studied islam and learned Conversational arabic.
5. The french revolution began in 1789, which was After the end of the American revolution.
6. I learned in american history class that the french and indian war was actually fought between the french and the english.
7. We celebrate july 4 because on that day the declaration of independence was adopted by the Continental Congress meeting in philadelphia.
8. leonardo da Vinci and michelangelo are famous artists of the renaissance Period, not Teenage mutant ninja turtles.

European History
The First Amendment
Bill of Rights
freedom of speech
governor history
I Islam
conversational Arabic
French Revolution after
Revolution
American History French
and Indian War
French English
July Declaration of
Independence
Philadelphia
Leonardo Michelangelo
Renaissance period
Mutant Ninja Turtles

Activity 30-8

DIRECTIONS: Proofread the following paragraph to find errors in capitalization. Change small letters into capitals and capitals into small letters wherever appropriate. Write the paragraph correctly on your own paper.

The answers to this *Activity* are in the Instructor's Section.

this week's copy of <u>Sports illustrated</u> arrived at my house on monday. i enjoyed one article in particular about Chicago bulls Star michael jordan. A Native of wilmington, North carolina, Jordan attended the university of north Carolina. At UNC, jordan set many University Records and helped the tar heels win the national Championship. after leaving the University, he played on the 1984 united states olympic team, leading the Americans to the Gold medal in los Angeles. the Bulls drafted him that year, and Jordan was on his way to becoming possibly the Most Popular Athlete in the country. his spectacular Slam dunks gained him world-wide fame; there are Jordan fans as far away at the soviet union and japan. he is also renowned for his clean style of living off the basketball court. this popularity has led to his becoming a spokesperson for many of america's most famous Companies. from nike to McDonald's to chevrolet and Coca-cola. i think it is difficult to turn on a Television set and not see a Michael Jordan Commercial. Jordan has said that because of his Position, he can influence many people, especially kids. that's why he thinks it's important to keep his Clean Image and help people any way he can. I think Michael Jordan is one of the greatest Basketball Players ever!

Part VI

Words

Chapter 31 Word Choice

In this chapter you will

- discover differences among dictionaries
- learn about a thesaurus
- distinguish between sound-alike words
- make correct choices between words often confused

Writing is, after all, a matter of choosing the right words for the right places. If you have done that, you have communicated what you wanted to.

Most of the words you will need to use are those thousands you already know. You have been learning them your whole life from people you know, from school, from hearing words on radio or television or film, and from reading. Often people set out to enlarge their present vocabularies, either through courses, self-help books, or personal planning. The most successful kind of vocabulary development is what you set out to do yourself: keeping careful records of words new to you, what they mean, and how they are used. No matter which of several ways a person learns new words, or how many words one knows, most writers keep a dictionary handy.

Word Reference Sources: Dictionaries

There are several kinds of dictionaries. For example, people in different businesses and professions have dictionaries especially for their work: chemistry, law, business, history, and so on. People who work with verse a great deal often have a rhyming dictionary. Those in government may have a dictionary of acronyms (letters that stand for the titles of organizations).

But every writer ought to have a **standard dictionary**, the kind that gives an alphabetical listing of words, their pronunciation, and their meanings. Most standard dictionaries also tell you the part of speech a word is, its principal parts (if it's a verb), and something about the source of the word. The larger the dictionary, the more information it will have room to give about each word entry. From now on, all mention of "dictionary" will refer to such a standard dictionary.

An **unabridged dictionary** is one that its editors and publisher have not shortened. It contains all the words that the people who compiled the dictionary believe will be useful to the wide variety of those who use such a dictionary. In fact, an unabridged dictionary may contain more than 400,000 words. Obviously, that is too big a book to carry around, so unabridged dictionaries are usually on sturdy stands in libraries, or in the homes or offices of people who have a special interest in language.

An **abridged dictionary** is a shortened dictionary, one that its editors and publisher have limited in length. Therefore, they have had to decide which words to omit and which of the many possibilities to include. The dictionaries most people use are abridged, and usually those are the following two kinds:

A **desk-size dictionary** is essential for anybody who does any amount of writing, whether for school or personal reasons. The 100,000- to 200,000-word entries are enough for most of us. However, they make a large book, and one not always convenient to carry around. You should certainly have a desk-size dictionary where you live so that you can refer to it when you do homework.

A paperback **pocket dictionary** is all right to carry to classes, but serious students—and writers—often need more information than it can provide. Only the most essential information can be printed about its usual 50,000- to 70,000-word entries.

All dictionaries contain much information besides words and meanings. But as a writer, you will almost certainly use a dictionary for these purposes:

- to read the definition and make sure to choose the most accurate word for a particular place in the writing
- to check the spelling of what you write (many writers do so, even though they have a spell checker computer program)
- to find out where to hyphenate words if they run out of space at the end of a line

The following *Activity* will help you see how dictionaries differ.

31-1

DIRECTIONS: On your own paper, follow these steps:

1. Locate a **pocket dictionary** and from it select a word that you will look up. A familiar noun or verb is usually a good choice.
2. Copy the complete entry for the word you selected. Record, also, the title of the dictionary and the year it was published or copyrighted. (If the date is not on the title page, it is undoubtedly on the back of that page.)
3. Locate a **desk-size dictionary** and from it copy the complete entry for the same word. (Underline once anything that is italicized in the entry; underline twice anything that is in bold face type.) Write down the title and publication or copyright date of the dictionary.

4. Locate an **unabridged dictionary** and copy from it the complete entry for the same word. Record the title and date of that dictionary.
5. Compare the entires you have recorded. Then answer the following questions. Use your own paper if you need more space.
   A) What word did you look up?______________________________
   B) What information (pronunciation, definition, etc.) did you discover about the word from the pocket dictionary?

      ____

      ____

   C) What additional information or details did you discover about the word from the desk-size dictionary?

      ____

   D) What additional information or details did you discover about the word from the unabridged dictionary?

      ____

Word Reference Sources: Thesauruses

A thesaurus is a book that gives writers additional word choices by listing synonyms and antonyms. "Synonyms" are words that have the same, or almost the same, meanings as other words. "Antonyms" are their opposites.

Some writers turn to a thesaurus to find synonyms for familiar words, believing that by substituting a word that sounds "difficult" or "big" the writing will sound more important or intelligent. That is far from the truth! First, good writing sounds natural, as if the author is, indeed, the true writer of the piece. Second, although the dictionary definitions of some words may *seem* to be alike, there are differences in what they suggest to a reader and in how they are customarily used in English.

EXAMPLES ▶ Both "number" and "amount" refer to quantities.

However, people do not ordinarily say or write,

"I have a small number of money in my bank account," nor do they usually say or write,

"A great amount of people attended the football game."

Words, then, are seldom interchangeable because they have slight differences of meaning and use.

The benefit of having a thesaurus is to use it as a reference source to learn about the many words available to you to use in writing, to enlarge your own vocabulary, and to use it to jog your memory so you think about using words you may not have thought of for a particular sentence.

Using Homophones (Sound-Alikes)

The word "homophone" is composed of the prefix "homo," meaning *the same* and the root "phon," meaning *sound.* Therefore, **homophones are words that sound the same (in pronunciation), but are spelled differently and have different meanings.** (Sometimes they are called homonyms.)

The "sound test" of homophones—that the words must have the same pronunciation—depends on crisp pronunciation and clear enunciation. It also requires that the speaker's dialect be what is called "broadcast standard," or very much the way a dictionary dictates.

There are many homophones in the English language, and usually they are word pairs. However, this section begins with two homophone "triples": three words that sound alike when spoken but look different when written, and all three within each group have different meanings. These triples are also among the words most-used by writers, which is probably why they are also so often confused with their homophones.

their–a plural possessive pronoun

They put **their** luggage in the car.

there–indicates direction or place/**or**/ a way of introducing a thought

Put the packages **there** on the table.

There is a light on the front porch.

they're–a contraction of *they* + *are*

Tell the neighbors **they're** playing the radio too loud.

They're putting **their** books on the table over **there**.

REMINDER: "There" answers the question "where?" Both words have to do with place or location and both end with the same letters: *–ere.*

to–toward / **or** / combine with a verb to form the infinitive

Move **to** the head of the line if you have your boarding pass.

Be sure **to** take the test you missed.

too–also /**or**/ very

Then **too,** holidays don't come often enough.

This is not **too** good a dinner for such a high price.

two–the number 2

I got **two** dinners for the price of one.

Two people said the prize was **too** good **to** be true.

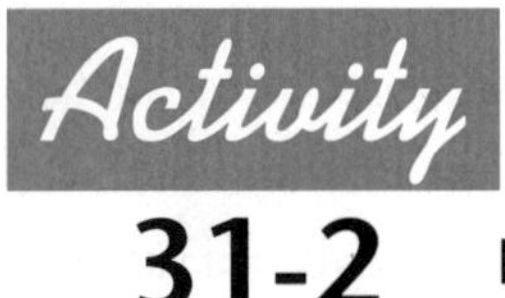

31-2

DIRECTIONS: Write the correct word from among the six above on each sentence blank.

EXAMPLE ▶ Don't go *too* near the edge of the cliff!

1. Most children would be anxious ______ go______ Disneyworld.
2. Many teachers feel ________ expected ________ keep discipline rather than __________ teach.
3. Is ______ really a light at the end of that tunnel?
4. Sympathetic friends arrived in __________ cars loaded with clothing for the tornado victims.
5. __________ were about 50 more people waiting ________ get into the auditorium than the room could hold.
6. If just _________ of the hundreds of people trying out for the quiz program get onto the show, I will not be __________ surprised.
7. Graduates must wear ___________ caps and gowns at the ceremony.
8. The lawyer felt lucky that ___________ of his clients were the top NFL draft choices.

Answers:
1. to to
2. they're to to
3. there
4. two
5. There to
6. two too
7. their
8. two

One homophone that has only two forms is sometimes mistakenly thought to have three forms:

its–the third person possessive pronoun (unlike nouns that need an *apostrophe* + *s* to show possession, pronouns that show possession are separate words)

The dog slipped **its** collar.

it's–a contraction of "it is" or "it has"

It's three weeks since I phoned my grandparents.

It's too bad you can't read, because the title of the book is on **its** spine.

There is no such word as its'.

capital–chief or major one, such as a city that is the center of government for a state or country /**or**/ money

A surprising number of people think New York City is the **capital** of New York state.

Attracting venture **capital** is not easy in a time of recession.

capitol–building in which a legislature meets

The dome of the **capitol** building in Denver really is covered with gold.

The **capitols** in many state **capitals** are badly in need of repairs.

REMINDER: Many capitols have a round dome—just like the "o" in the word "capitol."

complement–a completing element to make up a whole

The landscaping was designed to **complement** the architectural style of the house.

compliment–expression of praise

The teacher was sure to **compliment** pupils often.

A gracious **compliment** will often **complement** a good day.

REMINDER: "I like to receive compliments." The word for praise has an "I" in it.

passed–past tense of the verb *to pass*

The truck **passed** the car on the highway.

past–time before the present

My driver's license is **past** the renewal date and now I'll have to pay a fine.

Past successes should not be **passed** over in examining someone's qualifications for this job.

principal–chief, main, or most important / **or**/ the head of a school /**or** / a sum of money

The **principal** speaker at commencement was a self-made multimillionaire.

The **principal** escorted the queen on a tour of the school.

If the **principal** you invest is large enough, you can almost live on the interest it earns.

principle–rule or standard

A **principle** children should be taught is that honesty is the best policy.

Our **principal** believes that the **principles** of education should be enforced at this school.

REMINDER: "A school principal should be a pal to the students." The word meaning the head of a school ends in *-pal*.

31-3

DIRECTIONS: Underline the correct word for the sentence from those in parentheses.

EXAMPLE ▶ Quick! Grab the sponge before (its / it's / its') too late!

principle
its
compliment
capital
principal
passed
its
it's
complement
it's

1. "A person is innocent until proven otherwise" is a (principal / principle) of our legal system.
2. I don't like animals, so keep the dog in (its / it's / its') pen.
3. The gracious way to accept a (complement / compliment) is simply to say, "Thank you."
4. When Shielah was three years old she could name the (capital / capitol) cities of all 50 states.
5. The (principal / principle) speaker at the basketball banquet had never seen a basketball game played.
6. The center (passed / past) the football too quickly.
7. Herkimer thought the shirt was a smart purchase, but as soon as (its / it's / its') seams started pulling apart, he changed his mind.
8. I tried to register to vote, but because (its / it's / its') so close to election day, I couldn't.
9. Those blue suede shoes really (complement / compliment) your outfit.
10. Because of an upper air inversion, (its / it's / its') hailing the size of golf balls!

---

stationary–standing still

The stage furniture was **stationary**, although a moving background made the chairs and couch appear to move.

stationery–writing paper and envelopes

Be sure to have your full zip code on the **stationery** you order printed with your name and address.

Even though an office fan blew loose papers around, the new business **stationery** remained **stationary** because it was still in the box.

REMINDER: Both stationery and paper end in *–er*.

ware–articles of the same general kind

The wooden **ware** at the craft shop is all handmade.

wear–to have clothes on /**or**/ to reduce by constant rubbing /**or**/ to carry

Many people like to **wear** blue jeans for lounging.

You will **wear** the rug down if you always walk in the same place.

There's a saying that some people **wear** their heart on their sleeve, but that only means they show their emotions easily.

where–at or in what place

Please tell me **where** the sugar is stored.

Where you will find the latest fashions to **wear** is surely not at the hard**ware** store.

weather–atmospheric conditions

Weather conditions today do not look good for fishing.

whether–suggests a question

Please let me know **whether** or not you can attend the party.

Whether the **weather** is rain or shine, the mayor will give his outdoor reception tomorrow afternoon.

whose–a possessive pronoun

Whose hat is on the dining room table?

who's–the contraction of who + is or who + has

Who's that knocking at my door?

The person **who's** speaking tonight is a writer **whose** book I read.

your–a second person possessive pronoun

Did you remember **your** umbrella, in case of rain?

you're–a contraction of you + are

Make sure **you're** moved into the apartment by the weekend.

Don't push **your** luck; quit while **you're** ahead.

31-4

DIRECTIONS: Circle the correct word for the sentence from those in parentheses.

EXAMPLE ▶ **Humberto didn't know until the last minute (weather / whether) he could go on vacation at the time he had planned.**

Your
Who's
ware
wear
stationary
your
weather
who's
you're
where

1. (Your / You're) shirt tail should not be hanging out that way.
2. (Whose / Who's) at the door?
3. Please check the ads in the Sunday paper and let me know if there is any cooking (ware / wear / where) on special this week.
4. Annalee is about to (ware / wear / where) her parents down with her constant questions.
5. Mr. McAdoo bought a (stationary / stationery) bicycle for exercise.
6. Not doing the income tax on time is going to be (your / you're) problem, not mine!
7. Bugs keep moving into the house when the (weather / whether) gets wet and humid outside.
8. The person (whose / who's) substituting for me at work was not my first choice to do so.
9. If (your / you're) a good cook and like to sample as you go, you probably need to watch your waistline.
10. Be careful not to set up the aquarium (ware / wear / where) the fish can get too much heat.

Words Often Confused

Many words sound similar—but not exactly the same, as homophones do—and so they are confused when written. If it is hard to hear the difference between the first letters of *affect* and *effect,* one of the words may be written when the other should have been used.

There are also writers who forget, or never knew, the different meanings of words such as *affect* and *effect.*

The words paired in this section resemble each other in enough ways that separating them is difficult for many writers. The meanings and uses here will help you keep from confusing some of the many word pairs that often trouble writers.

Begin with the "**all**" pairs

all ready–everything is ready

The military installation was **all ready** for inspection.

already- before or previously

Anselm had **already** bought the tickets, so I paid him my share.

all right- everything is correct or acceptable

Micaela spoke with Jose and now everything is **all right** between them again.

***alright* — not considered a standard word**

all together–group of things or people in unison

Let's sing **all together** this time and make the song sound really great.

altogether–entirely or wholly

Many villages in Bangladesh were washed away **altogether** by the terrible cyclone.

all ways–in each direction

Be sure to look **all ways** when you come to an intersection.

always–at every time

Always set your alarm clock to be sure you get up on time.

Activity 31-5

DIRECTIONS: Cross off the wrong word in each pair in parentheses so the following paragraph makes sense.

alright
altogether
already all ready
altogether
all together
altogether
all right
always

Cynthia always felt it was (all right; alright) to eat whatever she wanted as long as she could pay for the food. But she was not (all together; altogether) correct. The results of a physical examination indicated she was (all ready; already) a high risk person and she should be (all ready; already) to change her poor eating habits (all together; altogether). She read about how people working (all together; altogether) could help individuals in a group. So she decided to change her way of living (all together; altogether) and determined she would be (all right; alright) in the future. Now Cynthia is (all ways; always) careful about what she eats.

Several conditional words are often written in impossible combinations, probably because the writer tries to record the sounds of speech on paper.

Sound	***Cannot Be Written***	***Should Be Written***
could've	could of	could **have**
should've	should of	should **have**
would've	would of	would **have**
might've	might of	might **have**

The sound is actually a contraction being pronounced. You can see in written form the apostrophe that represents letters omitted in the pronunciation.

These combinations are all helpers to the main verb in the sentence. The entire verb is underlined in the following sentence.

EXAMPLES ▶ Impala **could have** gone skating, but preferred to stay home.

I **should have** remembered to put out the garbage last night for today's pickup.

Medicines that **would have** helped the refugees arrived too late.

More paint **might have** covered the dark spots left by pictures hanging on the wall.

REMINDER: *Have* is a verb form and can only be used alone or as a helper with other verbs. *Of* is a preposition and can only be used in a prepositional phrase with a noun or noun substitute.

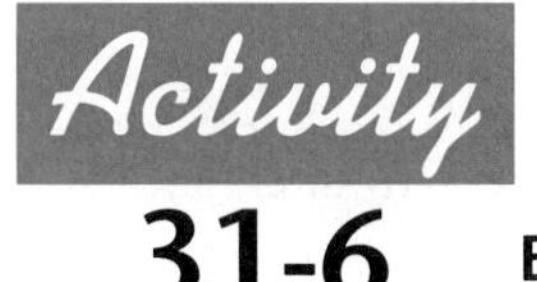

31-6

DIRECTIONS: On the line to the left of each sentence, write a **C** if the sentence is correct and an **I** if it in incorrect.

EXAMPLE ▶ C **The family upstairs should've paid its rent on the first of the month.**

C 1. Michael would've gone to the movies with me if he had the money.

I 2. The boss should of made sure all the workers were in the U.S. legally.

C 3. My grandfather should have earned more, but there was no minimum wage law when he was a young man.

C 4. Details of the visit have gone into the news article.

C 5. More details would've gone into the article if there had been more space available.

C 6. Mildred could've finished the report on time if the computer hadn't been down.

C 7. Office participation in the Community Chest drive should've been 100%, but it wasn't.

I 8. The judges for the talent contest might of chosen the singer, but they thought the dancer was a better performer.

Other words that are often confused by writers continue below.

accept–to receive, especially, willingly

The football player agreed to **accept** a $5 million contract.

except–to exclude

You can snack on any food you find in the kitchen **except** the cake that's on the counter.

You may **accept** any gifts **except** cash as long as you hold this job.

advice–opinion about what should or should not be done

Always listen to **advice** from those who know more than you do about a subject.

advise–to suggest or counsel

Be cautious of those people in the company who always want to **advise** you on how to do your job.

I **advise** you to accept her **advice.**

affect–to concern or influence

Too much water will **affect** the plant as much as too little water will.

effect–as a *noun:* result as a *verb:* cause or bring about

Hang the picture a little higher for a better **effect** in the room. *(noun)*

Nobody can **effect** change in the workplace without devoting time and effort to doing so. *(verb)*

alot–**NO SUCH WORD**

a lot–a quantity of something

Selma likes **a lot** of sugar in her coffee.

allot–to portion out

The boss will **allot** whatever work is available.

A lot of people do not want to **allot** their money to such foolishness.

been–past participle of "to be", and usually used after such helping verbs as "have", "has", or "had"

being–the *-ing* form of the verb "to be"; also used after helping verbs (such words as *are, am, was,* or *were.*)

I discovered that **being** there had **been** a real pleasure.

NEVER USE WITH THE WORD "THAT" AS IN "BEING THAT."

Activity 31-7

DIRECTIONS: In each blank space, write in the correct word from the pair shown after the sentence number.

EXAMPLE ▶ **accept, except Our company did not** *accept* **the lowest bid because it did not meet the specifications.**

1. **been, being** An animal seems to have __________ tracking through my vegetable garden.
2. **a lot, allot, alot** Prepare a personal budget so you can _________ money to pay monthly necessities.
3. **advice, advise** Older people can often give good _______________ to younger people.

been

allot

advice

accept	4. **accept, except** If you ____________ this check, the debt will be paid in full.
advise	5. **advice, advise** An accountant can ____________ you on tax savings.
accept	6. **accept, except** Do not ____________ any substitute product.
a lot	7. **a lot, allot, alot** If you drop a course in college, you stand to loose ____________ of money and time.
being	8. **been, being** You are ____________ foolish if you believe more building will not bring more traffic.
effect	9. **affect, effect** Special outdoor lighting gives a shimmering ________ in the garden.
except	10. **accept, except** Serve me anything ____________ spinach!
being	11. **been, being** Mario did not feel he was ____________ foolish to take the hairdresser to court for giving him a bad haircut.
affect	12. **affect, effect** Parents can only ____________ the education of their children if they keep in close touch with the schools.

continual- frequently repeated

Hernando could not stand the **continual** ringing of the phone when he was trying to work.

continuous–without interruption

The **continuous** rain kept many people from going out to vote last Tuesday.

Millie's **continuous** good work earned her **continual awards.**

good–an *adjective* (so it modifies a noun or pronoun)

Keep up the **good** work!

well–an *adverb* (so it modifies a verb, adjective, or another adverb)

Even as a new lawyer, she handled cases **well**.

Feel **good** and keep **well.**

imply–to hint or suggest

Maggie's behavior doesn't really **imply** her disapproval.

infer–to arrive at a conclusion

From that statement, I **infer** that you will not place an order this week.

Do not **imply** she is a cheat, although you may **infer** that from her present behavior.

lose–to misplace **/or/** fail to win (sounds like "Lou's")

I hope my child didn't **lose** the car keys.

If the team does **lose** this game, the championship will be impossible to win.

loose–not securely fastened (rhymes with "moose")

The **loose** shutter banged all night.

A hole in my pocket cause me to **lose** all my **loose** change.

quiet–silence

People accustomed to city noises sometimes say they can't sleep in the country because it's too **quiet** there at night.

quit–stop doing something

Lee **quit** that job when a promised raise never came.

quite–fully or exactly

The captain could never **quite** accept responsibility for running the ship aground.

I didn't **quite quit** that job, but I did stay **quiet** when the big deal was being discussed.

Activity 31-8

DIRECTIONS: In each blank space, write in the correct word from the pair shown after the sentence number.

EXAMPLE ▶ good, well This restaurant has a *good* **reputation.**

Continuousl
imply
loose
quite
well
continual
quit
good

1. **continual, continuous** _______________ worries about good child care keep many parents from continuing their education.
2. **imply, infer** To _______________ dishonesty will bring an immediate investigation.
3. **lose, loose** The paper must be a little _______________ as it feeds through the printer or it will jam.
4. **quiet, quit, quite** Sometimes a child tells _______________ a different story about an event than an adult does.
5. **good, well** How _______________ you do on the test will determine whether or not you can get a scholarship.
6. **continual, continuous** It's about time somebody fixed the _______________ drip in the bathroom sink.
7. **quiet, quit, quite** "Better _______________ while you're ahead" is a saying with a lot of truth in it.
8. **good, well** Maximo's _______________ friend from his country was about to arrive.

Activity 31-9

DIRECTIONS: Proofread the following paragraph by crossing off each word used incorrectly and writing above it the correct word.

Noah could have ~~excepted~~ accepted the ~~advise~~ advice of his friends and not gone to the seashore for his vacation. However, since he was ~~quiet~~ quite accustomed to making ~~alot~~ a lot of his own decisions, he went anyway. At first, Noah said the bad weather had no effect on his plans. But after it had been raining for several days, Noah thought he wasn't doing so ~~good~~ well after all. "Perhaps I ~~should of~~ should've listened to my friends after all. Now they may infer that I don't trust them. Besides, this ~~continual~~ continuous rain doesn't give me any chance to get outside. I ~~quite!~~ quit!" With that, Noah packed up, got in the car, and drove home.

DIRECTIONS: Proofread the following paragraph by crossing off each word used incorrectly and writing above it the correct word.

You ~~should of~~ should have watched the nature special on television last night because it was very interesting. It showed the ~~continual~~ continuous effect on animal life by people who ignore the ~~advise~~ advice of ecology experts. It is ~~quit~~ quite severe and causes the world to lose millions of animals every year. The show did more than ~~infer~~ imply some species of animals are almost extinct; it gave actual counts and showed maps of areas where all is not ~~good~~ well for some species. All together, the show was meant to ~~effect~~ affect the way people treat the environment and all life in it.

Chapter 32

Spelling

In this chapter you will

- learn tips to become a good speller
- review the building blocks of spelling
- determine how to spell plurals
- learn the rules that can help you spell many words
  - the *i* before *e* rule
  - the final *y* rule
  - the silent *e* rules
  - to double or not double final consonants
- practice with prefixes

Nothing about writing seems to mark someone as "dumb" or "careless" or "bad writer" as spelling errors do. Produce an effective letter, but let one spelling error pass and the letter is ignored and you, as the writer, may be laughed at. Write a clearly reasoned report, but let spelling errors pass and the entire work may be pushed aside as not worth real consideration. Words not spelled the way readers expect them to be are the easiest thing for most people to spot in writing and so they stand out more than any other element.

Our English spelling is not always regular and is therefore not always easy to learn. Part of the reason is historical—how words developed through history—and part is that there are many ways words come into the English language. Even today, there are differences in spelling between the United States and the countries which were or are part of the British empire. You may go to a **jewelry** store in the United States, but a **jewelery** store in

Canada. You read about **behavior** in this country but **behaviour** in the Bahamas. And there are other such differences. (In this book, you will be working with U.S. spelling customs.)

How to Become a Good Speller

Unless you have true dyslexia or another such disability that interferes with the ability to remember letters in sequence, you can become a good speller if you want to. Of course, like anything else you want to achieve, you have to work at it. Nobody can magically become a good speller. But by taking advantage of spelling aids and spending the time and effort this skill demands, you will never need to give that weakest of excuses, "Well, I never *was* a very good speller."

There are general aids to improve spelling:

- a dictionary
- a spell checker

and self-help aids

- learning clear, correct pronunciation
- your own spelling list
- original memory cards
- five learning steps

There are rules to help you through spelling, and many of them are detailed later in this chapter. Occasionally, there are exceptions to the rules, and some words you will simply have to memorize (if you don't already know them).

Finally—read, **read, READ!** The more you read, the better a reader *and* writer you will become. And the better a speller you will be!

GENERAL AIDS TO IMPROVE SPELLING

Begin with the most basic spelling aid: **a current standard dictionary.** Use it to check spelling, pronunciation, and syllabication (that is, where to put the hyphen when you have to break a word at the end of a line).

If you have to check the dictionary to find a correct spelling, circle that word (in red, if you can) so that should you look it up again you will know that you are repeating yourself and the word is one you should learn to spell without going to the dictionary each time

If you're not sure of how to spell a word and therefore can't find it in the dictionary, try to match the sound of the word when you say it as closely as possible. If that doesn't help, look for some possible alternates. If you can't find a word that begins with a vowel, try another vowel that sounds similar. If you think a word begins with a "c" but can't find it, try a "k" or even a "ch."

Another possibility is to check a **bad speller's dictionary.** In that book, the main entry shows how words are misspelled, either through mispronunciation or lack of attention to how the word looks. Then the conventional spelling is provided.

Computer or electronic typewriter spell checkers are very helpful—if you write on either of those devices. Many also offer suggestions when a word is flagged as being incorrectly spelled, and among the suggestions is usually the correct spelling.

SELF–HELP AIDS TO IMPROVE SPELLING

As you can tell, **clear pronunciation** of words helps you to spell them. Even though some words aren't spelled quite the way they sound, the sound of your pronunciation ought to be a guide. Make your pronunciation differentiate between a short *i* and an *a*, for instance. If you always mispronounce **ath'lete** as **ath–a–lete**, you will have a hard time learning to spell that word correctly. So if you sound out syllables clearly and pay attention to word endings, you will be helping yourself to spell.

Keep a **personal spelling list.** The words you use in writing but don't spell correctly are the ones you really need to learn, not words from a list. Set aside a page in a notebook that you can set up this easy way:

Misspellings	**Correct Spellings**
fedral	*federal*

On each line, write your error and its correction. Get the habit of adding to such a list every time anyone points out a spelling error to you. If repeating the correct spelling or writing a word correctly 10 or 20 times has worked for you in the past, use your correct spelling list with that self–help technique.

If your personal spelling list becomes long, analyze what kind of errors you seem to be making—such as one or more of the spelling rules later in this chapter—and work on eliminating that particular kind of error.

Make **original memory cards** for yourself as a way of remembering correct spelling. On one side of a 3x5 card, write out the correct spelling of a word you want to learn. On the other side, put a memory hint (such as "i before e" or "Poor grammar will mar your writing."). Or make a box around the word, with high and low extensions for tall letters or those that go below the line as a way of remembering how it looks. Or write any other associations or memory helps that have meaning to you. Keep these cards together, review both sides of them often, and occasionally have someone give you a spelling test on them so you can write out the words.

Finally, use the **five learning steps**, perhaps incorporating some of these other aids.

1. **SEE** the words you want to learn. Really look at them, especially when you see them in print. Doing so will help you recognize whether the way you write them is correct or not.
2. **SAY** the words. Hearing them—pronounced correctly, of course—helps you learn because you are using another of your senses.
3. **SPELL** the words aloud. Once isn't enough; you need to repeat them frequently.
4. **WRITE** the words as you customarily do, in longhand or on a typewriter or a computer. Using longhand is especially helpful because you get the muscles of your arm accustomed to the way writing a word correctly feels. But typing in the word gets your fingers accustomed to spelling, too.
5. **USE** the word whenever it's appropriate. Using the word in speaking is almost as helpful as using it in writing. But in writing you can always look back and check on yourself.

The Building Blocks of Spelling

In order to follow the rules about spelling that come later in this chapter, you must know the words that are going to be used to write about spelling. You probably know them, but here is a short review.

VOWELS are the letters *a, e, i, o,* and *u.* The letter *y* is also considered a vowel if it has an "ee" sound as in *daisy* or an "i" sound as in *sky.*

CONSONANTS are the remaining twenty letters in the alphabet. The *y* is considered a consonant if it has the sound of the letter, as in *yell.*

SYLLABLES are the sound units that make up a word. In most dictionaries, the first entry for a word shows how that word is divided into syllables. Marks that look something like an apostrophe are called "accent marks" and appear after syllables. A light accent mark means there is no stress on that syllable; a dark accent mark means you should put a voice stress on that syllable. In many dictionaries, a centered period after the second syllable means no stress should be put on that syllable.

EXAMPLES ▶ **der´ e · lict** **def´ i · lade´**

ROOT WORD is a basic word to which various beginnings or endings are sometimes added to create other words.

regret **mile** **plan**

SUFFIXES are groups of letters added to the **end** of a word. They create new words that are variations of or related to the root word.

(Suffixes are in bold face type.)
regret +**ful** mile + **age** plan + **n+ing**

PREFIXES are letters added to the **beginning** of a word. They create new words that are variations of or related to the root word.

(Prefixes are in bold face type.)
a + moral **mis** + spell **re** + cover

Forming Plurals Of Nouns

To Form REGULAR PLURALS

1. Add an *s* to the singular of most English nouns.
   stone + **s** = stones college + **s** = colleges
   program + **s** = programs toy + **s** = toys
   Smith + **s** = Smiths film + **s** = films

2. Add an *es* to nouns ending in *s* or *ss*, *x*, *ch*, or *sh*.
   chorus + **es** = choruses dress + **es** = dresses
   Ms. Jones + **es** = the Joneses fox + **es** = foxes
   church + **es** = churches bush + **es** = bushes

3. Words ending in *y*
   a) If a noun ends in a **consonant** + *y*, change the *y* to *i* and add *es*.
   study + **es** = studies city + **es** = cities
   country + **es** = countries enemy + **es** = enemies
   mentality + **es** = mentalities ruby + **es** = rubies

b) If noun ends in a **vowel + y**, add *s* to the singular.

holiday + s = holidays   boy + s = boys
valley + s = valleys   day + s = days
key + s = keys   play + s = plays

4. Words ending in ***o***
   a) Usually, add an *s* to form the plural.
   piano + s = pianos   igloo + s = igloos
   solo + s = solos   radio + s = radios
   b) Add ***es*** to form the plural of some nouns.
   tomato + **es** = tomatoes   potato + **es** = potatoes
   hero + **es** =heroes   echo + **es** = echoes

   If in doubt about whether to add an *s* or an *es*, check a dictionary.

5. Words ending in *f* or *f* + silent *e* change the *f* to a *v* and add ***es***.
   self + **es** = sel**ves**   wife + **es** = wi**ves**
   hoof + **es** = hoo**ves**   shelf + **es** = shel**ves**

To Form IRREGULAR PLURALS

1. Some words change completely from singular to plural. They don't follow a regular pattern, so you just have to memorize them.
   mouse – **mice**   foot – **feet**
   child – **children**   man – **men**
   tooth – **teeth**   woman – **women**

2. Some words don't change at all. They are the same in the singular and plural.
   deer   **fish**   **moose**   **sheep**

32-1

DIRECTIONS: Next to each singular word, show what you are adding to make the plural. Then write its plural form.

EXAMPLE ▶ **bank** +s banks

1.	box	+es boxes	11.	flash	+es flashes
2.	rose	+s roses	12.	nest	+s nests
3.	cemetery	+es cemeteries	13.	candy	+es candies
4.	automobile	+s automobiles	14.	buzz	+es buzzes
5.	patio	+s patios	15.	leaf	+es leaves
6.	day	+s days	16.	piano	+s pianos
7.	ray	+s rays	17.	fry	+es fries
8.	hero	+es heroes	18.	boat	+s boats
9.	calf	+es calves	19.	wish	+es wishes
10.	dish	+es dishes	20.	mess	+es messes

32-2

DIRECTIONS: Here are eight singular nouns.

loaf	baby	necessity	stereo
alley	biologist	tax	roach

Complete each sentence below by writing the plural of one of these words in the appropriate blank space.

EXAMPLE ▶ The *mosquitoes* **are out in force this summer.**

Biologists
taxes
roaches
stereos
babies
loaves
alleys
necessities

1. ________________ help us understand the plants and animals in our environment.
2. I am sure that ________ will keep going up faster than I can pay them.
3. Strangely, ________________ are among the oldest animals on earth.
4. When the ______________________ are on in all the apartments on my floor, you can hardly hear yourself talk.
5. Human ________________________ can't get along on their own as quickly as other animals can.
6. The restaurant served small ________________ of bread on each table.
7. Be careful walking down dark ____________________ at night!
8. Every culture has different ideas about their _______________ of life.

"SEED" Sound Words

In one unusual group of words that is spelled in three different ways, each word ends with the same sound: *seed.*

Only **one word** ends in ***–sede***
super**sede**

Three words end in ***–ceed***

ex**ceed**	pro**ceed**	suc**ceed**

Other words in the group end in ***–cede***

ac**cede**	con**cede**	inter**cede**
pre**cede**	re**cede**	se**cede**

32-3

DIRECTIONS: Use a dictionary or thesaurus as resource if you do not know the meanings of the "seed" sound words above. On the lines below each sentence, write the sentence using your own words instead of the bold type word printed. Circle your original wording in the sentence you write. Use your own paper if you need more space.

EXAMPLE  Bob's hairline continued to **recede** even though he used all kinds of ointments on it.

Bob's hairline continued to (move gradually backward) even though he used all kinds of ointments on it.

1. This memo is to **supersede** all others on the subject from my office.
   This memo is **to pass or override** all others on the subject from my office.

2. Certainly you may **precede** me in this line.
   Certainly you may **go ahead of me** in this line.

3. Please **proceed** with the reading of the minutes.
   Please **carry on** with the reading of the minutes.

4. A direct cause of the Civil War was that the South decided to **secede** from the Union.
   A direct cause of the Civil War was that the South decided **to part from** the Union.

5. Managers expect employees to **accede** to their directives.
   Managers expect employees to **consent** to their directives.

6. At 3 a.m. the present senator agreed to **concede** the election to his challenger.
   At 3 a.m. the present senator agreed **to give over** the election to his challenger.

7. Do not let your spending **exceed** your income, or you will be in big trouble!
   Do not let your spending **be more than** your income, or else you will be in big trouble!

8. Trying to **intercede** for me with the math teacher would be a waste of your time.
   Trying to **plead for** me with the math teacher would be a waste of your time.

9. When the flood waters **recede**, a rich layer of silt left behind makes the land good for crops.
   When the flood waters **go back**, a rich layer of silt left behind makes the land good for crops.

10. Here's hoping you **succeed** in learning to be a good speller.
    Here's hoping you **are successful** in learning to be a good speller.

Spelling Rules

The *I* BEFORE *E* RULE

Many people always remember the poem that goes with this spelling rule.

> ***I* before *e***
> **Except after *c***
> **Or when sounded as *ay***
> **As in neighbor and weigh.**

***i* before *e* words:**

believe	thief	achieve

***c* followed by *ei*:**

receive	deceive
receipt	ceiling

ei* if sounded as *ay:

weight	freight
eighty	sleigh

Exceptions to the "i before "e" rule include the following:

either	neither	leisure	species
weird	society	foreign	height
their	protein	veil	seize
ancient	conscience	efficient	sufficient

These are words you have to learn by memorizing them. The more you see and write them, the easier such memorizing will be.

32-4

DIRECTIONS: Fill in the missing letters for these words:

EXAMPLE ▶ p ie ce

1. brief	11. society
2. relief	12. pierce
3. vein	13. friend
4. conceit	14. cashier
5. perceive	15. chief
6. relieve	16. either
7. grief	17. eight
8. neither	18. eighth
9. field	19. ancient
10. their	20. conceive

1. br _____ f
2. rel _____ f
3. v _____ n
4. conc _____ t
5. perc _____ ve
6. rel _____ ve
7. gr _____ f
8. n _____ ther
9. f _____ ld
10. th _____ r
11. soc _____ ty
12. p _____ rce
13. fr _____ nd
14. cash _____ r
15. ch _____ f
16. _____ ther
17. _____ ght
18. _____ ghth
19. anc _____ nt
20. conc _____ ve

The SILENT FINAL "*E*" RULE

1. Drop the silent final *e* of a word root before a suffix beginning with a vowel.

enclose + **ure** = enclos**ure**	base + **ic** = bas**ic**
approve + **al** = approv**al**	file + **ing** = fil**ing**
ridicule + **ous** = ridicul**ous**	advise + **ory** = advis**ory**

An exception is that some words do not drop the ***e***
canoe + **ing** = cano**eing**
mile + **age** = mil**eage**

2. A word root that ends in –*ce* or –*ge* followed by a suffix that begins with *a* or *o* keeps the final *e*.

advantage + **ous** = advantag**eous**
manage + **able** = manag**eable**
enforce + **able** = enforc**eable**
change + **able** = chang**eable**

3. Keep the silent final *e* before a suffix beginning with a consonant.

encourage + **ment** = encourag**ement**
hope + **ful** = hop**eful**
love + **less** =lov**eless**
nine + **ty** = nin**ety**
sincere + **ly** = sincer**ely**
same + **ness** = sam**eness**

An exception to this rule is that some words drop the ***e***
nine + **th** = nin**th**
judge + **ment** = judg**ment**
acknowledge + **ment** = acknowledg**ment**
wise + **dom** =wis**dom**
gentle + **ly** = gent**ly**

Exceptions to rules such as these simply have to be memorized.

32-5

DIRECTIONS: Combine each word root and suffix to write the correct spelling of the word.

EXAMPLE ▶ **arrange + ment =** *arrangement*

1. hoped	9. surely
2. sincerely	10. liking
3. lonely	11. writing
4. changeable	12. notation
5. sharing	13. usage
6. shining	14. responsible
7. nervous	15. scary
8. coming	

1. hope + ed = ____________________
2. sincere + ly =____________________
3. lone + ly =____________________
4. change + able = ____________________
5. share + ing = ____________________
6. shine + ing = ____________________
7. nerve + ous = ____________________
8. come + ing = ____________________
9. sure + ly = ____________________
10. like + ing = ____________________
11. write + ing ____________________
12. note + ation = ____________________
13. use + age = ____________________
14. response + ible = ____________________
15. scare + y = ____________________

The FINAL "*Y*" RULE

1. If there is a consonant before the final *y*, change the *y* to *i*, before a suffix that doesn't begin with an *i*.

beauty + **ful** = beauti**ful**
penny + **es** = penni**es**
lady + **es** = ladi**es**
easy + **ly** = easi**ly**
carry + **ed** = carri**ed**
busy + **ness**=busi**ness**

2. Keep the final *y* if the suffix does begin with an *i*.

fly + **ing** = fl**ying** lobby + **ist** = lobb**yist**
deny + **ing** = den**ying** cry + **ing** = cr**ying**

3. If there is a vowel before the final *y*, simply add the suffix.

employ + **er** = employ**er** buy + **ing** = bu**ying**
annoy + **ed** = anno**yed** joy + **ful** = jo**yful**

Exceptions to this rule:
lay + **ed** = **laid** pay + **ed** = **paid**
say + **ed** = **said** day + **ly** = **daily**

32-6

DIRECTIONS: Circle the correctly spelled word in each pair.

EXAMPLE ▶ **(trying)** / **triing**

1. plaied / played
2. employable / employble
3. happly/ happily
4. cryed / cried
5. merciful / mercyfull
6. copiing / copying
7. certifycate / certificate
8. pennyless / penniless

played
employable
happily
cried
merciful
copying
certificate
penniless

32-7

DIRECTIONS: To each root word, add the suffixes shown and then write out the correctly spelled words.

EXAMPLE ▶ **marry** **(age)** = *marriage*
(ed) = *married*
(ing) = *marrying*

1. destroy (er) = ________
(ing) = ________
(ed) = ________
2. carry (ing) = ________
(ed) = ________
(er) = ________

destoyer
destroying
destroyed
carrying
carried
carrier

Answers	Word	Suffix
uglier	3. ugly	(er) = ________
ugliest		(est) = ________
ugliness		(ness) = ________
angrier	4. angry	(er) = ________
angriest		(est) = ________
angrily		(ly)= ________
happier	5. happy	(er) = ________
happiness		(ness) = ________
happiest		(est) = ________
happily		(ly) = ________
supplier	6. supply	(er) = ________
supplies		(es) = ________
supplied		(ed) = ________
supplying		(ing) = ________
enjoyment	7. enjoy	(ment) = ________
enjoying		(ing) = ________
enjoyed		(ed) = ________
enjoys		(s) = ________
employment	8. employ	(ment) = ________
employed		(ed) = ________
employer		(er) = ________
employing		(ing) = ________

Final Consonants

All the words covered by the next group of spelling rules end in one or more consonants. Many use the same suffixes because almost all the words in this group are verbs and many of the others are modifiers. Whether or not to double the final consonant of the root word before adding the suffix depends on one of two elements of the root word: its spelling or its pronunciation.

Root Word Spelling

> **1. IF the root word has only one syllable that ends in a single vowel and a single consonant (except *w, x,* or *z*)**
> **AND the suffix begins with a vowel**
> **THEN double the final consonant of a root word**

win + **n** + **ing** = winning
hop + **p** + **ing** = hopping
skin + **n** + **y** = skinny
slip + **p** + **ing** = slipping

EXCEPTIONS are words ending in *s, w, x, and y.*

pay + **able** = payable wax + **y** = waxy
tow + **ed** = towed gas + **es** = gases

> **2. IF the root word ends in a vowel and more than one consonant**
> **AND the suffix begins with a vowel**
> **THEN do not double the final consonant of the root word**

assess + **ing** = assessing sing + **er** = singer
persist + **ence** = persistence

> **3. IF the root word ends with more than one vowel before the final single consonant**
> **AND the suffix begins with a vowel**
> **THEN do not double the final consonant of the root word**

need + **y** = needy cool + **est** = coolest
root + **ed** = rooted sail + **ing** = sailing

The present participle of a verb is always formed by adding *–ing* to a root word. The past tense and the past participle of regular verbs are formed by adding *–ed* to the root word. Therefore, in this exercise, you will be practicing both spelling and grammar.

DIRECTIONS: Check the end of each word to see the vowel and consonant pattern it has. Then, follow Rule 1 (1 vowel, 1 consonant), Rule 2 (vowel, 1+ consonants), or Rule 3 (1+ vowels, 1 consonant) above to decide whether or not to double the final consonant of the root word. Write the correct spelling of each root word with the suffixes *–ing* and *–ed*.

EXAMPLE ▶

Root Word	Suffix: *–ing*	Suffix: *–ed*
stir	stirring	stirred
exist	existing	existed

	Root Word	Suffix: *–ing*	Suffix: *–ed*
1.	cram	________	________
2.	plan	________	________
3.	bat	________	________
4.	perform	________	________
5.	shift	________	________
6.	evict	________	________
7.	bail	________	________

cramming	crammed
planning	planned
batting	batted
performing	performed
shifting	shifted
evicting	evicted
bailing	bailed

sunning	sunned
sewing	sewed
dropping	dropped
boxing	boxed
confirming	confirm
wishing	wished
obtaining	obtained
crawling	crawled

8. sun ________________ ________________
9. sew ________________ ________________
10. drop________________ ________________
11. box ________________ ________________
12. confirm ________________ ________________
13. wish________________ ________________
14. obtain________________ ________________
15. crawl ________________ ________________

32-9

Comparative and superlative forms of modifiers are formed by adding suffixes to root words.

DIRECTIONS: Check the end of each word to see the vowel and consonant pattern it has. Then, follow Rule 1 (1 vowel, 1 consonant), Rule 2 (vowel, 1+ consonants), or Rule 3 (1+ vowels, 1 consonant) above to decide whether or not to double the final consonant of the root word. Write the correct spelling of each root word with the suffixes *–er* and *–est*.

EXAMPLE ▶

Root Word	Suffix: *–er*	Suffix: *–est*
sad	*sadder*	*saddest*
moist	*moister*	*moistest*

bigger	biggest
slimmer	slimmest
wetter	wettest
tighter	tightest
deeper	deepest
greener	greenest
fatter	fattest
straighter	straightest

Root Word **Suffix: *–er*** **Suffix: *–est***

1. big ________________ ________________
2. slim ________________ ________________
3. wet ________________ ________________
4. tight ________________ ________________
5. deep ________________ ________________
6. green________________ ________________
7. fat ________________ ________________
8. straight________________ ________________

4. IF the root word ends with a consonant
AND the suffix begins with a consonant
DO NOT CHANGE either the root or the suffix

royal + **ty** = royalty   hat + **less** = hatless
leader + **ship** = leadership

5. IF the root word ends in a double consonant ADD any suffix

skill + **ful** = skillful bright + **ly** = brightly
embarrass + **ment** = embarrassment

32-10

DIRECTIONS: Look at each of the following root words to see if it ends with one or two consonants. Then add a suffix depending on whether it begins with a vowel or a consonant. You will then be able to write a word spelled according to Rule 4 or Rule 5, above.

Root and Suffix	Spelling
glad + ly	gladly

development
enrolled
condemning
embarassment
sinful
stardom
sadness
gladness

	Root and Suffix	Spelling
1.	develop + ment	______
2.	enroll + ed	______
3.	condemn + ing	______
4.	embarrass + ment	______
5.	sin + ful	______
6.	star + dom	______
7.	sad + ness	______
8.	glad + ness	______

Root Word Pronunciation

Say each of these root words aloud so you can hear where the stressed and unstressed syllables come. If you are not sure about either the syllabication or the stressed sounds, check a dictionary for both.

6. IF the word is stressed on the last syllable and ends in a single vowel and a single consonant (except *w, x,* or *z*) AND the suffix begins with a vowel THEN double the final consonant of a root word

be gin′ + **ing** = beginning o mit′ + **ed** = omitted
oc cur′ + **ence** = occurrence

EXCEPTIONS are words that change the stressed syllable when a suffix is added:

de fer′ = def′ er + **ence** = deference
gas′ = gas′ + **eous** = gaseous
in fer′ = in′ fer + **ence** = inference

7. IF the word is stressed on any syllable except the last AND the suffix begins with a vowel THEN do not double the final consonant of the root word

dif′ fer + **ent** = different
en′ ter + **ing** = entering
lis′ ten + **ed** = listened
mar′ vel + **ous** = marvelous

EXCEPTIONS are some words that do **double the final consonant** before adding the suffix.

can′ cel + **ation** = cancellation
ques′ tion + **aire** = questionnaire
pro′ gram + **ed** = programmed
hand′ i cap + **ed** = handicapped
for′ mat + **ed** (or **ing)** = formatted (formatting)

32-11

This spelling activity requires you to pronounce each root word and know where the syllables divide and which syllable is stressed. If you are not sure of any, check a dictionary.

DIRECTIONS: All these suffixes begin with vowels. However, you must know on which syllable of the root word the pronunciation stress is put. That will help you decide whether or not to double the final consonant of the root word. In order to spell each word correctly, decide if you should follow Rule 6 (stress last syllable) or Rule 7 (stress any syllable except last).

EXAMPLE 

Root and Suffix	Spelling
control + ing	*controlling*

Word Box		Root and Suffix	Spelling
committed	1.	commit + ed	______________
submitting	2.	submit + ing	______________
counselor	3.	counsel + or	______________
cancellation	4.	cancel + ation	______________
traveler	5.	travel + er	______________
benefited	6.	benefit + ed	______________
compelling	7.	compel + ing	______________
admittance	8.	admit + ance	______________
answering	10.	answer + ing	______________
expelled	11.	expel + ed	______________
beginning	12.	begin + ing	______________
listener	13.	listen + er	______________
preferred	14.	prefer + ed	______________
budgeted	15.	budget + ed	______________

Prefixes

Add standard prefixes to root words, even if the end letter of the prefix is the same as the beginning letter of the root. Only a few of the many prefixes are shown below.

32-12

DIRECTIONS: Combine each prefix shown here with the root words listed and write the resulting word.

EXAMPLE ▶ dis + integrate *disintegrate*

Answers			
disappear	1. dis +	appear =	________
dissatisfy		satisfy =	________
disintegrate		integrate =	________
disinterested		interested =	________
disagree		agree =	________
cooperate	2. co +	operate =	________
unnatural	3. un +	natural =	________
unusual		usual =	________
unnerve		nerve =	________
unable		able =	________
uninterested		interested =	________
inaccurate	4. in +	accurate =	________
procreate	5. pro +	create =	________
preeminent	6. pre +	eminent =	________
misspell	7. mis +	spell =	________
misapply		apply =	________
illogical	8. il +	logical =	________
illegal		legal =	________
immoral	9. im +	moral =	________
immaterial		material =	________
recreate	10. re +	create =	________
recreation		creation =	________

32-13

DIRECTIONS: Draw a line through each word spelled incorrectly and write the correct spelling directly above it.

People all over the United States look forward to summer. In
weather finally
the central and northern states, the ~~whether~~ is ~~finaly~~ warm
enough for people to do many things outdoors. Children,
swimming succeed
especially, look forward to ~~swiming~~. When they ~~succeede~~ in
relieved
learning to swim, parents and other adults are ~~releived~~ because
safer Picnicking
then they will be ~~saffer~~ in the water. ~~Picnicing~~ is popular with
eight eighty
people from ~~aght~~ to ~~eigty~~. Those who have cars often like to go
traveling mileage
~~travelling~~ and the ~~milage~~ really piles up quickly. You can tell
canoeing
those people who like ~~canooing~~ in the summer, because they
canoes
often have ~~canos~~ on top of their cars. As people drive through
beautiful blooming
the countryside, often they spot ~~beautyfull~~ roses ~~bloomming~~,
beginning nests calves
birds ~~begining~~ to leave their ~~nestes~~, and ~~calfs~~ learning to stand
beginning
up and be on their own. Yes, the ~~beggining~~ of this new season is
a happy time for many people everywhere.

Activity

32-14

DIRECTIONS: Draw a line through each word spelled incorrectly and write the correct spelling directly above it.

embarrassment
Many people have felt the ~~embarasment~~ of not being able to
themselves running
perform simple tasks for ~~themselfes~~. Even such tasks as ~~runing~~,
batting petting
~~bating~~ a ball, ~~peting~~ an animal, or sewing are more than some
handicapped
~~handycaped~~ people can do. Fortunately, with more attention
paid handicapped
being ~~payed~~ to their needs, more ~~handycaped~~ people are
independence
gaining ~~independdance~~ these days. For instance, thanks to
marvelous developments
~~marvlous~~ ~~developements~~ with computers, many more people
employable
who never expected to be ~~employeable~~ are able to earn their
enjoyable
own livings. They find it satisfying and ~~enjoyible~~ to be on their
own. Employers are discovering that those people labeled
"handicapped" their
"~~handycapped~~" are usually among ~~thier~~ best employees.

Index

Q

R

S